# COMPLETE GUIDE

*to*

# Convenience Food
# *Counts*

## Lea Ann Holzmeister, RD, CDE

**American Diabetes Association**

*Director, Book Publishing,* John Fedor; *Book Acquisitions,* Sherrye Landrum; *Editor,* Abe Ogden; *Production Manager,* Peggy M. Rote; *Composition,* Circle Graphics, Inc.; *Text and Cover Design,* KSA Plus Communications; *Printer,* Transcontinental Printing.

Printed in Canada
1 3 5 7 9 10 8 6 4 2

The suggestions and information contained in this publication are generally consistent with the *Clinical Practice Recommendations* and other policies of the American Diabetes Association, but they do not represent the policy or position of the Association or any of its boards or committees. Reasonable steps have been taken to ensure the accuracy of the information presented. However, the American Diabetes Association cannot ensure the safety or efficacy of any product or service described in this publication. Individuals are advised to consult a physician or other appropriate health care professional before undertaking any diet or exercise program or taking any medication referred to in this publication. Professionals must use and apply their own professional judgment, experience, and training and should not rely solely on the information contained in this publication before prescribing any diet, exercise, or medication. The American Diabetes Association—its officers, directors, employees, volunteers, and members—assumes no responsibility or liability for personal or other injury, loss, or damage that may result from the suggestions or information in this publication.

⊗ The paper in this publication meets the requirements of the ANSI Standard Z39.48-1992 (permanence of paper).

ADA titles may be purchased for business or promotional use or for special sales. For information, please write to Lee Romano Sequeira, Special Sales & Promotions, at the address below.

American Diabetes Association
1701 North Beauregard Street
Alexandria, Virginia 22311

**Library of Congress Cataloging-in-Publication Data**

Holzmeister, Lea Ann.
  Complete guide to convenience food counts / Lea Ann Holzmeister.
    p. cm.
  ISBN 1-58040-042-6 (pbk.)
    1. Diabetes—Diet therapy. 2. Food exchange lists. 3. Convenience foods—Composition—Tables.   I. Title.

RC662 .H659 2001
616.4'620654—dc21

2001022563

*To Jeff, Erin, Adam, and Emily for your enduring support!*

# Contents

# Acknowledgments

Thanks to Madelyn L. Wheeler, MS, RD, FADA, CDE, and Patti Bazel Geil, MS, RD, FADA, CDE, for their valuable review comments.

# Introduction

## The Express Lane to Sensible Nutrition

Our lives have become increasingly busy—full of family, work, and community involvement. Finding ways to save time on domestic tasks, such as cooking, is a high priority in many households. As a result, many people choose to cook less, but still demand good-tasting, healthy food choices. To cater to this lifestyle change, food manufacturers are offering a wide variety of convenience foods, or foods that require little or no preparation before eating. They come in every form; from fully cooked meal-kits to washed, ready-to-eat bagged salads. They can be time-savers like canned vegetables and packaged mixes, or step-saving ingredients that make it unnecessary to keep supplies you rarely use. But whatever form they come in, convenience foods make cooking quick and easy.

In the past, however, this convenience came with a price. For most people, the mention of "convenience food" brings to mind frozen microwave pizzas, refrigerated burritos, and boxes of macaroni and cheese. These foods were soaked with calories, fat, and sodium. While this still holds true for some convenience foods, many consumers are now demanding easy meal solutions and shortcuts that can meet their nutritional needs. Markets are adding many healthy products, as well as those that are reduced-calorie, low-fat and low-salt, to their growing selection.

The *American Diabetes Association's Complete Guide to Convenience Food Counts* introduces you to the types of markets and the convenience foods they offer. Consumers are increasingly shopping "in-store" and "on-line" at a variety of markets for takeout food, giving them convenient home-served meals. Warehouse clubs even offer "select-assembly-only meals." Many on-line markets offer the same "in-store" selections with even less shopping time required. Salad bars, rotisserie chicken, steamed shrimp, deli sandwiches, as well as a variety of heat-only main dishes, appetizers, and side dishes are just a few of the items to choose from. If you're short on time, buy your main dish—or a whole meal— already prepared. Then, just heat-and-serve.

The tips in this book also show you how to combine convenience foods with your favorite side-dishes or toppings to add variety and improve your nutrition score card. Balance your lasagna dinner with bagged salad and refrigerated breadsticks. Create a hassle-free breakfast with frozen waffles and cut fresh fruit from the produce department. With the help of this book, you will be able to choose convenience foods carefully so that you can make any meal fit in with your healthy lifestyle.

Another bonus of convenience food is saving time in food planning, shopping, and preparation. The average supermarket carries more than 30,000 separate items and more than half of these are foods. No wonder planning, shopping, and preparing foods takes so long. When you try to compare the nutrients in all these food items to ensure a healthy menu, it takes even more time. But still, 90% of shoppers are concerned about the nutritional content of the food they eat. Fat, salt, and cholesterol are the three top areas of interest, followed by sugar. People with diabetes also must be concerned with carbohydrate intake. Some of these concerns may be yours, but you may not have enough time to plan the healthy menus, compare the labels, and prepare the foods. Now you have a resource to help you get organized.

With *Convenience Food Counts* you can create nutritious menus, compare food products before you even get near the food store, and save time in food preparation.

The *American Diabetes Association's Complete Guide to Convenience Food Counts* gives you supermarket strategies to make your shopping trip more time efficient, healthy, and hassle free. You'll learn how to navigate the food market to fill your "diabetes smart shopping cart" and how to get quick results in the kitchen. Now you will always have a smartly stocked pantry, freezer, and refrigerator with a quick something to eat. And with the supermarket meal solution tips and seven days of convenience menus, you'll soon be in the express lane to sensible nutrition.

# Turning Quick Eating into Healthy Eating

*What you need to know about healthy eating for diabetes*

Healthy eating is one of the best personal investments you can make! This is especially true for people with diabetes. Staying healthy with diabetes is influenced by many factors. Certainly your genes, your age, your lifestyle, your healthcare, your medications, and your exercise habits all make a difference. But what you eat is a key player in keeping you healthy and your diabetes in control. Of the many health factors influenced by food, just a few include:

- blood glucose levels
- blood fats
- blood pressure
- weight
- long-term diabetes complications
- your risk for developing heart disease, cancer, and hypertension

But healthy eating doesn't just happen. Reflecting on your present lifestyle and knowing that you are ready to make realistic changes are the first steps toward focusing on a more moderate and balanced diet. Making changes toward a more sensible eating style may even require help from a registered dietitian. There's never a better time than now to take control of your food choices and your diabetes. The sooner you invest in your health with good nutrition, the greater the benefit.

## Dietary guidelines for the whole family

The Dietary Guidelines for Americans are the established foundation of proper diet for all healthy Americans ages two and over. While consistency is a main concern, new advancements in dietary research can cause some minor changes in the model. But even though the guidelines may be tweaked every few years, the foundations remain the same. They are the basis of good eating and they are here to stay.

The dietary guidelines help you to take a step back and look at the "big picture" when you plan your diet. It's easy to become narrowly focused on one aspect of your meal plan, such as carbohydrates or fats, if you are working toward better blood glucose or blood lipid control. In the process it might slip your mind that you forgot to include enough fruits or vegetables.

It's important to remember that guidelines are just that— suggested steps that you can take to ensure good health. You should also remember that these recommendations are for eating patterns over several days, not for single meals or foods. For example, if you decide to eat a piece of birthday cake at your granddaughter's party, that's fine; you haven't ruined your diet or your eating habits. What counts is that over the course of several days, your eating habits are generally low in fat, high in fiber, include plenty of fruits, vegetables and whole grains, and are at an appropriate calorie level for you.

The following are the dietary guidelines for all Americans:

- Aim for a healthy weight.
- Be physically active each day.
- Let the Pyramid guide your food choices.
- Choose a variety of grains daily, especially whole grains.
- Choose a variety of fruits and vegetables daily.
- Keep food safe to eat.
- Choose a diet that is low in saturated fat and cholesterol, and moderate in total fat.
- Choose beverages and foods to moderate your intake of sugars.
- Choose and prepare foods with less salt.
- If you drink alcoholic beverages, do so in moderation.

## Diabetes Eating Goals

Every few years the American Diabetes Association (ADA) reviews the latest research and distributes nutrition recommendations. The 2000 recommendations stress an overall healthy eating plan with the goal of keeping your blood glucose in the normal range as much as possible. The following are the ADA's recommended nutrition guidelines:

- **Calories.** Calorie sources are carbohydrates, proteins, and fats. Most adults need 1,800 to 2,500 calories per day; however, there is no single amount of calories that is right for everyone. Your calorie needs will depend on many factors, such as your current weight and height, your age, whether you want to lose weight or are at a healthy weight, and your daily activity level. If you take in more calories from food than you use up each day doing physical work, you will store the extra calories as body fat. In other words, you will gain weight. The reverse is true if you spend more energy in a day than you take in as food. You will pull the extra energy you need out of stored fat and lose weight. Your registered dietitian can help you determine your body weight goals and calorie requirements to meet your goal.

- **Protein.** 10–20% of your calories should come from protein. The main sources of protein are meats, poultry, seafood, and dairy foods. Beans, grains, vegetables, and some fruits are plant sources of protein. Two 3-ounce servings of meat a day are enough for most people. Low-fat animal sources of protein will make it easier to eat less total fat, saturated fat, and cholesterol. Certain diabetes-related conditions, such as overt nephropathy, might benefit from a lower intake of protein. However, this should be discussed with a physician or a registered dietician before any action is taken.

- **Fat and cholesterol.** Fat can contribute to weight gain and risk for heart disease. Most people need no more than 30% of their daily calories from fat. A lower fat intake (especially saturated fat) may lower your risk for cardiovascular disease, a common complication of diabetes. Less than 10% of your total calories should come from saturated fat. Cholesterol is only found in foods of animal origin. Your intake of cholesterol should be less than 300 milligrams every day. Eating low fat meats, poultry, and dairy products means less saturated fat and cholesterol.

- **Carbohydrate.** The amount of carbohydrate you need will vary from 40–60% of your total calories. All sources of carbohydrate raise blood glucose. The bulk of your carbohydrate intake will come from grains, beans, starches, dairy products, fruits, as well as vegetables, which also give you essential vitamins and minerals. Sugars and sweets are also carbohydrate sources. Foods such as cakes, candy, and other desserts may be high in fat and calories and have few vitamins and minerals. Eat small servings of these foods only once in a while.

- **Fiber.** On average, most people consume only about 11 grams of fiber every day. To increase health benefits from fiber, 20–35 grams of fiber per day are recommended for all Americans. Whole-grains, fresh fruits, and vegetables are good sources of fiber. Beans, oats, and many fruits and vegetables are good sources of soluble fiber, which can improve blood glucose control. Dietary fiber may be helpful in the treatment and prevention of constipation and several gastrointestinal disorders. Soluble fiber has a beneficial effect on serum lipids and can work to fill you up faster. Dietary fibers are also usually bundled with other nutrients, which give foods high in fiber an excellent one-two combo.

- **Sodium.** Sodium helps your body maintain fluid balance and regulate blood pressure. A high sodium intake can contribute to high blood pressure. Most Americans consume 4000–6000 milligrams per day. However, the recommendation for sodium is between 2400–3000 milligrams per day, and if you have high blood pressure, 2400 milligrams or less per day. Eating more fruits and vegetables and using herbs and spices as your primary seasonings can help you take in moderate amounts of sodium.

- **Alcohol.** If you choose to drink alcoholic beverages, keep your intake moderate. This means not more than one drink a day for women and two for men. Alcoholic beverages offer calories, but few nutrients. In excess, alcohol can be harmful and may become a substitute for nutritious foods. Alcohol can raise blood triglycerides, and for people with diabetes taking insulin or diabetes pills, alcohol can lower blood glucose to unacceptably low levels.

- **Vitamins and minerals.** Variety, balance, and moderation in food choices are the keys to eating the right amount of vitamins and minerals. If you follow a very low-calorie diet, limit certain food groups, or have poor diabetes control, you may need a vitamin and mineral supplement. Check with your registered dietitian about your specialized vitamin and mineral needs.

Factors such as your age, length of time with diabetes, your current weight, and your blood fat levels will determine your diabetes nutrition goals. This may mean that you focus on certain nutrients in your diet but your friend or uncle with diabetes may focus on something completely different. Find out what your specific nutrition goals are by meeting with a registered dietitian. Forming a partnership with a registered dietitian can help you learn how your lifestyle and the food you eat affect your diabetes. Your dietitian can also help you find the diabetes meal planning method that works best for you, whether it is the food guide pyramid, carbohydrate counting, or food exchanges. Here are ways you can find a registered dietitian who specializes in diabetes:

- Find the nearest American Diabetes Association Recognized Education Program, as well as information on registered dietitians in these programs by calling 1-800-DIABETES (342-2383). Or on the web at *www.diabetes.org/education/edustate2.asp.*
- Find a diabetes educator who is a dietitian by calling the American Association of Diabetes Educators at 1-800TEAMUP4 (1-800-832-6874). Or on the web at *www.diabeteseducator.org.*
- Contact your doctor for a referral.

# Supermarket Strategy

## *Making Your Trip Efficient, Healthy, and Hassle Free*

With the pace of today's hectic household, just the thought of a routine trip to the market can spark feelings of grief and anxiety. To cope with this dilemma, many households visit their grocer up to seven times a week, spending countless minutes scanning the shelves for an appealing, quick dinner to throw together. If you're one of these everyday shoppers, you probably know that in addition to the items you're searching for, every aisle and corner of the market provides an array of enticing products and opportunities for impulsive, unhealthy food purchases. Beware! These products are expensive and usually don't fit into your eating plan, creating holes in your diet and your wallet!

Convenience foods are often the answer to those everyday meal dilemmas, but they don't have to be damaging to your health. With a little supermarket savvy and mindful planning, convenience foods can pull you through time crunches and menu problems.

## Types of Convenience Foods

Saving time in meal preparation is a high priority for many households. Eight in ten shoppers consider both preparation ease and time when selecting their foods. However, convenience food is no longer just frozen pizzas or "TV dinners." Consumers demand more variety and types of convenience in their food choices. The food industry has responded by increasing the availability of value-added and ready-to-eat or -heat foods. Labor-saving ingredients such as pizza crust or bread dough can save a lot of time in recipes and meal preparation. Ready-to-cook vegetables, ready-to-eat bagged salads, and frozen foods are the top convenience items used by consumers. Combine these side items with refrigerated or frozen fully cooked meat entrees such as pot roasts and chicken fillets, and you've got a meal in a flash.

Supermarket convenience take-out foods are also replacing fast food and restaurant dining. The number of shoppers who purchase takeout food for meals eaten at home from their supermarket delis and in-store restaurants has doubled in the past decade. The wider selection of healthy convenience items offered in supermarkets appeals to consumers who consider nutrition one of their top concerns when shopping for food.

### Ready-to-cook or ready-to-eat? Helpful definitions for convenience foods

To better understand what convenience foods are available and how you can use them to create delicious, quick, and healthy meals, you should become familiar with the terms used when talking about convenience foods. The following is a list of helpful definitions related to convenience foods:

- **Ready-to-eat:** fully cleaned, cooked and assembled food, such as deli platters, entrees, meats, dips, salads, cooked seafood, bakery desserts, breads, lunch kits, side dishes, salad bar, hot food bar
- **Ready-to-heat:** fully cooked entrée/side items such as frozen waffles/pancakes, bakery bread, canned chili,

canned soup, frozen egg rolls, pizza, frozen complete dinners and pot pies, frozen french fries/hash browns, canned gravy, frozen lasagna, canned pasta sauce, pocket sandwiches, toaster pastries

- **Ready-to-cook:** refrigerated/packaged pasta, pancake batter, pre-cut, marinated or pre-seasoned meat or poultry
- **Ready-to-assemble:** partially or fully cooked meal/side dish kits such as caesar salad kits, stir-fry meal kits, chip/dip kits
- **Refrigerated/frozen fully cooked:** entrees/side dishes with/without heating required such as mashed potatoes, meat entrees, appetizers, desserts
- **Partially cooked refrigerated/frozen:** frozen fish sticks, garlic bread
- **Step-saving ingredients:** partially prepared ingredients such as pie/pizza crust, bread dough, frosting, caramel dip, coating mixes, cookie dough
- **Boxed mixes/seasoning packets:** time saving rice/pasta/stuffing mixes, entrees seasoning packets, bakery mixes, salad dressing mixes, meal mixes, soup mixes
- **Pre-cut/cleaned ready-to-cook:** meats such as stir-fry beef, poultry such as boneless/skinless chicken breast, vegetables
- **Pre-cut/cleaned ready-to-eat:** fruits, fruit salads, vegetables, bagged salads
- **Single-serving:** hot or cold cereal, fruited yogurt, applesauce, canned fruit, boxed/canned juices

## Where can you get healthy convenience foods?

Everywhere. Convenience foods can be found in every type of market, from the corner market to online markets. Availability and selection will vary depending on the size and type of store.

- The **corner market** or **a limited assortment store** is becoming less and less apparent in our super-sized retail climate. These stores offer a narrow selection of foods-to-go and pre-packaged convenience foods but their location is often closer to home. This can be a timesaver.

- **Convenience stores** are compact, drive-to stores offering a limited line of high-convenience, low-nutrition items.
- **Gourmet or fine food markets** are becoming more popular and trendy, as the American shopper has become more liberal with their food dollar and taste preferences. These types of markets offer a varying selection of foods-to-go and pre-packaged convenience foods.
- **Grocery stores** are any stores selling a line of dry grocery, canned goods, or non-food items, plus some perishable items. Since grocery stores can come in all shapes and sizes, the convenience food selection will vary from store to store.
- **Supermarkets** are full-line, self-service grocery stores, often containing a pharmacy, deli, photo finishing, banking services, and dry cleaning. Many types of fresh, ready-to-eat carryout or refrigerated/frozen ready-to-heat convenience foods are available in various departments of the supermarket.
- A **super center** is a large food/drug combination store and mass merchandiser under a single roof. Super centers offer a wide variety of food, often with over 40% of the space devoted to grocery items. Brand-name convenience items are available in somewhat limited varieties. Carryout convenience foods from delis and hot food counters are found in certain super centers.
- A **warehouse store** is a store with primarily dry grocery and some perishables with limited service and a focus on price appeal. Brand name and house-brand convenience items are available in limited variety.
- A **wholesale club** is a membership retail/wholesale store with a limited variety of convenience products in a warehouse-type atmosphere. These stores have general merchandise and health and beauty care products, as well as a grocery line dedicated to large sizes and bulk

sales. Carryout hot and cold deli items for quick-assemble meals may also be available.

- **On-line markets** offer the convenience of filling your virtual cart online and having your groceries delivered directly to your kitchen counter. Many on-line markets offer recipes with shopping lists and order histories to save time. Many of the brand name convenience items that you might find in your favorite market can be obtained on-line.

## Getting "Quick" in Your Kitchen and "Healthy" in Your Shopping

Saving time with meal planning and preparation starts with a list in your hand and healthy eating on your mind. Jump-start your shopping trip with brief menus and a list of items you need.

### Going to the market with a plan

- **Your meal plan is your guide.** Use your individualized diabetes meal plan and the food pyramid when planning your menus. This will help you keep your eating goals in mind.
- **Plan your menus when you're hungry** (they'll be more interesting) and shop when you're not (you'll have more control). Shopping when you are hungry can tempt you to succumb to impulse items, including more expensive, less nutritious snack and dessert foods.
- **Map out your meals.** Planning your menus a week in advance saves time and is the template for your grocery list. You don't have to eat the meals in the order you list, but this meal planning can give you ideas for making shopping and preparation faster and easier. It also gives you the opportunity to be sure your choices are balanced and healthy over a period of time.
- **Clip coupons wisely.** Forget about using coupons unless they're for food items that you usually buy. Saving 35 cents

on a $4.00 item you don't normally purchase is costing you $3.65. And don't assume that items with coupons are always the best buy. Another brand or similar food might be cheaper even without a coupon.

- **Consider convenience.** Convenience foods, such as canned vegetables, frozen juice concentrates, and packaged mixes for muffins and cakes can be real time-savers. They also make it unnecessary to keep supplies of ingredients that you rarely use. Prepared, pre-sliced, and pre-cooked foods are also handy, but they usually cost more. Depending on your schedule, the timesavings may be worth the price.

## What makes a healthy grocery list?

Shoppers who use lists spend slightly more money per trip to the market than non-list-users, but they don't have to run back to the market as frequently to pick up forgotten items. This saves time and also offers fewer chances to face unhealthy temptations.

- **Keep a running list.** When you create your menus for the week, keep your list nearby and write down the foods you'll need. Add items to your list as you notice you run out. Remember to write down the form of the food you'll be buying. For example, if you are planning precooked chicken breast, indicate the number or weight needed for the meal.
- **Use the Pyramid as a guide.** Write your menus and your list with the Food Pyramid in mind. Load up with grains, vegetables, and fruit. Choose smaller amounts of low-fat dairy, meats, fish, poultry, and legumes. Think carefully about fats, oils, and sweets.
- **Check for specials.** Make note of sale items from grocery ads while your making your list. Realize that many of the sale items may not work into your food plan (and just like with coupons, don't be tempted to buy items you normally wouldn't just because they're on sale), but usually there are

2–3 items that fit nicely into your meals. Keep your list flexible and some options open. For example, list fresh fruit, and choose whatever looks best and is well priced.

- **Organize your list by category to match the store layout.** Learn the store's layout and write your list with this in mind. You'll be less likely to forget items. Or write your list according to categories: frozen foods, produce, meat, and dairy. Doing this can help you avoid the supermarket's favorite traps—impulse items—and it saves time, too. Grocery stores tend to have similar layouts, and there are a few tricks to getting the most out of your shopping time. Wheel your cart around the outside aisles first. You'll pass the fresh dairy products, fruits, vegetables, breads, meat, fish, and poultry. These foods are the ones that emphasize the Food Guide Pyramid. Fill your basket with these.

## Is it Fresh, Is it Safe, and Does it Taste Good?

Consumers report taste, quality, and safety as top factors when selecting where and what foods they buy. Of course taste is *the* number one consideration when shopping for food, but freshness and quality contribute to taste. With this in mind food developers are interested in convenience products that not only save you time but offer taste appeal and are of the highest quality. Ready-to-eat foods such as bagged salads, stir-fry meat/vegetable combinations, and deli salads must remain fresh and maintain quality. No matter where you shop or what you shop for, look for these basic qualities of excellence in a food store:

- The store (display cases, grocery shelves, floor) should be clean and neat. The store should have a pleasant smell.
- Produce, meat, poultry, fish, deli foods, and dairy foods should show qualities of freshness.
- Refrigerated cases should be cold, and freezer compartments should keep food solidly frozen.

## So That There's Always Something to Eat

Knowing the right foods and having them at your fingertips can make quick, healthy cooking almost effortless. Check your cupboards, freezer, and refrigerator in advance to avoid duplicating purchases. Keep your food storage areas neatly stocked with low-fat standbys. If you can find foods easily, it will speed up preparation time. And always make a list of items as you run out of them. The following lists are suggested foods that will keep a healthy variety of convenience foods on hand:

### In the pantry

- Canned or bottled fruit
- Canned or bottled vegetables
- Vegetable or fruit juices
- Pasta sauce
- Gravy
- Tomatoes: crushed, stewed, sauce
- Dry pasta
- Canned beans: chickpeas, black beans, black-eyed peas, baked beans
- Oil: olive oil and another vegetable oil, like corn or canola
- Vinegar: sweet-tart balsamic, cider, red wine, white wine vinegars
- Ketchup
- Soy sauce
- Salsa
- Coating mixes such as breadcrumbs, oatmeal
- Dried fruit: raisins, prunes, apricots
- Nuts: walnuts, peanuts, pecans
- Evaporated skim milk or powdered skim milk
- Canned or dried mushrooms
- Instant flavorings such as bouillon cubes or powder, granules and flavor packets
- Canned soup and stews
- Canned meats and seafood
- Cereal: hot and ready-to-eat
- Condiments
- Jam or jelly
- Tea, coffee
- Sugar-free or light syrups
- Dip mixes
- Pasta and rice mixes
- Bean and rice mixes
- Piecrust mixes
- Nonstick cooking sprays
- Low-fat or fat-free salad dressing

(continued)

- Packaged food such as 10-minute brown rice
- Crackers, low-fat cookies
- Worcestershire sauce
- Dijon mustard
- Relish

### In the refrigerator

- Fresh fruit including citrus
- Low-fat cheese: grated or sliced
- Butter, margarine, or other spread
- Vegetables: onions, garlic, potatoes, carrots, tomatoes, bagged salad
- Pickles
- Eggs, egg whites, egg substitutes
- Mayonnaise/salad dressing
- Low-fat or skim milk
- Low-fat plain or fruited yogurt
- Low-fat plain/fruited cottage cheese
- Low-fat pudding or tapioca
- Parmesan cheese
- Meat, poultry, fish, shellfish:
  - Fat-free or low-fat cold cuts, such as chicken breast, ham, bologna, or turkey breast
  - Ground meat and ground turkey

- Canadian bacon
- Boneless, skinless turkey/chicken breast
- Fish and shellfish
- Soft low-fat cheese: cottage cheese, ricotta and cream cheese
- Sour cream
- Tortillas

### In the freezer

- Bread: whole-grain bread, bagels, pita, English muffins
- Vegetables: green peas, mixed vegetables, corn, broccoli spears, asparagus
- Fruit: strawberries, raspberries, blueberries, peaches, cherries
- Frozen juice and juice drinks
- Frozen low-fat or fat-free yogurt
- Meat and poultry: hamburger or turkey patties, chicken pieces, boneless chicken breast
- Frozen pancakes and waffles
- Fat-free whipped topping
- Low-fat ready-to-heat dinners
- Phyllo or bread dough

- Follow the use-before/sell-by date available on products. "Sell by" tells you how long the grocer can safely sell the food (you can usually consider the food safe for another two to three days). "Use by" tells you how long the food remains safe to eat. "Best if used by" tells you how long the food looks and tastes best. If there are no dates, ask your grocer.
- Salad bars, bakery, and bulk bins, and other self-serve areas should be clean and properly covered.
- Look for evidence of safe, fresh foods in specific areas:
  - **Produce Department:** Look for a clean, organized department where fresh fruits and vegetables are held at a proper temperature. Most fruits and vegetables are kept chilled; lettuce and other greens are often sprayed with a fine mist of water to keep them crisp. Bruised or wilted fruits and vegetables suggest that they haven't been handled properly or that they are past their time. Bagged greens should be cleaned with use-by date available on the label.
  - **Meat/Poultry and Deli Case:** Recognize the qualities of fresh meat by its color. Beef is typically a bright red color, while young veal and pork are grayish pink. Fresh poultry should look creamy white to yellow and be free of bruises, tiny feathers, and torn or dry skin. Check the product dating and only buy fresh and processed meats that will still be fresh when you're ready to eat them. Or plan to freeze the food immediately for later use. Deli salads and salad bars must look fresh and be kept at the proper temperature. Ready-to-cook combination entrees at the meat counter (such as stir-fry meats and vegetables) must be stored at the proper temperature and handled with safe food handling techniques.
  - **Seafood:** Seafood should be displayed in clean display cases. Learn to recognize the qualities of fresh seafood. Use your nose when determining the freshness of fish. A strong, "fishy" odor is a sign that fish is no longer fresh.

Cooked seafood should not be displayed alongside raw seafood. Frozen seafood should be solidly frozen, mild in odor, and free of ice crystals and freezer burn.

- **Refrigerated Case:** Look for sell-by/use-by dates on dairy and eggs. Buy only refrigerated eggs and open the carton and examine the eggs for cracks before you buy. Avoid cartons with cracked eggs—they may be contaminated with salmonella.

- **Frozen Foods:** Purchase foods that are frozen solid and avoid foods with opened or damaged packages. Check for freezer burn or ice crystals.

- **Canned/Packaged Foods:** Inspect cans and packages for dents, damages, or opened containers. Look for use-by dates on packages.

- **Bakery Foods:** Check the product date on the package label for freshness. Packaged bakery products may have a longer shelf life than those baked in the in-store bakery.

- **Take-out Foods:** Many supermarket take-out foods are just as perishable as carryout from a restaurant and should be handled in the same way. For hot foods, make sure the food is hot when it's purchased and eaten within two hours. Hot foods need to be held above 140°F. If you don't plan to eat the food within two hours, be sure to refrigerate in a shallow, covered container. Then reheat it to 165°F, or until it's hot and steaming. Hot food can also be kept for two hours or less in the oven or crock-pot at 140°F or above. Cold foods need to be held at 40°F or below. Refrigerate any cold foods that are not eaten right away. Throw away *any* carry-out foods kept at room temperature for more than two hours.

## The Diabetes Smart Shopping Cart

When shopping, you juggle a number of variables in the decision-making process—including quality, convenience, nutrition, taste, presentation, and price. Your menus, shopping list and filled grocery cart should also be in the same proportion as the Food Guide Pyramid—bread, cereal, rice, and pasta should occupy the largest space and be the foundation on which the rest is built. Fruits and vegetables come next, with meat and dairy following. Fats, oils, and sugar are last on the list.

In a "Diabetes Smart Shopping Cart," let the actual shopping cart be your guide. Think of your grocery cart as having three separate parts. Fill the base, or the largest bin of your cart, with bread, cereal, rice, pasta, fruits, and vegetables. This will represent the foundation of your pyramid. Use the "seat," or front part, for low-fat dairy, meat, poultry, fish, beans, eggs, and nuts. This will be the smaller, middle portion of your pyramid. Finally, stash your carefully selected items from the "tip" of the pyramid in the lower part of your cart. This "sizing up" of your choices gives you a visible way to "fess up" to your eating habits.

## Smart Shopping Up and Down the Aisles

To shop "pyramid wise" follow these suggestions:

### Breads, cereals, rice, and pasta: Build from the base

Thick-sliced, thin-sliced, with sugar or without, whole-grain or white—the base of the pyramid has grown to be the most varied and confusing portion to shop for in the store. Shop carefully and keep these tips in mind:

- Look for wholegrain breads that list whole wheat, oats, or millet as the first ingredient. Note that rye and pumpernickel breads are not whole grain, even though their color may indicate otherwise.
- Baked goods should have 3 grams of fat or less per serving. Look for cereal with at least 3 grams of fiber per serving.

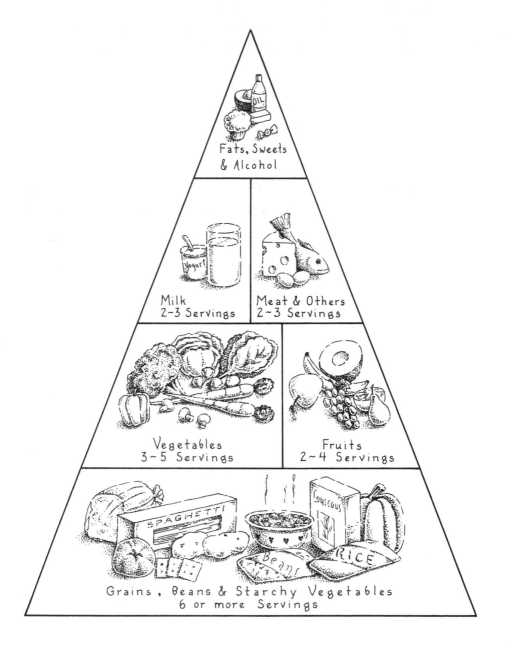

- In-store bakery items may not have nutrition facts labels. Refer to the ingredient lists for the type of flour and fat.
- Be aware of large muffins, scones, bagels, and biscuits. One serving may contain your carbohydrate goal for two meals! Split it with a friend or eat half and save the rest for later.
- When you read labels on packaged mixes, be sure to look at the "As prepared" column. Many mixes call for fats or eggs to be added in preparation.
- Brown rice has almost three times the fiber of white rice.

## Fruits and vegetables: Add solid footing

Eating more fruits and vegetables is the most common diet change consumers are saying they have made in the past years. There is no doubt that fruits and vegetables are important and will supply essential vitamins and minerals. But the fruits and vegetables you buy can make a big difference in how nutritious this section of the pyramid can be in your diet. Here's how to get more nutrition from the fruits and vegetables you choose:

- In general, the darker the color, the higher the nutrient content. Dark salad greens such as spinach, romaine, and watercress contain more nutrients than pale ones such as iceberg lettuce. Deep orange or red fruit, such as mangos, melon, and oranges, are richer in vitamins C and A than pears and bananas. However, pears are good sources of fiber and bananas are good sources of potassium.
- Buy fresh fruits and vegetables that are in season to get the best buy and best flavor. Unsweetened canned or frozen fruits are good substitutes.
- Fresh produce doesn't carry a nutrition facts label; look for nutrition information fliers or posters in the produce department for specifics. If there is no nutrition information for produce in your store, talk to your grocer about

providing some. Most produce is basically fat-free with the exception of avocado and coconut.

- Shop the salad bar when you need small amounts of ingredients and want to avoid buying large quantities.
- Bagged salad or salad kits that include dressing and garnishes can save time and energy. Substitute lower-fat salad dressing if desired.
- Dried fruits are a healthy, high-fiber snack food that can add variety and convenience. Keep in mind they are also concentrated sources of carbohydrate and calories, especially if they have added sugar.

### Dairy: To keep you sturdy

Dairy foods are good sources of bone-building calcium. Low-fat dairy products are among the best-tasting fat-reduced items in the supermarket, and they have all the calcium of the full-fat varieties. Here's what to look for:

- Buy low-fat (1% or 2%) or fat-free (skim) milk and buttermilk. Low-fat or fat-free milk is often fortified with non-fat milk protein to improve its texture.
- Buy low-fat or nonfat yogurt and cottage cheese.
- Buy low-fat cheeses that are labeled "part skim," "reduced fat," or "fat free."

### Meat, poultry, fish, dry beans, eggs, and nuts: Cut it down but not out

Meats and other protein foods are good sources of protein, B vitamins, iron, and zinc. Certain meats, poultry, and fish can also contribute significantly to your intake of saturated fat and cholesterol. Be careful of these pitfalls and shop smart instead.

- Read nutrition labels and familiarize yourself with the leanest cuts of the meat you enjoy. Here are some examples of lean cuts:

*Beef*: eye of round, top round steak, tenderloin steak, and chuck arm pot roast
*Veal*: cutlet, blade or arm steak, rib roast, and rib or loin chip
*Pork*: tenderloin, top loin roast, top loin chip, center loin chip, loin rib chip, and shoulder blade steak.
*Lamb*: leg, loin chip, arm chip, and fore shanks

- Choose leaner grades of meat and buy well-trimmed meat. "Select," "Choice," and "Prime" cuts of beef have the least marbled fat (thin streaks of fat between the muscle). Trim refers to the fat layer surrounding a steak or other cut of meat. Buy meat with 1/8-inch fat trim or less.
- Select whole cuts of meat rather than ground meat. Ground meat is a good place for the market to hide—and sell—fat. If you select ground meat, be sure that you get the leanest possible.
- Choose mostly lean varieties of turkey and chicken. Shop for skinless poultry and choose light meat as much as possible.
- Shop weekly meat sales with caution. The favorite sale items are usually the highest fat and saturated fat. Plus you're often paying for bone, skin, and lots of visible fat. Watch for good sales on skinless, boneless chicken breasts, lean cuts of beef, pork tenderloin, and boneless loin of pork.
- Use meat as a side dish that complements a meal of vegetables, grains, or legumes. Buy modest portions of meat; aim for individual servings of about 3 ounces.
- Choose beans and fish because they are more often lower in saturated fat.
- Look for weekly sales on fish and seafood. Salmon, tuna, and swordfish are particularly good sources of healthy omega-3 fatty acids.
- Buy water-packed tuna and sardines rather than those packed in oil.
- Buy fresh or frozen seafood without added breading or frying.

- Cold cuts should be the low-fat varieties. Turkey and chicken franks don't always have fewer calories than beef or pork; check the labels.

### Fats, oils and sweets: All pyramids have a tip

These foods add calories without contributing much in the way of other nutrients to your diet. Use them sparingly. But remember that when you plan carefully, you can make room for these foods.

- Keep an eye on visible fat, or the fat you can see. Visible fat is the fat you buy to add to your food. Oils, margarine, butter, salad dressing, and cream fall into this category.
- Use fats and oils low in saturated fat and trans fats.
- Watch out for invisible fat. Invisible fat is the fat hiding in your foods such as potato chips, bakery items, candy, and other sweets. Read labels to identify the type of added fat in your foods.
- Eat sweets in small portions and learn their effect on your blood glucose. Remember that high-sugar foods may also contain large amounts of fat and few vitamins and minerals.

# Reading Labels
# on Convenience Foods

*What Does All of This Mean?*

## Take a Look at Labels

In 1993, the Food and Drug Administration (FDA) and the U.S. Department of Agriculture (USDA) established extensive food labeling changes. It is now required that most foods list their ingredients and nutritional value per serving clearly and concisely on their packaging. These regulations also define the meaning of certain misleading terms that marketers love to use to entice you to buy their products.

Mastering the art of label scanning plays an important role in taking care of your diabetes. Knowing what you are eating helps you understand your blood glucose control and detect where food habit changes might be needed. The consumer-friendly food label is in a distinctive, easy-to-read format that enables you to quickly find the information you need to make good, healthy, personal food choices. To make sure you're eating right you need to read labels and take note of:

- ingredient lists
- Nutrition Facts
- nutrition descriptions
- health claims

By carefully studying these aspects, you can find out if the food is nutritionally sound, works with your health goals, and contains what you want.

## Run Each Item through Your "Nutrition Scanner"

Every time you buy groceries, you're investing in your family's long-term health. If you're responsible for food shopping in your house, you're making decisions and setting habits for all those under your roof by what you buy and bring home! If this sounds like serious business, it is! Each time you walk into a market you have hundreds of decisions to make. And yet the average shopper usually takes just seconds to consider what to buy.

Before you set foot in your supermarket reflect on your family's personal health goals and your buying patterns. Start with a "research trip" to the market when you can spend some time reviewing the products. Doing a little research during a quiet time at your usual store can help you shop just as quickly, but far more wisely. On your first tour of the market, get acquainted with food labels but don't buy a single thing. Just go aisle to aisle and examine your family's favorite items. Learn about Nutrition Facts, label lingo, ingredient listings, and health claims from this book. Then refine your "nutrition scanner" by using the healthy food selection guidelines listed below. Soon you will be answering these questions automatically as you make the best choices for your family.

### Nutrition Scanner: Healthy food selection guidelines

- Does the food fit with my health goals?
- Does the food satisfy one or more of my dietary goals?
- Will this food help me follow my meal plan or will it sabotage it?
- How often do I eat this food?

- Compared with similar products on the shelf, how does it stack up?
- Does it have more fat, salt, and sugar than other nutrients?

## Know Your Nutrition Facts

The Nutrition Facts panel gives specific information about calories and nutrients in a single serving of the food. You'll find these features on the Nutrition Facts label:

- **Serving size**. The serving size is the basis for reporting each food's nutrient content. In the past, the food manufacturer decided what made up a serving size. This is no longer true. They are now more uniform, but still may not reflect what you actually consider a serving. Serving sizes must be expressed in both common household terms and metric measures. Sometimes serving sizes differ only slightly. For example, one package of six bagels might have smaller bagels than another package of six bagels; however, both would say, "6 servings." Make sure that you look at the food label, as the nutrient information will be for the serving listed. (See box on page 30, *A Handy Trick*)
- **Calories**. This indicates the number of calories in a single serving and how many of these come from fat. This *does not* mean "percent of calories from fat." Percent of calories from fat does not appear on the label.
- **Daily Values**. These are nutrient reference values that help you see how a food fits into an overall daily diet. These numbers are set by the government and are based on a 2000-calorie diet. Values can also be given for an optional 2500-calorie diet. Keep in mind these values may not be your specific nutrient needs. The Daily Values for total fat, saturated fat, cholesterol, and sodium are the upper limits of how much to eat each day. Other Daily Values help you identify the best levels to aim for

## A Handy Trick

Sometimes, you'll find that ready-to-eat meals from your grocer's deli (as well as meals in a restaurant) will come without proper nutrition labeling. Many times, the ingredients will be listed, but serving sizes and other nutritional information won't. The following is a useful guide to determining serving sizes and the amounts of ingredients in unlabeled foods by using familiar objects for reference. It's not comprehensive, which means you probably won't be able to tell how much curry is in the prepared rice. But you can get an idea of how much beef you're getting with the steak.

**Thumb tip = 1 tsp**      *Example:* 1 tsp mayonnaise, salad dressing, or margarine

**Thumb = 1 oz**      *Example:* 1 oz cheese or meat

**Palm = 3 oz**      *Example:* 3 oz cooked meat (boneless)

**Tight fist = 1/2 cup**      *Example:* 1 serving noodles or rice, 1 serving canned fruit

**Loose fist = 1 cup**      *Example:* 1 cup vegetables

**Handful = 1 cup**      *Example:* 2 servings pasta, 2 servings cooked vegetable

*Note:* These guidelines hold true for most women's hands, but some men's hands are much larger and won't fit well into this scheme. This guide should also be limited to when you're eating out or when you don't have the option to measure your ingredients. When it comes to a healthy diet, serving size is very important. The more precise you are, the easier it is to properly regulate your diet.

each day. This applies to total carbohydrate, fiber, vitamins, and minerals.

- **Other nutrients**. The nutrients found on the Nutrition Facts panel are those that relate to today's most important health issues. Certain nutrients, such as fat, saturated fat, cholesterol, and sodium are included because people consume too much. Keep your intake at no more than 100% of your Daily Value for the day. Total fat includes all types of fat. Saturated fat and cholesterol are also listed because diets low in these nutrients may decrease the risk of heart disease. Trans fats are not listed separately, but are included in the total fat. Fat, saturated fat, cholesterol, total carbohydrate, fiber, sugars, protein, vitamins A and C, calcium, and iron are required on the label unless their amounts are insignificant. Other nutrients may be listed voluntarily.

### Foods without nutrition facts

Many fresh fruits and vegetables, as well as meat, poultry, and seafood, may be labeled voluntarily with nutrition information, too. Usually, this information is either on the package or on a poster or pamphlet displayed nearby. If you don't find this information in your supermarket, ask the supermarket manager to start providing it. Information about the nutrition content of these foods can also be obtained from resources such as the *The Diabetes Carbohydrate and Fat Gram Guide*, published by the American Diabetes Association.

## How Low is Low-Calorie?

### Deciphering nutrition descriptions

Table 4-1 lists the definitions of some common terms or nutritional key words that you may see on product packaging. If you're worried you'll never memorize all those numbers, don't worry; you don't have to. A little practice in

# Nutrition Facts

Serving Size 1 cup (228g)
Servings Per Container 2

**Amount Per Serving**

**Calories** 260  Calories from Fat 120

|  | % Daily Value* |
|---|---|
| **Total Fat** 13g | **20**% |
| Saturated Fat 5g | **25**% |
| **Cholesterol** 30mg | **10**% |
| **Sodium** 660mg | **28**% |
| **Total Carbohydrate** 31g | **10**% |
| Dietary Fiber 0g | **0**% |
| Sugars 5g | |
| **Protein** 5g | |

| | | |
|---|---|---|
| Vitamin A 4% | • | Vitamin C 2% |
| Calcium 15% | • | Iron 4% |

* Percent Daily Values are based on a 2,000
calorie diet. Your daily values may be higher
or lower depending on your calorie needs:

|  | Calories: | 2,000 | 2,500 |
|---|---|---|---|
| Total Fat | Less than | 65g | 80g |
| Sat Fat | Less than | 20g | 25g |
| Cholesterol | Less than | 300mg | 300mg |
| Sodium | Less than | 2,400mg | 2,400mg |
| Total Carbohydrate | | 300g | 375g |
| Dietary Fiber | | 25g | 30g |

Calories per gram:
Fat 9 • Carbohydrate 4 • Protein 4

scanning labels and actually noticing what you're buying
will help you automatically select more healthy foods.

## What is This Stuff?

### Reading the ingredients

Ingredient statements are on every package, can, or frozen
food, and they tell you what's actually included in the food

## TABLE 4-1 Definitions of Key Words on Food Labels

| Key Words | What They Mean |
|---|---|
| Calorie-free | Less than 5 calories per serving |
| Cholesterol-free | Less than 2 milligrams per serving and 2 grams or less of saturated fat per serving |
| Extra-lean | Less than 5 grams of fat, 2 grams of saturated fat, and 95 milligrams of cholesterol per serving |
| Fat-free | Less than 0.5 gram of fat per serving |
| Lean | Less than 10 grams of fat, 4 grams of saturated fat, and 95 milligrams of cholesterol per serving |
| Light or lite | 33% fewer calories, 50% less sodium, 50% less fat (all compared to the regular full-calorie, full-sodium, or full-fat product) |
| Low calorie | 40 calories or less per serving |
| Low-cholesterol | 20 milligrams or less of cholesterol per serving and 2 grams or less of saturated fat per serving |
| Low-fat | 3 grams (or less) of fat per serving |
| Low-saturated fat | 1 gram or less of saturated fat per serving and 15% or less of calories from saturated fat |
| Low-sodium | 140 milligrams per serving, with no sodium chloride |
| Reduced | 25% less per serving than comparison product |
| Saturated fat-free | Less than 0.5 grams of saturated fat per serving |
| Sodium-free | Less than 5 milligrams of sodium per serving |
| Sugar-free | Less than 0.5 milligrams of sugar per serving |
| High-fiber | 5 grams (or more) of fiber per serving |

you are eating. The ingredients on labels are listed according to amount by weight, starting with the heaviest and moving down to the lightest, so that you know relatively how much of one ingredient or another product it contains (although no exact amounts are given). For example, a certain multi-grain bread lists several types of flour in the ingredient listing and puts them in the following order—oat flour, wheat flour, and whole-wheat flour. From this listing all you can tell is that oat flour is the ingredient contributing the most weight. Unfortunately, you can't tell how much oat flour there is compared to the other types of flour.

The ingredient list, like a recipe, tells you what is in the food. This can be particularly useful for people with special food needs such as food allergies or food sensitivities. For people with diabetes it may be useful to know the type of sugar or sweetener and the type of fat or fat substitute in a product.

### Sugars and intense sweeteners

Sugar is a source of carbohydrate that can appear naturally in foods or be added to foods. Natural sugars are found in fruits, vegetables, and milk. Besides carbohydrate, these foods also give you vitamins and minerals. Added sugar comes in many forms, including:

- brown sugar
- confectioner's sugar
- corn syrup
- dextrin
- fruit juice concentrate
- honey
- invert sugar
- maple syrup
- raw sugar
- cane sugar
- corn sweeteners
- crystallized cane sugar
- evaporated cane juice

- high-fructose corn syrup
- malt
- molasses
- turbinado sugar

Added sugars are sources of carbohydrate and calories but rarely offer other valuable nutrients. As sources of carbohydrate, they, along with natural sugars, raise blood glucose similar to foods such as pasta, cereal, and bread.

Sugar alcohols such as sorbitol, mannitol, hydrogenated starch hydrolysate, and xylitol are ingredients used to add sweet flavors and texture to food. For some people, sugar alcohols have a laxative effect when they're consumed in large amounts; but that's about the only benefit. For people with diabetes there is no advantage to using sugar alcohols in place of sugar.

For individuals trying to be calorie or sugar conscious, intense sweeteners deliver sweet taste with just a fraction of the calories. Intense sweeteners also are known by other names, including:

- non-nutritive sweeteners
- sugar substitutes
- very-low-calorie sweeteners
- alternative sweeteners

All four of the intense sweeteners below meet the FDA guidelines for safety standards. These sweeteners may be identified using the following brand names:

| Sweetener | Other names |
| --- | --- |
| Saccharin | Sweet 'n Low |
| Aspartame | Nutrasweet, Equal |
| Acesulfame-K | Sunette, Sweet One |
| Sucralose | Splenda |

## Fat and fat substitutes

Fat contributes desirable flavors to foods and gives them a "rich" taste. But fat is also high in calories, and some fats (saturated in particular) can clog your arteries. Fat can be added to convenience foods in the form of oil, lard, and butter, but it also comes "attached" in certain foods, such as meat, poultry, and dairy foods. Foods that contain added fat from sour cream, cheese, mayonnaise, and salad dressing can be "reduced in fat" by the use of fat substitutes or by simply adding smaller amounts of the added fat ingredients. You can also make foods at home "reduced in fat" by removing skin or by the cooking method you select.

Check the ingredient listing for sources of saturated fat. Some sources include:

- tropical oils (coconut oil, palm oil, and palm kernel oil)
- butter lard
- shortening
- animal fats (beef, pork, and chicken)
- mono and diglycerides
- tallow
- hydrogenated oils
- shortenings

Locate where in the ingredient list these fats appear to determine how much is used in relation to the other ingredients. Also, refer to the Nutrition Facts panel for the saturated fat content in grams.

When "attached" fat has been removed, a fat substitute may be used to give the food a familiar texture, appearance, and taste. Removing some or all of the fat from a food often results in a product lower in calories, fat, saturated fat, and cholesterol. Unfortunately, this can also dramatically affect the taste of the food. To combat this, food manufacturers use different types of fat replacers to give the food a more familiar flavor. Fat replacers come in three varieties; carbohydrate-based, protein-based, and fat-based. Most types of fat

## TABLE 4-2  Fat Replacers

| Protein-based | Fat-based | Carbohydrate-based |
|---|---|---|
| Simplesse | caprenin | modified starches |
| K-Blazer | olestra (Olean) | dextrins |
| Whey protein concentrate | salatrim (Benefat) | polydextrose<br>cellulose gum<br>corn syrup solids<br>maltodextrin<br>hydrogenated starch hydrolysate<br>carrageenan<br>guar gum<br>pectin |

replacers contribute calories, but often less than if fat was used. But be careful; carbohydrate-based fat replacers can still raise your blood glucose. Some examples of fat replacers you will find on ingredient listings and their sources are listed in Table 4-2.

# Can this Food Actually Help Me?

## *Considering health claims*

In addition to ingredients and Nutrition Facts, a product label might include additional nutrition information called a health claim. A health claim describes the potential health benefit of a food or nutrient, such as fat intake and reduced cancer risk. They also link food in your overall diet with a lowered risk for some chronic diseases. Due to restrictions, only claims that are supported by scientific evidence are allowed on food labels. However, some foods that meet the criteria don't always carry a health claim. Currently, there are no health claims that link certain foods or nutrients with diabetes. Also keep in mind that diet is just one factor that can reduce your risk for certain health problems. Heredity, physical activity, and smoking are among other factors that affect your health and risk for disease.

When making a specific health claim, the food must also meet specific standards. Twelve health claims are allowed on labels. These are:

- **Calcium** may be linked to a reduced risk for osteoporosis.
- **Fiber-containing grain products, fruits, and vegetables** may be linked to a reduced risk for cancer.
- **Fruits and vegetables** that are low in fat and good sources of dietary fiber, vitamin A, or vitamin C, may help prevent some cancers.
- **Fruits, vegetables, and grain products** that contain fiber, especially soluble fiber, may be linked to a reduced risk of coronary heart disease.
- **Reduced fat** may be linked to a reduced risk of some types of cancer.
- **Reduced saturated fat and cholesterol** intake may be linked to a reduced risk for heart disease.
- **Reduced sodium** intake may help prevent hypertension, which is a risk factor for heart attacks and strokes.
- **Folic acid** intake of 0.4 milligrams per day reduces the risk of certain birth defects.
- **Reduced intake of foods high in sugars and starches** may reduce the risk of tooth decay.
- **Soluble fiber intake from whole oats and/or psyllium seed husk** of 3 grams per day, coupled with diets low in saturated fat and cholesterol, may reduce the risk of heart disease.
- **Soy protein intake** of 25 grams per day, coupled with diets low in saturated fat and cholesterol, may reduce the risk of heart disease.
- **A daily intake of at least 3.4 grams of plant stanol esters,** coupled with a diet low in saturated fat and cholesterol, may reduce the risk of heart disease.

# Turning Convenience Foods into Meals

*Easy in the Kitchen,*
*Easy Out of the Kitchen*

## Making the Most of Convenience Solutions

Convenience foods can be used in a variety of ways to speed up meal preparation so that you're not laboring over sauce or trying to figure out which spices to use. It's already done! Convenience foods can be a complete meal or meal solutions, ready to heat, or ingredient solutions that can be combined with other foods to save time. Some ingredient solutions, such as bacon bits and quick-cooking cereal, have been in markets so long they are not even thought of as convenience foods. However, they do take steps out of your preparation and save time. Keep the following ingredient solutions on hand for quick and easy food preparation.

| Ingredient solutions . . . | to use with . . . |
| --- | --- |
| Bacon bits | flavor salads, soups, vegetables |
| Bread dough | rolls, bread, sweet rolls, pocket sandwiches, pizza crust |

| | |
|---|---|
| Biscuit dough | dumplings and biscuits |
| Chopped fresh vegetables | salads, soups, sauces, pizza |
| Grated/shredded cheese | salads, tacos |
| Shredded cabbage, lettuce, carrots | salads, Mexican dishes, casseroles |
| Cut/cubed melons | desserts, salads |
| Bread cubes/crumbs | meat coatings, stuffing |
| Pastry crust | pie, cobbler, turnovers, entrée pies |
| Baking crumbs | casseroles, meat dishes |
| Pastry crust | pie, cobbler, turnovers, entrée pies |
| Baking crumbs | casseroles, meat dishes |
| Fully cooked and refrigerated meats/poultry | salads, burritos, tacos, casseroles, stir-fry |
| Canned chicken and turkey | salads, soups, stews |
| Canned seafood (tuna, crab, salmon, sardines) | dips, appetizers, salads, casseroles |
| Bottled or canned pasta sauce | pasta, pizza, appetizers |
| Meal mixes | stir-fry, casseroles |
| Seasoning packets | gravy, sauces, dips, salad dressing |

| | |
|---|---|
| Liquid egg substitutes | breakfast burritos, dessert recipes |
| Sun-dried vegetables | dips, sauces, casseroles, soups |
| Soup mixes | dips, salad dressing, marinades |
| Canned soups | casseroles, gravy, sauces |
| Canned beans | soups, salads, cooked dishes |
| Whipped topping or whipped dessert toppings | pies, desserts |
| Dessert/ice cream topping | ice cream, dessert, milk beverages |
| Dried fruit | muffins, breads, desserts |
| Canned sauces/salsa | marinates, gravy, dips |

### Enhancing your fast food

Convenience foods have their own taste appeal but it may not be yours. Often, these foods have with seasoning packets or ingredients you may choose not to use. Add your own fresh ingredients and maybe some of your own fresh or dried herbs and spices. If it's pasta alfredo, add fat-free skim milk, fat-free half-and-half, or nondairy creamer, plus fresh peas, mushrooms, and diced tomatoes. The high fat cream sauce is diluted without becoming thin, you get more fiber, it goes further, and it tastes better. Convenience foods may also contain high amounts of sodium. Read labels and compare the sodium content. Adding fresh, frozen, or canned low-sodium vegetables and maybe even your own cooked rice, barley, pasta, or canned, drained, and rinsed beans dilutes the salt. Fresh vegetables also add flavor and fiber. Consider these ideas to enhance convenience foods:

| To enhance . . . | add . . . |
|---|---|
| Bean dip | mashed canned beans, finely chopped onions, hot sauce, cilantro leaves, chopped black olives |
| Crab, salmon, or clam dip | additional fresh-cooked crab, salmon, clams, lemon juice, finely chopped chives or onions |
| Hummus dip | additional well-mashed garbanzo beans, lemon juice, minced garlic, chopped onions |
| Vegetable sour cream dip | additional vegetables such as chopped celery, onions, chives, peppers |
| Bagged salad | salad bar offerings such as baby corn, beets, carrots, canned beans (kidney, garbanzo, navy, red), dried fruit, lean meats, reduced-fat cheese, mushrooms, pickles, radishes, water chestnuts, tomatoes, peas, olives, onions, scallions, chives, nuts, other greens |
| Salad dressing | fresh garlic, Worcestershire, lemon juice, Parmesan cheese, vinegar (wine cider, balsamic), basil, oregano, tarragon, fresh parsley, finely chopped onions, shallots, leeks, raspberries, dill, chives, sage, thyme |

| | |
|---|---|
| Canned cream soups | fresh chopped vegetables |
| Canned broth-based soups | frozen vegetables or dinner mixes (mixed foods, not TV dinners), cooked rice or pasta, canned beans, cooked diced potatoes |
| Packaged soup mixes | fresh vegetables and cooked meat |
| Carrots, parsnips, turnips | citrus juice, vegetable broth, meat stock, ginger, onions, garlic |
| Sweet potatoes or yams | apricot juice, orange juice, cinnamon, nutmeg, Cajun spice blend, curry powder, Chinese five-spice powder |
| Baked potatoes | chili, reduced-fat or fat-free gravy, broccoli or cauliflower, low-fat or fat-free cream of mushroom soup, ready-to-eat sandwich toppings |
| Deli or packaged grilled chicken/turkey strips | chicken salad with chopped onions, celery, and mayonnaise or salad dressing: Serve cold, layer in strips over a lettuce salad or heated for a fast stir-fry, diced for a sauce, or warm to top rice or pasta. |
| Lean ham | Use with scrambled eggs, pancakes, quick soups, such as canned pea or bean, lettuce salads, potato salads, baked scalloped potatoes, and |

| | steamed broccoli or Brussels sprouts, cauliflower or green beans. Use as garnish to mashed or baked potatoes. |
|---|---|
| Canned/bottled sauces | garlic, onions, peppers, mushrooms, dried tomatoes, fresh tomatoes, carrots, parsley, chives, dried fruits, oregano, tarragon, sweet basil, lean meat or poultry, seafood |
| Cream-based sauces | Extend with skim milk, dry skim milk powder, fat-free nondairy creamers, fat-free half-and-half, a variety of low-fat and fat-free cheeses, sautéed vegetables, and mushrooms. |
| Pesto | Extend with chicken broth. |
| Lunch kits | side salad, fresh fruit |
| Pocket sandwich | fresh vegetables, salsa |
| Frozen pizza | fresh chopped vegetables or canned fruits |

## Convenience Food Check-up

We know convenience foods can be real timesavers while offering ease in the kitchen. But these foods must also provide nutritional variety and flavor. To evaluate how these foods benefit your eating plan and schedule, ask yourself these three questions:

- Did you use the food as an ingredient or meal solution?

- Did the food help you save time in food purchasing, planning, assembling, serving, and cleanup?
- When you used the convenience food did you satisfy your health and nutrition goals?

By keeping these questions in mind, you can ensure that you'll use convenience foods to effectively and nutritiously provide delicious meals for you and your family.

# One Week of Sample Menus
## *Convenience at Its Best*

To help you in your quest for convenience and ease in the kitchen, the following section contains seven days of sample menus using foods discussed in this book. The focus was to use foods that required as little preparation as possible. Most of the meals are assembly only, though some may require heating or combining.

The nutrition facts and exchange values for each meal have been listed so that you can determine how these foods fit into your eating plan. Everyone with diabetes has individual nutrition goals; therefore, you will find a range in the nutrition content of each meal. A Pyramid checklist indicates the food groups found in each meal. To provide a well-rounded meal, three or more food groups are found in each sample menu. The serving size listed in the sample menus may not be the serving size found in the food table (in this book) or on the food label. Be sure to refer to the serving size you are eating and compare with the nutrient values found in the food table or on the food label.

If your meal plan indicates different nutritional needs than those found in the sample meals, simply take off or add to the sample menus to satisfy your goals. You can also refer to the food tables in this book for alternative food choices. It may mean simply reducing or doubling the serving size. Some meals may seem high or low in certain nutrients, but remember; when combined with other meals throughout the day they'll work to satisfy your nutrition goals. Selecting an alternative product in the same food category may also help you meet your meal plan. For example, a meal may be higher in sodium than your nutrition goals. To correct this, you could select an alternate brand or variety of the same type of food.

## BREAKFAST MENUS

The following breakfast menus contain between 300–500 calories.

### Pancakes and Eggs

### Food Exchanges

| | |
|---|---|
| Fleishmann's Vegetable Omelet Egg Beaters (1/2 cup) | 1 very lean meat |
| Aunt Jemima Low Fat Microwave Pancakes (3) | 2 starch |
| Unsweetened Applesauce (1/2 cup) | 1 fruit |
| 1% Low-fat milk (1 cup) | 1 skim milk |

| Nutrition Facts | | Pyramid Checklist | |
|---|---|---|---|
| Calories | 354 | Grains | ■ |
| Fat (g) | 5 | Fruits | ■ |
| % Calories Fat | 15 | Vegetables | |
| Saturated Fat (g) | 2 | Dairy | ■ |
| Cholesterol (mg) | 15 | Meat & Meat Substitute | ■ |
| Sodium (mg) | 825 | Fats, Sweets, Oils | |
| Protein (g) | 20 | | |
| Fiber (g) | 10 | | |
| Carbohydrate (g) | 61 | | |
| Carbohydrate Choices | 4 | | |

## Fruit Shake and Toast

|  | **Food Exchanges** |
|---|---|
| No Sugar Added Vanilla Carnation Instant Breakfast (1 pkt). | 1 skim milk |
| Unsweetened Frozen Strawberries (2/3 cup) | 1 fruit |
| 1% Low-fat milk (1 cup) | 1 skim milk |
| Pepperidge Farm Light Style Oatmeal Bread, Toasted (1 slice) | 1/2 starch |
| Shedd's Spread Tub Margarine Spread (2 tsp) | 1 fat |

| Nutrition Facts | |
|---|---|
| Calories | 309 |
| Fat (g) | 10 |
| % Calories Fat | 29 |
| Saturated Fat (g) | 4 |
| Cholesterol (mg) | 15 |
| Sodium (mg) | 399 |
| Protein (g) | 16 |
| Fiber (g) | 4 |
| Carbohydrate (g) | 46 |
| Carbohydrate Choices | 3 |

| Pyramid Checklist | |
|---|---|
| Grains | ■ |
| Fruits | ■ |
| Vegetables | |
| Dairy | ■ |
| Meat & Meat Substitute | |
| Fats, Sweets, Oils | ■ |

## Cranberry Orange Scone and
## Pineapple Fruit Bowl

**Food Exchanges**

Health Valley Fat-Free Cranberry
Orange Scone (2)

2 starch

Dole Pineapple Fruit Bowls (1)

1 fruit

Fleishmann's Lightly Salted Whipped
Margarine (1 Tbsp)

1 fat

1% Low-fat Milk (1 cup)

1 milk

| Nutrition Facts | |
|---|---|
| Calories | 392 |
| Fat (g) | 10 |
| % Calories Fat | 23 |
| Saturated Fat (g) | 4 |
| Cholesterol (mg) | 10 |
| Sodium (mg) | 513 |
| Protein (g) | 15 |
| Fiber (g) | 15 |
| Carbohydrate (g) | 58 |
| Carbohydrate Choices | 4 |

| Pyramid Checklist | |
|---|---|
| Grains | ■ |
| Fruits | ■ |
| Vegetables | |
| Dairy | ■ |
| Meat & Meat Substitute | |
| Fats, Sweets, Oils | ■ |

# Breakfast Burrito with Fresh Melon

Swanson Burrito with Bacon &
    Scrambled Eggs (3.5 oz)
Fresh Honeydew Melon (1 cup)
1% Low-Fat Milk (1 cup)

# Food Exchanges

2 carb, 1 med-fat
    meat, 1 fat
1 fruit
1 skim milk

| Nutrition Facts | |
| --- | --- |
| Calories | 411 |
| Fat (g) | 14 |
| % Calories Fat | 31 |
| Saturated Fat (g) | 6 |
| Cholesterol (mg) | 100 |
| Sodium (mg) | 678 |
| Protein (g) | 18 |
| Fiber (g) | 3 |
| Carbohydrate (g) | 55 |
| Carbohydrate Choices | 3 1/2 |

| Pyramid Checklist | |
| --- | --- |
| Grains | ■ |
| Fruits | ■ |
| Vegetables | |
| Dairy | ■ |
| Meat & Meat Substitute | ■ |
| Fats, Sweets, Oils | |

# Hearty Oatmeal with Fresh Fruit     Food Exchanges

Quaker Quick 'N Hearty Microwave         1 starch
  Oatmeal (1 pkt)
Promise Vegetable Oil Spread (1 Tbsp)    2 fat
1% Low-fat Milk (1 cup)                  1 skim milk
Small Banana (1)                         1 fruit

| Nutrition Facts | |
|---|---|
| Calories | 366 |
| Fat (g) | 14 |
| % Calories Fat | 34 |
| Saturated Fat (g) | 4 |
| Cholesterol (mg) | 10 |
| Sodium (mg) | 319 |
| Protein (g) | 12 |
| Fiber (g) | 4 |
| Carbohydrate (g) | 47 |
| Carbohydrate Choices | 3 |

| Pyramid Checklist | |
|---|---|
| Grains | ■ |
| Fruits | ■ |
| Vegetables | |
| Dairy | ■ |
| Meat & Meat Substitute | |
| Fats, Sweets, Oils | ■ |

# Blueberry Waffles and Turkey Sausage

## Food Exchanges

| | |
|---|---|
| Kellogg's Low-fat Nutrigrain Blueberry Waffles (1) | 1 starch |
| Lite Pancake Syrup (2 Tbsp) | 1 carb |
| Promise Vegetable Oil Spread (2 tsp) | 1 fat |
| Blueberries, Frozen, Thawed (3/4 cup) | 1 fruit |
| Louis Rich Turkey Sausage Links (2) | 2 lean meat |

| Nutrition Facts | |
|---|---|
| Calories | 365 |
| Fat (g) | 14 |
| % Calories Fat | 35 |
| Saturated Fat (g) | 7 |
| Cholesterol (mg) | 35 |
| Sodium (mg) | 745 |
| Protein (g) | 14 |
| Fiber (g) | 6 |
| Carbohydrate (g) | 49 |
| Carbohydrate Choices | 3 |

| Pyramid Checklist | |
|---|---|
| Grains | ■ |
| Fruits | ■ |
| Vegetables | |
| Dairy | |
| Meat & Meat Substitute | ■ |
| Fats, Sweets, Oils | ■ |

# Cinnamon Bagel with Fruited Yogurt

## Food Exchanges

| | |
|---|---|
| Lender's Cinnamon Swirl Bagel (1) | 2 starch |
| Kraft Philadelphia Light Soft Strawberry Cream Cheese (2 Tbsp) | 1 fat |
| Yoplait Fruited Yogurt (6 oz) | 1 skim milk |
| Grapefruit Sections (1/2 cup) | 1 fruit |

| Nutrition Facts | |
|---|---|
| Calories | 360 |
| Fat (g) | 6 |
| % Calories Fat | 15 |
| Saturated Fat (g) | 4 |
| Cholesterol (mg) | 20 |
| Sodium (mg) | 495 |
| Protein (g) | 14 |
| Fiber (g) | 3 |
| Carbohydrate (g) | 62 |
| Carbohydrate Choices | 4 |

| Pyramid Checklist | |
|---|---|
| Grains | ■ |
| Fruits | ■ |
| Vegetables | |
| Dairy | ■ |
| Meat & Meat Substitute | |
| Fats, Sweets, Oils | ■ |

## LUNCH MENUS

The following lunch menus contain between 300–500 calories.

### Cheddar Baked Potato with Cottage Cheese

### Food Exchanges

Lean Cuisine Cheddar Potato (10.4 oz)  —  2 1/2 carb, 1 med-fat meat

Knudson On the Go! 2% Cottage Cheese (4 oz)  —  2 very lean meat

Fresh Apple (small)  —  1 fruit

Campbell's V-8 Light Tangy 100% Vegetable Juice (8 oz)  —  2 vegetables

| Nutrition Facts | |
|---|---|
| Calories | 483 |
| Fat (g) | 9 |
| % Calories Fat | 17 |
| Saturated Fat (g) | 6 |
| Cholesterol (mg) | 35 |
| Sodium (mg) | 1300 |
| Protein (g) | 27 |
| Fiber (g) | 10 |
| Carbohydrate (g) | 72 |
| Carbohydrate Choices | 5 |

| Pyramid Checklist | |
|---|---|
| Grains | |
| Fruits | ■ |
| Vegetables | ■ |
| Dairy | ■ |
| Meat & Meat Substitute | ■ |
| Fats, Sweets, Oils | |

# Hot Beef Sandwich with Mixed Fruit

# Food Exchanges

| | |
|---|---|
| Banquet Gravy & Sliced Beef Sandwich Toppers (2 4-oz pkg) | 1/2 carb, 2 lean meat |
| Pepperidge Farm Multi-Grain Sandwich Bun (1) | 1 1/2 starch, 1 fat |
| Del Monte Fruit-to-Go Fruit Combo (4 oz) | 1 fruit |
| 1% Low-fat Milk (1 cup) | 1 skim milk |

| Nutrition Facts | |
|---|---|
| Calories | 462 |
| Fat (g) | 10 |
| % Calories Fat | 19 |
| Saturated Fat (g) | 5 |
| Cholesterol (mg) | 60 |
| Sodium (mg) | 1243 |
| Protein (g) | 30 |
| Fiber (g) | 4 |
| Carbohydrate (g) | 64 |
| Carbohydrate Choices | 4 |

| Pyramid Checklist | |
|---|---|
| Grains | ■ |
| Fruits | ■ |
| Vegetables | |
| Dairy | ■ |
| Meat & Meat Substitute | ■ |
| Fats, Sweets, Oils | |

## Chicken Parmesan Pocket with a Fresh Pear

### Food Exchanges

Chef American Lean Pocket,
Chicken Parmesan (4.6 oz)

3 carb, 1 med-fat meat

Large Fresh Pear (1)

2 fruit

| Nutrition Facts | |
|---|---|
| Calories | 398 |
| Fat (g) | 7 |
| % Calories Fat | 16 |
| Saturated Fat (g) | 3 |
| Cholesterol (mg) | 25 |
| Sodium (mg) | 490 |
| Protein (g) | 15 |
| Fiber (g) | 7 |
| Carbohydrate (g) | 71 |
| Carbohydrate Choices | 5 |

| Pyramid Checklist | |
|---|---|
| Grains | ■ |
| Fruits | ■ |
| Vegetables | |
| Dairy | ■ |
| Meat & Meat Substitute | ■ |
| Fats, Sweets, Oils | |

## Cottage Doubles with Triscuit Thin Crisps

## Food Exchanges

| | |
|---|---|
| Knudson Cottage Cheese Doubles (1) | 1 fruit, 1 lean meat |
| Triscuit Thin Crisps (30) | 3 starch, 2 fat |
| 1% Low-fat Milk (1 cup) | 1 skim milk |

| Nutrition Facts | |
|---|---|
| Calories | 502 |
| Fat (g) | 16 |
| % Calories Fat | 29 |
| Saturated Fat (g) | 6 |
| Cholesterol (mg) | 25 |
| Sodium (mg) | 853 |
| Protein (g) | 26 |
| Fiber (g) | 7 |
| Carbohydrate (g) | 71 |
| Carbohydrate Choices | 5 |

| Pyramid Checklist | |
|---|---|
| Grains | ■ |
| Fruits | ■ |
| Vegetables | |
| Dairy | ■ |
| Meat & Meat Substitute | ■ |
| Fats, Sweets, Oils | |

## Black Bean Soup with Fruit Bowl     Food Exchanges

Nile Spice Single-Serving Black                2 1/2 carb
    Bean Soup (1 cup)
Zesta Unsalted Crackers (5)                    1/2 starch
Dole Diced Peaches Fruit Bowl (4 oz)           1 fruit

| Nutrition Facts | |
|---|---|
| Calories | 310 |
| Fat (g) | 4 |
| % Calories Fat | 12 |
| Saturated Fat (g) | <1 |
| Cholesterol (mg) | 0 |
| Sodium (mg) | 745 |
| Protein (g) | 13 |
| Fiber (g) | 14 |
| Carbohydrate (g) | 60 |
| Carbohydrate Choices | 4 |

| Pyramid Checklist | |
|---|---|
| Grains | ■ |
| Fruits | ■ |
| Vegetables | |
| Dairy | |
| Meat & Meat Substitute | ■ |
| Fats, Sweets, Oils | |

## Teriyaki Chicken Salad with Mini Bagels

Fresh Express Teriyaki Chicken
Lunch Salad (1 pkg)
Sara Lee Sun Dried Tomato &
Basil Bagel (1)
Philadelphia Light Soft Cream
Cheese (1 Tbsp)

## Food Exchanges

3 vegetable, 1 med-fat
meat, 2 fat
2 starch

1 fat

| Nutrition Facts | |
|---|---|
| Calories | 425 |
| Fat (g) | 19 |
| % Calories Fat | 40 |
| Saturated Fat (g) | 5 |
| Cholesterol (mg) | 33 |
| Sodium (mg) | 1135 |
| Protein (g) | 19 |
| Fiber (g) | 3 |
| Carbohydrate (g) | 48 |
| Carbohydrate Choices | 3 |

| Pyramid Checklist | |
|---|---|
| Grains | ■ |
| Fruits | |
| Vegetables | ■ |
| Dairy | |
| Meat & Meat Substitute | ■ |
| Fats, Sweets, Oils | ■ |

# Albacore Tuna on Crackers with Fruited Yogurt

## Food Exchanges

| | |
|---|---|
| Star Kist Solid White Albacore Tuna in Water (2.8 oz can) | 3 very lean meat |
| Nabisco Sociable Crackers (14) | 1 starch, 2 fat |
| Yoplait Original 99% Fat-Free Fruited Yogurt (6 oz) | 1 skim milk, 1 carb |
| Fresh Baby Carrots (1 cup) | 2 vegetables |

| Nutrition Facts | |
|---|---|
| Calories | 477 |
| Fat (g) | 11 |
| % Calories Fat | 21 |
| Saturated Fat (g) | 2 |
| Cholesterol (mg) | 45 |
| Sodium (mg) | 768 |
| Protein (g) | 29 |
| Fiber (g) | 3 |
| Carbohydrate (g) | 62 |
| Carbohydrate Choices | 4 |

| Pyramid Checklist | |
|---|---|
| Grains | ■ |
| Fruits | |
| Vegetables | ■ |
| Dairy | ■ |
| Meat & Meat Substitute | ■ |
| Fats, Sweets, Oils | |

# DINNER MENUS

The following dinner menus contain between 500–800 calories.

## Breaded Fish Fillets with Baked Beans and Coleslaw

## Food Exchanges

Van De Kamp's Breaded Garlic & Herb, Crispy & Healthy Fillets (4)  —  3 carb, 2 lean meat

B&M 99% Fat-Free Vegetarian Baked Beans (1/2 cup)  —  2 starch

Fresh Express Coleslaw Kit (2 cups)  —  2 vegetables, 2 fat

| Nutrition Facts | |
|---|---|
| Calories | 630 |
| Fat (g) | 15 |
| % Calories Fat | 21 |
| Saturated Fat (g) | 2 |
| Cholesterol (mg) | 55 |
| Sodium (mg) | 1256 |
| Protein (g) | 31 |
| Fiber (g) | 9 |
| Carbohydrate (g) | 93 |
| Carbohydrate Choices | 6 |

| Pyramid Checklist | |
|---|---|
| Grains | ■ |
| Fruits | |
| Vegetables | ■ |
| Dairy | |
| Meat & Meat Substitute | ■ |
| Fats, Sweets, Oils | |

## Chicken & Herb Rice with Steamed Broccoli

### Food Exchanges

| | |
|---|---|
| Betty Crocker Chicken Helper, Chicken & Herb Rice (1 cup) | 2 carb, 2 lean meat |
| Frozen Broccoli Spears, Cooked (1 cup) | 2 vegetables |
| Pepperidge Farm Heat & Serve Butter Crescent Rolls (1) | 1 starch, 1 fat |
| Breyer's Premium Vanilla Light Ice Cream (1/2 cup) | 1 carb, 1 fat |

| Nutrition Facts | |
|---|---|
| Calories | 542 |
| Fat (g) | 17 |
| % Calories Fat | 28 |
| Saturated Fat (g) | 7 |
| Cholesterol (mg) | 85 |
| Sodium (mg) | 754 |
| Protein (g) | 36 |
| Fiber (g) | 8 |
| Carbohydrate (g) | 67 |
| Carbohydrate Choices | 4 1/2 |

| Pyramid Checklist | |
|---|---|
| Grains | ■ |
| Fruits | |
| Vegetables | ■ |
| Dairy | ■ |
| Meat & Meat Substitute | ■ |
| Fats, Sweets, Oils | ■ |

## Teriyaki Stir-Fry with Brown Rice

## Food Exchanges

| | |
|---|---|
| Green Giant Create-A-Meal Teriyaki Stir-Fry Vegetables (1 3/4 cups) | 4 vegetables, 3 lean meats |
| Uncle Ben's Instant Whole Grain Brown Rice (1/2 cup) | 1 1/2 starch |
| Mrs. Smith's Apple Pie in Minutes (1/8 pie) | 2 carb, 2 fat |
| 1% Low-Fat Milk (1 cup) | 1 skim milk |

| Nutrition Facts | |
|---|---|
| Calories | 632 |
| Fat (g) | 19 |
| % Calories Fat | 27 |
| Saturated Fat (g) | 5 |
| Cholesterol (mg) | 65 |
| Sodium (mg) | 1304 |
| Protein (g) | 39 |
| Fiber (g) | 5 |
| Carbohydrate (g) | 80 |
| Carbohydrate Choices | 5 |

| Pyramid Checklist | |
|---|---|
| Grains | ■ |
| Fruits | |
| Vegetables | ■ |
| Dairy | ■ |
| Meat & Meat Substitute | ■ |
| Fats, Sweets, Oils | ■ |

# Vegetable Pizza and Pound Cake with Mixed Fruit

## Food Exchanges

| | |
|---|---|
| Tombstone Single-Serving Vegetable Pizza (1) | 3 carb, 2 med-fat meat |
| Pepperidge Farm Frozen All Butter Pound Cake (1 slice) | 1 carb, 1 fat |
| Frozen Unsweetened Berry Mix (1 cup) | 1 fruit |
| 1% Low-Fat Milk (1 cup) | 1 skim milk |

| Nutrition Facts | |
|---|---|
| Calories | 662 |
| Fat (g) | 18 |
| % Calories Fat | 24 |
| Saturated Fat (g) | 7 |
| Cholesterol (mg) | 20 |
| Sodium (mg) | 1088 |
| Protein (g) | 31 |
| Fiber (g) | 12 |
| Carbohydrate (g) | 93 |
| Carbohydrate Choices | 6 |

| Pyramid Checklist | |
|---|---|
| Grains | ■ |
| Fruits | ■ |
| Vegetables | ■ |
| Dairy | ■ |
| Meat & Meat Substitute | ■ |
| Fats, Sweets, Oils | ■ |

## Stuffed Shells and Italian Salad

## Food Exchanges

Michael Angelo Stuffed
Shells (8 oz)

2 1/2 carb, 3 med-fat meat

Di Giorno Plum Tomato &
Mushroom Pasta Sauce
(3/4 cup)

1 carb

Fresh Express Italian Salad
Blend (1 1/2 cup)

free

Kraft Presto Italian Salad
Dressing (2 Tbsp)

2 fat

| Nutrition Facts | |
|---|---|
| Calories | 615 |
| Fat (g) | 29 |
| % Calories Fat | 42 |
| Saturated Fat (g) | 14 |
| Cholesterol (mg) | 80 |
| Sodium (mg) | 1220 |
| Protein (g) | 29 |
| Fiber (g) | 5 |
| Carbohydrate (g) | 56 |
| Carbohydrate Choices | 4 |

| Pyramid Checklist | |
|---|---|
| Grains | ■ |
| Fruits | |
| Vegetables | ■ |
| Dairy | |
| Meat & Meat Substitute | ■ |
| Fats, Sweets, Oils | ■ |

# Chicken Caesar Salad with Breadsticks

## Food Exchanges

Fresh Express Chicken Caesar
  Dinner Salad (3 cups)
Pillsbury Breadsticks (1)
Weight Watchers Smart Ones
  Chocolate Chip Cookie
  Dough Sundae (1)

2 vegetables, 1 med-
  fat meat, 2 fat
1 starch
2 carb, 1 fat

| Nutrition Facts | |
|---|---|
| Calories | 560 |
| Fat (g) | 25 |
| % Calories Fat | 87 |
| Saturated Fat (g) | 6 |
| Cholesterol (mg) | 53 |
| Sodium (mg) | 1350 |
| Protein (g) | 20 |
| Fiber (g) | 2 |
| Carbohydrate (g) | 66 |
| Carbohydrate Choices | 4 1/2 |

| Pyramid Checklist | |
|---|---|
| Grains | ■ |
| Fruits | |
| Vegetables | ■ |
| Dairy | |
| Meat & Meat Substitute | ■ |
| Fats, Sweets, Oils | ■ |

## Beef Pot Roast with Home-style Potatoes and Creamed Onions

## Food Exchanges

| | |
|---|---|
| Harris Ranch Fully Cooked Beef Pot Roast (5 oz) | 4 very lean meat |
| Ore Ida Home-style Potato Wedges (6 oz) | 2 1/2 starch, 1 fat |
| Bird's Eye Small Onions with Cream Sauce (1/2 cup) | 2 vegetables |
| Dannon Non-fat Strawberry Frozen Yogurt (1/2 cup) | 1 carb |

| Nutrition Facts | |
|---|---|
| Calories | 760 |
| Fat (g) | 14 |
| % Calories Fat | 17 |
| Saturated Fat (g) | 4 |
| Cholesterol (mg) | 84 |
| Sodium (mg) | 1095 |
| Protein (g) | 41 |
| Fiber (g) | 10 |
| Carbohydrate (g) | 71 |
| Carbohydrate Choices | 6 |

| Pyramid Checklist | |
|---|---|
| Grains | |
| Fruits | |
| Vegetables | ■ |
| Dairy | ■ |
| Meat & Meat Substitute | ■ |
| Fats, Sweets, Oils | ■ |

# Using the Convenience Food Tables

Foods found in *Convenience Food Counts* are listed alphabetically to provide a timesaving reference as you work convenience foods into your eating plan. Most foods listed will be brand-name foods. However, some generic foods were listed when brand-name foods were not available or if all foods in the category were similar in nutritional value. When the nutrition information for all the flavors or varieties of a product is the same or similar, the values have been averaged. For example, Sara Lee Toaster Size bagels in the various flavors are very similar in nutritional value; therefore it is listed as Sara Lee Toaster Size bagels, all varieties (avg.).

The nutrient content information found in this book was obtained from food manufacturers, food labels, and the U.S. Department of Agricultural Research Service, 2000 USDA Nutrient Database for Standard Reference, Release 13. For each product listed, the information is listed exactly as it is on manufacturers or food label information. However, you may find minor variations between the listing in the book and the listing on the package. The information may have changed slightly or the label may have been redesigned. Nutrient information for foods from mixes (e.g., pasta side-dishes and muffin mixes) reflects values after the food has been prepared according to package directions.

This book lists the calories, fat, percent of calories for fat, saturated fat, cholesterol, sodium, protein, carbohydrate, carbohydrate choices, exchanges, and "best bet" rating. The nutrient values you use will depend on your eating goals and your meal planning approach. Values have been rounded to the nearest calorie, gram (g), or milligram (mg) per serving. Many of the terms and values you will need to know when using the food charts—including calories, fat, cholesterol, sodium, protein, and carbohydrates—were defined earlier in the section titled "Diabetes Eating Goals." Following is a list of additional facts to consider:

- **Serving size**. The serving size listed by each product is that which is provided by the food manufacturer or found on the food label. The serving size may be very different from the amount you serve yourself to eat.
- **Carbohydrate choices**. This value is useful for people who plan and monitor their carbohydrate intake. This type of meal plan will indicate the number of carbohydrate choices at each meal and snack. One carbohydrate choice is equal to 15 grams of carbohydrate. The carbohydrate choice can be determined from the Nutrition Facts food label by dividing the total carbohydrate in one serving by 15. This will be the number of "carbohydrate choices."
- **Food exchanges**. Food exchanges form a food planning system used for weight control or weight loss, or for diabetes. The exchange system is a method of grouping foods with similar nutritional value into lists with the goal of eating consistent amounts of nutrients. The exchange system groups foods into these main categories:
  - carbohydrate list (starches, fruits, milk, other carbohydrates, and vegetables)
  - the meat and meat substitute list (very lean, lean, medium-fat, and high-fat meats)

- the fat list (monounsaturated, polyunsaturated, and saturated fats)
- the free foods list

Each food exchange group has approximately the same number of calories, carbohydrate, protein, and fat as the other foods in the same group. Any food on a list can be traded or "exchanged" for any other food on the same list.

- ✔ **"Best Bet" (rating).** The "best bet" rating helps you quickly identify foods that are low in fat in each food category. In order for foods to be considered a "best bet" they must fit into certain fat, saturated fat, and sodium criteria. These criteria are listed below. Use these guidelines when selecting food items for a menu or when you are making up a healthy meal or snack. Keep in mind that foods that don't meet this criteria are not to be avoided entirely. When you're putting healthy meals together, mix and match the "best bets" with the not-so-healthy choices. Or adjust your portion size or how often you eat the food. Remember that it is a balance of what you eat over several days that makes up a healthy eating pattern.

### TABLE 7-1 "Best Bet" Guidelines

| Food Category | Criteria |
| --- | --- |
| Frozen meals and entrees, and other foods that make up most of a meal | 3 grams of fat or less per 100 calories, and no more than 1/3 of total fat from saturated fat, and less than 1000 milligrams of sodium |
| Milk and cheese | 5 grams of fat or less per serving |
| Side dishes, snacks, cereals, soups, breads, desserts, and other foods and beverages | 3 grams of fat or less per serving; less than 500 milligrams of sodium |

# Convenience
# Food Tables

| Product | Serving Size | Cal. | Fat (g) | % Cal. Fat | Sat. Fat (g) | Chol. (mg) | Sod. (mg) | Pro. (g) | Fiber (g) | Carb. (g) | Carb. Ch. | Servings/Exchanges |
|---|---|---|---|---|---|---|---|---|---|---|---|---|
| **ALCOHOLIC BEVERAGES** | | | | | | | | | | | | |
| Beer, Light | 12 oz | 100 | 0 | 0 | 0 | 0 | 11 | <1 | 0 | 5 | 0 | 2 fat |
| Beer, Regular | 12 oz | 146 | 0 | 0 | 0 | 0 | 18 | 0 | 0 | 13 | 0 | 3 fat |
| Wine, Dry Dessert | 4 oz | 88 | 0 | 0 | 0 | 0 | 6 | <1 | 0 | 3 | 0 | 2 fat |
| Wine, Medium White | 4 oz | 80 | 0 | 0 | 0 | 0 | 6 | <1 | 0 | <1 | 0 | 2 fat |
| Wine, Non Alcoholic, Light or Regular | 8 oz | 15 | 0 | 0 | 0 | 0 | 18 | <1 | 0 | 2 | 0 | free |
| Wine, Red | 4 oz | 85 | 0 | 0 | 0 | 0 | 6 | <1 | 0 | 2 | 0 | 2 fat |
| **APPETIZERS (CANNED)** | | | | | | | | | | | | |
| **Progresso** | | | | | | | | | | | | |
| ✓Artichoke Hearts, In Brine | | 30 | 0 | 0 | 0 | 0 | 240 | 2 | 1 | 6 | 1/2 | 1 vegetable |
| ✓Cherry Peppers, Drained | 2 Tbsp | 30 | 0 | 0 | 0 | 0 | 500 | 0 | 0 | 6 | 1/2 | 1 vegetable |
| ✓Eggplant Appetizer | 2 Tbsp | 25 | 2 | 72 | 0 | 0 | 130 | 0 | 2 | 2 | 0 | 1 fat |
| Fried Peppers, Drained | 2 Tbsp | 60 | 5 | 75 | <1 | 0 | 60 | 0 | 1 | 3 | 0 | 1 fat |
| ✓Olive Salad, Drained | 2 Tbsp | 25 | 3 | 100 | 0 | 0 | 360 | 0 | <1 | 1 | 0 | 1 fat |
| Olives, Oil Cured | 6 | 80 | 6 | 68 | <1 | 0 | 330 | 0 | 1 | 3 | 0 | 1 fat |
| ✓Pepper Salad, Drained | 2 Tbsp | 15 | 1 | 60 | 0 | 0 | 160 | 0 | <1 | 1 | 0 | free |
| ✓Peppers, Hot Cherry | 2 Tbsp | 25 | 2 | 72 | 0 | 0 | 30 | 0 | 1 | 2 | 0 | free |
| ✓Peppers, Sweet Fried w/Onion | 2 Tbsp | 20 | 2 | 90 | 0 | 0 | 130 | 0 | 1 | 2 | 0 | free |

| Products | Amount | Cal. | Fat (g) | % Cal. from Fat | Sat. Fat (g) | Chol. (mg) | Sod. (mg) | Carb. (g) | Fiber (g) | Prot. (g) | Carb. Ch. | Exchanges/Choices |
|---|---|---|---|---|---|---|---|---|---|---|---|---|
| ✔Roasted Peppers | 2 | 10 | 0 | 0 | 0 | 0 | 55 | 1 | 0 | 0 | 0 | free |
| ✔Tuscan Peppers, Drained | 3 | 10 | 0 | 0 | 0 | 0 | 450 | 1 | 0 | 0 | 0 | free |
| **APPETIZERS (FROZEN)** | | | | | | | | | | | | |
| **Anchor Foods** | | | | | | | | | | | | |
| Three Cheese Poppers | 1 | 100 | 6 | 54 | 3 | 0 | 290 | 8 | <1 | 3 | 1/2 | 1/2 carb, 1 fat |
| **Nancy's** | | | | | | | | | | | | |
| Florentine Puffs | 12 puffs | 400 | 21 | 47 | 11 | 165 | 1120 | 35 | 3 | 19 | 2 | 2 carb, 2 med-fat meat, 2 fat |
| Petite Quiche | 6 | 390 | 23 | 53 | 11 | 135 | 580 | 31 | 1 | 14 | 2 | 2 carb, 1 med-fat meat, 4 fat |
| Seafood Crab Cakes | 12 | 350 | 20 | 51 | 9 | 150 | 1140 | 28 | 2 | 16 | 2 | 2 carb, 1 med-fat meat, 3 fat |
| **Poppers** | | | | | | | | | | | | |
| Mozzarella Poppers | 3 | 90 | 5 | 50 | 2 | 10 | 170 | 8 | 0 | 5 | 1/2 | 1/2 carb, 1 fat |
| Mushroom Poppers | 6 | 140 | 5 | 32 | 1 | 0 | 260 | 19 | 2 | 4 | 1 | 1 carb, 1 fat |
| Zucchini Poppers | 5 | 200 | 11 | 50 | 2 | 0 | 230 | 22 | 2 | 4 | 1 1/2 | 1 1/2 carb, 2 fat |
| **TGI Friday's** | | | | | | | | | | | | |
| Buffalo Wings | 3 | 100 | 7 | 63 | 2 | 35 | 920 | 1 | 0 | 8 | 0 | 1 med-fat meat |

✔= Best Bet; NA = Not Available; Carb. Ch. = Carbohydrate Choices

| Appetizers (Frozen) (Continued) | Serving Size | Cal. | Fat (g) | % Cal. Fat | Sat. Fat (g) | Chol. (mg) | Sod. (mg) | Pro. (g) | Fiber (g) | Carb. (g) | Carb. Ch. | Servings/Exchanges |
|---|---|---|---|---|---|---|---|---|---|---|---|---|
| Potato Skins | 3 | 250 | 17 | 61 | 7 | 40 | 510 | 10 | 4 | 15 | 1 | 1 carb, 1 med-fat meat, 2 fat |

## APPLESAUCE

### (Generic)

| | Serving Size | Cal. | Fat (g) | % Cal. Fat | Sat. Fat (g) | Chol. (mg) | Sod. (mg) | Pro. (g) | Fiber (g) | Carb. (g) | Carb. Ch. | Servings/Exchanges |
|---|---|---|---|---|---|---|---|---|---|---|---|---|
| ✓Applesauce, Unsweetened | 1/2 cup | 52 | <1 | 0 | 0 | 0 | 2 | 0 | 2 | 14 | 1 | 1 fruit |
| ✓Chunky Applesauce | 1/2 cup | 100 | 0 | 0 | 0 | 0 | 0 | 0 | 2 | 24 | 1 1/2 | 1 1/2 fruit |
| ✓Cinnamon Applesauce | 1/2 cup | 110 | 0 | 0 | 0 | 0 | 0 | 0 | 1 | 28 | 2 | 2 fruit |
| ✓Regular Applesauce | 1/2 cup | 100 | 0 | 0 | 0 | 0 | 0 | 0 | 1 | 25 | 1 1/2 | 1 1/2 fruit |

### Motts

| | Serving Size | Cal. | Fat (g) | % Cal. Fat | Sat. Fat (g) | Chol. (mg) | Sod. (mg) | Pro. (g) | Fiber (g) | Carb. (g) | Carb. Ch. | Servings/Exchanges |
|---|---|---|---|---|---|---|---|---|---|---|---|---|
| ✓Blues Clues Berry Applesauce | 4 oz | 90 | 0 | 0 | 0 | 0 | 10 | 0 | 1 | 23 | 1 1/2 | 1 1/2 fruit |
| ✓Fruitsations Applesauce, All Flavors (Avg) | 4 oz | 90 | 0 | 0 | 0 | 0 | 5 | 0 | 1 | 23 | 1 1/2 | 1 1/2 fruit |

## BACON

### Louis Rich

| | Serving Size | Cal. | Fat (g) | % Cal. Fat | Sat. Fat (g) | Chol. (mg) | Sod. (mg) | Pro. (g) | Fiber (g) | Carb. (g) | Carb. Ch. | Servings/Exchanges |
|---|---|---|---|---|---|---|---|---|---|---|---|---|
| ✓Turkey Bacon | 1 slice | 35 | 3 | 77 | <1 | 15 | 185 | 2 | 0 | <1 | 0 | 1 fat |

### Oscar Mayer

| | Serving Size | Cal. | Fat (g) | % Cal. Fat | Sat. Fat (g) | Chol. (mg) | Sod. (mg) | Pro. (g) | Fiber (g) | Carb. (g) | Carb. Ch. | Servings/Exchanges |
|---|---|---|---|---|---|---|---|---|---|---|---|---|
| Bacon | 2 slices | 70 | 6 | 77 | 2 | 15 | 290 | 4 | 0 | 0 | 0 | 1 med-fat meat |
| Bacon, Lower Sodium | 2 slices | 70 | 5 | 64 | 2 | 15 | 200 | 5 | 0 | 0 | 0 | 1 med-fat meat |
| Bacon-1/8≤ Thick Cut | 1 slice | 60 | 5 | 75 | 2 | 10 | 250 | 4 | 0 | 0 | 0 | 1 med-fat meat |

## BACON BITS

### Betty Crocker

| | | | | | | | | | | | | |
|---|---|---|---|---|---|---|---|---|---|---|---|---|
| ✔BacOs | 1 1/2 Tbsp | 30 | 2 | 60 | 0 | 0 | 120 | 3 | 0 | 2 | 0 | 1 fat |
| ✔Bac-Os, Salad Topping Bits or Chips | 1 1/2 Tbsp | 30 | 2 | 60 | 0 | 0 | 120 | 3 | 0 | 2 | 0 | 1 fat |

### General Mills

| | | | | | | | | | | | | |
|---|---|---|---|---|---|---|---|---|---|---|---|---|
| ✔Bac-O-Bits | 1 Tbsp | 25 | <1 | 36 | NA | 0 | 103 | 3 | NA | 2 | 0 | free |

### Oscar Mayer

| | | | | | | | | | | | | |
|---|---|---|---|---|---|---|---|---|---|---|---|---|
| ✔Bacon Bits | 1 Tbsp | 25 | 2 | 72 | <1 | 5 | 220 | 3 | 0 | 0 | 0 | 1 fat |

## BAGELS

### Earth Grains

| | | | | | | | | | | | | |
|---|---|---|---|---|---|---|---|---|---|---|---|---|
| ✔Cinnamon Raisin Bagel | 1 | 230 | 2 | 6 | 0 | 0 | 310 | 10 | 2 | 56 | 4 | 4 strch |
| ✔Plain Bagel | 1 | 230 | 2 | 6 | 0 | 0 | 450 | 9 | 1 | 47 | 3 | 3 strch |

### Lender's Frozen Bagels

| | | | | | | | | | | | | |
|---|---|---|---|---|---|---|---|---|---|---|---|---|
| Big and Crusty Bagel | 1 | 250 | 1 | 4 | 0 | 0 | 540 | 9 | 1 | 52 | 3 1/2 | 3 1/2 strch |
| ✔Cinnamon Swirl | 1 | 150 | <1 | 3 | 0 | 0 | 270 | 5 | 1 | 32 | 2 | 2 strch |
| ✔Egg Bagel | 1 | 160 | 2 | 8 | 0 | 10 | 320 | 6 | 1 | 30 | 2 | 2 strch |
| Original Bagel | 1 | 210 | 4 | 15 | <1 | 10 | 330 | 6 | 2 | 37 | 2 1/2 | 2 1/2 strch, 1 fat |

### Sara Lee

| | | | | | | | | | | | | |
|---|---|---|---|---|---|---|---|---|---|---|---|---|
| Banana Nut Bagel | 1 | 350 | 7 | 18 | 2 | 0 | 440 | 12 | 4 | 61 | 4 | 4 strch, 1 fat |

✔= Best Bet; NA = Not Available; Carb. Ch. = Carbohydrate Choices

| | Serving Size | Cal. | Fat (g) | % Cal. Fat | Sat. Fat (g) | Chol. (mg) | Sod. (mg) | Pro. (g) | Fiber (g) | Carb. (g) | Carb. Ch. | Servings/Exchanges |
|---|---|---|---|---|---|---|---|---|---|---|---|---|
| **Bagels (*Continued*)** | | | | | | | | | | | | |
| ✓Blueberry Bagel | 1 | 260 | 1 | 4 | 0 | 0 | 490 | 9 | 2 | 53 | 3 1/2 | 3 1/2 strch |
| ✓Cinnamon Raisin Bagel | 1 | 260 | 1 | 4 | 0 | 0 | 460 | 9 | 4 | 55 | 3 1/2 | 3 1/2 strch |
| ✓Mini Plain Bagels | 1 | 70 | 0 | 0 | 0 | 0 | 130 | 3 | <1 | 15 | 1 | 1 strch |
| Sun Dried Tomato & Basil Bagel | 1 | 300 | 2 | 5 | 0 | 0 | 480 | 11 | 2 | 61 | 4 | 4 strch |
| The Works Bagel | 1 | 330 | 4 | 10 | 0 | 0 | 480 | 13 | 2 | 62 | 4 | 4 strch |
| ✓Toaster Size, Low-fat Bagel, All Varieties (Avg) | 1 | 160 | <1 | 3 | 0 | 0 | 310 | 6 | 1 | 33 | 2 | 2 strch |
| **Thomas** | | | | | | | | | | | | |
| ✓Cinnamon Raisin Swirl Bagel | 1 | 290 | 2 | 5 | <1 | 0 | 470 | 10 | 4 | 57 | 4 | 4 strch |
| ✓New York Style Plain Bagel | 1 | 280 | 2 | 5 | <1 | 0 | 530 | 10 | 2 | 56 | 4 | 4 strch |
| **BAKING CHIPS** | | | | | | | | | | | | |
| **M&M's** | | | | | | | | | | | | |
| Semi-Sweet Chocolate Mini Baking Bits | 1 Tbsp | 70 | 4 | 51 | 2 | 0 | 0 | 1 | 1 | 9 | 1/2 | 1/2 carb, 1 fat |
| **Nestle** | | | | | | | | | | | | |
| Butterscotch Morsels | 1 Tbsp | 80 | 4 | 45 | 4 | 0 | 15 | 0 | 0 | 9 | 1/2 | 1/2 carb, 1 fat |
| Peanut Butter & Milk Chocolate Morsels | 1 Tbsp | 80 | 5 | 56 | 3 | 0 | 25 | <1 | 0 | 8 | 1/2 | 1/2 carb, 1 fat |
| Premier White Morsels | 1 Tbsp | 80 | 4 | 45 | 4 | 0 | 20 | <1 | 0 | 9 | 1/2 | 1/2 carb, 1 fat |
| Semi-Sweet Chocolate Chips | 1 Tbsp | 70 | 4 | 51 | 3 | 0 | 0 | <1 | <1 | 9 | 1/2 | 1/2 carb, 1 fat |

| | | | | | | | | | | | | |
|---|---|---|---|---|---|---|---|---|---|---|---|---|
| Semi-Sweet Mini Chocolate Chip Morsels | 1 Tbsp | 70 | 4 | 51 | 3 | 0 | <1 | 0 | <1 | 9 | 1/2 | 1/2 carb, 1 fat |
| **Reese's** | | | | | | | | | | | | |
| Peanut Butter Chips | 1 Tbsp | 80 | 4 | 45 | 4 | 0 | 35 | 3 | 0 | 7 | 1/2 | 1/2 carb, 1 fat |
| **Skor** | | | | | | | | | | | | |
| English Toffee Bits | 1 Tbsp | 60 | 4 | 60 | 3 | 10 | 75 | 0 | 0 | 7 | 1/2 | 1/2 carb, 1 fat |

## BAKING CRUMBS

**Nabisco**

| | | | | | | | | | | | | |
|---|---|---|---|---|---|---|---|---|---|---|---|---|
| ✔Honey Maid Graham Cracker Crumbs | 2 1/2 Tbsp | 70 | 2 | 26 | 0 | 0 | 100 | 1 | 0 | 12 | 1 | 1 carb |
| Oreo Base Cake Crumbs | 1/4 cup | 140 | 5 | 32 | 1 | 0 | 260 | 2 | 1 | 23 | 1 1/2 | 1 1/2 strch, 1 fat |

## BARBEQUE SAUCE

**Healthy Choice**

| | | | | | | | | | | | | |
|---|---|---|---|---|---|---|---|---|---|---|---|---|
| ✔BBQ Sauce, All Varieties (Avg) | 2 Tbsp | 25 | <1 | 0 | 0 | 0 | 229 | <1 | <1 | 7 | 1/2 | 1/2 carb |

**Hunt's**

| | | | | | | | | | | | | |
|---|---|---|---|---|---|---|---|---|---|---|---|---|
| ✔All Varieties (Avg) | 2 Tbsp | 45 | <1 | 0 | 0 | 0 | 395 | <1 | <1 | 11 | 1 | 1 carb |
| ✔BBQ Sauce, Hickory & Brown Sugar | 2 Tbsp | 75 | <1 | 0 | 0 | 0 | 382 | <1 | 1 | 18 | 1 | 1 carb |
| ✔BBQ Sauce, Light | 2 Tbsp | 26 | <1 | 0 | 0 | 0 | 223 | <1 | <1 | 6 | 1/2 | 1/2 carb |

**Kraft**

| | | | | | | | | | | | | |
|---|---|---|---|---|---|---|---|---|---|---|---|---|
| ✔All Varieties (Avg) | 2 Tbsp | 50 | 0 | 0 | 0 | 0 | 400 | 0 | 0 | 11 | 1 | 1 carb |

✔= Best Bet; NA = Not Available; Carb. Ch. = Carbohydrate Choices

| | Serving Size | Cal. | Fat (g) | % Cal. Fat | Sat. Fat (g) | Chol. (mg) | Sod. (mg) | Pro. (g) | Fiber (g) | Carb. (g) | Carb. Ch. | Servings/Exchanges |
|---|---|---|---|---|---|---|---|---|---|---|---|---|
| **Barbeque Sauce** (*Continued*) | | | | | | | | | | | | |
| **Open Pit** | | | | | | | | | | | | |
| ✔All Varieties (Avg) | 2 Tbsp | 50 | 0 | 0 | 0 | 0 | 395 | 0 | 0 | 11 | 1 | 1 carb |
| **BEANS (CANNED)** | | | | | | | | | | | | |
| **B&M** | | | | | | | | | | | | |
| ✔Baked Beans w/Honey | 1/2 cup | 170 | 2 | 11 | 0 | 0 | 450 | 8 | 8 | 30 | 2 | 2 strch |
| ✔Baked Beans w/Pork | 1/2 cup | 180 | 2 | 10 | <1 | <5 | 430 | 8 | 7 | 33 | 2 | 2 strch |
| ✔Baked Beans, 99% Fat-Free Vegetarian | 1/2 cup | 170 | 1 | 5 | 0 | 0 | 220 | 8 | 7 | 31 | 2 | 2 strch |
| ✔Baked Beans, Bacon & Onion w/Brown Sugar | 1/2 cup | 190 | 2 | 9 | <1 | <5 | 450 | 8 | 8 | 36 | 2 1/2 | 2 1/2 strch |
| ✔Baked Beans, Barbeque | 1/2 cup | 170 | 1 | 5 | 0 | 0 | 460 | 7 | 6 | 33 | 2 | 2 strch |
| ✔Baked Beans, Red Kidney | 1/2 cup | 170 | 2 | 11 | <1 | <5 | 440 | 7 | 6 | 32 | 2 | 2 strch |
| ✔Baked Beans, Yellow Eye | 1/2 cup | 180 | 3 | 15 | <1 | <5 | 450 | 8 | 8 | 30 | 2 | 2 strch, 1 fat |
| **Campbells** | | | | | | | | | | | | |
| ✔Chili Beans in Zesty Sauce | 1/2 cup | 130 | 3 | 21 | 1 | 5 | 490 | 6 | 6 | 21 | 1 1/2 | 1 1/2 strch, 1 fat |
| ✔New England Style Baked Beans | 1/2 cup | 180 | 3 | 15 | 1 | 5 | 460 | 5 | 6 | 32 | 2 | 2 strch, 1 fat |
| ✔Old Fashioned Barbecue Beans | 1/2 cup | 170 | 3 | 16 | <1 | 5 | 460 | 7 | 6 | 29 | 2 | 2 strch, 1 fat |
| ✔Pork & Beans in Tomato Sauce | 1/2 cup | 130 | 2 | 14 | <1 | 5 | 420 | 5 | 6 | 24 | 1 1/2 | 1 1/2 strch |

**Friends**

| | Serving | Cal. | Fat (g) | % Cal. Fat | Sat. Fat (g) | Chol. (mg) | Sod. (mg) | Prot. (g) | Fiber (g) | Carb. (g) | Carb. Ch. | Exchanges |
|---|---|---|---|---|---|---|---|---|---|---|---|---|
| ✓Baked Beans, Original | 1/2 cup | 170 | 1 | 5 | 0 | <5 | 390 | 8 | 7 | 32 | 2 | 2 strch |
| Baked Beans, Red Kidney | 1/2 cup | 170 | 1 | 5 | 0 | <5 | 510 | 7 | 6 | 32 | 2 | 2 strch |

**Green Giant**

| | Serving | Cal. | Fat (g) | % Cal. Fat | Sat. Fat (g) | Chol. (mg) | Sod. (mg) | Prot. (g) | Fiber (g) | Carb. (g) | Carb. Ch. | Exchanges |
|---|---|---|---|---|---|---|---|---|---|---|---|---|
| Baked Beans | 1/2 cup | 160 | 2 | 11 | 1 | 5 | 580 | 6 | 7 | 31 | 2 | 2 strch |
| Baked Beans in Sauce | 1/2 cup | 160 | 2 | 11 | 1 | 5 | 580 | 6 | 7 | 31 | 2 | 2 strch |
| ✓Barbecue Beans | 1/2 cup | 140 | 1 | 6 | 0 | 0 | 460 | 6 | 5 | 28 | 2 | 2 strch |
| ✓Beans, Honey Bacon | 1/2 cup | 160 | 1 | 6 | 0 | 0 | 490 | 6 | 6 | 34 | 2 | 2 strch |
| Black Beans | 1/2 cup | 90 | 0 | 0 | 0 | 0 | 580 | 7 | 6 | 21 | 1 1/2 | 1 1/2 strch |
| ✓Black-Eyed Peas | 1/2 cup | 90 | 1 | 10 | 0 | 0 | 300 | 7 | 4 | 18 | 1 | 1 strch |
| Chili Beans in Spicy Sauce | 1/2 cup | 100 | 1 | 9 | 0 | 0 | 580 | 7 | 6 | 21 | 1 1/2 | 1 1/2 strch |
| ✓Garbanzo Beans | 1/2 cup | 110 | 2 | 16 | 0 | 0 | 380 | 6 | 5 | 18 | 1 | 1 strch |
| ✓Great North Beans | 1/2 cup | 80 | 1 | 11 | 0 | 0 | 290 | 6 | 5 | 18 | 1 | 1 strch |
| ✓Italian Beans | 1/2 cup | 130 | 1 | 7 | 0 | 0 | 480 | 5 | 5 | 24 | 1 1/2 | 1 1/2 strch |
| ✓Kidney Beans, Light or Dark Red | 1/2 cup | 90 | 1 | 10 | 0 | 0 | 330 | 7 | 5 | 20 | 1 | 1 strch, 1 very lean meat |
| Mexican Beans | 1/2 cup | 120 | 2 | 15 | 0 | 0 | 530 | 6 | 5 | 21 | 1 1/2 | 1 1/2 strch |
| ✓Pinto Beans | 1/2 cup | 90 | 1 | 10 | 0 | 0 | 280 | 6 | 5 | 20 | 1 | 1 strch |
| ✓Red Beans | 1/2 cup | 90 | 1 | 10 | 0 | 0 | 340 | 6 | 5 | 19 | 1 | 1 strch |

✓ = Best Bet; NA = Not Available; Carb. Ch. = Carbohydrate Choices

| Beans (Canned) (Continued) | Serving Size | Cal. | Fat (g) | % Cal. Fat | Sat. Fat (g) | Chol. (mg) | Sod. (mg) | Pro. (g) | Fiber (g) | Carb. (g) | Carb. Ch. | Servings/Exchanges |
|---|---|---|---|---|---|---|---|---|---|---|---|---|
| **Health Valley** | | | | | | | | | | | | |
| ✔ Honey-Baked Beans, Fat-Free, Salted | 1/2 cup | 110 | 0 | 0 | 0 | 0 | 135 | 7 | 7 | 24 | 1 1/2 | 1 1/2 strch |
| **Hunt's** | | | | | | | | | | | | |
| Chili Beans | 1/2 cup | 87 | 1 | 0 | 0 | 0 | 597 | 6 | 6 | 17 | 1 | 1 strch |
| ✔ Kidney Beans | 1/2 cup | 120 | 0 | 0 | 0 | 0 | 400 | 7 | NA | 21 | 1 1/2 | 1 1/2 strch |
| Navy Beans w/Ham | 1/2 cup | 239 | 3 | 11 | <1 | 10 | 735 | 16 | 10 | 38 | 2 1/2 | 2 1/2 strch, 1 lean meat |
| Red Beans, Small | 1/2 cup | 91 | 0 | 0 | 0 | 0 | 580 | 6 | NA | 18 | 1 | 1 strch |
| **Old El Paso** | | | | | | | | | | | | |
| ✔ Black Beans | 1/2 cup | 110 | 1 | 8 | 0 | 0 | 400 | 7 | 7 | 17 | 1 | 1 strch, 1 very lean meat |
| ✔ Garbanzo Beans | 1/2 cup | 100 | 2 | 18 | 0 | 0 | 340 | 6 | 4 | 16 | 1 | 1 strch, 1 lean meat |
| Mexe Beans | 1/2 cup | 110 | 0 | 0 | 0 | 0 | 630 | 7 | 7 | 19 | 1 | 1 strch, 1 very lean meat |
| ✔ Pinto Beans | 1/2 cup | 100 | <1 | 9 | 0 | 0 | 420 | 6 | 7 | 19 | 1 | 1 strch, 1 very lean meat |
| **Orval Kent** | | | | | | | | | | | | |
| Barbeque Beans | 1/2 cup | 160 | <1 | 6 | 0 | 0 | 700 | 6 | NA | 34 | 2 | 2 strch |
| ✔ Four Bean Salad | 1/2 cup | 100 | <1 | 9 | 0 | 0 | 300 | 4 | 3 | 19 | 1 | 1 strch |
| **Progresso** | | | | | | | | | | | | |
| ✔ Black Beans | 1/2 cup | 110 | 1 | 8 | 0 | 0 | 400 | 7 | 7 | 17 | 1 | 1 strch, 1 very lean meat |
| ✔ Cannellini Beans | 1/2 cup | 100 | <1 | 9 | 0 | 0 | 270 | 5 | 5 | 18 | 1 | 1 strch |

| | Serving Size | Cal. | Fat (g) | % Cal. Fat | Sat. Fat (g) | Chol. (mg) | Sod. (mg) | Carb. (g) | Fiber (g) | Prot. (g) | Carb. Ch. | Exchanges |
|---|---|---|---|---|---|---|---|---|---|---|---|---|
| ✓Chick Peas | 1/2 cup | 120 | 3 | 23 | 0 | 0 | 280 | 20 | 5 | 5 | 1 | 1 strch, 1 fat |
| ✓Fava Beans | 1/2 cup | 110 | <1 | 8 | 0 | 0 | 250 | 20 | 5 | 6 | 1 | 1 strch, 1 very lean meat |
| ✓Garbanzo Beans | 1/2 cup | 110 | 2 | 16 | 0 | 0 | 380 | 18 | 5 | 6 | 1 | 1 strch, 1 lean meat |
| ✓Kidney Beans, Red | 1/2 cup | 110 | <1 | 8 | 0 | 0 | 280 | 20 | 8 | 7 | 1 | 1 strch, 1 very lean meat |
| ✓Pinto Beans | 1/2 cup | 110 | 1 | 8 | 0 | 0 | 250 | 18 | 7 | 7 | 1 | 1 strch, 1 very lean meat |

## BEANS, REFRIED (CANNED)

### Gebhardt

| | Serving Size | Cal. | Fat (g) | % Cal. Fat | Sat. Fat (g) | Chol. (mg) | Sod. (mg) | Carb. (g) | Fiber (g) | Prot. (g) | Carb. Ch. | Exchanges |
|---|---|---|---|---|---|---|---|---|---|---|---|---|
| ✓Refried Beans, Jalapeno | 1/2 cup | 110 | 2 | 16 | NA | NA | 320 | 19 | NA | 7 | 1 | 1 strch, 1 fat |
| ✓Refried Beans, Traditional | 1/2 cup | 130 | 2 | 14 | 0 | NA | 490 | 20 | NA | 7 | 1 | 1 strch, 1 fat |

### Old El Paso

| | Serving Size | Cal. | Fat (g) | % Cal. Fat | Sat. Fat (g) | Chol. (mg) | Sod. (mg) | Carb. (g) | Fiber (g) | Prot. (g) | Carb. Ch. | Exchanges |
|---|---|---|---|---|---|---|---|---|---|---|---|---|
| Refried Beans | 1/2 cup | 100 | <1 | 9 | 0 | 0 | 570 | 17 | 6 | 6 | 1 | 1 strch, 1 very lean meat |
| Refried Beans & Cheese | 1/2 cup | 130 | 4 | 28 | 2 | 5 | 500 | 18 | 6 | 7 | 1 | 1 strch, 1 med-fat meat |
| Refried Beans w/Green Chili | 1/2 cup | 100 | <1 | 9 | 0 | <5 | 720 | 17 | 6 | 6 | 1 | 1 strch, 1 very lean meat |
| Refried Beans w/Sausage | 1/2 cup | 200 | 13 | 59 | 5 | 10 | 360 | 14 | 4 | 7 | 1 | 1 strch, 1 med-fat meat, 2 fat |
| ✓Refried Beans, Fat-Free | 1/2 cup | 100 | 0 | 0 | 0 | 0 | 480 | 18 | 6 | 6 | 1 | 1 strch, 1 very lean meat |
| Refried Beans, Fat-Free, Spicy | 1/2 cup | 100 | 0 | 0 | 0 | 0 | 720 | 18 | 6 | 6 | 1 | 1 strch, 1 very lean meat |
| ✓Refried Beans, Vegetarian | 1/2 cup | 100 | 1 | 0 | 0 | 0 | 490 | 17 | 6 | 6 | 1 | 1 strch |
| ✓Refried Black Beans | 1/2 cup | 110 | 2 | 16 | 0 | 0 | 340 | 18 | 7 | 6 | 1 | 1 strch, 1 lean meat |

✓ = Best Bet; NA = Not Available; Carb. Ch. = Carbohydrate Choices

| Beans, Refried (Canned) *(Continued)* | Serving Size | Cal. | Fat (g) | % Cal. Fat | Sat. Fat (g) | Chol. (mg) | Sod. (mg) | Pro. (g) | Fiber (g) | Carb. (g) | Carb. Ch. | Servings/Exchanges |
|---|---|---|---|---|---|---|---|---|---|---|---|---|
| **Ortega** | | | | | | | | | | | | |
| ✓Refried Beans/Frijoles | 1/2 cup | 140 | 3 | 19 | <1 | 0 | 480 | 8 | 6 | 23 | 1 1/2 | 1 1/2 strch, 1 lean meat |
| **Rosarita** | | | | | | | | | | | | |
| Refried Beans w/Zesty Salsa, No-Fat | 1/2 cup | 90 | 0 | 0 | 0 | 0 | 670 | 6 | 5 | 18 | 1 | 1 1/2 strch |
| Refried Beans, Bacon | 1/2 cup | 110 | 2 | 16 | <1 | 14 | 560 | 7 | 6 | 20 | 1 | 1 strch, 1 lean meat |
| ✓Refried Beans, Green Chili | 1/2 cup | 90 | 2 | 20 | <1 | 0 | 460 | 6 | 6 | 18 | 1 | 1 strch |
| ✓Refried Beans, Nacho Cheese | 1/2 cup | 110 | 2 | 16 | <1 | 2 | 490 | 7 | 6 | 20 | 1 | 1 strch, 1 lean meat |
| ✓Refried Beans, No-Fat | 1/2 cup | 180 | 0 | 0 | 0 | 0 | 490 | 7 | 6 | 18 | 1 | 1 strch, 1 very lean meat |
| ✓Refried Beans, Onion | 1/2 cup | 110 | 2 | 16 | <1 | 0 | 490 | 7 | 6 | 21 | 1 1/2 | 1 1/2 strch |
| ✓Refried Beans, Spicy | 1/2 cup | 120 | 2 | 15 | 1 | 0 | 465 | 8 | 6 | 20 | 1 | 1 strch, 1 lean meat |
| ✓Refried Beans, Traditional | 1/2 cup | 120 | 2 | 15 | NA | NA | 470 | 7 | 6 | 19 | 1 | 1 strch, 1 lean meat |
| Refried Beans, Vegetarian | 1/2 cup | 100 | 2 | 18 | 0 | 0 | 520 | 6 | 2 | 18 | 1 | 1 strch |
| Refried Beans, w/Green Chiles & Lime, No-Fat | 1/2 cup | 90 | 0 | 0 | 0 | 0 | 570 | 6 | 5 | 18 | 1 | 1 strch |
| **Taco Bell Home Originals** | | | | | | | | | | | | |
| ✓Fat-Free Refried Beans, All Varieties (Avg) | 1/2 cup | 110 | 0 | 0 | 0 | 0 | 460 | 7 | 6 | 21 | 1 1/2 | 1 1/2 strch |
| Refried Beans | 1/2 cup | 140 | 3 | 32 | <1 | 0 | 530 | 5 | 7 | 23 | 1 1/2 | 1 1/2 strch, 1 fat |

## BEEF JERKY

### Slim Jim

| | | | | | | | | | | | |
|---|---|---|---|---|---|---|---|---|---|---|---|
| ✔Big Jerk Beef Jerky | 0.25 oz | 25 | 1 | 36 | 0 | NA | 220 | 3 | 0 | 1 | 0 | 1 very lean meat |
| Giant Jerk Beef Jerky | 0.6 oz | 60 | 2 | 30 | NA | NA | 510 | 7 | 0 | 2 | 0 | 1 very lean meat |

## BEEF MEALS/ENTREES (FROZEN)

### Armour Classics

| | | | | | | | | | | | |
|---|---|---|---|---|---|---|---|---|---|---|---|
| Meat Loaf Dinner | 11.4 oz dinner | 300 | 10 | 30 | 5 | NA | 600 | 19 | NA | 33 | 2 | 2 carb, 2 med-fat meat |
| Salisbury Steak | 11.25 oz dinner | 350 | 17 | 44 | NA | 55 | 1430 | 22 | NA | 26 | 2 | 2 carb, 2 med-fat meat, 1 fat |
| Swedish Meatballs Dinner | 11.25 oz dinner | 330 | 18 | 49 | NA | 80 | 1140 | 19 | NA | 23 | 1 1/2 | 1 1/2 carb, 2 med-fat meat, 2 fat |
| Yankee Pot Roast | 10 oz dinner | 310 | 12 | 36 | NA | 85 | 670 | 25 | NA | 26 | 2 | 2 carb, 3 med-fat meat |

### Armour Classics Lite

| | | | | | | | | | | | |
|---|---|---|---|---|---|---|---|---|---|---|---|
| ✔Beef Steak Dinner | 10 oz dinner | 290 | 9 | 28 | NA | 80 | 440 | 27 | NA | 25 | 1 1/2 | 1 1/2 carb, 3 lean meat |
| Salisbury Steak | 11.5 oz dinner | 300 | 2 | 8 | NA | 35 | 1020 | 21 | NA | 29 | 2 | 2 carb, 2 very lean meat |
| ✔Sirloin Beef Tips | 10.25 oz dinner | 230 | 7 | 27 | NA | 70 | 820 | 22 | NA | 20 | 1 | 1 carb, 3 lean meat |
| ✔Stroganoff | 11.25 oz dinner | 250 | 6 | 21 | NA | 55 | 510 | 18 | NA | 33 | 2 | 2 carb, 2 lean meat |

✔= Best Bet; NA = Not Available; Carb. Ch. = Carbohydrate Choices

| Beef Meals/Entrees (Frozen) (*Continued*) | Serving Size | Cal. | Fat (g) | % Cal. Fat | Sat. Fat (g) | Chol. (mg) | Sod. (mg) | Pro. (g) | Fiber (g) | Carb. (g) | Carb. Ch. | Servings/Exchanges |
|---|---|---|---|---|---|---|---|---|---|---|---|---|
| **Banquet** | | | | | | | | | | | | |
| Beef Patty & Vegetables | 9.5 oz dinner | 310 | 20 | 58 | 8 | 40 | 1090 | 11 | 3 | 22 | 1 1/2 | 1 1/2 carb, 1 med-fat meat, 3 fat |
| Chicken Fried Beef Steak | 10 oz dinner | 420 | 23 | 49 | 12 | 35 | 1200 | 15 | 4 | 39 | 2 1/2 | 2 1/2 carb, 1 med-fat meat, 4 fat |
| Extra Helping Yankee Pot Roast | 14.5 oz dinner | 410 | 20 | 44 | 7 | 50 | 1680 | 25 | 3 | 33 | 2 | 2 carb, 3 med-fat meat, 1 fat |
| Extra Helping-Chicken Fried Beef Steak | 16 oz dinner | 820 | 50 | 55 | 23 | 70 | 2260 | 29 | 8 | 63 | 4 | 4 carb, 2 med-fat meat, 8 fat |
| Extra Helping-Meat Loaf | 16 oz dinner | 610 | 40 | 59 | 15 | 110 | 1940 | 29 | 6 | 24 | 1 1/2 | 1 1/2 carb, 3 med-fat meat, 5 fat |
| Extra Helping-Salisbury Steak | 16.5 oz dinner | 740 | 54 | 66 | 21 | 130 | 2200 | 27 | 7 | 37 | 2 1/2 | 2 1/2 carb, 3 med-fat meat, 8 fat |
| Family Size Beef Patties & Onion Gravy | 4.7 oz | 220 | 17 | 70 | 10 | 30 | 630 | 8 | 1 | 7 | 1/2 | 1/2 carb, 1 med-fat meat, 2 fat |
| Family Size Charbroiled Beef Patties & Mushroom Gravy | 4.7 oz | 230 | 18 | 70 | 8 | 30 | 700 | 11 | 2 | 6 | 1/2 | 1/2 carb, 1 med-fat meat, 3 fat |

| | Serving Size | Cal. | Fat (g) | % Cal. Fat | Sat. Fat (g) | Chol. (mg) | Sod. (mg) | Prot. (g) | Fiber (g) | Carb. (g) | Carb. Ch. | Exchanges/Choices |
|---|---|---|---|---|---|---|---|---|---|---|---|---|
| Family Size Egg Noodles w/Beef & Brown Gravy | 7 oz | 150 | 5 | 30 | 3 | 35 | 1120 | 11 | 2 | 16 | 1 | 1 carb, 1 med-fat meat |
| Family Size Hearty Beef Stew | 8.7 oz | 170 | 7 | 35 | 3 | 30 | 1120 | 10 | 4 | 18 | 1 | 1 carb, 1 med-fat meat |
| Family Size Meatloaf & Savory Gravy | 4.7 oz | 190 | 13 | 62 | 7 | 35 | 750 | 10 | 1 | 7 | 1/2 | 1/2 carb, 1 med-fat meat, 2 fat |
| Family Size Salisbury Steak & Brown Gravy | 4.7 oz | 230 | 17 | 65 | 8 | 30 | 630 | 11 | 1 | 7 | 1/2 | 1/2 carb, 2 med-fat meat, 1 fat |
| Family Size Sliced Beef & Brown Gravy | 5.6 oz | 140 | 8 | 50 | 4 | 40 | 850 | 13 | <1 | 5 | 0 | 2 med-fat meat |
| Meatloaf | 9.5 oz dinner | 280 | 16 | 61 | 6 | 60 | 1020 | 12 | 3 | 23 | 1 1/2 | 1 1/2 carb, 1 med-fat meat, 2 fat |
| Salisbury Steak | 9.5 oz dinner | 380 | 24 | 57 | 12 | 60 | 1140 | 12 | 4 | 28 | 2 | 2 carb, 2 med-fat meat, 1 fat |
| Sliced Beef | 9 oz dinner | 270 | 10 | 33 | 5 | 70 | 740 | 26 | 4 | 19 | 1 | 1 carb, 3 lean meat |
| Western Style Beef Patty | 9.5 oz dinner | 360 | 21 | 53 | 10 | 40 | 1400 | 14 | 5 | 28 | 2 | 2 carb, 1 med-fat meat, 3 fat |
| Yankee Pot Roast | 9.4 oz dinner | 230 | 10 | 39 | 4 | 60 | 1130 | 14 | 4 | 20 | 1 | 1 carb, 1 med-fat meat, 1 fat |

✓ = Best Bet; NA = Not Available; Carb. Ch. = Carbohydrate Choices

| Beef Meals/Entrees (Frozen) (Continued) | Serving Size | Cal. | Fat (g) | % Cal. Fat | Sat. Fat (g) | Chol. (mg) | Sod. (mg) | Pro. (g) | Fiber (g) | Carb. (g) | Carb. Ch. | Servings/Exchanges |
|---|---|---|---|---|---|---|---|---|---|---|---|---|
| **Boston Market** | | | | | | | | | | | | |
| Meatloaf | 16 oz meal | 720 | 42 | 53 | 16 | 90 | 2100 | 27 | 3 | 56 | 4 | 4 carb, 2 med-fat meat, 6 fat |
| **Budget Gourmet** | | | | | | | | | | | | |
| Beef Sirloin Tips w/Country Gravy | 10 oz meal | 310 | 18 | 52 | NA | 40 | 570 | 16 | NA | 21 | 1 1/2 | 1 1/2 carb, 2 med-fat meat, 2 fat |
| Beef Stroganoff | 8.6 oz dinner | 250 | 7 | 25 | 4 | 35 | 580 | 16 | 4 | 30 | 2 | 2 carb, 2 lean meat |
| Hearty Country Fried Beef Steak | 13 oz meal | 440 | 24 | 49 | 8 | 30 | 1350 | 13 | 4 | 42 | 3 | 3 carb, 1 med-fat meat, 4 fat |
| ✔Light & Healthy Beef Stir-Fry | 11 oz meal | 261 | 6 | 20 | 2 | 45 | 495 | 18 | 7 | 34 | 2 | 2 carb, 2 lean meat |
| Pepper Steak & Rice | 10 oz meal | 290 | 8 | 25 | 3 | 40 | 1060 | 18 | 4 | 38 | 2 1/2 | 2 1/2 carb, 2 med-fat meat |
| ✔Sirloin Salisbury Steak | 8.6 oz dinner | 240 | 8 | 30 | 3 | 40 | 550 | 16 | 2 | 27 | 2 | 2 carb, 2 med-fat meat |
| Sirloin Beef Tips in Burgundy Sauce | 11 oz meal | 310 | 11 | 32 | NA | 65 | 720 | 24 | NA | 28 | 2 | 2 carb, 3 lean meat |
| ✔Special Recipe Sirloin of Beef | 11 oz meal | 270 | 5 | 17 | 2 | 25 | 510 | 19 | 5 | 36 | 2 1/2 | 2 1/2 carb, 2 lean meat |
| Special Selections Beef Stroganoff | 9 oz meal | 260 | 8 | 28 | 4 | 35 | 500 | 18 | 3 | 28 | 2 | 2 carb, 2 med-fat meat |
| Swedish Meatballs | 11.2 oz dinner | 450 | 22 | 44 | NA | 70 | 1110 | 23 | NA | 40 | 2 1/2 | 2 1/2 carb, 2 med-fat meat, 2 fat |

| Product | Serving Size | Cal. | Fat (g) | % Cal. Fat | Sat. Fat (g) | Chol. (mg) | Sod. (mg) | Prot. (g) | Fiber (g) | Carb. (g) | Carb. Ch. | Exchanges/Choices |
|---|---|---|---|---|---|---|---|---|---|---|---|---|
| Swedish Meatballs | 11.2 oz meal | 450 | 22 | 44 | NA | 70 | 1110 | 23 | NA | 40 | 2 1/2 | 2 1/2 carb, 2 med-fat meat, 2 fat |
| ✔ Yankee Pot Roast | 10 oz meal | 230 | 5 | 20 | 2 | 30 | 650 | 15 | 4 | 30 | 2 | 2 carb, 2 med-fat meat |
| **Dining Lite** | | | | | | | | | | | | |
| Pepper Steak | 9 oz meal | 260 | 6 | 21 | NA | 40 | 1050 | 18 | NA | 33 | 2 | 2 carb, 2 lean meat |
| Salisbury Steak | 9 oz meal | 200 | 8 | 36 | NA | 55 | 1000 | 18 | NA | 14 | 1 | 1 carb, 2 med-fat meat |
| **Healthy Choice** | | | | | | | | | | | | |
| Beef Pepper Steak Oriental | 9.5 oz meal | 260 | 5 | 17 | 3 | 35 | 520 | 19 | 2 | 34 | 2 | 2 carb, 2 lean meat |
| ✔ Beef Stroganoff | 11 oz meal | 310 | 7 | 20 | 3 | 60 | 440 | 19 | 3 | 44 | 3 | 3 carb, 2 lean meat |
| ✔ Beef Tips Francais | 9.5 oz meal | 300 | 7 | 20 | 3 | 40 | 520 | 20 | 4 | 40 | 2 1/2 | 2 1/2 carb, 2 lean meat |
| ✔ Charbroiled Beef Patty | 11 oz meal | 310 | 9 | 26 | 3 | 45 | 550 | 16 | 4 | 40 | 2 1/2 | 2 1/2 carb, 1 med-fat meat, 1 fat |
| Grilled Peppercorn Beef Patty | 9 oz meal | 220 | 6 | 27 | 3 | 30 | 470 | 16 | 5 | 26 | 2 | 2 carb, 2 lean meat |
| ✔ Hearty Handfuls, Philly Beef Steak | 6.1 oz | 290 | 5 | 16 | 2 | 25 | 550 | 16 | 5 | 47 | 3 | 3 carb, 1 med-fat meat |
| ✔ Mesquite Beef Barbeque | 11 oz meal | 320 | 9 | 25 | 3 | 55 | 490 | 21 | 5 | 38 | 2 1/2 | 2 1/2 carb, 2 med-fat meat |
| ✔ Salisbury Steak | 11.5 oz meal | 330 | 7 | 19 | 3 | 50 | 470 | 18 | 6 | 48 | 3 | 3 carb, 1 med-fat meat |
| Swedish Meatballs | 9.1 oz meal | 280 | 6 | 19 | 3 | 50 | 590 | 22 | 3 | 35 | 2 | 2 carb, 2 lean meat |
| Traditional Beef Tips | 11.25 oz meal | 260 | 6 | 21 | 3 | 40 | 390 | 20 | 6 | 32 | 2 | 2 carb, 2 lean meat |

✔ = Best Bet; NA = Not Available; Carb. Ch. = Carbohydrate Choices

| Beef Meals/Entrees (Frozen) (*Continued*) | Serving Size | Cal. | Fat (g) | % Cal. Fat | Sat. Fat (g) | Chol. (mg) | Sod. (mg) | Pro. (g) | Fiber (g) | Carb. (g) | Carb. Ch. | Servings/Exchanges |
|---|---|---|---|---|---|---|---|---|---|---|---|---|
| Traditional Meatloaf Dinner | 12 oz meal | 330 | 7 | 19 | 4 | 35 | 460 | 15 | 6 | 52 | 3 | 3 carb, 2 med-fat meat |
| ✓Yankee Pot Roast | 11 oz meal | 290 | 7 | 22 | 3 | 55 | 460 | 19 | 4 | 38 | 2 1/2 | 2 1/2 carb, 2 lean meat |
| **Kirkland Signature** | | | | | | | | | | | | |
| Beef Meatballs, Fully Cooked | 6 (3.2 oz) | 230 | 15 | 59 | 6 | 45 | 680 | 14 | 0 | 9 | 1/2 | 1/2 carb, 2 med-fat meat, 1 fat |
| **Lean Cuisine** | | | | | | | | | | | | |
| ✓American Favorites, Beef Pot Roast | 9 oz meal | 210 | 6 | 26 | 2 | 30 | 570 | 13 | 6 | 25 | 1 1/2 | 1 1/2 carb, 2 lean meat |
| ✓American Favorites, Country Vegetables & Beef | 9 oz meal | 210 | 4 | 17 | 1 | 25 | 590 | 11 | 3 | 33 | 2 | 2 carb, 1 med-fat meat |
| American Favorites, Meatloaf & Whipped Potatoes | 9.4 oz meal | 250 | 6 | 22 | 3 | 50 | 590 | 18 | 4 | 30 | 2 | 2 carb, 2 lean meat |
| ✓American Favorites, Oven Roasted Beef | 9.3 oz meal | 260 | 8 | 27 | 3 | 50 | 590 | 18 | 4 | 28 | 2 | 2 carb, 2 med-fat meat |
| American Favorites, Salisbury Steak | 9.5 oz meal | 280 | 8 | 26 | 4 | 60 | 590 | 24 | 4 | 29 | 2 | 2 carb, 3 lean meat |
| ✓American Favorites, Southern Beef Tips | 8.8 oz meal | 290 | 6 | 17 | 2 | 30 | 560 | 13 | 7 | 47 | 3 | 3 carb, 1 med-fat meat |
| ✓Cafe Classics, Beef Peppercorn | 8.8 oz meal | 220 | 7 | 29 | 2 | 35 | 580 | 15 | 2 | 23 | 1 1/2 | 1 1/2 carb, 1 med-fat meat |

| | Serving Size | Cal. | Fat (g) | % Cal. Fat | Sat. Fat (g) | Chol. (mg) | Sod. (mg) | Pro. (g) | Fiber (g) | Carb. (g) | Carb. Ch. | Exchanges/Choices |
|---|---|---|---|---|---|---|---|---|---|---|---|---|
| Café Classics, Beef Portabello | 9 oz meal | 220 | 7 | 29 | 4 | 35 | 590 | 14 | 2 | 24 | 1 1/2 | 1 1/2 carb, 1 med-fat meat |
| ✔Hearty Portions, Homestyle Beef Stroganoff | 14.2 oz meal | 350 | 9 | 23 | 3 | 30 | 890 | 23 | 9 | 44 | 3 | 3 carb, 2 med-fat meat |
| ✔Hearty Portions, Sa,osbiru Steal | 15.5 oz meal | 340 | 7 | 19 | 3 | 50 | 850 | 28 | 10 | 40 | 2 1/2 | 2 1/2 carb, 3 lean meat |
| ✔Skillet Sensations, Roasted Beef & Potatoes | 12 oz meal | 290 | 7 | 22 | 3 | 35 | 760 | 18 | 9 | 38 | 2 1/2 | 2 1/2 carb, 2 lean meat |
| Swedish Meatballs w/Pasta | 9.1 oz meal | 290 | 6 | 19 | 3 | 45 | 580 | 21 | 3 | 38 | 2 1/2 | 2 1/2 carb, 2 lean meat |
| **Marie Callender** | | | | | | | | | | | | |
| Beef Stroganoff and Noodles | 13 oz meal | 610 | 27 | 40 | 11 | 70 | 1140 | 30 | 4 | 59 | 4 | 4 carb, 3 med-fat meat, 2 fat |
| Beef Tips in Mushroom Sauce | 13.6 oz meal | 430 | 19 | 40 | 7 | 50 | 1620 | 25 | 6 | 39 | 2 1/2 | 2 1/2 carb, 3 med-fat meat, 1 fat |
| Chicken Fried Beef Steak & Gravy | 15 oz meal | 650 | 37 | 51 | 13 | 50 | 2260 | 20 | 7 | 50 | 3 | 3 carb, 2 med-fat meat, 5 fat |
| Meatloaf & Gravy | 14 oz meal | 540 | 30 | 50 | 12 | 95 | 1570 | 23 | 5 | 42 | 3 | 3 carb, 2 med-fat meat, 4 fat |

✔ = Best Bet; NA = Not Available; Carb. Ch. = Carbohydrate Choices

| Beef Meals/Entrees (Frozen) (*Continued*) | Serving Size | Cal. | Fat (g) | % Cal. Fat | Sat. Fat (g) | Chol. (mg) | Sod. (mg) | Pro. (g) | Fiber (g) | Carb. (g) | Carb. Ch. | Servings/Exchanges |
|---|---|---|---|---|---|---|---|---|---|---|---|---|
| Old Fashioned Beef Pot Roast | 15 oz meal | 500 | 17 | 30 | 6 | 110 | 1460 | 23 | 3 | 55 | 3 1/2 | 3 1/2 carb, 2 med-fat meat, 1 fat |
| Pasta w/Beef & Broccoli | 15 oz meal | 570 | 15 | 25 | 4 | 70 | 1160 | 35 | 6 | 73 | 5 | 5 carb, 2 med-fat meat, 1 fat |
| Sirloin Salisbury Steak & Gravy | 14 oz meal | 550 | 25 | 40 | 11 | 85 | 680 | 30 | 6 | 51 | 4 1/2 | 4 1/2 carb, 2 med-fat meat, 3 fat |
| Swedish Meatballs | 12.5 oz meal | 520 | 26 | 44 | 12 | 65 | 1020 | 28 | 3 | 44 | 3 | 3 carb, 3 med-fat meat, 2 fat |
| **Morton** | | | | | | | | | | | | |
| Gravy & Charbroiled Beef Patty Meal | 9 oz meal | 310 | 18 | 52 | 9 | 30 | 1210 | 10 | 5 | 26 | 2 | 2 carb, 1 med-fat meat, 2 fat |
| Gravy & Salisbury Steak Meal | 9 oz meal | 310 | 20 | 58 | 8 | 30 | 1100 | 7 | 3 | 24 | 1 1/2 | 1 1/2 carb, 1 med-fat meat |
| Tomato Sauce w/Meat Loaf | 9 oz meal | 250 | 13 | 47 | 5 | 20 | 1200 | 9 | 3 | 24 | 1 1/2 | 1 1/2 carb, 1 med-fat meat, 2 fat |
| **Stouffer's** | | | | | | | | | | | | |
| Beef Stroganoff | 9.8 oz meal | 390 | 20 | 46 | 7 | 85 | 1100 | 23 | 2 | 30 | 2 | 2 carb, 2 med-fat meat, 2 fat |

| | | | | | | | | | | | | |
|---|---|---|---|---|---|---|---|---|---|---|---|---|
| Country Fried Beef Steak | 16 oz meal | 560 | 25 | 40 | 10 | 50 | 1750 | 22 | 7 | 61 | 4 | 4 carb, 2 med-fat meat, 3 fat |
| Creamed Chipped Beef | 4.4 oz | 160 | 10 | 56 | 5 | 35 | 620 | 10 | 0 | 8 | 1/2 | 1/2 carb, 1 med-fat meat, 1 fat |
| ✔Green Pepper Steak | 10.5 oz meal | 330 | 9 | 25 | 3 | 35 | 650 | 17 | 3 | 45 | 3 | 3 carb, 1 med-fat meat |
| Hearty Portions, Beef Pot Roast | 16 oz meal | 370 | 11 | 27 | 5 | 45 | 1410 | 23 | 8 | 44 | 3 | 3 carb, 2 med-fat meat |
| Hearty Portions, Meatloaf | 17 oz meal | 480 | 23 | 43 | 10 | 90 | 1580 | 23 | 8 | 46 | 3 | 3 carb, 2 med-fat meat, 3 fat |
| Home Style Salisbury Steak | 9.6 oz meal | 380 | 18 | 43 | 8 | 60 | 1170 | 26 | 1 | 28 | 2 | 2 carb, 3 med-fat meat, 1 fat |
| ✔Homestyle Beef Pot Roast | 8.9 oz meal | 250 | 8 | 29 | 3 | 35 | 780 | 16 | 4 | 29 | 2 | 2 carb, 2 med-fat meat |
| Homestyle Meatloaf | 9.9 oz meal | 390 | 21 | 48 | 11 | 90 | 840 | 22 | 3 | 28 | 2 | 2 carb, 2 med-fat meat, 2 fat |
| Meatloaf in Gravy | 5.5 oz meal | 190 | 10 | 47 | 5 | 50 | 550 | 15 | 0 | 10 | 1/2 | 1/2 carb, 2 med-fat meat |
| Salisbury Steak w/Pasta Shells | 16 oz meal | 570 | 24 | 38 | 10 | 100 | 1640 | 41 | 4 | 47 | 3 | 3 carb, 5 med-fat meat |
| Skillet Sensations, Broccoli and Beef | 12.5 oz | 310 | 3 | 9 | 2 | 25 | 1350 | 18 | 3 | 52 | 3 1/2 | 3 1/2 carb, 1 lean meat |
| Skillet Sensations, Cheddar Beef | 12.5 oz meal | 600 | 29 | 44 | 14 | 55 | 1340 | 26 | 5 | 58 | 4 | 4 carb, 2 med-fat meat, 4 fat |

✔= Best Bet; NA = Not Available; Carb. Ch. = Carbohydrate Choices

| Beef Meals/Entrees (Frozen) (Continued) | Serving Size | Cal. | Fat (g) | % Cal. Fat | Sat. Fat (g) | Chol. (mg) | Sod. (mg) | Pro. (g) | Fiber (g) | Carb. (g) | Carb. Ch. | Servings/Exchanges |
|---|---|---|---|---|---|---|---|---|---|---|---|---|
| Swedish Meatballs | 10.3 oz meal | 470 | 22 | 42 | 8 | 65 | 970 | 23 | 2 | 45 | 3 | 3 carb, 2 med-fat meat, 2 fat |
| **Swanson** | | | | | | | | | | | | |
| Chopped Sirloin Beef Steak | 10.5 oz meal | 370 | 17 | 41 | 7 | 50 | 640 | 20 | 4 | 35 | 2 | 2 carb, 2 med-fat meat, 1 fat |
| Country Fried Beef Steak | 10.8 oz meal | 460 | 22 | 43 | 10 | 45 | 910 | 17 | 3 | 47 | 3 | 3 carb, 1 med-fat meat, 3 fat |
| Roast Beef & Gravy | 10.5 oz meal | 370 | 15 | 36 | 6 | 40 | 700 | 19 | 6 | 40 | 3 1/2 | 3 1/2 carb, 1 med-fat meat, 2 fat |
| Salisbury Steak | 13 oz meal | 390 | 16 | 37 | 6 | 45 | 1160 | 26 | 12 | 35 | 2 | 2 carb, 3 med-fat meat |
| Sirloin Beef Tips | 10 oz meal | 290 | 11 | 34 | 5 | 50 | 530 | 16 | 5 | 34 | 3 | 3 carb, 1 med-fat meat, 1 fat |
| **Swanson Hungry-Man** | | | | | | | | | | | | |
| Beef Pot Roast | 18.5 oz meal | 390 | 8 | 19 | 3 | 40 | 1520 | 20 | 7 | 59 | 4 | 4 carb, 1 med-fat meat, 1 fat |
| Country Fried Beef Steak | 16 oz meal | 860 | 49 | 51 | 18 | 75 | 1600 | 30 | 2 | 75 | 5 | 5 carb, 2 med-fat meat, 8 fat |

| | Serving Size | Cal | Fat (g) | % Cal. Fat | Sat. Fat (g) | Chol. (mg) | Sod. (mg) | Prot. (g) | Fiber (g) | Carb. (g) | Carb. Ch. | Exchanges/Choices |
|---|---|---|---|---|---|---|---|---|---|---|---|---|
| Salisbury Steak | 16.3 oz meal | 610 | 34 | 50 | 13 | 95 | 1710 | 30 | 5 | 45 | 3 | 3 carb, 3 med-fat meat, 4 fat |
| Sirloin Beef Tips | 15.8 oz meal | 440 | 16 | 33 | 6 | 55 | 960 | 25 | 6 | 49 | 3 | 3 carb, 2 med-fat meat, 1 fat |
| **Weight Watchers Smart Ones** | | | | | | | | | | | | |
| Salisbury Steak | 9.5 oz meal | 260 | 6 | 21 | 3 | 30 | 790 | 22 | 4 | 25 | 1 1/2 | 1 1/2 carb, 2 lean meat |
| **White Castle** | | | | | | | | | | | | |
| Micro Cheeseburgers, Fully Cooked | 2 sandwich | 310 | 17 | 49 | 9 | 29 | 485 | 15 | 6 | 23 | 1 1/2 | 1 1/2 strch, 2 med-fat meat, 1 fat |

## BEEF MEALS/ENTREES (REFRIGERATED)

### Harris Ranch

| | Serving Size | Cal | Fat (g) | % Cal. Fat | Sat. Fat (g) | Chol. (mg) | Sod. (mg) | Prot. (g) | Fiber (g) | Carb. (g) | Carb. Ch. | Exchanges/Choices |
|---|---|---|---|---|---|---|---|---|---|---|---|---|
| Beef Pot Roast w/Natural Juices Fully Cooked | 5 oz | 200 | 6 | 27 | 3 | 80 | 670 | 31 | 0 | 4 | 0 | 4 very lean meat |
| Beef Stew w/Garden Vegetables/Beef Stock | 1 cup | 240 | 9 | 34 | 3 | 70 | 830 | 25 | 2 | 15 | 1 | 1 carb, 3 lean meat |
| Boneless Beef Short Ribs w/Tangy BBQ Sauce | 5 oz w/sauce | 380 | 16 | 38 | 6 | 130 | 540 | 38 | 0 | 16 | 1 | 1 carb, 5 lean meat |

✔= Best Bet; NA = Not Available; Carb. Ch. = Carbohydrate Choices

## BEVERAGE/DRINK MIX (AS PREPARED)

| Product | Serving Size | Cal. | Fat (g) | % Cal. Fat | Sat. Fat (g) | Chol. (mg) | Sod. (mg) | Pro. (g) | Fiber (g) | Carb. (g) | Carb. Ch. | Servings/Exchanges |
|---|---|---|---|---|---|---|---|---|---|---|---|---|
| **(Generic)** | | | | | | | | | | | | |
| ✔Fruit Drink Powder & Water, Low Calorie | 8 oz | 43 | 0 | 0 | 0 | 0 | 50 | 0 | 0 | 11 | 1 | 1 carb |
| ✔Fruit Punch Drink-Bottle/Can | 8 oz | 119 | <1 | 0 | <1 | 0 | 56 | 0 | <1 | 30 | 2 | 2 carb |
| ✔Lemonade-Frozen Concentrate & Water | | | | | | | | | | | | |
| **Country Time** | | | | | | | | | | | | |
| ✔Iced Tea Drink w/Sugar | 8 oz | 70 | 0 | 0 | 0 | 0 | 0 | 0 | 0 | 17 | 1 | 1 carb |
| ✔Lem'N Berry Sippers, All Varieties (Avg) | 8 oz | 90 | 0 | 0 | 0 | 0 | 0 | 0 | 0 | 21 | 1 1/2 | 1 1/2 carb |
| ✔Lem'N Berry Sippers, Sugar Free | 8 oz | 5 | 0 | 0 | 0 | 0 | 0 | 0 | 0 | 0 | 0 | free |
| ✔Lemonade | 8 oz | 70 | 0 | 0 | 0 | 0 | 15 | 0 | 0 | 15 | 1 | 1 carb |
| ✔Lemonade Drink, Sugar-Free, Low Calorie | 8 oz | 5 | 0 | 0 | 0 | 0 | 0 | 0 | 0 | 0 | 0 | free |
| **Crystal Light** | | | | | | | | | | | | |
| ✔Cranberry Breeze Drink | 8 oz | 5 | 0 | 0 | 0 | 0 | 0 | 0 | 0 | 0 | 0 | free |
| ✔Iced Lemon Tea Drink | 8 oz | 5 | 0 | 0 | 0 | 0 | 0 | 0 | 0 | 0 | 0 | free |
| ✔Lemonade Drink, Sugar Free | 8 oz | 5 | 0 | 0 | 0 | 0 | 0 | 0 | 0 | 0 | 0 | free |
| **New York Seltzer** | | | | | | | | | | | | |
| ✔Diet Sparkling Water, All Varieties (Avg) | 8 oz | 2 | 0 | 0 | 0 | 0 | 15 | 0 | 0 | 0 | 0 | free |

| | Serving | Cal | Fat (g) | % Cal Fat | Sat Fat (g) | Chol (mg) | Sodium (mg) | Prot (g) | Fiber (g) | Carb (g) | Carb Ch. | Exchanges |
|---|---|---|---|---|---|---|---|---|---|---|---|---|
| ✓Sparkling Flavored Water, All Varieties (Avg) | 8 oz | 90 | 0 | | 0 | 0 | 15 | | 0 | 22 | 1 1/2 | 1 1/2 carb |
| ✓Sparkling Iced Tea, All Varieties (Avg) | 8 oz | 95 | 0 | | 0 | 0 | 50 | | 0 | 21 | 1 1/2 | 1 1/2 carb |
| **Ross** | | | | | | | | | | | | |
| Glucerna, Chocolate or Vanilla | 8 oz | 220 | 11 | 45 | 1 | <5 | 210 | 10 | 2 | 22 | 1 1/2 | 1/2 carb, 1 low-fat milk |
| **Snapple** | | | | | | | | | | | | |
| ✓Diet, All Varieties (Avg) | 8 oz | 0 | 0 | | 0 | 0 | 10 | | 0 | 1 | 0 | free |
| ✓Elements, Lightning-Ginseng Black Tea | 8 oz | 90 | 0 | | 0 | 0 | 10 | | 0 | 22 | 1 1/2 | 1 1/2 carb |
| ✓Tea, All Varieties (Avg) | 8 oz | 100 | 0 | | 0 | 0 | 10 | | 0 | 26 | 2 | 2 carb |
| **Tang** | | | | | | | | | | | | |
| ✓Drink Mix, All Varieties (Avg) | 8 oz | 95 | 0 | | 0 | 0 | 0 | | 0 | 24 | 1 1/2 | 1 1/2 carb |
| ✓Orange Drink, Sugar-Free | 8 oz | 5 | 0 | | 0 | 0 | 0 | | 0 | 0 | 0 | free |

## BEVERAGES/DRINKS (CANNED/BOTTLED)

**(Generic)**

| | Serving | Cal | Fat (g) | % Cal Fat | Sat Fat (g) | Chol (mg) | Sodium (mg) | Prot (g) | Fiber (g) | Carb (g) | Carb Ch. | Exchanges |
|---|---|---|---|---|---|---|---|---|---|---|---|---|
| ✓Tonic Water, Sugar Free | 12 oz | 0 | 0 | | 0 | 0 | 57 | | 0 | <1 | 0 | free |
| ✓Tonic Water/Quinine Water | 12 oz | 124 | 0 | | 0 | 0 | 15 | | 0 | 32 | 2 | 2 carb |
| **Capri Sun** | | | | | | | | | | | | |
| ✓Natural Juice Drink, All Varieties (Avg) | 9.6 oz | 110 | 0 | | 0 | 0 | 20 | | 0 | 26 | 2 | 2 carb |

✓= Best Bet; NA = Not Available; Carb. Ch. = Carbohydrate Choices

| Beverages/Drinks (Canned/Bottled) (Continued) | Serving Size | Cal. | Fat (g) | % Cal. Fat | Sat. Fat (g) | Chol. (mg) | Sod. (mg) | Pro. (g) | Fiber (g) | Carb. (g) | Carb. Ch. | Servings/Exchanges |
|---|---|---|---|---|---|---|---|---|---|---|---|---|
| **Nestea** | | | | | | | | | | | | |
| ✔Cool From Nestea | 12 oz | 120 | 0 | 0 | 0 | 0 | 100 | 0 | 0 | 33 | 2 | 2 carb |
| **Powerade** | | | | | | | | | | | | |
| ✔Sports Drink, All Varieties (Avg) | 8 oz | 72 | 0 | 0 | 0 | 0 | 53 | 0 | 0 | 19 | 1 | 1 carb |
| **Snapple** | | | | | | | | | | | | |
| ✔Elements, Moon-Green Tea | 8 oz | 80 | 0 | 0 | 0 | 0 | 10 | 0 | 0 | 19 | 1 1/2 | 1 carb |
| **Sunny Delight** | | | | | | | | | | | | |
| ✔Orange Drink/Ade | 8 oz | 130 | 0 | 0 | 0 | 0 | 130 | 0 | 0 | 32 | 2 | 2 carb |
| **Tropicana** | | | | | | | | | | | | |
| ✔Twister, All Varieties (Avg) | 8 oz | 125 | 0 | 0 | 0 | 0 | 33 | <1 | <1 | 32 | 2 | 2 carb |
| ✔Twister, Light | 8 oz | 40 | 0 | 0 | 0 | 0 | 100 | 0 | <1 | 10 | 1/2 | 1/2 carb |
| **BISCUIT MIX (AS PREPARED)** | | | | | | | | | | | | |
| **Bisquick** | | | | | | | | | | | | |
| Baking Mix | 1/3 cup | 170 | 6 | 32 | 2 | 0 | NA | 3 | <1 | 25 | 1 1/2 | 1 1/2 carb, 1 fat |
| ✔Reduced Fat Baking Mix | 1/3 cup | 150 | 3 | 18 | <1 | 0 | 460 | 3 | <1 | 28 | 2 | 2 carb, 1 fat |
| Sweet Baking Mix | 1/4 cup | 170 | 4 | 21 | 2 | 0 | 260 | 1 | 0 | 31 | 2 | 2 carb, 1 fat |
| **Gold Medal/General Mills** | | | | | | | | | | | | |
| Baking Powder Biscuit Mix | 1 | 160 | 5 | 28 | 1 | 0 | 460 | 4 | <1 | 25 | 1 1/2 | 1 1/2 strch, 1 fat |

|  |  |  |  |  |  |  |  |  |  | Carb. Ch. | Exchanges |
|---|---|---|---|---|---|---|---|---|---|---|---|
| Buttermilk Biscuit Mix | 1 | 170 | 8 | 42 | 3 | 0 | 420 | 3 | <1 | 24 | 1 1/2 | 1 1/2 strch, 2 fat |
| Cinnamon Raisin Biscuit Mix | 1 | 260 | 9 | 28 | 3 | 0 | 560 | 4 | 1 | 41 | 3 | 3 strch, 2 fat |
| Regular Biscuit Mix | 1 | 160 | 7 | 39 | 2 | 0 | 420 | 3 | <1 | 22 | 1 1/2 | 1 1/2 strch, 1 fat |

## BISCUITS (REFRIGERATED)

### Ballard

|  |  |  |  |  |  |  |  |  |  | Carb. Ch. | Exchanges |
|---|---|---|---|---|---|---|---|---|---|---|---|
| ✓Xtra Light Oven Ready Biscuit Dough, Regular or Buttermilk | 1 | 50 | <1 | 18 | <1 | 0 | 165 | 1 | <1 | 10 | 1/2 | 1/2 strch |

### Big Country

|  |  |  |  |  |  |  |  |  |  | Carb. Ch. | Exchanges |
|---|---|---|---|---|---|---|---|---|---|---|---|
| Butter Tastin' Biscuit Dough | 1 | 100 | 4 | 36 | 1 | 0 | 360 | 2 | 0 | 13 | 1 | 1 strch, 1 fat |

### Grands

|  |  |  |  |  |  |  |  |  |  | Carb. Ch. | Exchanges |
|---|---|---|---|---|---|---|---|---|---|---|---|
| Butter Tastin' Biscuit Dough | 1 | 200 | 10 | 45 | 3 | 0 | 620 | 4 | <1 | 24 | 1 1/2 | 1 1/2 strch, 2 fat |
| Buttermilk Refrigerated Biscuits | 1 | 200 | 10 | 45 | 3 | 0 | 573 | 4 | 1 | 23 | 1 1/2 | 1 1/2 strch, 2 fat |
| Extra Rich Biscuit Dough | 1 | 220 | 12 | 49 | 3 | 0 | 580 | 4 | <1 | 25 | 1 1/2 | 1 1/2 strch, 2 fat |
| Flaky Biscuit Dough | 1 | 200 | 9 | 41 | 2 | 0 | 580 | 4 | <1 | 25 | 1 1/2 | 1 1/2 strch, 2 fat |
| Homestyle Refrigerated Biscuits | 1 | 190 | 9 | 43 | 2 | 0 | 595 | 4 | 1 | 24 | 1 1/2 | 1 1/2 strch, 2 fat |
| Reduced Fat Buttermilk Biscuit Dough | 1 | 190 | 7 | 33 | 2 | 0 | 620 | 4 | <1 | 27 | 2 | 2 strch, 1 fat |
| Southern Refrigerated Biscuits | 1 | 200 | 10 | 45 | 3 | 0 | 573 | 4 | 1 | 23 | 1 1/2 | 1 1/2 strch, 2 fat |

✓= Best Bet; NA = Not Available; Carb. Ch. = Carbohydrate Choices

| Biscuits (Refrigerated) (*Continued*) | Serving Size | Cal. | Fat (g) | % Cal. Fat | Sat. Fat (g) | Chol. (mg) | Sod. (mg) | Pro. (g) | Fiber (g) | Carb. (g) | Carb. Ch. | Servings/Exchanges |
|---|---|---|---|---|---|---|---|---|---|---|---|---|
| **Pillsbury** | | | | | | | | | | | | |
| Big Country Buttermilk Biscuit Dough | 1 | 100 | 4 | 36 | 1 | 0 | 360 | 2 | 0 | 14 | 1 | 1 strch, 1 fat |
| Big Country Southern Biscuit Dough | 1 | 100 | 4 | 36 | 1 | 0 | 360 | 2 | 0 | 14 | 1 | 1 strch, 1 fat |
| Country Biscuit Dough | 1 | 150 | 2 | 12 | 0 | 0 | 540 | 4 | <1 | 29 | 2 | 2 strch |
| Tender Layer Buttermilk Biscuit Dough | 1 | 160 | 5 | 28 | 1 | 0 | 520 | 4 | 3 | 27 | 2 | 2 strch |
| **Pillsbury/Hungry Jack** | | | | | | | | | | | | |
| Biscuit Dough, Flaky Buttermilk | 1 | 100 | 5 | 45 | 1 | 0 | 360 | 2 | 0 | 14 | 1 | 1 strch, 1 fat |
| Butter Tastin Flaky Biscuit Dough | 1 | 100 | 5 | 45 | 1 | 0 | 350 | 2 | 0 | 14 | 1 | 1 strch, 1 fat |
| Cinnamon & Sugar Biscuit Dough | 1 | 110 | 4 | 33 | 1 | 0 | 280 | 2 | <1 | 17 | 1 | 1 strch, 1 fat |
| Fluffy Refrigerated Biscuits | 1 | 81 | 5 | 56 | 1 | 0 | 350 | 2 | 0 | 14 | 1 | 1 strch, 1 fat |
| **BREAD (READY-TO-EAT)** | | | | | | | | | | | | |
| **Earthgrains** | | | | | | | | | | | | |
| ✔Iron Kids Bread | 1 slice | 60 | <1 | 8 | 0 | 0 | 130 | 2 | 1 | 13 | 1 | 1 strch |
| **Holsum** | | | | | | | | | | | | |
| ✔Smart Kids Bread | 1 slice | 60 | <1 | 8 | 0 | 0 | 140 | 3 | 1 | 12 | 1 | 1 strch |
| **Oro Wheat** | | | | | | | | | | | | |
| ✔100% Whole Wheat Light Bread | 2 slices | 80 | <1 | 6 | 0 | 0 | 230 | 4 | 7 | 18 | 1 | 1 strch |
| ✔9 Grain Light Bread | 2 slices | 80 | <1 | 6 | 0 | 0 | 220 | 4 | 5 | 18 | 1 | 1 strch |

| Food | Serving Size | Cal. | Fat (g) | % Cal. Fat | Sat. Fat (g) | Chol. (mg) | Sod. (mg) | Carb. (g) | Fiber (g) | Pro. (g) | Carb. Ch. | Exchanges |
|---|---|---|---|---|---|---|---|---|---|---|---|---|
| ✓ Country Potato Light Bread | 2 slices | 80 | <1 | 6 | 0 | 0 | 240 | 20 | 6 | 3 | 1 | 1 strch |
| **Pepperidge Farm** | | | | | | | | | | | | |
| ✓ 100% Whole-Wheat Bread | 1 slice | 90 | 1 | 10 | 0 | 0 | 160 | 15 | 2 | 4 | 1 | 1 strch |
| ✓ 1-1/2 lb Natural Wheat Bread | 1 slice | 90 | 2 | 20 | 0 | 0 | 170 | 16 | 1 | 4 | 1 | 1 strch |
| ✓ 1-1/2 lb Wheat Bread | 1 slice | 90 | 2 | 20 | 0 | 0 | 190 | 16 | 1 | 3 | 1 | 1 strch |
| 2 lb Family Wheat Bread | 1 slice | 70 | 1 | 13 | 0 | 0 | 135 | 13 | 1 | 2 | 1 | 1 strch |
| ✓ Apple Walnut Swirl Bread | 1 slice | 80 | 2 | 23 | <1 | 0 | 120 | 14 | 1 | 2 | 1 | 1 strch |
| ✓ Cinnamon Bread | 1 slice | 80 | 3 | 34 | <1 | 0 | 115 | 14 | 1 | 3 | 1 | 1 strch, 1 fat |
| ✓ Classic Dark Pumpernickel Bread | 1 slice | 80 | 1 | 11 | <1 | 0 | 230 | 15 | 1 | 3 | 1 | 1 strch |
| ✓ Cracked Wheat Thin Slice Bread | 1 slice | 70 | 1 | 13 | 0 | 0 | 140 | 12 | <1 | 2 | 1 | 1 strch |
| Garlic Bread | 1 slice | 160 | 10 | 56 | 3 | 30 | 250 | 14 | 1 | 5 | 1 | 1 strch, 2 fat |
| Garlic Parmesan Bread | 1 slice | 160 | 7 | 39 | 2 | 10 | 260 | 19 | 2 | 6 | 1 | 1 strch, 1 fat |
| ✓ Golden Swirl Vermont Maple Bread | 1 slice | 90 | 3 | 30 | 1 | 0 | 100 | 15 | <1 | 2 | 1 | 1 strch, 1 fat |
| ✓ Hearty Country White Bread | 1 slice | 90 | 1 | 10 | 0 | 0 | 190 | 19 | 2 | 3 | 1 | 1 strch |
| ✓ Hearty Crunchy Oat Bread | 1 slice | 100 | 2 | 18 | 0 | 0 | 180 | 17 | 2 | 4 | 1 | 1 strch |
| ✓ Hearty Honey Wheatberry Bread | 1 slice | 100 | 2 | 18 | 0 | 0 | 200 | 18 | 2 | 3 | 1 | 1 strch |
| ✓ Hearty Russet Potato Bread | 1 slice | 90 | 2 | 20 | <1 | <5 | 260 | 18 | 3 | 4 | 1 | 1 strch |
| ✓ Hearty Sesame Wheat Bread | 1 slice | 100 | 2 | 18 | 0 | 0 | 180 | 17 | 2 | 4 | 1 | 1 strch |

✓ = Best Bet; NA = Not Available; Carb. Ch. = Carbohydrate Choices

| Bread (Ready-to-Eat) (Continued) | Serving Size | Cal. | Fat (g) | % Cal. Fat | Sat. Fat (g) | Chol. (mg) | Sod. (mg) | Pro. (g) | Fiber (g) | Carb. (g) | Carb. Ch. | Servings/Exchanges |
|---|---|---|---|---|---|---|---|---|---|---|---|---|
| ✓Hearty Slice 7-Grain Bread | 1 slice | 100 | 2 | 18 | 0 | 0 | 180 | 3 | 2 | 18 | 1 | 1 strch |
| ✓Hearty White Bread | 1 slice | 90 | 1 | 10 | 0 | 0 | 190 | 3 | 2 | 19 | 1 | 1 strch |
| ✓Jewish Seeded Rye Bread | 1 slice | 80 | 1 | 11 | <1 | 0 | 210 | 3 | 1 | 15 | 1 | 1 strch |
| ✓Jewish Seedless Family Rye Bread | 1 slice | 80 | 1 | 11 | <1 | 0 | 210 | 3 | 1 | 15 | 1 | 1 strch |
| ✓Large Family White Thin Slice Bread | 1 slice | 80 | 2 | 23 | 0 | 0 | 160 | 2 | 0 | 14 | 1 | 1 strch |
| ✓Light Style Seven-Grain Bread | 1 slice | 47 | <1 | 19 | 0 | 0 | 107 | 2 | 2 | 9 | 1/2 | 1/2 strch |
| ✓Light Style Sourdough Bread | 1 slice | 43 | <1 | 21 | 0 | 0 | 107 | 2 | 1 | 9 | 1/2 | 1/2 strch |
| ✓Light Vienna Bread | 1 slice | 43 | <1 | 21 | <1 | 0 | 100 | 2 | 2 | 9 | 1/2 | 1/2 strch |
| ✓Light-Style Oatmeal Bread | 1 slice | 47 | <1 | 19 | 0 | 0 | 103 | 2 | 2 | 9 | 1/2 | 1/2 strch |
| ✓Light-Style Wheat Bread | 1 slice | 43 | <1 | 21 | <1 | 0 | 97 | 2 | 2 | 9 | 1/2 | 1/2 strch |
| Monterey Jack w/Jalapeno Cheese Bread | 1 slice | 200 | 10 | 45 | 4 | 40 | 280 | 5 | 1 | 22 | 1 1/2 | 1 1/2 strch, 2 fat |
| ✓Old Fashioned Honey Bran Bread | 1 slice | 90 | 1 | 10 | 0 | 0 | 160 | 3 | 2 | 17 | 1 | 1 strch |
| ✓Onion Rye Bread | 1 slice | 80 | 1 | 11 | <1 | 0 | 210 | 3 | 1 | 15 | 1 | 1 strch |
| ✓Party Pumpernickel Bread | 3 slices | 110 | 2 | 16 | 0 | 0 | 320 | 6 | 4 | 22 | 1 1/2 | 1 1/2 strch |
| ✓Raisin with Cinnamon Bread | 1 slice | 80 | 2 | 23 | 0 | 0 | 105 | 3 | 1 | 14 | 1 | 1 strch |
| ✓Soft Oatmeal Bread | 1 slice | 60 | 1 | 15 | 0 | 0 | 2 | 2 | 0 | 12 | 1 | 1 strch |
| ✓Thin Sliced Dijon Rye Bread | 2 slices | 100 | 2 | 18 | <1 | 0 | 340 | 4 | 2 | 18 | 1 | 1 strch |
| Two Cheddar Cheese Bread | 1 slice | 210 | 11 | 47 | 5 | 50 | 280 | 5 | 1 | 21 | 1 1/2 | 1 1/2 strch, 2 fat |

| | | | | | | | | | | | | |
|---|---|---|---|---|---|---|---|---|---|---|---|---|
| ✔Very Thin Sliced White Bread | 3 slices | 110 | 2 | 16 | 0 | 0 | 270 | 4 | 2 | 23 | 1 1/2 | 1 1/2 strch |
| ✔Vienna Thick Sliced Bread | 1 slice | 70 | 1 | 13 | 0 | 0 | 150 | 3 | <1 | 12 | 1 | 1 strch |
| ✔White Sandwich Bread | 1 slices | 65 | 1 | 14 | <1 | 0 | 130 | 2 | <1 | 12 | 1 | 1 strch |
| ✔White Thin Sliced Bread | 1 slice | 80 | 2 | 23 | 0 | 0 | 135 | 2 | 0 | 13 | 1 | 1 strch |
| ✔Whole Wheat Thin Sliced Bread | 1 slice | 60 | 1 | 15 | 0 | 0 | 120 | 3 | <1 | 11 | 1 | 1 strch |
| **Rainbo** | | | | | | | | | | | | |
| ✔Thin Slice White | 1 slice | 70 | 1 | 13 | 0 | 0 | 160 | 2 | 1 | 14 | 1 | 1 strch |

## BREAD DOUGH (FROZEN)

### Rhodes

| | | | | | | | | | | | | |
|---|---|---|---|---|---|---|---|---|---|---|---|---|
| ✔White Bread Dough | 1 slice | 140 | 2 | 13 | 0 | 0 | 280 | 5 | 2 | 24 | 1 1/2 | 1 1/2 carb |
| ✔White Texas Rolls | 1 | 150 | 3 | 18 | 0 | 0 | 220 | 5 | 1 | 27 | 2 | 2 carb, 1 fat |

## BREAD DOUGH (REFRIGERATED)

### Pillsbury

| | | | | | | | | | | | | |
|---|---|---|---|---|---|---|---|---|---|---|---|---|
| Cornbread Twist Roll/Bread Dough | 1 | 140 | 6 | 39 | 2 | 0 | 310 | 3 | 0 | 18 | 1 | 1 strch, 1 fat |
| Crescent Roll/Bread Dough | 1 | 110 | 6 | 49 | 2 | 0 | 220 | 2 | 0 | 11 | 1 | 1 carb, 1 fat |
| Garlic & Herb Bread Sticks | 1 | 180 | 7 | 35 | 2 | 0 | 580 | 4 | <1 | 25 | 1 1/2 | 1 1/2 strch, 1 fat |
| Reduced Fat Crescents Roll/Bread Dough | 1 | 100 | 5 | 45 | 1 | 0 | 230 | 2 | 0 | 12 | 1 | 1 strch, 1 fat |

✔= Best Bet; NA = Not Available; Carb. Ch. = Carbohydrate Choices

| Product | Serving Size | Cal. | Fat (g) | % Cal. Fat | Sat. Fat (g) | Chol. (mg) | Sod. (mg) | Pro. (g) | Fiber (g) | Carb. (g) | Carb. Ch. | Servings/Exchanges |
|---|---|---|---|---|---|---|---|---|---|---|---|---|
| **BREAD MIX (AS PREPARED)** | | | | | | | | | | | | |
| **Betty Crocker** | | | | | | | | | | | | |
| Banana Quickbread Mix (pouch) | 1/12 loaf | 170 | 7 | 37 | 2 | 35 | 200 | 3 | 0 | 25 | 1 1/2 | 1 1/2 carb, 1 fat |
| Cinnamon Streusel Quickbread Mix (pouch) | 1/14 loaf | 180 | 7 | 35 | 2 | 30 | 160 | 2 | 0 | 28 | 2 | 2 carb, 1 fat |
| Cranberry Orange Quickbread Mix (pouch) | 1/12 loaf | 180 | 6 | 30 | 1 | 35 | 180 | 3 | 0 | 29 | 2 | 2 carb, 1 fat |
| Lemon Poppyseed Quickbread Mix (pouch) | 1/12 loaf | 170 | 7 | 37 | 2 | 35 | 200 | 3 | 0 | 25 | 1 1/2 | 1 1/2 carb, 1 fat |
| **Pillsbury** | | | | | | | | | | | | |
| Apple Cinnamon Quick Bread Mix | 1 slice | 180 | 6 | 30 | 1 | 20 | 170 | 2 | 1 | 30 | 2 | 2 strch, 1 fat |
| Ballard Corn Bread | 1 slice | 130 | 3 | 21 | 1 | 25 | 520 | 4 | <1 | 23 | 1 1/2 | 1 1/2 strch, 1 fat |
| Banana Quick Bread Mix | 1 slice | 170 | 6 | 32 | 1 | 35 | 200 | 3 | <1 | 26 | 2 | 2 strch, 1 fat |
| Blueberry Quick Bread Mix | 1 slice | 180 | 6 | 30 | 1 | 20 | 160 | 2 | <1 | 29 | 2 | 2 carb, 1 fat |
| Carrot Quick Bread Mix | 1 slice | 140 | 5 | 32 | 1 | 25 | 150 | 2 | <1 | 22 | 1 1/2 | 1 1/2 strch, 1 fat |
| ✓Cracker Wheat Bread Machine Mix | 1 slice | 130 | 2 | 14 | 0 | 0 | 260 | 4 | 2 | 25 | 1 1/2 | 1 1/2 strch |
| Cranberry Quickl Bread Mix | 1 slice | 160 | 4 | 23 | 1 | 20 | 150 | 2 | <1 | 30 | 2 | 2 strch, 1 fat |

| | Serving | Cal. | Fat (g) | % Cal. Fat | Sat. Fat (g) | Chol. (mg) | Sod. (mg) | Prot. (g) | Fiber (g) | Carb. (g) | Carb. Ch. | Exchanges |
|---|---|---|---|---|---|---|---|---|---|---|---|---|
| ✔Crusty White Bread Machine Mix | 1 slice | 130 | 2 | 14 | 0 | 0 | 250 | 4 | 2 | 25 | 1 1/2 | 1 1/2 strch |
| Date Quick Bread Mix | 1 slice | 180 | 4 | 20 | 1 | 20 | 160 | 3 | 1 | 32 | 2 | 2 strch, 1 fat |
| Gingerbread Mix | 1 slice | 220 | 5 | 21 | 2 | 0 | 340 | 3 | <1 | 40 | 2 1/2 | 2 1/2 strch, 1 fat |
| Nut Quick Bread Mix | 1 slice | 170 | 6 | 32 | 1 | 20 | 190 | 3 | 1 | 27 | 2 | 2 strch, 1 fat |
| Pumpkin Quick Bread Mix | 1 slice | 170 | 6 | 32 | 1 | 35 | 200 | 3 | <1 | 27 | 2 | 2 strch, 1 fat |

## BREADSTICKS

### Pepperidge Farm

| | Serving | Cal. | Fat (g) | % Cal. Fat | Sat. Fat (g) | Chol. (mg) | Sod. (mg) | Prot. (g) | Fiber (g) | Carb. (g) | Carb. Ch. | Exchanges |
|---|---|---|---|---|---|---|---|---|---|---|---|---|
| ✔Brown & Serve Breadsticks | 1 | 150 | 2 | 12 | <1 | 0 | 290 | 7 | 1 | 28 | 2 | 2 strch |

### Pillsbury

| | Serving | Cal. | Fat (g) | % Cal. Fat | Sat. Fat (g) | Chol. (mg) | Sod. (mg) | Prot. (g) | Fiber (g) | Carb. (g) | Carb. Ch. | Exchanges |
|---|---|---|---|---|---|---|---|---|---|---|---|---|
| ✔Breadsticks | 1 | 110 | 2 | 16 | 0 | 0 | 290 | 3 | <1 | 19 | 1 | 1 strch |

## BREAKFAST MEALS/ENTREES (FROZEN)

### Red Baron

| | Serving | Cal. | Fat (g) | % Cal. Fat | Sat. Fat (g) | Chol. (mg) | Sod. (mg) | Prot. (g) | Fiber (g) | Carb. (g) | Carb. Ch. | Exchanges |
|---|---|---|---|---|---|---|---|---|---|---|---|---|
| Bacon Scramble Breakfast Sandwich | 1 | 420 | 24 | 53 | 9 | 65 | 830 | 16 | 2 | 34 | 2 | 2 carb, 1 med-fat meat, 4 fat |
| Ham Scramble Breakfast Sandwich | 1 | 370 | 19 | 47 | 7 | 65 | 770 | 15 | 2 | 34 | 2 | 2 carb, 1 med-fat meat, 3 fat |
| Sausage Scramble Breakfast Sandwich | 1 | 380 | 21 | 50 | 8 | 65 | 730 | 15 | 2 | 34 | 2 | 2 carb, 1 med-fat meat, 3 fat |

✔ = Best Bet; NA = Not Available; Carb. Ch. = Carbohydrate Choices

## Swanson Great Starts

| Breakfast Meals/Entrees (Frozen) (Continued) | Serving Size | Cal. | Fat (g) | % Cal. Fat | Sat. Fat (g) | Chol. (mg) | Sod. (mg) | Pro. (g) | Fiber (g) | Carb. (g) | Carb. Ch. | Servings/Exchanges |
|---|---|---|---|---|---|---|---|---|---|---|---|---|
| Burrito w/Bacon & Scrambled Eggs | 3.5 oz | 250 | 11 | 40 | 4 | 90 | 540 | 10 | 2 | 27 | 2 | 2 carb, 1 med-fat meat, 1 fat |
| Burrito w/Scrambled Eggs | 3.5 oz | 200 | 8 | 36 | 3 | 60 | 510 | 8 | 2 | 25 | 1 1/2 | 1 1/2 carb, 1 med-fat meat, 1 fat |
| Canadian Bacon/Cheese/Egg Sandwich | 5.2 oz | 420 | 22 | 48 | NA | NA | 1845 | 16 | NA | 37 | 2 1/2 | 2 1/2 carb, 1 med-fat meat, 3 fat |
| Cinnamon French Toast | 5.6 oz | 440 | 28 | 57 | 12 | 150 | 580 | 14 | 2 | 34 | 2 | 2 carb, 1 med-fat meat, 5 fat |
| Egg & Cheese Sandwich | 4.3 oz | 350 | 20 | 51 | 8 | 110 | 890 | 12 | 1 | 30 | 2 | 2 carb, 1 med-fat meat, 3 fat |
| Egg Bacon Cheese Muffin | 4 oz | 290 | 15 | 47 | 6 | 95 | 750 | 14 | 2 | 25 | 1 1/2 | 1 1/2 carb, 1 med-fat meat, 2 fat |
| Eggs & Silver Dollar Pancake | 4.3 oz | 250 | 14 | 50 | 6 | 290 | 540 | 9 | 1 | 22 | 1 1/2 | 1 1/2 carb, 1 med-fat meat, 2 fat |
| Ham & Cheese Bagel Pancake | 3 oz | 240 | 8 | 31 | NA | NA | 600 | 12 | NA | 28 | 2 | 2 carb, 1 med-fat meat, 1 fat |
| Pancakes w/Bacon | 4.6 oz | 400 | 20 | 45 | 7 | 100 | 1030 | 12 | 1 | 42 | 3 | 3 carb, 4 fat |

| | Serving Size | Cal. | Fat (g) | % Cal. Fat | Sat. Fat (g) | Chol. (mg) | Sod. (mg) | Pro. (g) | Fiber (g) | Carb. (g) | Carb. Choices | Exchanges/Choices |
|---|---|---|---|---|---|---|---|---|---|---|---|---|
| Pancakes w/Sausage | 6 oz | 490 | 25 | 46 | 11 | 90 | 950 | 14 | 3 | 52 | 3 1/2 | 3 1/2 carb, 1 med-fat meat, 4 fat |
| Sausage Burrito | 3.5 oz | 240 | 12 | 45 | 4 | 90 | 500 | 9 | 1 | 24 | 1 1/2 | 1 1/2 carb, 1 med-fat meat, 1 fat |
| Scrambled Eggs & Bacon | 5.3 oz | 290 | 19 | 59 | 9 | 240 | 700 | 11 | 1 | 17 | 1 | 1 carb, 1 med-fat meat, 3 fat |
| Scrambled Eggs & Sausage | 6.3 oz | 360 | 26 | 65 | 10 | 280 | 800 | 12 | 3 | 21 | 1 1/2 | 1 1/2 carb, 1 med-fat meat, 5 fat |

## BROWNIE MIX (AS PREPARED)

### Betty Crocker

| | Serving Size | Cal. | Fat (g) | % Cal. Fat | Sat. Fat (g) | Chol. (mg) | Sod. (mg) | Pro. (g) | Fiber (g) | Carb. (g) | Carb. Choices | Exchanges/Choices |
|---|---|---|---|---|---|---|---|---|---|---|---|---|
| Chocolate Chunk Brownie Supreme | 1 brownie | 180 | 9 | 45 | 3 | 20 | 95 | 2 | 0 | 25 | 1 1/2 | 1 1/2 carb, 2 fat |
| Dark Chocolate Fudge Supreme Brownie Mix | 1 brownie | 170 | 7 | 37 | 2 | 20 | 110 | 2 | 0 | 24 | 1 1/2 | 1 1/2 carb, 1 fat |
| Dark Chocolate w/Hershey's Syrup Supreme Brownies | 1 brownie | 170 | 7 | 37 | 2 | 20 | 110 | 2 | 0 | 25 | 1 1/2 | 1 1/2 carb, 1 fat |
| Fall Frosted Supreme Brownie Mix | 1 brownie | 210 | 9 | 39 | 2 | 20 | 125 | 2 | <1 | 31 | 2 | 2 carb, 2 fat |
| Frosted Brownie Supreme | 1 brownie | 210 | 9 | 39 | 2 | 20 | 135 | 2 | 1 | 30 | 2 | 2 carb, 2 fat |
| Fudge Brownie Pouch Mix | 1 brownie | 190 | 8 | 38 | 2 | 25 | 130 | 2 | 1 | 27 | 2 | 2 carb, 2 fat |
| Fudge Supreme Brownie Mix | 1 brownie | 190 | 7 | 33 | 2 | 20 | 130 | 2 | 1 | 30 | 2 | 2 carb, 1 fat |

✓ = Best Bet; NA = Not Available; Carb. Ch. = Carbohydrate Choices

| Brownie Mix (As Prepared) (*Continued*) | Serving Size | Cal. | Fat (g) | % Cal. Fat | Sat. Fat (g) | Chol. (mg) | Sod. (mg) | Pro. (g) | Fiber (g) | Carb. (g) | Carb. Ch. | Servings/Exchanges |
|---|---|---|---|---|---|---|---|---|---|---|---|---|
| German Chocolate Supreme | 1 brownie | 200 | 8 | 36 | 2 | 0 | 115 | 1 | 1 | 29 | 2 | 2 carb, 2 fat |
| Hot Fudge Supreme | 1 brownie | 170 | 8 | 42 | 2 | 20 | 110 | 2 | 0 | 23 | 1 1/2 | 1 1/2 carb, 2 fat |
| Original Fudge Supreme | 1 brownie | 160 | 6 | 34 | 1 | 20 | 110 | 2 | 0 | 27 | 2 | 2 carb, 1 fat |
| Peanut Butter Chunk w/Reese's Pieces | 1 brownie | 180 | 9 | 45 | 3 | 20 | 105 | 3 | 0 | 23 | 1 1/2 | 1 1/2 carb, 2 fat |
| Stir 'n Bake Brownie w/Mini Kisses | 1/6 pkg | 220 | 7 | 29 | 3 | 0 | 160 | 2 | 1 | 36 | 2 1/2 | 2 1/2 carb, 1 fat |
| Turtle | 1 brownie | 170 | 8 | 42 | 2 | 20 | 100 | 2 | 0 | 23 | 1 1/2 | 1 1/2 carb, 2 fat |
| Walnut Supreme | 1 brownie | 180 | 9 | 45 | 2 | 20 | 95 | 2 | 0 | 22 | 1 1/2 | 1 1/2 carb, 2 fat |
| **Betty Crocker/Sweet Rewards** | | | | | | | | | | | | |
| ✔Low Fat Fudge | 1 brownie | 130 | 3 | 21 | 1 | 0 | 115 | 2 | 1 | 27 | 2 | 2 carb, 1 fat |
| Reduced Fat Fudge | 1 brownie | 140 | 4 | 26 | 1 | 20 | 110 | 2 | 0 | 27 | 2 | 2 carb, 1 fat |
| **Pillsbury** | | | | | | | | | | | | |
| Chocolate Deluxe Brownie Mix | 1/20 recipe | 180 | 7 | 35 | 2 | 10 | 110 | 2 | <1 | 28 | 2 | 2 carb, 1 fat |
| Deluxe Chocolate Brownie Mix | 1/16 recipe | 150 | 6 | 36 | 1 | 15 | 80 | 2 | <1 | 22 | 1 1/2 | 1 1/2 carb, 1 fat |
| ✔Snackwell's Devil's Food Brownie Mix | 1/12 recipe | 140 | 3 | 19 | <1 | 0 | 105 | 2 | <1 | 28 | 2 | 2 carb, 1 fat |
| ✔Snackwell's Fudge Brownie Mix | 1/12 recipe | 150 | 3 | 18 | <1 | 0 | 115 | 2 | 1 | 29 | 2 | 2 carb, 1 fat |
| **BROWNIES (READY-TO-EAT)** | | | | | | | | | | | | |
| **Pepperidge Farm** | | | | | | | | | | | | |
| Old-Fashioned Brownie | 2 | 110 | 7 | 57 | 2 | 5 | 45 | 1 | NA | 11 | 1 | 1 carb, 1 fat |

## BUNS/ROLLS, SANDWICH (READY-TO-EAT)

### Pepperidge Farm

| Product | Amount | Cal. | Fat (g) | % Cal. Fat | Sat. Fat (g) | Chol. (mg) | Sod. (mg) | Carb. (g) | Fiber (g) | Prot. (g) | Carb. Ch. | Exchanges |
|---|---|---|---|---|---|---|---|---|---|---|---|---|
| 5-inch Sandwich Hearty Buns/Rolls | 1 | 210 | 5 | 21 | 2 | 0 | 346 | 36 | 2 | 7 | 2 1/2 | 2 1/2 strch, 1 fat |
| ✔ 7-Grain French Rolls | 1 | 80 | 2 | 23 | 0 | 0 | 270 | 19 | 2 | 4 | 1 | 1 strch |
| ✔ Baked French-Style Sliced Rolls | 1 | 120 | 2 | 15 | <1 | 0 | 260 | 24 | 1 | 4 | 1 1/2 | 1 1/2 strch |
| Deli Classic Soft Hoagie Rolls | 1 | 200 | 5 | 23 | 3 | 0 | 340 | 32 | 2 | 7 | 2 | 2 strch, 1 fat |
| ✔ Dijon Frankfurter Rolls | 1 | 140 | 3 | 19 | 2 | 0 | 240 | 23 | 2 | 6 | 1 1/2 | 1 1/2 strch, 1 fat |
| ✔ European Bake Shop French Rolls | 1 | 100 | 1 | 9 | 0 | 0 | 230 | 19 | 1 | 4 | 1 | 1 strch |
| ✔ Finger Dinner Rolls w/Poppy Seed | 1 | 50 | 2 | 36 | <1 | <5 | 77 | 7 | <1 | 2 | 1/2 | 1/2 strch |
| ✔ Frankfurter Rolls | 1 | 140 | 3 | 19 | 1 | 0 | 270 | 24 | <1 | 5 | 1 1/2 | 1 1/2 strch, 1 fat |
| Garlic & Cheese Rolls | 1 | 130 | 5 | 35 | 5 | 15 | 280 | 16 | 2 | 6 | 1 | 1 strch, 1 fat |
| Heat & Serve Butter Crescent Rolls | 1 | 110 | 5 | 41 | 3 | 15 | 160 | 13 | 1 | 3 | 1 | 1 strch, 1 fat |
| ✔ Heat & Serve Golden Twist Rolls | 1 | 110 | 4 | 33 | 2 | <5 | 160 | 13 | 1 | 2 | 1 | 1 strch, 1 fat |
| ✔ Multi-grain Sandwich Bun | 1 | 150 | 3 | 18 | <1 | 0 | 230 | 24 | 3 | 6 | 1 1/2 | 1 1/2 strch, 1 fat |
| ✔ Onion Sliced Sandwich Rolls | 1 | 150 | 3 | 18 | 2 | 0 | 270 | 26 | 1 | 5 | 2 | 2 strch, 1 fat |
| Party Enriched Rolls | 1 | 240 | 7 | 26 | 2 | 10 | 240 | 26 | 2 | 6 | 2 | 2 strch, 1 fat |
| ✔ Party Rye Bread | 3 slices | 170 | 2 | 16 | 0 | 0 | 410 | 22 | 3 | 6 | 1 1/2 | 1 1/2 strch |
| Petite Croissants | 1 | 130 | 8 | 55 | 4 | 20 | 180 | 13 | <1 | 3 | 1 | 1 strch, 2 fat |
| ✔ Potato Sandwich Buns/Rolls | 1 | 160 | 4 | 23 | <1 | <1 | 260 | 28 | <1 | 4 | 2 | 2 strch, 1 fat |

✔ = Best Bet; NA = Not Available; Carb. Ch. = Carbohydrate Choices

| Buns/Rolls, Sandwich (Ready-to-Eat) (*Continued*) | Serving Size | Cal. | Fat (g) | % Cal. Fat | Sat. Fat (g) | Chol. (mg) | Sod. (mg) | Pro. (g) | Fiber (g) | Carb. (g) | Carb. Ch. | Servings/Exchanges |
|---|---|---|---|---|---|---|---|---|---|---|---|---|
| ✓Sandwich Sliced w/Sesame Seeds Rolls | 1 | 140 | 3 | 19 | 2 | 0 | 240 | 5 | 1 | 23 | 1 1/2 | 1 1/2 strch, 1 fat |
| ✓Sliced Hamburger Rolls | 1 | 130 | 3 | 21 | 1 | 0 | 230 | 5 | 1 | 22 | 1 1/2 | 1 1/2 strch, 1 fat |
| Sourdough Sandwich Bun | 1 | 170 | 4 | 21 | 2 | 0 | 290 | 6 | 1 | 28 | 2 | 2 strch, 1 fat |
| **BUTTER** | | | | | | | | | | | | |
| **(Generic)** | | | | | | | | | | | | |
| Reduced-Fat Butter | 1 Tbsp | 50 | 6 | 90 | 4 | 20 | 70 | 0 | 0 | 0 | 0 | 1 fat |
| Stick Butter | 1 tsp | 36 | 4 | 100 | 3 | 11 | 41 | 0 | 0 | 0 | 0 | 1 fat |
| Whipped Butter | 2 tsp | 40 | 5 | 100 | 3 | 13 | 50 | 0 | 0 | 0 | 0 | 1 fat |
| **CAKE (FROZEN)** | | | | | | | | | | | | |
| **Mrs. Smith's** | | | | | | | | | | | | |
| Carrot Cake | 1/6 cake | 300 | 16 | 48 | 4 | 30 | 360 | 3 | 1 | 37 | 2 1/2 | 2 1/2 carb, 3 fat |
| **Pepperidge Farm** | | | | | | | | | | | | |
| All Butter Pound Cake | 1 slice | 110 | 6 | 49 | 1 | 0 | 85 | 1 | 1 | 13 | 1 | 1 carb, 1 fat |
| Boston Creme | 1 slice | 290 | 14 | 43 | 6 | 50 | 190 | 3 | NA | 39 | 2 1/2 | 2 1/2 carb, 3 fat |
| Chocolate Fudge Layer Cake | 1 slice | 170 | 9 | 48 | 3 | 20 | 140 | 2 | NA | 20 | 1 | 1 carb, 2 fat |
| Chocolate Mousse Cake | 1 slice | 190 | 9 | 43 | 3 | 5 | 260 | 3 | NA | 25 | 1 1/2 | 1 1/2 carb, 2 fat |
| Coconut Layer Cake | 1 slice | 230 | 11 | 43 | 4 | 20 | 160 | 2 | NA | 31 | 2 | 2 carb, 2 fat |
| Devil's Food Cake | 1 slice | 180 | 9 | 45 | 3 | 20 | 135 | 1 | NA | 24 | 1 1/2 | 1 1/2 carb, 2 fat |

| | Amount | Cal. | Fat (g) | % Cal. Fat | Sat. Fat (g) | Chol. (mg) | Sod. (mg) | Prot. (g) | Fiber (g) | Carb. (g) | Carb. Ch. | Exchanges |
|---|---|---|---|---|---|---|---|---|---|---|---|---|
| German Chocolate Layer Cake | 1 slice | 250 | 13 | 47 | 4 | 45 | 230 | 2 | NA | 29 | 2 | 2 carb, 3 fat |
| Lemon Cake | 1 slice | 170 | 5 | 26 | 1 | 50 | 100 | 4 | NA | 26 | 2 | 2 carb, 1 fat |
| Old Fashioned Carrot Cake | 1 slice | 150 | 9 | 54 | 3 | 15 | 160 | 1 | NA | 19 | 1 | 1 carb, 2 fat |
| Strawberry Cream | 1 slice | 190 | 7 | 33 | 3 | 20 | 120 | 1 | NA | 30 | 2 | 2 carb, 1 fat |
| Strawberry Stripe Layer Cake | 1 slice | 160 | 8 | 45 | 3 | 20 | 120 | 1 | NA | 21 | 1 1/2 | 1 1/2 carb, 2 fat |
| **Sara Lee** | | | | | | | | | | | | |
| All Butter Pound Cake | 1/6 cake | 320 | 16 | 45 | 9 | 85 | 280 | 4 | <1 | 38 | 2 1/2 | 2 1/2 carb, 3 fat |
| Carrot Cake Bites | 5 | 370 | 25 | 61 | 17 | 25 | 180 | 4 | 1 | 32 | 2 | 2 carb, 5 fat |

## CAKE (READY-TO-EAT)

### Entenmann's

| | Amount | Cal. | Fat (g) | % Cal. Fat | Sat. Fat (g) | Chol. (mg) | Sod. (mg) | Prot. (g) | Fiber (g) | Carb. (g) | Carb. Ch. | Exchanges |
|---|---|---|---|---|---|---|---|---|---|---|---|---|
| All-Butter French Crumb Cake | 1 slice | 210 | 10 | 43 | 6 | 60 | 240 | 3 | 0 | 29 | 2 | 2 carb, 2 fat |
| All-Butter Loaf Cake | 1 slice | 220 | 10 | 41 | 6 | 80 | 290 | 3 | 0 | 31 | 2 | 2 carb, 2 fat |
| Banana Crunch Cake | 1 slice | 220 | 9 | 33 | 2 | 40 | 280 | 2 | <1 | 32 | 2 | 2 carb, 2 fat |
| Carrot Cake | 1 slice | 290 | 16 | 50 | 4 | 35 | 240 | 3 | <1 | 35 | 2 | 2 carb, 3 fat |
| Cheese Topped Coffeecake | 1 slice | 190 | 8 | 38 | 3 | 30 | 180 | 3 | 1 | 26 | 2 | 2 carb, 2 fat |
| Chocolate Fudge Cake | 1 slice | 310 | 14 | 41 | 5 | 45 | 260 | 3 | 2 | 47 | 3 | 3 carb, 3 fat |
| ✔Fat-Free Apple Spice Crumb Cake | 1 slice | 130 | 0 | 0 | 0 | 0 | 140 | 2 | 2 | 30 | 2 | 2 carb |
| ✔Fat-Free Banana Crunch Cake | 1 slice | 140 | 0 | 0 | 0 | 0 | 150 | 2 | 2 | 33 | 2 | 2 carb |
| ✔Fat-Free Banana Loaf Cake | 1 slice | 150 | 0 | 0 | 0 | 0 | 190 | 2 | 1 | 34 | 2 | 2 carb |

✔ = Best Bet; NA = Not Available; Carb. Ch. = Carbohydrate Choices

| Cake (Ready-to-Eat) (Continued) | Serving Size | Cal. | Fat (g) | % Cal. Fat | Sat. Fat (g) | Chol. (mg) | Sod. (mg) | Pro. (g) | Fiber (g) | Carb. (g) | Carb. Ch. | Servings/Exchanges |
|---|---|---|---|---|---|---|---|---|---|---|---|---|
| ✔Fat-Free Blueberry Crunch Cake | 1 slice | 140 | 0 | 0 | 0 | 0 | 200 | 2 | 2 | 32 | 2 | 2 carb |
| ✔Fat-Free Carrot Cake | 1 slice | 170 | 0 | 0 | 0 | 0 | 230 | 3 | NA | 40 | 2 1/2 | 2 1/2 carb |
| ✔Fat-Free Chocolate Crunch Cake | 1 slice | 130 | 0 | 0 | 0 | 0 | 170 | 2 | 2 | 32 | 2 | 2 carb |
| ✔Fat-Free Chocolate Loaf Cake | 1 slice | 130 | 0 | 0 | 0 | 0 | 250 | 3 | 1 | 30 | 2 | 2 carb |
| ✔Fat-Free Fudge Chocolate Cake | 1 slice | 210 | 0 | 0 | 0 | 0 | 270 | 3 | 2 | 51 | 3 1/2 | 3 1/2 carb |
| ✔Fat-Free Fudge Gold Cake | 1 slice | 220 | 0 | 0 | 0 | 0 | 200 | 3 | 2 | 52 | 3 1/2 | 3 1/2 carb |
| ✔Fat-Free Gold Chocolate Chip Cake | 1 slice | 130 | 0 | 0 | 0 | 0 | 220 | 3 | 1 | 31 | 2 | 2 carb |
| ✔Fat-Free Marble Loaf Cake | 1 slice | 130 | 0 | 0 | 0 | 0 | 190 | 2 | 1 | 29 | 2 | 2 carb |
| ✔Fat-Free Raisin Loaf Cake | 1 slice | 140 | 0 | 0 | 0 | 0 | 150 | 2 | 1 | 33 | 2 | 2 carb |
| Louisiana Crunch Cake | 1 slice | 310 | 13 | 38 | 4 | 50 | 290 | 3 | <1 | 45 | 3 | 3 carb, 3 fat |
| Marble Loaf Cake | 1 slice | 200 | 10 | 45 | 6 | 65 | 230 | 2 | <1 | 25 | 1 1/2 | 1 1/2 carb, 2 fat |
| Marshmallow Iced Devil's Food Cake | 1 slice | 350 | 18 | 46 | 5 | 45 | 290 | 3 | 1 | 45 | 3 | 3 carb, 4 fat |
| Thick Fudge Golden Cake | 1 slice | 330 | 16 | 44 | 4 | 50 | 270 | 3 | 2 | 48 | 3 | 3 carb, 3 fat |

## CAKE MIX (AS PREPARED)

### Betty Crocker

| | Serving Size | Cal. | Fat (g) | % Cal. Fat | Sat. Fat (g) | Chol. (mg) | Sod. (mg) | Pro. (g) | Fiber (g) | Carb. (g) | Carb. Ch. | Servings/Exchanges |
|---|---|---|---|---|---|---|---|---|---|---|---|---|
| Classic Dessert Pineapple Upside Down Cake | 1/6 cake | 400 | 15 | 34 | 4 | 35 | 330 | 3 | 0 | 64 | 4 | 4 carb, 3 fat |
| Classic Dessert Pound Cake | 1/8 cake | 260 | 8 | 28 | 3 | 55 | 210 | 4 | 0 | 45 | 3 | 3 carb, 2 fat |

| | Serving | Cal. | Fat (g) | % Cal. Fat | Sat. Fat (g) | Chol. (mg) | Sod. (mg) | Prot. (g) | Fiber (g) | Carb. (g) | Carb. Ch. | Exchanges |
|---|---|---|---|---|---|---|---|---|---|---|---|---|
| Stir 'n Bake Carrot Cake | 1/6 pkg | 250 | 7 | 25 | 2 | 0 | 300 | 2 | 0 | 47 | 3 | 3 carb, 1 fat |
| Stir 'n Bake Devils Food Cake w/Chocolate Frosting | 1/6 pkg | 240 | 7 | 26 | 2 | 1 | 270 | 2 | 1 | 42 | 3 | 3 carb, 1 fat |
| Stir 'n Bake Yellow Cake w/Choc. Frosting | 1/6 pkg | 240 | 7 | 26 | 2 | 10 | 240 | 2 | <1 | 43 | 3 | 3 carb, 1 fat |
| **Betty Crocker/Sweet Rewards** | | | | | | | | | | | | |
| ✔Fat-Free Cake Mix, All Varieties (Avg) | 1/8 cake | 170 | 0 | 0 | 0 | 0 | 290 | 3 | <1 | 39 | 2 1/2 | 2 1/2 carb |
| Reduced Fat Cake Mix, All Varieties (Avg) | 1/12 cake | 210 | 6 | 26 | 2 | 35 | 325 | 3 | <1 | 35 | 2 | 2 carb, 1 fat |
| Reduced Fat Devils Food | 1/12 cake | 200 | 5 | 23 | 2 | 55 | 380 | 4 | 1 | 36 | 2 1/2 | 2 1/2, 1 fat |
| Reduced Fat White | 1/12 cake | 190 | 4 | 19 | 1 | 0 | 310 | 3 | 0 | 36 | 2 1/2 | 2 1/2, 1 fat |
| Reduced Fat Yellow | 1/12 cake | 200 | 5 | 23 | 1 | 55 | 300 | 3 | 0 | 37 | 2 1/2 | 2 1/2, 1 fat |
| **General Mills** | | | | | | | | | | | | |
| SuperMoist Butter Chocolate | 1/12 cake | 125 | 11 | 79 | 6 | 75 | 420 | 4 | 1 | 35 | 2 | 2 carb, 2 fat |
| SuperMoist Butter Pecan | 1/12 cake | 240 | 10 | 38 | 2 | 55 | 280 | 3 | 0 | 35 | 2 | 2 carb, 2 fat |
| SuperMoist Butter Yellow | 1/12 cake | 260 | 11 | 38 | 6 | 75 | 370 | 3 | 0 | 36 | 2 1/2 | 2 1/2 carb, 2 fat |
| SuperMoist Carrot Cake | 1/10 cake | 320 | 15 | 42 | 3 | 65 | 340 | 4 | 0 | 42 | 3 | 3 carb, 3 fat |
| SuperMoist Cherry Chip | 1/10 cake | 300 | 13 | 39 | 3 | 65 | 340 | 4 | 0 | 41 | 3 | 3 carb, 3 fat |
| SuperMoist Chocolate Chip | 1/12 cake | 250 | 11 | 40 | 3 | 55 | 270 | 3 | 0 | 35 | 2 | 2 carb, 2 fat |
| SuperMoist Chocolate Fudge | 1/12 cake | 270 | 12 | 40 | 3 | 55 | 340 | 3 | 1 | 35 | 2 | 2 carb, 2 fat |
| ✔SuperMoist Chocolate Swirl | 1/12 cake | 150 | 0 | 0 | 0 | 0 | 310 | 3 | 0 | 34 | 2 | 2 carb |

✔= Best Bet; NA = Not Available; Carb. Ch. = Carbohydrate Choices

| Cake Mix (As Prepared) (*Continued*) | Serving Size | Cal. | Fat (g) | % Cal. Fat | Sat. Fat (g) | Chol. (mg) | Sod. (mg) | Pro. (g) | Fiber (g) | Carb. (g) | Carb. Ch. | Servings/Exchanges |
|---|---|---|---|---|---|---|---|---|---|---|---|---|
| SuperMoist Chocolate w/ Creamy Swirls of Fudge | 1/9 cake | 210 | 8 | 34 | 2 | 50 | 250 | 3 | 0 | 32 | 2 | 2 carb, 2 fat |
| ✔SuperMoist Confetti | 1/12 cake | 150 | 0 | 0 | 0 | 0 | 320 | 3 | 0 | 34 | 2 | 2 carb |
| SuperMoist Devils Food | 1/12 cake | 270 | 13 | 43 | 3 | 55 | 340 | 3 | 1 | 35 | 2 | 2 carb, 3 fat |
| SuperMoist Double Chocolate Swirl | 1/12 cake | 270 | 13 | 43 | 3 | 55 | 330 | 4 | 1 | 35 | 2 | 2 carb, 3 fat |
| ✔SuperMoist Easy Angel Food | 1/4 cake | 170 | 0 | 0 | 0 | 0 | 330 | 3 | 0 | 37 | 2 1/2 | 2 1/2 carb |
| SuperMoist French Vanilla | 1/12 cake | 240 | 10 | 38 | 3 | 55 | 290 | 3 | 0 | 35 | 2 | 2 carb, 2 fat |
| SuperMoist Fudge Marble | 1/10 cake | 290 | 12 | 28 | 3 | 65 | 330 | 4 | 0 | 43 | 3 | 3 carb, 2 fat |
| SuperMoist German Chocolate | 1/12 cake | 270 | 13 | 43 | 3 | 55 | 330 | 3 | 0 | 36 | 2 1/2 | 2 1/2 carb, 3 fat |
| SuperMoist Golden Vanilla | 1/12 cake | 240 | 10 | 38 | 3 | 55 | 290 | 3 | 0 | 35 | 2 | 2 carb, 2 fat |
| SuperMoist Lemon | 1/12 cake | 240 | 10 | 38 | 3 | 55 | 290 | 3 | 0 | 36 | 2 1/2 | 2 1/2 carb, 2 fat |
| SuperMoist Milk Chocolate | 1/12 cake | 240 | 10 | 38 | 3 | 55 | 300 | 4 | 1 | 34 | 2 | 2 carb, 2 fat |
| ✔SuperMoist One-Step White | 1/12 cake | 140 | 0 | 0 | 0 | 0 | 320 | 3 | 0 | 32 | 2 | 2 carb |
| SuperMoist Party Swirl | 1/12 cake | 250 | 11 | 40 | 3 | 55 | 280 | 3 | 0 | 35 | 2 | 2 carb, 2 fat |
| SuperMoist Pineapple | 1/12 cake | 250 | 10 | 40 | 3 | 55 | 290 | 3 | 0 | 35 | 2 | 2 carb, 2 fat |
| SuperMoist Rainbow Chip | 1/10 cake | 300 | 13 | 39 | 3 | 65 | 340 | 4 | 0 | 41 | 3 | 3 carb, 3 fat |
| SuperMoist Sour Cream White | 1/10 cake | 280 | 12 | 39 | 3 | 0 | 370 | 3 | 0 | 41 | 3 | 3 carb, 2 fat |
| SuperMoist Spice | 1/12 cake | 240 | 10 | 38 | 2 | 55 | 290 | 3 | 0 | 35 | 2 | 2 carb, 2 fat |

| Item | Serving | Cal. | Fat (g) | % Fat Cal. | Sat. Fat (g) | Chol. (mg) | Sod. (mg) | Pro. (g) | Fiber (g) | Carb. (g) | Carb. Ch. | Exchanges |
|---|---|---|---|---|---|---|---|---|---|---|---|---|
| SuperMoist Strawberry | 1/12 cake | 250 | 10 | 36 | 2 | 55 | 280 | 3 | 0 | 35 | 2 | 2 carb, 2 fat |
| SuperMoist Strawberry Swirl | 1/10 cake | 300 | 13 | 39 | 3 | 65 | 350 | 4 | 0 | 41 | 3 | 3 carb, 3 fat |
| ✔SuperMoist Traditional White | 1/12 cake | 130 | 0 | 0 | 0 | 0 | 150 | 3 | 0 | 30 | 2 | 2 carb |
| SuperMoist White | 1/12 cake | 230 | 10 | 39 | 2 | 0 | 300 | 3 | 0 | 34 | 2 | 2 carb, 2 fat |
| SuperMoist White Chocolate Swirl | 1/12 cake | 250 | 11 | 40 | 3 | 55 | 310 | 4 | 1 | 34 | 2 | 2 carb, 2 fat |
| SuperMoist Yellow | 1/12 cake | 250 | 10 | 36 | 3 | 55 | 290 | 3 | 0 | 35 | 2 | 2 carb, 2 fat |
| SuperMoist Yellow w/ Creamy Swirls of Fudge | 1/9 cake | 210 | 8 | 34 | 2 | 50 | 230 | 3 | 0 | 32 | 2 | 2 carb, 2 fat |
| **Pillsbury** | | | | | | | | | | | | |
| Bundt Hot Fudge Cake Mix | 1/12 recipe | 350 | 20 | 51 | 6 | 55 | 280 | 4 | 1 | 39 | 2 1/2 | 2 1/2 carb, 4 fat |
| Moist Supreme Chocolate | 1/12 recipe | 250 | 11 | 40 | 3 | 35 | 280 | 3 | <1 | 35 | 2 | 2 carb, 2 fat |
| Moist Supreme French Vanilla Cake Mix | 1/10 recipe | 300 | 13 | 39 | 3 | 45 | 350 | 3 | 1 | 42 | 3 | 3 carb, 3 fat |
| Moist Supreme Funfetti Cake Mix | 1/12 recipe | 240 | 9 | 34 | 2 | 0 | 290 | 3 | <1 | 36 | 2 1/2 | 2 1/2 carb, 2 fat |
| Snackwell's Devil's Food Cake Mix | 1/6 recipe | 200 | 4 | 18 | 2 | 12 | 380 | 3 | 2 | 38 | 2 1/2 | 2 1/2 carb, 1 fat |
| Snackwell's White Cake Mix | 1/6 recipe | 210 | 5 | 21 | 2 | 35 | 320 | 3 | 1 | 39 | 2 1/2 | 2 1/2 carb, 1 fat |
| Snackwell's Yellow Cake Mix | 1/6 recipe | 210 | 5 | 21 | 2 | 35 | 320 | 3 | 1 | 39 | 2 1/2 | 2 1/2 carb, 1 fat |

✔ = Best Bet; NA = Not Available; Carb. Ch. = Carbohydrate Choices

| Product | Serving Size | Cal. | Fat (g) | % Cal. Fat | Sat. Fat (g) | Chol. (mg) | Sod. (mg) | Pro. (g) | Fiber (g) | Carb. (g) | Carb. Ch. | Servings/Exchanges |
|---|---|---|---|---|---|---|---|---|---|---|---|---|
| **CATSUP/KETCHUP** | | | | | | | | | | | | |
| **(Generic)** | | | | | | | | | | | | |
| ✔Catsup/Ketchup | 1 Tbsp | 16 | <1 | 0 | <1 | 0 | 182 | <1 | 4 | 0 | | free |
| ✔Catsup/Ketchup, Low Sodium | 1 Tbsp | 16 | <1 | 0 | <1 | 0 | 3 | <1 | 4 | 0 | | free |
| **CEREAL, HOT** | | | | | | | | | | | | |
| **Arrowhead Mills** | | | | | | | | | | | | |
| ✔Rise & Shine, Uncooked Brown Rice Cereal | 1.5 oz | 160 | 1 | 6 | NA | 0 | 1 | 3 | 2 | 35 | 2 | 2 strch |
| ✔Uncooked Bulgar Wheat Cereal | 2 oz | 200 | 1 | 4 | NA | 0 | 0 | 6 | 5 | 43 | 3 | 3 strch |
| **Krusteaz** | | | | | | | | | | | | |
| ✔Ala Hot Cereal | 1/4 cup | 150 | 0 | 0 | 0 | 0 | 0 | 4 | 7 | 33 | 2 | 2 strch |
| ✔Farina Hot Cereal | 1 oz | 100 | 0 | 0 | 0 | 0 | 1 | 3 | 1 | 22 | 1 1/2 | 1 1/2 strch |
| ✔Zoom Hot Cereal | 1/3 cup | 120 | 0 | 0 | 0 | 0 | 0 | 5 | 4 | 24 | 1 1/2 | 1 1/2 strch |
| **Malt-o-Meal** | | | | | | | | | | | | |
| ✔Hot Wheat Cereal, Chocolate | 3 Tbsp dry | 120 | 0 | 0 | 0 | 0 | 0 | 3 | 1 | 28 | 2 | 2 strch |
| ✔Hot Wheat Cereal, Maple & Brown Sugar | 3 Tbsp dry | 120 | 0 | 0 | 0 | 0 | 0 | 3 | 1 | 28 | 2 | 2 strch |
| ✔Hot Wheat Cereal, Quick Original | 3 Tbsp dry | 120 | 0 | 0 | 0 | 0 | 0 | 4 | 1 | 27 | 2 | 2 strch |

| | Serving Size | Cal. | Fat (g) | % Cal. from Fat | Sat. Fat (g) | Chol. (mg) | Sod. (mg) | Carb. (g) | Fiber (g) | Prot. (g) | Carb. Ch. | Exchanges |
|---|---|---|---|---|---|---|---|---|---|---|---|---|
| **Nabisco** | | | | | | | | | | | | |
| ✓Cream of Rice Hot Cereal | 1/4 cup | 170 | 0 | 0 | 0 | 0 | 0 | 38 | 0 | 3 | 2 1/2 | 2 1/2 strch |
| ✓Cream of Wheat Hot Cereal | 3 Tbsp. | 120 | 0 | 0 | 0 | 0 | 90 | 25 | 1 | 3 | 1 1/2 | 1 1/2 strch |
| **Quaker** | | | | | | | | | | | | |
| ✓Hot Oat Bran | 1/2 cup | 150 | 3 | 18 | <1 | 0 | 230 | 25 | 6 | 7 | 1 1/2 | 1 1/2 strch, 1 fat |
| ✓Multi-Grain Hot Cereal | 1/2 cup | 130 | 2 | 14 | 0 | 0 | 10 | 29 | 5 | 5 | 2 | 2 strch |
| ✓Old-Fashioned Hot Oats | 1/2 cup | 150 | 3 | 18 | <1 | 0 | 0 | 27 | 4 | 5 | 2 | 2 strch, 1 fat |
| ✓Quick Hot Oats | 1/2 cup | 150 | 3 | 18 | <1 | 0 | 0 | 27 | 4 | 5 | 2 | 2 strch, 1 fat |
| Whole-Wheat Natural Hot Cereal | 1/2 cup | 130 | 1 | 7 | 0 | 0 | 0 | 30 | 4 | 5 | 2 | 2 strch |
| **Roman Meal** | | | | | | | | | | | | |
| ✓Multi-Grain Hot Cereal, Apples & Cinnamon | 2/3 cup | 112 | 3 | 19 | NA | 1 | 14 | 24 | 6 | 4 | 1 1/2 | 1 1/2 strch |
| ✓Multi-Grain Hot Cereal, Plain | 1/3 cup | 100 | <1 | 6 | 0 | 0 | 2 | 22 | 6 | 5 | 1 1/2 | 1 1/2 strch |

## CEREAL, HOT, SINGLE-SERVING

| | Serving Size | Cal. | Fat (g) | % Cal. from Fat | Sat. Fat (g) | Chol. (mg) | Sod. (mg) | Carb. (g) | Fiber (g) | Prot. (g) | Carb. Ch. | Exchanges |
|---|---|---|---|---|---|---|---|---|---|---|---|---|
| **Malt-to-Meal** | | | | | | | | | | | | |
| ✓Big Bowl Oatmeal, Apple & Cinnamon | 1 pkt | 190 | 2 | 9 | <1 | 0 | 260 | 41 | 5 | 4 | 3 | 3 strch |
| ✓Big Bowl Oatmeal, Cinnamon & Spice | 1 pkt | 250 | 3 | 11 | <1 | 0 | 360 | 54 | 5 | 6 | 3 1/2 | 3 1/2 strch, 1 fat |
| ✓Big Bowl Oatmeal, Maple & Brown Sugar | 1 pkt | 230 | 3 | 12 | <1 | 0 | 360 | 49 | 5 | 6 | 3 | 3 strch, 1 fat |

✓ = Best Bet; NA = Not Available; Carb. Ch. = Carbohydrate Choices

| Cereal, Hot, Single-Serving (Continued) | Serving Size | Cal. | Fat (g) | % Cal. Fat | Sat. Fat (g) | Chol. (mg) | Sod. (mg) | Pro. (g) | Fiber (g) | Carb. (g) | Carb. Ch. | Servings/Exchanges |
|---|---|---|---|---|---|---|---|---|---|---|---|---|
| **Nabisco** | | | | | | | | | | | | |
| ✔Harvest Mornings Instant Multigrain Hot Cereal, Raspberry Danish | 1 pkt | 140 | 2 | 13 | 0 | 0 | 115 | 3 | 3 | 32 | 2 | 2 strch |
| ✔Instant Cream of Wheat, Original | 1 pkt | 100 | 0 | 0 | 0 | 0 | 170 | 3 | 1 | 21 | 1 1/2 | 1 1/2 strch |
| **Quaker** | | | | | | | | | | | | |
| ✔Instant Hot Oatmeal | 1 pkt | 100 | 2 | 18 | 0 | 0 | 80 | 4 | 3 | 19 | 1 | 1 strch |
| ✔Instant Hot Oatmeal, Apple & Cinnamon | 1 pkt | 130 | 2 | 14 | <1 | 0 | 170 | 3 | 3 | 27 | 2 | 2 strch |
| ✔Instant Hot Oatmeal, Bananas & Cream | 1 pkt | 140 | 3 | 19 | <1 | 0 | 160 | 3 | 2 | 26 | 2 | 2 strch, 1 fat |
| ✔Instant Hot Oatmeal, Blueberry & Cream | 1 pkt | 140 | 3 | 19 | <1 | 0 | 180 | 3 | 2 | 26 | 2 | 2 strch, 1 fat |
| ✔Instant Hot Oatmeal, Chocolate Chip Cookie | 1 pkt | 160 | 3 | 17 | <1 | 0 | 200 | 4 | 3 | 32 | 2 | 2 strch, 1 fat |
| ✔Instant Hot Oatmeal, Cinnamon Spice | 1 pkt | 170 | 2 | 11 | 0 | 0 | 240 | 4 | 3 | 36 | 2 1/2 | 2 1/2 strch |
| ✔Instant Hot Oatmeal, Cookies 'n Cream | 1 pkt | 160 | 3 | 17 | <1 | 0 | 200 | 4 | 2 | 31 | 2 | 2 strch, 1 fat |
| Instant Hot Oatmeal, Dinosaur Eggs | 1 pkt | 200 | 4 | 18 | 2 | 0 | 240 | 4 | 3 | 38 | 2 1/2 | 2 1/2 strch, 1 fat |
| ✔Instant Hot Oatmeal, Maple/Brown Sugar | 1 pkt | 160 | 2 | 11 | 0 | 0 | 240 | 4 | 3 | 33 | 2 | 2 strch |
| ✔Instant Hot Oatmeal, Peaches & Cream | 1 pkt | 140 | 3 | 19 | <1 | 0 | 180 | 3 | 2 | 27 | 2 | 2 strch, 1 fat |
| ✔Instant Hot Oatmeal, Raisin/Date/Walnut | 1 pkt | 140 | 3 | 19 | <1 | 0 | 240 | 3 | 3 | 27 | 2 | 2 strch, 1 fat |

| | Serving | Cal. | Fat (g) | % Cal. Fat | Sat. Fat (g) | Chol. (mg) | Sod. (mg) | Fiber (g) | Prot. (g) | Carb. (g) | Carb. Ch. | Exchanges |
|---|---|---|---|---|---|---|---|---|---|---|---|---|
| Instant Hot Oatmeal, S'mores | 1 pkt | 160 | 3 | 17 | <1 | 0 | 220 | 4 | 2 | 32 | 2 | 2 strch, 1 fat |
| ✔Instant Hot Oatmeal, Strawberries & Cream | 1 pkt | 140 | 3 | 19 | <1 | 0 | 180 | 3 | 2 | 27 | 2 | 2 strch, 1 fat |
| ✔Instant Oatmeal, Cinnamon Roll | 1 pkt | 160 | 3 | 17 | 2 | 0 | 240 | 3 | 3 | 33 | 2 | 2 strch, 1 fat |
| ✔Instant Oatmeal, French Vanilla | 1 pkt | 160 | 2 | 11 | 0 | 0 | 250 | 4 | 3 | 33 | 2 | 2 strch |
| ✔Quick ' N Hearty Microwave Oatmeal, Apple Spice | 1 pkt | 170 | 2 | 11 | <1 | 0 | 310 | 4 | 3 | 35 | 2 | 2 strch |
| ✔Quick 'N Hearty Microwave Oatmeal, Brown Sugar Cinn | 1 pkt | 150 | 2 | 12 | <1 | 0 | 260 | 4 | 3 | 31 | 2 | 2 strch |
| ✔Quick 'N Hearty Microwave Oatmeal, Cinn Raisin | 1 pkt | 170 | 2 | 11 | <1 | 0 | 270 | 4 | 3 | 35 | 2 | 2 strch |
| ✔Quick 'N Hearty Microwave Oatmeal, Honey Bran | 1 pkt | 150 | 2 | 12 | <1 | 0 | 250 | 4 | 3 | 31 | 2 | 2 strch |
| ✔Quick 'N Hearty Microwave Oatmeal, Regular | 1 pkt | 110 | 2 | 16 | <1 | 0 | 150 | 4 | 2 | 19 | 1 | 1 strch |

## CEREAL, READY-TO-EAT

### Breadshop

| | Serving | Cal. | Fat (g) | % Cal. Fat | Sat. Fat (g) | Chol. (mg) | Sod. (mg) | Fiber (g) | Prot. (g) | Carb. (g) | Carb. Ch. | Exchanges |
|---|---|---|---|---|---|---|---|---|---|---|---|---|
| ✔Puffs'n Honey | 3/4 cup | 120 | 3 | 23 | 0 | 0 | 10 | 1 | 1 | 21 | 1 1/2 | 1 1/2 strch, 1 fat |

### General Mills

| | Serving | Cal. | Fat (g) | % Cal. Fat | Sat. Fat (g) | Chol. (mg) | Sod. (mg) | Fiber (g) | Prot. (g) | Carb. (g) | Carb. Ch. | Exchanges |
|---|---|---|---|---|---|---|---|---|---|---|---|---|
| ✔Basic 4 | 1 cup | 200 | 3 | 14 | 0 | 0 | 320 | 4 | 3 | 43 | 3 | 3 strch, 1 fat |

✔= Best Bet; NA = Not Available; Carb. Ch. = Carbohydrate Choices

| Cereal, Ready-to-Eat (Continued) | Serving Size | Cal. | Fat (g) | % Cal. Fat | Sat. Fat (g) | Chol. (mg) | Sod. (mg) | Pro. (g) | Fiber (g) | Carb. (g) | Carb. Ch. | Servings/Exchanges |
|---|---|---|---|---|---|---|---|---|---|---|---|---|
| ✓Berry Berry Kix | 3/4 cup | 120 | 1 | 8 | 0 | 0 | 170 | 1 | 0 | 26 | 2 | 2 strch |
| ✓Body Buddies Natural Fruit | 1 cup | 120 | 1 | 8 | 0 | 0 | 290 | 2 | 0 | 26 | 2 | 2 strch |
| ✓Boo Berry | 1 cup | 120 | 1 | 8 | 0 | 0 | 210 | 1 | 0 | 27 | 2 | 2 strch |
| ✓Cheerios | 1 cup | 110 | 2 | 16 | 0 | 0 | 280 | 3 | 3 | 22 | 1 1/2 | 1 1/2 strch |
| ✓Cheerios Plus, Multi-Grain | 1 cup | 110 | 1 | 8 | 0 | 0 | 200 | 3 | 3 | 24 | 1 1/2 | 1 1/2 strch |
| Cheerios, Apple Cinnamon | 3/4 cup | 120 | 2 | 15 | 0 | 0 | 160 | 2 | 1 | 25 | 1 1/2 | 1 1/2 strch |
| ✓Cheerios, Honey Nut | 1 cup | 120 | 2 | 15 | 0 | 0 | 270 | 3 | 2 | 24 | 1 1/2 | 1 1/2 strch |
| ✓Chex Multi-Bran | 1 cup | 200 | 2 | 9 | 0 | 0 | 390 | 4 | 7 | 49 | 3 | 3 strch |
| ✓Cinnamon Grahams | 3/4 cup | 120 | 1 | 8 | 0 | 0 | 230 | 1 | 1 | 26 | 2 | 2 strch |
| Cinnamon Toast Crunch | 3/4 cup | 130 | 4 | 28 | <1 | 0 | 210 | 1 | 1 | 24 | 1 1/2 | 1 1/2 strch |
| ✓Cocoa Puffs | 1 cup | 120 | 1 | 8 | 0 | 0 | 170 | 1 | 0 | 26 | 2 | 2 strch |
| ✓Cookie Crisp | 1 cup | 120 | 1 | 8 | 0 | 0 | 180 | 1 | 0 | 27 | 2 | 2 strch |
| ✓Corn Chex | 1 cup | 110 | 0 | 0 | 0 | 0 | 280 | 2 | 0 | 26 | 2 | 2 strch |
| ✓Count Chocula | 1 cup | 120 | 1 | 8 | 0 | 0 | 180 | 1 | 0 | 26 | 2 | 2 strch |
| ✓Country Corn Flakes | 1 cup | 110 | 0 | 0 | 0 | 0 | 260 | 2 | 0 | 26 | 2 | 2 strch |
| ✓Crispy Wheat 'N Raisins | 1 cup | 190 | 1 | 5 | 0 | 0 | 270 | 4 | 4 | 45 | 3 | 3 strch |
| ✓Fiber One | 1/2 cup | 60 | 1 | 15 | 0 | 0 | 130 | 2 | 13 | 24 | 1 1/2 | 1 1/2 strch |
| ✓Frankenberry | 1 cup | 120 | 1 | 8 | 0 | 0 | 210 | 1 | 0 | 27 | 2 | 2 strch |

| | | | | | | | | | | | | |
|---|---|---|---|---|---|---|---|---|---|---|---|---|
| ✓French Toast Crunch | 3/4 cup | 120 | 2 | 15 | 0 | 0 | 180 | 1 | 0 | 26 | 2 | 2 strch |
| ✓Frosted Cheerios | 1 cup | 120 | 1 | 8 | 0 | 0 | 210 | 2 | 1 | 26 | 2 | 2 strch |
| ✓Golden Grahams | 3/4 cup | 120 | 1 | 8 | 0 | 0 | 270 | 1 | 1 | 25 | 1 1/2 | 1 1/2 strch |
| ✓Honey Nut Chex | 3/4 cup | 110 | 1 | 8 | 0 | 0 | 220 | 1 | 0 | 26 | 2 | 2 strch |
| ✓Honey Nut Clusters | 3/4 cup | 210 | 2 | 9 | 0 | 0 | 210 | 4 | 3 | 47 | 3 | 3 strch |
| ✓Kaboom | 1 1/4 cup | 120 | 1 | 8 | 0 | 0 | 290 | 2 | 1 | 24 | 1 1/2 | 1 1/2 strch |
| ✓Kix | 1 1/3 cup | 120 | <1 | 8 | 0 | 0 | 270 | 2 | 1 | 26 | 2 | 2 strch |
| ✓Lucky Charms | 1 cup | 120 | 1 | 8 | 0 | 0 | 210 | 2 | 1 | 25 | 1 1/2 | 1 1/2 strch |
| ✓Millenios | 1 cup | 120 | 1 | 8 | 0 | 0 | 180 | 2 | 1 | 25 | 1 1/2 | 1 1/2 strch |
| ✓Nature Valley Low Fat Fruit Granola | 2/3 cup | 210 | 3 | 13 | 0 | 0 | 210 | 4 | 3 | 44 | 3 | 3 strch, 1 fat |
| ✓Nesquik Chocolate | 3/4 cup | 120 | 2 | 15 | 0 | 0 | 190 | 1 | 0 | 25 | 1 1/2 | 1 1/2 strch |
| Oatmeal Crisp, Almond | 1 cup | 220 | 5 | 20 | <1 | 0 | 240 | 5 | 4 | 42 | 3 | 3 strch, 1 fat |
| ✓Oatmeal Crisp, Apple Cinnamon | 1 cup | 210 | 2 | 9 | 0 | 0 | 250 | 5 | 4 | 45 | 3 | 3 strch |
| ✓Oatmeal Crisp, Raisins | 1 cup | 210 | 2 | 9 | 0 | 0 | 210 | 5 | 4 | 44 | 3 | 3 strch |
| Raisin Nut Bran | 3/4 cup | 200 | 4 | 18 | <1 | 0 | 250 | 4 | 5 | 41 | 3 | 3 strch |
| ✓Reese's Peanut Butter Puffs | 3/4 cup | 130 | 3 | 21 | <1 | 0 | 200 | 2 | 0 | 24 | 1 1/2 | 1 1/2 strch, 1 fat |
| ✓Rice Chex | 1 1/4 cup | 120 | 0 | 0 | 0 | 0 | 290 | 2 | 0 | 27 | 2 | 2 strch |
| ✓Sunrise | 3/4 cup | 110 | <1 | 8 | 0 | 0 | 190 | 1 | 1 | 26 | 2 | 2 strch |
| ✓Sunrise Organic Cereal | 3/4 cup | 110 | <1 | 8 | 0 | 0 | 190 | 1 | 1 | 26 | 2 | 2 strch |

✓= Best Bet; NA = Not Available; Carb. Ch. = Carbohydrate Choices

| Cereal, Ready-to-Eat (Continued) | Serving Size | Cal. | Fat Cal. (g) | % Fat | Sat. Fat (g) | Chol. (g) | Sod. (mg) | Pro. (mg) | Fiber (g) | Carb. (g) | Ch. | Servings/Exchanges |
|---|---|---|---|---|---|---|---|---|---|---|---|---|
| ✓Team Cheerios | 1 cup | 120 | 1 | 8 | 0 | 0 | 210 | 2 | 1 | 25 | 1 1/2 | 1 1/2 strch |
| ✓Total Brown Sugar & Oat | 3/4 cup | 110 | 1 | 8 | 0 | 0 | 170 | 2 | 1 | 25 | 1 1/2 | 1 1/2 strch |
| ✓Total Corn Flakes | 1 13/ cup | 110 | 0 | 0 | 0 | 0 | 200 | 2 | 0 | 26 | 2 | 2 strch |
| ✓Total Raisin Bran | 1 cup | 180 | 1 | 5 | 0 | 0 | 240 | 4 | 5 | 43 | 3 | 3 strch |
| ✓Total Whole Grain | 3/4 cup | 110 | 1 | 8 | <1 | 0 | 200 | 3 | 3 | 24 | 1 1/2 | 1 1/2 strch |
| ✓Trix | 1 cup | 120 | 1 | 8 | 0 | 0 | 200 | 1 | 1 | 27 | 2 | 2 strch |
| ✓Wheat Chex | 1 cup | 180 | 1 | 5 | 0 | 0 | 420 | 5 | 5 | 40 | 2 1/2 | 2 1/2 strch |
| ✓Wheat Hearts | 1/4 cup dry | 130 | 1 | 7 | 0 | 0 | 0 | 5 | 2 | 26 | 2 | 2 strch |
| ✓Wheaties | 1 cup | 110 | 1 | 8 | 0 | 0 | 220 | 3 | 3 | 24 | 1 1/2 | 1 1/2 strch |
| ✓Wheaties Raisin Bran | 1 cup | 180 | 1 | 5 | 0 | 0 | 250 | 4 | 5 | 45 | 3 | 3 strch |
| ✓Wheaties, Frosted | 3/4 cup | 110 | 0 | 0 | 0 | 0 | 200 | 1 | 0 | 27 | 2 | 2 strch |
| **Health Valley** | | | | | | | | | | | | |
| ✓Fat-Free Granola O's, Apple Cinnamon | 1 oz | 90 | 0 | 0 | 0 | 0 | 5 | 3 | 5 | 19 | 1 | 1 strch |
| ✓Fat-Free High Fiber O's | 1 oz | 90 | 0 | 0 | 0 | 0 | 5 | 3 | 5 | 19 | 1 | 1 strch |
| ✓Organic Amaranth Flakes | 1 oz | 90 | 0 | 0 | 0 | 0 | 10 | 3 | 3 | 20 | 1 | 1 strch |
| ✓Organic Apple Crunch | 3/4 cup | 160 | 0 | 0 | 0 | 0 | 10 | 5 | 7 | 41 | 3 | 3 strch |
| ✓Organic Raisin Bran Flakes | 1 1/4 cup | 190 | 0 | 0 | 0 | 0 | 90 | 5 | 6 | 47 | 3 | 3 strch |

## Kashi

| | | | | | | | | | | | | |
|---|---|---|---|---|---|---|---|---|---|---|---|---|
| ✔Kashi | 1/2 cup | 170 | 3 | 16 | 0 | 0 | 15 | 6 | 6 | 30 | 2 | 2 strch |
| ✔Kashi Medley | 1/2 cup | 100 | 1 | 9 | 0 | 0 | 50 | 4 | 2 | 20 | 1 | 1 strch |
| ✔Puffed Kashi | 1 cup | 70 | <1 | 13 | 0 | 0 | 0 | 3 | 2 | 13 | 1 | 1 strch |

## Kellogg's

| | | | | | | | | | | | | |
|---|---|---|---|---|---|---|---|---|---|---|---|---|
| ✔All-Bran | 1/2 cup | 80 | 1 | 11 | 0 | 0 | 65 | 4 | 10 | 24 | 1 1/2 | 1 1/2 strch |
| ✔All-Bran w/Extra Fiber | 1/2 cup | 50 | 1 | 18 | 0 | 0 | 120 | 3 | 13 | 20 | 1 | 1 strch |
| ✔Apple Jack's | 1 cup | 120 | 0 | 0 | 0 | 0 | 150 | 1 | 1 | 30 | 2 | 2 strch |
| ✔Bran Buds | 1/3 cup | 80 | 1 | 11 | 0 | 0 | 200 | 2 | 13 | 24 | 1 1/2 | 1 1/2 strch |
| ✔Cocoa Frosted Flakes | 3/4 cup | 120 | 0 | 0 | 0 | 0 | 170 | 1 | 0 | 28 | 2 | 2 strch |
| ✔Cocoa Krispies | 3/4 cup | 120 | 1 | 8 | <1 | 0 | 190 | 1 | 1 | 27 | 2 | 2 strch |
| ✔Complete Oat Bran Flakes | 3/4 cup | 110 | 1 | 8 | 0 | 0 | 210 | 3 | 4 | 23 | 1 1/2 | 1 1/2 strch |
| ✔Complete Wheat Bran Flakes | 3/4 cup | 90 | 0 | 0 | 0 | 0 | 210 | 3 | 5 | 23 | 1 1/2 | 1 1/2 strch |
| ✔Corn Flakes | 1 cup | 100 | 0 | 0 | 0 | 0 | 200 | 2 | 1 | 24 | 1 1/2 | 1 1/2 strch |
| ✔Corn Pops | 1 cup | 120 | 0 | 0 | 0 | 0 | 120 | 1 | 0 | 28 | 2 | 2 strch |
| ✔Country Inn Specialties, Green Gables Inn Blend | 1/2 cup | 210 | 6 | 26 | 0 | 0 | 160 | 4 | 4 | 37 | 2 1/2 | 2 1/2 strch, 1 fat |
| Country Inn Specialties, Greyfield Inn Blend | 3/4 cup | 210 | 6 | 26 | 1 | 0 | 220 | 3 | 3 | 38 | 2 1/2 | 2 1/2 strch, 1 fat |

✔= Best Bet; NA = Not Available; Carb. Ch. = Carbohydrate Choices

| Cereal, Ready-to-Eat (*Continued*) | Serving Size | Cal. | Fat (g) | % Cal. Fat | Sat. Fat (g) | Chol. (mg) | Sod. (mg) | Pro. (g) | Fiber (g) | Carb. (g) | Carb. Ch. | Servings/Exchanges |
|---|---|---|---|---|---|---|---|---|---|---|---|---|
| ✔Country Inn Specialties, Inn at Ormsby Hill Blend | 1 cup | 220 | 2 | 8 | 1 | 0 | 300 | 4 | 3 | 49 | 3 | 3 strch |
| Cracklin' Oat Bran | 3/4 cup | 190 | 7 | 33 | 2 | 0 | 170 | 4 | 6 | 35 | 2 | 2 strch, 1 fat |
| ✔Crispix | 1 cup | 110 | 0 | 0 | 0 | 0 | 210 | 2 | 1 | 25 | 1 1/2 | 1 1/2 strch |
| ✔Froot Loops | 1 cup | 120 | 1 | 8 | <1 | 0 | 150 | 1 | 1 | 28 | 2 | 2 strch |
| ✔Froot Loops, Marshmallow Blasted | 1 cup | 120 | <1 | 8 | 0 | 0 | 105 | 1 | 0 | 27 | 2 | 2 strch |
| ✔Frosted Flakes | 3/4 cup | 120 | 0 | 0 | 0 | 0 | 150 | 1 | 1 | 28 | 2 | 2 strch |
| ✔Golden Crispix | 1 cup | 120 | 0 | 0 | 0 | 0 | 250 | 2 | <1 | 29 | 2 | 2 strch |
| ✔Healthy Choice Almond Crunch w/Raisins | 1 cup | 210 | 3 | 13 | 0 | 0 | 230 | 5 | 5 | 45 | 3 | 3 strch, 1 fat |
| ✔Healthy Choice Low Fat Granola | 1/2 cup | 190 | 3 | 14 | <1 | 0 | 120 | 4 | 3 | 39 | 2 1/2 | 2 1/2 strch, 1 fat |
| ✔Healthy Choice Low Fat Granola w/Raisins | 2/3 cup | 220 | 3 | 12 | 1 | 0 | 150 | 5 | 3 | 48 | 3 | 3 strch, 1 fat |
| ✔Healthy Choice Mueslix Raisin & Almond Crunch | 2/3 cup | 200 | 3 | 14 | 0 | 0 | 160 | 5 | 4 | 41 | 3 | 3 strch, 1 fat |
| ✔Healthy Choice Toasted Brown Sugar Squares | 1 cup | 190 | 1 | 5 | 0 | 0 | 5 | 5 | 5 | 44 | 3 | 3 strch |
| ✔Honey Crunch Flakes | 3/4 cup | 120 | 1 | 8 | 0 | 0 | 210 | 2 | 1 | 26 | 2 | 2 strch |

| Food | Serving | | | | | | | | | | | Carb. Ch. |
|---|---|---|---|---|---|---|---|---|---|---|---|---|
| ✔ Just Right w/Fruit & Nut | 1 cup | 220 | 2 | 8 | 0 | 0 | 280 | 4 | 3 | 49 | 3 | 3 strch |
| ✔ Mini-Wheats, Honey Frosted | 24 biscuits | 200 | 1 | 5 | 0 | 0 | 5 | 5 | 6 | 48 | 3 | 3 strch |
| ✔ Mini-Wheats, Apple Cinnamon | 3/4 cup | 180 | 1 | 5 | 0 | 0 | 20 | 4 | 5 | 44 | 3 | 3 strch |
| ✔ Mini-Wheats, Frosted Bite Size | 24 biscuits | 200 | 1 | 0 | 0 | 0 | 0 | 6 | 6 | 48 | 3 | 3 strch |
| ✔ Mini-Wheats, Frosted Original | 5 biscuits | 180 | 1 | 5 | 0 | 0 | 5 | 5 | 5 | 41 | 3 | 3 strch |
| ✔ Mini-Wheats-Blueberry | 3/4 cup | 180 | 1 | 5 | 0 | 0 | 20 | 4 | 5 | 43 | 3 | 3 strch |
| ✔ Nut & Honey Crunch | 1 1/4 cup | 223 | 3 | 12 | <1 | 0 | 370 | 4 | <1 | 45 | 3 | 3 strch, 1 fat |
| ✔ Pokemon | 1 cup | 110 | <1 | 8 | 0 | 0 | 160 | 2 | 1 | 25 | 1 1/2 | 1 1/2 strch |
| ✔ Product 19 | 1 cup | 100 | 0 | 0 | 0 | 0 | 210 | 2 | 1 | 25 | 1 1/2 | 1 1/2 strch |
| ✔ Raisin Bran | 1 cup | 190 | 2 | 9 | 0 | 0 | 350 | 5 | 8 | 45 | 3 | 3 strch |
| ✔ Raisin Bran Crunch | 1 cup | 190 | 1 | 5 | 0 | 0 | 200 | 3 | 4 | 44 | 3 | 3 strch |
| ✔ Rice Krispies | 1 1/4 cup | 120 | 0 | 0 | 0 | 0 | 320 | 2 | <1 | 29 | 2 | 2 strch |
| ✔ Rice Krispies Treats | 3/4 cup | 120 | 2 | 0 | 0 | 0 | 190 | 1 | 0 | 26 | 2 | 2 strch |
| ✔ Rice Krispies, Apple Cinnamon | 3/4 cup | 110 | 0 | 0 | 0 | 0 | 223 | 2 | <1 | 27 | 2 | 2 strch |
| ✔ Rice Krispies, Razzle Dazzle | 3/4 cup | 110 | 0 | 0 | 0 | 0 | 170 | 1 | 0 | 25 | 1 1/2 | 1 1/2 strch |
| ✔ Smacks | 3/4 cup | 100 | <1 | 9 | 0 | 0 | 50 | 2 | 1 | 24 | 1 1/2 | 1 1/2 strch |
| ✔ Smart Start | 1 cup | 180 | <1 | 5 | 0 | 0 | 330 | 3 | 2 | 43 | 3 | 3 strch |
| ✔ Smart Start, Soy Protein | 1 cup | 200 | 2 | 9 | 0 | 0 | 250 | 10 | 4 | 40 | 2 1/2 | 2 1/2 strch |
| ✔ Special K | 1 cup | 110 | 0 | 0 | 0 | 0 | 220 | 6 | 1 | 23 | 1 1/2 | 1 1/2 strch |

✔ = Best Bet; NA = Not Available; Carb. Ch. = Carbohydrate Choices

| Cereal, Ready-to-Eat (Continued) | Serving Size | Cal. | Fat (g) | % Cal. Fat | Sat. Fat (g) | Chol. (mg) | Sod. (mg) | Pro. (g) | Fiber (g) | Carb. (g) | Carb. Ch. | Servings/Exchanges |
|---|---|---|---|---|---|---|---|---|---|---|---|---|
| ✓Special K Plus | 1 cup | 210 | 2 | 9 | 0 | 0 | 250 | 4 | 3 | 47 | 3 | 3 strch |
| **Malt-0-Meal** | | | | | | | | | | | | |
| ✓Berry Colossal Crunch | 3/4 cup | 120 | 2 | 15 | 0 | 0 | 220 | 1 | 1 | 26 | 2 | 2 strch |
| ✓Cocoa Comets | 3/4 cup | 120 | 1 | 8 | 0 | 0 | 190 | 1 | <1 | 27 | 2 | 2 strch |
| ✓Colossal Crunch | 3/4 cup | 120 | 2 | 15 | 0 | 0 | 230 | 1 | 1 | 25 | 1 1/2 | 1 1/2 strch |
| ✓Corn Bursts | 1 cup | 120 | 0 | 0 | 0 | 0 | 120 | 1 | 0 | 29 | 2 | 2 strch |
| ✓Crispy Rice | 1 cup | 110 | 0 | 0 | 0 | 0 | 320 | 2 | 0 | 26 | 2 | 2 strch |
| ✓Frosted Flakes | 3/4 cup | 110 | 0 | 0 | 0 | 0 | 200 | 1 | <1 | 27 | 2 | 2 strch |
| ✓Frosted Mini Spooners | 1 cup | 190 | 1 | 5 | 0 | 0 | 0 | 5 | 6 | 45 | 3 | 3 strch |
| ✓Golden Puffs | 3/4 cup | 100 | 0 | 0 | 0 | 0 | 40 | 2 | <1 | 26 | 2 | 2 strch |
| ✓Puffed Rice | 1 cup | 60 | 0 | 0 | 0 | 0 | 0 | 1 | 0 | 13 | 1 | 1 strch |
| ✓Puffed Wheat | 1 cup | 50 | 0 | 0 | 0 | 0 | 0 | 2 | 1 | 11 | 1 | 1 strch |
| ✓Toasty O's | 1 cup | 110 | 2 | 16 | 0 | 0 | 260 | 3 | 3 | 22 | 1 1/2 | 1 1/2 strch |
| ✓Toasty O's, Apple & Cinnamon | 3/4 cup | 120 | 2 | 15 | 0 | 0 | 160 | 2 | 1 | 25 | 1 1/2 | 1 1/2 strch |
| ✓Toasty O's, Frosted | 1 cup | 120 | 1 | 8 | 0 | 0 | 210 | 7 | 1 | 25 | 1 1/2 | 1 1/2 strch |
| ✓Toasty O's, Honey & Nut | 1 cup | 110 | 1 | 8 | 0 | 0 | 270 | 3 | 2 | 24 | 1 1/2 | 1 1/2 strch |
| ✓Tootie Fruities | 1 cup | 120 | 1 | 8 | 0 | 0 | 140 | 1 | <1 | 26 | 2 | 2 strch |

## Nabisco

| | | | | | | | | | | | | |
|---|---|---|---|---|---|---|---|---|---|---|---|---|
| ✔100% Bran Cereal | 1/3 cup | 80 | <1 | 11 | 0 | 0 | 120 | 4 | 8 | 23 | 1 1/2 | 1 1/2 strch |
| ✔Shredded Wheat | 2 biscuits | 160 | <1 | 6 | 0 | 0 | 0 | 5 | 5 | 38 | 2 1/2 | 2 1/2 strch |
| ✔Shredded Wheat & Bran | 1 1/4 cup | 200 | 1 | 5 | 0 | 0 | 0 | 7 | 8 | 47 | 3 | 3 strch |
| ✔Shredded Wheat Bites, Frosted | 1 cup | 190 | 1 | 9 | 0 | 0 | 10 | 4 | 5 | 44 | 3 | 3 strch |
| ✔Shredded Wheat Bites, Honey Nut | 1 cup | 200 | 2 | 9 | 0 | 0 | 40 | 5 | 4 | 43 | 3 | 3 strch |
| ✔Shredded Wheat, Spoon Size | 1 cup | 170 | <1 | 5 | 0 | 0 | 0 | 5 | 5 | 41 | 3 | 3 strch |

## Nature Valley

| | | | | | | | | | | | | |
|---|---|---|---|---|---|---|---|---|---|---|---|---|
| Granola, Cinnamon Raisin | 1/3 cup | 120 | 4 | 30 | <1 | 0 | 50 | 2 | 1 | 20 | 1 | 1 strch, 1 fat |
| ✔Granola, Fruit & Nut | 1 oz | 130 | 5 | 35 | 1 | 0 | 45 | 2 | 1 | 19 | 1 | 1 strch, 1 fat |

## Post

| | | | | | | | | | | | | |
|---|---|---|---|---|---|---|---|---|---|---|---|---|
| ✔Alpha-Bits | 1 cup | 130 | 2 | 14 | 0 | 0 | 210 | 3 | 1 | 27 | 2 | 2 strch |
| ✔Alpha-Bits, Marshmallow | 1 cup | 120 | 1 | 8 | 0 | 0 | 160 | 2 | 0 | 25 | 1 1/2 | 1 1/2 strch |
| Banana Nut Crunch | 1 cup | 250 | 6 | 22 | 1 | 0 | 240 | 5 | 4 | 43 | 3 | 3 strch, 1 fat |
| ✔Blueberry Morning | 1 1/4 | 220 | 3 | 12 | <1 | 0 | 250 | 4 | 2 | 43 | 3 | 3 strch, 1 fat |
| ✔Bran Flakes | 3/4 cup | 100 | <1 | 9 | 0 | 0 | 220 | 3 | 5 | 24 | 1 1/2 | 1 1/2 strch |
| ✔Cinna-Cluster Raisin Bran | 1 cup | 220 | 3 | 12 | 0 | 0 | 260 | 4 | 7 | 48 | 3 | 3 strch, 1 fat |
| ✔Cocoa Pebbles | 3/4 cup | 120 | 1 | 8 | 1 | 0 | 160 | 1 | 0 | 26 | 2 | 2 strch |
| ✔Cranberry Almond Crunch | 1 cup | 220 | 3 | 12 | 0 | 0 | 200 | 4 | 3 | 44 | 3 | 3 strch, 1 fat |

✔ = Best Bet; NA = Not Available; Carb. Ch. = Carbohydrate Choices

| Cereal, Ready-to-Eat (*Continued*) | Serving Size | Cal. | Fat (g) | % Cal. Fat | Sat. Fat (g) | Chol. (mg) | Sod. (mg) | Pro. (g) | Fiber (g) | Carb. (g) | Carb. Ch. | Servings/Exchanges |
|---|---|---|---|---|---|---|---|---|---|---|---|---|
| ✔Fruit & Fiber, Date/Raisin/Walnut | 1 cup | 210 | 3 | 13 | <1 | 0 | 250 | 4 | 5 | 42 | 3 | 3 strch, 1 fat |
| ✔Fruit & Fiber, Peach/Raisin/Almond | 1 cup | 210 | 3 | 13 | <1 | 0 | 260 | 4 | 5 | 42 | 3 | 3 strch, 1 fat |
| ✔Fruity Pebbles | 3/4 cup | 110 | 1 | 8 | <1 | 0 | 160 | <1 | 0 | 24 | 1 1/2 | 1 1/2 strch |
| ✔Golden Crisp | 3/4 cup | 110 | 0 | 0 | 0 | 0 | 40 | 1 | 0 | 25 | 1 1/2 | 1 1/2 strch |
| ✔Grape Nuts | 1/2 cup | 200 | 1 | 5 | 0 | 0 | 350 | 6 | 5 | 47 | 3 | 3 strch |
| ✔Grape Nuts Flakes | 3/4 cup | 100 | 1 | 9 | 0 | 0 | 140 | 6 | 5 | 24 | 1 1/2 | 1 1/2 strch |
| ✔Grape Nuts O's | 1 cup | 120 | 0 | 0 | 0 | 0 | 150 | 3 | 2 | 28 | 2 | 2 strch |
| Great Grains Crunchy Pecan | 2/3 cup | 220 | 6 | 25 | 1 | 0 | 190 | 5 | 4 | 38 | 2 1/2 | 2 1/2 strch, 1 fat |
| Great Grains, Raisin/Date/Pecan | 2/3 cup | 210 | 5 | 21 | .5 | <1 | 160 | 4 | 4 | 39 | 2 1/2 | 2 1/2 strch, 1 fat |
| ✔Honey Bunches of Oats | 3/4 cup | 120 | 2 | 15 | <1 | 0 | 190 | 2 | 1 | 25 | 1 1/2 | 1 1/2 strch |
| ✔Honey Bunches of Oats & Almond | 3/4 cup | 130 | 3 | 21 | <1 | 0 | 190 | 2 | 1 | 24 | 1 1/2 | 1 1/2 strch, 1 fat |
| ✔Honeycombs | 1 1/3 cup | 110 | <1 | 8 | 0 | 0 | 220 | 2 | <1 | 26 | 2 | 2 strch |
| ✔Oreo O's | 3/4 cup | 110 | 3 | 25 | <1 | 0 | 105 | 1 | 1 | 22 | 1 1/2 | 1 1/2 strch, 1 fat |
| ✔Raisin Bran | 1 cup | 190 | 1 | 5 | 0 | 0 | 300 | 4 | 8 | 47 | 3 | 3 strch |
| ✔Toasties Corn Flakes | 1 cup | 100 | 0 | 0 | 0 | 0 | 270 | 2 | 1 | 24 | 1 1/2 | 1 1/2 strch |
| ✔Waffle Crisp | 1 cup | 130 | 3 | 21 | 0 | 0 | 120 | 2 | 0 | 24 | 1 1/2 | 1 1/2 strch, 1 fat |
| **Quaker** | | | | | | | | | | | | |
| ✔100% Natural Granola, Low Fat | 2/3 cup | 210 | 3 | 13 | NA | 0 | 140 | 5 | 3 | 44 | 3 | 3 strch, 1 fat |

| | | | | | | | | | | | | |
|---|---|---|---|---|---|---|---|---|---|---|---|---|
| 100% Natural Granola, Raisin | 1/2 cup | 230 | 9 | 35 | 4 | 0 | 20 | 5 | 3 | 34 | 2 | 2 strch, 2 fat |
| 100% Natural Granola, Regular | 1/2 cup | 220 | 9 | 37 | NA | 0 | 20 | 5 | 3 | 31 | 2 | 2 strch, 2 fat |
| ✔Apple Zaps | 1 cup | 120 | 1 | 8 | NA | 0 | 135 | 1 | 1 | 27 | 2 | 2 strch |
| ✔Cap'n Crunch | 3/4 cup | 110 | 2 | 16 | 0 | 0 | 200 | 1 | 1 | 23 | 1 1/2 | 1 1/2 strch |
| ✔Cap'n Crunch Oops! All Berries | 1 cup | 130 | 2 | 14 | NA | 0 | 180 | 2 | 1 | 27 | 2 | 2 strch |
| ✔Cap'n Crunch Peanut Butter | 3/4 cup | 110 | 3 | 25 | <1 | 0 | 200 | 2 | 1 | 22 | 1 1/2 | 1 1/2 strch, 1 fat |
| ✔Cap'n Crunch w/Crunchberries | 3/4 cup | 100 | 2 | 18 | 0 | 0 | 180 | 1 | 1 | 22 | 1 1/2 | 1 1/2 strch |
| ✔Cinnamon Crunch | 1 cup | 120 | 2 | 15 | NA | 0 | 230 | 2 | 1 | 25 | 1 1/2 | 1 1/2 strch |
| ✔Crunchy Corn Bran | 1 cup | 90 | 1 | 10 | <1 | 0 | 250 | 5 | 5 | 23 | 1 1/2 | 1 1/2 strch |
| ✔Frosted Flakers | 3/4 cup | 120 | 0 | 0 | NA | 0 | 200 | 1 | 0 | 28 | 2 | 2 strch |
| ✔Frosted Oats | 1 cup | 110 | 2 | 16 | NA | 0 | 230 | 2 | 1 | 23 | 1 1/2 | 1 1/2 strch |
| ✔Frosted Shredded Wheat | 1 cup | 200 | 1 | 5 | NA | 0 | 0 | 5 | 4 | 45 | 3 | 3 strch |
| ✔Fruitangy Oh's | 1 cup | 120 | 1 | 8 | NA | 0 | 150 | 2 | 1 | 27 | 2 | 2 strch |
| ✔Honey Crisp Corn Flakes | 3/4 cup | 110 | 0 | 0 | NA | 0 | 260 | 2 | 1 | 27 | 2 | 2 strch |
| ✔Honey Graham | 3/4 cup | 110 | 2 | 16 | NA | 0 | 230 | 2 | 1 | 23 | 1 1/2 | 1 1/2 strch |
| ✔Honey Nut Oats | 3/4 cup | 110 | 1 | 8 | NA | 0 | 220 | 2 | 1 | 24 | 1 1/2 | 1 1/2 strch |
| ✔King Vitamin | 1 1/2 Tbsp | 120 | 1 | 8 | 0 | 0 | 260 | 2 | 1 | 26 | 2 | 2 strch |
| ✔Kretschmer Honey Crunch Wheat Germ | 1 2/3 Tbsp | 50 | 1 | 18 | 0 | 0 | 0 | 4 | 1 | 8 | 1/2 | 1/2 strch |

✔ = Best Bet; NA = Not Available; Carb. Ch. = Carbohydrate Choices

| Cereal, Ready-to-Eat (*Continued*) | Serving Size | Cal. | Fat (g) | % Cal. Fat | Sat. Fat (g) | Chol. (mg) | Sod. (mg) | Pro. (g) | Fiber (g) | Carb. (g) | Carb. Ch. | Servings/Exchanges |
|---|---|---|---|---|---|---|---|---|---|---|---|---|
| ✓Kretschmer Toasted Wheat Bran | 1/4 cup | 30 | 1 | 30 | 0 | 0 | 0 | 3 | 7 | 10 | 1/2 | 1/2 strch |
| ✓Kretschmer Wheat Germ | 2 Tbsp | 50 | 1 | 18 | 0 | 0 | 0 | 4 | 2 | 6 | 1 1/2 | 1/2 strch |
| ✓Life | 3/4 cup | 120 | 2 | 15 | 0 | 0 | 160 | 3 | 2 | 25 | 1 1/2 | 1 1/2 strch |
| ✓Life, Cinnamon | 3/4 cup | 120 | 1 | 8 | 0 | 0 | 150 | 3 | 2 | 26 | 2 | 2 strch |
| ✓Marshmallow Safari | 3/4 cup | 140 | 2 | 13 | NA | 0 | 210 | 2 | 1 | 29 | 2 | 2 strch |
| ✓Mother's Butter Bumpers | 1.2 oz | 130 | 3 | 21 | <1 | 0 | 270 | 3 | 1 | 26 | 2 | 2 strch, 1 fat |
| ✓Mother's Cinnamon Oat Crunch | 2 oz | 230 | 3 | 12 | <1 | 0 | 250 | 6 | 5 | 48 | 3 | 3 strch, 1 fat |
| ✓Mother's Groovy Grahams | 1 oz | 100 | <1 | 9 | 0 | 0 | 240 | 2 | 1 | 24 | 1 1/2 | 1 1/2 strch |
| ✓Mother's Harvest Oat Flakes w/Apples & Almonds | 1 oz | 120 | 2 | 15 | 0 | 0 | 170 | 3 | 2 | 24 | 1 1/2 | 1 1/2 strch |
| ✓Mother's Harvest Oat Flakes | 1 oz | 110 | 1 | 8 | 0 | 0 | 200 | 3 | 2 | 23 | 1 1/2 | 1 1/2 strch |
| ✓Mother's Honey Roundups | 1 oz | 110 | <1 | 8 | 0 | 0 | 170 | 2 | 1 | 24 | 1 1/2 | 1 1/2 strch |
| ✓Mother's Toasted Oat Bran | 1.1 oz | 120 | 2 | 15 | 0 | 0 | 200 | 4 | 3 | 24 | 1 1/2 | 1 1/2 strch |
| ✓Oat Bran | 1 1/4 cup | 210 | 3 | 13 | <1 | 0 | 210 | 7 | 6 | 43 | 3 | 3 strch, 1 fat |
| ✓Oh's, Honey Graham | 3/4 cup | 110 | 2 | 16 | <1 | 0 | 180 | 1 | 1 | 23 | 1 1/2 | 1 1/2 strch |
| ✓Popeye Cocoa Blasts | 1 cup | 130 | 2 | 14 | <1 | 0 | 140 | 1 | 1 | 29 | 2 | 2 strch |
| ✓Popeye Puffed Rice | 1 cup | 50 | 0 | 0 | 0 | 0 | 0 | 1 | 0 | 12 | 1 | 1 strch |
| ✓Popeye Puffed Wheat | 1 1/4 cup | 50 | 0 | 0 | 0 | 0 | 0 | 2 | 1 | 11 | 1 | 1 strch |

| | Serving | Cal. | Fat (g) | % Cal. Fat | Sat. Fat (g) | Chol. (mg) | Sod. (mg) | Carb. (g) | Fiber (g) | Prot. (g) | Carb. Ch. | Exchanges |
|---|---|---|---|---|---|---|---|---|---|---|---|---|
| ✔Quick Hot Oats | 1/2 cup | 150 | 3 | <1 | 0 | 0 | 5 | 27 | | | | 2 strch, 1 fat |
| ✔Quisp | 1 cup | 110 | 2 | 16 | NA | 0 | 190 | 1 | 23 | 1 | 1 1/2 | 1 1/2 strch |
| ✔Rice Crisps | 1 cup | 110 | 0 | 0 | NA | 0 | 290 | 2 | 26 | 0 | 2 | 2 strch |
| ✔Shredded Wheat | 3 biscuits | 220 | 2 | 8 | <1 | 0 | 0 | 7 | 50 | 7 | 3 | 3 strch |
| ✔Sweet Crunch | 1 cup | 110 | 2 | 16 | <1 | 0 | 190 | 1 | 23 | 1 | 1 1/2 | 1 1/2 strch |
| ✔Sweet Puffs | 1 cup | 130 | 1 | 7 | 0 | 0 | 80 | 2 | 30 | 2 | 2 | 2 strch |
| ✔Toasted Oatmeal Squares, Cinnamon | 1 cup | 230 | 3 | 12 | NA | 0 | 270 | 8 | 47 | 5 | 3 | 3 strch, 1 fat |
| ✔Toasted Oatmeal Squares, Regular | 1 cup | 220 | 3 | 12 | NA | 0 | 260 | 7 | 43 | 4 | 3 | 3 strch, 1 fat |
| ✔Toasted Oatmeal, Honey Nut | 1 cup | 190 | 3 | 14 | NA | 0 | 180 | 4 | 40 | 3 | 2 1/2 | 2 1/2 strch, 1 fat |
| ✔Toasted Oatmeal, Original | 1 cup | 190 | 2 | 9 | NA | 0 | 220 | 5 | 40 | 4 | 2 1/2 | 2 1/2 strch |
| ✔Toasted Oats | 1 cup | 110 | 2 | 16 | NA | 0 | 280 | 3 | 23 | 2 | 1 1/2 | 1 1/2 strch |
| ✔Unprocessed Bran | 1/3 cup | 35 | 1 | 26 | 0 | 0 | 0 | 3 | 11 | 8 | 1 | 1 strch |

## CHEESE BLEND

### Kraft

| | Serving | Cal. | Fat (g) | % Cal. Fat | Sat. Fat (g) | Chol. (mg) | Sod. (mg) | Carb. (g) | Fiber (g) | Prot. (g) | Carb. Ch. | Exchanges |
|---|---|---|---|---|---|---|---|---|---|---|---|---|
| ✔Grated Parm Plus!, Garlic Herb | 2 tsp | 15 | 0 | 0 | 0 | 0 | 75 | <1 | 0 | 2 | 0 | free |
| ✔Grated Parm Plus!, Zesty Red Pepper | 2 tsp | 15 | 0 | 0 | 0 | 0 | 110 | <1 | 0 | 2 | 0 | free |

### Valley Fine Foods

| | Serving | Cal. | Fat (g) | % Cal. Fat | Sat. Fat (g) | Chol. (mg) | Sod. (mg) | Carb. (g) | Fiber (g) | Prot. (g) | Carb. Ch. | Exchanges |
|---|---|---|---|---|---|---|---|---|---|---|---|---|
| ✔Herb Cheese Delight | 1 Tbsp | 34 | 2 | 53 | 1 | 3 | 70 | 2 | 1 | 2 | 0 | 1 fat |

✔ = Best Bet; NA = Not Available; Carb. Ch. = Carbohydrate Choices

| Product | Serving Size | Cal. | Fat (g) | % Cal. Fat | Sat. Fat (g) | Chol. (mg) | Sod. (mg) | Pro. (g) | Fiber (g) | Carb. (g) | Carb. Ch. | Servings/Exchanges |
|---|---|---|---|---|---|---|---|---|---|---|---|---|
| **CHEESE SAUCE** | | | | | | | | | | | | |
| **Chef Mate** | | | | | | | | | | | | |
| Basic Cheese Sauce | 1/2 cup | 82 | 5 | 55 | 2 | 6 | 471 | 2 | 0 | 8 | 1/2 | 1/2 carb, 1 fat |
| Golden Cheese Sauce | 1/4 cup | 139 | 11 | 71 | 6 | 29 | 501 | 7 | <1 | 2 | 0 | 1 med-fat meat, 1 fat |
| Sharp Cheddar Cheese Sauce | 1/4 cup | 133 | 12 | 81 | 5 | 23 | 473 | 6 | <1 | 2 | 0 | 1 med-fat meat, 1 fat |
| **Ortega** | | | | | | | | | | | | |
| Nacho Cheese Sauce | 1/4 cup | 80 | 6 | 68 | 3 | 0 | 360 | 3 | 0 | 4 | 0 | 1 med-fat meat |
| **Que Bueno** | | | | | | | | | | | | |
| ✓Jalapeno Cheese Sauce | 2 Tbsp | 33 | 2 | 55 | <1 | 3 | 248 | 1 | 0 | 3 | 0 | 1 fat |
| Nacho Cheese Sauce | 1/2 cup | 63 | 5 | 71 | 3 | 15 | 290 | 3 | <1 | 2 | 0 | 1 fat |
| **CHEESE SPREAD** | | | | | | | | | | | | |
| **Kraft** | | | | | | | | | | | | |
| Cheese Spread w/Bacon | 2 Tbsp | 90 | 8 | 80 | 5 | 25 | 570 | 5 | 0 | <1 | 0 | 1 high-fat meat |
| Cheez Whiz Cheese Sauce | 2 Tbsp | 90 | 7 | 70 | 5 | 20 | 540 | 4 | 0 | 3 | 0 | 1 med-fat meat |
| Cheez Whiz Jalapeno Pepper Cheese Spread | 2 Tbsp | 90 | 7 | 70 | 5 | 25 | 510 | 4 | 0 | 0 | 0 | 1 med-fat meat |
| Cheez Whiz Light Cheese | 2 Tbsp | 80 | 3 | 34 | 2 | 15 | 540 | 6 | 0 | 6 | 1/2 | 1/2 carb, 1 lean meat |

| | | | | | | | | | | | | |
|---|---|---|---|---|---|---|---|---|---|---|---|---|
| Cheez Whiz Squeezable Cheese Sauce | 2 Tbsp | 100 | 8 | 72 | 4 | 15 | 470 | 2 | 0 | 4 | 0 | 2 fat |
| Cheez Whiz, Mild Salsa Cheese Spread | 2 Tbsp | 100 | 7 | 63 | 5 | 25 | 530 | 4 | 0 | 3 | 0 | 1 high-fat meat |
| Cracker Barrel Sharp Cheddar Cheese | 2 Tbsp | 80 | 5 | 56 | 5 | 20 | 180 | 3 | 0 | <1 | 0 | 1 high-fat meat |
| Pimiento Cheese Spread | 2 Tbsp | 80 | 6 | 68 | 4 | 20 | 170 | 2 | 0 | 3 | 0 | 1 med-fat meat |
| Pineapple Cheese Spread | 2 Tbsp | 70 | 5 | 64 | 4 | 15 | 115 | 2 | 0 | 4 | 0 | 1 med-fat meat |
| Roka Brand Blue Cheese Spread | 2 Tbsp | 80 | 7 | 79 | 5 | 20 | 340 | 3 | 0 | 2 | 0 | 1 med-fat meat |
| **Sargento** | | | | | | | | | | | | |
| Brick Cheese Spread "Cracker Snacks" | 1 oz | 100 | 9 | 81 | NA | 25 | 430 | 6 | 0 | 1 | 0 | 1 high-fat meat |
| Port Wine Cheese-Log | 1 oz | 100 | 7 | 63 | NA | 18 | 250 | 6 | NA | 3 | 0 | 1 high-fat meat |
| Sharp American Cheese "Cracker Snacks" | 1 oz | 110 | 9 | 74 | NA | 27 | 410 | 6 | 0 | <1 | 0 | 1 high-fat meat |
| **Weight Watchers** | | | | | | | | | | | | |
| ✔Sharp Cheddar Cheese Spread | 2 Tbsp | 70 | 3 | 39 | 2 | 10 | 190 | 4 | 0 | 7 | 1/2 | 1/2 carb, 1/2 med-fat meat |
| **CHEESE, NATURAL** | | | | | | | | | | | | |
| **Alpine Lace** | | | | | | | | | | | | |
| American | 1 oz | 90 | 7 | 70 | 4 | 20 | 200 | 6 | 0 | 2 | 0 | 1 high-fat meat |
| ✔Mozzarella Part Skim | 1 oz | 70 | 5 | 64 | 3 | 15 | 75 | 7 | 0 | 1 | 0 | 1 med-fat meat |
| Natural Swiss Cheese | 1 oz | 90 | 6 | 60 | 4 | 1 | 35 | 8 | 0 | 1 | 0 | 1 med-fat meat |
| ✔Provolone Cheese | 1 oz | 70 | 5 | 64 | 5 | 15 | 85 | 7 | 0 | 1 | 0 | 1 med-fat meat |

✔= Best Bet; NA = Not Available; Carb. Ch. = Carbohydrate Choices

| Cheese, Natural (*Continued*) | Serving Size | Cal. | Fat (g) | % Cal. Fat | Sat. Fat (g) | Chol. (mg) | Sod. (mg) | Pro. (g) | Fiber (g) | Carb. (g) | Carb. Ch. | Servings/Exchanges |
|---|---|---|---|---|---|---|---|---|---|---|---|---|
| ✓Reduced Fat Cheddar Cheese | 1 oz | 80 | 5 | 56 | 3 | 20 | 95 | 7 | 0 | 1 | 0 | 1 med-fat meat |
| ✓Reduced Fat Colby Cheese | 1/4 cup | 80 | 5 | 56 | 4 | 20 | 85 | 7 | 0 | 1 | 0 | 1 med-fat meat |
| ✓Reduced Fat Monterey Jack | 1 oz | 80 | 5 | 56 | 4 | 15 | 75 | 7 | 0 | 1 | 0 | 1 med-fat meat |
| Reduced Fat Swiss Cheese | 1 oz | 100 | 7 | 63 | 4 | 20 | 35 | 8 | 0 | 1 | 0 | 1 high-fat meat |
| Reduced Sodium Muenster Cheese | 1 oz | 100 | 9 | 81 | 6 | 25 | 85 | 7 | 0 | 1 | 0 | 1 high-fat meat |
| **Breakstone** | | | | | | | | | | | | |
| Ricotta Cheese | 1/4 cup | 110 | 8 | 65 | 5 | 25 | 90 | 7 | 0 | 3 | 0 | 1 high-fat meat |
| **Di Giorno** | | | | | | | | | | | | |
| ✓100% Parmesan Cheese, Shredded | 2 Tbsp | 20 | 2 | 90 | 1 | 5 | 75 | 2 | 0 | 0 | 0 | free |
| ✓100% Romano Cheese, Shredded or Grated | 2 Tbsp | 20 | 2 | 90 | 1 | 5 | 70 | 2 | 0 | 0 | 0 | free |
| **Healthy Choice** | | | | | | | | | | | | |
| ✓Fat-Free Mozzarella, Shredded | 1 oz | 40 | 0 | 0 | 0 | 5 | 200 | 9 | 0 | 1 | 0 | 1 very lean meat |
| ✓Fat-Free Natural Cheddar Cheese, Shredded | 1 oz | 40 | 0 | 0 | 0 | 0 | 200 | 9 | 0 | 1 | 0 | 1 very lean meat |
| ✓Mozzarella Stick, Fat-Free | 1 oz | 40 | 0 | 0 | 0 | 5 | 200 | 9 | 0 | 1 | 0 | 1 very lean meat |
| ✓Pizza Cheese, Fat-Free Shredded | 1 oz | 40 | 0 | 0 | 0 | 5 | 200 | 9 | 0 | 1 | 0 | 1 very lean meat |

## Kraft

| | Serving Size | Cal. | Fat (g) | % Fat Cal. | Sat. Fat (g) | Chol. (mg) | Sod. (mg) | Carb. (g) | Fiber (g) | Prot. (g) | Carb. Ch. | Exchanges/Choices |
|---|---|---|---|---|---|---|---|---|---|---|---|---|
| Baby Swiss Cheese | 1 oz | 110 | 9 | 74 | 6 | 25 | 110 | 0 | 0 | 7 | 0 | 1 high-fat meat |
| Cheddar Cheese | 1 oz | 110 | 9 | 74 | 6 | 30 | 180 | <1 | 0 | 7 | 0 | 1 high-fat meat |
| Cheddar Cheese-Shredded | 1/4 cup | 100 | 8 | 72 | 6 | 30 | 170 | <1 | 0 | 6 | 0 | 1 high-fat meat |
| ✔ Cheddar, Fat-Free, Shredded | 1/4 cup | 40 | 0 | 0 | 0 | <5 | 270 | 1 | 0 | 9 | 0 | 1 very lean meat |
| Colby & Monterey Jack Cheese-Shredded | 1/4 cup | 100 | 8 | 72 | 6 | 25 | 170 | <1 | 0 | 6 | 0 | 1 high-fat meat |
| Colby Cheese | 1 oz | 110 | 9 | 74 | 6 | 30 | 180 | <1 | 0 | 7 | 0 | 1 high-fat meat |
| ✔ Fat-Free Mozzarella Cheese, Shredded | 1/4 cup | 45 | 0 | 0 | 0 | <5 | 340 | 2 | <1 | 9 | 0 | 1 very lean meat |
| Four Cheese-Pizza Style-Shredded | 1/4 cup | 90 | 7 | 70 | 5 | 20 | 220 | <1 | 0 | 6 | 0 | 1 high-fat meat |
| ✔ Grated Nonfat Topping | 2 tsp | 15 | 0 | 0 | 0 | 0 | 75 | 3 | 0 | <1 | 0 | free |
| ✔ Grated Parmesan Cheese | 2 tsp | 20 | 2 | 90 | 1 | <5 | 75 | 0 | 0 | 2 | 0 | free |
| ✔ Grated Romano Cheese | 2 tsp | 20 | 2 | 90 | 1 | <5 | 70 | 0 | 0 | 2 | 0 | free |
| Monterey Jack Cheese | 1 oz | 110 | 9 | 74 | 6 | 30 | 190 | 0 | 0 | 6 | 0 | 1 high-fat meat |
| Monterey Jack Cheese & Jalapeno Pepper | 1 oz | 110 | 9 | 82 | 6 | 30 | 190 | <1 | <1 | 7 | 0 | 1 high-fat meat |
| Monterey Jack Cheese Shredded | 1/4 cup | 100 | 8 | 80 | 6 | 20 | 170 | <1 | 0 | 6 | 0 | 1 high-fat meat |
| ✔ Mozzarella Part Skim Cheese | 1 oz | 80 | 5 | 56 | 4 | 15 | 200 | <1 | 0 | 8 | 0 | 1 med-fat meat |
| Mozzarella Part Skim String Cheese | 1 piece | 80 | 6 | 68 | 4 | 20 | 240 | 0 | 0 | 7 | 0 | 1 med-fat meat |
| Mozzarella Whole Milk Shredded Cheese | 1/3 cup | 160 | 8 | 72 | 5 | 25 | 220 | 1 | 0 | 7 | 0 | 1 high-fat meat |

✔ = Best Bet; NA = Not Available; Carb. Ch. = Carbohydrate Choices

| Cheese, Natural (*Continued*) | Serving Size | Cal. | Fat (g) | % Cal. Fat | Sat. Fat (g) | Chol. (mg) | Sod. (mg) | Pro. (g) | Fiber (g) | Carb. (g) | Carb. Ch. | Servings/Exchanges |
|---|---|---|---|---|---|---|---|---|---|---|---|---|
| Provolone Cheese | 1 oz | 100 | 7 | 63 | 4 | 25 | 260 | 7 | 0 | 1 | 0 | 1 high-fat meat |
| Reduced Fat 2% Cheddar Cheese | 1 oz | 90 | 6 | 60 | 4 | 20 | 240 | 7 | 0 | <1 | 0 | 1 med-fat met |
| Reduced Fat 2% Colby Cheese | 1 oz | 80 | 6 | 68 | 4 | 20 | 220 | 7 | 0 | 0 | 0 | 1 med-fat meat |
| Reduced Fat 2% Mild Cheddar Cheese, Shredded | 1/4 cup | 80 | 6 | 68 | 4 | 20 | 220 | 7 | 0 | <1 | 0 | 1 med-fat meat |
| Reduced Fat 2% Monterey Jack Cheese | 1 oz | 80 | 6 | 68 | 4 | 20 | 240 | 7 | 0 | <1 | 0 | 1 med-fat meat |
| Reduced Fat 2% Sharp Cheddar Cheese | 1 oz | 90 | 6 | 60 | 4 | 20 | 240 | 7 | 0 | <1 | 0 | 1 med-fat meat |
| Smoke Flavored Mozzarella & Provolone Pizza Cheese | 1/4 cup | 90 | 7 | 70 | 5 | 20 | 200 | 6 | 0 | <1 | 0 | 1 high-fat meat |
| Swiss Cheese | 1 oz | 110 | 8 | 67 | 5 | 25 | 40 | 8 | 0 | 1 | 0 | 1 high-fat meat |
| Swiss Cheese Slices, 2% Reduced Fat | 1 slice | 130 | 9 | 62 | 6 | 25 | 90 | 11 | 0 | <1 | 0 | 1 1/2 med-fat meat |
| Swiss Cheese, Shredded | 1/3 cup | 100 | 8 | 72 | 5 | 25 | 45 | 7 | 0 | <1 | 0 | 1 high-fat meat |
| Taco Cheese, Shredded | 1/3 cup | 120 | 10 | 75 | 7 | 30 | 240 | 7 | 0 | 1 | 0 | 1 high-fat meat |

**Lifetime**

| | | | | | | | | | | | | |
|---|---|---|---|---|---|---|---|---|---|---|---|---|
| ✔Fat-Free Cheddar Cheese | 1/4 cup | 45 | 0 | 0 | 0 | 5 | 245 | 9 | 0 | 1 | 0 | 1 very lean meat |
| ✔Fat-Free Cheddar Cheese | 1 oz | 40 | 0 | 0 | 0 | 5 | 225 | 8 | 0 | 1 | 0 | 1 very lean meat |
| ✔Fat-Free Mild Mexican Cheese | 1 oz | 40 | 0 | 0 | 0 | 5 | 225 | 8 | 0 | 1 | 0 | 1 very lean meat |
| ✔Fat-Free Monterey Jack Cheese | 1 oz | 40 | 0 | 0 | 0 | 5 | 225 | 8 | 0 | 1 | 0 | 1 very lean meat |

| Food | Serving | Cal. | Fat (g) | % Fat | Sat. Fat | Chol. | Sod. | | | Carb. Ch. | | Exchanges |
|---|---|---|---|---|---|---|---|---|---|---|---|---|
| ✓Fat-Free Mozzarella Cheese | 1/4 cup | 44 | 0 | 0 | 0 | 5 | 245 | 9 | 0 | 1 | 0 | 1 very lean meat |
| ✓Fat-Free Swiss Cheese | 1 oz | 40 | 0 | 0 | 0 | 5 | 225 | 8 | 0 | 1 | 0 | 1 very lean meat |
| **Sargento** | | | | | | | | | | | | |
| 4 Cheese Mexican | 1/4 cup | 110 | 9 | 74 | <1 | NA | 200 | 6 | 0 | 6 | 0 | 1 high-fat meat |
| Blue Cheese | 1 oz | 100 | 8 | 72 | NA | 21 | 400 | 6 | 0 | 1 | 0 | 1 high-fat meat |
| Edam Cheese | 1 oz | 100 | 8 | 72 | NA | 25 | 270 | 7 | 0 | <1 | 0 | 1 high-fat meat |
| Feta Cheese | 1 oz | 80 | 6 | 68 | NA | 25 | 320 | 4 | 0 | 1 | 0 | 1 high-fat meat |
| Italian Style Cheese, Grated | 1 oz | 110 | 8 | 65 | NA | 26 | 105 | 8 | 0 | 1 | 0 | 1 med-fat meat |
| Limburger Cheese | 1 oz | 90 | 8 | 80 | NA | 25 | 230 | 4 | 0 | <1 | 0 | 1 high-fat meat |
| Parmesan Cheese | 1 oz | 110 | 7 | 57 | NA | 19 | 450 | 10 | 0 | 1 | 0 | 1 high-fat meat |
| ✓Part-Skim Ricotta Cheese | 1 oz | 30 | 2 | 60 | NA | 10 | 30 | 3 | 0 | 1 | 0 | 1/2 med-fat meat |
| ✓Ricotta Cheese | 1 oz | 40 | 3 | 68 | NA | 13 | 25 | 3 | 0 | 1 | 0 | 1/2 med-fat meat |
| Taco Cheese | 1 oz | 110 | 9 | 74 | NA | 27 | 160 | 7 | 0 | <1 | 0 | 1 high-fat meat |
| **Stella Foods** | | | | | | | | | | | | |
| Aged Provolone Cheese | 1 oz | 100 | 8 | 72 | 5 | 20 | 290 | 7 | 0 | <1 | 0 | 1 high-fat meat |
| Blue Cheese | 1 oz | 100 | 8 | 72 | 5 | 20 | 390 | 6 | 0 | <1 | 0 | 1 high-fat meat |
| ✓Dried Grated Romano Cheese | 1 Tbsp | 35 | 3 | 77 | 2 | 10 | 130 | 3 | 0 | 0 | 0 | 1 fat |
| Feta Cheese | 1 oz | 80 | 6 | 68 | 5 | 25 | 310 | 5 | 0 | 1 | 0 | 1 med-fat meat |
| Fontinella Cheese | 1 oz | 100 | 7 | 63 | 4 | 30 | 330 | 8 | 0 | <1 | 0 | 1 high-fat meat |

✓ = Best Bet; NA = Not Available; Carb. Ch. = Carbohydrate Choices

| Cheese, Natural (*Continued*) | Serving Size | Cal. | Fat (g) | % Cal. Fat | Sat. Fat (g) | Chol. (mg) | Sod. (mg) | Pro. (g) | Fiber (g) | Carb. (g) | Carb. Ch. | Servings/Exchanges |
|---|---|---|---|---|---|---|---|---|---|---|---|---|
| ✔Fresh Grated Romano | 1 Tbsp | 30 | 2 | 60 | 2 | 5 | 75 | 2 | 0 | 0 | 0 | 1 fat |
| Lite Provolone Cheese | 1 oz | 70 | 4 | 51 | 2 | 20 | 120 | 8 | 0 | <1 | 0 | 1 med-fat meat |
| Lorraine Cheese w/Chive & Onion | 1 oz | 110 | 9 | 74 | 5 | 25 | 30 | 7 | 0 | <1 | 0 | 1 high-fat meat |
| Lorranie Cheese, Smoked | 1 oz | 110 | 9 | 74 | 5 | 25 | 30 | 7 | 0 | <1 | 0 | 1 high-fat meat |
| Mello Provolone Cheese | 1 oz | 100 | 7 | 63 | 4 | 20 | 290 | 7 | 0 | <1 | 0 | 1 high-fat meat |
| Mozzarella Cheese | 1 oz | 80 | 6 | 68 | 4 | 15 | 180 | 8 | 0 | <1 | 0 | 1 med-fat meat |
| ✔Part-Skim Ricotta Cheese | 1/4 cup | 85 | 5 | 53 | 3 | 20 | 75 | 7 | 0 | 3 | 0 | 1 med-fat meat |
| Sharp Italian Cheese | 1 oz | 100 | 7 | 63 | 5 | 30 | 330 | 8 | 0 | <1 | 0 | 1 high-fat meat |
| Whole Milk Mozzarella Cheese | 1 oz | 90 | 7 | 70 | 5 | 20 | 180 | 6 | 0 | <1 | 0 | 1 high-fat meat |
| **Weight Watchers** | | | | | | | | | | | | |
| ✔Fat-Free Grated Parmesan ItalianTopping | 1 tsp | 15 | 0 | 0 | 0 | 0 | 45 | 2 | 0 | 2 | 0 | free |
| ✔Fat-Free Sharp Cheddar Cheese Slices | 2 slices | 30 | 0 | 0 | 0 | 0 | 310 | 5 | 0 | 2 | 0 | 1 very lean meat |
| ✔Natural Colby Cheese | 1 oz | 80 | 5 | 56 | 2 | 15 | 130 | 8 | 0 | 1 | 0 | 1 med-fat meat |
| ✔Natural Mild Yellow Cheddar Cheese | 1 oz | 80 | 5 | 56 | 3 | 15 | 150 | 8 | 0 | 1 | 0 | 1 med-fat meat |
| ✔Natural Monterey Jack Cheese | 1 oz | 80 | 5 | 56 | 2 | 15 | 120 | 8 | 0 | 1 | 0 | 1 med-fat meat |
| ✔Shredded Mozzarella Cheese | 1 oz | 80 | 4 | 45 | 2 | 15 | 150 | 8 | 0 | 1 | 0 | 1 med-fat meat |
| ✔Swiss Cheese Slices | 1 oz | 90 | 5 | 50 | 3 | 15 | 50 | 9 | 0 | 1 | 0 | 1 med-fat meat |

## CHEESE, PROCESS, LOAF

### Kraft

| | | | | | | | | | | | | |
|---|---|---|---|---|---|---|---|---|---|---|---|---|
| Old English Sharp American Cheese | 1 oz | 100 | 9 | 81 | 6 | 25 | 370 | 6 | 0 | <1 | 0 | 1 high-fat meat |
| Velveeta Cheese | 1 oz | 90 | 6 | 60 | 4 | 25 | 420 | 5 | 0 | 3 | 0 | 1 med-fat meat |
| Velveeta Cheese Spread, Mexican, Milk or Hot | 1 oz | 90 | 6 | 60 | 4 | 20 | 420 | 5 | 0 | 3 | 0 | 1 med-fat meat |
| ✔Velveeta Reduced Fat | 1 oz | 60 | 3 | 45 | 2 | 10 | 440 | 5 | 0 | 3 | 0 | 1 lean meat |
| Velveeta, Shredded | 1/4 cup | 130 | 9 | 62 | 6 | 30 | 500 | 8 | 0 | 3 | 0 | 1 high-fat meat |

## CHEESE, PROCESS, SLICES

### Alpine Lace

| | | | | | | | | | | | | |
|---|---|---|---|---|---|---|---|---|---|---|---|---|
| ✔Fat-Free Free N' Lean Singles | 1 oz | 40 | 0 | 0 | 0 | 5 | 260 | 8 | 0 | 1 | 0 | 1 very lean meat |

### Healthy Choice

| | | | | | | | | | | | | |
|---|---|---|---|---|---|---|---|---|---|---|---|---|
| ✔Cheese Food, Fat-Free Singles | 1 oz | 40 | 0 | 0 | 0 | 5 | 390 | 6 | 0 | 3 | 0 | 1 very lean meat |

### Kraft

| | | | | | | | | | | | | |
|---|---|---|---|---|---|---|---|---|---|---|---|---|
| ✔American Cheese | 3/4 oz | 70 | 5 | 64 | 4 | 15 | 280 | 4 | 0 | 2 | 0 | 1 med-fat meat |
| ✔American Cheese Light N' Lively | 3/4 oz | 45 | 3 | 60 | 2 | 10 | 280 | 5 | 0 | 2 | 0 | 1 lean meat |
| ✔American Cheese w/Pimento | 3/4 oz | 70 | 5 | 64 | 4 | 15 | 290 | 4 | 0 | 2 | 0 | 1 med-fat meat |
| ✔Fat-Free Cheese Slice | 3/4 oz | 30 | 0 | 0 | 0 | <5 | 290 | 5 | 0 | 2 | 0 | 1 very lean meat |
| ✔Fat-Free Sharp Cheddar Cheese | 2/3 oz | 35 | 0 | 0 | 0 | <5 | 300 | 5 | 0 | 3 | 0 | 1 very lean meat |

✔= Best Bet; NA = Not Available; Carb. Ch. = Carbohydrate Choices

| Cheese, Process, Slices (Continued) | Serving Size | Cal. | Fat (g) | % Cal. Fat | Sat. Fat (g) | Chol. (mg) | Sod. (mg) | Pro. (g) | Fiber (g) | Carb. (g) | Carb. Ch. | Servings/Exchanges |
|---|---|---|---|---|---|---|---|---|---|---|---|---|
| ✓Fat-Free Swiss Cheese | 3/4 oz | 30 | 0 | 0 | 0 | 0 | 270 | 5 | 0 | 3 | 0 | 1 very lean meat |
| ✓Fat-Free White Cheese | 3/4 oz | 30 | 0 | 0 | 0 | <5 | 300 | 5 | 0 | 3 | 0 | 1 very lean meat |
| ✓Monterey Cheese Food Singles | 3/4 oz | 70 | 5 | 64 | 4 | 15 | 290 | 4 | 0 | 2 | 0 | 1 med-fat meat |
| ✓Sharp Cheddar Cheese Singles | 3/4 oz | 70 | 5 | 64 | 4 | 15 | 290 | 4 | 0 | 2 | 0 | 1 med-fat meat |
| ✓Singles, American 2% Reduced Fat | 3/4 oz | 50 | 3 | 54 | 2 | 10 | 320 | 5 | 0 | 2 | 0 | 1 lean meat |
| ✓Swiss Cheese Singles | 3/4 oz | 70 | 5 | 64 | 4 | 15 | 320 | 4 | 0 | 1 | 0 | 1 med-fat meat |
| ✓White American Cheese | 3/4 oz | 70 | 5 | 64 | 4 | 2 | 280 | 4 | 0 | 2 | 0 | 1 med-fat meat |
| **CHEESECAKE (FROZEN)** | | | | | | | | | | | | |
| **Sara Lee** | | | | | | | | | | | | |
| Chocolate-Dipped Original Cheesecake Bites | 5 | 480 | 33 | 62 | 24 | 75 | 290 | 6 | 2 | 40 | 2 1/2 | 2 1/2 carb, 7 fat |
| Chocolate-Dipped Praline Cheesecake Bites | 5 | 390 | 30 | 69 | 20 | 80 | 290 | 6 | 3 | 42 | 2 | 2 carb, 6 fat |
| Toasted Almond Crunch Cheesecake Bites | 5 | 450 | 29 | 58 | 21 | 75 | 300 | 6 | 2 | 42 | 3 | 3 carb, 6 fat |
| **CHICKEN (CANNED)** | | | | | | | | | | | | |
| **Hormel** | | | | | | | | | | | | |
| ✓Breast of Chicken in Water | 2 oz | 60 | 1 | 15 | 0 | 25 | 290 | 13 | 0 | 0 | 0 | 2 very lean meat |
| ✓Chunk Chicken in Water | 2 oz | 70 | 3 | 39 | 1 | 35 | 250 | 11 | 0 | 0 | 0 | 2 lean meat |
| ✓No Added Salt Breast of Chicken in Water | 2 oz | 60 | 1 | 15 | 0 | 30 | 35 | 12 | 0 | 0 | 0 | 2 very lean meat |

## Swanson

| Food | Serving | Cal. | Fat (g) | % Cal. Fat | Sat. Fat (g) | Chol. (mg) | Sod. (mg) | Carb. (g) | Fiber (g) | Prot. (g) | Carb. Ch. | Exchanges |
|---|---|---|---|---|---|---|---|---|---|---|---|---|
| Chunk Chicken White in Water | 2.5 oz | 100 | 4 | 36 | NA | 35 | 240 | 15 | 0 | 0 | 0 | 2 lean meat |
| White/Dark Chunk Chicken | 2.5 oz | 100 | 4 | 36 | NA | 40 | 240 | 16 | 0 | 0 | 0 | 2 lean meat |

## CHICKEN MEAL/ENTREES (REFRIGERATED)

### Fresh Selections

| Food | Serving | Cal. | Fat (g) | % Cal. Fat | Sat. Fat (g) | Chol. (mg) | Sod. (mg) | Carb. (g) | Fiber (g) | Prot. (g) | Carb. Ch. | Exchanges |
|---|---|---|---|---|---|---|---|---|---|---|---|---|
| Cheddar Broccoli Chicken Breast w/Mashed Potatoes | 1 piece chicken, 6 oz potatoes | 500 | 27 | 49 | 11 | 100 | 1160 | 35 | 2 | 31 | 2 | 2 carb, 4 med-fat meat, 1 fat |

## CHICKEN MEAL/ENTREES (FROZEN)

### Armour Classics

| Food | Serving | Cal. | Fat (g) | % Cal. Fat | Sat. Fat (g) | Chol. (mg) | Sod. (mg) | Carb. (g) | Fiber (g) | Prot. (g) | Carb. Ch. | Exchanges |
|---|---|---|---|---|---|---|---|---|---|---|---|---|
| ✔Chicken & Noodle Dinner | 11 oz dinner | 230 | 7 | 27 | NA | 50 | 160 | 19 | NA | 23 | 1 1/2 | 1 1/2 carb, 2 med-fat meat |
| Chicken Fettucini Dinner | 11 oz dinner | 260 | 9 | 31 | NA | 50 | 660 | 17 | NA | 28 | 2 | 2 carb, 2 med-fat meat |
| Chicken Mesquite Dinner | 9.5 oz dinner | 370 | 16 | 39 | NA | 55 | 660 | 15 | NA | 42 | 3 | 3 carb, 2 med-fat meat, 1 fat |
| Chicken Parmigiana Dinner | 11.5 oz dinner | 370 | 19 | 46 | NA | 75 | 1060 | 22 | NA | 27 | 2 | 2 carb, 2 med-fat meat, 2 fat |
| ✔Chicken-Wine & Mushroom Dinner | 10.75 oz dinner | 280 | 11 | 29 | NA | 50 | 900 | 22 | NA | 24 | 1 1/2 | 1 1/2 carb, 3 med-fat meat |

✔ = Best Bet; NA = Not Available; Carb. Ch. = Carbohydrate Choices

| Chicken Meal/Entrees (Frozen) (Continued) | Serving Size | Cal. | Fat (g) | % Cal. Fat | Sat. Fat (g) | Chol. (mg) | Sod. (mg) | Pro. (g) | Fiber (g) | Carb. (g) | Carb. Ch. | Servings/Exchanges |
|---|---|---|---|---|---|---|---|---|---|---|---|---|
| Glazed Chicken Dinner | 10.75 oz meal | 300 | 16 | 48 | NA | 60 | 960 | 15 | NA | 24 | 1 1/2 | 1 1/2 carb, 2 med-fat meat, 1 fat |
| **Armour Classics Lite** | | | | | | | | | | | | |
| ✔Chicken Burgundy Dinner | 10 oz dinner | 210 | 2 | 9 | NA | 45 | 780 | 23 | NA | 25 | 1 1/2 | 1 1/2 carb, 3 very lean meat |
| ✔Chicken Marsala | 10.5 oz dinner | 250 | 7 | 25 | NA | 80 | 930 | 20 | NA | 27 | 2 | 2 carb, 2 med-fat meat |
| ✔Sweet & Sour Chicken | 11 oz dinner | 240 | 2 | 8 | NA | 35 | 870 | 18 | NA | 39 | 2 1/2 | 2 1/2 carb, 1 very lean meat |
| **Banquet** | | | | | | | | | | | | |
| ✔Chicken & Dumplings w/Gravy | 10 oz dinner | 270 | 9 | 30 | 3 | 40 | 780 | 13 | 3 | 35 | 2 | 2 carb, 1 med-fat meat, 1 fat |
| Chicken Fettuccine Alfredo | 10.25 oz dinner | 420 | 24 | 51 | 10 | 70 | 1000 | 15 | 4 | 37 | 2 1/2 | 2 1/2 carb, 1 med-fat meat, 4 fat |
| Chicken Fingers & BBQ Sauce | 9 oz dinner | 340 | 16 | 42 | 4 | 60 | 800 | 13 | 3 | 36 | 2 1/2 | 2 1/2 carb, 1 med-fat meat, 2 fat |
| Chicken Parmigiana | 9.5 oz dinner | 320 | 15 | 42 | 5 | 50 | 900 | 10 | 3 | 29 | 2 | 2 carb, 2 med-fat meat, 1 fat |

| | Amount | Cal. | Fat (g) | % Cal. Fat | Sat. Fat (g) | Chol. (mg) | Sod. (mg) | Carb. (g) | Fiber (g) | Pro. (g) | Carb. Ch. | Exchanges |
|---|---|---|---|---|---|---|---|---|---|---|---|---|
| Extra Helping Fried Chicken | 14.7 oz dinner | 910 | 55 | 54 | 13 | 160 | 2600 | 34 | 5 | 70 | 4 1/2 | 4 1/2 carb, 3 med-fat meat, 8 fat |
| Family Size Chicken & Broccoli Alfredo | 6.9 oz | 270 | 12 | 41 | 7 | 40 | 540 | 11 | 3 | 28 | 2 | 2 carb, 1 med-fat meat, 1 fat |
| Family Size Chicken Parmigiana Patties w/Tomato Sauce | 4.7 oz | 240 | 13 | 49 | 5 | 20 | 690 | 11 | 2 | 18 | 1 | 1 carb, 1 med-fat meat, 2 fat |
| Family Size Country-Style Chicken & Dumplings | 7 oz | 290 | 14 | 45 | 5 | 40 | 1270 | 12 | 2 | 30 | 2 | 2 carb, 1 med-fat meat, 2 fat |
| Family Size Creamy Broccoli, Chicken, Cheese & Rice | 8 oz | 280 | 14 | 46 | 7 | 45 | 980 | 14 | 2 | 25 | 2 | 2 carb, 1 med-fat meat, 2 fat |
| Grilled Chicken | 9.9 oz dinner | 330 | 13 | 35 | 3 | 50 | 1210 | 16 | 3 | 37 | 2 1/2 | 2 1/2 carb, 1 med-fat meat, 2 fat |
| Our Original Fried Chicken | 9 oz dinner | 470 | 27 | 52 | 9 | 90 | 1500 | 21 | 2 | 35 | 2 | 2 carb, 2 med-fat meat, 3 fat |
| Southern Fried Chicken | 8.75 oz dinner | 560 | 33 | 53 | 8 | 100 | 1540 | 26 | 3 | 40 | 2 1/2 | 2 1/2 carb, 3 med-fat meat, 4 fat |
| White Meat Fried Chicken | 8.75 oz | 480 | 28 | 53 | 11 | 100 | 1100 | 18 | 3 | 40 | 2 1/2 | 2 1/2 carb, 2 med-fat meat, 4 fat |

✔ = Best Bet; NA = Not Available; Carb. Ch. = Carbohydrate Choices

| Chicken Meal/Entrees (Frozen) (Continued) | Serving Size | Cal. | Fat (g) | % Cal. Fat | Sat. Fat (g) | Chol. (mg) | Sod. (mg) | Pro. (g) | Fiber (g) | Carb. (g) | Carb. Ch. | Servings/Exchanges |
|---|---|---|---|---|---|---|---|---|---|---|---|---|
| **Boston Market** | | | | | | | | | | | | |
| Country Fried Chicken | 13.6 oz meal | 580 | 29 | 45 | 7 | 75 | 1910 | 20 | 2 | 56 | 4 | 4 carb, 1 med-fat meat, 5 fat |
| Oven Roasted Chicken | 6 oz | 180 | 7 | 35 | 3 | 105 | 800 | 23 | 0 | 0 | 0 | 3 lean meat |
| **Budget Gourmet** | | | | | | | | | | | | |
| Chicken & Fettuccine | 10 oz dinner | 380 | 19 | 45 | 10 | 85 | 810 | 20 | 3 | 33 | 2 | 2 carb, 2 med-fat meat, 2 fat |
| Chicken & Noodles | 10 oz meal | 450 | 26 | 52 | NA | 130 | 1110 | 23 | NA | 31 | 2 | 2 carb, 2 med-fat meat, 3 fat |
| ✓Chicken & Pasta in Wine & Mushroom Sauce | 9.1 oz meal | 280 | 7 | 22 | 2 | 25 | 890 | 15 | 3 | 40 | 2 1/2 | 2 1/2 carb, 1 med-fat meat |
| Chicken Cacciatore | 11 oz meal | 300 | 13 | 38 | NA | 60 | 810 | 20 | NA | 27 | 2 | 2 carb, 2 med-fat meat, 1 fat |
| ✓Chicken Meals/Entrees | 10 oz meal | 250 | 5 | 18 | NA | 65 | 660 | 15 | NA | 37 | 2 1/2 | 2 1/2 carb, 1 med-fat meat |
| Fettucini Primavera w/Chicken | 9.1 oz meal | 280 | 8 | 26 | 4 | 30 | 650 | 14 | 3 | 38 | 2 1/2 | 2 1/2 carb, 1 med-fat meat, 1 fat |

| | Serving | | | | | | | | | | | Carb. Ch. |
|---|---|---|---|---|---|---|---|---|---|---|---|---|
| Hearty Broccoli Chicken Bake | 13 oz meal | 320 | 10 | 28 | 3 | 25 | 1350 | 14 | 5 | 42 | 3 | 3 carb, 1 med-fat meat, 1 fat |
| Hearty Chicken A La King | 14 oz meal | 520 | 21 | 36 | 9 | 55 | 1450 | 26 | 3 | 56 | 4 | 4 carb, 2 med-fat meat, 2 fat |
| Hearty Golden Fried Chicken Supreme | 13 oz meal | 390 | 19 | 44 | 5 | 35 | 1550 | 13 | 6 | 42 | 3 | 3 carb, 1 med-fat meat, 3 fat |
| ✔Herbed Chicken w/Fettucini | 10.1 oz meal | 260 | 8 | 27 | 3 | 80 | 640 | 19 | 4 | 29 | 2 | 2 carb, 2 med-fat meat |
| ✔Italian Style Vegetables w/Chicken | 10.25 oz meal | 310 | 8 | 22 | 2 | 30 | 690 | 14 | NA | 50 | 3 | 3 carb, 1 med-fat meat, 1 fat |
| ✔Light & Healthy French Chicken Breast | 9.1 oz meal | 180 | 6 | 28 | 2 | 25 | 865 | 23 | 6 | 9 | 1/2 | 1/2 carb, 3 lean meat |
| ✔Light & Healthy Teriyaki Chicken Breast & Oriental Vegetables | 11.1 oz meal | 315 | 4 | 11 | <1 | 25 | 675 | 19 | 4 | 52 | 3 1/2 | 3 1/2 carb, 1 med-fat meat |
| ✔Orange Glazed Chicken Breast | 9.1 oz meal | 280 | 3 | 9 | 1 | 30 | 790 | 11 | 2 | 51 | 3 1/2 | 3 1/2 carb, 1 fat |
| Roasted Chicken | 11.2 oz meal | 280 | 7 | 23 | NA | 40 | 1110 | 19 | NA | 34 | 2 | 2 carb, 2 lean meat, 2 fat |
| Special Selections, French Recipe Chicken | 9 oz dinner | 200 | 8 | 36 | 3 | 30 | 950 | 13 | 4 | 19 | 1 | 1 carb, 1 med-fat meat, 1 fat |
| ✔Teriyaki Chicken | 12 oz meal | 360 | 12 | 30 | 2 | 55 | 610 | 20 | 3 | 44 | 3 | 3 carb, 2 med-fat meat |

✔ = Best Bet; NA = Not Available; Carb. Ch. = Carbohydrate Choices

| Chicken Meal/Entrees (Frozen) (*Continued*) | Serving Size | Cal. | Fat (g) | % Cal. Fat | Sat. Fat (g) | Chol. (mg) | Sod. (mg) | Pro. (g) | Fiber (g) | Carb. (g) | Carb. Ch. | Servings/Exchanges |
|---|---|---|---|---|---|---|---|---|---|---|---|---|
| **Casual Gourmet** | | | | | | | | | | | | |
| Chicken Burgers w/ Red Bell Pepper & Basil | 1 burger (3.5 oz) | 120 | 5 | 38 | 2 | 55 | 690 | 18 | 0 | 1 | 0 | 3 lean meat |
| **Dining Lite** | | | | | | | | | | | | |
| ✓Chicken and Noodles | 9 oz meal | 240 | 7 | 26 | NA | 50 | 570 | 17 | NA | 28 | 2 | 2 carb, 2 lean meat |
| ✓Glazed Chicken | 9 oz meal | 220 | 4 | 16 | NA | 45 | 680 | 17 | NA | 30 | 2 | 2 carb, 2 lean meat |
| **Healthy Choice** | | | | | | | | | | | | |
| ✓Breaded Chicken Breast Strips | 8 oz meal | 270 | 5 | 19 | 3 | 40 | 600 | 22 | 1 | 34 | 2 | 2 carb, 2 lean meat |
| ✓Cacciatore Chicken | 10.8 oz meal | 340 | 5 | 13 | 2 | 20 | 590 | 21 | 6 | 52 | 3 1/2 | 3 1/2 carb, 1 med-fat meat |
| Chicken & Vegetables Marsala | 11.5 oz meal | 240 | 4 | 15 | 2 | 30 | 440 | 20 | 3 | 32 | 2 | 2 carb, 2 very lean meat |
| ✓Chicken Broccoli Alfredo | 11.5 oz meal | 300 | 7 | 21 | 3 | 50 | 530 | 25 | 2 | 34 | 2 | 2 carb, 3 lean meat |
| ✓Chicken Dijon | 11 oz meal | 270 | 5 | 17 | 2 | 40 | 470 | 23 | 6 | 33 | 2 | 2 carb, 2 lean meat |
| Chicken Francesca | 12.5 oz meal | 330 | 6 | 16 | 3 | 30 | 600 | 23 | 4 | 46 | 3 | 3 carb, 2 lean meat |
| ✓Chicken Parmigiana | 11.5 oz meal | 330 | 8 | 22 | 3 | 40 | 490 | 19 | 3 | 46 | 3 | 2 carb, 2 med-fat meat |
| ✓Country Breaded Chicken | 10.3 oz meal | 350 | 9 | 23 | 2 | 45 | 480 | 16 | 5 | 51 | 3 1/2 | 3 1/2 carb, 1 med-fat meat, 1 fat |

| | | | | | | | | | | | | |
|---|---|---|---|---|---|---|---|---|---|---|---|---|
| Country Glazed Chicken | 8.5 oz meal | 230 | 4 | 16 | 2 | 45 | 480 | 17 | 3 | 30 | 2 | 2 carb, 2 lean meat |
| ✓Country Herb Chicken | 12.2 oz meal | 320 | 8 | 22 | 3 | 45 | 540 | 18 | 3 | 44 | 3 | 3 carb, 1 med-fat meat, 1 fat |
| ✓Country Herb Chicken | 12 oz meal | 320 | 8 | 23 | 3 | 45 | 540 | 18 | 3 | 44 | 3 | 3 carb, 1 med-fat meat |
| Garlic Chicken Milano | 9.5 oz meal | 260 | 6 | 19 | 3 | 35 | 510 | 18 | 3 | 34 | 2 | 2 carb, 2 lean meat |
| ✓Grilled Chicken Sonoma | 9 oz meal | 230 | 4 | 15 | 1 | 45 | 530 | 18 | 3 | 30 | 2 | 2 carb, 2 lean meat |
| ✓Grilled Chicken w/Mashed Potatoes | 8 oz meal | 170 | 4 | 18 | 2 | 40 | 600 | 18 | 3 | 18 | 1 | 1 carb, 2 lean meat |
| ✓Hearty Handfuls, Chicken & Brocolli | 6.1 oz | 320 | 5 | 14 | 2 | 20 | 580 | 17 | 5 | 51 | 3 1/2 | 3 1/2 carb, 1 med-fat meat |
| Homestyle Chicken and Pasta | 9 oz meal | 270 | 6 | 19 | 3 | 35 | 570 | 21 | 5 | 32 | 2 | 2 carb, 2 lean meat |
| Honey Mustard Chicken | 9.5 oz meal | 290 | 6 | 19 | 3 | 40 | 520 | 21 | 1 | 38 | 2 1/2 | 2 1/2 carb, 2 lean meat |
| ✓Mesquite Chicken Barbeque | 10.5 oz meal | 310 | 5 | 15 | 2 | 55 | 480 | 18 | 6 | 48 | 3 | 3 1/2 carb, 2 lean meat |
| ✓Roasted Chicken | 11 oz meal | 230 | 5 | 20 | 3 | 45 | 480 | 20 | 6 | 25 | 1 1/2 | 1 1/2 carb, 2 lean meat |
| Southwestern Glazed Chicken | 10.2 oz meal | 260 | 6 | 21 | 3 | 40 | 450 | 21 | 4 | 30 | 2 | 2 carb, 2 lean meat |
| **Lean Cuisine** | | | | | | | | | | | | |
| American Favorites, Baked Chicken | 8.6 oz meal | 230 | 4 | 16 | 2 | 35 | 520 | 18 | 5 | 31 | 2 | 2 carb, 2 lean meat |
| American Favorites, Chicken Medallions | 9.4 oz meal | 260 | 9 | 31 | 3 | 25 | 520 | 17 | 3 | 27 | 2 | 2 carb, 2 med-fat meat |

✔= Best Bet; NA = Not Available; Carb. Ch. = Carbohydrate Choices

| Chicken Meal/Entrees (Frozen) (Continued) | Serving Size | Cal. | Fat (g) | % Cal. Fat | Sat. Fat (g) | Chol. (mg) | Sod. (mg) | Pro. (g) | Fiber (g) | Carb. (g) | Carb. Ch. | Servings/Exchanges |
|---|---|---|---|---|---|---|---|---|---|---|---|---|
| ✓American Favorites, Honey Roasted Chicken | 8 1/2 oz | 270 | 6 | 20 | 2 | 25 | 590 | 13 | 4 | 42 | 3 | 3 carb, 1 med-fat meat |
| ✓Cafe Classics, Bow Tie Pasta & Chicken | 9.5 oz meal | 250 | 5 | 18 | 1 | 45 | 530 | 16 | 3 | 34 | 2 | 2 carb, 2 lean meat |
| ✓Café Classics, Chicken a l'Orange | 9 oz meal | 260 | 1 | 3 | <1 | 40 | 320 | 22 | 2 | 40 | 2 1/2 | 2 1/2 carb, 2 very lean meat |
| ✓Cafe Classics, Chicken Breast in Wine Sauce | 8.1 oz meal | 210 | 6 | 26 | 2 | 35 | 560 | 15 | 2 | 23 | 1 1/2 | 1 1/2 carb, 2 lean meat |
| ✓Cafe Classics, Chicken Carbonara | 9 oz meal | 280 | 8 | 26 | 2 | 30 | 580 | 18 | 2 | 33 | 2 | 2 carb, 2 med-fat meat |
| ✓Cafe Classics, Chicken Mediterranean | 10 oz meal | 260 | 4 | 14 | 1 | 25 | 590 | 17 | 2 | 38 | 2 1/2 | 2 1/2 carb, 2 lean meat |
| ✓Cafe Classics, Chicken Parmesan | 10.8 oz meal | 260 | 7 | 24 | 3 | 30 | 590 | 19 | 4 | 31 | 2 | 2 carb, 2 lean meat |
| ✓Cafe Classics, Chicken Piccata | 9 oz meal | 270 | 6 | 20 | 2 | 25 | 530 | 13 | 2 | 41 | 3 | 3 carb, 1 med-fat meat |
| ✓Café Classics, Chicken w/Basil Cream Sauce | 8 1/2 oz | 270 | 7 | 23 | 2 | 35 | 580 | 16 | 3 | 35 | 2 | 2 carb, 1 med-fat meat |
| ✓Café Classics, Fiesta Chicken | 8.5 oz meal | 200 | 5 | 23 | <1 | 30 | 590 | 19 | 4 | 36 | 2 1/2 | 2 1/2 carb, 2 lean meat |
| ✓Café Classics, Glazed Chicken | 8.5 oz meal | 240 | 6 | 23 | 1 | 55 | 480 | 22 | 0 | 25 | 1 1/2 | 1 1/2 carb, 2 lean meat |
| ✓Cafe Classics, Grilled Chicken Salsa | 8.9 oz meal | 270 | 7 | 23 | 3 | 45 | 570 | 15 | 4 | 36 | 2 1/2 | 2 1/2 carb, 1 med-fat meat |

| Product | Serving Size | Cal. | Fat (g) | % Cal. Fat | Sat. Fat (g) | Chol. (mg) | Sod. (mg) | Carb. (g) | Fiber (g) | Prot. (g) | Carb. Ch. | Exchanges/Choices |
|---|---|---|---|---|---|---|---|---|---|---|---|---|
| ✓ Cafe Classics, Herb-Roasted Chicken | 8 oz meal | 200 | 5 | 23 | 1 | 25 | 510 | 24 | 3 | 15 | 1 1/2 | 1 1/2 carb, 2 lean meat |
| ✓ Cafe Classics, Honey Mustard Chicken | 8 oz meal | 260 | 4 | 14 | 1 | 35 | 550 | 40 | 3 | 15 | 2 1/2 | 2 1/2 carb, 1 med-fat meat |
| Chicken Fettucine | 9.3 oz meal | 300 | 6 | 18 | 3 | 50 | 590 | 38 | 3 | 24 | 2 1/2 | 2 1/2 carb, 2 lean meat |
| ✓ Chicken in Peanut Sauce | 9 oz meal | 290 | 6 | 19 | 2 | 30 | 590 | 35 | 2 | 23 | 2 | 2 carb, 2 lean meat |
| ✓ Glazed Chicken w/Vegetable Rice | 10.5 oz meal | 270 | 6 | 20 | 2 | 25 | 590 | 33 | 4 | 20 | 2 | 2 carb, 2 lean meat |
| ✓ Hearty Portions, Chicken & BBQ Sauce | 13.9 oz meal | 380 | 8 | 19 | 2 | 50 | 790 | 54 | 6 | 24 | 3 1/2 | 3 1/2 carb, 2 med-fat meat |
| ✓ Hearty Portions, Grilled Chicken & Penne Pasta | 14 oz | 380 | 7 | 17 | 3 | 40 | 850 | 50 | 6 | 30 | 3 | 3 carb, 3 lean meat |
| ✓ Hearty Portions, Roasted Chicken w/Mushrooms | 12.5 oz meal | 340 | 6 | 16 | 2 | 35 | 850 | 44 | 4 | 27 | 3 | 3 carb, 3 lean meat |
| **Marie Callender** | | | | | | | | | | | | |
| Breaded Chicken Parmigiana | 16 oz meal | 660 | 32 | 44 | 8 | 50 | 920 | 63 | 5 | 30 | 4 | 4 carb, 3 med-fat meat, 3 fat |
| Cheesy Rice w/Chicken & Broccoli | 12 oz meal | 390 | 13 | 31 | 9 | 55 | 1220 | 44 | 6 | 24 | 3 | 3 carb, 2 med-fat meat, 1 fat |
| Chicken and Dumplings | 14 oz meal | 390 | 20 | 46 | 8 | 130 | 1650 | 34 | 4 | 17 | 2 | 2 carb, 2 med-fat meat, 2 fat |

✓ = Best Bet; NA = Not Available; Carb. Ch. = Carbohydrate Choices

| Chicken Meal/Entrees (Frozen) (Continued) | Serving Size | Cal. | Fat (g) | % Cal. Fat | Sat. Fat (g) | Chol. (mg) | Sod. (mg) | Pro. (g) | Fiber (g) | Carb. (g) | Carb. Ch. | Servings/Exchanges |
|---|---|---|---|---|---|---|---|---|---|---|---|---|
| Chicken and Noodles | 13 oz meal | 520 | 30 | 52 | 11 | 80 | 1320 | 21 | 5 | 42 | 3 | 3 carb, 2 med-fat meat, 4 fat |
| Chicken Cordon Bleu | 13 oz meal | 610 | 28 | 41 | 9 | 75 | 1920 | 33 | 6 | 58 | 4 | 4 carb, 3 med-fat meat, 3 fat |
| Chicken Marsala | 14 oz meal | 450 | 17 | 33 | 7 | 70 | 1260 | 33 | 6 | 42 | 3 | 3 carb, 3 med-fat meat |
| Chicken Pasta Fiesta | 12.5 oz meal | 640 | 40 | 56 | 26 | 80 | 860 | 27 | 4 | 44 | 3 | 3 carb, 3 med-fat meat, 5 fat |
| Country Fried Chicken & Gravy | 16 oz meal | 620 | 30 | 44 | 9 | 75 | 2300 | 24 | 6 | 63 | 4 | 4 carb, 2 med-fat meat, 4 fat |
| Escalloped Noodles & Chicken | 13 oz meal | 740 | 46 | 57 | 16 | 90 | 1600 | 21 | 5 | 60 | 4 | 4 carb, 1 med-fat meat, 8 fat |
| Grilled Chicken in Mushroom Sauce | 14 oz meal | 480 | 15 | 29 | 6 | 65 | 1030 | 33 | 7 | 54 | 4 | 4 carb, 3 med-fat meat |
| Herb Roasted Chicken | 14 oz meal | 580 | 34 | 53 | 16 | 205 | 2100 | 42 | 7 | 26 | 2 | 2 carb, 5 med-fat meat, 2 fat |
| **Morton** | | | | | | | | | | | | |
| Breaded Chicken Patty Meal | 6.8 oz meal | 290 | 17 | 53 | 4 | 35 | 840 | 10 | 4 | 24 | 1 1/2 | 1 1/2 carb, 1 med-fat meat, 2 fat |

| | Serving | Cal. | Fat (g) | % Cal. Fat | Sat. Fat (g) | Chol. (mg) | Sod. (mg) | Prot. (g) | Fiber (g) | Carb. (g) | Carb. Ch. | Exchanges per Serving |
|---|---|---|---|---|---|---|---|---|---|---|---|---|
| Chicken Nuggets Meal | 7 oz meal | 340 | 19 | 51 | 5 | 30 | 470 | 12 | 2 | 31 | 2 | 2 carb, 1 med-fat meat, 3 fat |
| Fried Chicken | 9 oz meal | 470 | 30 | 57 | 10 | 90 | 1100 | 20 | 3 | 30 | 2 | 2 carb, 2 med-fat meat, 4 fat |
| **Pierre** | | | | | | | | | | | | |
| ✓Flame Broiled Chicken Breast Sandwich | 1 (3.75 oz) | 260 | 8 | 28 | 2 | 30 | 440 | 14 | 3 | 32 | 2 | 2 strch, 1 med-fat meat, 1 fat |
| **Stouffer's** | | | | | | | | | | | | |
| Chicken a la King | 9.5 oz meal | 350 | 13 | 33 | 4 | 40 | 800 | 17 | 2 | 41 | 3 | 3 carb, 1 med-fat meat, 2 fat |
| Escalloped Chicken and Noodles | 10 oz meal | 460 | 29 | 57 | 5 | 100 | 1310 | 18 | 3 | 31 | 2 | 2 carb, 2 med-fat meat, 4 fat |
| ✓Glazed Chicken w/Rice | 11.8 oz meal | 290 | 6 | 19 | 1 | 45 | 810 | 21 | 2 | 39 | 2 1/2 | 2 1/2 carb, 2 lean meat |
| Homestyle Baked Chicken Breast | 8.9 oz | 260 | 11 | 38 | 6 | 65 | 680 | 22 | 3 | 18 | 1 | 1 carb, 3 lean meat |
| Homestyle Chicken and Dumplings | 10 oz meal | 280 | 8 | 26 | 4 | 55 | 1000 | 19 | 0 | 33 | 2 | 2 carb, 2 med-fat meat |
| Homestyle Chicken Fettucine | 10.5 oz meal | 350 | 14 | 36 | 4 | 50 | 1040 | 28 | 2 | 28 | 2 | 2 carb, 3 med-fat meat |
| Homestyle Chicken Parmigiana | 12 oz meal | 460 | 16 | 31 | 4 | 45 | 1060 | 24 | 5 | 54 | 3 1/2 | 3 1/2 carb, 2 med-fat meat, 1 fat |

✓= Best Bet; NA = Not Available; Carb. Ch. = Carbohydrate Choices

| Chicken Meal/Entrees (Frozen) (Continued) | Serving Size | Cal. | Fat (g) | % Cal. Fat | Sat. Fat (g) | Chol. (mg) | Sod. (mg) | Pro. (g) | Fiber (g) | Carb. (g) | Carb. Ch. | Servings/Exchanges |
|---|---|---|---|---|---|---|---|---|---|---|---|---|
| Homestyle Fried Chicken | 8.9 oz meal | 400 | 17 | 38 | 6 | 55 | 950 | 23 | 2 | 38 | 2 1/2 | 2 1/2 carb, 2 med-fat meat, 1 fat |
| Skillet Sensations, Chicken Alfredo | 12.5 oz meal | 490 | 16 | 29 | 6 | 30 | 1240 | 23 | 9 | 63 | 4 | 4 carb, 2 med-fat meat, 1 fat |
| Skillet Sensations, Chicken and Grilled Vegetables | 12.5 oz meal | 440 | 9 | 18 | 4 | 30 | 1330 | 27 | 6 | 62 | 4 | 4 carb, 2 med-fat meat |
| Skillet Sensations, Homestyle Chicken | 12.5 oz meal | 390 | 13 | 30 | 4 | 50 | 1040 | 22 | 7 | 47 | 3 | 3 carb, 2 med-fat meat, 1 fat |
| **Swanson** | | | | | | | | | | | | |
| Boneless Roast Chicken w/Herb Gravy | 11 oz meal | 320 | 7 | 20 | 2 | 40 | 1020 | 18 | 3 | 46 | 3 | 3 carb, 1 med-fat meat |
| Boneless White Meat Fried Chicken | 11 oz meal | 430 | 16 | 33 | 5 | 40 | 1010 | 23 | 5 | 49 | 3 | 3 carb, 2 med-fat meat, 1 fat |
| Chicken Nuggets | 10 oz meal | 590 | 25 | 38 | 7 | 35 | 990 | 20 | 5 | 71 | 4 1/2 | 4 1/2 carb, 1 med-fat meat, 4 fat |
| Classic Fried Chicken | 11.5 oz meal | 600 | 31 | 47 | 8 | 70 | 1360 | 24 | 5 | 58 | 4 | 4 carb, 2 med-fat meat, 4 fat |

## Swanson Hungry-Man

| | Serving | Cal. | Fat (g) | % Cal. Fat | Sat. Fat (g) | Chol. (mg) | Sod. (mg) | Prot. (g) | Fiber (g) | Carb. (g) | Carb. Ch. | Exchanges/Choices |
|---|---|---|---|---|---|---|---|---|---|---|---|---|
| Boneless White Meat Fried Chicken | 13.8 oz meal | 660 | 26 | 35 | 7 | 60 | 1740 | 34 | 5 | 73 | 5 | 5 carb, 3 med-fat meat, 2 fat |
| Classic Fried Chicken | 16.5 oz meal | 790 | 40 | 46 | 10 | 80 | 1940 | 33 | 6 | 75 | 5 | 5 carb, 3 med-fat meat, 5 fat |
| **Trio's** | | | | | | | | | | | | |
| Chicken Tenders & Cheese | 10 oz | 550 | 31 | 51 | 12 | 95 | 970 | 33 | 4 | 35 | 2 | 2 carb, 4 med-fat meat, 2 fat |
| Tortellini in Pesto Alfredo Sauce | | | | | | | | | | | | |
| **Tyson** | | | | | | | | | | | | |
| Chicken Cordon Bleu | 1 piece (7 oz) | 460 | 30 | 59 | 11 | 115 | 1390 | 31 | 0 | 17 | 1 | 1 strch, 4 med-fat meat, 2 fat |
| ✓Low Fat Marco Polo | 1 (6 oz) | 190 | 5 | 24 | 2 | 60 | 820 | 31 | 1 | 8 | 1/2 | 1/2 strch, 4 very lean meat |
| Stuffed Chicken Breasts | | | | | | | | | | | | |
| **Weight Watchers Smart Ones** | | | | | | | | | | | | |
| ✓Creamy Rigatoni w/Broccoli & Chicken | 9 oz meal | 240 | 4 | 15 | 1 | 25 | 780 | 16 | 4 | 39 | 2 1/2 | 2 1/2 carb, 1 med-fat meat |
| ✓Lemon Herb | 9 oz meal | 250 | 5 | 18 | 2 | 45 | 510 | 15 | 2 | 36 | 2 1/2 | 2 1/2 carb, 1 med-fat meat |
| Chicken Piccata | | | | | | | | | | | | |

✓= Best Bet; NA = Not Available; Carb. Ch. = Carbohydrate Choices

## CHICKEN PIECES (FROZEN)

### Banquet

| Product | Serving Size | Cal. | Fat (g) | % Cal. Fat | Sat. Fat (g) | Chol. (mg) | Sod. (mg) | Pro. (g) | Fiber (g) | Carb. (g) | Carb. Ch. | Servings/Exchanges |
|---|---|---|---|---|---|---|---|---|---|---|---|---|
| Boneless Chicken Patties | 1 | 190 | 14 | 66 | 3 | 30 | 440 | 7 | 1 | 10 | 1/2 | 1/2 carb, 1 med-fat meat, 2 fat |
| Chicken Breast Patties, Grilled Honey Mustard | 1 | 120 | 5 | 38 | 2 | 25 | 500 | 13 | 0 | 5 | 0 | 2 lean meat |
| Chicken Tenders | 3 | 250 | 15 | 54 | 4 | 40 | 480 | 12 | <1 | 15 | 1 | 1 carb, 2 med-fat meat, 2 fat |
| Country Fried Chicken | 3 oz | 270 | 18 | 60 | 5 | 45 | 620 | 14 | 1 | 13 | 1 | 1 carb, 2 med-fat meat, 2 fat |
| Drums & Thighs Fried Chicken | 3 oz | 260 | 18 | 62 | 5 | 65 | 540 | 15 | 2 | 10 | 1/2 | 1/2 carb, 2 med-fat meat, 2 fat |
| ✔ Fat-Free Baked Breast Tenders | 3 | 120 | 0 | 0 | 0 | 30 | 480 | 13 | 2 | 16 | 1 | 1 carb, 1 very lean meat |
| ✔ Fat-Free Baked Chicken Breast Patty | 1 | 100 | 0 | 0 | 0 | 0 | 400 | 9 | 1 | 15 | 1 | 1 carb, 1 very lean meat |
| Fried Chicken Breast | 1 | 410 | 26 | 57 | 13 | 85 | 600 | 23 | 4 | 18 | 1 | 1 carb, 3 med-fat meat, 2 fat |

| | Serving | Cal. | Fat (g) | % Fat Cal. | Sat. Fat (g) | Chol. (mg) | Sod. (mg) | Carb. (g) | Fiber (g) | Sugar (g) | Carb. Ch. | Exchanges |
|---|---|---|---|---|---|---|---|---|---|---|---|---|
| Grilled Honey BBQ Chicken Breast Patties | 1 | 110 | 5 | 41 | 2 | 40 | 440 | 13 | 0 | 3 | 0 | 2 lean meat |
| Honey BBQ Skinless Fried Chicken | 3 oz | 230 | 13 | 52 | 3 | 55 | 480 | 18 | 2 | 9 | 1/2 | 1/2 carb, 2 med-fat meat, 1 fat |
| Hot Bites Chicken Nuggets w/Sweet & Sour Sauce | 6 nuggets w/sauce | 320 | 18 | 50 | 4 | 45 | 670 | 16 | 2 | 25 | 1 1/2 | 1 1/2 carb, 2 med-fat meat, 2 fat |
| Hot 'n Spicy Breaded Chicken Wing Sections | 4 | 290 | 20 | 62 | 5 | 90 | 450 | 18 | <1 | 9 | 1/2 | 1/2 carb, 2 med-fat meat, 2 fat |
| Hot 'n Spicy Fried Chicken | 3 oz | 260 | 18 | 62 | 5 | 65 | 490 | 14 | 1 | 13 | 1 | 1 carb, 2 med-fat meat, 2 fat |
| Lemon Pepper Skinless Fried Chicken | 3 oz | 210 | 13 | 56 | 3 | 55 | 560 | 18 | 2 | 7 | 1/2 | 1/2 carb, 2 med-fat meat, 1 fat |
| Original Fried Chicken | 3 oz | 280 | 18 | 58 | 5 | 65 | 620 | 14 | 1 | 15 | 1 | 1 carb, 2 med-fat meat, 2 fat |
| Skinless Fried Chicken | 3 oz | 210 | 13 | 56 | 3 | 55 | 480 | 18 | 2 | 7 | 1/2 | 1/2 carb, 2 med-fat meat, 1 fat |
| Southern Fried Chicken | 3 oz | 260 | 18 | 62 | 5 | 65 | 700 | 14 | 1 | 15 | 1 | 1 carb, 2 med-fat meat, 1 fat |
| Southern Fried Chicken Nuggets | 6 | 270 | 18 | 60 | 4 | 35 | 570 | 12 | 2 | 16 | 1 | 1 carb, 1 med-fat meat, 2 fat |

✔ = Best Bet; NA = Not Available; Carb. Ch. = Carbohydrate Choices

| Chicken Pieces (Frozen) (Continued) | Serving Size | Cal. | Fat (g) | % Cal. Fat | Sat. Fat (g) | Chol. (mg) | Sod. (mg) | Pro. (g) | Fiber (g) | Carb. (g) | Carb. Ch. | Servings/Exchanges |
|---|---|---|---|---|---|---|---|---|---|---|---|---|
| Southern Fried Chicken Patties | 1 | 190 | 13 | 62 | 3 | 25 | 430 | 8 | <1 | 10 | 1/2 | 1 carb, 1 med-fat meat, 1 fat |
| Southern Fried Chicken Tenders | 3 | 250 | 16 | 58 | 4 | 40 | 460 | 12 | 1 | 16 | 1 | 1 carb, 2 med-fat meat, 1 fat |
| **Country Skillet** | | | | | | | | | | | | |
| Chicken Chunks | 5 | 270 | 18 | 60 | 3 | 20 | 720 | 12 | 1 | 18 | 1 | 1 carb, 2 med-fat meat, 2 fat |
| Chicken Nuggets | 10 | 280 | 17 | 55 | 4 | 25 | 610 | 14 | 1 | 16 | 1 | 1 carb, 2 med-fat meat, 1 fat |
| Chicken Patties | 1 | 190 | 11 | 52 | 3 | 20 | 490 | 9 | 1 | 12 | 1 | 1 carb, 1 med-fat meat, 1 fat |
| Fried Chicken | 3 oz | 270 | 18 | 60 | 5 | 65 | 620 | 14 | 1 | 13 | 1 | 1 carb, 2 med-fat meat, 2 fat |
| Southern Fried Chicken Chunks | 5 | 270 | 16 | 53 | 4 | 20 | 550 | 11 | 1 | 17 | 1 | 1 carb, 1 med-fat meat, 2 fat |
| Southern Fried Chicken Patties | 1 | 190 | 12 | 57 | 3 | 20 | 440 | 9 | 1 | 12 | 1 | 1 carb, 1 med-fat meat, 1 fat |

## Michael Toshio

| Product | Amount | Cal. | Fat (g) | % Cal. Fat | Sat. Fat (g) | Chol. (mg) | Sod. (mg) | Prot. (g) | Fiber (g) | Carb. (g) | Carb. Ch. | Exchanges/Choices |
|---|---|---|---|---|---|---|---|---|---|---|---|---|
| Teriyaki Chicken, Skewered, Seasoned | 3 skewers (3 oz) | 190 | 7 | 33 | 2 | 45 | 1090 | 16 | 0 | 16 | 1 | 1 carb, 2 med-fat meat |

## Tyson

| Product | Amount | Cal. | Fat (g) | % Cal. Fat | Sat. Fat (g) | Chol. (mg) | Sod. (mg) | Prot. (g) | Fiber (g) | Carb. (g) | Carb. Ch. | Exchanges/Choices |
|---|---|---|---|---|---|---|---|---|---|---|---|---|
| ✔ Baked Chicken Breasts | 3 oz | 115 | 2 | 16 | NA | 70 | 65 | 24 | 0 | 0 | 0 | 3 very lean meat |
| Breaded Chicken Breast Patties | 1 piece (3.2 oz) | 220 | 14 | 57 | 4 | 20 | 430 | 12 | 1 | 12 | 1 | 1 strch, 1 med-fat meat, 2 fat |
| ✔ Breaded Chicken Breast Tenderloins | 2 pieces (5.1 oz) | 250 | 7 | 25 | 2 | 30 | 330 | 26 | 2 | 22 | 1 1/2 | 1 1/2 carb, 3 lean meats |
| Breaded Chicken Nuggets | 4 pieces | 240 | 14 | 53 | 4 | 40 | 330 | 12 | 2 | 16 | 1 | 1 strch, 1 med-fat meat, 2 fat |
| Buffalo Style Tenders | 2 pieces (3 oz) | 190 | 9 | 43 | 2 | 20 | 1050 | 12 | 1 | 17 | 1 | 1 carb, 1 med-fat meat, 1 fat |
| Chicken Nuggets | 3 oz | 205 | 14 | 61 | 4 | 50 | 385 | 11 | <1 | 9 | 1/2 | 1/2 carb, 1 med-fat meat, 2 fat |
| Cornish Hen | 3.5 oz | 240 | 14 | 53 | NA | 75 | 70 | 28 | 0 | 0 | 0 | 4 lean meat |
| ✔ Grilled Chicken Breast Strips | 3 oz | 120 | 4 | 30 | 1 | 60 | 500 | 21 | 0 | 1 | 0 | 3 very lean meat |
| Honey BBQ Drums | 1 piece (3 oz) | 140 | 6 | 39 | 2 | 80 | 370 | 17 | 0 | 5 | 0 | 2 lean meat |

✔ = Best Bet; NA = Not Available; Carb. Ch. = Carbohydrate Choices

| Chicken Pieces (Frozen) (Continued) | Serving Size | Cal. | Fat (g) | % Cal. Fat | Sat. Fat (g) | Chol. (mg) | Sod. (mg) | Pro. (g) | Fiber (g) | Carb. (g) | Carb. Ch. | Servings/Exchanges |
|---|---|---|---|---|---|---|---|---|---|---|---|---|
| Honey BBQ Wings | 3 pieces (3 oz) | 180 | 10 | 50 | 3 | 85 | 400 | 16 | 0 | 7 | 1/2 | 1/2 carb, 2 med-fat meat |
| Honey Mustard Flavored Chicken Breast Fillets | 1 piece (3 oz) | 130 | 5 | 35 | 2 | 45 | 520 | 17 | 0 | 3 | 0 | 2 lean meat |
| Mesquite Flavored Chicken Breast Fillets | 1 piece (3 oz) | 130 | 7 | 48 | 2 | 45 | 540 | 17 | 0 | 1 | 0 | 2 med-fat meat |
| Southwestern Seasoned Popcorn Chicken Bites | 3 oz | 230 | 12 | 47 | 2 | 25 | 630 | 16 | 0 | 16 | 1 | 1 strch, 2 med-fat meat |
| Teriyaki Glazed Chicken Breast Fillets | 1 fillet, 3 oz | 170 | 7 | 37 | 2 | 55 | 620 | 20 | 0 | 7 | 1/2 | 1/2 carb, 3 lean meat |
| Wings of Fire | 2 pieces (3.75 oz) | 140 | 9 | 58 | 3 | 70 | 480 | 13 | 0 | 2 | 0 | 2 med-fat meat |

## CHICKEN, FULLY COOKED (REFRIGERATED)

### Louis Rich Carving Board Meats

| | Serving Size | Cal. | Fat (g) | % Cal. Fat | Sat. Fat (g) | Chol. (mg) | Sod. (mg) | Pro. (g) | Fiber (g) | Carb. (g) | Carb. Ch. | Servings/Exchanges |
|---|---|---|---|---|---|---|---|---|---|---|---|---|
| ✓Grilled Chicken Breast Strips | 3 oz | 110 | 4 | 33 | 1 | 55 | 770 | 19 | 0 | 1 | 0 | 3 very lean meat |

### Tyson

| | Serving Size | Cal. | Fat (g) | % Cal. Fat | Sat. Fat (g) | Chol. (mg) | Sod. (mg) | Pro. (g) | Fiber (g) | Carb. (g) | Carb. Ch. | Servings/Exchanges |
|---|---|---|---|---|---|---|---|---|---|---|---|---|
| Oven Roasted Chicken Leg Quarters, Fully Cooked | 1 piece (6 oz) | 380 | 25 | 59 | 7 | 215 | 780 | 35 | 0 | 1 | 0 | 5 med-fat meat |
| Oven Roasted Half Chicken Breast, Fully Cooked | 1 piece (5 oz) | 260 | 13 | 45 | 4 | 110 | 670 | 34 | 0 | 1 | 0 | 5 lean meat |

## CHILI (CANNED)

| | | | | | | | | | | | | |
|---|---|---|---|---|---|---|---|---|---|---|---|---|
| **Chef Mate** | | | | | | | | | | | | |
| Chili w/o Beans | 1 cup | 430 | 32 | 67 | 14 | 85 | 1590 | 19 | 3 | 18 | 1 | 1 strch, 2 med-fat meat, 5 fat |
| Chili with Beans | 1 cup | 410 | 25 | 55 | 11 | 55 | 1170 | 18 | 11 | 29 | 2 | 2 strch, 2 med-fat meat, 3 fat |
| Spice Chili | 1/2 cup | 423 | 24 | 51 | 11 | 56 | 1485 | 17 | 4 | 33 | 2 | 2 strch, 2 med-fat meat, 3 fat |
| **Healthy Choice** | | | | | | | | | | | | |
| ✔Chili Beef | 1 cup | 189 | 2 | 10 | <1 | 12 | 440 | 15 | 5 | 32 | 2 | 2 strch, 1 very lean meat |
| **Libby's** | | | | | | | | | | | | |
| Chili & Beans | 7.5 oz | 270 | 13 | 43 | NA | NA | 390 | 13 | NA | 25 | 1 1/2 | 1 1/2 strch, 1 med-fat meat, 2 fat |
| Chili, No Beans | 7.5 oz | 390 | 30 | 69 | NA | NA | 800 | 18 | NA | 11 | 1 | 1 strch, 2 med-fat meat, 4 fat |
| **Old El Paso** | | | | | | | | | | | | |
| Chili w/Beans | 1 cup | 240 | 11 | 41 | 3 | 30 | 770 | 17 | 6 | 19 | 1 | 1 carb, 2 med-fat meat |
| Tamales in Chili Gravy | 3 | 320 | 19 | 53 | 7 | 30 | 590 | 7 | 5 | 31 | 2 | 2 carb, 4 fat |

✔= Best Bet; NA = Not Available; Carb. Ch. = Carbohydrate Choices

| Product | Serving Size | Cal. | Fat (g) | % Cal. Fat | Sat. Fat (g) | Chol. (mg) | Sod. (mg) | Pro. (g) | Fiber (g) | Carb. (g) | Carb. Ch. | Servings/Exchanges |
|---|---|---|---|---|---|---|---|---|---|---|---|---|
| **CHILI (FROZEN)** | | | | | | | | | | | | |
| **Healthy Choice** | | | | | | | | | | | | |
| ✓Bowl Creations, Chili & Cornbread | 9.5 oz bowl | 340 | 7 | 19 | 3 | 30 | 600 | 21 | 11 | 49 | 3 | 3 carb, 2 lean meat |
| **Lean Cuisine** | | | | | | | | | | | | |
| ✓Three Bean Chili w/Rice | 10 oz | 250 | 6 | 22 | 2 | 5 | 590 | 10 | 9 | 38 | 2 1/2 | 2 1/2 carb, 1 fat |
| **Marie Callender** | | | | | | | | | | | | |
| Chili & Cornbread | 16 oz | 540 | 21 | 35 | 9 | 60 | 2110 | 21 | 7 | 67 | 4 1/2 | 4 1/2 carb, 1 med-fat meat, 3 fat |
| **Stouffer's** | | | | | | | | | | | | |
| Chili w/Beans | 8.75 oz | 270 | 10 | 33 | 4 | 35 | 1130 | 15 | 8 | 29 | 2 | 2 carb, 2 fat |
| **CHIPS, CORN** | | | | | | | | | | | | |
| **Frito-Lay** | | | | | | | | | | | | |
| 3D's Doritos, All Varieties (Avg) | 1 oz | 140 | 6 | 39 | 2 | <5 | 355 | 2 | 1 | 18 | 1 | 1 strch, 1 fat |
| Doritos, All Varieties (Avg) | 1 oz | 145 | 7 | 43 | 2 | 0 | 190 | 2 | 1 | 19 | 1 | 1 strch, 1 fat |
| ✓Doritos, WOW Nacho Cheesier | 1 oz | 90 | 1 | 10 | 0 | 0 | 240 | 2 | 1 | 18 | 1 | 1 strch |
| Fritos, All Varieties (Avg) | 1 oz | 160 | 10 | 56 | 2 | 0 | 150–290 | 2 | 1 | 16 | 1 | 1 strch, 2 fat |
| Santitas 100% White Corn Chips | 1 oz | 130 | 6 | 42 | 1 | 0 | 110 | 2 | 1 | 19 | 1 | 1 strch, 1 fat |
| Santitas Restaurant Style Chips | 1 oz | 130 | 6 | 42 | 1 | 0 | 110 | 2 | 1 | 19 | 1 | 1 strch, 1 fat |

| | Amount | Cal. | Fat (g) | % Fat Cal. | Sat. Fat (g) | Chol. (mg) | Sod. (mg) | Prot. (g) | Fiber (g) | Carb. (g) | Carb. Choices | Exchanges |
|---|---|---|---|---|---|---|---|---|---|---|---|---|
| ✓Tostitos WOW Original Tortilla Chips | 1 oz | 90 | 1 | 10 | 0 | 0 | 105 | 2 | 1 | 20 | 1 | 1 strch |
| Tostitos, All Varieties (Avg) | 1 oz | 145 | 7 | 43 | 1 | 0 | 110 | 2 | 2 | 18 | 1 | 1 strch, 1 fat |
| ✓Tostitos, Baked, All Varieties (Avg) | 1 oz | 115 | 2 | 16 | <1 | <5 | 195 | 3 | 2 | 23 | 1 1/2 | 1 1/2 strch |
| **Old El Paso** | | | | | | | | | | | | |
| Nachips Tortilla Chips | 1 oz | 150 | 8 | 48 | 2 | 0 | 85 | 3 | 2 | 17 | 1 | 1 strch, 2 fat |
| White Corn Tortilla Chips | 1 oz | 140 | 8 | 51 | 1 | 0 | 60 | 2 | 1 | 16 | 1 | 1 strch, 2 fat |

## CHIPS, POTATO

**Frito-Lay**

| | Amount | Cal. | Fat (g) | % Fat Cal. | Sat. Fat (g) | Chol. (mg) | Sod. (mg) | Prot. (g) | Fiber (g) | Carb. (g) | Carb. Choices | Exchanges |
|---|---|---|---|---|---|---|---|---|---|---|---|---|
| Adobadas Potato Chips | 1 oz | 170 | 10 | 53 | 3 | 0 | 240 | 2 | 1 | 18 | 1 | 1 strch, 2 fat |
| Lay's Potato Chips, All Flavors (Avg) | 1 oz | 155 | 10 | 58 | 3 | 0 | 180–380 | 2 | 1 | 16 | 1 | 1 carb, 2 fat |
| ✓Lay's Potato Chips-Baked, All Varieties (Avg) | 1 oz | 120 | 3 | 23 | 0 | 0 | 190 | 2 | 2 | 23 | 1 1/2 | 1 1/2 strch, 1 fat |
| ✓Lay's WOW Potato Chips, All Varieties (Avg) | 1 oz | 75 | 0 | 0 | 0 | 0 | 225 | 2 | 1 | 17 | 1 | 1 strch |
| Ruffles Potato Chips, All Varieties (Avg) | 1 oz | 150 | 10 | 60 | 3 | 0 | 205 | 2 | 1 | 15 | 1 | 1 strch, 2 fat |
| ✓Ruffles WOW Original Potato Chips | 1 oz | 75 | 0 | 0 | 0 | 0 | 200 | 2 | 1 | 17 | 1 | 1 strch |
| Ruffles, Reduced-Fat Potato Chips | 1 oz | 130 | 7 | 48 | 1 | 0 | 160 | 2 | 1 | 18 | 1 | 1 strch, 1 fat |
| Sunchips, All Varieties (Avg) | 1 oz | 140 | 7 | 45 | 1 | 0 | 115 | 2 | 2 | 19 | 1 | 1 strch, 1 fat |

## CHIPS, SNACK

**Betty Crocker**

| | Amount | Cal. | Fat (g) | % Fat Cal. | Sat. Fat (g) | Chol. (mg) | Sod. (mg) | Prot. (g) | Fiber (g) | Carb. (g) | Carb. Choices | Exchanges |
|---|---|---|---|---|---|---|---|---|---|---|---|---|
| Bugles, All Varieties (Avg) | 1 1/2 cup | 155 | 9 | 52 | 8 | 0 | 940 | 2 | 0 | 19 | 1 | 1 carb, 2 fat |

✓= Best Bet; NA = Not Available; Carb. Ch. = Carbohydrate Choices

| Chips, Snack (*Continued*) | Serving Size | Cal. | Fat (g) | % Cal. Fat | Sat. Fat (g) | Chol. (mg) | Sod. (mg) | Pro. (g) | Fiber (g) | Carb. (g) | Carb. Ch. | Servings/Exchanges |
|---|---|---|---|---|---|---|---|---|---|---|---|---|
| Bugles, Baked, All Varieties (Avg) | 1 1/2 cup | 130 | 4 | 28 | <1 | 0 | 410 | 2 | 0 | 23 | 1 1/2 | 1 1/2 carb, 1 fat |
| **Frito-Lay** | | | | | | | | | | | | |
| Baken-ets Fried Pork Rind-Regular Cracklins | 8 | 40 | 6 | 100 | 2 | 15 | 550 | 7 | <1 | <1 | 0 | 1 med-fat meat |
| Baken-ets, Fried Pork Rind, All Flavors (Avg) | 8 | 75 | 5 | 60 | 2 | 20 | 375 | 8 | <1 | <1 | 0 | 1 med-fat meat |
| Cheetos, All Varieties (Avg) | 1 oz | 155 | 10 | 58 | 3 | 0 | 285 | 2 | <1 | 15 | 1 | 1 strch, 2 fat |
| Funyuns | 1 oz | 140 | 7 | 45 | 2 | 0 | 270 | 2 | <1 | 18 | 1 | 1 strch, 1 fat |
| Munchos, All Varieties (Avg) | 1 oz | 160 | 10 | 56 | 2 | 0 | 240 | 1 | 1 | 16 | 1 | 1 strch, 2 fat |
| **Health Valley** | | | | | | | | | | | | |
| ✔Fat-Free Cheese Flavor Puffs, All Varieties (Avg) | 1 oz | 100 | 0 | 0 | 0 | 0 | 75 | 3 | <1 | 21 | 1 1/2 | 1 1/2 strch |
| **Pepperidge Farm** | | | | | | | | | | | | |
| Three Cheese Bagel Chips | 1 oz | 250 | 12 | 43 | 2 | 10 | 425 | 7 | <1 | 28 | 2 | 2 strch, 2 fat |
| **CLAMS (CANNED)** | | | | | | | | | | | | |
| **(Generic)** | | | | | | | | | | | | |
| ✔Chopped Clams | 1/4 cup | 25 | 0 | 0 | 0 | 10 | 320 | 4 | 0 | 2 | 0 | 1 very lean meat |

## COATING MIXES

| Product | Serving | Cal. | Fat (g) | % Cal. Fat | Sat. Fat (g) | Chol. (mg) | Sod. (mg) | Prot. (g) | Carb. (g) | Fiber (g) | Carb. Choices |
|---|---|---|---|---|---|---|---|---|---|---|---|
| **Contadina** | | | | | | | | | | | |
| Seasoned Italian Style Bread Crumbs | 1/4 cup | 100 | 2 | 18 | 0 | 0 | 720 | 3 | 19 | 1 | 1 strch |
| **Kellogg's** | | | | | | | | | | | |
| ✓ Corn Flake Crumbs | 2 Tbsp | 40 | 0 | 0 | 0 | 0 | 80 | 1 | 9 | 1/2 | 1/2 strch |
| **Kraft/Shake 'N Bake** | | | | | | | | | | | |
| ✓ BBQ Chicken or Pork Coating Mix | 1/8 pkt | 45 | 1 | 20 | 0 | 0 | 410 | 0 | 9 | 1/2 | 1/2 strch |
| ✓ Classic Italian Herb Coating Mix | 1/8 pkt | 40 | <1 | 23 | 0 | 0 | 270 | 1 | 7 | 1/2 | 1/2 strch |
| ✓ Crispy Cheddar Potato Mix | 1/6 pkt | 30 | 2 | 60 | 2 | 5 | 380 | 2 | 2 | 0 | 1 fat |
| ✓ Herb & Garlic for Boneless/Skinless Chicken | 2 tsp | 20 | <1 | 23 | 0 | 0 | 160 | 0 | 4 | 0 | free |
| ✓ Herb & Garlic Potato Mix | 1/6 pkt | 20 | 0 | 0 | 0 | 0 | 380 | 0 | 5 | 0 | free |
| ✓ Honey Mustard Coating Mix | 1/8 pkt | 45 | 1 | 20 | 0 | 0 | 300 | 0 | 9 | 1/2 | 1/2 strch |
| ✓ Hot Spicy Chicken or Pork Coating Mix | 1/8 pkt | 40 | 1 | 23 | 0 | 0 | 170 | 1 | 7 | 1/2 | 1/2 strch |
| ✓ Mild Country Coating Mix | 1/8 pkt | 35 | 2 | 51 | 1 | 0 | 240 | 0 | 5 | 0 | 1 fat |
| ✓ Original Chicken Coating Mix | 1/8 pkt | 40 | 1 | 23 | 0 | 0 | 220 | 1 | 7 | 1/2 | 1/2 strch |
| ✓ Original Fish Coating Mix | 1/4 pkt | 80 | 2 | 23 | 0 | 0 | 350 | 2 | 14 | 1 | 1 strch |
| ✓ Original Pork Coating Mix | 1/8 pkt | 45 | <1 | 20 | 0 | 0 | 230 | 1 | 8 | 1/2 | 1/2 strch |
| ✓ Tangy Honey Coating Mix | 1/8 pkt | 45 | 1 | 20 | 0 | 0 | 300 | 0 | 9 | 1/2 | 1/2 strch |

✓ = Best Bet; NA = Not Available; Carb. Ch. = Carbohydrate Choices

| Coating Mixes (*Continued*) | Serving Size | Cal. | Fat (g) | % Cal. Fat | Sat. Fat (g) | Chol. (mg) | Sod. (mg) | Pro. (g) | Fiber (g) | Carb. (g) | Carb. Ch. | Servings/Exchanges |
|---|---|---|---|---|---|---|---|---|---|---|---|---|
| **Old London** | | | | | | | | | | | | |
| Bread Crumbs, All Varieties (Avg) | 1/4 cup | 110 | 1 | 8 | 0 | 0 | 510 | 4 | 1 | 19 | 1 | 1 strch |
| **Oven Fry** | | | | | | | | | | | | |
| ✔Seasoned Coating-Chicken/ Pork, All Varieties (Avg) | 1/8 pkt | 53 | 1 | 17 | 0 | 0 | 410 | <1 | 0 | 7 | 1/2 | 1/2 strch |
| **Progresso** | | | | | | | | | | | | |
| ✔Italian Style Bread Crumbs | 1/4 cup | 110 | 2 | 16 | 0 | 0 | 430 | 4 | 1 | 20 | 1 | 1 strch |
| Parmesan Bread Crumbs | 1/4 cup | 100 | 2 | 18 | 0 | 0 | 870 | 4 | 1 | 17 | 1 | 1 strch |
| ✔Plain Bread Crumbs | 1/4 cup | 110 | 2 | 16 | 0 | 0 | 210 | 4 | 1 | 19 | 1 | 1 strch |
| **COBBLER (FROZEN)** | | | | | | | | | | | | |
| **Marie Callenders** | | | | | | | | | | | | |
| Apple Crumb Cobbler | 4 oz | 320 | 17 | 48 | 3 | 0 | 170 | 2 | 3 | 41 | 3 | 3 carb, 3 fat |
| Cherry Crumb Cobbler | 4 oz | 330 | 18 | 49 | 5 | 0 | 190 | 2 | 3 | 43 | 3 | 3 carb, 4 fat |
| Peach Cobbler | 4 oz | 350 | 22 | 57 | 3 | 0 | 150 | 2 | 4 | 37 | 2 1/2 | 2 1/2 carb, 4 fat |
| **COCKTAIL SAUCE** | | | | | | | | | | | | |
| **(Generic)** | | | | | | | | | | | | |
| Cocktail Sauce | 1/4 cup | 60 | 0 | 0 | 0 | 0 | 690 | 1 | 1 | 15 | 1 | 1 carb |

## COCOA MIX (AS PREPARED)

| Product | Serving | Cal. | Fat (g) | % Cal. Fat | Sat. Fat (g) | Chol. (mg) | Sod. (mg) | Prot. (g) | Fiber (g) | Carb. (g) | Carb. Ch. | Exchanges/Choices |
|---|---|---|---|---|---|---|---|---|---|---|---|---|
| **Carnation** | | | | | | | | | | | | |
| ✓ Hot Cocoa Mix w/Marshmallow | 1 pkt | 120 | 3 | 23 | 2 | <5 | 170 | 1 | <1 | 23 | 1 1/2 | 1 1/2 carb |
| ✓ Hot Cocoa, Rich Chocolate | 1 pkt | 120 | 3 | 23 | 2 | <5 | 180 | 1 | <1 | 23 | 1 1/2 | 1 1/2 carb, 1 fat |
| **Swiss Miss** | | | | | | | | | | | | |
| ✓ Fat-Free Cocoa Mix | 1 pkt | 50 | 0 | 0 | 0 | 0 | 230 | 3 | 1 | 9 | 1/2 | 1 reduced-fat milk |
| ✓ Milk Chocolate Cocoa | 1 pkt | 120 | 3 | 23 | 1 | 0 | 130 | 2 | 1 | 22 | 1 1/2 | 1 1/2 carb, 1 fat |
| **Weight Watchers** | | | | | | | | | | | | |
| ✓ Cocoa Mix w/Marshmallows | 1 pkt | 60 | 0 | 0 | 0 | 0 | 160 | 6 | 0 | 10 | 1 | 1 skim milk |

## COFFEE CAKE

| Product | Serving | Cal. | Fat (g) | % Cal. Fat | Sat. Fat (g) | Chol. (mg) | Sod. (mg) | Prot. (g) | Fiber (g) | Carb. (g) | Carb. Ch. | Exchanges/Choices |
|---|---|---|---|---|---|---|---|---|---|---|---|---|
| **Betty Crocker** | | | | | | | | | | | | |
| Stir 'n Bake Cinnamon Streusel Coffee Cake | 1/6 pkg | 200 | 7 | 32 | 2 | 10 | 220 | 2 | 0 | 36 | 2 1/2 | 2 1/2 carb, 1 fat |
| **Entenmann's** | | | | | | | | | | | | |
| Cheese Coffee Cake | 1 slice | 190 | 8 | 38 | 4 | 30 | 160 | 4 | 0 | 24 | 1 1/2 | 1 1/2 carb, 2 fat |
| Cheese Topped Coffeecake | 1 slice | 190 | 8 | 38 | 3 | 30 | 180 | 3 | 1 | 26 | 2 | 2 carb, 2 fat |
| Cheese-Filled Crumb Coffeecake | 1 slice | 210 | 10 | 43 | 4 | 40 | 190 | 4 | <1 | 25 | 1 1/2 | 1 1/2 carb, 2 fat |
| Cinnamon Filbert Ring Pastry | 1 slice | 270 | 17 | 57 | 3 | NA | 190 | 4 | NA | 27 | 2 | 2 strch, 3 fat |
| Crumb Coffee Cake | 1 slice | 250 | 12 | 43 | 3 | 15 | 210 | 4 | 1 | 33 | 2 | 2 carb, 2 fat |

✓ = Best Bet; NA = Not Available; Carb. Ch. = Carbohydrate Choices

| | Serving Size | Cal. | Fat (g) | % Cal. Fat | Sat. Fat (g) | Chol. (mg) | Sod. (mg) | Pro. (g) | Fiber (g) | Carb. (g) | Carb. Ch. | Servings/Exchanges |
|---|---|---|---|---|---|---|---|---|---|---|---|---|
| **Coffee Cake** (*Continued*) | | | | | | | | | | | | |
| ✔Fat-Free Cheese Filled Crumb Coffeecake | 1 slice | 130 | 0 | 0 | 0 | 0 | 230 | 4 | 1 | 29 | 2 | 2 carb |
| ✔Fat-Free Cinnamon Apple Coffee Cake (1 slice) | 1 slice | 130 | 0 | 0 | 0 | 0 | 110 | 2 | 2 | 29 | 2 | 2 carb |
| York Crumb Coffeecake | 1 slice | 250 | 12 | 43 | 3 | 15 | 200 | 4 | 1 | 33 | 2 | 2 carb, 2 fat |
| **Weight Watchers** | | | | | | | | | | | | |
| Cinnamon Streusel Coffee Cake | 1 slice | 190 | 7 | 33 | 1 | 5 | 250 | 3 | NA | 28 | 2 | 2 carb, 1 fat |
| **COFFEE CREAMER** | | | | | | | | | | | | |
| **Carnation Coffee-Mate** | | | | | | | | | | | | |
| ✔Non-Dairy Creamer | 1 Tbsp | 16 | 1 | 56 | <1 | 0 | 5 | 0 | 0 | 2 | 0 | free |
| ✔Non-Fat, Non-Dairy Creamer | 1 Tbsp | 10 | 0 | 0 | 0 | 0 | 0 | 0 | 0 | 2 | 0 | free |
| **Cremora** | | | | | | | | | | | | |
| ✔Lite Non-Dairy Creamer, Powder | 1 tsp | 8 | <1 | 0 | 0 | 0 | 3 | 0 | 0 | 2 | 0 | free |
| ✔Non-Dairy Creamer | 1 tsp | 10 | 1 | 90 | NA | 0 | 5 | 0 | 0 | 1 | 0 | free |
| **COFFEE/TEA BEVERAGES** | | | | | | | | | | | | |
| **(Generic)** | | | | | | | | | | | | |
| ✔Brewed Coffee | 8 oz | 5 | <1 | 0 | <1 | 0 | 5 | <1 | 0 | <1 | 0 | free |
| ✔Brewed Tea | 8 oz | 2 | <1 | 0 | <1 | 0 | 7 | 0 | 0 | <1 | 0 | free |
| ✔Cappuccino Coffee | 6 oz | 61 | 2 | 30 | 2 | 0 | 104 | <1 | 0 | 11 | 1 | 1 carb |

| | Serving | Cal. | Fat (g) | % Cal. from Fat | Sat. Fat (g) | Chol. (mg) | Sod. (mg) | Pro. (g) | Fiber (g) | Carb. (g) | Carb. Ch. | Exchanges |
|---|---|---|---|---|---|---|---|---|---|---|---|---|
| ✓Demi Tasse Coffee | 8 oz | 5 | 0 | 0 | <1 | 0 | 5 | <1 | 0 | <1 | 0 | free |
| ✓Espresso Coffee | 8 oz | 5 | 0 | 0 | <1 | 0 | 5 | <1 | 0 | <1 | 0 | free |
| ✓Instant Coffee-Prepared | 8 oz | 5 | <1 | 0 | <1 | 0 | 7 | 0 | 0 | <1 | 0 | free |
| **General Foods** | | | | | | | | | | | | |
| ✓Flavored Teas, All Varieties (Avg) | 8 oz | 70 | 2 | 26 | <1 | 4 | 65 | 0 | 0 | 13 | 1 | 1 carb |
| ✓International Coffee, All Varieties | 8 oz | 65 | 3 | 42 | <1 | 0 | 70 | <1 | <1 | 10 | 1/2 | 1/2 carb |
| ✓International Coffee, Sugar-Free, All Varieties (Avg) | 8 oz | 25 | 0 | 0 | 0 | 0 | 50 | 0 | <1 | 5 | 0 | free |
| **Lipton** | | | | | | | | | | | | |
| ✓Iced Tea Mix, Sugar Sweetened Lemon | 4 tsp | 70 | 0 | 0 | 0 | 0 | 0 | 0 | 0 | 18 | 1 | 1 carb |
| **Maxwell House** | | | | | | | | | | | | |
| ✓Cappuccino Mix, All Varieties (Avg) | 1 envelope | 95 | 2 | 19 | <1 | 0 | 65 | 2 | 0 | 18 | 1 | 1 carb |
| ✓Coffee, Cappuccino, All Varieties except Iced (Avg) | 8 oz | 95 | 2 | 19 | <1 | 0 | 65 | 2 | 0 | 18 | 1 | 1 carb |
| ✓Coffee, Cappuccino, Sugar-Free, All Varieties (Avg) | 8 oz | 60 | 3 | 45 | <1 | 0 | 83 | <1 | <1 | 7 | 1/2 | 1/2 carb |
| Coffee, Iced Cappuccino | 8 oz | 180 | 5 | 25 | 3 | 20 | 125 | 8 | <1 | 27 | 2 | 2 carb, 1 fat |
| **Nescafe** | | | | | | | | | | | | |
| ✓Frothe Mix, All Varieties (Avg) | 1/4 cup | 100 | 1 | 9 | 0 | 0 | 145 | 3 | 0 | 21 | 1 1/2 | 1 1/2 carb |

✓ = Best Bet; NA = Not Available; Carb. Ch. = Carbohydrate Choices

| Coffee/Tea Beverages (*Continued*) | Serving Size | Cal. | Fat (g) | % Cal. Fat | Sat. Fat (g) | Chol. (mg) | Sod. (mg) | Pro. (g) | Fiber (g) | Carb. (g) | Carb. Ch. | Servings/Exchanges |
|---|---|---|---|---|---|---|---|---|---|---|---|---|
| **Nestea** | | | | | | | | | | | | |
| ✓Iced Tea Mix, Sugar Sweetened Lemon | 2 Tbsp | 80 | 0 | 0 | 0 | 0 | 0 | 0 | 0 | 19 | 1 | 1 carb |
| **COOKIE DOUGH** | | | | | | | | | | | | |
| **Pillsbury** | | | | | | | | | | | | |
| Refrigerated Cookie Dough, Chocolate Chip | 1 oz | 130 | 6 | 42 | 3 | <5 | 85 | 1 | <1 | 17 | 1 | 1 carb, 1 fat |
| Refrigerated Cookie Dough, M&M's | 1 oz | 130 | 6 | 42 | 2 | <5 | 75 | 1 | <1 | 18 | 1 | 1 carb, 1 fat |
| ✓Refrigerated Cookie Dough, Reduced Fat Choc Chip | 1 oz | 110 | 3 | 25 | 2 | <5 | 85 | 1 | <1 | 19 | 1 | 1 carb, 1 fat |
| Refrigerated One Step Chocolate Chip Cookies Pan | 1/8 recipe | 130 | 6 | 42 | 2 | <5 | 100 | 1 | <1 | 19 | 1 | 1 carb, 1 fat |
| Refrigerated One Step M&M's Pan Cookies | 1/8 recipe | 130 | 6 | 42 | 2 | <5 | 85 | 1 | <1 | 19 | 1 | 1 carb, 1 fat |
| Refrigerated Sugar Cookie Dough | 2 | 130 | 5 | 35 | 2 | <5 | 125 | 1 | 0 | 19 | 1 | 1 carb, 1 fat |
| **COOKIE MIX (AS PREPARED)** | | | | | | | | | | | | |
| **Betty Crocker** | | | | | | | | | | | | |
| Chocolate Chip | 2 cookies | 160 | 8 | 45 | 3 | 10 | 105 | 2 | 0 | 21 | 1 1/2 | 1 1/2 carb, 2 fat |
| Chocolate Peanut Butter | 2 cookies | 160 | 7 | 39 | 3 | 10 | 120 | 3 | 0 | 20 | 1 | 1 carb, 1 fat |

| | | | | | | | | | | | |
|---|---|---|---|---|---|---|---|---|---|---|---|
| Double Chocolate Chunk | 2 cookies | 150 | 6 | 36 | 2 | 10 | 100 | 2 | 0 | 21 | 1 1/2 | 1 1/2 carb, 1 fat |
| Gingerbread Classic Cookie Mix | 1/8 pkg | 230 | 6 | 23 | 2 | 25 | 350 | 3 | 0 | 39 | 2 1/2 | 2 1/2 carb, 1 fat |
| Oatmeal Chocolate Chip | 2 cookies | 150 | 7 | 42 | 2 | 10 | 135 | 2 | 0 | 21 | 1 1/2 | 1 1/2 carb, 1 fat |
| Peanut Butter | 2 cookies | 160 | 8 | 45 | 2 | 10 | 135 | 3 | 0 | 20 | 1 | 1 carb, 2 fat |
| Sugar | 2 cookies | 160 | 8 | 45 | 2 | 10 | 115 | 2 | 0 | 22 | 1 1/2 | 1 1/2 carb, 2 fat |

**Pillsbury**

| | | | | | | | | | | | |
|---|---|---|---|---|---|---|---|---|---|---|---|
| ✔Snackwell's Chocolate Fudge Cookie Mix | 1 oz | 90 | 2 | 20 | 0 | <5 | 95 | 1 | <1 | 18 | 1 | 1 carb |
| ✔Snackwell's Reduced Fat | 1 oz | 110 | 3 | 25 | 2 | <5 | 85 | 1 | <1 | 19 | 1 | 1 carb, 1 fat |
| Chocolate Chip Cookie Mix | | | | | | | | | | | | |

## COOKIES

### Archway

| | | | | | | | | | | | |
|---|---|---|---|---|---|---|---|---|---|---|---|
| ✔Apple Filled Cookies | 1 | 100 | 3 | 27 | <1 | <5 | 105 | 1 | <1 | 16 | 1 | 1 carb, 1 fat |
| ✔Apple N' Raisin Cookies | 1 | 120 | 3 | 23 | NA | 10 | 170 | 2 | 1 | 20 | 1 | 1 carb, 1 fat |
| Chocolate Chip & Toffee Cookies | 1 | 130 | 6 | 41 | 2 | 5 | 125 | 1 | <1 | 18 | 1 | 1 carb, 1 fat |
| ✔Chocolate Chip Cookies | 1 | 50 | 3 | 54 | NA | 5 | 40 | 1 | NA | 7 | 1/2 | 1/2 carb, 1 fat |
| Cinnamon Apple Cookies | 1 | 105 | 4 | 43 | <1 | 0 | 130 | 1 | <1 | 17 | 1 | 1 carb, 1 fat |
| ✔Cinnamon Honey Heart Fat-Free Cookies | 3 | 105 | 0 | 0 | 0 | 0 | 125 | 1 | <1 | 25 | 1 1/2 | 1 1/2 carb |
| Coconut Macaroon Cookies | 5 | 105 | 6 | 51 | 5 | 0 | 40 | <1 | <1 | 15 | 1 | 1 carb, 1 fat |
| ✔Cookie Jar Hermits | 1 | 95 | 3 | 28 | <1 | 5 | 145 | <1 | 1 | 17 | 1 | 1 carb, 1 fat |

✔= Best Bet; NA = Not Available; Carb. Ch. = Carbohydrate Choices

| Cookies (*Continued*) | Serving Size | Cal. | Fat (g) | % Cal. Fat | Sat. Fat (g) | Chol. (mg) | Sod. (mg) | Pro. (g) | Fiber (g) | Carb. (g) | Carb. Ch. | Servings/Exchanges |
|---|---|---|---|---|---|---|---|---|---|---|---|---|
| ✔Dark Molasses Cookies | 1 | 115 | 3 | 23 | <1 | 0 | 150 | 1 | <1 | 20 | 1 | 1 carb, 1 fat |
| ✔Date Filled Oatmeal Cookies | 1 | 100 | <1 | 9 | <1 | <5 | 100 | 1 | <1 | 18 | 1 | 1 carb, 1 fat |
| ✔Dutch Cocoa Cookies | 1 | 100 | 3 | 27 | <1 | <5 | 85 | 1 | <1 | 17 | 1 | 1 carb, 1 fat |
| ✔Fat-Free Devil's Food | 1 | 70 | <1 | 13 | <1 | 0 | 80 | <1 | <1 | 16 | 1 | 1 carb |
| ✔Fat-Free Sugar Cookies | 1 | 70 | 0 | 0 | 0 | 0 | 80 | <1 | <1 | 17 | 1 | 1 carb |
| Frosty Lemon Cookies | 1 | 110 | 5 | 41 | 2 | 0 | 110 | 1 | <1 | 17 | 1 | 1 carb, 1 fat |
| Frosty Orange Cookies | 1 | 115 | 5 | 39 | 1 | 0 | 95 | 1 | <1 | 17 | 1 | 1 carb, 1 fat |
| ✔Fruit & Honey Bar Cookies | 1 | 105 | 3 | 26 | <1 | 5 | 105 | 1 | <1 | 18 | 1 | 1 carb, 1 fat |
| ✔Iced Gingersnaps | 3 | 170 | 7 | 37 | 2 | 0 | 130 | 1 | <1 | 26 | 2 | 2 carb, 1 fat |
| Iced Molasses Cookies | 1 | 115 | 4 | 32 | 1 | 0 | 130 | 1 | <1 | 20 | 1 | 1 carb, 1 fat |
| Iced Oatmeal Cookies | 1 | 125 | 5 | 36 | 2 | <5 | 90 | 2 | <1 | 18 | 1 | 1 carb, 1 fat |
| ✔Lemon Drop Cookies | 1 | 95 | 3 | 28 | <1 | 10 | 95 | 1 | <1 | 15 | 1 | 1 carb, 1 fat |
| Mud Pie Cookies | 1 | 110 | 5 | 41 | 2 | 5 | 105 | 1 | <1 | 15 | 1 | 1 carb, 1 fat |
| Oatmeal Cookies | 1 | 110 | 4 | 33 | <1 | <5 | 90 | 2 | <1 | 17 | 1 | 1 carb, 1 fat |
| Oatmeal Pecan Cookies | 1 | 135 | 7 | 47 | 2 | 5 | 100 | 2 | <1 | 16 | 1 | 1 carb, 1 fat |
| Oatmeal Raisin Cookies | 1 | 110 | 4 | 33 | <1 | <5 | 100 | 2 | <1 | 17 | 1 | 1 carb, 1 fat |
| ✔Oatmeal Raisin, Fat-Free Cookies | 1 | 105 | 0 | 0 | 0 | 0 | 165 | 1 | <1 | 24 | 1 1/2 | 1 1/2 carb |
| ✔Old Fashioned Molasses Cookies | 1 | 105 | 3 | 26 | <1 | 10 | 140 | 1 | <1 | 18 | 1 | 1 carb, 1 fat |

| | | | | | | | | | | | | |
|---|---|---|---|---|---|---|---|---|---|---|---|---|
| Old Fashioned Windmill Cookies | 1 | 90 | 4 | 40 | <1 | 0 | 95 | 1 | <1 | 14 | 1 | 1 carb, 1 fat |
| Peanut Butter Cookies | 1 | 100 | 5 | 45 | 1 | 8 | 85 | 2 | <1 | 12 | 1 | 1 carb, 1 fat |
| Peanut Jumble Cookies | 1 | 115 | 6 | 47 | 2 | <5 | 75 | 2 | <1 | 13 | 1 | 1 carb, 1 fat |
| Pecan Ice-Box Cookies | 1 | 120 | 6 | 45 | 1 | 5 | 75 | 1 | <1 | 15 | 1 | 1 carb, 1 fat |
| Pineapple Filled Cookies | 1 | 110 | 4 | 33 | 1 | 5 | 65 | 1 | <1 | 17 | 1 | 1 carb, 1 fat |
| ✔Plain Molasses Cookies | 1 | 105 | 3 | 26 | <1 | 10 | 145 | 1 | <1 | 18 | 1 | 1 carb, 1 fat |
| Raspberry Filled Cookies | 1 | 100 | 4 | 36 | 1 | 5 | 85 | 1 | <1 | 16 | 1 | 1 carb, 1 fat |
| ✔Raspberry Oatmeal Fat Free Cookies | 1 | 110 | 0 | 0 | 0 | 0 | 165 | 1 | <1 | 25 | 1 1/2 | 1 1/2 carb |
| Reduced Fat Gingersnaps | 3 | 140 | 4 | 26 | <1 | 0 | 140 | 1 | <1 | 24 | 1 1/2 | 1 1/2 carb, 1 fat |
| Ruth's Golden Oatmeal Cookies | 1 | 110 | 4 | 33 | <1 | <5 | 115 | 2 | <1 | 17 | 1 | 1 carb, 1 fat |
| ✔Soft Sugar Cookies | 1 | 110 | 3 | 25 | <1 | 5 | 160 | 1 | <1 | 17 | 1 | 1 carb, 1 fat |
| Strawberry/Cherry Filled Cookies | 1 | 100 | 4 | 36 | 1 | 5 | 85 | 1 | <1 | 16 | 1 | 1 carb, 1 fat |
| Sugar Free Oatmeal Raisin Cookies | 1 | 105 | 5 | 43 | 1 | 0 | 75 | 1 | <1 | 16 | 1 | 1 carb, 1 fat |
| Sugar Free Rocky Road Cookies | 1 | 100 | 5 | 45 | 1 | <1 | 65 | 1 | <1 | 15 | 1 | 1 carb, 1 fat |
| Sugar Free Chocolate Chip | 1 | 105 | 5 | 43 | 1 | <1 | 65 | 1 | <1 | 16 | 1 | 1 carb, 1 fat |
| **Betty Crocker** | | | | | | | | | | | | |
| Dunk Aroos | 1 tray | 120 | 4 | 30 | 1 | 0 | 55 | 0 | 0 | 21 | 1 1/2 | 1 1/2 carb, 1 fat |

✔= Best Bet; NA = Not Available; Carb. Ch. = Carbohydrate Choices

| Cookies (*Continued*) | Serving Size | Cal. | Fat (g) | % Cal. Fat | Sat. Fat (g) | Chol. (mg) | Sod. (mg) | Pro. (g) | Fiber (g) | Carb. (g) | Carb. Ch. | Servings/Exchanges |
|---|---|---|---|---|---|---|---|---|---|---|---|---|
| **Estee** | | | | | | | | | | | | |
| No Sucrose Added Vanilla or Lemon Thins | 4 | 140 | 6 | 39 | 1 | 0 | 25 | 2 | <1 | 19 | 1 | 1 carb, 1 fat |
| No Sucrose Added Chocolate Sandwich Cookies | 3 | 160 | 6 | 34 | 2 | 0 | 60 | 2 | 1 | 24 | 1 1/2 | 1 1/2 carb, 1 fat |
| ✓No Sucrose Added Fig Bars, All Flavors (average) | 2 bars | 100 | 1 | 9 | 0 | 0 | 20 | 1 | 3 | 23 | 1 1/2 | 1 1/2 carb |
| No Sucrose Added Oatmeal Raisin | 4 | 130 | 5 | 35 | 1 | 0 | 25 | 2 | 1 | 19 | 1 | 1 carb, 1 fat |
| No Sucrose Added Original Sandwich Cookie | 3 | 160 | 6 | 34 | 2 | 0 | 45 | 2 | 1 | 24 | 1 1/2 | 1 1/2 carb, 1 fat |
| No Sucrose Added Peanut Butter Sandwich Cookies | 3 | 160 | 7 | 39 | 1 | 0 | 55 | 4 | 1 | 22 | 1 1/2 | 1 1/2 carb, 1 fat |
| No Sucrose Added Shortbread Cookies | 4 | 130 | 4 | 28 | 1 | 0 | 150 | 2 | <1 | 22 | 1 1/2 | 1 1/2 carb, 1 fat |
| No Sucrose Added Vanilla Sandwich Cookies | 3 | 160 | 5 | 28 | 1 | 0 | 35 | 2 | <1 | 25 | 1 1/2 | 1 1/2 carb, 1 fat |
| Sugar Free Chocolate Chip Cookies | 3 | 110 | 4 | 33 | <1 | 0 | 70 | 2 | 1 | 22 | 1 1/2 | 1 1/2 carb, 1 fat |
| Sugar Free Chocolate Walnut Cookies | 3 | 110 | 4 | 33 | 0 | 0 | 95 | 2 | 1 | 22 | 1 1/2 | 1 1/2 carb, 1 fat |
| Sugar Free Coconut Cookies | 3 | 110 | 4 | 33 | 1 | 0 | 110 | 2 | 1 | 22 | 1 1/2 | 1 1/2 carb, 1 fat |

|  | | | | | | | | | | | | |
|---|---|---|---|---|---|---|---|---|---|---|---|---|
| Sugar Free Creme Wafers, Vanilla & Chocolate | 5 | 150 | 8 | 48 | 2 | 0 | 10 | 1 | 0 | 21 | 1 1/2 | 1 1/2 carb, 2 fat |
| ✔Sugar Free Lemon Cookies | 3 | 110 | 3 | 25 | 0 | 0 | 90 | 2 | 1 | 22 | 1 1/2 | 1 1/2 carb, 1 fat |
| **Frookie** | | | | | | | | | | | | |
| ✔7-Grain Oatmeal Cookies | 1 | 45 | 2 | 38 | <1 | 0 | 35 | 1 | NA | 7 | 1/2 | 1/2 carb |
| ✔Apple Cinnamon Oat Bran Cookies | 1 | 45 | 2 | 40 | <1 | 0 | 35 | 1 | NA | 7 | 1/2 | 1/2 carb |
| ✔Chocolate Animal Crackers | 6 | 60 | 2 | 31 | 0 | 0 | 70 | 1 | NA | 9 | 1/2 | 1/2 carb |
| ✔Chocolate Frookwich Sandwich Cookies | 1 | 50 | 2 | 36 | 0 | 0 | 30 | 1 | NA | 7 | 1/2 | 1/2 carb |
| ✔Cinnamon Animal Crackers | 6 | 60 | 2 | 31 | 0 | 0 | 45 | 1 | NA | 9 | 1/2 | 1/2 carb |
| ✔Fat-Free Banana Cookies | 1 | 45 | 0 | 0 | 0 | 0 | 90 | 1 | 1 | 10 | 1/2 | 1/2 carb |
| ✔Fat-Free Cranberry Orange Cookies | 1 | 45 | 0 | 0 | 0 | 0 | 75 | 1 | 1 | 10 | 1/2 | 1/2 carb |
| ✔Fat-Free Fruitins Fig Cookies | 2 | 90 | 0 | 0 | 0 | 0 | 75 | 1 | 1 | 21 | 1 1/2 | 1 1/2 carb |
| ✔Fat-Free Oatmeal Raisin Cookies | 1 | 50 | 0 | 0 | 0 | 0 | 75 | 1 | 1 | 11 | 1 | 1 carb |
| ✔Lemon Cookies | 1 | 50 | 2 | 36 | 0 | 0 | 30 | 1 | NA | 7 | 1/2 | 1/2 carb |
| ✔Mint Chocolate Chip Cookies | 1 | 45 | 2 | 38 | <1 | 0 | 35 | 1 | NA | 7 | 1/2 | 1/2 carb |
| ✔Trolls | 11 | 60 | 2 | 29 | 0 | 0 | 65 | 1 | NA | 10 | 1/2 | 1/2 carb |
| **Grandma's** | | | | | | | | | | | | |
| Big Chocolate Chip Cookie | 1 | 190 | 9 | 43 | 3 | 0 | 135 | 2 | <1 | 25 | 1 1/2 | 1 1/2 carb, 2 fat |
| Big Fudge Chocolate Chip Cookie | 1 | 170 | 7 | 37 | 3 | <5 | 160 | 1 | 1 | 26 | 2 | 2 carb, 1 fat |

✔= Best Bet; NA = Not Available; Carb. Ch. = Carbohydrate Choices

| Cookies (*Continued*) | Serving Size | Cal. | Fat (g) | % Cal. Fat | Sat. Fat (g) | Chol. (mg) | Sod. (mg) | Pro. (g) | Fiber (g) | Carb. (g) | Carb. Ch. | Servings/Exchanges |
|---|---|---|---|---|---|---|---|---|---|---|---|---|
| Big Oatmeal Raisin Cookie | 1 | 160 | 6 | 34 | 2 | 5 | 250 | 1 | 1 | 26 | 2 | 2 carb, 1 fat |
| Big Old Time Molasses Cookie | 1 | 160 | 4 | 23 | 2 | <5 | 230 | 2 | <1 | 29 | 2 | 2 carb, 1 fat |
| Big Peanut Butter Chocolate Chip Cookie | 1 | 190 | 9 | 43 | 3 | <5 | 170 | 4 | 1 | 23 | 1 1/2 | 1 1/2 carb, 2 fat |
| Big Peanut Butter Cookie | 1 | 190 | 9 | 43 | 2 | 5 | 200 | 2 | 1 | 22 | 1 1/2 | 1 1/2 carb, 2 fat |
| Mini Fudge Cookies | 9 | 150 | 7 | 42 | 2 | 0 | 180 | 2 | 1 | 21 | 1 1/2 | 1 1/2 carb, 1 fat |
| Mini Peanut Butter Cookies | 9 | 150 | 7 | 42 | 2 | 0 | 140 | 2 | 1 | 21 | 1 1/2 | 1 1/2 carb, 1 fat |
| Mini Vanilla Cookies | 9 | 150 | 7 | 42 | 2 | <5 | 85 | 2 | <1 | 22 | 1 1/2 | 1 1/2 carb, 1 fat |
| Peanut Butter Sandwich Cookies | 5 | 210 | 10 | 43 | 3 | 0 | 200 | 3 | 1 | 28 | 2 | 2 carb, 2 fat |
| Vanilla Sandwich Cookies | 5 | 210 | 10 | 43 | 3 | 5 | 125 | 2 | <1 | 30 | 2 | 2 carb, 2 fat |
| **Health Valley** | | | | | | | | | | | | |
| ✔Almond Fruit Jumbos | 1 | 70 | 3 | 39 | NA | 0 | 30 | 2 | 1 | 10 | 1/2 | 1/2 carb, 1 fat |
| Apricot Fancy Fruit Chunks | 2 | 90 | 4 | 36 | NA | 0 | 45 | 2 | 2 | 14 | 1 | 1 carb, 1 fat |
| ✔Fat-Free Apple Spice | 3 | 80 | 0 | 0 | 0 | 0 | 80 | 2 | 3 | 18 | 1 | 1 carb |
| ✔Fat-Free Breakfast Bar Raspberry Cookie | 1 | 80 | 0 | 0 | 0 | 0 | 80 | 2 | 2 | 17 | 1 | 1 carb |
| ✔Fat-Free Date Fruit Center Cookie | 1 | 70 | 0 | 0 | 0 | 0 | 35 | 2 | 4 | 16 | 1 | 1 carb |
| ✔Fat-Free Date Snack Bar Cookie | 1 | 140 | 0 | 0 | 0 | 0 | 10 | 3 | 4 | 33 | 2 | 2 carb |
| ✔Fat-Free Oatmeal Raisin | 3 | 80 | 0 | 0 | 0 | 0 | 80 | 2 | 3 | 18 | 1 | 1 carb |
| ✔Fat-Free Oatmeal Raisin | 3 | 85 | 0 | 0 | 0 | 0 | 80 | 2 | 3 | 19 | 1 | 1 carb |

|  | | | | | | | | | | | |
|---|---|---|---|---|---|---|---|---|---|---|---|
| ✔Fat-Free Strawberry Fruit Centers Cookie | 1 | 75 | 0 | 0 | 0 | 0 | 60 | 2 | 3 | 17 | 1 | 1 carb |
| ✔Fat-Free Banana Fruit Chunks | 3 | 85 | 0 | 0 | 0 | 0 | 80 | 2 | 3 | 19 | 1 | 1 carb |
| ✔Fat-Free Fruit Centers Apple Cookies | 1 | 80 | 0 | 0 | 0 | 0 | 80 | 2 | 2 | 17 | 1 | 1 carb |
| ✔Fat-Free Healthy Carob Chips | 3 | 80 | 0 | 0 | 0 | 0 | 80 | 2 | 2 | 18 | 1 | 1 carb |
| ✔Granola Cookies | 3 | 75 | 0 | 0 | 0 | 0 | 60 | 2 | 3 | 17 | 1 | 1 carb |
| ✔Honey Jumbos | 1 | 70 | 2 | 29 | NA | 0 | 35 | 1 | 3 | 10 | 1/2 | 1/2 carb |
| ✔Oat Bran Cookies | 1 | 70 | 2 | 26 | NA | 0 | 20 | 1 | 2 | 10 | 1/2 | 1/2 carb |
| ✔Oatbran Graham w/Honey | 7 | 130 | 2 | 14 | NA | 0 | 45 | 3 | 3 | 25 | 1 1/2 | 1 1/2 carb |
| ✔Peach Apricot Mini Fruit Centers | 3 | 75 | 0 | 0 | 0 | 0 | 60 | 2 | 3 | 17 | 1 | 1 carb |
| Peanut Cookies | 2 | 100 | 3 | 27 | NA | 0 | 585 | 2 | 2 | 14 | 1 | 1 carb, 1 fat |
| ✔Tofu Cookies | 2 | 90 | 3 | 30 | NA | 0 | 30 | 2 | 1 | 16 | 1 | 1 carb |
| **Keebler** | | | | | | | | | | | |
| Animal Crackers | 10 | 130 | 4 | 28 | 1 | 0 | 140 | 2 | <1 | 22 | 1 1/2 | 1 1/2 carb, 1 fat |
| Chips Deluxe | 1 | 80 | 5 | 56 | 2 | 0 | 60 | 1 | 0 | 9 | 1/2 | 1/2 carb, 1 fat |
| Chips Deluxe, Rainbow | 1 | 80 | 4 | 45 | 2 | <5 | 45 | 1 | <1 | 10 | 1/2 | 1/2 carb, 1 fat |
| Chocolate Chip Cookie Stix | 4 | 130 | 5 | 35 | 2 | 5 | 100 | 2 | <1 | 19 | 1 | 1 carb, 1 fat |
| ✔Cinnamon Crisp Cookies | 8 | 130 | 3 | 21 | 1 | 0 | 230 | 1 | <1 | 24 | 1 1/2 | 1 1/2 carb, 1 fat |
| Classic Collection French Vanilla Crème | 1 | 80 | 4 | 45 | 1 | 0 | 65 | 1 | 0 | 12 | 1 | 1 carb, 1 fat |
| Deluxe Grahams | 3 | 140 | 7 | 45 | 5 | 0 | 105 | 1 | <1 | 19 | 1 | 1 carb, 1 fat |

✔ = Best Bet; NA = Not Available; Carb. Ch. = Carbohydrate Choices

| Cookies (Continued) | Serving Size | Cal. | Fat (g) | % Cal. Fat | Sat. Fat (g) | Chol. (mg) | Sod. (mg) | Pro. (g) | Fiber (g) | Carb. (g) | Carb. Ch. | Servings/Exchanges |
|---|---|---|---|---|---|---|---|---|---|---|---|---|
| E.L. Fudge Chocolate Sandwich Cookies | 2 | 120 | 6 | 45 | 1 | 0 | 70 | 2 | <1 | 17 | 1 | 1 carb, 1 fat |
| E.L. Fudge, Butter Sandwich Cookies | 2 | 120 | 6 | 45 | 1 | <5 | 70 | 1 | <1 | 17 | 1 | 1 carb, 1 fat |
| Fudge Shoppe Fudge Strips | 3 | 160 | 8 | 45 | 5 | 0 | 140 | 1 | <1 | 21 | 1 1/2 | 1 1/2 carb, 2 fat |
| Fudge Shoppe Reduced-Fat Fudge Strips | 3 | 140 | 5 | 32 | 3 | 0 | 120 | 1 | 0 | 21 | 1 1/2 | 1 1/2 carb, 1 fat |
| Ginger Snaps | 5 | 150 | 6 | 36 | 1 | 0 | 120 | 2 | 0 | 24 | 1 1/2 | 1 1/2 carb, 1 fat |
| ✓Golden Fruit Cranberry Biscuits | 1 | 80 | 2 | 23 | 0 | 0 | 55 | 1 | <1 | 14 | 1 | 1 carb |
| Golden Vanilla Wafers | 8 | 150 | 7 | 42 | 2 | 0 | 120 | 1 | <1 | 20 | 1 | 1 carb, 1 fat |
| Pecan Sandies | 1 | 80 | 5 | 56 | 1 | <5 | 75 | <1 | <1 | 9 | 1/2 | 1/2 carb, 1 fat |
| ✓Sandies, 25% Reduced Fat | 1 | 80 | 3 | 34 | <1 | 0 | 60 | <1 | 0 | 11 | 1 | 1 carb, 1 fat |
| Soft Batch Chocolate Chip Cookies | 1 | 80 | 4 | 45 | 1 | 0 | 70 | <1 | <1 | 10 | 1/2 | 1/2 carb, 1 fat |
| ✓Soft Batch, Oatmeal Raisin | 1 | 70 | 3 | 39 | 1 | 0 | 65 | <1 | <1 | 10 | 1/2 | 1/2 carb, 1 fat |
| Soft 'N Chewy Chips Deluxe | 1 | 80 | 4 | 45 | 1 | 5 | 60 | 1 | 0 | 11 | 1 | 1 carb, 1 fat |
| Vanilla Wafers, 30% Reduced Fat | 8 | 130 | 4 | 28 | <1 | 0 | 140 | 2 | <1 | 25 | 1 1/2 | 1 1/2 carb, 1 fat |

**Kraft**

| | | | | | | | | | | | | |
|---|---|---|---|---|---|---|---|---|---|---|---|---|
| ✓Handi-Snacks Cookie Jammers | 1 | 130 | 3 | 21 | 0 | 0 | 125 | 1 | <1 | 26 | 2 | 2 carb, 1 fat |

**La Choy**

| | | | | | | | | | | | | |
|---|---|---|---|---|---|---|---|---|---|---|---|---|
| ✓Fortune Cookies | 4 | 110 | <1 | 8 | <1 | 0 | 11 | 2 | <1 | 26 | 2 | 2 carb |

## Nabisco

| | | | | | | | | | | Carb. Ch. | Exchanges |
|---|---|---|---|---|---|---|---|---|---|---|---|
| Barnum's Animal Cracker Cookies | 10 | 120 | 4 | 30 | <1 | 0 | 140 | 2 | NA | 22 | 1 1/2 | 1 1/2 strch, 1 fat |
| Bugs Bunny Graham Cracker Cookies | 10 | 120 | 4 | 30 | 0 | 0 | 140 | 2 | NA | 22 | 1 1/2 | 1/2 carb, 1 fat |
| ✔ Cameo w/Crème | 1 | 70 | 3 | 39 | 0 | 0 | 50 | 1 | 0 | 10 | 1/2 | 1/2 carb, 1 fat |
| Chips Ahoy! Chocolate Chip Cookies | 3 | 160 | 8 | 45 | 3 | 0 | 105 | 2 | 1 | 21 | 1 1/2 | 1 1/2 carb, 2 fat |
| Chips Ahoy! Reduced Fat | 3 | 140 | 5 | 32 | 2 | 0 | 150 | 2 | <1 | 22 | 1 1/2 | 1 1/2 carb, 1 fat |
| Famous Chocolate Wafer Cookies | 5 | 140 | 4 | 26 | 2 | 5 | 110 | 2 | NA | 22 | 1 1/2 | 1 1/2 carb, 1 fat |
| ✔ Fat-Free Apple Newton Cookies | 2 | 90 | 0 | 0 | 0 | 0 | 65 | 1 | <1 | 21 | 1 1/2 | 1 1/2 carb |
| ✔ Fat-Free Fig Newton Cookie | 2 | 90 | 0 | 0 | 0 | 0 | 115 | 1 | 1 | 22 | 1 1/2 | 1 1/2 carb |
| ✔ Fat-Free Newton Cookie, Raspberry | 2 | 90 | 0 | 0 | 0 | 0 | 100 | 1 | <1 | 21 | 1 1/2 | 1 1/2 carb |
| ✔ Fat-Free Newton Cookie, Strawberry | 2 | 90 | 0 | 0 | 0 | 0 | 95 | 1 | 0 | 21 | 1 1/2 | 1 1/2 carb |
| ✔ Fig Newton Cookies | 2 | 110 | 3 | 25 | 0 | 0 | 115 | 1 | 1 | 22 | 1 1/2 | 1 1/2 carb, 1 fat |
| ✔ Ginger Snaps | 4 | 120 | 3 | 23 | <1 | 0 | 230 | 1 | 0 | 22 | 1 1/2 | 1 1/2 carb, 1 fat |
| Lorna Doone Shortbread Cookie | 4 | 140 | 7 | 45 | 1 | 5 | 130 | 2 | <1 | 19 | 1 | 1 carb, 1 fat |
| Nilla Wafers | 8 | 140 | 5 | 32 | 1 | <5 | 100 | 1 | 0 | 24 | 1 1/2 | 1 1/2 carb, 1 fat |
| Nutter Butter Bites | 10 | 150 | 4 | 24 | <1 | 0 | 125 | 2 | <1 | 20 | 1 | 1 carb, 1 fat |
| Nutter Butters | 2 | 140 | 6 | 39 | 2 | 0 | 50 | 2 | 0 | 18 | 1 | 1 carb, 1 fat |
| Oreo Sandwich Cookies | 3 | 160 | 7 | 39 | 2 | 0 | 220 | 1 | 1 | 23 | 1 1/2 | 1 1/2 carb, 1 fat |
| Reduced Fat Oreo Sandwich Cookies | 3 | 130 | 4 | 28 | 1 | 0 | 190 | 2 | 1 | 25 | 1 1/2 | 1 1/2 carb, 1 fat |

✔ = Best Bet; NA = Not Available; Carb. Ch. = Carbohydrate Choices

| Cookies (Continued) | Serving Size | Cal. | Fat (g) | % Cal. Fat | Sat. Fat (g) | Chol. (mg) | Sod. (mg) | Pro. (g) | Fiber (g) | Carb. (g) | Carb. Ch. | Servings/Exchanges |
|---|---|---|---|---|---|---|---|---|---|---|---|---|
| ✔Reduced Fat Vanilla Wafers | 8 | 120 | 2 | 15 | <1 | 0 | 105 | 1 | 0 | 24 | 1 1/2 | 1 1/2 carb |
| Snackwell's Chocolate Chip Cookies | 13 | 130 | 4 | 28 | 2 | 0 | 160 | 2 | <1 | 22 | 1 1/2 | 1 1/2 carb, 1 fat |
| ✔Snackwell's Creme Sandwich Cookie | 2 | 110 | 3 | 25 | <1 | 0 | 130 | 1 | 0 | 20 | 1 | 1 carb, 1 fat |
| ✔Snackwell's Devil's Food Cookie Cakes | 1 | 50 | 0 | 0 | 0 | 0 | 30 | 1 | 0 | 12 | 1 | 1 carb |
| Snackwell's Mint Creme Cookies | 1 | 110 | 4 | 33 | 1 | 0 | 70 | 1 | <1 | 19 | 1 | 1 carb, 1 fat |
| ✔Snackwell's, Caramel Delights | 1 | 70 | 2 | 26 | <1 | 0 | 35 | 1 | 0 | 13 | 1 | 1 carb |
| ✔Sweet Crispers Chocolate | 18 | 130 | 3 | 21 | <1 | 0 | 130 | 2 | 1 | 25 | 1 1/2 | 1 1/2 carb, 1 fat |
| Teddy Grahams, All Varieties (Avg) | 24 | 130 | 4 | 28 | 1 | 0 | 160 | 2 | 1 | 23 | 1 1/2 | 1 1/2 carb, 1 fat |
| **Pepperidge Farm** | | | | | | | | | | | | |
| Beacon Hill Chocolate Chocolate Walnut | 1 | 120 | 7 | 53 | 2 | 65 | 65 | 2 | 1 | 14 | 1 | 1 carb, 1 fat |
| Chesapeake Chocolate Chunk Pecan | 1 | 120 | 7 | 53 | 2 | 5 | 60 | 1 | 1 | 14 | 1 | 1 carb, 1 fat |
| ✔Distinctive Bordeaux Cookies | 2 | 70 | 3 | 39 | 1 | 0 | 40 | 1 | NA | 11 | 1/2 | 1/2 carb, 1 fat |
| Distinctive Brussels | 2 | 110 | 5 | 41 | 2 | 0 | 65 | 1 | NA | 13 | 1 | 1 carb, 1 fat |
| Distinctive Brussels Mint Cookies | 2 | 130 | 7 | 48 | 2 | 0 | 40 | 1 | NA | 17 | 1 | 1 carb, 1 fat |
| Distinctive Chessman Cookies | 2 | 90 | 4 | 40 | 2 | 10 | 60 | 2 | NA | 12 | 1 | 1 carb, 1 fat |
| Distinctive Chocolate Walnut | 1 | 130 | 6 | 42 | 2 | 5 | 45 | 1 | NA | 11 | 1 | 1 carb, 1 fat |
| Distinctive Double Chocolate Milano | 2 | 150 | 8 | 48 | 3 | 10 | 45 | 2 | NA | 18 | 1 | 1 carb, 2 fat |
| Distinctive Geneva Cookies | 2 | 130 | 6 | 42 | 2 | 5 | 50 | 1 | NA | 14 | 1 | 1 carb, 1 fat |

| | | | | | | | | | | | | |
|---|---|---|---|---|---|---|---|---|---|---|---|---|
| Distinctive Hazelnut Milano | 2 | 130 | 8 | 55 | 2 | 5 | 30 | 2 | NA | 15 | 1 | 1 carb, 2 fat |
| Distinctive Lido Cookies | 2 | 90 | 5 | 50 | 1 | 5 | 30 | 1 | NA | 10 | 1/2 | 1/2 carb, 1 fat |
| Distinctive Milano Cookies | 2 | 120 | 6 | 45 | 2 | 5 | 45 | 1 | NA | 15 | 1 | 1 carb, 1 fat |
| Distinctive Milk Chocolate Macadamia | 1 | 130 | 7 | 48 | 2 | 10 | 45 | 1 | NA | 16 | 1 | 1 carb, 1 fat |
| Distinctive Mint Milano | 2 | 150 | 7 | 42 | 2 | 5 | 60 | 1 | NA | 17 | 1 | 1 carb, 1 fat |
| Distinctive Orange Milano Cookies | 2 | 150 | 7 | 42 | 2 | 5 | 60 | 1 | NA | 17 | 1 | 1 carb, 1 fat |
| Milk Chocolate Milano Distinctive Cookies | 3 | 170 | 9 | 48 | 4 | 10 | 110 | 2 | <1 | 21 | 1 1/2 | 1 1/2 carb, 2 fat |
| Mini Chocolate Chip Cookies | 4 | 150 | 8 | 48 | 3 | 10 | 70 | 0 | 0 | 20 | 1 | 1 carb, 2 fat |
| Nantucket Chocolate Chunk | 1 | 120 | 6 | 45 | 2 | 5 | 60 | 1 | 1 | 15 | 1 | 1 carb, 1 fat |
| Oatmeal Raisin | 2 | 110 | 5 | 41 | 2 | 10 | 115 | 1 | NA | 15 | 1 | 1 carb, 1 fat |
| ✔ Old Fashioned Chocolate Chip | 2 | 100 | 5 | 45 | 2 | 5 | 45 | 1 | NA | 12 | 1 | 1 carb, 1 fat |
| Old Fashioned Gingerman Cookies | 2 | 70 | 3 | 39 | 0 | 5 | 30 | 1 | NA | 10 | 1/2 | 1/2 carb, 1 fat |
| Old Fashioned Lemon Nut Crunch Cookies | 2 | 110 | 7 | 57 | 2 | 5 | 50 | 1 | NA | 13 | 1 | 1 carb, 1 fat |
| ✔ Old Fashioned Molasses Crisps | 2 | 70 | 3 | 39 | 0 | 0 | 50 | 1 | NA | 8 | 1/2 | 1/2 carb, 1 fat |
| Old Fashioned Oatmeal Raisin | 2 | 90 | 5 | 50 | 1 | 5 | 80 | 1 | NA | 13 | 1 | 1 carb, 1 fat |
| Old Fashioned Pecan Shortbread | 1 | 70 | 5 | 64 | 2 | 10 | 55 | 1 | NA | 7 | 1/2 | 1/2 carb, 1 fat |
| Old Fashioned Sugar Cookie | 2 | 100 | 5 | 45 | 2 | 10 | 55 | 1 | NA | 13 | 1 | 1 carb, 1 fat |
| Sausalito Milk Chocolate Macadamia | 1 | 120 | 7 | 53 | 2 | 5 | 65 | 1 | NA | 14 | 1 | 1 carb, 1 fat |
| Soft Baked Chocolate Chunk | 1 | 130 | 6 | 42 | 2 | 10 | 45 | 2 | NA | 17 | 1 | 1 carb, 1 fat |

✔ = Best Bet; NA = Not Available; Carb. Ch. = Carbohydrate Choices

| Cookies *(Continued)* | Serving Size | Cal. | Fat (g) | % Cal. Fat | Sat. Fat (g) | Chol. (mg) | Sod. (mg) | Pro. (g) | Fiber (g) | Carb. (g) | Carb. Ch. | Servings/Exchanges |
|---|---|---|---|---|---|---|---|---|---|---|---|---|
| ✔Wholesome Choice Cookie Raspberry Tart | 1 | 60 | 1 | 15 | 1 | 0 | 35 | 1 | NA | 11 | 1 | 1 carb |
| **Sunshine** | | | | | | | | | | | | |
| Animal Crackers | 14 | 140 | 4 | 26 | 1 | 0 | 125 | 2 | <1 | 24 | 1 1/2 | 1 1/2 carb, 1 fat |
| Country Style Oatmeal | 2 | 120 | 5 | 38 | 1 | 0 | 115 | 2 | <1 | 17 | 1 | 1 carb, 1 fat |
| Ginger Snaps | 7 | 130 | 5 | 35 | 1 | 0 | 150 | 2 | <1 | 22 | 1 1/2 | 1 1/2 carb, 1 fat |
| Hydrox Reduced Fat Sandwich Cookies | 3 | 140 | 5 | 32 | 2 | 0 | 150 | 2 | 1 | 23 | 1 1/2 | 1 1/2 carb, 1 fat |
| Hydrox Sandwich Cookies | 3 | 150 | 7 | 42 | 2 | 0 | 125 | 2 | 1 | 21 | 1 1/2 | 1 1/2 carb, 1 fat |
| Lemon Coolers | 5 | 140 | 6 | 39 | 2 | 0 | 100 | 1 | <1 | 21 | 1 1/2 | 1 1/2 carb, 1 fat |
| Vanilla Sugar Wafers | 3 | 130 | 6 | 42 | 2 | 0 | 20 | 1 | <1 | 18 | 1 | 1 carb, 1 fat |
| Vanilla Wafers | 7 | 150 | 7 | 42 | 2 | 3 | 110 | 2 | <1 | 21 | 1 1/2 | 1 1/2 carb, 1 fat |
| Vienna Fingers | 2 | 140 | 6 | 39 | 2 | 0 | 105 | 2 | <1 | 21 | 1 1/2 | 1 1/2 carb, 1 fat |
| Vienna Fingers 25% Reduced Fat | 2 | 130 | 5 | 35 | 1 | 0 | 105 | 1 | <1 | 22 | 1 1/2 | 1 1/2 carb, 1 fat |
| **Weight Watchers** | | | | | | | | | | | | |
| ✔Chocolate Chip | 2 | 90 | 2 | 20 | 1 | 0 | 65 | 1 | NA | 18 | 1 | 1 carb |
| ✔Chocolate Cookie | 3 | 80 | 3 | 34 | 1 | 0 | 70 | 1 | NA | 13 | 1 | 1 carb, 1 fat |
| ✔Chocolate Sandwich Cookies | 2 | 90 | 3 | 30 | 1 | 0 | 90 | 1 | NA | 15 | 1 | 1 carb, 1 fat |
| ✔Oatmeal Raisin Cookie | 2 | 90 | 1 | 10 | NA | 0 | 75 | 1 | NA | 20 | 1 | 1 carb |
| ✔Raspberry Fruit Cookie | 2 | 80 | 1 | 11 | NA | 0 | 45 | 1 | NA | 22 | 1 1/2 | 1 1/2 carb |

| Item | Serving | | | | | | | | | | | |
|---|---|---|---|---|---|---|---|---|---|---|---|---|
| ✔Vanilla Sandwich Cookie | 2 | 90 | 3 | 30 | 1 | 0 | 50 | 1 | NA | 15 | 1 | 1 carb, 1 fat |

## COOKING SPRAY

**(Generic)**

| Item | Serving | | | | | | | | | | | |
|---|---|---|---|---|---|---|---|---|---|---|---|---|
| ✔All Varieties, All Brands | 1 spray | 0 | 0 | 0 | 0 | 0 | 0 | 0 | 0 | 0 | 0 | free |

## CORNBREAD MIX (AS PREPARED)

### Gold Medal/General Mills

| Item | Serving | | | | | | | | | | | |
|---|---|---|---|---|---|---|---|---|---|---|---|---|
| Corn Bread Muffin Mix | 1 | 140 | 4 | 26 | 1 | 5 | 290 | 2 | <1 | 25 | 1 1/2 | 1 1/2 strch, 1 fat |
| ✔Honey Cornbread Mix | 1 slice | 140 | 3 | 19 | 1 | 10 | 290 | 2 | 0 | 26 | 2 | 2 strch, 1 fat |

## CORNUTS

**Cornuts**

| Item | Serving | | | | | | | | | | | |
|---|---|---|---|---|---|---|---|---|---|---|---|---|
| All Flavors (Avg) | 1 oz | 130 | 5 | 35 | 1 | 0 | 210 | 3 | 2 | 20 | 1 | 1 strch, 1 fat |

## COTTAGE CHEESE

**(Generic)**

| Item | Serving | | | | | | | | | | | |
|---|---|---|---|---|---|---|---|---|---|---|---|---|
| ✔2% Reduced Fat Cottage Cheese | 1/4 cup | 50 | 1 | 18 | <1 | 5 | 227 | 8 | 0 | 2 | 0 | 1 very lean meat |
| ✔4.5% Cottage Cheese | 1/4 cup | 54 | 2 | 33 | 2 | 8 | 213 | 7 | 1 | 0 | 1 | 1 lean meat |
| ✔Dry Cottage Cheese | 1/4 cup | 31 | <1 | 29 | <1 | 2 | 5 | 6 | 0 | <1 | 0 | 1 very lean meat |
| ✔Non-Fat Cottage Cheese, All Varieties (Avg) | 1/4 cup | 35 | 0 | 0 | 0 | 5 | 210 | 7 | 0 | 3 | 0 | 1 very lean meat |

✔ = Best Bet; NA = Not Available; Carb. Ch. = Carbohydrate Choices

| Cottage Cheese (*Continued*) | Serving Size | Cal. | Fat (g) | % Cal. Fat | Sat. Fat (g) | Chol. (mg) | Sod. (mg) | Pro. (g) | Fiber (g) | Carb. (g) | Carb. Ch. | Servings/Exchanges |
|---|---|---|---|---|---|---|---|---|---|---|---|---|
| **Knudsen** | | | | | | | | | | | | |
| ✔Cottage Cheese Doubles, All Varieties (Avg) | 1 | 140 | 3 | 19 | 2 | 15 | 390 | 12 | <1 | 17 | 1 | 1 fruit, 1 lean meat |
| ✔Cottage Cheese On The Go! 2% Lowfat | 4 oz | 90 | 2 | 20 | 2 | 15 | 370 | 13 | 0 | 5 | 0 | 2 very lean meat |
| ✔Cottage Cheese On The Go!, 2% Lowfat w/Pineapple | 4 oz | 110 | 2 | 16 | 1 | 10 | 300 | 10 | 0 | 13 | 1 | 1 fruit, 1 lean meat |
| ✔Cottage Cheese, 1 1/2% Lowfat w/Pineapple | 1/2 cup | 120 | 2 | 15 | 1 | 10 | 330 | 11 | 0 | 14 | 1 | 1 fruit, 2 very lean meat |
| ✔Knudson On The Go! 1.5% Cottage Cheese/Fruit, All Flavors (Avg) | 4 oz | 110 | 2 | 16 | 1 | 10 | 300 | 10 | 0 | 13 | 1 | 1 fruit, 1 lean meat |
| ✔Knudson On The Go! 2% Cottage Cheese | 4 oz | 90 | 2 | 20 | 2 | 15 | 370 | 13 | 0 | 5 | 0 | 2 very lean meat |
| ✔Knudson On The Go! Fat-Free Cottage Cheese | 4 oz | 70 | 0 | 0 | 0 | 5 | 350 | 13 | 0 | 4 | 0 | 2 very lean meat |
| **Light N' Lively** | | | | | | | | | | | | |
| ✔1% Cottage Cheese, Garden Salad | 1/2 cup | 80 | 2 | 23 | 1 | 10 | 380 | 12 | 0 | 5 | 0 | 2 very lean meat |
| ✔1% Cottage Cheese, Peach & Pineapple | 1/2 cup | 110 | 1 | 8 | <1 | 10 | 340 | 11 | 0 | 15 | 1 | 1 fruit, 2 very lean meat |

# CRACKERS

| Food | Amount | Cal. | Fat (g) | % Cal. Fat | Sat. Fat (g) | Chol. (mg) | Sod. (mg) | Prot. (g) | Fiber (g) | Carb. (g) | Carb. Ch. | Exchanges |
|---|---|---|---|---|---|---|---|---|---|---|---|---|
| **Estee** | | | | | | | | | | | | |
| ✔Cracked Pepper Crackers | 18 | 120 | 2 | 15 | 0 | 0 | 200 | 3 | 1 | 24 | 1 1/2 | 1 1/2 strch |
| ✔Golden Crackers | 10 | 130 | 2 | 14 | 0 | 0 | 200 | 3 | 1 | 28 | 2 | 2 strch |
| ✔Graham Crackers, Sugar Free, All Varieties (Avg) | 2 | 90 | 2 | 20 | 0 | 0 | 105 | 3 | 2 | 21 | 1 1/2 | 1 1/2 carb |
| ✔Wheat Crackers | 17 | 100 | 2 | 18 | 0 | 0 | 200 | 3 | 2 | 18 | 1 | 1 strch |
| **Health Valley** | | | | | | | | | | | | |
| ✔Fat-Free Amaranth Graham Crackers | 8 | 100 | 0 | 0 | 0 | 0 | 30 | 4 | 3 | 23 | 1 1/2 | 1 1/2 strch |
| ✔Fat-Free Fire Crackers, All Varieties (Avg) | 6 | 50 | 0 | 0 | 0 | 0 | 80 | 2 | 2 | 11 | 1 | 1 strch |
| ✔Fat-Free Healthy Pizza Crackers, Garlic/Cheese | 6 | 50 | 0 | 0 | 0 | 0 | 140 | 2 | 2 | 11 | 1 | 1 strch |
| ✔Fat-Free Oat Bran Graham Crackers | 8 | 100 | 0 | 0 | 0 | 0 | 30 | 4 | 3 | 23 | 1 1/2 | 1 1/2 strch |
| ✔Fat-Free Whole-Wheat Cracker, All Varieties (Avg) | 5 | 50 | 0 | 0 | 0 | 0 | 80 | 2 | 2 | 11 | 1 | 1 strch |
| **Keebler** | | | | | | | | | | | | |
| ✔33% Reduced-Fat Club Crackers | 5 | 70 | 2 | 26 | 0 | 0 | 200 | 1 | 0 | 12 | 1 | 1 strch |
| Cheese & Peanut Butter Cracker Sandwiches | 1 pkg | 190 | 9 | 43 | 2 | <5 | 420 | 6 | <1 | 22 | 1 1/2 | 1 1/2 strch, 2 fat |
| Chocolate Grahams | 8 | 130 | 4 | 28 | 1 | 0 | 115 | 2 | 0 | 23 | 1 1/2 | 1 1/2 carb, 1 fat |
| Club & Cheddar Cracker Sandwiches | 1 pkg | 190 | 11 | 52 | 3 | 10 | 320 | 3 | <1 | 20 | 1 | 1 strch, 2 fat |

✔= Best Bet; NA = Not Available; Carb. Ch. = Carbohydrate Choices

| Crackers (Continued) | Serving Size | Cal. | Fat (g) | % Cal. Fat | Sat. Fat (g) | Chol. (mg) | Sod. (mg) | Pro. (g) | Fiber (g) | Carb. (g) | Carb. Ch. | Servings/Exchanges |
|---|---|---|---|---|---|---|---|---|---|---|---|---|
| ✓Club 50% Reduced-Sodium Crackers | 4 | 70 | 3 | 39 | 1 | 0 | 80 | 1 | 0 | 9 | 1/2 | 1/2 strch, 1 fat |
| Honey Grahams | 8 | 140 | 5 | 32 | 1 | 0 | 170 | 2 | 0 | 23 | 1 1/2 | 1 1/2 carb, 1 fat |
| ✓Honey Grahams, Low-Fat | 9 | 120 | 2 | 15 | <1 | 0 | 210 | 2 | 1 | 25 | 1 1/2 | 1 1/2 carb |
| ✓Low-Fat Cinnamon Crisp | 8 | 110 | 2 | 16 | <1 | 0 | 160 | 2 | 1 | 23 | 1 1/2 | 1 1/2 strch |
| Munch'ems, Seasoned Original | 41 | 140 | 5 | 32 | 1 | 0 | 220 | 2 | 1 | 21 | 1 1/2 | 1 1/2 strch, 1 fat |
| ✓Original Club Partners Crackers | 4 | 70 | 3 | 39 | 1 | 0 | 160 | 1 | 0 | 9 | 1/2 | 1/2 strch, 1 fat |
| ✓Original Grahams | 8 | 130 | 3 | 21 | 1 | 0 | 135 | 2 | <1 | 23 | 1 1/2 | 1 1/2 carb, 1 fat |
| ✓Reduced-Fat Sesame Toasteds | 5 | 60 | 2 | 30 | 0 | 0 | 160 | 1 | <1 | 10 | 1/2 | 1/2 strch |
| ✓Snackin' Cinnamon Crisp Grahams | 21 | 130 | 3 | 21 | 1 | 0 | 210 | 2 | 1 | 23 | 1 1/2 | 1 1/2 carb, 1 fat |
| Snackin' Honey Grahams | 23 | 130 | 4 | 28 | 1 | 0 | 120 | 2 | <1 | 22 | 1 1/2 | 1 1/2 carb, 1 fat |
| Toast & Peanut Butter Cracker Sandwiches | 1 pkg | 190 | 9 | 43 | 2 | 30 | 300 | 5 | 1 | 23 | 1 1/2 | 1 1/2 strch, 2 fat |
| Toasteds Buttercrisps | 5 | 80 | 4 | 45 | 1 | 0 | 150 | 1 | 0 | 10 | 1/2 | 1/2 strch, 1 fat |
| ✓Toasteds Wheat Crackers | 5 | 80 | 3 | 34 | <1 | 0 | 160 | 1 | 0 | 11 | 1 | 1 strch, 1 fat |
| ✓Toasteds, Onion | 5 | 80 | 3 | 34 | <1 | 0 | 230 | 1 | 0 | 10 | 1/2 | 1/2 strch, 1 fat |
| Toasteds, Sesame | 5 | 80 | 4 | 45 | <1 | 0 | 160 | 1 | <1 | 10 | 1/2 | 1/2 strch, 1 fat |
| Town House 50% Reduced-Sodium Crackers | 5 | 80 | 5 | 56 | 1 | 0 | 75 | 1 | <1 | 10 | 1/2 | 1/2 strch, 1 fat |
| Town House Crackers | 5 | 80 | 5 | 56 | 1 | 0 | 150 | 1 | <1 | 9 | 1/2 | 1/2 strch, 1 fat |
| ✓Town House Reduced-Fat Crackers | 6 | 70 | 2 | 26 | <1 | 0 | 180 | 1 | <1 | 11 | 1 | 1 strch |

| | | | | | | | | | | | | |
|---|---|---|---|---|---|---|---|---|---|---|---|---|
| Wheat & Cheddar Cracker Sandwiches | 1 pkg | 180 | 10 | 50 | 3 | 5 | 300 | 2 | 0 | 17 | 1 | 1 strch, 2 fat |
| Wheatables, Original | 12 | 140 | 6 | 39 | 6 | 0 | 210 | 2 | 1 | 19 | 1 | 1 strch, 1 fat |
| Wheatables-33% Reduced Fat | 13 | 130 | 4 | 28 | 1 | 0 | 230 | 2 | 2 | 21 | 1 1/2 | 1 1/2 strch, 1 fat |
| ✔Zesta Crackers, Unsalted Tops | 5 | 70 | 2 | 26 | <1 | 0 | 90 | 1 | <1 | 10 | 1 | 1/2 strch |
| ✔Zesta Fat-Free Saltines | 5 | 50 | 0 | 0 | 0 | 0 | 150 | 1 | 0 | 11 | 1 | 1 strch |
| ✔Zesta Saltine Crackers, Original | 5 | 60 | 2 | 30 | <1 | 0 | 190 | 1 | <1 | 10 | 1 | 1 strch |
| ✔Zesta Saltine Crackers- 50% Reduced-Sodium | 5 | 70 | 2 | 26 | <1 | 0 | 95 | 1 | <1 | 11 | 1 | 1 strch |
| ✔Zesta Soup & Oyster Crackers | 45 | 70 | 3 | 39 | 1 | 0 | 220 | 1 | 0 | 9 | 1/2 | 1/2 strch, 1 fat |
| **Kraft** | | | | | | | | | | | | |
| Handi-Snacks, Cheez 'n Breadstick | 1 pkg | 120 | 6 | 45 | 3 | 15 | 320 | 4 | 0 | 12 | 1 | 1 strch, 1 fat |
| Handi-Snacks, Cheez 'n Crackers | 1 pkg | 110 | 7 | 57 | 3 | 15 | 300 | 3 | 0 | 9 | 1/2 | 1/2 strch, 1 fat |
| Handi-Snacks, Cheez 'n Pretzels | 1 pkg | 100 | 5 | 45 | 3 | 15 | 410 | 4 | <1 | 11 | 1 | 1 strch, 1 fat |
| Handi-Snacks, Mozzarella String Cheese | 1 pkg | 80 | 6 | 68 | 4 | 0 | 240 | 7 | 0 | 0 | 0 | 1 med-fat meat |
| Handi-Snacks, Nacho Stix'n Cheez | 1 | 110 | 6 | 49 | 3 | 15 | 320 | 4 | 0 | 11 | 1 | 1 strch, 1 fat |
| **Nabisco** | | | | | | | | | | | | |
| Air Crisps Wheat Thins | 24 | 130 | 5 | 35 | 1 | 0 | 290 | 2 | 1 | 21 | 1 1/2 | 1 1/2 strch, 1 fat |
| Better Cheddars | 22 | 150 | 8 | 48 | 2 | <5 | 290 | 4 | <1 | 17 | 1 | 1 strch, 1 fat |
| Better Cheddars, Reduced-Fat | 24 | 140 | 6 | 39 | 2 | <5 | 350 | 4 | <1 | 19 | 1 | 1 strch, 1 fat |

✔ = Best Bet; NA = Not Available; Carb. Ch. = Carbohydrate Choices

| Crackers (*Continued*) | Serving Size | Cal. | Fat (g) | % Cal. Fat | Sat. Fat (g) | Chol. (mg) | Sod. (mg) | Pro. (g) | Fiber (g) | Carb. (g) | Carb. Ch. | Servings/Exchanges |
|---|---|---|---|---|---|---|---|---|---|---|---|---|
| Cheese Nips | 27 | 140 | 6 | 39 | 2 | <5 | 350 | 3 | <1 | 19 | 1 | 1 strch, 1 fat |
| Cheese Nips Air Crisp | 32 | 130 | 4 | 28 | 1 | <5 | 300 | 3 | <1 | 21 | 1 1/2 | 1/2 strch, 1 fat |
| Chicken In A Biskit | 12 | 160 | 9 | 51 | 2 | 0 | 270 | 2 | <1 | 17 | 1 | 1 strch, 2 fat |
| Harvest Crisps-5 Grain | 13 | 130 | 4 | 28 | <1 | 0 | 270 | 3 | 1 | 23 | 1 1/2 | 1 1/2 strch, 1 fat |
| ✓Honey Maid Chocolate Graham Crackers | 8 | 120 | 3 | 23 | <1 | 0 | 170 | 2 | 1 | 22 | 1 1/2 | 1 1/2 carb, 1 fat |
| ✓Honey Maid Honey Graham Crackers | 8 | 120 | 3 | 23 | 0 | 0 | 180 | 2 | 1 | 22 | 1 1/2 | 1 1/2 carb, 1 fat |
| ✓Honey Maid Low-fat Cinnamon Graham Crackers | 8 | 110 | 2 | 16 | 0 | 0 | 170 | 2 | <1 | 23 | 1 1/2 | 1 1/2 strch |
| ✓Honey Maid Low-fat Graham Crackers | 8 | 110 | 2 | 16 | 0 | 0 | 200 | 2 | <1 | 23 | 1 1/2 | 1 1/2 carb |
| Original Ritz Air Crisps | 24 | 140 | 5 | 32 | 1 | 0 | 240 | 2 | <1 | 22 | 1 1/2 | 1 1/2 strch, 1 fat |
| ✓Premium Saltine Crackers | 5 | 60 | 2 | 30 | <1 | 0 | 180 | 1 | 0 | 10 | 1/2 | 1/2 strch |
| ✓Premium Saltine Crackers, Unsalted Tops | 5 | 60 | 2 | 30 | 0 | 0 | 105 | 1 | 0 | 10 | 1/2 | 1/2 strch |
| Reduced-Fat Cheese Nips | 31 | 130 | 4 | 28 | 1 | 0 | 310 | 3 | <1 | 21 | 1 1/2 | 1 1/2 strch, 1 fat |
| ✓Reduced-Fat Ritz Crackers | 5 | 70 | 2 | 26 | 0 | 0 | 140 | 1 | 0 | 11 | 1 | 1 strch |
| ✓Reduced-Fat Triscuits | 8 | 130 | 3 | 21 | <1 | 0 | 170 | 3 | 4 | 24 | 1 1/2 | 1 1/2 strch, 1 fat |
| Reduced-Fat Wheat Thins Crackers | 18 | 120 | 4 | 30 | <1 | 0 | 270 | 3 | 1 | 21 | 1 1/2 | 1 1/2 strch, 1 fat |
| Ritz Bitz Sandwiches w/Cheese | 14 | 170 | 10 | 53 | 3 | 5 | 300 | 3 | 0 | 17 | 1 | 1 strch, 2 fat |
| Ritz Bitz Sandwiches w/Peanut Butter | 14 | 150 | 8 | 48 | 2 | 0 | 200 | 3 | 1 | 18 | 1 | 1 strch, 2 fat |

| Food | | | | | | | | | | Carb. Ch. | Exchanges |
|---|---|---|---|---|---|---|---|---|---|---|---|
| Ritz Crackers | 5 | 80 | 4 | 45 | <1 | 10 | 135 | 1 | 0 | 10 | 1/2 | 1/2 strch, 1 fat |
| ✔Snackwell's French Onion Crackers | 28 | 130 | 3 | 21 | <1 | 0 | 270 | 2 | <1 | 23 | 1 1/2 | 1 1/2 strch, 1 fat |
| ✔Snackwell's, Fat-Free Cracked Pepper Crackers | 5 | 60 | 0 | 0 | 0 | 0 | 115 | 1 | 0 | 10 | 1/2 | 1 strch |
| ✔Snackwell's, Wheat Crackers | 5 | 70 | 0 | 0 | 0 | 0 | 150 | 1 | <1 | 11 | 1 | 1 strch |
| ✔Snackwell's, Zesty Cheese Crackers | 38 | 130 | 3 | 21 | <1 | 0 | 320 | 2 | <1 | 23 | 1 1/2 | 1 1/2 strch, 1 fat |
| Sociables | 7 | 80 | 4 | 45 | <1 | 0 | 150 | 1 | 0 | 9 | 1/2 | 1/2 strch, 1 fat |
| Swiss Cheese Crackers | 15 | 140 | 7 | 45 | 2 | 0 | 350 | 2 | <1 | 18 | 1 | 1 strch, 1 fat |
| Triscuit Thin Crisps | 15 | 130 | 5 | 35 | 1 | 0 | 170 | 3 | 3 | 21 | 1 1/2 | 1 1/2 strch, 1 fat |
| Triscuits | 7 | 140 | 5 | 32 | 1 | 0 | 170 | 3 | 4 | 22 | 1 1/2 | 1/2 strch, 1 fat |
| Twigs Snack Sticks | 15 | 150 | 7 | 42 | 2 | 0 | 310 | 2 | 1 | 17 | 1 | 1 strch, 1 fat |
| Vegetable Thins Crackers | 14 | 160 | 9 | 51 | 2 | 0 | 310 | 2 | 1 | 19 | 1 | 1 strch, 2 fat |
| Wheat Thins Crackers, Original | 16 | 140 | 6 | 39 | 1 | 0 | 260 | 2 | 1 | 19 | 1 | 1 strch, 1 fat |
| Wheatsworth Wheat Crackers | 5 | 80 | 4 | 45 | <1 | 0 | 170 | 2 | 1 | 10 | 1/2 | 1/2 strch, 1 fat |
| **Pepperidge Farm** | | | | | | | | | | | | |
| ✔Butter-Flavored Thins Crackers | 4 | 70 | 3 | 39 | 1 | 10 | 95 | 1 | 0 | 10 | 1/2 | 1/2 strch, 1 fat |
| Cracked Wheat Crackers | 3 | 105 | 4 | 34 | 2 | 0 | 225 | 2 | <1 | 14 | 1 | 1 strch, 1 fat |
| ✔Cracker Trio | 4 | 70 | 3 | 39 | 0 | 0 | 100 | 1 | 1 | 10 | 1/2 | 1/2 strch, 1 fat |
| Goldfish Crackers, All Flavors (Avg) | 55 | 145 | 6 | 37 | 2 | 5 | 230 | 3 | 1 | 19 | 1 | 1 strch, 1 fat |
| Goldfish Crackers, Cheddar, Low-Salt | 60 | 150 | 6 | 36 | 2 | 10 | 175 | 3 | <1 | 18 | 1 | 1 strch, 1 fat |

✔= Best Bet; NA = Not Available; Carb. Ch. = Carbohydrate Choices

| Crackers (*Continued*) | Serving Size | Cal. | Fat (g) | % Cal. Fat | Sat. Fat (g) | Chol. (mg) | Sod. (mg) | Pro. (g) | Fiber (g) | Carb. (g) | Carb. Ch. | Servings/Exchanges |
|---|---|---|---|---|---|---|---|---|---|---|---|---|
| Hearty Wheat, Distinctive | 3 | 80 | 4 | 45 | 0 | 0 | 90 | 2 | 1 | 10 | 1/2 | 1/2 strch, 1 fat |
| Assortment Crackers | | | | | | | | | | | | |
| Sesame Snack Sticks | 9 | 140 | 5 | 32 | 1 | 0 | 280 | 4 | 1 | 19 | 1 | 1 strch, 1 fat |
| **Ry Krisp** | | | | | | | | | | | | |
| ✔Seasoned Rye Crackers | 2 | 60 | 2 | 30 | 0 | 0 | 90 | 1 | 3 | 10 | 1/2 | 1/2 strch |
| ✔Sesame Crackers | 2 | 60 | 2 | 30 | 0 | 0 | 80 | 2 | 3 | 11 | 1 | 1 strch |
| **Sunshine** | | | | | | | | | | | | |
| Big Cheez It | 13 | 150 | 8 | 48 | 2 | 0 | 230 | 4 | <1 | 16 | 1 | 1 strch, 2 fat |
| Big Cheez It, Reduced-Fat | 15 | 140 | 5 | 32 | 1 | 0 | 280 | 4 | <1 | 20 | 1 | 1 strch, 1 fat |
| Cheez It Heads and Tails | 37 | 140 | 6 | 39 | 2 | 0 | 330 | 3 | 1 | 18 | 1 | 1 strch, 1 fat |
| Cheez It, Reduced-Fat | 29 | 140 | 5 | 32 | 1 | 0 | 280 | 4 | <1 | 20 | 1 | 1 strch, 1 fat |
| Cheez It, White Cheddar | 26 | 150 | 7 | 42 | 2 | <5 | 280 | 3 | <1 | 18 | 1 | 1 strch, 1 fat |
| Cheez Its, Original | 27 | 160 | 8 | 45 | 2 | 0 | 240 | 4 | <1 | 16 | 1 | 1 strch, 2 fat |
| Hi Ho Crackers | 4 | 70 | 4 | 51 | 1 | 0 | 130 | 1 | <1 | 8 | 1/2 | 1/2 strch, 1 fat |
| ✔Hi Ho, Reduced-Fat | 5 | 70 | 3 | 39 | <1 | 0 | 140 | 1 | <1 | 10 | 1/2 | 1/2 strch, 1 fat |
| ✔Krispy Saltines, Fat-Free | 5 | 50 | 0 | 0 | 0 | 0 | 150 | 1 | 0 | 11 | 1 | 1 strch |
| ✔Krispy Saltines, Original | 5 | 60 | 2 | 30 | 0 | 0 | 180 | 2 | <1 | 10 | 1/2 | 1/2 strch |

# CRANBERRY SAUCE

**(Generic)**

| Food | Serving | Cal. | Fat (g) | % Fat Cal. | Sat. Fat (g) | Chol. (mg) | Sod. (mg) | Prot. (g) | Carb. (g) | Carb. Ch. | Exchanges/Choices |
|------|---------|------|---------|-----------|------|------|------|------|------|------|------|
| ✔Cranberry Sauce-Canned | 1/4 cup | 105 | 0 | 0 | 0 | 0 | 20 | <1 | 27 | 2 | 2 fruit |

**Ocean Spray**

| Food | Serving | Cal. | Fat (g) | % Fat Cal. | Sat. Fat (g) | Chol. (mg) | Sod. (mg) | Prot. (g) | Carb. (g) | Carb. Ch. | Exchanges/Choices |
|------|---------|------|---------|-----------|------|------|------|------|------|------|------|
| ✔Whole Berry Cranberry Sauce | 1/4 cup | 110 | 0 | 0 | 0 | 0 | 35 | 0 | 28 | 2 | 2 carb |

# CREAM CHEESE

**Breakstone**

| Food | Serving | Cal. | Fat (g) | % Fat Cal. | Sat. Fat (g) | Chol. (mg) | Sod. (mg) | Prot. (g) | Carb. (g) | Carb. Ch. | Exchanges/Choices |
|------|---------|------|---------|-----------|------|------|------|------|------|------|------|
| Cream Cheese, Temp-Tee Whipped | 2 Tbsp | 80 | 8 | 90 | 5 | 25 | 70 | 2 | <1 | 0 | 2 fat |

**Kraft**

| Food | Serving | Cal. | Fat (g) | % Fat Cal. | Sat. Fat (g) | Chol. (mg) | Sod. (mg) | Prot. (g) | Carb. (g) | Carb. Ch. | Exchanges/Choices |
|------|---------|------|---------|-----------|------|------|------|------|------|------|------|
| ✔Cream Cheese, Philadelphia Fat-Free Brick | 1 oz | 30 | 0 | 0 | 0 | <5 | 140 | 4 | 2 | 0 | 1 very lean meat |
| Philadelphia Brick Cream Cheese | 1 oz | 100 | 10 | 90 | 6 | 30 | 90 | 2 | <1 | 0 | 2 fat |
| Philadelphia Brick Cream Cheese w/Chives | 1 oz | 90 | 9 | 100 | 6 | 25 | 135 | 2 | <1 | 0 | 2 fat |
| ✔Philadelphia Free Nonfat Cream Cheese | 2 Tbsp | 30 | 0 | 0 | 0 | <5 | 200 | 5 | 2 | 0 | 1 very lean meat |
| ✔Philadelphia Light Soft Cream Cheese | 2 Tbsp | 70 | 5 | 64 | 4 | 15 | 150 | 3 | 2 | 0 | 1 fat |
| Philadelphia Neufchatel Cheese | 1 oz | 70 | 6 | 77 | 4 | 20 | 120 | 3 | <1 | 0 | 1 med-fat meat |
| Philadelphia Soft Cream Cheese | 2 Tbsp | 100 | 10 | 90 | 7 | 30 | 100 | 2 | 1 | 0 | 2 fat |
| Philadelphia Soft Cream Cheese-Chive & Onion | 2 Tbsp | 110 | 10 | 82 | 7 | 30 | 135 | 1 | 2 | 0 | 2 fat |

✔= Best Bet; NA = Not Available; Carb. Ch. = Carbohydrate Choices

| Cream Cheese (*Continued*) | Serving Size | Cal. | Fat (g) | % Cal. Fat | Sat. Fat (g) | Chol. (mg) | Sod. (mg) | Pro. (g) | Fiber (g) | Carb. (g) | Carb. Ch. | Servings/Exchanges |
|---|---|---|---|---|---|---|---|---|---|---|---|---|
| Philadelphia Soft Cream Cheese–Herb & Garlic | 2 Tbsp | 110 | 10 | 82 | 7 | 25 | 180 | 1 | 0 | 2 | 0 | 2 fat |
| Philadelphia Soft Cream Cheese–Pineapple | 2 Tbsp | 100 | 9 | 90 | 6 | 25 | 100 | 1 | 0 | 4 | 0 | 2 fat |
| Philadelphia Soft Cream Cheese–Smoked Salmon | 2 Tbsp | 100 | 9 | 90 | 6 | 30 | 200 | 2 | 0 | 1 | 0 | 2 fat |
| Philadelphia Soft Cream Cheese–Strawberry | 2 Tbsp | 110 | 9 | 41 | 6 | 25 | 100 | 1 | 0 | 5 | 0 | 2 fat |
| Philadelphia Soft, Cheesecake | 2 Tbsp | 110 | 9 | 74 | 6 | 25 | 95 | 2 | 0 | 4 | 0 | 2 fat |
| Philadelphia Soft, Honey Nut | 2 Tbsp | 110 | 10 | 82 | 6 | 30 | 150 | 2 | 0 | 4 | 0 | 2 fat |
| Philadelphia Whipped Cream Cheese | 2 Tbsp | 70 | 7 | 90 | 7 | 25 | 85 | 1 | 0 | <1 | 0 | 1 fat |
| **Weight Watchers** | | | | | | | | | | | | |
| ✔Cream Cheese Substitute | 1 oz | 35 | 2 | 51 | 1 | NA | 40 | 3 | 0 | 1 | 0 | 1 fat |

## CROUTONS

### Fresh Gourmet

| | Serving Size | Cal. | Fat (g) | % Cal. Fat | Sat. Fat (g) | Chol. (mg) | Sod. (mg) | Pro. (g) | Fiber (g) | Carb. (g) | Carb. Ch. | Servings/Exchanges |
|---|---|---|---|---|---|---|---|---|---|---|---|---|
| ✔Fat-Free Seasoned Croutons, All Varieties (Avg) | 7 | 20 | 0 | 0 | 0 | 0 | 65 | 1 | 0 | 3 | 0 | free |
| ✔Seasoned Croutons, All Varieties (Avg) | 7 | 25 | 1 | 36 | 0 | 0 | 70 | 0 | 0 | 3 | 0 | free |

## Mrs. Cubbison's

| Products | Amount | Cal. | Fat (g) | % Cal. Fat | Sat. Fat (g) | Chol. (mg) | Sod. (mg) | Carb. (g) | Fiber (g) | Prot. (g) | Carb. Ch. | Exchanges |
|---|---|---|---|---|---|---|---|---|---|---|---|---|
| ✓ Fat-Free Seasoned Croutons, All Varieties (Avg) | 5 | 30 | 0 | 0 | 0 | 0 | 90 | 5 | 0 | 1 | 1/2 | 1/2 strch |
| ✓ Seasoned Croutons, All Varieties (Avg) | 5 | 30 | 1 | 30 | 0 | 0 | 100 | 5 | 0 | 0 | 1/2 | 1/2 strch |
| **Pepperidge Farm** | | | | | | | | | | | | |
| ✓ Caesar Homestyle Croutons | 1/2 oz | 71 | 3 | 38 | 0 | 0 | 183 | 8 | 0 | 2 | 1/2 | 1/2 strch, 1 fat |
| ✓ Cheddar & Romano Cheese Croutons | 1/2 oz | 61 | 2 | 30 | 0 | 0 | 193 | 8 | 0 | 2 | 1/2 | 1/2 strch |
| ✓ Cheese & Garlic Croutons | 1/2 oz | 71 | 3 | 38 | 0 | 0 | 162 | 8 | 0 | 4 | 1/2 | 1/2 strch, 1 fat |
| ✓ Italian Homestyle Croutons | 1/2 oz | 71 | 3 | 38 | 1 | 5 | 132 | 8 | 0 | 2 | 1/2 | 1/2 strch, 1 fat |
| ✓ Olive Oil & Garlic Homestyle Croutons | 1/2 oz | 61 | 2 | 30 | 0 | 0 | 162 | 10 | 0 | 2 | 1/2 | 1/2 strch |
| ✓ Onion & Garlic Croutons | 1/2 oz | 61 | 2 | 30 | 0 | 0 | 162 | 10 | 0 | 2 | 1/2 | 1/2 strch |
| ✓ Seasoned Croutons | 1/2 oz | 71 | 3 | 38 | 0 | 0 | 172 | 8 | 0 | 2 | 1/2 | 1/2 strch, 1 fat |
| ✓ Sourdough Cheese Homestyle Croutons | 1/2 oz | 61 | 2 | 30 | 0 | 5 | 162 | 8 | 0 | 2 | 1/2 | 1/2 strch |
| **Toastettes** | | | | | | | | | | | | |
| ✓ Gourmet Round Croutons, All Varieties (Avg) | 10 | 25 | 1 | 36 | 0 | 0 | 55 | 3 | 0 | 0 | 0 | free |

## DESSERT BAR MIX (AS PREPARED)

| Products | Amount | Cal. | Fat (g) | % Cal. Fat | Sat. Fat (g) | Chol. (mg) | Sod. (mg) | Carb. (g) | Fiber (g) | Prot. (g) | Carb. Ch. | Exchanges |
|---|---|---|---|---|---|---|---|---|---|---|---|---|
| **Betty Crocker** | | | | | | | | | | | | |
| Date Bar Classic Dessert Mix | 1/12 pkg | 230 | 6 | 23 | 2 | 0 | 90 | 23 | 1 | 1 | 1 1/2 | 1 1/2 carb, 1 fat |

✓ = Best Bet; NA = Not Available; Carb. Ch. = Carbohydrate Choices

| Dessert Bar Mix (As Prepared) (Continued) | Serving Size | Cal. | Fat (g) | % Cal. Fat | Sat. Fat (g) | Chol. (mg) | Sod. (mg) | Pro. (g) | Fiber (g) | Carb. (g) | Carb. Ch. | Servings/Exchanges |
|---|---|---|---|---|---|---|---|---|---|---|---|---|
| Supreme Chocolate Peanut Butter Bars | 1 bar | 200 | 9 | 41 | 3 | 20 | 190 | 3 | 0 | 26 | 2 | 2 carb, 2 fat |
| Supreme Easy Layer Dessert Bar | 1 bar | 140 | 6 | 39 | 3 | 0 | 105 | 1 | 0 | 21 | 1 1/2 | 1 1/2 carb, 1 fat |
| Supreme Hershey Cookie Bar | 1 bar | 150 | 6 | 36 | 2 | 15 | 110 | 2 | 0 | 21 | 1 1/2 | 1 1/2 carb, 1 fat |
| Supreme Sunkist Lemon Bar | 1 bar | 140 | 5 | 32 | 1 | 40 | 90 | 2 | 0 | 24 | 1 1/2 | 1 1/2 carb, 1 fat |
| **Pillsbury** | | | | | | | | | | | | |
| Fudge Swirl Cookie Deluxe Bar Mixes | 1/20 recipe | 180 | 8 | 40 | 2 | 10 | 110 | 1 | <1 | 25 | 1 1/2 | 1 1/2 carb, 2 fat |
| Lemon Cheesecake Deluxe Bar Mixes | 1/24 recipe | 190 | 10 | 47 | 3 | 25 | 105 | 2 | 0 | 22 | 1 1/2 | 1 1/2 carb, 2 fat |
| **DESSERT MIX (AS PREPARED)** | | | | | | | | | | | | |
| **Jell-O** | | | | | | | | | | | | |
| No-Bake Cherry Cheesecake | 1/8 recipe | 340 | 12 | 32 | 5 | 5 | 400 | 5 | <1 | 52 | 3 1/2 | 3 1/2 carb, 2 fat |
| No-Bake Chocolate Silk Pie | 1/8 recipe | 320 | 16 | 45 | 6 | 5 | 490 | 5 | <1 | 37 | 2 1/2 | 2 1/2 carb, 3 fat |
| No-Bake Double Layer Lemon | 1/8 recipe | 260 | 12 | 42 | 4 | <5 | 370 | 4 | <1 | 36 | 2 1/2 | 2 1/2 carb, 2 fat |
| **DESSERTS, INDIVIDUAL (FROZEN)** | | | | | | | | | | | | |
| **Weight Watchers** | | | | | | | | | | | | |
| Boston Cream Pie | 1 slice | 160 | 4 | 23 | 1 | 5 | 260 | 3 | NA | 34 | 2 | 2 carb, 1 fat |
| Chocolate Eclair | 1 | 150 | 4 | 24 | 2 | 15 | 110 | 3 | 1 | 26 | 2 | 2 carb, 1 fat |
| Smart Ones New York Style Cheesecake | 1 | 150 | 5 | 30 | 3 | 15 | 140 | 6 | 1 | 21 | 1 1/2 | 1 1/2 carb, 1 fat |

| | | | | | | | | | | | | |
|---|---|---|---|---|---|---|---|---|---|---|---|---|
| Smart Ones, Chocolate Chip Cookie Dough Sundae | 1 | 190 | 5 | 24 | 2 | 5 | 120 | 3 | 1 | 35 | 2 | 2 carb, 1 fat |

## DIPS

### Breakstone

| | | | | | | | | | | | | |
|---|---|---|---|---|---|---|---|---|---|---|---|---|
| ✔Fat-Free French Onion Dip | 2 Tbsp | 25 | 0 | 0 | 0 | <5 | 260 | 2 | 0 | 4 | 0 | free |
| ✔Fat-Free Ranch Dip | 2 Tbsp | 25 | 0 | 0 | 0 | <5 | 330 | 2 | 0 | 4 | 0 | free |
| Sour Cream Dip, Bacon & Onion | 2 Tbsp | 60 | 5 | 75 | 3 | 20 | 180 | 2 | 0 | 2 | 0 | 1 fat |
| Sour Cream Dip, French Onion | 2 Tbsp | 50 | 5 | 90 | 3 | 20 | 160 | 1 | 0 | 2 | 0 | 1 fat |
| Sour Cream Dip, Toasted Onion | 2 Tbsp | 50 | 5 | 90 | 3 | 20 | 170 | 1 | 0 | 2 | 0 | 1 fat |

### Cheez Whiz

| | | | | | | | | | | | | |
|---|---|---|---|---|---|---|---|---|---|---|---|---|
| Cheese & Salsa Dip, All Varieties | 2 Tbsp | 100 | 8 | 72 | 5 | 20 | 490 | 3 | 0 | 3 | 0 | 2 fat |

### Eagle

| | | | | | | | | | | | | |
|---|---|---|---|---|---|---|---|---|---|---|---|---|
| ✔Black Bean Dip | 2 Tbsp | 35 | 1 | 26 | 0 | 0 | 220 | 2 | 1 | 5 | 1/2 | 1/2 carb |
| ✔Cheese & Salsa Dip | 2 Tbsp | 40 | 3 | 68 | 1 | 5 | 300 | 1 | 0 | 3 | 0 | 1 fat |

### Frito-Lay

| | | | | | | | | | | | | |
|---|---|---|---|---|---|---|---|---|---|---|---|---|
| French Onion Dip | 2 Tbsp | 60 | 5 | 75 | 3 | 15 | 230 | 1 | 0 | 4 | 0 | 1 fat |
| ✔Fritos Bean Dip | 2 Tbsp | 40 | 1 | 23 | <1 | 0 | 140 | 2 | 0 | 6 | 1/2 | 1/2 strch |
| ✔Fritos Chili Cheese | 2 Tbsp | 45 | 3 | 60 | 1 | <5 | 310 | 1 | 0 | 3 | 0 | 1 fat |
| ✔Fritos Hot Bean Dip | 2 Tbsp | 40 | 1 | 23 | 0 | 0 | 170 | 2 | 1 | 5 | 1/2 | 1/2 carb |

✔ = Best Bet; NA = Not Available; Carb. Ch. = Carbohydrate Choices

| Dips (*Continued*) | Serving Size | Cal. | Fat (g) | % Cal. Fat | Sat. Fat (g) | Chol. (mg) | Sod. (mg) | Pro. (g) | Fiber (g) | Carb. (g) | Carb. Ch. | Servings/Exchanges |
|---|---|---|---|---|---|---|---|---|---|---|---|---|
| Jalapeno & Cheddar Cheese Dip | 2 Tbsp | 50 | 4 | 72 | 1 | 5 | 300 | 1 | 0 | 4 | 0 | 1 fat |
| Mild Cheddar Cheese Dip | 2 Tbsp | 60 | 4 | 60 | 2 | 5 | 330 | 1 | 0 | 3 | 0 | 1 fat |
| **Frito-Lay/Tostitos** | | | | | | | | | | | | |
| Beef Fiesta Nacho Topping | 1/4 cup | 120 | 8 | 60 | 3 | 10 | 500 | 4 | <2 | 6 | 1/2 | 1/2 carb, 2 fat |
| Chicken Quesadilla Topping | 1/4 cup | 90 | 6 | 60 | 2 | 10 | 600 | 4 | <2 | 6 | 1/2 | 1/2 carb, 1 fat |
| Low-Fat Salsa Con Queso | 1/4 cup | 70 | 3 | 39 | 2 | <10 | 560 | 2 | <2 | 8 | 1/2 | 1/2 carb, 1 fat |
| Salsa Conqueso | 1/4 cup | 80 | 5 | 56 | 2 | <10 | 560 | 2 | <2 | 10 | 1/2 | 1/2 carb, 1 fat |
| **Guiltless Gourmet** | | | | | | | | | | | | |
| ✔Nonfat Black Bean Dip | 2 Tbsp | 35 | 0 | 0 | 0 | 0 | 125 | 2 | 1 | 6 | 1/2 | 1/2 carb |
| ✔Nonfat Cheddar Cheese Queso Dip | 1 oz | 20 | 0 | 0 | 0 | 0 | 150 | 1 | 0 | 5 | 1/2 | 1/2 carb |
| ✔Nonfat Pinto Bean Dip | 2 Tbsp | 35 | 0 | 0 | 0 | 0 | 100 | 2 | 2 | 6 | 1/2 | 1/2 carb |
| **IMO** | | | | | | | | | | | | |
| Avocado Dip | 2 Tbsp | 110 | 11 | 90 | 3 | <5 | 210 | 1 | 0 | 2 | 0 | 2 fat |
| ✔Fat-Free French Onion | 2 Tbsp | 30 | 0 | 0 | 0 | 0 | 290 | 2 | 0 | 4 | 0 | free |
| French Onion Dip | 2 Tbsp | 70 | 6 | 77 | 3 | <5 | 160 | 1 | 0 | 2 | 0 | 1 fat |
| Green Chili Dip | 2 Tbsp | 70 | 6 | 77 | 3 | <5 | 180 | <1 | 0 | 1 | 0 | 1 fat |
| Ranch Dip | 2 Tbsp | 110 | 11 | 90 | 2 | 10 | 160 | 1 | 0 | 2 | 0 | 2 fat |
| Zesty Guacamole Dip | 2 Tbsp | 90 | 9 | 90 | 3 | <5 | 190 | 1 | 0 | 2 | 0 | 2 fat |

## Knudsen

| | Amount | | | | | | | | | | Carb. Ch. | |
|---|---|---|---|---|---|---|---|---|---|---|---|---|
| ✔ Fat-Free Creamy Salsa Dip | 2 Tbsp | 20 | 0 | | 0 | 0 | <5 | 240 | 1 | 0 | 3 | 0 | free |
| ✔ Fat-Free French Onion Dip | 2 Tbsp | 25 | 0 | | 0 | 0 | <5 | 260 | 2 | 0 | 4 | 0 | free |
| ✔ Fat-Free Ranch Dip | 2 Tbsp | 25 | 0 | | 0 | 0 | <5 | 330 | 2 | 0 | 4 | 0 | free |

## Kraft

| | Amount | | | | | | | | | | Carb. Ch. | |
|---|---|---|---|---|---|---|---|---|---|---|---|---|
| Avocado Dip | 2 Tbsp | 60 | 4 | 0 | 60 | 3 | 0 | 240 | 1 | 0 | 4 | 0 | 1 fat |
| Bacon & Horseradish Dip | 2 Tbsp | 60 | 5 | 0 | 75 | 3 | 0 | 220 | 1 | 0 | 3 | 0 | 1 fat |
| Clam Dip | 2 Tbsp | 60 | 4 | 0 | 60 | 3 | 0 | 250 | 1 | 0 | 3 | 0 | 1 fat |
| ✔ Fat-Free French Onion Dip | 2 Tbsp | 25 | 0 | 0 | 0 | 0 | <5 | 330 | 2 | 0 | 4 | 0 | free |
| ✔ Fat-Free Ranch Dip | 2 Tbsp | 25 | 0 | 0 | 0 | 0 | <5 | 330 | 2 | 0 | 4 | 0 | free |
| French Onion Dip | 2 Tbsp | 60 | 4 | 0 | 60 | 3 | 0 | 230 | 1 | 0 | 4 | 0 | 1 fat |
| Green Onion Dip | 2 Tbsp | 60 | 4 | 0 | 60 | 3 | 0 | 190 | 1 | 0 | 4 | 0 | 1 fat |
| Premium Bacon & Horseradish Dip | 2 Tbsp | 60 | 5 | 0 | 75 | 3 | 15 | 240 | 2 | 0 | 2 | 0 | 1 fat |
| Premium Bacon & Onion Dip | 2 Tbsp | 60 | 5 | 0 | 75 | 3 | 20 | 180 | 2 | 0 | 2 | 0 | 1 fat |
| Premium Clam Dip | 2 Tbsp | 50 | 4 | 0 | 72 | 3 | 20 | 180 | 1 | 0 | 1 | 0 | 1 fat |
| Premium Creamy Onion Dip | 2 Tbsp | 45 | 4 | 0 | 80 | 3 | 15 | 160 | 1 | 0 | 2 | 0 | 1 fat |
| Premium French Onion Dip | 2 Tbsp | 45 | 4 | 0 | 80 | 3 | 15 | 160 | <1 | 0 | 2 | 0 | 1 fat |
| Premium Jalapeno Cheese Dip | 2 Tbsp | 60 | 4 | 0 | 60 | 3 | 0 | 260 | 1 | 0 | 3 | 0 | 1 fat |
| Ranch Dip | 2 Tbsp | 60 | 5 | 0 | 75 | 3 | 0 | 210 | 1 | 0 | 3 | 0 | 1 fat |

✔= Best Bet; NA = Not Available; Carb. Ch. = Carbohydrate Choices

| Dips (*Continued*) | Serving Size | Cal. | Fat (g) | % Cal. Fat | Sat. Fat (g) | Chol. (mg) | Sod. (mg) | Pro. (g) | Fiber (g) | Carb. (g) | Carb. Ch. | Servings/Exchanges |
|---|---|---|---|---|---|---|---|---|---|---|---|---|
| **Marie's** | | | | | | | | | | | | |
| Bacon Ranch Dip | 2 Tbsp | 150 | 16 | 96 | 2 | 15 | 200 | 1 | 0 | 3 | 0 | 3 fat |
| Fiesta Bean Dip | 2 Tbsp | 140 | 14 | 90 | 2 | 10 | 160 | <1 | <1 | 2 | 0 | 3 fat |
| Homestyle Ranch Dip | 2 Tbsp | 150 | 15 | 90 | 2 | 15 | 140 | 0 | 0 | 3 | 0 | 3 fat |
| Parmesan Garlic Dip | 2 Tbsp | 140 | 14 | 90 | 2 | 10 | 140 | <1 | <1 | 2 | 0 | 3 fat |
| Spinach Dip | 2 Tbsp | 140 | 14 | 90 | 2 | 10 | 200 | 0 | 0 | 3 | 0 | 3 fat |
| Sun Dried Tomato Dip | 2 Tbsp | 140 | 14 | 90 | 2 | 15 | 135 | <1 | <1 | 2 | 0 | 3 fat |
| **Marzetti** | | | | | | | | | | | | |
| Vegetable Dip | 1 Tbsp | 88 | 10 | 100 | NA | 2 | 120 | 0 | 0 | 1 | 0 | 2 fat |
| **Old El Paso** | | | | | | | | | | | | |
| ✔Black Bean Dip | 2 Tbsp | 25 | 0 | 0 | 0 | 0 | 280 | 1 | 1 | 5 | 0 | free |
| ✔Cheese 'n Salsa Dip-Mild/Medium | 2 Tbsp | 40 | 3 | 68 | 1 | <5 | 300 | <1 | 0 | 3 | 0 | 1 fat |
| ✔Jalapeno Dip | 2 Tbsp | 30 | 1 | 30 | 0 | <5 | 125 | 1 | 2 | 4 | 0 | 1 vegetable |
| ✔Low Fat Cheese 'n Salsa Dip | 2 Tbsp | 30 | 2 | 60 | 1 | 5 | 240 | 0 | 0 | 3 | 0 | 1 fat |
| **Orval Kent** | | | | | | | | | | | | |
| Pimento Spread | 2 Tbsp | 130 | 12 | 83 | 2 | 10 | 280 | 2 | 1 | 3 | 0 | 2 fat |
| **Poore Brothers** | | | | | | | | | | | | |
| ✔Sante Fe Black Bean Dip | 2 Tbsp | 20 | 0 | 0 | 0 | 0 | 410 | 1 | <1 | 4 | 0 | free |

| | Serving | Cal. | Fat (g) | % Cal. from Fat | Sat. Fat (g) | Chol. (mg) | Sod. (mg) | Prot. (g) | Fiber (g) | Carb. (g) | Carb. Ch. | Choices/Exch. |
|---|---|---|---|---|---|---|---|---|---|---|---|---|
| ✔Sour Cream & Jalapeno Dip | 2 Tbsp | 35 | 3 | 77 | 2 | 10 | 490 | 0 | 0 | 2 | 0 | 1 fat |
| **Taco Bell Home Originals** | | | | | | | | | | | | |
| ✔Fat-Free Black Bean Dip | 2 Tbsp | 30 | 0 | 0 | 0 | 0 | 220 | 2 | 2 | 6 | 1/2 | 1/2 strch |
| ✔Salsa con Queso, All Varieties (Avg) | 2 Tbsp | 45 | 3 | 60 | <1 | <5 | 270 | <1 | <1 | 5 | 0 | 1 fat |
| **DONUTS** | | | | | | | | | | | | |
| **Dolly Madison Bakery** | | | | | | | | | | | | |
| Plain Donut | 1 | 170 | 10 | 53 | 6 | 10 | 210 | 2 | <1 | 18 | 1 | 1 carb, 2 fat |
| **Entenmann's** | | | | | | | | | | | | |
| Glazed 50% Less Fat Donuts | 1 | 190 | 5 | 24 | 2 | 15 | 240 | 2 | <1 | 34 | 2 | 2 carb, 1 fat |
| Glazed Chocolate POPEMS | 4 | 260 | 15 | 52 | 4 | 10 | 150 | 2 | 2 | 32 | 2 | 2 carb, 3 fat |
| Glazed POPEMS | 4 | 240 | 12 | 45 | 3 | 15 | 230 | 2 | 1 | 31 | 2 | 2 carb, 2 fat |
| Rich Frosted Popettes Donuts | 3 | 280 | 18 | 58 | 5 | 15 | 220 | 3 | 1 | 26 | 2 | 2 carb |
| Rich Frosted Variety Donuts | 1 | 310 | 19 | 55 | 5 | 15 | 170 | 3 | 2 | 34 | 2 | 2 carb, 4 fat |
| Soft Powdered Cinnamon Popettes Donuts | 3 | 240 | 15 | 56 | 4 | 15 | 220 | 2 | <1 | 24 | 1 1/2 | 1 1/2 carb, 3 fat |
| **Hostess** | | | | | | | | | | | | |
| Crumb Donettes | 4 | 220 | 8 | 33 | 4 | 10 | 260 | 3 | 1 | 34 | 2 | 2 carb, 2 fat |
| Frosted Donettes | 3 | 230 | 14 | 55 | 9 | 15 | 210 | 2 | 0 | 24 | 1 1/2 | 1 1/2 carb, 2 fat |
| Powdered Donettes | 4 | 250 | 11 | 40 | 4 | 15 | 270 | 3 | 0 | 34 | 2 | 2 carb, 2 fat |
| Raspberry Filled Donuts | 1 | 230 | 8 | 31 | 4 | 5 | 230 | 3 | 1 | 34 | 2 | 2 carb, 2 fat |

✔= Best Bet; NA = Not Available; Carb. Ch. = Carbohydrate Choices

| Product | Serving Size | Cal. | Fat (g) | % Cal. Fat | Sat. Fat (g) | Chol. (mg) | Sod. (mg) | Pro. (g) | Fiber (g) | Carb. (g) | Carb. Ch. | Servings/Exchanges |
|---|---|---|---|---|---|---|---|---|---|---|---|---|
| **EGG PRODUCTS** | | | | | | | | | | | | |
| **Fleischmann's** | | | | | | | | | | | | |
| ✔Egg Beaters | 1/4 cup | 25 | 0 | 0 | 0 | 0 | 80 | 5 | 0 | 1 | 0 | 1 very lean meat |
| Egg Beaters w/Cheez | 1/2 cup | 110 | 5 | 41 | 2 | 5 | 480 | 14 | 0 | 2 | 0 | 2 lean meat |
| ✔Egg Beaters, Vegetable Omelet | 1/2 cup | 50 | 0 | 0 | 0 | 0 | 170 | 7 | 0 | 5 | 0 | 1 very lean meat |
| **Morningstar** | | | | | | | | | | | | |
| ✔Scramblers | 1/4 cup | 60 | 3 | 45 | NA | 0 | NA | 6 | 0 | 3 | 0 | 1 lean meat |
| **Second Nature** | | | | | | | | | | | | |
| ✔Real Egg Product | 1/4 cup | 60 | 2 | 30 | 0 | 0 | 110 | 6 | 0 | 3 | 0 | 1 lean meat |
| ✔Real Egg Product, Nonfat | 1/4 cup | 40 | 0 | 0 | 0 | 0 | 115 | 6 | 0 | 3 | 0 | 1 lean meat |
| **Tofutti** | | | | | | | | | | | | |
| ✔Egg Watchers, Egg Substitute | 1/4 cup | 50 | 2 | 36 | NA | 0 | 100 | 7 | 0 | 2 | 0 | 1 lean meat |
| **EGG ROLLS (FROZEN)** | | | | | | | | | | | | |
| **Chun King** | | | | | | | | | | | | |
| Egg Rolls, Chicken | 1 | 190 | 9 | 43 | 5 | 20 | 650 | 6 | 2 | 22 | 1 1/2 | 1 1/2 carb, 2 fat |
| Egg Rolls, Shrimp | 1 | 180 | 7 | 35 | 3 | 15 | 490 | 5 | 2 | 24 | 1 1/2 | 1 1/2 carb, 1 fat |
| Mini Egg Rolls, Chicken | 6 | 210 | 9 | 39 | 3 | 8 | 650 | 6 | 2 | 25 | 1 1/2 | 1 1/2 carb, 2 fat |

| | Amount | Cal. | Fat (g) | % Cal. from Fat | Sat. Fat (g) | Chol. (mg) | Sod. (mg) | Carb. (g) | Fiber (g) | Pro. (g) | Carb. Choices | Exchanges/Choices |
|---|---|---|---|---|---|---|---|---|---|---|---|---|
| Mini Egg Rolls, Pork & Shrimp | 6 | 210 | 9 | 39 | 3 | 15 | 540 | 27 | 2 | 6 | 2 | 2 carb, 2 fat |
| Mini Egg Rolls, Shrimp | 6 | 190 | 9 | 43 | 2 | 10 | 730 | 28 | 2 | 5 | 2 | 2 carb, 2 fat |
| **Golden Tiger** | | | | | | | | | | | | |
| Gourmet Chicken Egg Rolls | 1 | 160 | 7 | 39 | 2 | 20 | 430 | 19 | 1 | 7 | 1 | 1 carb, 1 med-fat meat |
| **La Choy** | | | | | | | | | | | | |
| Egg Rolls, Chicken | 1 | 170 | 9 | 48 | 5 | 15 | 550 | 15 | 4 | 6 | 1 | 1 carb, 1 med-fat meat, 1 fat |
| Egg Rolls, Pork | 1 | 220 | 7 | 35 | 2 | 15 | 490 | 25 | 2 | 5 | 1 1/2 | 1 1/2 carb, 1 fat |
| Egg Rolls, Shrimp | 1 | 180 | 7 | 35 | 2 | 15 | 490 | 25 | 2 | 5 | 1 1/2 | 1 1/2 carb, 1 fat |
| Egg Rolls, Sweet & Sour Chicken | 1 | 220 | 9 | 37 | 2 | 15 | 350 | 29 | 2 | 5 | 2 | 2 carb, 2 fat |
| Mini Egg Rolls, Chicken | 6 | 210 | 9 | 39 | 3 | 15 | 650 | 25 | 2 | 6 | 1 1/2 | 1 1/2 carb, 2 fat |
| Mini Egg Rolls, Chinese-Style Vegetables w/Lobster | 6 | 190 | 7 | 33 | 2 | 5 | 440 | 27 | 2 | 5 | 2 | 2 carb, 1 fat |
| Mini Egg Rolls, Pork & Shrimp | 5 | 210 | 5 | 24 | 2 | 10 | 730 | 29 | 2 | 5 | 2 | 2 carb, 1 fat |
| Mini Egg Rolls, Shrimp | 5 | 190 | 5 | 24 | 2 | 10 | 730 | 29 | 2 | 5 | 2 | 2 carb, 1 fat |
| **EGGS** | | | | | | | | | | | | |
| **(Generic)** | | | | | | | | | | | | |
| ✓ Egg Whites | 2 | 34 | 0 | 0 | 0 | 0 | 110 | <1 | 0 | 7 | 0 | 1 very lean meat |
| Egg-Boiled/Cooked (1 Jumbo) | 1 | 99 | 7 | 64 | 2 | 271 | 79 | <1 | <1 | 8 | <1 | 1 med-fat meat |

✓= Best Bet; NA = Not Available; Carb. Ch. = Carbohydrate Choices

| Eggs (*Continued*) | Serving Size | Cal. | Fat (g) | % Cal. Fat | Sat. Fat (g) | Chol. (mg) | Sod. (mg) | Pro. (g) | Fiber (g) | Carb. (g) | Carb. Ch. | Servings/Exchanges |
|---|---|---|---|---|---|---|---|---|---|---|---|---|
| Egg-Boiled/Cooked (1 Small) | 1 | 57 | 4 | 63 | 1 | 157 | 46 | 5 | 0 | <1 | 0 | 1 med-fat meat |
| Egg-Boiled/Cooked Egg (1 Extra Large) | 1 | 90 | 6 | 60 | 2 | 246 | 72 | 7 | 0 | <1 | 0 | 1 med-fat meat |
| Egg-Boiled/Cooked Egg (1 Medium) | 1 | 68 | 5 | 66 | 1 | 187 | 55 | 6 | 0 | <1 | 0 | 1 med-fat meat |
| **ENGLISH MUFFINS** | | | | | | | | | | | | |
| **Pepperidge Farm** | | | | | | | | | | | | |
| ✔7-Grain English Muffin | 1 | 130 | 1 | 7 | 0 | 0 | 230 | 5 | 2 | 26 | 2 | 2 strch |
| ✔Cinnamon Raisin English Muffin | 1 | 140 | 1 | 6 | 0 | 0 | 230 | 5 | 2 | 28 | 2 | 2 strch |
| ✔Plain English Muffin | 1 | 130 | 1 | 7 | 0 | 0 | 250 | 5 | 2 | 26 | 2 | 2 strch |
| ✔Sourdough English Muffins | 1 | 130 | 1 | 7 | 0 | 0 | 250 | 5 | 2 | 26 | 2 | 2 strch |
| **Thomas** | | | | | | | | | | | | |
| ✔Blueberry English Muffins | 1 | 140 | 0 | 0 | 0 | 0 | 210 | 4 | 1 | 29 | 2 | 2 strch |
| ✔Cinnamon Raisin English Muffins | 1 | 140 | 1 | 6 | 0 | 0 | 180 | 4 | 2 | 30 | 2 | 2 strch |
| ✔Honey Wheat English Muffins | 1 | 130 | <1 | 3 | 0 | 0 | 180 | 4 | 1 | 27 | 2 | 2 strch |
| ✔Original English Muffins | 1 | 120 | 1 | 8 | 0 | 0 | 200 | 4 | 1 | 25 | 1 1/2 | 1 1/2 strch |
| ✔Sourdough English Muffins | 1 | 120 | 1 | 8 | 0 | 0 | 190 | 4 | 1 | 25 | 1 1/2 | 1 1/2 strch |
| ✔Super Size English Muffins | 1 | 190 | 2 | 9 | 0 | 0 | 280 | 7 | 2 | 38 | 2 1/2 | 2 1/2 strch |

# ENTRÉE POT PIE (FROZEN)

| | Serving | Cal. | Fat (g) | % Cal. Fat | Sat. Fat (g) | Chol. (mg) | Sod. (mg) | Prot. (g) | Fiber (g) | Carb. (g) | Carb. Ch. | Exchanges/Choices |
|---|---|---|---|---|---|---|---|---|---|---|---|---|
| **Banquet** | | | | | | | | | | | | |
| Beef Pot Pie | 7 oz | 400 | 23 | 52 | 11 | 30 | 1000 | 9 | 1 | 38 | 2 1/2 | 2 1/2 carb, 5 fat |
| Cheesy Potato & Broccoli w/Ham | 7 oz pie | 400 | 23 | 52 | 11 | 25 | 1220 | 9 | 3 | 39 | 2 1/2 | 2 1/2 carb, 5 fat |
| Chicken & Broccoli | 7 oz pie | 350 | 20 | 51 | 9 | 35 | 830 | 10 | 2 | 32 | 2 | 2 carb, 1 med-fat meat, 3 fat |
| Chicken Pot Pie | 7 oz | 380 | 22 | 52 | 9 | 40 | 950 | 10 | 1 | 36 | 2 1/2 | 2 1/2 carb, 4 fat |
| Family Size Hearty Chicken Pie | 8 oz | 460 | 29 | 57 | 11 | 35 | 1010 | 11 | 2 | 39 | 2 1/2 | 2 1/2 carb, 1 med-fat meat, 5 fat |
| ✓Macaroni & Cheese | 6.5 oz pie | 210 | 5 | 21 | 3 | 10 | 750 | 7 | 1 | 34 | 2 | 2 carb, 1 fat |
| Turkey | 7 oz pie | 370 | 20 | 49 | 8 | 45 | 850 | 10 | 3 | 38 | 2 1/2 | 2 1/2 carb, 1 med-fat meat, 3 fat |
| Vegetable Cheese Pot Pie | 7 oz | 340 | 17 | 45 | 7 | 10 | 920 | 6 | 1 | 39 | 2 1/2 | 2 1/2 carb, 3 fat |
| **Lean Cuisine** | | | | | | | | | | | | |
| ✓Chicken Pie | 9.5 oz meal | 290 | 9 | 28 | 3 | 30 | 570 | 18 | 5 | 35 | 2 1/2 | 2 1/2 carb, 1 med-fat meat, 1 fat |
| **Marie Callendar's** | | | | | | | | | | | | |
| Chicken Pot Pie | 9.5 oz | 680 | 46 | 62 | 21 | 20 | 1100 | 14 | 3 | 53 | 3 1/2 | 3 1/2 carb, 9 fat |

✓= Best Bet; NA = Not Available; Carb. Ch. = Carbohydrate Choices

| Entrée Pot Pie (Frozen) (Continued) | Serving Size | Cal. | Fat (g) | % Cal. Fat | Sat. Fat (g) | Chol. (mg) | Sod. (mg) | Pro. (g) | Fiber (g) | Carb. (g) | Carb. Ch. | Servings/Exchanges |
|---|---|---|---|---|---|---|---|---|---|---|---|---|
| Country Style Chicken Pot Pies | 1 pie (10.1 oz) | 650 | 39 | 54 | 11 | 30 | 1060 | 18 | 5 | 57 | 4 | 4 strch, 1 med-fat meat, 7 fat |
| Turkey Pot Pie | 9.5 oz | 690 | 46 | 61 | 19 | 15 | 1100 | 13 | 5 | 56 | 4 | 4 carb, 9 fat |
| Yankee Pot Pie | 9.5 oz | 660 | 42 | 58 | 21 | 20 | 1430 | 16 | 1 | 53 | 3 1/2 | 3 1/2 carb, 1 med-fat meat, 7 fat |
| **Morton** | | | | | | | | | | | | |
| Vegetable Pot Pie w/Beef | 7 oz | 340 | 21 | 56 | 9 | 20 | 1380 | 8 | 2 | 35 | 2 | 2 carb, 4 fat |
| Vegetable Pot Pie w/Chicken | 7 oz | 320 | 18 | 51 | 7 | 25 | 1040 | 8 | 2 | 32 | 2 | 2 carb, 3 fat |
| Vegetable Pot Pie w/Turkey | 7 oz | 310 | 18 | 52 | 9 | 25 | 1060 | 8 | 2 | 29 | 2 | 2 carb, 3 fat |
| **Mrs. Paterson's** | | | | | | | | | | | | |
| Aussie Chicken Pie | 1 pie (6.6 oz) | 480 | 27 | 51 | 9 | 50 | 840 | 15 | 2 | 43 | 3 | 3 strch, 1 med-fat meat, 4 fat |
| **Stouffer's** | | | | | | | | | | | | |
| Beef Pie | 10 oz | 440 | 25 | 51 | 10 | 55 | 1140 | 18 | 4 | 36 | 2 1/2 | 2 1/2 carb, 2 med-fat meat, 3 fat |
| Chicken Pie | 8 oz | 430 | 25 | 52 | 8 | 40 | 1150 | 17 | 5 | 35 | 2 | 2 carb, 2 med-fat meat, 3 fat |

| | | | | | | | | | | | | |
|---|---|---|---|---|---|---|---|---|---|---|---|---|
| Hearty Portions, Chicken Pot Pie | 8 oz | 590 | 37 | 56 | 12 | 40 | 1240 | 15 | 4 | 49 | 3 | 3 carb, 1 med-fat meat, 6 fat |
| Turkey Pie | 10 oz | 530 | 33 | 56 | 9 | 65 | 1040 | 21 | 3 | 36 | 2 1/2 | 2 1/2 carb, 2 med-fat meat, 5 fat |
| **Swanson** | | | | | | | | | | | | |
| Beef Pot Pie | 7 oz | 420 | 22 | 47 | 9 | 25 | 730 | 13 | 2 | 42 | 3 | 3 carb, 1 med-fat meat, 3 fat |
| Chicken Pot Pie | 7 oz | 410 | 22 | 48 | 9 | 25 | 780 | 10 | 2 | 43 | 3 | 3 carb, 4 fat |
| Turkey Pot Pie | 7 oz | 400 | 21 | 47 | 8 | 25 | 700 | 10 | 3 | 42 | 3 | 3 carb, 4 fat |
| **Taverna Classics** | | | | | | | | | | | | |
| Spinach Pie | 1/5 pie | 190 | 6 | 28 | 4 | 30 | 420 | 11 | 2.5 | 24 | 1 1/2 | 1 carb, 2 vegetable, 1 med-fat meat |
| **FISH (FROZEN)** | | | | | | | | | | | | |
| **Mrs. Paul's** | | | | | | | | | | | | |
| Battered Fish Portions | 2 | 250 | 16 | 58 | 5 | 30 | 430 | 9 | 2 | 20 | 1 | 1 carb, 1 med-fat meat, 2 fat |
| Breaded Fish Portions | 2 | 190 | 10 | 47 | 3 | 15 | 280 | 9 | 1 | 16 | 1 | 1 carb, 1 med-fat meat, 1 fat |

✔= Best Bet; NA = Not Available; Carb. Ch. = Carbohydrate Choices

| Fish (Frozen) *(Continued)* | Serving Size | Cal. | Fat (g) | % Cal. Fat | Sat. Fat (g) | Chol. (mg) | Sod. (mg) | Pro. (g) | Fiber (g) | Carb. (g) | Carb. Ch. | Servings/Exchanges |
|---|---|---|---|---|---|---|---|---|---|---|---|---|
| Breaded Fish Stick-Minis | 12 | 220 | 11 | 45 | 3 | 30 | 330 | 11 | 2 | 20 | 1 | 1 carb, 1 med-fat meat, 1 fat |
| Breaded Fish Sticks | 6 | 210 | 11 | 47 | 2 | 20 | 370 | 9 | 1 | 19 | 1 | 1 carb, 1 med-fat meat, 1 fat |
| ✔Healthy Treasure Breaded Fish Sticks | 4 | 170 | 3 | 16 | 2 | 20 | 350 | 10 | 2 | 20 | 1 | 1 carb, 1 lean meat |
| Premium Fillets Sole | 1 | 250 | 13 | 47 | 4 | 40 | 510 | 14 | 2 | 22 | 1 1/2 | 1 1/2 carb, 2 med-fat meat, 1 fat |
| Premium Haddock Fillets | 1 | 230 | 11 | 43 | 3 | 35 | 450 | 16 | 2 | 18 | 1 | 1 carb, 2 med-fat meat |
| Sea Pals Breaded Fish Shapes | 5 | 190 | 9 | 43 | 3 | 20 | 320 | 9 | 1 | 18 | 1 | 1 carb, 1 med-fat meat, 1 fat |
| **Van De Kamp's** | | | | | | | | | | | | |
| Battered Fish Fillet | 1 | 170 | 10 | 53 | 2 | 20 | 390 | 8 | 0 | 13 | 1 | 1 carb, 1 med-fat meat, 1 fat |
| Battered Fish Portions | 2 | 350 | 22 | 57 | 4 | 20 | 710 | 6 | 0 | 26 | 2 | 2 carb, 1 med-fat meat, 3 fat |
| Battered Fish Tenders | 4 | 290 | 17 | 53 | 3 | 25 | 590 | 11 | 0 | 24 | 1 1/2 | 1 1/2 carb, 1 med-fat meat, 2 fat |

| | | | | | | | | | | | |
|---|---|---|---|---|---|---|---|---|---|---|---|
| Battered Haddock Fillet | 2 | 240 | 12 | 45 | 2 | 25 | 530 | 12 | 0 | 19 | 1 | 1 carb, 1 med-fat meat, 1 fat |
| Battered Halibut Filets | 3 | 220 | 10 | 41 | 2 | 25 | 530 | 13 | 0 | 19 | 1 | 1 carb, 1 med-fat meat, 1 fat |
| Battered Ocean Perch Fillets | 2 | 240 | 13 | 49 | 3 | 25 | 510 | 11 | 0 | 20 | 1 | 1 carb, 1 med-fat meat, 2 fat |
| ✔Breaded Lemon Pepper Crisp & Healthy Fillets | 2 | 170 | 3 | 16 | <1 | 25 | 450 | 11 | 0 | 24 | 1 1/2 | 1 1/2 carb, 1 med-fat meat, 1 fat |
| Breaded Fish Fillets | 2 | 260 | 17 | 59 | 3 | 25 | 380 | 10 | 0 | 17 | 1 | 1 carb, 1 med-fat meat, 2 fat |
| Breaded Fish Sticks | 6 | 290 | 17 | 53 | 3 | 30 | 420 | 12 | 0 | 22 | 1 1/2 | 1 1/2 carb, 1 med-fat meat, 2 fat |
| ✔Breaded Garlic & Herb Crisp & Healthy Fillets | 2 | 170 | 3 | 16 | <1 | 25 | 450 | 11 | 0 | 25 | 1 1/2 | 1 1/2 carb, 1 med-fat meat |
| Fish Sticks Snack Pack | 6 | 260 | 15 | 52 | 3 | 25 | 350 | 11 | 0 | 20 | 1 | 1 carb, 1 med-fat meat, 2 fat |
| Grilled Garlic Butter Fillets | 1 | 120 | 6 | 45 | 1 | 60 | 210 | 17 | 0 | 0 | 0 | 2 lean meat |
| Grilled Lemon Butter Fillets | 1 | 120 | 6 | 45 | 1 | 60 | 190 | 17 | 0 | 0 | 0 | 2 lean meat |

✔= Best Bet; NA = Not Available; Carb. Ch. = Carbohydrate Choices

| Fish (Frozen) (Continued) | Serving Size | Cal. | Fat (g) | % Cal. Fat | Sat. Fat (g) | Chol. (mg) | Sod. (mg) | Pro. (g) | Fiber (g) | Carb. (g) | Carb. Ch. | Servings/Exchanges |
|---|---|---|---|---|---|---|---|---|---|---|---|---|
| Mini, Breaded Fish Sticks | 13 | 250 | 14 | 50 | 2 | 30 | 330 | 11 | 0 | 19 | 1 | 1 carb, 1 med-fat meat, 2 fat |
| Premium Breaded Cod Fillets | 1 | 230 | 11 | 43 | 2 | 35 | 400 | 14 | 0 | 18 | 1 | 1 carb, 2 med-fat meat |
| Premium Breaded Flounder Fillet | 1 | 230 | 11 | 43 | 2 | 40 | 390 | 14 | 0 | 18 | 1 | 1 carb, 2 lean meat |
| Premium Breaded Haddock Fillet | 2 | 230 | 11 | 43 | 2 | 35 | 410 | 14 | 0 | 18 | 1 | 1 carb, 2 med-fat meat |

## FISH MEALS/ENTREES (FROZEN)

### Banquet

| | | | | | | | | | | | | |
|---|---|---|---|---|---|---|---|---|---|---|---|---|
| Fish Sticks | 6.6 oz dinner | 290 | 13 | 40 | 5 | 30 | 820 | 11 | 4 | 33 | 2 | 2 carb, 1 med-fat meat, 2 fat |

### Healthy Choice

| | | | | | | | | | | | | |
|---|---|---|---|---|---|---|---|---|---|---|---|---|
| ✔Herb Baked Fish | 10.9 oz | 340 | 7 | 19 | 2 | 35 | 480 | 16 | 5 | 54 | 3 1/2 | 3 1/2 carb, 1 med-fat meat |
| ✔Lemon Pepper Fish | 10.7 oz meal | 320 | 7 | 19 | 2 | 30 | 480 | 14 | 5 | 50 | 3 | 3 carb, 1 med-fat meat |
| ✔Tuna Casserole | 9 oz meal | 240 | 5 | 19 | 2 | 25 | 580 | 16 | 4 | 33 | 2 | 2 carb, 1 med-fat meat |

### Lean Cuisine

| | | | | | | | | | | | | |
|---|---|---|---|---|---|---|---|---|---|---|---|---|
| ✔American Favorites, Baked Fish | 9 oz meal | 270 | 6 | 20 | 2 | 45 | 540 | 17 | 3 | 36 | 2 1/2 | 2 1/2 carb, 2 lean meat |

## Marie Callender

| | Amount | Cal. | Fat (g) | % Cal. Fat | Sat. Fat (g) | Chol. (mg) | Sod. (mg) | Prot. (g) | Fiber (g) | Carb. (g) | Carb. Ch. | Exchanges/Choices |
|---|---|---|---|---|---|---|---|---|---|---|---|---|
| Breaded Fish w/Macaroni and Cheese | 12 oz meal | 550 | 28 | 46 | 9 | 60 | 1400 | 22 | 3 | 53 | 3 1/2 | 3 1/2 carb, 2 med-fat meat, 4 fat |

## Stouffer's

| | Amount | Cal. | Fat (g) | % Cal. Fat | Sat. Fat (g) | Chol. (mg) | Sod. (mg) | Prot. (g) | Fiber (g) | Carb. (g) | Carb. Ch. | Exchanges/Choices |
|---|---|---|---|---|---|---|---|---|---|---|---|---|
| Homestyle Fish & Macaroni & Cheese | 9 oz meal | 430 | 21 | 44 | 5 | 70 | 930 | 24 | 2 | 37 | 2 1/2 | 2 1/2 car, 1 med-fat meat, 2 fat |
| Tuna Noodle Casserole | 10 oz meal | 320 | 10 | 28 | 4 | 40 | 1130 | 20 | 0 | 37 | 2 1/2 | 2 1/2 carb, 2 med-fat meat |

## Swanson

| | Amount | Cal. | Fat (g) | % Cal. Fat | Sat. Fat (g) | Chol. (mg) | Sod. (mg) | Prot. (g) | Fiber (g) | Carb. (g) | Carb. Ch. | Exchanges/Choices |
|---|---|---|---|---|---|---|---|---|---|---|---|---|
| Fish 'n Chips | 10 oz meal | 490 | 20 | 37 | 4 | 45 | 1030 | 19 | 5 | 59 | 4 | 4 carb, 1 med-fat meat, 3 fat |

## Swanson Hungry-Man

| | Amount | Cal. | Fat (g) | % Cal. Fat | Sat. Fat (g) | Chol. (mg) | Sod. (mg) | Prot. (g) | Fiber (g) | Carb. (g) | Carb. Ch. | Exchanges/Choices |
|---|---|---|---|---|---|---|---|---|---|---|---|---|
| Fisherman's Platter | 13 oz meal | 640 | 25 | 35 | 6 | 55 | 1580 | 22 | 3 | 80 | 5 | 5 carb, 1 med-fat meat, 4 fat |

# FRENCH FRIES/TATOR TOTS (FROZEN)

## Ore Ida

| | Amount | Cal. | Fat (g) | % Cal. Fat | Sat. Fat (g) | Chol. (mg) | Sod. (mg) | Prot. (g) | Fiber (g) | Carb. (g) | Carb. Ch. | Exchanges/Choices |
|---|---|---|---|---|---|---|---|---|---|---|---|---|
| Cottage Fries | 3 oz | 125 | 4 | 29 | <1 | 0 | 17 | 2 | NA | 20 | 1 | 1 strch, 1 fat |
| Country Fries | 3 oz | 120 | 4 | 30 | <1 | 0 | 240 | 2 | 1 | 19 | 1 | 1 strch, 1 fat |
| ✔Crinkle Cuts, Lite | 3 oz | 90 | 2 | 20 | <1 | 0 | 20 | 2 | NA | 16 | 1 | 1 strch |

✔ = Best Bet; NA = Not Available; Carb. Ch. = Carbohydrate Choices

| French Fries/Tator Tots (Frozen) (Continued) | Serving Size | Cal. | Fat (g) | % Cal. Fat | Sat. Fat (g) | Chol. (mg) | Sod. (mg) | Pro. (g) | Fiber (g) | Carb. (g) | Carb. Ch. | Servings/Exchanges |
|---|---|---|---|---|---|---|---|---|---|---|---|---|
| Crispers | 3 oz | 140 | 6 | 39 | 1 | 0 | 210 | 2 | 2 | 20 | 1 1/2 | 1 1/2 strch, 3 fat |
| Crispy Crowns | 3 oz | 170 | 9 | 48 | 2 | 0 | 410 | 2 | NA | 20 | 1 | 1 strch, 2 fat |
| Crispy Crunchies | 3 oz | 160 | 9 | 51 | 2 | 0 | 310 | 2 | 2 | 18 | 1 | 1 strch, 2 fat |
| Fast Fries | 3 oz | 140 | 6 | 39 | 2 | 0 | 230 | 2 | 2 | 20 | 1 | 1 strch, 1 fat |
| Golden Crinkles | 3 oz | 120 | 4 | 30 | <1 | 0 | 360 | 2 | 2 | 20 | 1 | 1 strch, 1 fat |
| Golden Fries | 3 oz | 125 | 4 | 29 | <1 | 0 | 15 | 2 | NA | 20 | 1 | 1 strch, 1 fat |
| Golden Twirls | 3 oz | 160 | 7 | 39 | 1 | 0 | 25 | 2 | 2 | 22 | 1 1/2 | 1 1/2 strch, 1 fat |
| Hot Tots | 3 oz | 150 | 6 | 36 | 1 | 0 | 385 | 2 | 2 | 21 | 1 1/2 | 1 1/2 strch, 1 fat |
| Microwave Tater Tots | 1 pkg | 200 | 9 | 41 | 2 | 0 | 350 | 2 | NA | 29 | 2 | 2 strch, 2 fat |
| Onion Tater Tots | 3 oz | 145 | 7 | 43 | 1 | 0 | 520 | 2 | NA | 16 | 1 | 1 strch, 1 fat |
| Pixie Crinkles | 3 oz | 140 | 5 | 32 | 1 | 0 | 30 | 2 | NA | 21 | 1 1/2 | 1 1/2 strch, 1 fat |
| Shoestrings | 3 oz | 150 | 6 | 36 | 1 | 0 | 15 | 2 | NA | 22 | 1 1/2 | 1 1/2 strch, 1 fat |
| Snackin' Fries | 1 pkg | 340 | 20 | 53 | 4 | 0 | 590 | 4 | 3 | 36 | 2 1/2 | 2 1/2 strch, 4 fat |
| ✓Steak Fries | 3 oz | 110 | 3 | 25 | <1 | 0 | 360 | 2 | 2 | 19 | 1 | 1 carb, 1 fat |
| Tater Tots | 9 pieces | 170 | 8 | 42 | 2 | 0 | 440 | 1 | 2 | 21 | 1 1/2 | 1 1/2 strch, 2 fat |
| Texas Crispers | 3 oz | 170 | 10 | 53 | 3 | 0 | 280 | 2 | 2 | 19 | 1 | 1 strch, 2 fat |
| Waffle Fries | 3 oz | 140 | 5 | 32 | 2 | 0 | 35 | 2 | 2 | 22 | 1 1/2 | 1 1/2 strch, 1 fat |
| Zesties | 3 oz | 150 | 7 | 42 | 2 | 0 | 340 | 2 | 1 | 21 | 1 1/2 | 1 1/2 strch, 1 fat |

## FRENCH TOAST (FROZEN)

| | Serving Size | Calories | Fat (g) | % Cal. from Fat | Sat. Fat (g) | Chol. (mg) | Sodium (mg) | Carb. (g) | Fiber (g) | Protein (g) | Carb. Ch. | Exchanges |
|---|---|---|---|---|---|---|---|---|---|---|---|---|
| **Aunt Jemima** | | | | | | | | | | | | |
| French Toast | 2 | 240 | 7 | 26 | 2 | 95 | 310 | 35 | 8 | 10 | 2 | 2 strch, 1 fat |
| French Toast, Cinnamon | 2 | 240 | 7 | 26 | 1 | 30 | 330 | 35 | 8 | 10 | 2 | 2 strch, 1 fat |
| **Krusteaz** | | | | | | | | | | | | |
| Cinnamon Swirl French Toast | 2 slices | 230 | 5 | 20 | 1 | 95 | 540 | 36 | 2 | 9 | 2 1/2 | 2 1/2 carb, 1 fat |

## FROSTING (FROM MIX)

| | Serving Size | Calories | Fat (g) | % Cal. from Fat | Sat. Fat (g) | Chol. (mg) | Sodium (mg) | Carb. (g) | Fiber (g) | Protein (g) | Carb. Ch. | Exchanges |
|---|---|---|---|---|---|---|---|---|---|---|---|---|
| **Betty Crocker** | | | | | | | | | | | | |
| Coconut Pecan (As Prepared) | 2 Tbsp | 160 | 8 | 45 | 3 | 0 | 55 | 21 | 0 | <1 | 1 1/2 | 1 1/2 carb, 2 fat |
| ✔Fluffy White (As Prepared) | 6 Tbsp | 100 | 0 | 0 | 0 | 0 | 60 | 24 | 0 | <1 | 1 1/2 | 1 1/2 carb |

## FROSTING (READY-TO-SPREAD)

| | Serving Size | Calories | Fat (g) | % Cal. from Fat | Sat. Fat (g) | Chol. (mg) | Sodium (mg) | Carb. (g) | Fiber (g) | Protein (g) | Carb. Ch. | Exchanges |
|---|---|---|---|---|---|---|---|---|---|---|---|---|
| **Betty Crocker** | | | | | | | | | | | | |
| Creamy Deluxe Party Frostings, All Varieties (Avg) | 2 Tbsp | 140 | 5 | 32 | 1.5 | 0 | 80 | 23 | 0 | 0 | 1 1/2 | 1 1/2 carb, 1 fat |
| Creamy Deluxe, All Varieties except Coconut Pecan (Avg) | 2 Tbsp | 140 | 5 | 32 | 2 | 0 | 80 | 23 | 0 | <1 | 1 1/2 | 1 1/2 carb, 1 fat |
| Creamy Deluxe, Coconut Pecan | 2 Tbsp | 140 | 8 | 51 | 3 | 0 | 50 | 17 | 0 | 1 | 1 | 1 carb, 2 fat |
| Whipped Deluxe, All Varieties (Avg) | 2 Tbsp | 100 | 5 | 45 | 1.5 | 0 | 35 | 15 | 0 | 0 | 1 | 1 carb, 1 fat |

✔ = Best Bet; NA = Not Available; Carb. Ch. = Carbohydrate Choices

| Frosting (Ready-to-Spread) *(Continued)* | Serving Size | Cal. | Fat (g) | % Cal. Fat | Sat. Fat (g) | Chol. (mg) | Sod. (mg) | Pro. (g) | Fiber (g) | Carb. (g) | Carb. Ch. | Servings/Exchanges |
|---|---|---|---|---|---|---|---|---|---|---|---|---|
| **Betty Crocker/Sweet Rewards** | | | | | | | | | | | | |
| ✔Reduced Fat Frosting, All Varieties (Avg) | 2 Tbsp | 125 | 2 | 14 | <1 | 0 | 55 | 0 | 0 | 25 | 1 1/2 | 1 1/2 carb |
| **Pillsbury** | | | | | | | | | | | | |
| Chocolate Frosting Supreme | 2 Tbsp | 140 | 6 | 39 | 2 | 0 | 80 | 0 | 0 | 21 | 1 1/2 | 1 1/2 carb, 1 fat |
| French Vanilla Frosting Supreme | 2 Tbsp | 150 | 6 | 36 | 2 | 0 | 80 | 0 | 0 | 25 | 1 1/2 | 1 1/2 carb, 1 fat |
| ✔Snackwell's Chocolate Frostings | 2 Tbsp | 120 | 3 | 23 | 1 | 0 | 65 | 0 | 0 | 22 | 1 1/2 | 1 1/2 carb, 1 fat |
| ✔Snackwell's Vanilla Frosting | 2 Tbsp | 130 | 3 | 21 | <1 | 0 | 65 | 0 | 0 | 25 | 1 1/2 | 1 1/2 carb, 1 fat |
| **FRUIT (CANNED)** | | | | | | | | | | | | |
| **(Generic)** | | | | | | | | | | | | |
| ✔Apricots, extra light syrup | 1/2 cup | 60 | <1 | 0 | 0 | 0 | 2 | <1 | 2 | 15 | 1 | 1 fruit |
| ✔Apricots, juice pack | 1/2 cup | 60 | 0 | 0 | 0 | 0 | 5 | <1 | 2 | 15 | 1 | 1 fruit |
| ✔Cheeries, sweet, juice pack | 1/2 cup | 68 | 0 | 0 | 0 | 0 | 4 | 1 | <1 | 17 | 1 | 1 fruit |
| ✔Fruit Cocktail, extra light syrup | 1/2 cup | 55 | <1 | 0 | 0 | 0 | 5 | <1 | 1 | 14 | 1 | 1 fruit |
| ✔Fruit Cocktail, juice pack | 1/2 cup | 57 | 0 | 0 | 0 | 0 | 5 | <1 | 1 | 15 | 1 | 1 fruit |
| ✔Mandarin Oranges, juice pack | 3/4 cup | 69 | <1 | 0 | 0 | 0 | 9 | 1 | 1 | 18 | 1 | 1 fruit |
| ✔Peaches, extra light syrup | 1/2 cup | 52 | <1 | 0 | 0 | 0 | 6 | <1 | 1 | 14 | 1 | 1 fruit |
| ✔Peaches, juice pack | 1/2 cup | 55 | 0 | 0 | 0 | 0 | 5 | <1 | 1 | 14 | 1 | 1 fruit |
| ✔Pears, canned | 1/2 cup | 60 | 0 | 0 | 0 | 0 | 10 | 0 | 1 | 15 | 1 | 1 fruit |

| Food | Serving Size | Cal. | Fat (g) | Sat. Fat (g) | Chol. (mg) | Sod. (mg) | Prot. (g) | Fiber (g) | Carb. (g) | Carb. Ch. | Exch. |
|---|---|---|---|---|---|---|---|---|---|---|---|
| ✔Pears, light syrup | 1/2 cup | 58 | <1 | 0 | 0 | 3 | <1 | 3 | 15 | 1 | 1 fruit |
| ✔Pineapple, juice pack | 1/2 cup | 74 | 0 | 0 | 0 | 1 | 0 | <1 | 20 | 1 | 1 fruit |
| ✔Plums, juice pack | 1/2 cup | 73 | 0 | 0 | 0 | 2 | <1 | 1 | 19 | 1 | 1 fruit |
| **Del Monte** | | | | | | | | | | | |
| ✔Fruit-to-Go, Banana Berry Peaches | 4 oz | 70 | 0 | 0 | 0 | 10 | <1 | <1 | 17 | 1 | 1 fruit |
| ✔Fruit-to-Go, Fruity Combo | 4 oz | 70 | 0 | 0 | 0 | 10 | <1 | <1 | 18 | 1 | 1 fruit |
| ✔Fruit-to-Go, Peachy Peaches | 4 oz | 70 | 0 | 0 | 0 | 10 | <1 | <1 | 17 | 1 | 1 fruit |
| **Dole** | | | | | | | | | | | |
| ✔Fruit Bowls, Diced Peaches | 4 oz bowl | 70 | 0 | 0 | 0 | 15 | <1 | 1 | 14 | 1 | 1 fruit |
| ✔Fruit Bowls, Pineapple | 4 oz bowl | 60 | 0 | 0 | 0 | 10 | <1 | 1 | 16 | 1 | 1 fruit |
| ✔Fruit Bowls, Tropical Fruit | 4 oz bowl | 60 | 0 | 0 | 0 | 10 | <1 | 2 | 16 | 1 | 1 fruit |
| ✔Mixed Fruit | 4 oz bowl | 80 | 0 | 0 | 0 | 10 | <1 | 1 | 19 | 1 | 1 fruit |
| **FRUIT (FRESH)** | | | | | | | | | | | |
| **(Generic)** | | | | | | | | | | | |
| ✔Apple, unpeeled, large | 1 | 125 | <1 | 0 | 0 | 0 | <1 | 6 | 32 | 2 | 2 fruit |
| ✔Apple, unpeeled, small | 1 | 63 | <1 | 0 | <1 | 0 | 0 | 3 | 16 | 1 | 1 fruit |
| ✔Apples, dried | 4 rings | 63 | 0 | 0 | 0 | 23 | 0 | 2 | 17 | 1 | 1 fruit |
| ✔Apricots, dried | 8 halves | 66 | 0 | 0 | 0 | 2 | 1 | 3 | 17 | 1 | 1 fruit |
| ✔Apricots, fresh | 4 | 68 | 1 | 0 | 2 | 0 | 1 | 3 | 16 | 1 | 1 fruit |

✔ = Best Bet; NA = Not Available; Carb. Ch. = Carbohydrate Choices

| Fruit (Fresh) *(Continued)* | Serving Size | Cal. | Fat (g) | % Cal. Fat | Sat. Fat (g) | Chol. (mg) | Sod. (mg) | Pro. (g) | Fiber (g) | Carb. (g) | Carb. Ch. | Servings/Exchanges |
|---|---|---|---|---|---|---|---|---|---|---|---|---|
| ✔Banana, small | 1 | 64 | <1 | 0 | <1 | 0 | 1 | <1 | 2 | 16 | 1 | 1 fruit |
| ✔Blackberries, fresh | 3/4 cup | 56 | <1 | 0 | 0 | 0 | 0 | <1 | 5 | 14 | 1 | 1 fruit |
| ✔Blueberries, fresh | 3/4 cup | 61 | <1 | 0 | 0 | 0 | 7 | <1 | 3 | 15 | 1 | 1 fruit |
| ✔Cantaloupe, fresh | 1 cup | 56 | <1 | 0 | 0 | 0 | 14 | 1 | 1 | 13 | 1 | 1 fruit |
| ✔Cherries, sweet, fresh | 12 | 59 | <1 | 0 | <1 | 0 | 0 | 1 | 2 | 14 | 1 | 1 fruit |
| ✔Cranberries | 1 cup | 47 | <1 | 0 | <1 | 0 | <1 | <1 | 4 | 12 | 1 | 1 fruit |
| ✔Grapefruit, fresh | 1/2 cup | 51 | <1 | 0 | 0 | 0 | 0 | 1 | 2 | 13 | 1 | 1 fruit |
| ✔Grapes, fresh seedless | 17 | 60 | <1 | 0 | <1 | 0 | 2 | <1 | <1 | 15 | 1 | 1 fruit |
| ✔Honeydew Melon, fresh | 1 cup | 59 | <1 | 0 | 0 | 0 | 15 | <1 | 1 | 16 | 1 | 1 fruit |
| ✔Kiwi, fresh | 1 | 56 | <1 | 0 | 0 | 0 | 5 | <1 | 3 | 14 | 1 | 1 fruit |
| ✔Mango, fresh | 1/2 mango | 68 | <1 | 0 | <1 | 0 | 2 | <1 | 2 | 18 | 1 | 1 fruit |
| ✔Nectarine, fresh | 1 | 67 | <1 | 0 | 0 | 0 | 0 | 1 | 2 | 16 | 1 | 1 fruit |
| ✔Orange, fresh | 1 | 62 | <1 | 0 | 0 | 0 | 0 | 1 | 3 | 15 | 1 | 1 fruit |
| ✔Papaya, fresh, medium | 1/2 papaya | 59 | <1 | 0 | <1 | 0 | 4 | 1 | 3 | 15 | 1 | 1 fruit |
| ✔Peach, fresh, medium | 1 | 57 | <1 | 0 | 0 | 0 | 0 | <1 | 3 | 15 | 1 | 1 fruit |
| Pear, fresh | 1/2 large | 59 | <1 | 0 | 0 | 0 | 0 | <1 | 2 | 15 | 1 | 1 fruit |
| ✔Pineapple, fresh | 3/4 cup | 57 | <1 | 0 | 0 | 0 | 1 | <1 | 1 | 14 | 1 | 1 fruit |
| ✔Plums, fresh, small | 2 plums | 73 | <1 | 0 | 0 | 0 | 0 | 1 | 2 | 17 | 1 | 1 fruit |

| Food | Amount | Cal. | Fat (g) | Sat. Fat (g) | Chol. (mg) | Sod. (mg) | Fiber (g) | Prot. (g) | Carb. (g) | Carb. Ch. | Exch. |
|---|---|---|---|---|---|---|---|---|---|---|---|
| ✔ Prunes, dried, uncooked | 3 prunes | 60 | <1 | 0 | 0 | 1 | <1 | 2 | 16 | 1 | 1 fruit |
| ✔ Raisins, dark, seedless | 2 Tbsp | 54 | <1 | 0 | 0 | 2 | <1 | 1 | 14 | 1 | 1 fruit |
| ✔ Raspberries, black, fresh | 1 cup | 60 | <1 | 0 | 0 | 0 | 1 | 5 | 14 | 1 | 1 fruit |
| ✔ Strawberries, fresh | 1 1/4 cup | 56 | <1 | 0 | 0 | 2 | 1 | 4 | 13 | 1 | 1 fruit |
| ✔ Tangerine, fresh, small | 2 tangerines | 74 | <1 | 0 | 0 | 2 | 1 | 4 | 19 | 1 | 1 fruit |
| ✔ Watermelon, fresh | 1 1/4 cup | 64 | <1 | 0 | NA | 4 | 1 | 1 | 15 | 1 | 1 fruit |

## FRUIT (FROZEN)

### (Generic)

| Food | Amount | Cal. | Fat (g) | Sat. Fat (g) | Chol. (mg) | Sod. (mg) | Fiber (g) | Prot. (g) | Carb. (g) | Carb. Ch. | Exch. |
|---|---|---|---|---|---|---|---|---|---|---|---|
| ✔ Berry Mix, Unsweetened | 1 cup | 90 | 0 | 0 | 0 | 20 | 1 | 6 | 20 | 1 | 1 fruit |
| ✔ Blackberries, Unsweetened | 1 cup | 110 | 0 | 0 | 0 | 0 | 1 | 4 | 26 | 2 | 2 fruit |
| ✔ Cherries, Pitted, Unsweetened | 1 cup | 110 | 0 | 0 | 0 | 0 | 1 | 3 | 25 | 1 1/2 | 1 1/2 fruit |
| ✔ Cranberries, Unsweetened | 1/2 cup | 25 | 0 | 0 | 0 | 0 | <1 | <1 | 5 | 0 | free |
| ✔ Red Raspberries, Unsweetened | 1 cup | 80 | 0 | 0 | 0 | 0 | 1 | 5 | 20 | 1 | 1 fruit |
| ✔ Sliced Peaches, Unsweetened | 2/3 cup | 50 | 0 | 0 | 0 | 0 | <1 | 1 | 13 | 1 | 1 fruit |
| ✔ Strawberries, Unsweetened | 2/3 cup | 50 | 0 | 0 | 0 | 0 | <1 | 2 | 13 | 1 | 1 fruit |
| ✔ Tropical Fruit Mix | 1 1/4 cup | 100 | 0 | 0 | 0 | 0 | <1 | 3 | 25 | 1 1/2 | 1 1/2 fruit |
| ✔ Whole Blueberries, Unsweetened | 3/4 cup | 80 | 0 | 0 | 0 | 0 | 0 | 4 | 20 | 1 | 1 fruit |

✔ = Best Bet; NA = Not Available; Carb. Ch. = Carbohydrate Choices

| Product | Serving Size | Cal. | Fat (g) | % Cal. Fat | Sat. Fat (g) | Chol. (mg) | Sod. (mg) | Pro. (g) | Fiber (g) | Carb. (g) | Carb. Ch. | Servings/Exchanges |
|---|---|---|---|---|---|---|---|---|---|---|---|---|
| **FRUIT SNACKS** | | | | | | | | | | | | |
| **Betty Crocker** | | | | | | | | | | | | |
| ✔Fruit By The Foot | 1 roll | 80 | 2 | 23 | <1 | 0 | 50 | 0 | 0 | 17 | 1 | 1 carb |
| ✔Fruit Gushers | 1 pouch | 90 | 1 | 10 | 0 | 0 | 45 | 0 | 0 | 20 | 1 | 1 carb |
| ✔Fruit Roll-Ups | 1 | 50 | <1 | 0 | 0 | 0 | 55 | 0 | 0 | 12 | 1 | 1 carb |
| ✔Fruit Snacks, All Varieties | 1 pouch | 80 | 0 | 0 | 0 | 0 | 50 | 0 | 0 | 21 | 1 1/2 | 1 1/2 carb |
| ✔Fruit String Ling | 1 pouch | 80 | 1 | 11 | 0 | 0 | 45 | 0 | 0 | 17 | 1 | 1 carb |
| ✔Fruitfield's Adult Fruit Shapes, All Varieties (Avg) | 10 pieces | 100 | 0 | 0 | 0 | 0 | 80 | 0 | 0 | 23 | 1 1/2 | 1 1/2 carb |
| **Ocean Spray** | | | | | | | | | | | | |
| ✔Craisins | 1/3 cup | 130 | 0 | 0 | 0 | 0 | 0 | 0 | 2 | 33 | 2 | 2 carb |
| ✔Cran Fruit | 1/4 cup | 120 | 0 | 0 | 0 | 0 | 35 | 0 | 2 | 29 | 2 | 2 carb |
| **GARLIC BREAD** | | | | | | | | | | | | |
| **Marie Callender's** | | | | | | | | | | | | |
| Original Garlic Bread, Frozen | 1 slice | 190 | 8 | 38 | 2 | 0 | 290 | 4 | 2 | 25 | 1 1/2 | 1 1/2 strch, 2 fat |
| Parmesan Romano Garlic Bread, Frozen | 1 slice | 200 | 10 | 45 | 3 | 5 | 430 | 5 | 2 | 23 | 1 1/2 | 1 1/2 strch, 2 fat |
| **Pepperidge Farm** | | | | | | | | | | | | |
| Mozzarella Garlic Bread | 1slice | 200 | 10 | 45 | 5 | 40 | 280 | 6 | 1 | 21 | 1 1/2 | 1 1/2 strch, 2 fat |

| | Serving | Cal. | Fat (g) | % Cal. Fat | Sat. Fat | Chol. | Sod. | Carb | Fiber | Sugar | Carb. Ch. | Exchanges |
|---|---|---|---|---|---|---|---|---|---|---|---|---|
| Sourdough Garlic Bread | 1 slice | 180 | 9 | 45 | 3 | 10 | 220 | 5 | 2 | 20 | 1 | 1 strch, 2 fat |

### GELATIN

#### Jell-O

| | Serving | Cal. | Fat (g) | % Cal. Fat | Sat. Fat | Chol. | Sod. | Carb | Fiber | Sugar | Carb. Ch. | Exchanges |
|---|---|---|---|---|---|---|---|---|---|---|---|---|
| ✔Gelatin Dessert, Cherry | 1/2 cup | 80 | 0 | 0 | 0 | 0 | 100 | 2 | 0 | 19 | 1 | 1 carb |
| ✔Gelatin Snacks, Cherry | 1 | 70 | 0 | 0 | 0 | 0 | 40 | 1 | 0 | 17 | 1 | 1 carb |
| ✔Gelatin Snacks, Sugar Free, Strawberry | 1 | 10 | 0 | 0 | 0 | 0 | 45 | 1 | 0 | 0 | 0 | free |
| ✔SugarFree Gelatin Dessert, All Flavors (Avg) | 1/2 cup | 10 | 0 | 0 | 0 | 0 | 70 | 1 | 0 | 0 | 0 | free |

#### Kraft

| | Serving | Cal. | Fat (g) | % Cal. Fat | Sat. Fat | Chol. | Sod. | Carb | Fiber | Sugar | Carb. Ch. | Exchanges |
|---|---|---|---|---|---|---|---|---|---|---|---|---|
| ✔Handi-Snacks Gel Snacks, Cherry | 1 | 80 | 0 | 0 | 0 | 0 | 45 | 0 | 0 | 20 | 1 | 1 carb |

### GRANOLA/SNACK BAR

#### Health Valley

| | Serving | Cal. | Fat (g) | % Cal. Fat | Sat. Fat | Chol. | Sod. | Carb | Fiber | Sugar | Carb. Ch. | Exchanges |
|---|---|---|---|---|---|---|---|---|---|---|---|---|
| ✔Apple Snack Bar | 1 | 100 | 3 | 27 | NA | 0 | 27 | 2 | 3 | 16 | 1 | 1 carb, 1 fat |
| ✔Apricot Oat Bran Snack Bar | 1 | 100 | 2 | 18 | NA | 0 | 20 | 2 | 3 | 19 | 1 | 1 carb |
| ✔Blueberry Apple Cereal Bar | 1 | 140 | 0 | 0 | 0 | 0 | 10 | 3 | 4 | 33 | 2 | 2 carb |
| ✔Date Almond Cereal Bar | 1 | 140 | 0 | 0 | 0 | 0 | 10 | 3 | 4 | 33 | 2 | 2 carb |
| ✔Date Snack Bar | 1 | 100 | 3 | 27 | NA | 0 | 25 | 3 | 3 | 16 | 1 | 1 carb, 1 fat |
| ✔Fat-Free Raisin Fruit Snack Bar | 1 | 140 | 0 | 0 | 0 | 0 | 10 | 3 | 4 | 33 | 2 | 2 carb |

✔= Best Bet; NA = Not Available; Carb. Ch. = Carbohydrate Choices

| Granola/Snack Bar (Continued) | Serving Size | Cal. | Fat (g) | % Cal. Fat | Sat. Fat (g) | Chol. (mg) | Sod. (mg) | Pro. (g) | Fiber (g) | Carb. (g) | Carb. Ch. | Servings/Exchanges |
|---|---|---|---|---|---|---|---|---|---|---|---|---|
| ✔Fat-Free Raspberry Cereal Bar | 1 | 140 | 0 | 0 | 0 | 0 | 10 | 3 | 4 | 33 | 1 | 2 carb |
| ✔Fat-Free Apple Snack Bar | 1 | 140 | 0 | 0 | 0 | 0 | 10 | 3 | 4 | 33 | 2 | 2 carb |
| ✔Fat-Free Apricot Snack Bar | 1 | 140 | 0 | 0 | 0 | 0 | 10 | 3 | 4 | 33 | 2 | 2 carb |
| ✔Fig Oat Bran Snack Bar | 1 | 110 | 3 | 25 | NA | 0 | 20 | 2 | 3 | 19 | 1 | 1 carb, 1 fat |
| Fruit Nut Oat Bran Snack Bar | 1 | 150 | 4 | 24 | NA | 0 | 10 | 4 | 8 | 29 | 2 | 2 carb, 1 fat |
| ✔Fruit Snack Bar | 1 | 200 | 3 | 14 | NA | 0 | 235 | 4 | 5 | 39 | 2 1/2 | 2 1/2 carb, 1 fat |
| Jumbo Fruit Oat Bran Snack Bar | 1 | 170 | 5 | 26 | NA | 0 | 10 | 4 | 7 | 28 | 2 | 2 carb, 1 fat |
| ✔Raisin & Cinnamon Oat Bran Snack Bar | 1 | 140 | 2 | 13 | NA | 0 | 12 | 3 | 6 | 32 | 2 | 2 carb |
| ✔Raisin Snack Bar | 1 | 100 | 3 | 27 | NA | 0 | 20 | 2 | 3 | 16 | 1 | 1 carb, 1 fat |
| **Kellogg's** | | | | | | | | | | | | |
| ✔Nutri-Grain Bars, All Varieties (Avg) | 1 | 140 | 3 | 19 | <1 | 0 | 110 | 2 | 1 | 27 | 2 | 2 carb, 1 fat |
| Nutri-Grain Fruit-full Squares, All Varieties (Avg) | 1 | 185 | 5 | 24 | <1 | 0 | 95 | 3 | 1 | 35 | 2 | 2 carb, 1 fat |
| ✔Nutri-Grain Twists Cereal Bar, All Varieties (Avg) | 1 | 140 | 3 | 19 | <1 | 0 | 110 | 1 | 1 | 27 | 2 | 2 carb, 1 fat |
| Pop-Tarts Snack-Stix, All Varieties (Avg) | 1 | 190 | 4 | 19 | 1 | 0 | 240 | 2 | 1 | 37 | 2 1/2 | 2 1/2 carb, 1 fat |
| ✔Rice Krispies Treats, All Varieties (Avg) | 1 | 100 | 3 | 27 | 1 | 0 | 100 | 2 | 0 | 17 | 1 | 1 carb, 1 fat |
| ✔Snack 'Ums, All Varieties (Avg) | 1 cup | 125 | 1 | 7 | 0 | 0 | 10-150 | 2 | 1 | 27 | 2 | 2 carb |

## M&M Mars

|  | | | | | | | | | | | | |
|---|---|---|---|---|---|---|---|---|---|---|---|---|
| Kudos Granola Bars, Chocolate Chip | 1 | 120 | 5 | 38 | 3 | 0 | 70 | 2 | 1 | 20 | 1 | 1 carb, 1 fat |
| Kudos Granola Bars, Peanut Butter | 1 | 130 | 5 | 35 | 2 | 0 | 85 | 2 | 1 | 19 | 1 | 1 carb, 1 fat |

## Medical Foods

|  | | | | | | | | | | | | |
|---|---|---|---|---|---|---|---|---|---|---|---|---|
| Choice DM Bar, All Varieties (Avg) | 1 | 140 | 5 | 32 | 3 | <5 | 80 | 6 | 3 | 19 | 1 | 1 carb, 1 fat |
| Crunchy Granola Bars, All Varieties (Avg) | 2 | 180 | 6 | 30 | <1 | 0 | 165 | 5 | 2 | 29 | 2 | 2 carb, 1 fat |
| Nit-Bite, Chocolate Fudge or Peanut Butter | 1 | 100 | 4 | 36 | 1 | 5 | 40-80 | 3 | 0 | 15 | 1 | 1 carb, 1 fat |

## Nabisco

|  | | | | | | | | | | | | |
|---|---|---|---|---|---|---|---|---|---|---|---|---|
| ✓Snackwell's Cereal Bar, All Varieties (Avg) | 1 | 125 | 2 | 14 | <1 | 0 | 90 | 1 | 1 | 27 | 2 | 2 carb |

## Nature Valley

|  | | | | | | | | | | | | |
|---|---|---|---|---|---|---|---|---|---|---|---|---|
| ✓Low-Fat Chewy Granola Bars | 1 | 110 | 2 | 16 | 0 | 0 | 65 | 2 | 1 | 21 | 1 1/2 | 1 1/2 strch |

## Nestle

|  | | | | | | | | | | | | |
|---|---|---|---|---|---|---|---|---|---|---|---|---|
| Sweet Success Snack Bar, All Varieties (Avg) | 1 | 120 | 4 | 30 | 2 | 0 | 35 | 2 | 3 | 18 | 1 | 1 carb, 1 fat |

## Quaker

|  | | | | | | | | | | | | |
|---|---|---|---|---|---|---|---|---|---|---|---|---|
| ✓Chewy Granola Bars, All Varieties | 1 | 110 | 2 | 16 | <1 | 0 | 80 | 2 | 1 | 22 | 1 1/2 | 1 1/2 strch |
| ✓Fruit & Oatmeal Cereal Bars, All Varieties (Avg) | 1 | 140 | 3 | 19 | 0 | 0 | 100 | 2 | 1 | 26 | 2 | 2 carb, 1 fat |

## Ross

|  | | | | | | | | | | | | |
|---|---|---|---|---|---|---|---|---|---|---|---|---|
| Ensure Glucerna Bar, Chocolate Graham | 1 | 140 | 4 | 26 | 1 | <5 | 100 | 5 | 4 | 24 | 1 1/2 | 1 1/2 carb, 1 fat |

✓ = Best Bet; NA = Not Available; Carb. Ch. = Carbohydrate Choices

| Granola/Snack Bar (Continued) | Serving Size | Cal. | Fat (g) | % Cal. Fat | Sat. Fat (g) | Chol. (mg) | Sod. (mg) | Pro. (g) | Fiber (g) | Carb. (g) | Carb. Ch. | Servings/Exchanges |
|---|---|---|---|---|---|---|---|---|---|---|---|---|
| **Slim Fast** | | | | | | | | | | | | |
| Breakfast/Lunch Bar, Peanut Butter | 1 | 150 | 5 | 90 | 3 | 5 | 80 | 6 | 2 | 19 | 1 | 1 carb, 1 fat |
| Breakfast/Lunch Bars, Dutch Chocolate | 1 | 140 | 5 | 32 | 3 | 5 | 80 | 5 | 2 | 20 | 1 | 1 carb, 1 fat |
| Energy Snack Bars, Peanut Butter Crunch | 1 | 130 | 4 | 28 | 2 | <5 | 80 | 1 | <1 | 21 | 1 1/2 | 1 1/2 carb, 1 fat |
| Energy Snack Bars, Rich Chewy Caramel | 1 | 120 | 4 | 30 | 3 | <5 | 80 | <1 | 2 | 22 | 1 1/2 | 1 1/2 carb, 1 fat |
| Meal-On-The-Go Bars, Oatmeal Raisin | 1 | 220 | 5 | 21 | 4 | <5 | 110 | 8 | 2 | 36 | 2 1/2 | 2 1/2 carb, 1 med-fat meat |
| Meal-On-The-Go Bars, Rich Chocolate Brownie | 1 | 220 | 5 | 21 | 3 | <5 | 110 | 8 | 2 | 34 | 2 | 2 carb, 1 med-fat meat |
| **GRAVY (CAN OR JAR)** | | | | | | | | | | | | |
| **Chef Mate** | | | | | | | | | | | | |
| Country Sausage Gravy | 1/4 cup | 96 | 8 | 75 | 2 | 13 | 236 | 3 | <1 | 4 | 0 | 2 fat |
| **Franco American** | | | | | | | | | | | | |
| ✔Au Jus Gravy | 1/4 cup | 10 | 0 | 0 | 0 | 0 | 330 | 0 | 0 | 2 | 0 | free |
| ✔Beef Gravy | 1/4 cup | 25 | 1 | 36 | NA | NA | 340 | 0 | 0 | 4 | 0 | free |
| ✔Brown Gravy w/Onions | 1/2 cup | 25 | 1 | 36 | 0 | 5 | 340 | 0 | 0 | 4 | 0 | free |
| ✔Chicken Giblet Gravy | 1/4 cup | 30 | 2 | 60 | 0 | NA | 310 | 1 | 0 | 3 | 0 | 1 fat |
| Chicken Gravy | 1/4 cup | 45 | 4 | 80 | NA | NA | 240 | 0 | 0 | 3 | 0 | 1 fat |

| Food | Amount | Cal. | Fat (g) | % Cal. from Fat | Sat. Fat (g) | Chol. (mg) | Sod. (mg) | Carb. (g) | Fiber (g) | Prot. (g) | Carb. Ch. | Exchanges/Choices |
|---|---|---|---|---|---|---|---|---|---|---|---|---|
| ✔Golden Pork Gravy | 1/4 cup | 40 | 3 | 68 | 2 | NA | 330 | 0 | 0 | 3 | 0 | 1 fat |
| ✔Mushroom Gravy | 1/4 cup | 25 | 1 | 36 | NA | NA | 290 | 0 | 0 | 3 | 0 | free |
| ✔Turkey Gravy | 1/4 cup | 30 | 2 | 60 | 0 | NA | 290 | 0 | 0 | 3 | 0 | 1 fat |
| **La Choy** | | | | | | | | | | | | |
| Brown Gravy Sauce | 1 Tbsp | 90 | 6 | 60 | 0 | 0 | 90 | 6 | 1 | 24 | 1 1/2 | 1 1/2 carb, 1 fat |
| **Libby's** | | | | | | | | | | | | |
| Country Chicken Gravy | 1/4 cup | 60 | 4 | 60 | <1 | 5 | 330 | 1 | 0 | 3 | 0 | 1 fat |
| Country Sausage Gravy | 1/4 cup | 90 | 7 | 70 | 2 | 5 | 280 | 1 | 0 | 3 | 0 | 2 fat |

## HASH BROWNS / HOME FRIES (FROZEN)

### Ore Ida

| Food | Amount | Cal. | Fat (g) | % Cal. from Fat | Sat. Fat (g) | Chol. (mg) | Sod. (mg) | Carb. (g) | Fiber (g) | Prot. (g) | Carb. Ch. | Exchanges/Choices |
|---|---|---|---|---|---|---|---|---|---|---|---|---|
| ✔Cheddar Browns | 1 patty | 85 | 2 | 21 | 1 | 3 | 365 | 3 | NA | 14 | 1 | 1 strch |
| Golden Patties | 1 patty | 130 | 8 | 55 | 2 | 0 | 120 | 1 | 1 | 14 | 1 | 1 strch, 2 fat |
| Microwave Hash Browns | 2 oz | 115 | 7 | 55 | 1 | 0 | 135 | 1 | NA | 13 | 1 | 1 strch, 1 fat |
| ✔Potatoes O'Brien | 3/4 cup | 60 | 0 | 0 | 0 | 0 | 20 | <1 | 1 | 14 | 1 | 1 strch |
| ✔Shredded Hash Browns | 1 cup | 70 | 0 | 0 | 0 | 0 | 15 | 2 | 1 | 15 | 1 | 1 strch |
| ✔Southern Style Hash Browns | 2/3 cup | 70 | 0 | 0 | 0 | 0 | 25 | 2 | 1 | 16 | 1 | 1 strch |
| Toaster Hash Browns | 1 patty | 100 | 6 | 54 | 3 | 3 | 175 | 1 | NA | 12 | 1 | 1 strch, 1 fat |

✔ = Best Bet; NA = Not Available; Carb. Ch. = Carbohydrate Choices

| Product | Serving Size | Cal. | Fat (g) | % Cal. Fat | Sat. Fat (g) | Chol. (mg) | Sod. (mg) | Pro. (g) | Fiber (g) | Carb. (g) | Carb. Ch. | Servings/Exchanges |
|---|---|---|---|---|---|---|---|---|---|---|---|---|
| **HORSERADISH SAUCE** | | | | | | | | | | | | |
| **(Generic)** | | | | | | | | | | | | |
| ✔Horseradish Sauce | 1 tsp | 0 | 0 | 0 | 0 | 0 | 10 | 0 | 0 | 0 | 0 | free |
| **HOT DOGS** | | | | | | | | | | | | |
| **Foster Farms** | | | | | | | | | | | | |
| Jumbo Corn Dogs | 1 | 270 | 15 | 50 | 4 | 50 | 730 | 10 | 1 | 22 | 1 1/2 | 1 1/2 carb, 1 med-fat meat, 2 fat |
| **Healthy Choice** | | | | | | | | | | | | |
| ✔Low-Fat Franks | 1 | 70 | 3 | 39 | 1 | 15 | 440 | 6 | 0 | 7 | 1/2 | 1/2 carb, 1 lean meat |
| **Louis Rich** | | | | | | | | | | | | |
| Bun Length Turkey & Chicken Frank | 1 | 130 | 10 | 69 | 3 | 55 | 640 | 7 | 0 | 2 | 0 | 1 high-fat meat |
| Turkey & Cheese Franks | 1 | 110 | 9 | 74 | 3 | 45 | 525 | 6 | 0 | 1 | 0 | 1 high-fat meat |
| Turkey & Chicken Frank | 1 | 100 | 8 | 72 | 3 | 40 | 505 | 6 | 0 | 1 | 0 | 1 med-fat meat |
| **Oscar Mayer** | | | | | | | | | | | | |
| Beef Franks | 1 | 140 | 13 | 84 | 6 | 30 | 460 | 5 | 0 | 1 | 0 | 1 high-fat meat, 1 fat |
| Big & Juicy Deli-Style Franks | 1 | 230 | 22 | 86 | 10 | 50 | 680 | 9 | 0 | 1 | 0 | 2 high-fat meat, 1 fat |
| Big & Juicy Original Beef Franks | 1 | 240 | 22 | 83 | 9 | 45 | 700 | 9 | 0 | 1 | 0 | 2 high-fat meat, 1 fat |
| Big & Juicy-Hot 'N Spicy Wieners | 1 | 220 | 20 | 82 | 8 | 45 | 750 | 10 | 0 | 1 | 0 | 2 high-fat meat, 1 fat |

| | Serving Size | Cal. | Fat (g) | % Cal. Fat | Sat. Fat (g) | Chol. (mg) | Sod. (mg) | Pro. (g) | Fiber (g) | Carb. (g) | Carb. Choices | Exchanges |
|---|---|---|---|---|---|---|---|---|---|---|---|---|
| Big & Juicy-Original Wieners | 1 | 240 | 22 | 83 | 9 | 45 | 690 | 9 | 0 | 1 | 0 | 2 high-fat meat, 1 fat |
| Big & Juicy-Quarter Pound Beef Franks | 1 | 350 | 33 | 85 | 13 | 65 | 1050 | 13 | 0 | 2 | 0 | 2 high-fat meat, 3 fat |
| Big & Juicy-Smokie Links Wieners | 1 | 220 | 19 | 78 | 7 | 50 | 770 | 10 | 0 | 1 | 0 | 2 high-fat meat, 1 fat |
| Bun Length Beef Franks | 1 | 180 | 17 | 85 | 7 | 35 | 580 | 6 | 0 | 2 | 0 | 1 high-fat meat, 2 fat |
| Bun-Length Wieners | 1 | 190 | 17 | 81 | 6 | 40 | 550 | 6 | 0 | 2 | 0 | 1 high-fat meat, 2 fat |
| Cheese Hot Dogs | 1 | 140 | 13 | 84 | 5 | 1 | 510 | 5 | 0 | 1 | 0 | 1 high-fat meat, 1 fat |
| ✔Fat-Free Beef Franks | 1 | 40 | 0 | 0 | 0 | 15 | 460 | 7 | 0 | 3 | 0 | 1 very lean meat |
| ✔Fat-Free Hot Dogs | 1 | 50 | 0 | 0 | 0 | 15 | 490 | 6 | 0 | 2 | 0 | 1 very lean meat |
| Light Beef Franks | 1 | 110 | 8 | 72 | 4 | 30 | 620 | 6 | 0 | 2 | 0 | 1 high-fat meat |
| Light Wieners | 1 | 110 | 8 | 65 | 3 | 35 | 590 | 7 | 0 | 2 | 0 | 1 high-fat meat |
| Little Wieners | 6 | 180 | 17 | 85 | 6 | 35 | 570 | 6 | 0 | 2 | 0 | 1 high-fat meat, 2 fat |
| Old Fashioned Loaf | 1 slice | 70 | 5 | 64 | 2 | 15 | 330 | 4 | 0 | 2 | 0 | 1 med-fat meat |
| Wieners | 1 | 150 | 13 | 78 | 5 | 35 | 430 | 5 | 0 | 1 | 0 | 1 high-fat meat, 1 fat |

## ICE CREAM

### Ben & Jerry's

| | Serving Size | Cal. | Fat (g) | % Cal. Fat | Sat. Fat (g) | Chol. (mg) | Sod. (mg) | Pro. (g) | Fiber (g) | Carb. (g) | Carb. Choices | Exchanges |
|---|---|---|---|---|---|---|---|---|---|---|---|---|
| Butter Pecan | 1/2 cup | 330 | 25 | 68 | 12 | 65 | 140 | 6 | 2 | 22 | 1 1/2 | 1 1/2 carb, 5 fat |
| Cherry Garcia | 1/2 cup | 260 | 16 | 55 | 11 | 70 | 60 | 5 | 0 | 26 | 2 | 2 carb, 3 fat |
| Chocolate Almond Fudge Chip | 1/2 cup | 310 | 22 | 64 | 14 | 40 | 70 | 5 | 2 | 24 | 1 1/2 | 1 1/2 carb, 4 fat |
| Chocolate Chip Cookie Dough | 1/2 cup | 300 | 16 | 48 | 10 | 65 | 95 | 5 | 0 | 34 | 2 | 2 carb, 3 fat |

✔ = Best Bet; NA = Not Available; Carb. Ch. = Carbohydrate Choices

| Ice Cream (Continued) | Serving Size | Cal. | Fat (g) | % Cal. Fat | Sat. Fat (g) | Chol. (mg) | Sod. (mg) | Pro. (g) | Fiber (g) | Carb. (g) | Carb. Ch. | Servings/Exchanges |
|---|---|---|---|---|---|---|---|---|---|---|---|---|
| Chocolate Fudge Brownie | 1/2 cup | 280 | 15 | 48 | 10 | 45 | 90 | 5 | 2 | 32 | 2 | 2 carb, 3 fat |
| Chubby Hubby | 1/2 cup | 350 | 21 | 54 | 12 | 55 | 250 | 6 | 1 | 33 | 2 | 2 carb, 4 fat |
| Chunky Monkey | 1/2 cup | 310 | 19 | 55 | 11 | 55 | 55 | 5 | 3 | 32 | 2 | 2 carb, 4 fat |
| Coffee Heath Bar Crunch | 1/2 cup | 310 | 18 | 52 | 12 | 65 | 125 | 4 | 0 | 32 | 2 | 2 carb, 4 fat |
| ✔Low-Fat Blackberry Cobbler | 1/2 cup | 180 | 3 | 15 | 2 | 20 | 70 | 3 | <1 | 34 | 2 | 2 carb, 1 fat |
| ✔Low-Fat Chocolate Comfort | 1/2 cup | 150 | 2 | 12 | 2 | 10 | 85 | 4 | <1 | 29 | 2 | 2 carb |
| ✔Low-Fat S'mores | 1/2 cup | 190 | 2 | 9 | 1 | 15 | 85 | 5 | 1 | 35 | 3 | 2 carb |
| Mint Chocolate Cookie | 1/2 cup | 280 | 17 | 55 | 11 | 70 | 130 | 4 | 1 | 28 | 2 | 2 carb, 3 fat |
| New York Super Fudge Crunch | 1/2 cup | 220 | 21 | 86 | 12 | 50 | 65 | 5 | 4 | 28 | 2 | 2 carb, 4 fat |
| Orange and Cream | 1/2 cup | 230 | 14 | 55 | 10 | 40 | 50 | 3 | 0 | 23 | 1 1/2 | 1 1/2 carb, 3 fat |
| Peanut Butter Cup | 1/2 cup | 380 | 25 | 59 | 13 | 65 | 130 | 7 | 2 | 32 | 2 | 2 carb, 5 fat |
| Triple Carmel Chunk | 1/2 cup | 290 | 17 | 53 | 12 | 40 | 105 | 4 | 0 | 32 | 2 | 2 carb, 3 fat |
| Vanilla Carmel Fudge Swirl | 1/2 cup | 300 | 17 | 51 | 10 | 70 | 115 | 4 | 1 | 33 | 2 | 2 carb, 3 fat |
| Wavy Gravy | 1/2 cup | 340 | 20 | 53 | 10 | 60 | 120 | 7 | 9 | 32 | 2 | 2 carb, 5 fat |
| World's Best Vanilla | 1/2 cup | 250 | 16 | 58 | 11 | 75 | 60 | 4 | 0 | 22 | 1 1/2 | 1 1/2 carb, 3 fat |

**Breyers**

| | Serving Size | Cal. | Fat (g) | % Cal. Fat | Sat. Fat (g) | Chol. (mg) | Sod. (mg) | Pro. (g) | Fiber (g) | Carb. (g) | Carb. Ch. | Servings/Exchanges |
|---|---|---|---|---|---|---|---|---|---|---|---|---|
| Butter Pecan | 1/2 cup | 180 | 12 | 60 | 5 | 25 | 125 | 3 | 0 | 15 | 1 | 1 carb, 2 fat |
| Chocolate | 1/2 cup | 160 | 8 | 45 | 5 | 20 | 30 | 3 | 0 | 20 | 1 | 1 carb, 2 fat |

| | Serving | Cal. | Fat (g) | % Cal. Fat | Sat. Fat (g) | Chol. (mg) | Sod. (mg) | Prot. (g) | Fiber (g) | Carb. (g) | Carb. Ch. | Exchanges |
|---|---|---|---|---|---|---|---|---|---|---|---|---|
| Chocolate Chip Ice Cream | 1/2 cup | 170 | 10 | 52 | NA | 35 | 45 | 3 | 0 | 18 | 1 | 1 carb, 2 fat |
| Coffee | 1/2 cup | 150 | 8 | 49 | 5 | 30 | 50 | 3 | 0 | 16 | 1 | 1 carb, 2 fat |
| Cookies 'N Cream | 1/2 cup | 170 | 9 | 48 | 5 | 20 | 60 | 3 | 0 | 19 | 1 | 1 carb, 2 fat |
| Mint Chocolate | 1/2 cup | 170 | 10 | 52 | 6 | 25 | 45 | 3 | 0 | 18 | 1 | 1 carb, 2 fat |
| Mocha Almond Fudge | 1/2 cup | 190 | 10 | 48 | NA | NA | 60 | 4 | 0 | 20 | 1 | 1 carb, 2 fat |
| Premium Chocolate Light Ice Milk | 1/2 cup | 120 | 4 | 30 | 2 | 15 | 55 | 3 | 0 | 18 | 1 | 1 carb, 1 fat |
| ✔ Premium Strawberry Light Ice Milk | 1/2 cup | 110 | 3 | 25 | 2 | 15 | 50 | 3 | 0 | 18 | 1 | 1 carb, 1 fat |
| Premium Vanilla Light Ice Milk | 1/2 cup | 120 | 4 | 30 | 2 | 10 | 60 | 3 | 0 | 18 | 1 | 1 carb, 1 fat |
| Strawberry | 1/2 cup | 130 | 6 | 42 | 4 | 20 | 40 | 2 | 0 | 16 | 1 | 1 carb, 1 fat |
| Vanilla | 1/2 cup | 150 | 8 | 48 | 5 | 25 | 50 | 3 | 0 | 15 | 1 | 1 carb, 2 fat |
| Vanilla Fudge Swirl | 1/2 cup | 160 | 8 | 45 | 4 | 20 | 55 | 3 | 0 | 19 | 1 | 1 carb, 2 fat |
| **Haagen Dazs** | | | | | | | | | | | | |
| Butter Pecan | 1/2 cup | 390 | 24 | 61 | 9 | 110 | 100 | 5 | 0 | 29 | 2 | 2 carb, 5 fat |
| Chocolate & Almond | 1/2 cup | 310 | 22 | 64 | 12 | <5 | 50 | 6 | 0 | 23 | 1 1/2 | 1 1/2 carb, 4 fat |
| Chocolate Chip | 1/2 cup | 290 | 20 | 58 | 10 | 105 | 40 | 5 | 0 | 28 | 2 | 2 carb, 4 fat |
| Chocolate Fudge | 1/2 cup | 290 | 14 | 50 | NA | NA | 70 | 5 | 0 | 26 | 2 | 2 carb, 3 fat |
| Chocolate Ice Cream | 1/2 cup | 270 | 18 | 60 | 11 | 115 | 75 | 5 | 1 | 22 | 1 1/2 | 1 1/2 carb, 4 fat |
| Chocolate Mint | 1/2 cup | 300 | 20 | 59 | NA | NA | 50 | 5 | 0 | 26 | 2 | 2 carb, 4 fat |
| Coffee | 1/2 cup | 270 | 17 | 58 | 8 | 55 | 120 | 5 | 0 | 26 | 2 | 2 carb, 3 fat |

✔= Best Bet; NA = Not Available; Carb. Ch. = Carbohydrate Choices

| Ice Cream (Continued) | Serving Size | Cal. | Fat (g) | % Cal. Fat | Sat. Fat (g) | Chol. (mg) | Sod. (mg) | Pro. (g) | Fiber (g) | Carb. (g) | Carb. Ch. | Servings/Exchanges |
|---|---|---|---|---|---|---|---|---|---|---|---|---|
| Cookie Dough Dynamo | 1/2 cup | 300 | 18 | 54 | NA | NA | 110 | 4 | 0 | 31 | 2 | 2 carb, 3 fat |
| ✔Low-Fat Cookies & Fudge | 1/2 cup | 180 | 3 | 15 | 2 | 15 | 115 | 7 | <1 | 33 | 2 | 2 carb, 1 fat |
| ✔Low-Fat Vanilla | 1/2 cup | 170 | 3 | 16 | 2 | 20 | 50 | 7 | 0 | 29 | 2 | 2 carb, 1 fat |
| Strawberry | 1/2 cup | 250 | 15 | 56 | 8 | 95 | 40 | 4 | 0 | 23 | 1 1/2 | 1 1/2 carb, 3 fat |
| Vanilla | 1/2 cup | 270 | 18 | 60 | 11 | 120 | 85 | 5 | 0 | 21 | 1 1/2 | 1 1/2 carb, 4 fat |
| Vanilla Peanut Butter Swirl | 1/2 cup | 280 | 21 | 66 | 8 | 110 | 120 | 5 | 0 | 19 | 1 | 1 carb, 4 fat |
| **Healthy Choice** | | | | | | | | | | | | |
| ✔Black Forest | 1/2 cup | 120 | 2 | 15 | 1 | 5 | 50 | 3 | 1 | 23 | 1 1/2 | 1 1/2 carb |
| ✔Chocolate | 1/2 cup | 130 | 2 | 14 | 1 | 5 | 70 | 3 | 0 | 24 | 1 1/2 | 1 1/2 carb |
| ✔Chocolate Chocolate Chunk | 1/2 cup | 120 | 2 | 15 | 1 | <5 | 45 | 3 | 2 | 21 | 1 1/2 | 1 1/2 carb |
| ✔Coffee & Toffee | 1/2 cup | 130 | 2 | 14 | 1 | 5 | 80 | 3 | 0 | 25 | 1 1/2 | 1 1/2 carb |
| ✔Cookies & Cream | 1/2 cup | 120 | 2 | 15 | 1 | <5 | 90 | 3 | <1 | 21 | 1 1/2 | 1 1/2 carb |
| ✔Fudge Brownie | 1/2 cup | 120 | 2 | 15 | 1 | 5 | 55 | 3 | 2 | 22 | 1 1/2 | 1 1/2 carb |
| ✔Mint Chocolate Chip | 1/2 cup | 120 | 2 | 15 | 1 | <5 | 50 | 3 | <1 | 21 | 1 1/2 | 1 1/2 carb |
| ✔Old Fashioned Butter Pecan | 1/2 cup | 120 | 2 | 15 | 1 | <5 | 60 | 3 | 1 | 22 | 1 1/2 | 1 1/2 carb |
| ✔Old Fashioned Strawberry | 1/2 cup | 110 | 2 | 16 | 1 | 0 | 35 | 2 | 1 | 20 | 1 | 1 carb |
| ✔Praline & Caramel | 1/2 cup | 130 | 2 | 14 | 2 | <1 | 70 | 3 | <1 | 25 | 1 1/2 | 1 1/2 carb |

| | Amount | Cal | Fat (g) | % Cal Fat | Sat Fat (g) | Chol (mg) | Sod (mg) | Carb (g) | Fiber (g) | Prot (g) | Carb Ch | Exchanges |
|---|---|---|---|---|---|---|---|---|---|---|---|---|
| ✓ Rocky Road | 1/2 cup | 140 | 2 | 13 | 1 | <5 | 60 | 28 | 2 | 3 | 2 | 2 carb |
| ✓ Vanilla Ice Cream | 1/2 cup | 100 | 2 | 18 | 1 | 5 | 50 | 18 | 1 | 3 | 1 | 1 carb |
| **Weight Watchers** | | | | | | | | | | | | |
| Chocolate Chip | 1/2 cup | 120 | 4 | 30 | NA | 10 | 80 | 19 | NA | 3 | 1 | 1 carb, 1 fat |
| ✓ Chocolate Ice Milk | 1/2 cup | 120 | 3 | 23 | 2 | 5 | 75 | 19 | NA | 3 | 1 | 1 carb, 1 fat |
| ✓ Heavenly Hash | 1/2 cup | 130 | 3 | 21 | 2 | 10 | 90 | 22 | NA | 4 | 1 1/2 | 1 1/2 carb, 1 fat |
| ✓ Neopolitan Reckless Rocky Road Ice Milk | 1/2 cup | 110 | 3 | 25 | 1 | 10 | 75 | 18 | NA | 3 | 1 | 1 carb, 1 fat |
| Pralines 'n Crème | 1/2 cup | 120 | 4 | 30 | NA | 10 | 110 | 19 | NA | 3 | 1 | 1 carb, 1 fat |

## ICE CREAM CONES

### (Generic)

| | Amount | Cal | Fat (g) | % Cal Fat | Sat Fat (g) | Chol (mg) | Sod (mg) | Carb (g) | Fiber (g) | Prot (g) | Carb Ch | Exchanges |
|---|---|---|---|---|---|---|---|---|---|---|---|---|
| ✓ Cake Cone | 1 | 20 | 0 | 0 | 0 | 0 | 5 | 3 | 0 | 0 | 0 | free |
| ✓ Sugar Cone | 1 | 50 | 0 | 0 | 0 | 0 | 15 | 11 | 0 | <1 | 1 | 1 carb |

## ICE CREAM TOPPINGS

### Hershey's

| | Amount | Cal | Fat (g) | % Cal Fat | Sat Fat (g) | Chol (mg) | Sod (mg) | Carb (g) | Fiber (g) | Prot (g) | Carb Ch | Exchanges |
|---|---|---|---|---|---|---|---|---|---|---|---|---|
| ✓ Chocolate Syrup | 2 Tbsp | 100 | 0 | 0 | 0 | 0 | 25 | 25 | 0 | <1 | 1 1/2 | 1 1/2 carb |
| ✓ Lite Chocolate Syrup | 2 Tbsp | 50 | 0 | 0 | 0 | 0 | 35 | 12 | 0 | 0 | 1 | 1 carb |
| Shell Chocolate | 2 Tbsp | 230 | 18 | 70 | 7 | 0 | 15 | 16 | 1 | 1 | 1 | 1 carb, 3 fat |
| ✓ Strawberry Syrup | 2 Tbsp | 100 | 0 | 0 | 0 | 0 | 10 | 26 | 0 | 0 | 2 | 2 carb |

✓ = Best Bet; NA = Not Available; Carb. Ch. = Carbohydrate Choices

| Ice Cream Toppings (*Continued*) | Serving Size | Cal. | Fat (g) | % Cal. Fat | Sat. Fat (g) | Chol. (mg) | Sod. (mg) | Pro. (g) | Fiber (g) | Carb. (g) | Carb. Ch. | Servings/Exchanges |
|---|---|---|---|---|---|---|---|---|---|---|---|---|
| **Kraft** | | | | | | | | | | | | |
| ✓Butterscotch Topping | 2 Tbsp | 130 | 2 | 14 | 1 | <5 | 150 | <1 | 0 | 28 | 2 | 2 carb |
| ✓Caramel Topping | 2 Tbsp | 120 | 0 | 0 | 0 | 0 | 90 | 2 | 0 | 28 | 2 | 2 carb |
| ✓Chocolate Topping | 2 Tbsp | 110 | 0 | 0 | 0 | 0 | 30 | 2 | 1 | 26 | 2 | 2 carb |
| Hot Fudge Topping | 2 Tbsp | 140 | 5 | 32 | 2 | 0 | 100 | 1 | <1 | 24 | 1 1/2 | 1 1/2 carb, 1 fat |
| ✓Pineapple Topping | 2 Tbsp | 110 | 0 | 0 | 0 | 0 | 15 | 0 | 0 | 28 | 2 | 2 carb |
| ✓Strawberry Topping | 2 Tbsp | 110 | 0 | 0 | 0 | 0 | 15 | 0 | 0 | 29 | 2 | 2 carb |
| **Reese's** | | | | | | | | | | | | |
| Chocolate & Peanut Butter Shell | 2 Tbsp | 220 | 17 | 70 | 8 | 0 | 70 | <1 | 1 | 17 | 1 | 1 carb, 3 fat |
| **Smucker's** | | | | | | | | | | | | |
| ✓Butterscotch Topping | 2 Tbsp | 130 | 0 | 0 | 0 | 0 | 110 | 0 | <1 | 31 | 2 | 2 carb |
| ✓Caramel Sundae Syrup | 2 Tbsp | 100 | 0 | 0 | 0 | 0 | 110 | 1 | 0 | 25 | 1 1/2 | 1 1/2 carb |
| ✓Caramel Topping | 2 Tbsp | 130 | 0 | 0 | 0 | 0 | 110 | 0 | <1 | 31 | 2 | 2 carb |
| ✓Chocolate Sundae Syrup | 2 Tbsp | 110 | 0 | 0 | 0 | 0 | 20 | 1 | 1 | 26 | 2 | 2 carb |
| Hot Fudge Topping | 2 Tbsp | 140 | 4 | 26 | 1 | 0 | 60 | 2 | 1 | 24 | 1 1/2 | 1 1/2 carb |
| Magic Shell Chocolate Fudge | 2 Tbsp | 200 | 14 | 63 | 8 | 0 | 50 | 1 | 1 | 19 | 1 | 1 carb, 3 fat |
| ✓Pineapple Topping | 2 Tbsp | 110 | 0 | 0 | 0 | 0 | 0 | 0 | 0 | 28 | 2 | 2 carb |
| ✓Strawberry Topping | 2 Tbsp | 100 | 0 | 0 | 0 | 0 | 0 | 0 | 0 | 26 | 2 | 2 carb |

# ICE CREAM TREAT/FRUIT BAR

## Weight Watchers

|  | | | | | | | | | | | | |
|---|---|---|---|---|---|---|---|---|---|---|---|---|
| ✔ Sugar Free Chocolate Mousse Ice Cream Bar | 1 | 35 | 1 | 26 | 0 | 5 | 30 | 2 | NA | 9 | 1/2 | 1/2 carb |
| ✔ Sugar Free Orange Ice Cream Bar | 1 | 30 | 1 | 30 | 0 | 5 | 40 | 2 | NA | 8 | 1/2 | 1/2 carb |

# ICE CREAM TREAT/FRUIT POPS

## Ben & Jerry's

|  | | | | | | | | | | | | |
|---|---|---|---|---|---|---|---|---|---|---|---|---|
| Cherry Garcia Yogurt Pop | 1 | 250 | 13 | 47 | 8 | 15 | 85 | 6 | 2 | 32 | 2 | 2 carb, 3 fat |
| Cookie Dough Pop | 1 | 410 | 24 | 53 | 11 | 45 | 140 | 5 | <1 | 45 | 3 | 3 carb, 5 fat |
| ✔ Strawberry Banana Manna Smoothies | 12 oz | 290 | 0 | 0 | 0 | 0 | 45 | 4 | 5 | 68 | 4 1/2 | 4 1/2 carb |
| ✔ Tropic of Mango Smoothie | 12 oz | 300 | <1 | 3 | 0 | 0 | 50 | 3 | 5 | 75 | 3 | 5 carb |
| Vanilla Heath Bar Crunch Pop | 1 | 320 | 21 | 59 | 13 | 50 | 105 | 4 | <1 | 32 | 2 | 2 carb, 4 fat |

## Dole

|  | | | | | | | | | | | | |
|---|---|---|---|---|---|---|---|---|---|---|---|---|
| Chocolate & Banana Fruit/Cream Bar | 1 | 175 | 9 | 46 | NA | NA | 20 | 2 | 0 | 22 | 1 1/2 | 1 1/2 carb, 2 fat |
| ✔ Fruit 'N Cream Bar, Strawberry | 1 | 90 | 1 | 10 | 0 | 5 | 22 | 1 | 0 | 19 | 1 | 1 carb |
| ✔ Fruit 'N Juice Bar, Strawberry | 1 | 70 | 0 | 0 | 0 | 0 | 6 | <1 | 0 | 16 | 1 | 1 carb |
| ✔ Raspberry Fruit & Yogurt Bar | 1 | 70 | 1 | 8 | NA | NA | 18 | 1 | 0 | 17 | 1 | 1 carb |
| ✔ Strawberry No Sugar Added Juice Bar | 1 | 25 | 0 | 0 | 0 | 0 | 5 | 0 | 0 | 6 | 1/2 | 1/2 carb |

## Dove

|  | | | | | | | | | | | | |
|---|---|---|---|---|---|---|---|---|---|---|---|---|
| ✔ Vanilla w/Milk Chocolate Ice Cream Bar | 1 | 260 | 17 | 59 | 11 | 30 | 45 | 3 | 0 | 24 | 1 1/2 | 1 1/2 carb, 3 fat |

✔ = Best Bet; NA = Not Available; Carb. Ch. = Carbohydrate Choices

| Ice Cream Treat/Fruit Pops (*Continued*) | Serving Size | Cal. | Fat (g) | % Cal. Fat | Sat. Fat (g) | Chol. (mg) | Sod. (mg) | Pro. (g) | Fiber (g) | Carb. (g) | Carb. Ch. | Servings/Exchanges |
|---|---|---|---|---|---|---|---|---|---|---|---|---|
| **Eskimo Pie** | | | | | | | | | | | | |
| Arctic Madness Ice Cream Sandwich | 1 | 230 | 15 | 59 | 10 | 15 | 75 | 3 | 1 | 23 | 1 1/2 | 1 1/2 carb, 3 fat |
| No Sugar Added Ice Cream Bar | 1 | 120 | 8 | 60 | 6 | 10 | 40 | 3 | 0 | 13 | 1 | 1 carb, 2 fat |
| Original Ice Cream Bar | 1 | 160 | 10 | 56 | 8 | 15 | 35 | 2 | 0 | 15 | 1 | 1 carb, 2 fat |
| **Haagen Dazs** | | | | | | | | | | | | |
| Chocolate & Dark Chocolate Ice Cream Bar | 1 | 350 | 24 | 62 | 15 | 85 | 60 | 5 | 2 | 28 | 2 | 2 carb, 5 fat |
| ✔Raspberry Stick Bars | 1 | 100 | <1 | 9 | 0 | 0 | NA | <1 | 0 | 24 | 1 1/2 | 1 1/2 carb |
| **Heath** | | | | | | | | | | | | |
| English Toffee Ice Cream Bar | 1 | 205 | 15 | 66 | 12 | 25 | 43 | 2 | <1 | 17 | 1 | 1 carb, 3 fat |
| **Klondike** | | | | | | | | | | | | |
| Light Vanilla Ice Cream Bar | 1 | 140 | 10 | 64 | NA | 10 | 45 | 3 | 0 | 10 | 1/2 | 1/2 carb, 2 fat |
| ✔Light Vanilla Ice Cream Sandwich | 1 | 100 | 2 | 18 | 1 | 5 | 110 | 2 | 0 | 18 | 1 | 1 carb |
| Vanilla Ice Cream Bar | 1 | 280 | 19 | 61 | 14 | NA | 65 | 4 | 0 | 23 | 1 1/2 | 1 1/2 carb, 4 fat |
| Vanilla Ice Cream Sandwich | 1 | 230 | 9 | 27 | 9 | NA | 220 | 5 | 0 | 33 | 2 | 2 carb, 2 fat |
| **Mr. Freeze** | | | | | | | | | | | | |
| ✔Freezer Bars, Assorted Flavors (Avg) | 2 bars | 45 | 0 | 0 | 0 | 0 | 20 | 0 | 0 | 11 | 1 | 1 carb |
| **Nestle** | | | | | | | | | | | | |
| Crunch Bar | 1 | 200 | 13 | 59 | 9 | 15 | 40 | 2 | 0 | 20 | 1 1/2 | 1 1/2 carb, 3 fat |

| | Serving Size | Cal. | Fat (g) | % Cal. Fat | Sat. Fat (g) | Chol. (mg) | Sod. (mg) | Prot. (g) | Fiber (g) | Carb. (g) | Carb. Ch. | Exchanges Per Serving |
|---|---|---|---|---|---|---|---|---|---|---|---|---|
| Drumstick | 1 | 340 | 19 | 50 | 11 | 20 | 90 | 6 | 2 | 35 | 2 | 2 carb, 4 fat |
| Reduced Fat, No Sugar Added Crunch Bar | 1 | 120 | 8 | 60 | 6 | 5 | 35 | 1 | 0 | 15 | 1 | 1 carb, 2 fat |
| **Yoplait** | | | | | | | | | | | | |
| ✔Vanilla Orange Crème Frozen Yogurt Bar | 1 | 30 | <1 | 30 | 0 | 0 | 25 | 1 | 0 | 8 | 1/2 | 1/2 carb |
| **ICE CREAM, NON-DAIRY SUBSTITUTES** | | | | | | | | | | | | |
| **Life Lite** | | | | | | | | | | | | |
| ✔Tofutti-All Flavors | 1/2 cup | 200 | 1 | 5 | NA | 0 | 80 | 2 | NA | 20 | 1 | 1 carb, 2 fat |
| **Mocha Mix** | | | | | | | | | | | | |
| Non-Dairy Mocha Mix Strawberry Swirl Frozen Dessert | 1/2 cup | 140 | 6 | 39 | 2 | 0 | 55 | 1 | 0 | 20 | 1 | 1 carb, 1 fat |
| Non-Dairy Mocha Mix Vanilla Frozen Dessert | 1/2 cup | 140 | 7 | 45 | 2 | 0 | 70 | 1 | 0 | 18 | 1 | 1 carb, 1 fat |
| **JAM/JELLY/FRUIT SPREAD (Generic)** | | | | | | | | | | | | |
| ✔Apple Butter | 2 Tbsp | 65 | <1 | 0 | 0 | 0 | 0 | 0 | <1 | 17 | 1 | 1 carb |
| ✔Honey | 1 Tbsp | 64 | 0 | 0 | 0 | 0 | <1 | <1 | 0 | 17 | 1 | 1 carb |
| ✔Jam/Marmalade, Artificially Sweetened | 1 Tbsp | 2 | <1 | 0 | 0 | 0 | 0 | <1 | 0 | 0 | 0 | free |
| ✔Jam/Marmalade/Preserves, Reduced Sugar | 1 Tbsp | 36 | <1 | <1 | 0 | <1 | 5 | <1 | | 9 | 1/2 | 1/2 carb |

✔ = Best Bet; NA = Not Available; Carb. Ch. = Carbohydrate Choices

| Jam/Jelly/Fruit Spread (Continued) | Serving Size | Cal. | Fat (g) | % Cal. Fat | Sat. Fat (g) | Chol. (mg) | Sod. (mg) | Pro. (g) | Fiber (g) | Carb. (g) | Carb. Ch. | Servings/Exchanges |
|---|---|---|---|---|---|---|---|---|---|---|---|---|
| ✔Jam/Preserves | 1 Tbsp | 48 | <1 | 0 | <1 | 0 | 8 | <1 | <1 | 13 | 1 | 1 carb |
| ✔Jam-Cherry/Strawberry | 1 Tbsp | 54 | <1 | 0 | 0 | 0 | 2 | 0 | <1 | 14 | 1 | 1 carb |
| ✔Jam-Not Cherry or Strawberry | 1 Tbsp | 54 | <1 | 0 | 0 | 0 | 2 | <1 | <1 | 14 | 1 | 1 carb |
| ✔Jelly | 1 Tbsp | 52 | <1 | 0 | <1 | 0 | 7 | <1 | <1 | 14 | 1 | 1 carb |
| ✔Orange Marmalade | 1 Tbsp | 49 | 0 | 0 | 0 | 0 | 11 | <1 | <1 | 13 | 1 | 1 carb |
| ✔Reduced Sugar Jelly | 1 Tbsp | 34 | <1 | 0 | <1 | 0 | 0 | 0 | <1 | 9 | 1/2 | 1/2 carb |
| **JUICE** | | | | | | | | | | | | |
| **(Generic)** | | | | | | | | | | | | |
| ✔Apple juice/cider, Canned/bottled | 1/2 cup | 58 | <1 | 0 | 0 | 0 | 4 | 0 | <1 | 15 | 1 | 1 fruit |
| ✔Apricot Nectar, Canned | 1/2 cup | 71 | <1 | 0 | <1 | 0 | 4 | 0 | <1 | 18 | 1 | 1 fruit |
| ✔Fruit Juice Blends, 100% Juice | 1/3 cup | 50 | <1 | 0 | 0 | 0 | 10 | <1 | <1 | 12 | 1 | 1 fruit |
| ✔Grape, Bottled | 1/3 cup | 51 | <1 | 0 | 0 | 0 | 3 | <1 | <1 | 13 | 1 | 1 fruit |
| ✔Grapefruit, Canned | 1/2 cup | 47 | <1 | 0 | 0 | 0 | 1 | <1 | <1 | 11 | 1 | 1 fruit |
| ✔Orange, Canned | 1/2 cup | 52 | <1 | 0 | <1 | 0 | 3 | <1 | <1 | 12 | 1 | 1 fruit |
| ✔Orange, Fresh | 1/2 cup | 56 | <1 | 0 | 0 | 0 | 1 | 1 | <1 | 13 | 1 | 1 fruit |
| ✔Orange, Frozen, Reconstituted | 1/2 cup | 56 | 0 | 0 | 0 | 0 | 1 | <1 | <1 | 13 | 1 | 1 fruit |
| ✔Pineapple, Canned | 1/2 cup | 70 | <1 | 0 | 0 | 0 | 1 | <1 | <1 | 17 | 1 | 1 fruit |
| ✔Prune, Bottled | 1/3 cup | 60 | 0 | 0 | 0 | 0 | 3 | <1 | <1 | 15 | 1 | 1 fruit |

## JUICE DRINKS

| | | | | | | | | | | |
|---|---|---|---|---|---|---|---|---|---|---|
| **Betty Crocker** | | | | | | | | | | |
| ✔Squeezit 100, All Varieties (Avg) | 1 bottle | 90 | 0 | 0 | 0 | 0 | 15 | 0 | 22 | 1 1/2 | 1 1/2 carb |
| ✔Squeezit, All Varieties (Avg) | 1 bottle | 110 | 0 | 0 | 0 | 0 | 0 | 0 | 27 | 2 | 2 carb |
| **Capri Sun** | | | | | | | | | | |
| ✔Coolers, All Flavors (Avg) | 6.75 oz pouch | 95 | 0 | 0 | 0 | 0 | 20 | 0 | 26 | 2 | 2 carb |
| **Fruitopia** | | | | | | | | | | |
| ✔Fruit Drink, All Varieties (Avg) | 8 oz | 110 | 0 | 0 | 0 | 0 | 78 | 0 | 29 | 2 | 2 carb |
| ✔Juice Blends, All Flavors (Avg) | 8 oz | 110 | 0 | 0 | 0 | 0 | 75 | 0 | 29 | 2 | 2 carb |
| **Fruitworks** | | | | | | | | | | |
| ✔Fruit Drink, All Varieties (Avg) | 12 oz | 160 | 0 | 0 | 0 | 0 | 90 | 0 | 43 | 3 | 3 carb |
| **HI C** | | | | | | | | | | |
| ✔Coolers, All Flavors (Avg) | 6.75 oz box | 100 | 0 | 0 | 0 | 0 | 25 | 0 | 27 | 2 | 2 carb |
| ✔Fruit Punch | 8 oz | 120 | 0 | 0 | 0 | 0 | 140 | 0 | 33 | 2 | 2 carb |
| **Kool-Aid** | | | | | | | | | | |
| ✔Bursts Soft Drink, All Varieties | 6.7 oz | 100 | 0 | 0 | 0 | 0 | 30 | 0 | 25 | 1 1/2 | 1 1/2 carb |
| ✔Cherry Drink, Sugar-Free, Low Calorie | 8 oz | 5 | 0 | 0 | 0 | 0 | 5 | 0 | 0 | 0 | free |
| ✔Fruit Drink Powder & Water | 8 oz | 89 | <1 | <1 | 0 | 0 | 34 | 0 | 23 | 1 1/2 | 1 1/2 carb |
| ✔Splash Soft Drink, Blue Raspberry | 8 oz | 120 | 0 | 0 | 0 | 0 | 35 | 0 | 30 | 2 | 2 carb |

✔ = Best Bet; NA = Not Available; Carb. Ch. = Carbohydrate Choices

| Juice Drinks *(Continued)* | Serving Size | Cal. | Fat (g) | % Cal. Fat | Sat. Fat (g) | Chol. (mg) | Sod. (mg) | Pro. (g) | Fiber (g) | Carb. (g) | Carb. Ch. | Servings/Exchanges |
|---|---|---|---|---|---|---|---|---|---|---|---|---|
| **Minute Maid** | | | | | | | | | | | | |
| ✔Coolers, All Flavors (Avg) | 6.75 oz pkg | 95 | 0 | 0 | 0 | 0 | 20 | 0 | 0 | 26 | 2 | 2 carb |
| ✔Fruit Punch Drinks, All Varieties (Avg) | 8 oz | 117 | 0 | 0 | 0 | 0 | 22 | 0 | 0 | 31 | 2 | 2 carb |
| **Ocean Spray** | | | | | | | | | | | | |
| ✔Cranberry Juice Cocktail, All Flavors (Avg) | 8 oz | 140 | 0 | 0 | 0 | 0 | 35 | 0 | 0 | 35 | 2 | 2 carb |
| ✔Cranberry Juice Cocktail, Light | 8 oz | 40 | 0 | 0 | 0 | 0 | 75 | 0 | 0 | 10 | 1/2 | 1/2 |
| ✔Mauna La'i Island Grove | 8 oz | 130 | 0 | 0 | 0 | 0 | 35 | 0 | 0 | 32 | 0 | 2 carb |
| ✔Ruby Red Grapefruit Juice Drink | 8 oz | 130 | 0 | 0 | 0 | 0 | 35 | 0 | 0 | 33 | 2 | 2 carb |
| **Snapple** | | | | | | | | | | | | |
| ✔Elements, Fruit Drinks, All Varieties (Avg) | 8 oz | 125 | 0 | 0 | 0 | 0 | 10 | 0 | 0 | 30 | 2 | 2 carb |
| ✔Hydro Fruit Drinks, All Varieties (Avg) | 8 oz | 90 | 0 | 0 | 0 | 0 | 40 | 0 | 0 | 22 | 1 1/2 | 1 1/2 carb |
| ✔Juice Drinks, All Varieties (Avg) | 8 oz | 115 | 0 | 0 | 0 | 0 | 10 | 0 | 0 | 29 | 2 | 2 carb |
| ✔Lemonade, All Varieties (Avg) | 8 oz | 120 | 0 | 0 | 0 | 0 | 10 | 0 | 0 | 30 | 2 | 2 carb |
| ✔Pink Lemonade, Diet | 8 oz | 20 | 0 | 0 | 0 | 0 | 10 | 0 | 0 | 4 | 0 | free |
| ✔WhipperSnapple, All Varieties (Avg) | 10 oz | 150 | 0 | 0 | 0 | 0 | 60 | 0 | 0 | 38 | 0 | 2 1/2 carb |
| **Tang** | | | | | | | | | | | | |
| ✔Juice Blend | 6.75 oz pouch | 100 | 0 | 0 | 0 | 0 | 30 | 0 | 0 | 26 | 2 | 2 carb |

## Tropicana Twister

| Item | Serving | Cal | Fat (g) | % Cal Fat | Sat Fat (g) | Chol (mg) | Sod (mg) | Prot (g) | Fiber (g) | Carb (g) | Carb Ch | Exchanges |
|---|---|---|---|---|---|---|---|---|---|---|---|---|
| ✓ Juice Beverage | 8 oz | 130 | 0 | 0 | 0 | 0 | 30 | <1 | 0 | 32 | 2 | 2 carb |
| ✓ Light Juice Beverage | 8 oz | 40 | 0 | 0 | 0 | 0 | 100 | <1 | 0 | 10 | 1/2 | 1/2 carb |

## V-8 Splash

| Item | Serving | Cal | Fat (g) | % Cal Fat | Sat Fat (g) | Chol (mg) | Sod (mg) | Prot (g) | Fiber (g) | Carb (g) | Carb Ch | Exchanges |
|---|---|---|---|---|---|---|---|---|---|---|---|---|
| ✓ Diet Blends | 8 oz | 10 | 0 | 0 | 0 | 0 | 35 | 0 | 0 | 3 | 0 | free |
| ✓ Regular Blends | 8 oz | 110 | 0 | 0 | 0 | 0 | 40 | 0 | 0 | 27 | 2 | 2 carb |

## KIDS MEALS/ENTREES (FROZEN)

### Hormel

| Item | Serving | Cal | Fat (g) | % Cal Fat | Sat Fat (g) | Chol (mg) | Sod (mg) | Prot (g) | Fiber (g) | Carb (g) | Carb Ch | Exchanges |
|---|---|---|---|---|---|---|---|---|---|---|---|---|
| Kid's Kitchen, Beans & Weiners | 7.5 oz | 310 | 13 | 38 | 4 | 45 | 730 | 13 | NA | 36 | 2 1/2 | 2 1/2 carb, 1 med-fat meat, 2 fat |
| Kid's Kitchen, Cheezy Mac'n Cheese | 7.5 oz | 260 | 11 | 38 | 6 | 45 | 660 | 12 | NA | 28 | 2 | 2 carb, 1 med-fat meat, 1 fat |
| Kid's Kitchen, Spaghetti & Mini Meat Balls | 7.5 oz | 220 | 8 | 32 | 4 | 20 | 880 | 11 | NA | 26 | 2 | 2 carb, 1 med-fat meat, 1 fat |
| ✓ Kid's Kitchen, Beefy Mac | 7.5 oz | 200 | 6 | 27 | 2 | 25 | 780 | 11 | NA | 25 | 1 1/2 | 1 1/2 carb, 1 med-fat meat |

### Kids Cuisine

| Item | Serving | Cal | Fat (g) | % Cal Fat | Sat Fat (g) | Chol (mg) | Sod (mg) | Prot (g) | Fiber (g) | Carb (g) | Carb Ch | Exchanges |
|---|---|---|---|---|---|---|---|---|---|---|---|---|
| ✓ Big League Hamburger Pizza (8.3 oz) | 8.3 oz | 400 | 11 | 25 | 4 | 25 | 530 | 14 | 6 | 61 | 4 | 4 carb, 1 med-fat meat, 1 fat |

✓ = Best Bet; NA = Not Available; Carb. Ch. = Carbohydrate Choices

| Kids Meals/Entrees (Frozen) (*Continued*) | Serving Size | Cal. | Fat (g) | % Cal. Fat | Sat. Fat (g) | Chol. (mg) | Sod. (mg) | Pro. (g) | Fiber (g) | Carb. (g) | Carb. Ch. | Servings/Exchanges |
|---|---|---|---|---|---|---|---|---|---|---|---|---|
| Buckaroo Beef Patty Sandwich w/Cheese | 8.5 oz | 410 | 15 | 32 | 7 | 30 | 500 | 12 | 4 | 58 | 4 | 4 carb, 1 med-fat meat, 2 fat |
| Circus Show Corn Dog | 8.8 oz | 490 | 20 | 37 | 7 | 30 | 800 | 8 | 5 | 70 | 4 1/2 | 4 1/2 carb, 4 fat |
| Cosmic Chicken Nuggets | 9.1 oz | 500 | 25 | 45 | 10 | 45 | 1070 | 18 | 5 | 50 | 3 | 3 carb, 1 med-fat meat, 4 fat |
| Funtastic Fish Sticks | 8.3 oz | 410 | 16 | 35 | 4 | 20 | 550 | 9 | 4 | 57 | 4 | 4 carb, 3 fat |
| Game Time Taco Roll Up | 7.4 oz | 420 | 18 | 67 | 7 | 25 | 740 | 9 | 4 | 55 | 3 1/2 | 3 1/2 carb, 4 fat |
| High-Flying Fried Chicken | 10.1 oz | 440 | 20 | 41 | 9 | 70 | 940 | 18 | 5 | 48 | 3 | 3 carb, 2 med-fat meat, 2 fat |
| Magical Macaroni & Cheese | 10.6 oz meal | 440 | 13 | 27 | 8 | 15 | 870 | 10 | 4 | 72 | 5 | 5 carb, 3 fat |
| Parachuting Pork Ribettes | 7.6 oz | 380 | 15 | 37 | 7 | 50 | 760 | 16 | 3 | 43 | 3 | 3 carb, 1 med-fat meat, 2 fat |
| ✔Pirate Pizza w/Cheese | 8 oz | 430 | 11 | 23 | 3 | 30 | 480 | 12 | 5 | 71 | 5 | 5 carb, 1 med-fat meat, 1 fat |
| ✔Raptor Ravioli w/Cheese | 9.8 oz | 320 | 5 | 14 | 2 | 15 | 780 | 7 | 5 | 60 | 4 | 4 carb, 1 fat |
| ✔Wave Rider Waffle Sticks | 6.6 oz | 380 | 8 | 18 | 2 | 30 | 580 | 3 | 3 | 75 | 5 | 5 carb, 2 fat |

# LUNCH KIT

## Bumble Bee

| | Amount | Cal. | Fat (g) | % Fat Cal. | Sat. Fat (g) | Chol. (mg) | Sod. (mg) | Prot. (g) | Fiber (g) | Carb. (g) | Carb. Ch. | Exchanges |
|---|---|---|---|---|---|---|---|---|---|---|---|---|
| Ready-to-Eat Fat-Free Tuna Salad with Crackers | 1 kit | 160 | 2 | 11 | 0 | 15 | 510 | 9 | 0 | 25 | 1 1/2 | 1 1/2 carb, 1 lean meat |
| Ready-to-Eat Regular Tuna Salad with Crackers | 1 kit | 280 | 18 | 58 | 3 | 15 | 400 | 10 | 1 | 21 | 1 1/2 | 1 1/2 carb, 1 med-fat meat, 3 fat |

## Eckrich

| | Amount | Cal. | Fat (g) | % Fat Cal. | Sat. Fat (g) | Chol. (mg) | Sod. (mg) | Prot. (g) | Fiber (g) | Carb. (g) | Carb. Ch. | Exchanges |
|---|---|---|---|---|---|---|---|---|---|---|---|---|
| Lunch Makers Bologna Fun Kit | 1 | 410 | 20 | 44 | 9 | 45 | 830 | 9 | 2 | 48 | 3 | 3 carb, 4 fat |
| Lunch Makers Cheese Pizza Fun Kit | 1 | 380 | 13 | 31 | 8 | 30 | 670 | 12 | 3 | 54 | 3 1/2 | 3 1/2 carb, 1 med-fat meat, 2 fat |
| Lunch Makers Chicken & Crackers | 1 | 230 | 13 | 51 | 6 | 30 | 780 | 12 | 1 | 15 | 1 | 1 carb, 1 med-fat meat, 2 fat |
| Lunch Makers Ham Fun Kit | 1 | 360 | 14 | 35 | 7 | 35 | 850 | 10 | 1 | 48 | 3 | 3 carb, 3 fat |
| Lunch Makers Nacho Fun Kit | 1 | 420 | 18 | 39 | 5 | 5 | 680 | 4 | 4 | 62 | 4 | 4 carb, 4 fat |
| Lunch Makers Pepperoni Pizza | 1 | 220 | 10 | 41 | 5 | 20 | 510 | 12 | 2 | 21 | 1 1/2 | 1 1/2 carb, 1 med-fat meat, 1 fat |
| Lunch Makers Pepperoni Pizza Fun Kit | 1 | 390 | 14 | 32 | 7 | 30 | 650 | 11 | 2 | 55 | 3 1/2 | 3 1/2 carb, 3 fat |
| Lunch Makers Turkey | 1 | 230 | 13 | 51 | 7 | 30 | 700 | 10 | 2 | 18 | 1 | 1 carb, 1 med-fat meat, 2 fat |

✔ = Best Bet; NA = Not Available; Carb. Ch. = Carbohydrate Choices

| Lunch Kit (Continued) | Serving Size | Cal. | Fat (g) | % Cal. Fat | Sat. Fat (g) | Chol. (mg) | Sod. (mg) | Pro. (g) | Fiber (g) | Carb. (g) | Carb. Ch. | Servings/Exchanges |
|---|---|---|---|---|---|---|---|---|---|---|---|---|
| Lunch Makers Turkey Fun Kit | 1 | 360 | 14 | 35 | 8 | 35 | 860 | 10 | 1 | 48 | 3 | 3 carb, 3 fat |
| **Oscar Mayer** | | | | | | | | | | | | |
| Lunchables Bologna & American | 1 | 480 | 38 | 71 | 17 | 80 | 1520 | 18 | 4 | 20 | 1 | 1 carb, 2 med-fat meat, 5 fat |
| Lunchables Deluxe Turkey/Ham | 1 | 370 | 20 | 49 | 10 | 60 | 1760 | 23 | NA | 23 | 1 1/2 | 1 1/2 carb, 2 med-fat meat, 2 fat |
| Lunchables Fun Pack Extra Cheesy Pizza | 1 | 450 | 15 | 30 | 9 | 30 | 720 | 17 | 2 | 61 | 4 | 4 carb, 1 med-fat meat, 2 fat |
| Lunchables Fun Pack Ham | 1 | 440 | 20 | 41 | 9 | 50 | 1270 | 15 | 1 | 48 | 3 | 3 carb, 2 med-fat meat, 2 fat |
| Lunchables Fun Pack Low-fat Turkey & Cheddar | 1 | 250 | 9 | 32 | 5 | 35 | 1600 | 18 | 2 | 18 | 1 | 1 carb, 2 med-fat meat |
| Lunchables Fun Pack Pizza Pepperoni | | 460 | 16 | 31 | 8 | 35 | 830 | 16 | 2 | 55 | 3 1/2 | 3 1/2 carb, 1 med-fat meat, 2 fat |
| ✓Lunchables Fun Pack Taco Bell Tacos | 1 | 460 | 13 | 25 | 6 | 35 | 950 | 20 | 2 | 69 | 4 1/2 | 4 1/2 carb, 2 med-fat meat, 1 fat |
| Lunchables Fun Pack Turkey | 1 | 450 | 20 | 40 | 9 | 50 | 1340 | 15 | 1 | 51 | 3 1/2 | 3 1/2 carb, 1 med-fat meat, 3 fat |

| | | | | | | | | | | | |
|---|---|---|---|---|---|---|---|---|---|---|---|
| Lunchables Fun Pack w/ Bologna/Wild Cherry | 1 | 530 | 28 | 48 | 13 | 70 | 1140 | 12 | 2 | 48 | 3 | 3 carb, 1 med-fat meat, 5 fat |
| Lunchables Grilled Burgers | 1 | 460 | 14 | 27 | 8 | 40 | 1060 | 15 | 1 | 67 | 4 1/2 | 4 1/2 carb, 1 med-fat meat, 2 fat |
| Lunchables Ham & Cheddar | 1 | 370 | 25 | 61 | 11 | 70 | 1680 | 21 | 2 | 18 | 1 | 1 carb, 3 med-fat meat, 2 fat |
| Lunchables Ham & Swiss | 1 | 340 | 21 | 56 | 10 | 65 | 1660 | 22 | NA | 18 | 1 | 1 carb, 3 med-fat meat, 1 fat |
| Lunchables Low Fat-Turkey | 1 | 360 | 9 | 23 | 5 | 30 | 1190 | 15 | <1 | 56 | 2 | 2 carb, 2 fruit, 1 med-fat meat, 1 fat |
| Lunchables Low-Fat Ham | 1 | 330 | 9 | 25 | 5 | 35 | 1120 | 17 | <1 | 54 | 3 1/2 | 3 1/2 carb, 2 med-fat meat |
| ✓Lunchables Pancakes & Bac'n Bites | 1 | 560 | 11 | 18 | 3 | 70 | 480 | 8 | <1 | 107 | 7 | 7 carb, 2 fat |
| Lunchables Pizza Extra Cheesy | 1 | 300 | 13 | 39 | 7 | 30 | 690 | 17 | 2 | 28 | 2 | 2 carb, 1 med-fat meat, 2 fat |
| Lunchables Pizza-Pepperoni/ Mozzarella | 1 | 310 | 15 | 44 | 7 | 35 | 790 | 15 | 2 | 28 | 2 | 2 carb, 1 med-fat meat, 2 fat |

✓= Best Bet; NA = Not Available; Carb. Ch. = Carbohydrate Choices

| Lunch Kit (*Continued*) | Serving Size | Cal. | Fat (g) | % Cal. Fat | Sat. Fat (g) | Chol. (mg) | Sod. (mg) | Pro. (g) | Fiber (g) | Carb. (g) | Carb. Ch. | Servings/Exchanges |
|---|---|---|---|---|---|---|---|---|---|---|---|---|
| Lunchables Taco Bell Nachos | 1 | 380 | 21 | 50 | 5 | 10 | 1060 | 19 | 3 | 39 | 2 1/2 | 2 1/2 carb, 2 med-fat meat, 2 fat |
| ✓Lunchables Waffles & Sausage | 1 | 550 | 14 | 23 | 3 | 55 | 520 | 9 | <1 | 100 | 7 | 7 carb, 3 fat |
| Lunchables Turkey & Monterey Jack | 1 | 360 | 22 | 55 | 11 | 75 | 1600 | 21 | NA | 18 | 1 | 1 carb, 2 med-fat meat, 2 fat |
| Salami for Beer | 2 slices | 110 | 9 | 74 | 3 | 30 | 580 | 6 | 0 | 1 | 0 | 1 high-fat meat |
| **Star Kist** | | | | | | | | | | | | |
| ✓Tuna Salad Lunch Kit, Chunk Light Tuna | 1 kit | 210 | 7 | 30 | 1 | 40 | 720 | 20 | 1 | 17 | 1 | 1 carb, 2 lean meat |
| ✓Tuna Salad Lunch Kit, Chunk White Tuna | 1 kit | 210 | 7 | 30 | 1 | 35 | 720 | 20 | 1 | 17 | 1 | 1 carb, 2 lean meat |

## LUNCH MEATS

**Bryan Foods**

| | Serving Size | Cal. | Fat (g) | % Cal. Fat | Sat. Fat (g) | Chol. (mg) | Sod. (mg) | Pro. (g) | Fiber (g) | Carb. (g) | Carb. Ch. | Servings/Exchanges |
|---|---|---|---|---|---|---|---|---|---|---|---|---|
| Beef & Pork Bologna | 1 oz | 91 | 9 | 89 | 3 | 14 | 298 | 3 | NA | <1 | 0 | 1 high-fat meat |
| ✓Boned Chicken & Broth | 1 oz | 74 | 3 | 36 | NA | NA | 153 | 6 | 0 | 0 | 0 | 1 med-fat meat |
| ✓Cubed Beef in Broth | 1 oz | 60 | 1 | 15 | NA | NA | 234 | 7 | 0 | 0 | 0 | 1 lean meat |
| ✓Deli Classics Turkey Breast | 1 oz | 54 | 2 | 33 | <1 | 17 | 17 | 7 | 0 | 0 | 0 | 1 lean meat |
| Pepperoni | 1 oz | 162 | 13 | 72 | 5 | 23 | 581 | 6 | 0 | 1 | 0 | 1 high-fat meat, 1 fat |
| Salami | 2 oz | 71 | 6 | 77 | 2 | 20 | 284 | 4 | 0 | <1 | 0 | 1 med-fat meat |
| ✓Smoked 95% Fat-Free Ham | 1 oz | 31 | 1 | 29 | <1 | 14 | 357 | 5 | 0 | <1 | 0 | 1 very lean meat |

## Butterball

| | | | | | | | | | | | | |
|---|---|---|---|---|---|---|---|---|---|---|---|---|
| ✔Chicken Breast | 6 slices | 50 | 0 | 0 | 0 | 20 | 480 | 10 | 0 | 3 | 0 | 1 very lean meat |
| ✔Turkey Breast | 6 slices | 50 | 0 | 0 | 0 | 20 | 470 | 10 | 0 | 3 | 0 | 1 very lean meat |

## Healthy Choice

| | | | | | | | | | | | | |
|---|---|---|---|---|---|---|---|---|---|---|---|---|
| ✔Deli Traditions Ocean Roasted Chicken Breast | 6 slices | 60 | 2 | 30 | <1 | 25 | 470 | 9 | 0 | 3 | 0 | 1 lean meat |
| ✔Deli-Thin Turkey Breast | 6 slices | 60 | 2 | 30 | <1 | 20 | 470 | 9 | 0 | 2 | 0 | 1 lean meat |
| ✔Savory Selections Honey Ham | 6 slices | 60 | 2 | 30 | <1 | 25 | 470 | 10 | 0 | 2 | 0 | 1 lean meat |
| ✔Savory Selections Honey Roasted Turkey Breast | 6 slices | 60 | 2 | 30 | <1 | 25 | 470 | 10 | 0 | 4 | 0 | 1 lean meat |

## Hillshire Farm

| | | | | | | | | | | | | |
|---|---|---|---|---|---|---|---|---|---|---|---|---|
| Baked Ham | 6 slices | 60 | 2 | 30 | <1 | 25 | 620 | 10 | 0 | 1 | 0 | 1 lean meat |
| Deli Select Honey Ham | 6 slices | 60 | 2 | 30 | <1 | 25 | 600 | 10 | 0 | 2 | 0 | 1 lean meat |
| Deli Select Honey Roasted Turkey | 6 slices | 70 | <1 | 13 | 0 | 25 | 540 | 11 | 0 | 4 | 0 | 2 very lean meat |
| Deli Select Smoked Chicken Breast | 6 slices | 60 | 0 | 0 | 0 | 25 | 570 | 12 | 0 | 2 | 0 | 2 very lean meat |
| Pastrami | 6 slices | 60 | 1 | 15 | <1 | 20 | 560 | 11 | 0 | 1 | 0 | 2 very lean meat |
| Roast Beef | 6 slices | 60 | 1 | 15 | 0 | 25 | 810 | 11 | 0 | 2 | 0 | 2 very lean meat |

✔ = Best Bet; NA = Not Available; Carb. Ch. = Carbohydrate Choices

| Lunch Meats (*Continued*) | Serving Size | Cal. | Fat (g) | % Cal. Fat | Sat. Fat (g) | Chol. (mg) | Sod. (mg) | Pro. (g) | Fiber (g) | Carb. (g) | Carb. Ch. | Servings/Exchanges |
|---|---|---|---|---|---|---|---|---|---|---|---|---|
| **Louis Rich** | | | | | | | | | | | | |
| Breaded Turkey Sticks | 3 | 230 | 15 | 59 | 3 | 35 | 580 | 12 | 0 | 12 | 1 | 1 strch, 1 med-fat meat, 2 fat |
| ✔Chicken Breast-Deluxe Roasted-Cold Cut | 1 slice | 30 | 1 | 30 | NA | 15 | 330 | 5 | 0 | 1 | 0 | 1 very lean meat |
| ✔Chicken Breast-Hickory Smoked-Cold Cut | 1 slice | 30 | <1 | 30 | <1 | 14 | 360 | 5 | 0 | <1 | 0 | 1 very lean meat |
| ✔Ham-Baked in Juices | 2 slices | 45 | 1 | 20 | <1 | 10 | 250 | 8 | 0 | 1 | 0 | 1 very lean meat |
| Ham-Dinner Slice-Baked | 1 slice | 85 | 2 | 21 | <1 | 40 | 1135 | 16 | 0 | 0 | 0 | 2 very lean meat |
| Ham-Honey-Thin Cut | 6 slices | 70 | 2 | 26 | 1 | 35 | 760 | 11 | 0 | 2 | 0 | 1 lean meat |
| Ham-Honey-Traditional | 2 slices | 70 | 2 | 26 | <1 | 35 | 760 | 11 | 0 | 2 | 0 | 1 lean meat |
| ✔Ham-Smoked | 2 slices | 35 | 1 | 26 | <1 | 15 | 370 | 5 | 0 | 0 | 0 | 1 very lean meat |
| Turkey Bologna | 1 slice | 50 | 4 | 72 | 1 | 20 | 270 | 3 | 0 | 1 | 0 | 1 med-fat meat |
| Turkey Bologna-Chunk | 2 oz | 51 | 4 | 71 | 1 | 19 | 270 | 3 | 0 | 1 | 0 | 1 med-fat meat |
| ✔Turkey Breast-Carving Board | 2 slices | 40 | <1 | 23 | 0 | 20 | 560 | 9 | 0 | 0 | 0 | 1 very lean meat |
| ✔Turkey Breast-Fat Free-Hickory Smoke | 1 slice | 25 | <1 | 36 | <1 | 10 | 300 | 4 | 0 | 1 | 0 | 1 very lean meat |
| ✔Turkey Breast-Fat Free-Roasted | 1 slice | 25 | <1 | 36 | <1 | 10 | 335 | 4 | 0 | 1 | 0 | 1 very lean meat |
| Turkey Breast-Hickory Smoked-Dinner Slice | 1 slice | 80 | 1 | 11 | 0 | 35 | 1060 | 16 | 0 | 2 | 0 | 2 very lean meat |
| Turkey Breast-Honey Roast-Dinner Slice | 1 slice | 80 | 1 | 11 | <1 | 35 | 940 | 16 | 0 | 3 | 0 | 2 very lean meat |

| Food | Serving | Cal. | Fat (g) | % Cal. Fat | Sat. Fat (g) | Chol. (mg) | Sod. (mg) | Prot. (g) | Fiber (g) | Carb. (g) | Carb. Ch. | Exchanges/Choices |
|---|---|---|---|---|---|---|---|---|---|---|---|---|
| Turkey Breast-Oven Roast-Dinner Slice | 1 slice | 70 | 1 | 13 | 0 | 35 | 910 | 16 | 0 | 1 | 0 | 2 very lean meat |
| Turkey Breast-Roasted-Chunk | 2 oz | 60 | 2 | 30 | <1 | 25 | 640 | 10 | 0 | 2 | 0 | 2 very lean meat |
| Turkey Breast-Roasted-Deli Thin | 4 slices | 40 | 4 | 90 | NA | 20 | 500 | 8 | 0 | 4 | 0 | 1 med-fat meat |
| Turkey Breast-Skinless-Hickory Smoke | 2 oz | 55 | <1 | 16 | <1 | 25 | 745 | 11 | 0 | 1 | 0 | 2 very lean meat |
| Turkey Breast-Smoked-Carving Board | 2 slices | 40 | <1 | 23 | <1 | 20 | 545 | 9 | 0 | <1 | 0 | 1 very lean meat |
| ✔Turkey Breast-Smoked-Cold Cut | 1 slice | 21 | <1 | 43 | <1 | 9 | 210 | 5 | 0 | <1 | 0 | 1 very lean meat |
| Turkey Breast-Smoked-Deli Thin | 4 slices | 40 | 4 | 90 | 0 | 20 | 440 | 8 | 0 | 4 | 0 | 1 med-fat meat |
| ✔Turkey Cotto Salami | 1 slice | 40 | 3 | 68 | <1 | 20 | 285 | 4 | 0 | <1 | 0 | 1 lean meat |
| ✔Turkey Ham | 1 slice | 30 | 1 | 30 | <1 | 20 | 315 | 5 | 0 | <1 | 0 | 1 very lean meat |
| ✔Turkey Ham-Chopped | 1 slice | 46 | 3 | 59 | <1 | 19 | 289 | 5 | 0 | <1 | 0 | 1 lean meat |
| Turkey Ham-Chunk | 2 oz | 70 | 2 | 26 | 1 | 40 | 600 | 10 | 0 | <1 | 0 | 1 lean meat |
| ✔Turkey Ham-Deli Thin | 4 slices | 50 | 2 | 36 | <1 | 30 | 445 | 8 | 0 | <1 | 0 | 1 lean meat |
| ✔Turkey Ham-Honey Cured | 1 slice | 25 | 1 | 36 | <1 | 15 | 215 | 4 | 0 | 1 | 0 | 1 lean meat |
| Turkey Pastrami-Chunk | 2 oz | 65 | 2 | 28 | <1 | 35 | 575 | 10 | 0 | <1 | 0 | 1 lean meat |
| ✔Turkey Salami | 1 slice | 40 | 3 | 68 | <1 | 20 | 280 | 4 | 0 | <1 | 0 | 1 lean meat |
| Turkey Salami-Chunk | 2 oz | 110 | 8 | 65 | 3 | 40 | 530 | 8 | 0 | 2 | 0 | 1 med-fat meat |
| ✔TurkeyBreast-Honey Roasted-Cold Cut | 1 slice | 35 | 1 | 26 | NA | 10 | 315 | 5 | 0 | 1 | 0 | 1 very lean meat |
| ✔White Chicken-Oven Roasted-Cold Cut | 1 slice | 35 | 2 | 50 | <1 | 15 | 335 | 5 | 0 | <1 | 0 | 1 lean meat |

✔= Best Bet; NA = Not Available; Carb. Ch. = Carbohydrate Choices

| Lunch Meats (Continued) | Serving Size | Cal. | Fat (g) | % Cal. Fat | Sat. Fat (g) | Chol. (mg) | Sod. (mg) | Pro. (g) | Fiber (g) | Carb. (g) | Carb. Ch. | Servings/Exchanges |
|---|---|---|---|---|---|---|---|---|---|---|---|---|
| **Oscar Mayer** | | | | | | | | | | | | |
| Beef Bologna | 1 slice | 90 | 8 | 80 | 4 | 20 | 310 | 3 | 0 | 1 | 0 | 1 high-fat meat |
| Beef Salami Cotto | 2 slices | 60 | 5 | 75 | 2 | 25 | 370 | 4 | 0 | 1 | 0 | 1 med-fat meat |
| Bologna | 1 slice | 90 | 8 | 80 | 3 | 30 | 290 | 3 | 0 | 1 | 0 | 1 high-fat meat |
| Bologna, Garlic | 1 slice | 130 | 12 | 83 | 5 | 40 | 420 | 4 | 0 | 1 | 0 | 1 high-fat meat, 1 fat |
| Bologna, Light | 1 slice | 60 | 4 | 60 | 2 | 15 | 310 | 3 | 0 | 2 | 0 | 1 med-fat meat |
| Bologna, Wisconsin Made Ring | 2 oz | 180 | 16 | 18 | 6 | 35 | 460 | 6 | 0 | 2 | 0 | 1 high-fat meat, 2 fat |
| Canadian-Style Bacon | 2 slices | 50 | 2 | 36 | 1 | 25 | 620 | 8 | 0 | 0 | 0 | 1 lean meat |
| Chicken Breast, Oven Roasted, Fat-Free | 4 slices | 45 | 0 | 0 | 0 | 0 | 650 | 10 | 0 | 1 | 0 | 1 very lean meat |
| ✓Deli-Thin Cooked Ham | 6 slices | 60 | 2 | 30 | <1 | 25 | 470 | 9 | 0 | 1 | 0 | 1 lean meat |
| ✓Fat-Free Bologna | 1 slice | 20 | 0 | 0 | 0 | 0 | 280 | 4 | 0 | 2 | 0 | 1 very lean meat |
| Ham & Cheese Loaf | 1 slice | 70 | 5 | 64 | 3 | 20 | 350 | 4 | 0 | 1 | 0 | 1 med-fat meat |
| ✓Ham Chopped w/Natural Juices | 1 slice | 50 | 3 | 54 | 2 | 15 | 340 | 4 | 0 | 1 | 0 | 1 lean meat |
| Ham, Boiled | 3 slices | 60 | 3 | 45 | 1 | 30 | 820 | 10 | 0 | 0 | 0 | 1 lean meat |
| Ham, Lower Sodium | 3 slices | 70 | 3 | 39 | 1 | 30 | 520 | 10 | 0 | 2 | 0 | 1 lean meat |
| Ham-Baked | 3 slices | 70 | 3 | 39 | 1 | 30 | 790 | 11 | 0 | 2 | 0 | 1 lean meat |
| Ham-Baked-Fat-Free | 3 slices | 35 | 0 | 0 | 0 | 0 | 520 | 7 | 0 | 1 | 0 | 1 very lean meat |
| Ham-Honey | 3 slices | 70 | 3 | 39 | 1 | 30 | 760 | 10 | 0 | 2 | 0 | 1 lean meat |

| | Amount | | | | | | | | | | | Exchanges/Choices |
|---|---|---|---|---|---|---|---|---|---|---|---|---|
| Ham-Honey-Fat-Free | 3 slices | 35 | 0 | 0 | 0 | 15 | 580 | 7 | 0 | 2 | 0 | 1 very lean meat |
| Ham-Smoked | 3 slices | 60 | 2 | 30 | 1 | 30 | 760 | 11 | 0 | 0 | 0 | 1 lean meat |
| Ham-Smoked-Fat-Free | 3 slices | 35 | 0 | 0 | 0 | 15 | 550 | 7 | 0 | 1 | 0 | 1 very lean meat |
| Head Cheese | 1 slice | 50 | 4 | 72 | 2 | 25 | 360 | 5 | 0 | 0 | 0 | 1 med-fat meat |
| Light Beef Bologna | 1 slice | 60 | 4 | 60 | 2 | 15 | 310 | 3 | 0 | 2 | 0 | 1 med-fat meat |
| Liver Cheese | 1 slice | 120 | 10 | 75 | 4 | 80 | 420 | 6 | 0 | 1 | 0 | 1 high-fat meat |
| Olive Loaf | 1 slice | 70 | 6 | 77 | 2 | 20 | 370 | 3 | 0 | 2 | 0 | 1 med-fat meat |
| Pepperoni | 15 slices | 140 | 13 | 84 | 5 | 25 | 550 | 6 | 0 | 0 | 0 | 1 high-fat meat, 1 fat |
| Pickle & Pimiento Loaf | 1 slice | 80 | 6 | 68 | 2 | 20 | 360 | 3 | 0 | 3 | 0 | 1 med-fat meat |
| Salami Cotto | 2 slices | 70 | 5 | 64 | 2 | 25 | 280 | 3 | 0 | 1 | 0 | 1 med-fat meat |
| Salami Genoa | 3 slices | 100 | 9 | 81 | 3 | 25 | 490 | 5 | 0 | 0 | 0 | 1 high-fat meat |
| Salami-Hard | 3 slices | 100 | 9 | 81 | 3 | 25 | 510 | 6 | 0 | 0 | 0 | 1 high-fat meat |
| Sandwich Spread | 2 oz | 130 | 10 | 69 | 4 | 25 | 460 | 4 | 0 | 8 | 1/2 | 1/2 carb, 1 high-fat meat |
| Spices Luncheon Loaf | 1 slice | 70 | 5 | 64 | 2 | 20 | 340 | 4 | 0 | 2 | 0 | 1 med-fat meat |
| Turkey Breast-Oven Roasted | 4 slices | 40 | 0 | 0 | 0 | 15 | 670 | 8 | 0 | 2 | 0 | 1 very lean meat |
| Turkey Breast-Smoked-Fat Free | 4 slices | 40 | 0 | 0 | 0 | 15 | 570 | 8 | 0 | 2 | 0 | 1 very lean meat |
| ✔Turkey-White-Oven Roasted | 1 slice | 30 | 1 | 30 | 0 | 10 | 300 | 4 | 0 | 1 | 0 | 1 very lean meat |
| ✔Turkey-White-Smoked | 1 slice | 30 | 1 | 30 | 0 | 10 | 310 | 4 | 0 | 1 | 0 | 1 very lean meat |

✔= Best Bet; NA = Not Available; Carb. Ch. = Carbohydrate Choices

## MACARONI AND CHEESE (DRY, AS PREPARED)

| Product | Serving Size | Cal. | Fat (g) | % Cal. Fat | Sat. Fat (g) | Chol. (mg) | Sod. (mg) | Pro. (g) | Fiber (g) | Carb. (g) | Carb. Ch. | Servings/Exchanges |
|---|---|---|---|---|---|---|---|---|---|---|---|---|
| **Betty Crocker** | | | | | | | | | | | | |
| Bowl Appetit, Macaroni and Cheese | 1 bowl | 370 | 12 | 29 | 4 | 15 | 1230 | 12 | 1 | 54 | 3 1/2 | 3 1/2 carb, 2 fat |
| **Kraft** | | | | | | | | | | | | |
| All Shapes Macaroni & Cheese | 1 cup | 410 | 18 | 40 | 5 | 10 | 750 | 12 | 1 | 49 | 3 | 3 carb, 4 fat |
| Deluxe Original Macaroni & Cheese | 1 cup | 320 | 10 | 28 | 6 | 25 | 730 | 14 | 1 | 44 | 3 | 3 carb, 1 med-fat meat, 1 fat |
| Macaroni & Cheese | 1 cup | 410 | 18 | 40 | 5 | 10 | 750 | 12 | 1 | 49 | 3 | 3 carb, 3 fat |
| Macaroni & Cheese Deluxe, Four Cheese Blend | 1 cup | 320 | 10 | 28 | 7 | 25 | 910 | 14 | 1 | 44 | 3 | 3 carb, 1 med-fat meat, 1 fat |
| ✓Macaroni & Cheese, Light | 1 cup | 290 | 6 | 19 | 2 | 10 | 580 | 12 | 2 | 48 | 3 | 2 carb, 1 fat |
| Macaroni & Cheese, Light Deluxe | 1 cup | 290 | 5 | 16 | 3 | 15 | 810 | 14 | 1 | 48 | 3 | 3 carb, 1 med-fat meat |
| Thick'n Creamy Macaroni & Cheese | 1 cup | 420 | 19 | 41 | 5 | 15 | 760 | 13 | 2 | 50 | 3 | 3 carb, 4 fat |
| Velveeta Rotini & Cheese w/Broccoli | 1 cup | 400 | 16 | 36 | 10 | 50 | 1230 | 18 | 2 | 47 | 3 | 3 carb, 1 med-fat meat, 2 fat |
| Velvetta Shells & Cheese Original | 1 cup | 360 | 13 | 33 | 8 | 40 | 1030 | 16 | 1 | 44 | 3 | 3 carb, 1 med-fat meat, 2 fat |

| Product | Serving Size | Cal. | Fat (g) | % Cal. Fat | Sat. Fat (g) | Chol. (mg) | Sod. (mg) | Prot. (g) | Fiber (g) | Carb. (g) | Carb. Ch. | Exchanges per Serving |
|---|---|---|---|---|---|---|---|---|---|---|---|---|
| Velveeta Shells & Cheese Salsa | 1 cup | 380 | 14 | 33 | 9 | 40 | 1180 | 17 | 2 | 47 | 3 | 3 carb, 1 med-fat meat, 2 fat |
| Velveeta Shells & Cheese w/Bacon | 1 cup | 360 | 14 | 35 | 8 | 40 | 1140 | 17 | 1 | 43 | 3 | 3 carb, 1 med-fat meat, 2 fat |
| White Cheddar Macaroni & Cheese | 1 cup | 410 | 19 | 42 | 4 | 10 | 740 | 12 | 1 | 49 | 3 | 3 carb, 3 fat |

## MACARONI AND CHEESE MEALS/ENTREES (FROZEN)

### Banquet

| Product | Serving Size | Cal. | Fat (g) | % Cal. Fat | Sat. Fat (g) | Chol. (mg) | Sod. (mg) | Prot. (g) | Fiber (g) | Carb. (g) | Carb. Ch. | Exchanges per Serving |
|---|---|---|---|---|---|---|---|---|---|---|---|---|
| Family Size Macaroni and Cheese | 7 oz | 230 | 7 | 26 | 3 | 10 | 1290 | 8 | 3 | 33 | 2 | 2 carb, 1 fat |
| Macaroni & Cheese | 9.5 oz dinner | 320 | 11 | 31 | 4 | 20 | 970 | 11 | 4 | 44 | 3 | 3 carb, 1 med-fat meat, 1 fat |

### Boston Market

| Product | Serving Size | Cal. | Fat (g) | % Cal. Fat | Sat. Fat (g) | Chol. (mg) | Sod. (mg) | Prot. (g) | Fiber (g) | Carb. (g) | Carb. Ch. | Exchanges per Serving |
|---|---|---|---|---|---|---|---|---|---|---|---|---|
| Macaroni and Cheese | 1 cup | 290 | 10 | 31 | 4 | 15 | 810 | 8 | 1 | 39 | 2 1/2 | 2 1/2 carb, 2 fat |

### Budget Gourmet

| Product | Serving Size | Cal. | Fat (g) | % Cal. Fat | Sat. Fat (g) | Chol. (mg) | Sod. (mg) | Prot. (g) | Fiber (g) | Carb. (g) | Carb. Ch. | Exchanges per Serving |
|---|---|---|---|---|---|---|---|---|---|---|---|---|
| Macaroni and Cheese Entrée | 8 oz meal | 270 | 6 | 20 | 3 | 10 | 520 | 10 | 2 | 45 | 3 | 3 carb, 1 fat |

### Healthy Choice

| Product | Serving Size | Cal. | Fat (g) | % Cal. Fat | Sat. Fat (g) | Chol. (mg) | Sod. (mg) | Prot. (g) | Fiber (g) | Carb. (g) | Carb. Ch. | Exchanges per Serving |
|---|---|---|---|---|---|---|---|---|---|---|---|---|
| ✔ Macaroni and Cheese | 9 oz meal | 320 | 7 | 19 | 3 | 25 | 580 | 15 | 4 | 50 | 3 | 3 carb, 1 med-fat meat |

### Lean Cuisine

| Product | Serving Size | Cal. | Fat (g) | % Cal. Fat | Sat. Fat (g) | Chol. (mg) | Sod. (mg) | Prot. (g) | Fiber (g) | Carb. (g) | Carb. Ch. | Exchanges per Serving |
|---|---|---|---|---|---|---|---|---|---|---|---|---|
| Macaroni and Cheese | 10 oz | 290 | 6 | 19 | 4 | 15 | 560 | 14 | 4 | 45 | 3 | 3 carb, 1 med-fat meat |

✔ = Best Bet; NA = Not Available; Carb. Ch. = Carbohydrate Choices

| Macaroni and Cheese Meals/Entrees (Frozen) (*Continued*) | Serving Size | Cal. | Fat (g) | % Cal. Fat | Sat. Fat (g) | Chol. (mg) | Sod. (mg) | Pro. (g) | Fiber (g) | Carb. (g) | Carb. Ch. | Servings/Exchanges |
|---|---|---|---|---|---|---|---|---|---|---|---|---|
| **Marie Callender** | | | | | | | | | | | | |
| Macaroni and Cheese | 13.5 oz meal | 510 | 18 | 31 | 9 | 35 | 2020 | 22 | 5 | 65 | 4 | 4 carb, 1 med-fat meat, 3 fat |
| **Morton** | | | | | | | | | | | | |
| Macaroni & Cheese | 6.5 oz | 240 | 8 | 30 | 4 | 20 | 1190 | 9 | 3 | 34 | 2 | 2 carb, 2 fat |
| **Stouffer's** | | | | | | | | | | | | |
| Macaroni & Cheese | 6 oz | 320 | 16 | 45 | 7 | 30 | 990 | 13 | 3 | 31 | 2 | 2 carb, 1 med-fat meat, 2 fat |
| **Weight Watchers Smart Ones** | | | | | | | | | | | | |
| ✓Macaroni and Cheese | 10 oz meal | 240 | 3 | 11 | 1 | 10 | 800 | 10 | 3 | 45 | 3 | 3 carb, 1 fat |
| **MARGARINE** | | | | | | | | | | | | |
| **Benecol** | | | | | | | | | | | | |
| Margarine Spread | 1 Tbsp | 80 | 9 | 100 | 1 | 0 | 110 | 0 | 0 | 0 | 0 | 2 fat |
| ✓Margarine Spread, Light | 1 container | 30 | 3 | 90 | 0 | 0 | 65 | 0 | 0 | 0 | 0 | 1 fat |
| **Blue Bonnet** | | | | | | | | | | | | |
| Soft Better Blend Vegetable Oil Spread | 1 Tbsp | 90 | 11 | 100 | 2 | 0 | 95 | 0 | 0 | 0 | 0 | 2 fat |
| Soft Margarine | 1 Tbsp | 100 | 11 | 99 | 2 | 0 | 95 | 0 | 0 | 0 | 0 | 2 fat |

| | | | | | | | | | | | |
|---|---|---|---|---|---|---|---|---|---|---|---|
| Whipped Margarine | 1 Tbsp | 70 | 7 | 90 | 1 | 0 | 70 | 0 | 0 | 0 | 1 fat |

**Fleischmann's**

| | | | | | | | | | | | |
|---|---|---|---|---|---|---|---|---|---|---|---|
| Extra Light Corn Oil Spread | 1 Tbsp | 50 | 6 | 100 | 1 | 0 | 5 | 0 | 0 | 0 | 1 fat |
| Light Corn Oil Spread | 1 Tbsp | 80 | 8 | 90 | 1 | 0 | 70 | 0 | 0 | 0 | 2 fat |
| Lightly Salted Whipped Margarine | 1 Tbsp | 70 | 7 | 90 | 2 | 0 | 60 | 0 | 0 | 0 | 1 fat |
| Move Over Butter Vegetable Oil Spread | 1 Tbsp | 90 | 10 | 100 | 2 | 0 | 100 | 0 | 0 | 0 | 2 fat |
| Reduced Calorie Diet Margarine | 1 Tbsp | 50 | 6 | 100 | 1 | 0 | 50 | 0 | 0 | 0 | 1 fat |
| Soft Margarine | 1 Tbsp | 100 | 11 | 99 | 2 | 0 | 95 | 0 | 0 | 0 | 2 fat |
| Stick Margarine | 1 Tbsp | 100 | 11 | 99 | 2 | 0 | 95 | 0 | 0 | 0 | 2 fat |
| Unsalted Whipped Margarine | 1 Tbsp | 70 | 7 | 90 | 2 | 0 | 0 | 0 | 0 | 0 | 2 fat |

**Imperial**

| | | | | | | | | | | | |
|---|---|---|---|---|---|---|---|---|---|---|---|
| Light Vegetable Oil Spread | 1 Tbsp | 60 | 6 | 90 | 2 | 0 | 110 | 0 | 0 | 0 | 1 fat |
| Reduced Calorie Diet Margarine | 1 Tbsp | 50 | 6 | 100 | 1 | 0 | 140 | 0 | 0 | 0 | 1 fat |
| Soft Margarine | 1 Tbsp | 60 | 7 | 100 | 2 | 0 | 85 | 0 | 0 | 0 | 2 fat |

**Kraft**

| | | | | | | | | | | | |
|---|---|---|---|---|---|---|---|---|---|---|---|
| Chiffon Soft Margarine | 1 Tbsp | 100 | 11 | 99 | 2 | 0 | 105 | 0 | 0 | 0 | 2 fat |
| Chiffon Whipped Margarine | 1 Tbsp | 70 | 8 | 100 | 1 | 0 | 80 | 0 | 0 | 0 | 2 fat |
| Touch Of Butter Margarine Spread | 1 Tbsp | 50 | 6 | 100 | 1 | 0 | 110 | 0 | 0 | 0 | 1 fat |
| Touch-Of-Butter Stick Margarine | 1 Tbsp | 90 | 10 | 100 | 2 | 0 | 110 | 0 | 0 | 0 | 2 fat |

✔ = Best Bet; NA = Not Available; Carb. Ch. = Carbohydrate Choices

| Margarine *(Continued)* | Serving Size | Cal. | Fat (g) | % Cal. Fat | Sat. Fat (g) | Chol. (mg) | Sod. (mg) | Pro. (g) | Fiber (g) | Carb. (g) | Carb. Ch. | Servings/Exchanges |
|---|---|---|---|---|---|---|---|---|---|---|---|---|
| **Kraft Parkay** | | | | | | | | | | | | |
| Margarine-Squeeze | 1 Tbsp | 90 | 10 | 100 | 2 | 0 | 110 | 0 | 0 | 0 | 0 | 2 fat |
| Soft Diet Margarine | 1 Tbsp | 50 | 6 | 100 | 1 | 0 | 110 | 0 | 0 | 0 | 0 | 1 fat |
| Soft Tub Margarine | 1 Tbsp | 100 | 11 | 99 | 2 | 0 | 105 | 0 | 0 | 0 | 0 | 2 fat |
| Stick Margarine | 1 Tbsp | 100 | 11 | 99 | 2 | 0 | 105 | 0 | 0 | 0 | 0 | 2 fat |
| Whipped Margarine | 1 Tbsp | 70 | 7 | 90 | 1 | 0 | 70 | 0 | 0 | 0 | 0 | 1 fat |
| **Nucoa** | | | | | | | | | | | | |
| ✔Heart Beat Margarine | 1 Tbsp | 25 | 3 | 100 | 1 | 0 | 110 | 0 | 0 | 0 | 0 | 1 fat |
| Stick Margarine | 1 Tbsp | 100 | 11 | 99 | 2 | 0 | 160 | 0 | 0 | 0 | 0 | 2 fat |
| **Promise** | | | | | | | | | | | | |
| ✔Fat-Free Ultra Tub Margarine Spread | 1 Tbsp | 5 | 0 | 0 | 0 | 0 | 90 | 0 | 0 | 0 | 0 | 1 fat |
| Vegetable Oil Spread, Tub | 1 Tbsp | 90 | 10 | 100 | 2 | 0 | 90 | 0 | 0 | 0 | 0 | 2 fat |
| **Saffola** | | | | | | | | | | | | |
| Soft Tub Margarine | 1 Tbsp | 100 | 11 | 99 | 2 | 0 | 95 | 0 | 0 | 0 | 0 | 2 fat |
| Stick Margarine | 1 Tbsp | 100 | 11 | 99 | 2 | 0 | 95 | 0 | 0 | 0 | 0 | 2 fat |
| Unsalted Margarine Stick | 1 Tbsp | 100 | 11 | 99 | 2 | 0 | 0 | 0 | 0 | 0 | 0 | 2 fat |
| **Shedd's Spread** | | | | | | | | | | | | |
| Tub Margarine Spread | 1 Tbsp | 60 | 7 | 100 | 1 | 0 | 110 | 0 | 0 | 0 | 0 | 1 fat |

| | Serving | Cal. | Fat (g) | % Cal. Fat | Sat. Fat (g) | Chol. (mg) | Sod. (mg) | Carb. (g) | Carb. Ch. | Exchanges |
|---|---|---|---|---|---|---|---|---|---|---|
| **Take Control** | | | | | | | | | | |
| Vegetable Spread | 1 Tbsp | 50 | 6 | 100 | <1 | 0 | 110 | 0 | 0 | 1 fat |
| **Weight Watchers** | | | | | | | | | | |
| Extra Light Margarine Spread | 1 Tbsp | 50 | 6 | 100 | 1 | 0 | 130 | 2 | 0 | 1 fat |
| ✔ Light Margarine Spread | 1 Tbsp | 50 | 6 | 100 | 1 | 0 | 130 | 2 | 0 | 1 fat |
| Reduced-Fat Margarine Stick | 1 Tbsp | 60 | 7 | 100 | 1 | 0 | 130 | 0 | 0 | 1 fat |
| Sodium-Free Light Margarine | 1 Tbsp | 50 | 6 | 100 | 1 | 0 | 0 | 0 | 0 | 1 fat |
| **MARSHMALLOWS** | | | | | | | | | | |
| **Kraft** | | | | | | | | | | |
| ✔ Jet Puffed Marshmallows | 5 | 125 | 0 | 0 | 0 | 0 | 25 | 30 | 2 | 2 carb |
| ✔ Marshmallow Creme | 1 oz | 90 | 0 | 0 | 0 | 0 | 23 | 23 | 1 1/2 | 1 1/2 carb |
| ✔ Miniature Marshmallows | 30 | 55 | 0 | 0 | 0 | 0 | 15 | 15 | 1 | 1 carb |
| **MAYONNAISE** | | | | | | | | | | |
| **Kraft** | | | | | | | | | | |
| Fat-Free Mayonnaise Dressing | 1 Tbsp | 10 | 0 | 0 | 0 | 0 | 120 | 2 | 0 | free |
| Light Mayonnaise | 1 Tbsp | 50 | 5 | 90 | 1 | 5 | 90 | 2 | 0 | 1 fat |
| Real Mayonnaise | 1 Tbsp | 100 | 11 | 99 | 2 | 5 | 75 | 0 | 0 | 2 fat |
| **Kraft Miracle Whip** | | | | | | | | | | |
| ✔ Miracle Whip Dressing | 1 Tbsp | 70 | 7 | 90 | 1 | 5 | 95 | 2 | 0 | 1 fat |

✔ = Best Bet; NA = Not Available; Carb. Ch. = Carbohydrate Choices

| | Serving Size | Cal. | Fat (g) | % Cal. Fat | Sat. Fat (g) | Chol. (mg) | Sod. (mg) | Pro. (g) | Fiber (g) | Carb. (g) | Carb. Ch. | Servings/Exchanges |
|---|---|---|---|---|---|---|---|---|---|---|---|---|
| **Margarine** (*Continued*) | | | | | | | | | | | | |
| ✓Miracle Whip Free Nonfat Dressing | 1 Tbsp | 15 | 0 | 0 | 0 | 0 | 120 | 0 | 0 | 3 | 0 | free |
| ✓Miracle Whip Light Dressing | 1 Tbsp | 35 | 3 | 77 | 0 | <5 | 130 | 0 | 0 | 2 | 0 | 1 fat |
| **Weight Watchers** | | | | | | | | | | | | |
| ✓Fat-Free Whipped Salad Dressing | 1 Tbsp | 12 | 0 | 0 | 0 | 0 | 125 | 0 | 0 | 4 | 0 | free |
| Light Mayonnaise | 1 Tbsp | 50 | 5 | 90 | 1 | 5 | 100 | 0 | 0 | 1 | 0 | 1 fat |
| Low-Sodium Reduced Calorie Mayonnaise | 1 Tbsp | 50 | 5 | 90 | 1 | 5 | 45 | 0 | 0 | 1 | 0 | 1 fat |
| **MEAL MIXES (FROZEN, AS PREPARED)** | | | | | | | | | | | | |
| **Green Giant** | | | | | | | | | | | | |
| ✓Create A Meal Oven Roasted, Roasted, Garlic Herb | 1 3/4 cup | 360 | 9 | 23 | 2 | 70 | 760 | 32 | 6 | 37 | 2 1/2 | 2 strch, 1 vegetable, 3 lean meatx |
| Create A Meal, Broccoli Stir Fry | 1 1/3 cup | 290 | 13 | 40 | 3 | 60 | 1160 | 27 | 4 | 16 | 1 | 3 vegetables, 3 med-fat meat |
| ✓Create A Meal, Cheese & Herb Primavera Vegetables | 1 1/4 cup | 330 | 11 | 30 | 4 | 65 | 920 | 30 | 4 | 27 | 2 | 1 1/2 strch, 1 vegetable, 3 lean meat |
| ✓Create A Meal, Creamy Alfredo Vegetables | 1 1/4 cup | 380 | 12 | 28 | 5 | 75 | 990 | 34 | 3 | 33 | 2 | 1 1/2 strch, 2 vegetables, 2 med-fat meat |

| Food | Serving | | | | | | | | | | | Exchanges/Choices |
|---|---|---|---|---|---|---|---|---|---|---|---|---|
| ✔Create A Meal, Creamy Vegetable & Chicken Noodle | 1 1/4 cup | 340 | 11 | 29 | 5 | 65 | 960 | 28 | 3 | 31 | 2 | 2 strch, 1 vegetable, 3 lean meat |
| Create A Meal, Garlic Herb Vegetables | 1 1/4 cup | 330 | 14 | 38 | 5 | 145 | 660 | 24 | 3 | 27 | 2 | 1 strch, 2 vegetables, 2 med-fat meat, 1 fat |
| Create A Meal, Ground Beef w/Cheesy Pasta & Vegetables | 1 1/4 cup | 440 | 23 | 47 | 12 | 100 | 1220 | 31 | 2 | 27 | 2 | 1 1/2 strch, 1 vegetable, 3 med-fat meat |
| Create A Meal, Ground Beef, Beefy Noodle | 1 1/4 cup | 350 | 14 | 36 | 5 | 70 | 1130 | 26 | 3 | 31 | 2 | 1 1/2 strch, 1 vegetable, 3 med-fat meat |
| Create A Meal, Ground Beef, Homestyle Stew | 1 cup | 340 | 16 | 42 | 6 | 70 | 1310 | 24 | 4 | 25 | 1 1/2 | 1 strch, 1 vegetable, 3 med-fat meat |
| Create A Meal, Ground Beef, Skillet Lasagna | 1 1/4 cup | 350 | 13 | 33 | 5 | 70 | 830 | 26 | 3 | 33 | 2 | 2 strch, 1 vegetable, 3 med-fat meat |
| ✔Create A Meal, Hearty Vegetable Stew | 1 1/4 cup | 280 | 9 | 29 | 2 | 55 | 1000 | 23 | 16 | 25 | 1 1/2 | 1 strch, 2 vegetable, 2 med-fat meat |
| ✔Create A Meal, Lemon Herb Vegetables | 1 1/2 cup | 360 | 11 | 28 | 4 | 65 | 830 | 28 | 3 | 37 | 2 1/2 | 2 strch, 1 vegetable, 3 lean meat |

✔= Best Bet; NA = Not Available; Carb. Ch. = Carbohydrate Choices

| Meal Mixes (Frozen, As Prepared) (Continued) | Serving Size | Cal. | Fat (g) | % Cal. Fat | Sat. Fat (g) | Chol. (mg) | Sod. (mg) | Pro. (g) | Fiber (g) | Carb. (g) | Carb. Ch. | Servings/Exchanges |
|---|---|---|---|---|---|---|---|---|---|---|---|---|
| ✔Create A Meal, Lo Mein Stir Fry Vegetables | 2 1/2 cup | 320 | 7 | 20 | 2 | 60 | 980 | 30 | 4 | 35 | 2 | 1 strch, 4 vegetable, 2 lean meat |
| Create A Meal, Mushroom & Wine Sauce | 1 1/4 cup | 390 | 16 | 37 | 6 | 75 | 910 | 28 | 3 | 38 | 2 1/2 | 1 1/2 strch, 2 vegetable, 3 med-fat meat |
| Create A Meal, Oven Roasted, Parmesan Herb | 1 3/4 cup | 330 | 11 | 30 | 3 | 75 | 1080 | 31 | 5 | 27 | 2 | 1 1/2 strch, 1 vegetable, 3 lean meat |
| Create A Meal, Oven, Roasted Homestyle Pot Roast | 2 cup | 370 | 13 | 32 | 3 | 70 | 860 | 29 | 5 | 33 | 2 | 2 strch, 1 vegetable, 3 med-fat meat |
| Create A Meal, Savory Onion & Vegetables | 1 3/4 cup | 340 | 13 | 35 | 3 | 70 | 1130 | 28 | 5 | 28 | 2 | 1 strch, 2 vegetable, 3 med-fat meat |
| ✔Create A Meal, Sweet & Sour Stir Fry Vegetables | 1 1/4 cup | 290 | 7 | 22 | 1 | 60 | 460 | 27 | 5 | 29 | 2 | 1 strch, 3 vegetable, 3 lean meat |
| Create A Meal, Szechuan Stir Fry Vegetables | 1 3/4 cup | 310 | 14 | 41 | 3 | 60 | 1390 | 26 | 4 | 20 | 1 1/2 | 1/2 strch, 2 vegetable, 3 med-fat meat |
| ✔Create A Meal, Teriyaki Stir-Fry Vegetables | 1 3/4 cup | 230 | 6 | 23 | 1 | 55 | 920 | 27 | 4 | 18 | 1 | 4 vegetables, 3 lean meat |
| Create A Meal, Vegetable Almond Stir-Fry | 1 1/3 cup | 320 | 12 | 34 | 2 | 65 | 1070 | 32 | 5 | 20 | 1 1/2 | 1 strch, 1 vegetable, 4 lean meat |

# MEAL MIXES, DRY (AS PREPARED)

## Betty Crocker/Chicken Helper

| Food | Serving | | | | | | | | | | | Exchanges |
|---|---|---|---|---|---|---|---|---|---|---|---|---|
| ✓Cheddar & Broccoli | 1 cup | 310 | 9 | 26 | 3 | 65 | 780 | 28 | 1 | 30 | 2 | 2 carb, 3 lean meat |
| ✓Chicken Fried Rice | 1 cup | 260 | 8 | 28 | 2 | 120 | 730 | 24 | 1 | 23 | 1 1/2 | 1 1/2 carb, 3 lean meat |
| ✓Chicken & Herb Rice | 1 cup | 260 | 7 | 24 | 2 | 60 | 490 | 24 | <1 | 26 | 2 | 2 carb, 3 lean meat |
| ✓Chicken Potato AuGratin | 1 cup | 280 | 8 | 26 | 3 | 60 | 750 | 26 | 2 | 28 | 2 | 2 carb, 3 lean meat |
| ✓Chicken & Stuffing | 1 cup | 290 | 9 | 28 | 2 | 60 | 830 | 25 | 1 | 28 | 2 | 2 carb, 3 lean meat |
| ✓Fettuccini Alfredo | 1 cup | 290 | 8 | 25 | 3 | 65 | 830 | 26 | 1 | 28 | 2 | 2 carb, 3 lean meat |
| ✓Roasted Garlic | 1 cup | 290 | 8 | 25 | 3 | 65 | 730 | 27 | 1 | 29 | 2 | 2 carb, 3 lean meat |

## Betty Crocker/Hamburger Helper

| Food | Serving | | | | | | | | | | | Exchanges |
|---|---|---|---|---|---|---|---|---|---|---|---|---|
| ✓BBQ Beef | 1 cup | 320 | 10 | 28 | 4 | 55 | 760 | 21 | 1 | 37 | 2 1/2 | 2 1/2 carb, 2 med-fat meat |
| Beef Pasta | 1 cup | 270 | 10 | 33 | 4 | 50 | 910 | 20 | 1 | 26 | 2 | 2 carb, 2 med-fat meat |
| Beef Romanoff | 1 cup | 300 | 11 | 33 | 5 | 55 | 950 | 21 | 0 | 29 | 2 | 2 carb, 2 med-fat meat |
| Beef Stew | 1 cup | 260 | 10 | 35 | 4 | 50 | 760 | 18 | 2 | 26 | 2 | 2 carb, 2 med-fat meat |
| Beef Taco | 1 cup | 280 | 10 | 32 | 4 | 50 | 960 | 19 | 2 | 31 | 2 | 2 carb, 2 med-fat meat |
| Beef Teriyaki | 1 cup | 290 | 10 | 31 | 4 | 50 | 990 | 18 | 2 | 34 | 2 | 2 carb, 2 med-fat meat |
| Cheddar & Broccoli | 1 cup | 350 | 15 | 39 | 6 | 60 | 830 | 22 | 0 | 33 | 2 | 2 carb, 2 med-fat meat |
| Cheddar Melt | 1 cup | 310 | 12 | 35 | 5 | 55 | 890 | 20 | 1 | 31 | 2 | 2 carb, 2 med-fat meat |

✓= Best Bet; NA = Not Available; Carb. Ch. = Carbohydrate Choices

| Meal Mixes, Dry (As Prepared) (Continued) | Serving Size | Cal. | Fat (g) | % Cal. Fat | Sat. Fat (g) | Chol. (mg) | Sod. (mg) | Pro. (g) | Fiber (g) | Carb. (g) | Carb. Ch. | Servings/Exchanges |
|---|---|---|---|---|---|---|---|---|---|---|---|---|
| Cheddar 'n Bacon | 1 cup | 330 | 15 | 41 | 6 | 65 | 980 | 23 | 2 | 27 | 2 | 2 carb, 2 med-fat meat, 1 fat |
| Cheeseburger Macaroni | 1 cup | 360 | 16 | 40 | 6 | 65 | 940 | 23 | 1 | 33 | 33 | 2 carb, 2 med-fat meat, 1 fat |
| Cheesy Hashbrowns | 1 cup | 400 | 19 | 43 | 6 | 60 | 530 | 21 | 2 | 39 | 2 1/2 | 2 1/2 carb, 2 med-fat meat, 2 fat |
| Cheesy Italian | 1 cup | 320 | 14 | 39 | 6 | 60 | 920 | 22 | 1 | 28 | 2 | 2 carb, 2 med-fat meat, 1 fat |
| Cheesy Shells | 1 cup | 330 | 15 | 41 | 6 | 60 | 840 | 21 | <1 | 30 | 2 | 2 carb, 2 med-fat meat, 1 fat |
| Chili Macaroni | 1 cup | 290 | 10 | 31 | 4 | 55 | 870 | 20 | 2 | 30 | 2 | 2 carb, 2 med-fat meat |
| Fettuccine Alfredo | 1 cup | 300 | 13 | 39 | 6 | 55 | 860 | 20 | 0 | 26 | 2 | 2 carb, 2 med-fat meat, 1 fat |
| Four Cheese Lasagne | 1 cup | 330 | 14 | 38 | 5 | 55 | 860 | 21 | 0 | 31 | 2 | 2 carb, 2 med-fat meat, 1 fat |
| Italian Parmesan w/Rigatoni | 1 cup | 300 | 11 | 33 | 4 | 50 | 870 | 20 | <1 | 31 | 2 | 2 carb, 2 med-fat meat |
| Lasagne | 1 cup | 270 | 10 | 33 | 4 | 50 | 1000 | 19 | 2 | 29 | 2 | 2 carb, 2 med-fat meat |
| Meat Loaf | 1/6 loaf | 270 | 14 | 47 | 6 | 110 | 580 | 24 | 0 | 11 | 1 | 1 carb, 3 med-fat meat |

| | | | | | | | | | | | | |
|---|---|---|---|---|---|---|---|---|---|---|---|---|
| Meaty Spaghetti & Cheese | 1 cup | 290 | 10 | 31 | 4 | 50 | 970 | 20 | 1 | 30 | 2 | 2 carb, 2 med-fat meat, |
| Mushroom & Wild Rice | 1 cup | 310 | 12 | 35 | 5 | 55 | 880 | 20 | 2 | 30 | 2 | 2 carb, 2 med-fat meat |
| Nacho Cheese | 1 cup | 320 | 13 | 37 | 5 | 55 | 930 | 22 | <1 | 30 | 2 | 2 carb, 2 med-fat meat, 1 fat |
| Pizza Pasta w/Cheese Topping | 1 cup | 280 | 10 | 32 | 4 | 50 | 750 | 19 | 2 | 31 | 2 | 2 carb, 2 med-fat meat |
| Pizzabake | 1/6 pan | 270 | 10 | 33 | 4 | 45 | 720 | 17 | <1 | 28 | 2 | 2 carb, 2 med-fat meat |
| Potato Stroganoff | 1 cup | 260 | 11 | 38 | 5 | 50 | 880 | 18 | 2 | 24 | 1 1/2 | 1 1/2 carb, 2 med-fat meat |
| Potatoes Au Gratin | 1 cup | 280 | 13 | 42 | 5 | 55 | 730 | 18 | 2 | 25 | 1 1/2 | 1 1/2 carb, 2 med-fat meat, 1 fat |
| Ravioli | 1 cup | 280 | 10 | 32 | 4 | 50 | 840 | 20 | 1 | 30 | 2 | 2 carb, 2 med-fat meat |
| ✔ Ravioli w/White Cheese Topping | 1 cup | 310 | 10 | 29 | 4 | 50 | 960 | 20 | 1 | 34 | 2 | 2 carb, 2 med-fat meat |
| Rice Oriental | 1 cup | 280 | 10 | 32 | 4 | 50 | 990 | 18 | 0 | 32 | 2 | 2 carb, 2 med-fat meat |
| Salisbury | 1 cup | 270 | 10 | 33 | 4 | 50 | 790 | 19 | 1 | 26 | 2 | 2 carb, 2 med-fat meat |
| Spaghetti | 1 cup | 270 | 10 | 33 | 4 | 50 | 940 | 19 | 1 | 27 | 2 | 2 carb, 2 med-fat meat |
| Stroganoff | 1 cup | 320 | 13 | 37 | 5 | 55 | 830 | 21 | 0 | 30 | 2 | 2 carb, 2 med-fat meat, 1 fat |
| Swedish Meatballs | 1 cup | 290 | 14 | 43 | 5 | 55 | 780 | 19 | 2 | 25 | 1 1/2 | 1 1/2 carb, 2 med-fat meat, 1 fat |

✔= Best Bet; NA = Not Available; Carb. Ch. = Carbohydrate Choices

| Meal Mixes, Dry (As Prepared) (Continued) | Serving Size | Cal. | Fat (g) | % Cal. Fat | Sat. Fat (g) | Chol. (mg) | Sod. (mg) | Pro. (g) | Fiber (g) | Carb. (g) | Carb. Ch. | Servings/Exchanges |
|---|---|---|---|---|---|---|---|---|---|---|---|---|
| Three Cheese | 1 cup | 340 | 15 | 40 | 5 | 55 | 830 | 21 | <1 | 32 | 2 | 2 carb, 2 med-fat meat, 1 fat |
| ✓Zesty Italian | 1 cup | 300 | 10 | 30 | 4 | 50 | 580 | 20 | 2 | 32 | 2 | 2 carb, 2 med-fat meat |
| Zesty Mexican | 1 cup | 280 | 10 | 32 | 4 | 50 | 690 | 19 | 2 | 31 | 2 | 2 carb, 2 med-fat meat |
| **Betty Crocker/Hamburger Helper, Reduced Sodium** | | | | | | | | | | | | |
| Cheddar Spirals | 1 cup | 300 | 13 | 39 | 5 | 55 | 590 | 20 | 0 | 27 | 2 | 2 carb, 2 med-fat meat, 1 fat |
| Italian Herb | 1 cup | 270 | 10 | 33 | 4 | 50 | 630 | 19 | 2 | 29 | 2 | 2 carb, 2 med-fat meat |
| ✓Southwestern Beef | 1 cup | 300 | 10 | 30 | 4 | 50 | 620 | 20 | 2 | 32 | 2 | 2 carb, 2 med-fat meat |
| **Betty Crocker/Skillet Chicken Helper** | | | | | | | | | | | | |
| ✓Stir-Fried Chicken | 1 cup | 270 | 9 | 30 | 2 | 105 | 760 | 18 | 1 | 30 | 2 | 2 carb, 2 med-fat meat |
| **Betty Crocker/Tuna Helper** | | | | | | | | | | | | |
| Au Gratin | 1 cup | 300 | 11 | 33 | 3 | 20 | 890 | 13 | 1 | 37 | 2 1/2 | 2 1/2 carb, 1 med-fat meat, 1 fat |
| ✓Cheesy Broccoli | 1 cup | 290 | 9 | 28 | 3 | 20 | 860 | 15 | 1 | 38 | 2 1/2 | 2 1/2 carb, 1 med-fat meat, 1 fat |
| Cheesy Pasta | 1 cup | 280 | 11 | 35 | 3 | 20 | 890 | 14 | <1 | 32 | 2 | 2 carb, 1 med-fat meat, 1 fat |

| | | | | | | | | | | | |
|---|---|---|---|---|---|---|---|---|---|---|---|
| Creamy Broccoli | 1 cup | 310 | 12 | 35 | 3 | 20 | 880 | 14 | 1 | 35 | 2 | 2 carb, 1 med-fat meat, 1 fat |
| Creamy Pasta | 1 cup | 300 | 13 | 39 | 4 | 20 | 910 | 14 | 1 | 31 | 2 | 2 carb, 1 med-fat meat, 2 fat |
| Fettuccine Alfredo | 1 cup | 310 | 14 | 41 | 4 | 15 | 950 | 14 | 1 | 32 | 2 | 2 carb, 1 med-fat meat, 2 fat |
| Garden Cheddar | 1 cup | 290 | 11 | 34 | 3 | 20 | 1030 | 13 | 1 | 36 | 2 1/2 | 2 1/2, 1 med-fat meat, 1 fat |
| Pasta Salad | 2/3 cup | 380 | 27 | 64 | 3 | 10 | 730 | 10 | 1 | 26 | 2 | 2 carb, 1 med-fat meat, 4 fat |
| Tetrazzini | 1 cup | 300 | 12 | 36 | 4 | 20 | 1040 | 14 | 1 | 34 | 2 | 2 carb, 1 med-fat meat, 1 fat |
| Tuna Melt | 1 cup | 300 | 13 | 39 | 4 | 20 | 900 | 12 | 1 | 34 | 2 | 2 carb, 1 med-fat meat, 2 fat |
| Tuna Pot Pie | 1 cup | 440 | 24 | 49 | 7 | 110 | 1080 | 18 | 1 | 40 | 2 1/2 | 2 1/2 carb, 2 med-fat meat, 3 fat |
| ✔Tuna Romanoff | 1 cup | 280 | 8 | 26 | 2 | 20 | 800 | 15 | 1 | 38 | 2 1/2 | 2 1/2 carb, 1 med-fat meat, 1 fat |

✔= Best Bet; NA = Not Available; Carb. Ch. = Carbohydrate Choices

| Meal Mixes, Dry (As Prepared) (*Continued*) | Serving Size | Cal. | Fat (g) | % Cal. Fat | Sat. Fat (g) | Chol. (mg) | Sod. (mg) | Pro. (g) | Fiber (g) | Carb. (g) | Carb. Ch. | Servings/Exchanges |
|---|---|---|---|---|---|---|---|---|---|---|---|---|
| **Old El Paso** | | | | | | | | | | | | |
| Burrito Dinner Kit | 1 | 290 | 14 | 43 | 5 | 40 | 780 | 15 | 1 | 26 | 2 | 2 carb, 1 med-fat meat, 2 fat |
| Fajita Dinner Kit | 2 | 300 | 12 | 36 | 4 | 25 | 810 | 15 | 1 | 34 | 2 | 2 carb, 1 med-fat meat, 1 fat |
| One Skillet Mexican, Nacho Sheese Tacos | 2 | 490 | 19 | 35 | 7 | 65 | 1470 | 24 | 2 | 55 | 4 | 4 carb, 2 med-fat meat, 2 fat |
| One Skillet Mexican, Salsa Flavored Tacos | 2 | 460 | 16 | 31 | 5 | 55 | 1390 | 23 | 3 | 57 | 4 | 4 carb, 2 med-fat meat, 1 fat |
| Soft Taco Dinner Kit | 2 | 400 | 20 | 45 | 8 | 65 | 1360 | 22 | 1 | 33 | 2 | 2 carb, 2 med-fat meat, 2 fat |
| Taco Dinner Kit | 2 | 330 | 20 | 55 | 7 | 55 | 950 | 17 | 2 | 20 | 1 1/2 | 1 1/2 carb, 2 med-fat meat, 2 fat |
| **MEAT SPREAD (CANNED)** | | | | | | | | | | | | |
| **Red Devil** | | | | | | | | | | | | |
| Chunky Chicken Snackers | 1/4 cup | 140 | 10 | 64 | 3 | 30 | 400 | 10 | 0 | 2 | 0 | 1 high-fat meat, 1 fat |
| Deviled Ham Snackers | 1/4 cup | 140 | 11 | 71 | 4 | 30 | 410 | 7 | 0 | 3 | 0 | 1 high-fat meat, 1 fat |

## Underwood

| | Serving | Cal. | | | | | | | | Carb. Ch. | Exchanges/Choices |
|---|---|---|---|---|---|---|---|---|---|---|---|
| Chunky Chicken Spread | 1/4 cup | 120 | 8 | 60 | 3 | 40 | 390 | 9 | 0 | 2 | 0 | 1 high-fat meat |
| Deviled Ham Spread | 1/4 cup | 160 | 14 | 79 | 5 | 45 | 440 | 8 | 0 | 0 | 0 | 1 high-fat meat, 1 fat |
| Honey Ham Spread | 1/4 cup | 140 | 11 | 71 | 4 | 30 | 370 | 6 | 0 | 1 | 0 | 1 med-fat meat, 1 fat |
| Liverwurst Spread | 1/4 cup | 170 | 14 | 74 | 5 | 65 | 380 | 7 | 1 | 3 | 0 | 1 high-fat meat, 1 fat |
| Roast Beef Spread | 1/4 cup | 140 | 11 | 71 | 5 | 45 | 390 | 9 | 0 | 0 | 0 | 1 high-fat meat, 1 fat |
| ✔Tuna Spread, Lightly Seasoned | 1/4 cup | 50 | 1 | 18 | 0 | 30 | 480 | 9 | 0 | 2 | 0 | 1 very lean meat |

## MEXICAN MEALS/ENTREES (AS PREPARED)

### Taco Bell Home Originals

| | Serving | Cal. | | | | | | | | Carb. Ch. | Exchanges/Choices |
|---|---|---|---|---|---|---|---|---|---|---|---|
| Chicken Fajita Dinner | 2 fajitas | 340 | 9 | 24 | 2 | 40 | 1120 | 21 | 3 | 45 | 3 | 3 carb, 2 med-fat meat |
| Soft Taco Dinner | 2 tacos | 410 | 18 | 40 | 7 | 60 | 1090 | 21 | 2 | 41 | 3 | 3 carb, 2 med-fat meat, 2 fat |
| Taco Dinner | 2 tacos | 280 | 15 | 48 | 5 | 50 | 580 | 16 | 2 | 19 | 1 | 1 carb, 2 med-fat meat, 1 fat |
| ✔Ultimate Bean Burrito Dinner | 1 burrito | 200 | 5 | 23 | 2 | 0 | 710 | 6 | 3 | 34 | 2 | 2 carb, 1 fat |
| Ultimate Nachos | 12 nachos | 240 | 11 | 41 | 3 | 0 | 680 | 6 | 4 | 31 | 2 | 2 carb, 2 fat |

✔ = Best Bet; NA = Not Available; Carb. Ch. = Carbohydrate Choices

## MEXICAN MEALS/ENTREES (FROZEN)

| Product | Serving Size | Cal. | Fat (g) | % Cal. Fat | Sat. Fat (g) | Chol. (mg) | Sod. (mg) | Pro. (g) | Fiber (g) | Carb. (g) | Carb. Ch. | Servings/Exchanges |
|---|---|---|---|---|---|---|---|---|---|---|---|---|
| **Banquet** | | | | | | | | | | | | |
| Beef Enchilada | 11 oz dinner | 370 | 12 | 29 | 5 | 20 | 1330 | 10 | 8 | 54 | 3 1/2 | 3 1/2 carb, 1 med-fat meat, 1 fat |
| Cheese Enchilada | 11 oz dinner | 380 | 10 | 24 | 4 | 20 | 1500 | 12 | 9 | 56 | 4 | 4 carb, 1 med-fat meat, 1 fat |
| Chicken Enchiladas | 11 oz dinner | 350 | 10 | 26 | 3 | 25 | 1580 | 12 | 9 | 54 | 3 1/2 | 3 1/2 carb, 1 med-fat meat, 1 fat |
| Chimichanga | 9.5 oz dinner | 500 | 24 | 43 | 8 | 20 | 1180 | 13 | 9 | 56 | 4 | 4 carb, 1 med-fat meat, 4 fat |
| Extra Helping Beef Enchilada | 15.7 oz dinner | 520 | 16 | 29 | 4 | 20 | 2320 | 20 | 7 | 73 | 5 | 5 carb, 1 med-fat meat, 2 fat |
| Mexican-Style Enchilada Combination | 11 oz dinner | 360 | 11 | 28 | 5 | 20 | 1390 | 10 | 9 | 55 | 3 1/2 | 3 1/2 carb, 1 med-fat meat, 1 fat |
| **Budget Gourmet** | | | | | | | | | | | | |
| ✔Mexican Chicken | 12.8 oz meal | 510 | 15 | 27 | NA | 40 | 1210 | 23 | NA | 70 | 4 1/2 | 4 1/2 carb, 2 med-fat meat, 1 fat |

| Product | Serving | Cal. | Fat (g) | % Cal. Fat | Sat. Fat (g) | Chol. (mg) | Sod. (mg) | Prot. (g) | Fiber (g) | Carb. (g) | Carb Ch. | Exchanges/Choices |
|---|---|---|---|---|---|---|---|---|---|---|---|---|
| Mexicana Beef | 12.8 oz meal | 560 | 23 | 37 | NA | 50 | 1290 | 33 | NA | 56 | 4 | 4 carb, 3 med-fat meat, 2 fat |
| **Delimex** | | | | | | | | | | | | |
| Beef Tamales | 1 | 240 | 12 | 45 | 2 | 15 | 710 | 11 | 3 | 23 | 1 1/2 | 1 1/2 carb, 1 med-fat meat, 1 fat |
| Beef Taquitos | 5 | 340 | 12 | 32 | 2 | 25 | 590 | 17 | 3 | 43 | 3 | 3 carb, 1 med-fat meat, 1 fat |
| Chicken Taquitos | 5 | 360 | 14 | 35 | 3 | 40 | 560 | 17 | 3 | 43 | 3 | 3 carb, 1 med-fat meat, 2 fat |
| Grilled Chicken & Cheese Quesadillas | 1 | 220 | 9 | 37 | 4 | 20 | 510 | 11 | 1 | 24 | 1 1/2 | 1 1/2 carb, 1 med-fat meat, 1 fat |
| **El Monterey** | | | | | | | | | | | | |
| Grilled Chicken & Cheese Taquitos | 3 | 310 | 13 | 38 | 3 | 20 | 540 | 11 | 1 | 36 | 2 1/2 | 2 1/2 carb, 1 med-fat meat, 2 fat |
| Monterey Shredded Beef & Cheese Burrito | 1 | 290 | 10 | 31 | 4 | 30 | 410 | 13 | 1 | 37 | 2 1/2 | 2 1/2 carb, 1 med-fat meat, 1 fat |
| **Healthy Choice** | | | | | | | | | | | | |
| Chicken Breast Con Queso Burrito | 10.6 oz meal | 350 | 6 | 14 | 3 | 35 | 590 | 14 | 6 | 60 | 4 | 4 carb, 1 fat |
| ✔ Chicken Enchilada Suprema | 11.3 oz meal | 300 | 7 | 20 | 3 | 40 | 560 | 13 | 4 | 46 | 3 | 3 carb, 1 med-fat meat |

✔ = Best Bet; NA = Not Available; Carb. Ch. = Carbohydrate Choices

| Mexican Meals/Entrees (Frozen) (Continued) | Serving Size | Cal. | Fat (g) | % Cal. Fat | Sat. Fat (g) | Chol. (mg) | Sod. (mg) | Pro. (g) | Fiber (g) | Carb. (g) | Carb. Ch. | Servings/Exchanges |
|---|---|---|---|---|---|---|---|---|---|---|---|---|
| Chicken Enchiladas Suiza | 10 oz meal | 280 | 6 | 21 | 3 | 40 | 440 | 14 | 5 | 43 | 3 | 3 carb, 1 med-fat meat |
| ✓Chicken Picante | 10.8 oz meal | 250 | 7 | 24 | 3 | 45 | 550 | 18 | 4 | 30 | 2 | 2 carb, 2 lean meat |
| ✓Fiesta Chicken Fajitas | 7 oz meal | 260 | 4 | 14 | 1 | 30 | 410 | 21 | 4 | 36 | 2 1/2 | 2 1/2 carb, 2 lean meat |
| **Lean Cuisine** | | | | | | | | | | | | |
| ✓Chicken Enchilada Suiza w/Mexican-Style Rice | 9 oz meal | 280 | 5 | 16 | 2 | 25 | 520 | 11 | 3 | 48 | 3 | 3 carb, 1 med-fat meat |
| ✓Skillet Sensations, Beef Fajita | 12 oz meal | 300 | 4 | 12 | 2 | 25 | 760 | 19 | 6 | 48 | 3 | 3 carb, 1 med-fat meat |
| **Morton** | | | | | | | | | | | | |
| ✓Chili Gravy w/Beef Enchilada & Tamale | 10 oz meal | 260 | 7 | 24 | 3 | 5 | 1000 | 8 | 4 | 40 | 2 1/2 | 2 1/2 carb, 1 fat |
| **Old El Paso** | | | | | | | | | | | | |
| Bean and Cheese Burrito | 3.5 oz | 300 | 9 | 27 | 5 | 15 | 840 | 12 | 3 | 44 | 3 | 3 carb, 1 med-fat meat, 1 fat |
| ✓Beef & Bean Burrito | 5 oz | 320 | 10 | 28 | 4 | 5 | 800 | 12 | 3 | 46 | 3 | 3 carb, 1 med-fat meat, 1 fat |
| Beef Chimichanga | 4.5 oz | 360 | 20 | 50 | 5 | 10 | 470 | 9 | 3 | 37 | 2 1/2 | 2 1/2 carb, 4 fat |
| Chicken Chimichanga | 4.5 oz | 340 | 16 | 42 | 4 | 20 | 540 | 11 | 2 | 39 | 2 1/2 | 2 1/2 carb, 1 med-fat meat, 2 fat |

| | Amount | Cal. | Fat (g) | % Fat Cal. | Sat. Fat (g) | Chol. (mg) | Sod. (mg) | Carb. (g) | Fiber (g) | Prot. (g) | Carb. Ch. | Exchanges |
|---|---|---|---|---|---|---|---|---|---|---|---|---|
| Pizza Burrito-Cheese | 3.5 oz | 240 | 9 | 34 | 4 | 20 | 430 | 27 | 0 | 13 | 2 | 2 carb, 1 med-fat meat, 1 fat |
| Pizza Burrito-Pepperoni | 3.5 oz | 260 | 10 | 31 | 5 | 20 | 510 | 31 | 0 | 12 | 2 | 2 carb, 1 med-fat meat, 1 fat |
| Pizza Burrito-Sausage | 3.5 oz | 250 | 9 | 32 | 4 | 15 | 420 | 32 | 0 | 11 | 2 | 2 carb, 1 med-fat meat, 1 fat |
| **Ortega** | | | | | | | | | | | | |
| Bean & Cheese Burrito | 10.3 oz meal | 390 | 9 | 21 | 3 | 10 | 1440 | 66 | 6 | 11 | 4 1/2 | 4 1/2 carb, 2 fat |
| Beef Enchilada | 9.4 oz meal | 360 | 13 | 33 | 5 | 25 | 1460 | 49 | 5 | 12 | 3 | 3 carb, 3 fat |
| Beef Taco Filling | 1/3 cup | 100 | 6 | 54 | 3 | 20 | 290 | 4 | 1 | 7 | 0 | 1 med-fat meat |
| Cheese Enchilada | 9.8 oz meal | 410 | 15 | 33 | 6 | 20 | 1780 | 56 | 4 | 12 | 4 | 4 carb, 3 fat |
| Chicken Enchilada | 9.5 oz meal | 400 | 16 | 36 | 6 | 35 | 1450 | 51 | 4 | 13 | 3 1/2 | 3 1/2 carb, 3 fat |
| Creamy Chicken Monterey Skillet Meals | 11.6 oz meal | 430 | 17 | 36 | 6 | 50 | 1210 | 48 | 8 | 20 | 3 | 3 carb, 2 med-fat meat, 1 fat |
| Nacho Beef Bake | 9.1 oz meal | 400 | 20 | 45 | 8 | 30 | 1510 | 36 | 3 | 19 | 2 1/2 | 2 1/2 carb, 2 med-fat meat, 2 fat |
| Nacho Chicken Supreme Skillet Meals | 11.6 oz meal | 380 | 11 | 26 | 5 | 50 | 1810 | 49 | 8 | 20 | 3 | 3 carb, 2 med-fat meat |
| ✔Skillet Fajitas, Chicken | 3/4 cup | 45 | 1 | 20 | <1 | 10 | 170 | 4 | 1 | 5 | 0 | 1 very lean meat |

✔= Best Bet; NA = Not Available; Carb. Ch. = Carbohydrate Choices

| Mexican Meals/Entrees (Frozen) (*Continued*) | Serving Size | Cal. | Fat (g) | % Cal. Fat | Sat. Fat (g) | Chol. (mg) | Sod. (mg) | Pro. (g) | Fiber (g) | Carb. (g) | Carb. Ch. | Servings/Exchanges |
|---|---|---|---|---|---|---|---|---|---|---|---|---|
| ✔Skillet Fajitas, Steak | 3/4 cup | 45 | 1 | 20 | <1 | 10 | 240 | 5 | 1 | 4 | 0 | 1 very lean meat |
| Spanish Rice & Beans w/Chicken | 10 oz meal | 400 | 17 | 38 | 5 | 45 | 1400 | 17 | 4 | 44 | 3 | 3 carb, 1 med-fat meat, 2 fat |
| **Patio** | | | | | | | | | | | | |
| Bean & Cheese Burrito | 5 oz | 300 | 9 | 27 | 5 | 15 | 690 | 9 | 4 | 46 | 3 | 3 carb, 2 fat |
| Beef & Bean Burrito-Medium | 5 oz | 320 | 12 | 34 | 5 | 25 | 840 | 10 | 4 | 43 | 3 | 3 carb, 3 fat |
| Beef Enchilada Dinner | 12 oz meal | 370 | 12 | 29 | 5 | 25 | 1700 | 12 | 8 | 52 | 3 1/2 | 3 1/2 carb, 1 med-fat meat, 1 fat |
| Cheese Enchilada Dinner | 12 oz meal | 370 | 12 | 29 | 5 | 25 | 1570 | 11 | 7 | 54 | 3 1/2 | 3 1/2, 1 med-fat meat, 1 fat |
| ✔Chicken Burrito | 5 oz | 290 | 8 | 25 | 3 | 20 | 740 | 11 | 2 | 44 | 3 | 3 carb, 2 fat |
| Chicken Enchilada Dinner | 12 oz meal | 400 | 12 | 27 | 4 | 35 | 1470 | 13 | 8 | 60 | 4 | 4 carb, 1 med-fat meat, 1 fat |
| Fiesta Dinner | 12 oz meal | 350 | 11 | 28 | 6 | 25 | 1760 | 11 | 7 | 53 | 3 1/2 | 3 1/2 carb, 1 med-fat meat, 1 fat |
| Mexican Style Dinner | 13.3 oz meal | 470 | 19 | 36 | 8 | 30 | 2210 | 15 | 10 | 59 | 4 | 4 carb, 1 med-fat meat, 2 fat |

| | Serving Size | Cal. | Fat (g) | % Cal. Fat | Sat. Fat (g) | Chol. (mg) | Sod. (mg) | Prot. (g) | Fiber (g) | Carb. (g) | Carb. Ch. | Exchanges/Choices |
|---|---|---|---|---|---|---|---|---|---|---|---|---|
| Ranchera Dinner | 13 oz meal | 470 | 22 | 42 | 10 | 35 | 2670 | 13 | 9 | 55 | 3 1/2 | 3 1/2 carb, 1 med-fat meat, 3 fat |
| **Posada** | | | | | | | | | | | | |
| Beef Chimichangas | 1 | 400 | 18 | 41 | 6 | 30 | 910 | 14 | 2 | 43 | 3 | 3 carb, 1 med-fat meat, 3 fat |
| **Rio Colorado** | | | | | | | | | | | | |
| Chili Relleno | 1 | 175 | 13 | 67 | 9 | 45 | 360 | 20 | 2 | 11 | 1 | 1 carb, 1 med-fat meat, 1 fat |
| **Stouffer's** | | | | | | | | | | | | |
| Chicken Enchilada | 4.8 oz meal | 220 | 11 | 45 | 5 | 30 | 570 | 8 | 2 | 22 | 1 1/2 | 1 1/2 carb, 1 med-fat meat, 1 fat |
| **Swanson** | | | | | | | | | | | | |
| Mexican Style Combination | 13.3 oz meal | 470 | 18 | 34 | 6 | 25 | 1610 | 18 | 5 | 59 | 4 | 4 carb, 1 med-fat meat, 3 fat |
| **Swanson Hungry-Man** | | | | | | | | | | | | |
| Mexican Style Meal | 20 oz meal | 710 | 29 | 37 | 10 | 40 | 2160 | 26 | 13 | 87 | 6 | 6 carb, 1 med-fat meat, 5 fat |

✔ = Best Bet; NA = Not Available; Carb. Ch. = Carbohydrate Choices

| Product | Serving Size | Cal. | Fat (g) | % Cal. Fat | Sat. Fat (g) | Chol. (mg) | Sod. (mg) | Pro. (g) | Fiber (g) | Carb. (g) | Carb. Ch. | Servings/Exchanges |
|---|---|---|---|---|---|---|---|---|---|---|---|---|
| **MILK** | | | | | | | | | | | | |
| **(Generic)** | | | | | | | | | | | | |
| ✓1% Low-Fat | 1 cup | 102 | 3 | 26 | 2 | 10 | 123 | 8 | 0 | 12 | 1 | 1 skim milk |
| ✓2% Reduced-Fat Milk | 1 cup | 121 | 5 | 37 | 3 | 18 | 122 | 8 | 0 | 12 | 1 | 1 reduced-fat milk |
| ✓Fat-Free Milk | 1 cup | 86 | <1 | 10 | <1 | 4 | 126 | 8 | 0 | 12 | 1 | 1 skim milk |
| Whole Milk | 1 cup | 150 | 8 | 48 | 5 | 33 | 120 | 8 | 0 | 11 | 1 | 1 whole milk |
| **Lactaid** | | | | | | | | | | | | |
| ✓Lactaid 100, Fat-Free Milk | 1 cup | 80 | 0 | 0 | 0 | 0 | 125 | 8 | 0 | 13 | 1 | 1 skim milk |
| ✓Lactaid 100, Reduced-Fat Milk | 1 cup | 130 | 5 | 35 | 3 | 20 | 125 | 8 | 0 | 12 | 1 | 1 reduced-fat milk |
| **MILK DRINKS/MILK REPLACEMENTS** | | | | | | | | | | | | |
| **Alba** | | | | | | | | | | | | |
| ✓Chocolate or Vanilla Shake Mix & Water | 1 pkt | 65 | 0 | 0 | 0 | 0 | 150 | 5 | NA | 11 | 1 | 1 carb |
| **Carnation** | | | | | | | | | | | | |
| ✓Instant Breakfast-Cafe Mocha | 1 pkt | 130 | <1 | 7 | 0 | 3 | 100 | 5 | <1 | 28 | 2 | 2 carb |
| ✓Instant Breakfast-French Vanilla | 1 pkt | 130 | 0 | 0 | 0 | 3 | 110 | 5 | 0 | 27 | 2 | 2 carb |
| ✓Instant Breakfast-Milk Chocolate | 1 pkt | 130 | 1 | 7 | <1 | <5 | 100 | 4 | 1 | 28 | 2 | 2 carb |
| ✓Instant Breakfast-Strawberry Cream | 1 pkt | 130 | 0 | 0 | 0 | 0 | NA | 5 | 0 | 28 | 2 | 2 carb |

## Carnation Sweet Success

| | Amount | Cal. | Fat (g) | % Cal. Fat | Sat. Fat (g) | Chol. (mg) | Sod. (mg) | Carb. (g) | Fiber (g) | Pro. (g) | Carb. Ch. | Exchanges |
|---|---|---|---|---|---|---|---|---|---|---|---|---|
| ✓ Creamy Milk Chocolate Powder | 1 scoop | 90 | <1 | 10 | <1 | 2 | 125 | 24 | 6 | 3 | 1 1/2 | 1 1/2 carb |
| ✓ Creamy Milk Chocolate Shake | 10 oz | 200 | 3 | 14 | <1 | 5 | 230 | 32 | 6 | 11 | 2 | 1 skim milk, 1 1/2 carb |
| ✓ Creamy Vanilla Delight | 10 oz | 200 | 3 | 14 | <1 | NA | 230 | 32 | 6 | 11 | 2 | 2 skim milk, 1 1/2 carb |
| No Sugar Added Instant Breakfast, All Flavors (Avg) | 1 pkt | 70 | 1 | 13 | 1 | <5 | 100 | 12 | 1 | 5 | 1 | 1 skim milk |
| **Health Valley** | | | | | | | | | | | | |
| ✓ Fat-Free Soy Moo Milk | 1 cup | 110 | 0 | 0 | 0 | 0 | 25 | 19 | 0 | 7 | 1 | 1 carb |
| **Mocha Mix** | | | | | | | | | | | | |
| ✓ Fat-Free Mocha Mix | 1 Tbsp | 10 | 0 | 0 | 0 | 0 | 5 | 1 | 0 | 0 | 0 | free |
| ✓ Light Mocha Mix | 1 Tbsp | 20 | 2 | 90 | 0 | 0 | 5 | 1 | 0 | 0 | 0 | free |
| ✓ Mocha Mix, Regular | 1 Tbsp | 20 | 2 | 90 | 0 | 0 | 5 | 1 | 0 | 0 | 0 | free |
| ✓ Soy Milk, Vanilla | 1 cup | 110 | 3 | 25 | <1 | 0 | 135 | 14 | 3 | 6 | 1 | 1 carb, 1 lean meat |
| **Ovaltine** | | | | | | | | | | | | |
| ✓ Malted Milk Drink, Chocolate Malt/Rich Chocolate | 4 Tbsp | 80 | 0 | 0 | 0 | 0 | 115 | 18 | <1 | 1 | 1 | 1 carb |
| **Pillsbury** | | | | | | | | | | | | |
| ✓ Instant Breakfast Chocolate/Strawberry | 1 pkt | 130 | <1 | 7 | 0 | NA | 135 | 26 | 0 | 6 | 2 | 2 carb |

✓ = Best Bet; NA = Not Available; Carb. Ch. = Carbohydrate Choices

| Milk Drinks/Milk Replacements (Continued) | Serving Size | Cal. | Fat (g) | % Cal. Fat | Sat. Fat (g) | Chol. (mg) | Sod. (mg) | Pro. (g) | Fiber (g) | Carb. (g) | Carb. Ch. | Servings/Exchanges |
|---|---|---|---|---|---|---|---|---|---|---|---|---|
| **Regular Slim Fast** | | | | | | | | | | | | |
| ✓Chocolate Powder w/Skim Milk | 1 cup | 190 | 1 | 5 | 1 | NA | NA | 14 | 2 | 32 | 2 | 2 skim milk, 1/2 carb |
| ✓Vanilla Powder w/Skim Milk | 1 cup | 190 | 1 | 5 | <1 | NA | 220 | 14 | 2 | 32 | 2 | 2 skim milk, 1/2 carb |
| **Ultra Slim Fast** | | | | | | | | | | | | |
| ✓Chocolate Royale Powder w/Skim Milk | 1 cup | 200 | 2 | 9 | 1 | 5 | 130 | 14 | 5 | 36 | 2 1/2 | 2 skim milk, 1 carb |
| ✓French Vanilla | 11 oz | 220 | 3 | 12 | <1 | 5 | 220 | 10 | 5 | 40 | 2 1/2 | 1 1/2 skim milk, 1 1/2 carb |
| ✓Orange Pineapple | 11 oz | 220 | 2 | 8 | <1 | 10 | 200 | 7 | 5 | 46 | 3 | 1 skim milk, 2 carb |
| ✓Rich Chocolate Royale | 11 oz | 220 | 3 | 12 | 1 | 5 | 220 | 10 | 5 | 38 | 2 1/2 | 1 1/2 skim milk, 1 carb |
| ✓Vanilla Powder w/Skim Milk | 1 cup | 200 | 1 | 5 | <1 | 5 | 130 | 14 | 5 | 37 | 2 1/2 | 2 skim milk, 1 carb |

## MUFFIN MIX (AS PREPARED)

| Betty Crocker | Serving Size | Cal. | Fat (g) | % Cal. Fat | Sat. Fat (g) | Chol. (mg) | Sod. (mg) | Pro. (g) | Fiber (g) | Carb. (g) | Carb. Ch. | Servings/Exchanges |
|---|---|---|---|---|---|---|---|---|---|---|---|---|
| Apple Cinnamon Muffin Mix (Pouch) | 1 muffin | 170 | 7 | 37 | 2 | 35 | 220 | 3 | 0 | 24 | 1 1/2 | 1 1/2 carb, 1 fat |
| Apple Streusel Muffin Mix | 1 muffin | 210 | 8 | 34 | 2 | 20 | 220 | 2 | 0 | 33 | 2 | 2 carb, 2 fat |
| Banana Nut Muffin Mix | 1 muffin | 170 | 6 | 32 | 1 | 20 | 250 | 3 | 1 | 27 | 2 | 2 carb, 1 fat |
| Banana Nut Muffin Mix (Pouch) | 1 muffin | 170 | 7 | 37 | 2 | 35 | 250 | 3 | 0 | 22 | 1 1/2 | 1 1/2, 1 fat |
| Blueberry Muffin Mix (Pouch) | 1 muffin | 160 | 6 | 34 | 2 | 35 | 220 | 3 | 0 | 25 | 1 1/2 | 1 1/2 carb, 1 fat |
| Chocolate Chip Muffin Mix (Pouch) | 1 muffin | 170 | 8 | 42 | 3 | 35 | 220 | 3 | 0 | 23 | 1 1/2 | 1 1/2 carb, 2 fat |

| | | | | | | | | | | | | |
|---|---|---|---|---|---|---|---|---|---|---|---|---|
| Corn Muffin Mix (Pouch) | 1 muffin | 160 | 5 | 28 | 2 | 35 | 260 | 3 | 0 | 25 | 1 1/2 | 1 1/2 carb, 1 fat |
| Cranberry Orange Muffin Mix | 1 muffin | 150 | 5 | 30 | 1 | 20 | 180 | 2 | 0 | 25 | 1 1/2 | 1 1/2 carb, 1 fat |
| Double Chocolate Muffin Mix | 1 muffin | 200 | 8 | 36 | 3 | 20 | 220 | 3 | 0 | 30 | 2 | 2 carb, 2 fat |
| Lemon Poppyseed Muffin Mix | 1 muffin | 190 | 7 | 33 | 1 | 20 | 230 | 2 | 0 | 29 | 2 | 2 carb, 1 fat |
| Lemon Poppyseed Muffin Mix (Pouch) | 1 muffin | 180 | 8 | 40 | 2 | 35 | 190 | 3 | 0 | 25 | 1 1/2 | 1 1/2 carb, 2 fat |
| Twice the Blueberry Muffin Mix | 1 muffin | 140 | 4 | 26 | 1 | 20 | 180 | 2 | 1 | 25 | 1 1/2 | 1 1/2 carb, 1 fat |
| Wild Blueberry Muffin Mix | 1 muffin | 170 | 5 | 26 | 1 | 20 | 220 | 2 | <1 | 28 | 2 | 2 carb, 1 fat |
| **Betty Crocker/Sweet Rewards** | | | | | | | | | | | | |
| ✔Apple Cinnamon Low Fat Muffin Mix | 1 muffin | 140 | 2 | 13 | 0 | 20 | 200 | 2 | 0 | 28 | 2 | 2 carb |
| ✔Fat-Free Muffin Mix, All Varieties (Avg) | 1 muffin | 120 | 0 | 0 | 0 | 0 | 200 | 2 | 0 | 28 | 2 | 2 carb |
| ✔Wild Blueberry Low Fat Muffin Mix | 1 muffin | 130 | 2 | 14 | 0 | 20 | 190 | 2 | 0 | 26 | 2 | 2 carb |
| **Gold Medal/General Mills** | | | | | | | | | | | | |
| Blueberry Muffin Mix | 1 | 260 | 7 | 24 | 2 | 10 | 320 | 3 | <1 | 44 | 3 | 3 strch, 1 fat |
| Raisin Bran Muffin Mix | 1 | 270 | 8 | 27 | 2 | 10 | 450 | 3 | 2 | 46 | 3 | 3 strch, 2 fat |
| **Pillsbury** | | | | | | | | | | | | |
| Blueberry Muffins | 1 | 180 | 5 | 25 | 2 | 5 | 190 | 3 | 0 | 31 | 2 | 2 strch, 1 fat |
| Chocolate Chip | 1/3 cup | 190 | 6 | 28 | 3 | 5 | 190 | 3 | <1 | 31 | 2 | 2 strch, 1 fat |
| Chocolate Chip Muffins | 1 | 190 | 6 | 28 | 3 | 5 | 190 | 3 | <1 | 31 | 2 | 2 strch, 1 fat |
| ✔Low Fat Blueberry Muffins | 1 | 160 | 2 | 11 | 1 | 0 | 210 | 2 | <1 | 34 | 2 | 2 strch |

✔= Best Bet; NA = Not Available; Carb. Ch. = Carbohydrate Choices

# MUFFINS/SCONES

| Product | Serving Size | Cal. | Fat (g) | % Cal. Fat | Sat. Fat (g) | Chol. (mg) | Sod. (mg) | Pro. (g) | Fiber (g) | Carb. (g) | Carb. Ch. | Servings/Exchanges |
|---|---|---|---|---|---|---|---|---|---|---|---|---|
| **Entenmann's** | | | | | | | | | | | | |
| Blueberry Muffins | 1 | 160 | 7 | 39 | 2 | 40 | 210 | 2 | <1 | 24 | 1 1/2 | 1 1/2 carb, 1 fat |
| ✔Fat-Free Blueberry Muffins | 1 | 120 | 0 | 0 | 0 | 0 | 220 | 2 | <1 | 26 | 2 | 2 carb |
| **Health Valley** | | | | | | | | | | | | |
| ✔Fat-Free Apple Kiwi Scones | 1 | 80 | 0 | 0 | 0 | 0 | 160 | 7 | 7 | 15 | 1 | 1 strch |
| ✔Fat-Free Cinnamon Raisin Scones | 1 | 80 | 0 | 0 | 0 | 0 | 160 | 7 | 7 | 15 | 1 | 1 strch |
| ✔Fat-Free Cranberry Orange Scones | 1 | 80 | 0 | 0 | 0 | 0 | 160 | 7 | 7 | 15 | 1 | 1 strch |
| ✔Fat-Free Mountain Blueberry Scones | 1 | 80 | 0 | 0 | 0 | 0 | 160 | 7 | 7 | 15 | 1 | 1 strch |
| ✔Fat-Free Pineapple Raisin Scones | 1 | 80 | 0 | 0 | 0 | 0 | 160 | 7 | 7 | 15 | 1 | 1 strch |
| **Kellogg's Eggo** | | | | | | | | | | | | |
| Blueberry Toaster Muffins | 1 | 120 | 4 | 30 | <1 | 15 | 250 | 3 | 0 | 19 | 1 | 1 strch, 1 fat |
| Cinnamon Toaster Muffins | 1 | 130 | 5 | 35 | 1 | 15 | 270 | 3 | 0 | 20 | 1 | 1 strch, 1 fat |
| Strawberry Toaster Muffins | 1 | 130 | 5 | 35 | 1 | 15 | 260 | 3 | 0 | 20 | 1 | 1 strch, 1 fat |
| **Otis Spunkmeyer** | | | | | | | | | | | | |
| Almond Poppy Seed Muffin | 1/2 of 2 oz | 210 | 12 | 51 | 3 | 40 | 230 | 3 | <1 | 23 | 1 1/2 | 1 1/2 carb, 2 fat |
| Banana Nut Muffin | 1/2 of 2 oz | 240 | 12 | 45 | 2 | 25 | 190 | 3 | <1 | 30 | 2 | 2 carb, 2 fat |
| Chocolate, Chocolate Chip Muffin | 1/2 of 2 oz | 230 | 12 | 47 | 3 | 35 | 170 | 3 | <1 | 29 | 2 | 2 carb, 2 fat |

|  | | | | | | | | | | | | |
|---|---|---|---|---|---|---|---|---|---|---|---|---|
| Wild Blueberry Muffin | 1/2 of 2 oz | 210 | 11 | 47 | 3 | 40 | 200 | 3 | <1 | 24 | 1 1/2 | 1 1/2 carb, 2 fat |
| **Pepperidge Farm** | | | | | | | | | | | | |
| Apple Oatmeal Muffins | 1 | 160 | 4 | 23 | <1 | 0 | 190 | 4 | 3 | 28 | 2 | 2 strch, 1 fat |
| ✔Blueberry Muffins | 1 | 140 | 3 | 19 | 0 | 0 | 190 | 3 | 2 | 27 | 2 | 2 strch, 1 fat |
| ✔Bran w/Raisins Muffins | 1 | 150 | 3 | 18 | <1 | 0 | 260 | 4 | 4 | 30 | 2 | 2 strch, 1 fat |
| ✔Corn Muffins | 1 | 150 | 3 | 18 | 0 | 0 | 190 | 4 | 1 | 27 | 2 | 2 strch, 1 fat |
| **Weight Watchers** | | | | | | | | | | | | |
| Apple Spice Muffins | 1 | 160 | 5 | 28 | 1 | NA | 260 | 3 | NA | 29 | 2 | 2 strch, 1 fat |
| Banana Nut Muffins | 1 | 170 | 5 | 26 | 1 | 10 | 250 | 3 | NA | 32 | 2 | 2 strch, 1 fat |
| Blueberry Muffins | 1 | 170 | 5 | 26 | 1 | 10 | 220 | 3 | NA | 32 | 2 | 2 strch, 1 fat |
| Honey Bran Muffins | 1 | 160 | 4 | 23 | 1 | 5 | 150 | 3 | NA | 32 | 2 | 2 strch, 1 fat |
| **MUSHROOMS, CANNED** | | | | | | | | | | | | |
| **(Generic)** | | | | | | | | | | | | |
| ✔Mushrooms, Canned | 1/2 cup | 25 | 0 | 0 | 0 | 0 | 480 | 2 | 1 | 4 | 0 | free |
| **MUSTARD** | | | | | | | | | | | | |
| **(Generic)** | | | | | | | | | | | | |
| ✔Dijon Mustard | 1 Tbsp | 19 | 1 | 47 | <1 | 0 | 379 | <1 | <1 | 2 | 0 | free |
| ✔Prepared Mustard | 1 Tbsp | 12 | <1 | 0 | <1 | 0 | 196 | 0 | 0 | 1 | 0 | free |

✔ = Best Bet; NA = Not Available; Carb. Ch. = Carbohydrate Choices

| Product | Serving Size | Cal. | Fat (g) | % Cal. Fat | Sat. Fat (g) | Chol. (mg) | Sod. (mg) | Pro. (g) | Fiber (g) | Carb. (g) | Carb. Ch. | Servings/Exchanges |
|---|---|---|---|---|---|---|---|---|---|---|---|---|
| **NOODLES, FLAVORED (DRY, AS PREPARED)** | | | | | | | | | | | | |
| **Marchan** | | | | | | | | | | | | |
| Beef Ramen Noodle Soup | 1/2 pkg | 190 | 8 | 38 | 4 | 0 | 770 | 5 | 1 | 26 | 2 | 2 carb, 2 fat |
| Chicken Ramen Noodle Soup | 1/2 pkg | 190 | 8 | 38 | 4 | 0 | 780 | 5 | 1 | 26 | 2 | 2 carb, 2 fat |
| Creamy Chicken Ramen Noodle Soup | 1/2 pkg | 200 | 9 | 41 | 4 | 0 | 710 | 4 | 1 | 27 | 2 | 2 carb, 2 fat |
| Oriental Ramen Noodle Soup | 1/2 pkg | 190 | 8 | 38 | 4 | 0 | 900 | 4 | 1 | 26 | 2 | 2 carb, 2 fat |
| Pork Ramen Noodle Soup | 1/2 pkg | 190 | 8 | 38 | 4 | 0 | 890 | 5 | 1 | 26 | 2 | 2 carb, 2 fat |
| **Top Ramen** | | | | | | | | | | | | |
| Beef Ramen Noodle Soup | 1/2 pkg | 190 | 7 | 33 | 4 | 0 | 700 | 4 | 1 | 28 | 2 | 2 carb, 1 fat |
| Chicken Ramen Noodle Soup | 1/2 pkg | 180 | 7 | 35 | 4 | 0 | 800 | 4 | 1 | 26 | 2 | 2 carb, 1 fat |
| Oriental Ramen Noodle Soup | 1/2 pkg | 190 | 7 | 33 | 4 | 0 | 830 | 4 | 1 | 28 | 2 | 2 carb, 1 fat |
| Picante Ramen Noodle Soup | 1/2 pkg | 180 | 7 | 35 | 4 | 0 | 830 | 4 | 1 | 26 | 2 | 2 carb, 1 fat |
| **NUTS** | | | | | | | | | | | | |
| **(Generic)** | | | | | | | | | | | | |
| Almonds, Dry Roasted | 1 oz | 166 | 15 | 81 | 1 | 0 | 221 | 5 | 4 | 7 | 1/2 | 1/2 carb, 1 med-fat meat, 2 fat |
| Cashews, Dry Roasted | 1 oz | 161 | 13 | 73 | 3 | 0 | 179 | 5 | <1 | 9 | 1/2 | 1/2 carb, 3 fat |
| English Walnuts Halves, Dried | 1 oz | 182 | 18 | 89 | 2 | 0 | 3 | 4 | 1 | 5 | 0 | 1 med-fat meat, 3 fat |

| | Amount | Cal. | Fat (g) | % Cal. Fat | Sat. Fat (g) | Chol. (mg) | Sod. (mg) | Carb. (g) | Fiber (g) | Prot. (g) | Carb. Ch. | Exchanges per Serving |
|---|---|---|---|---|---|---|---|---|---|---|---|---|
| Macadamia Nuts | 1 oz | 199 | 21 | 95 | 3 | 0 | 1 | 0 | 4 | 3 | | 4 fat |
| Mixed Nuts, Dry Roasted | 1 oz | 168 | 15 | 80 | 2 | 0 | 190 | 7 | 3 | 5 | 1/2 | 1/2 strch, 3 fat |
| Peanuts, Oil Roasted | 1 oz | 165 | 14 | 76 | 2 | 0 | 123 | 5 | 3 | 8 | 0 | 1 med-fat meat, 2 fat |
| Pecan, Dry Roasted | 1 oz | 187 | 18 | 87 | 2 | 0 | 222 | 6 | 3 | 2 | 1/2 | 1/2 carb, 3 fat |
| **OIL** | | | | | | | | | | | | |
| **(Generic)** | | | | | | | | | | | | |
| Vegetable Oil, All Varieties (Avg) | 1 tsp | 42 | 5 | 100 | 1 | 0 | 0 | 0 | 0 | 0 | | 1 fat |
| **OLIVES** | | | | | | | | | | | | |
| **(Generic)** | | | | | | | | | | | | |
| Green Olives-Pitted | 10 | 45 | 5 | 100 | <1 | 0 | 936 | <1 | <1 | <1 | 0 | 1 fat |
| ✔ Small Ripe Olives-Canned | 10 | 37 | 3 | 73 | <1 | 0 | 279 | 2 | 1 | <1 | 0 | 1 fat |
| Stuffed Green Olives | 10 | 41 | 5 | 100 | <1 | 0 | 827 | <1 | <1 | <1 | 0 | 1 fat |
| **ONION RINGS (FROZEN)** | | | | | | | | | | | | |
| **Ore Ida** | | | | | | | | | | | | |
| Gourmet Onion Rings | 4 | 210 | 10 | 43 | 2 | 0 | 590 | 28 | 1 | 3 | 2 | 2 carb, 2 fat |
| Onion Rings | 6 | 220 | 12 | 49 | 2 | 0 | 350 | 25 | 3 | 3 | 1 1/2 | 1 1/2 carb, 2 fat |
| Vidalia O's | 5 | 240 | 15 | 56 | 3 | 0 | 420 | 20 | 1 | 3 | 1 | 1 carb, 3 fat |

✔ = Best Bet; NA = Not Available; Carb. Ch. = Carbohydrate Choices

| Product | Serving Size | Cal. | Fat (g) | % Cal. Fat | Sat. Fat (g) | Chol. (mg) | Sod. (mg) | Pro. (g) | Fiber (g) | Carb. (g) | Carb. Ch. | Servings/Exchanges |
|---|---|---|---|---|---|---|---|---|---|---|---|---|
| **ORIENTAL MEALS/ENTREES (CANNED)** | | | | | | | | | | | | |
| **Chef Mate** | | | | | | | | | | | | |
| Oriental Beef & Vegetables | 1 cup | 190 | 6 | 28 | <1 | 15 | 1150 | 9 | 1 | 25 | 1 1/2 | 1 1/2 carb, 1 med-fat meat |
| Oriental Chicken & Vegetables | 1 cup | 210 | 8 | 34 | 2 | 40 | 1170 | 11 | 1 | 24 | 1 1/2 | 1 1/2 carb, 1 med-fat meat, 1 fat |
| **La Choy** | | | | | | | | | | | | |
| Almond Chicken w/Rice Entrée, Canned | 9.8 oz | 270 | 8 | 27 | NA | 40 | 1090 | 14 | 3 | 40 | 2 1/2 | 2 1/2 carb, 1 med-fat meat, 1 fat |
| Chicken Chow Mein Entrée, Canned | 3/4 cup | 240 | 2 | 8 | <1 | 19 | 1420 | 8 | 1 | 47 | 3 | 3 carb |
| Oriental Chicken w/Noodles Entrée | 9 oz | 160 | 4 | 23 | 1 | 13 | 1165 | 11 | 4 | 23 | 1 1/2 | 1 1/2 carb, 1 med-fat meat |
| ✔Shrimp Chow Mein Entrée, Canned | 3/4 cup | 50 | 1 | 18 | 0 | 20 | 860 | 3 | 2 | 7 | 1/2 | 1/2 carb |
| Sweet & Sour Noodles w/Pork Entrée, Canned | 3/4 cup | 250 | 4 | 14 | 1 | 20 | 1540 | 6 | 1 | 48 | 3 | 3 carb, 1 fat |

# ORIENTAL MEALS/ENTREES (FROZEN)

## Armour Classics Lite

| | | | | | | | | | | | | |
|---|---|---|---|---|---|---|---|---|---|---|---|---|
| ✓Oriental Chicken A La King | 11.25 oz dinner | 290 | 7 | 22 | NA | 55 | 630 | 19 | NA | 38 | 2 1/2 | 2 1/2 carb, 2 med-fat meat |

## Banquet

| | | | | | | | | | | | | |
|---|---|---|---|---|---|---|---|---|---|---|---|---|
| ✓Chicken Chow Mein | 9 oz dinner | 210 | 7 | 30 | 2 | 30 | 850 | 9 | 3 | 28 | 2 | 2 carb, 1 med-fat meat |
| Chicken Lo Mein | 10.5 oz dinner | 270 | 6 | 20 | 1 | NA | 1060 | 11 | NA | 43 | 3 | 3 carb, 1 fat |
| Oriental-Style Chicken w/Egg Rolls | 9 oz dinner | 260 | 9 | 31 | 3 | 40 | 790 | 10 | 3 | 36 | 2 | 2 carb, 1 med-fat meat, 1 fat |

## Budget Gourmet

| | | | | | | | | | | | | |
|---|---|---|---|---|---|---|---|---|---|---|---|---|
| ✓Chicken Oriental w/Vegetables | 9.1 oz meal | 290 | 8 | 25 | 3 | 25 | 730 | 11 | 3 | 43 | 3 | 3 carb, 1 med-fat meat, 1 fat |
| ✓Chinese Style Vegetables w/Chicken | 10 oz meal | 280 | 7 | 23 | 1 | 10 | 590 | 11 | NA | 47 | 3 | 3 carb, 1 fat |
| Hearty Oriental Style Rice w/Vegetables & Chicken | 14 oz meal | 640 | 33 | 46 | 7 | 50 | 1450 | 18 | 6 | 67 | 4 1/2 | 4 1/2 carb, 1 med-fat meat, 6 fat |
| ✓Light & Healthy Oriental Chicken | 9 oz meal | 280 | 6 | 19 | 1 | 20 | 690 | 19 | NA | 44 | 3 | 3 carb, 1 med-fat meat |
| ✓Light & Healthy Oriental Chicken and Vegetables | 9 oz meal | 280 | 6 | 18 | 1 | 20 | 690 | 19 | NA | 44 | 3 | 3 carb, 1 med-fat meat |

✓ = Best Bet; NA = Not Available; Carb. Ch. = Carbohydrate Choices

| Oriental Meals/Entrees (Frozen) (Continued) | Serving Size | Cal. | Fat (g) | % Cal. Fat | Sat. Fat (g) | Chol. (mg) | Sod. (mg) | Pro. (g) | Fiber (g) | Carb. (g) | Carb. Ch. | Servings/Exchanges |
|---|---|---|---|---|---|---|---|---|---|---|---|---|
| ✓Special Selections, Mandarin Chicken | 10 oz dinner | 250 | 5 | 18 | 1 | 45 | 850 | 16 | 4 | 37 | 2 1/2 | 2 1/2 carb, 1 med-fat meat |
| ✓Sweet & Sour Chicken and Rice | 10 oz meal | 350 | 7 | 18 | NA | 40 | 640 | 18 | NA | 53 | 3 1/2 | 3 1/2 carb, 1 med-fat meat |
| **Chun King** | | | | | | | | | | | | |
| Chicken Chow Mein | 13 oz meal | 370 | 6 | 15 | NA | NA | 1560 | 25 | NA | 53 | 3 1/2 | 3 1/2 carb, 2 lean meat |
| Chicken Imperial | 13 oz meal | 300 | 1 | 3 | NA | NA | 1540 | 17 | NA | 54 | 3 1/2 | 3 1/2 carb, lean meat |
| Crunchy Walnut Chicken | 13 oz meal | 310 | 5 | 15 | NA | NA | 1700 | 16 | NA | 49 | 3 | 3 carb, 1 med-fat meat |
| Pepper Beef | 13 oz meal | 310 | 3 | 9 | NA | NA | 1300 | 17 | NA | 53 | 3 | 3 carb, 1 fat |
| Sweet & Sour Pork | 13 oz meal | 400 | 5 | 11 | NA | NA | 1460 | 11 | NA | 78 | 5 | 5 carb, 1 med-fat meat |
| Szechwan Beef | 13 oz meal | 340 | 3 | 8 | NA | NA | 1810 | 20 | NA | 57 | 3 1/2 | 3 1/2 carb, 1 lean meat |
| **Dining Lite** | | | | | | | | | | | | |
| ✓Chicken a la King | 9 oz meal | 240 | 7 | 26 | NA | 40 | 780 | 14 | NA | 30 | 2 | 2 carb, 1 med-fat meat |
| ✓Chicken Chow Mein | 9 oz meal | 180 | 2 | 10 | NA | 30 | 650 | 10 | NA | 31 | 2 | 2 carb, 1 lean meat |
| Oriental Pepper Steak | 9 oz meal | 260 | 6 | 21 | NA | 40 | 1050 | 18 | NA | 33 | 2 | 2 carb, 2 lean meat |
| ✓Teriyaki Beef | 9 oz meal | 270 | 5 | 17 | NA | 45 | 850 | 20 | NA | 36 | 2 1/2 | 2 1/2 carb, 2 lean meat |
| **Healthy Choice** | | | | | | | | | | | | |
| ✓Beef & Peppers Cantonese | 11.5 oz meal | 280 | 7 | 23 | 3 | 55 | 480 | 22 | 5 | 32 | 2 | 2 carb, 2 lean meat |

| | Serving | Cal. | Fat (g) | % Cal. Fat | Sat. Fat (g) | Chol. (mg) | Sod. (mg) | Prot. (g) | Fiber (g) | Carb. (g) | Carb. Ch. | Exchanges/Choices |
|---|---|---|---|---|---|---|---|---|---|---|---|---|
| ✔Beef Broccoli Beijing | 12 oz meal | 300 | 5 | 15 | 2 | 25 | 420 | 21 | 6 | 45 | 3 | 3 carb, 2 lean meat |
| ✔Chicken Imperial | 9 oz meal | 250 | 6 | 24 | 2 | 50 | 470 | 17 | 3 | 31 | 2 | 2 carb, 2 lean meat |
| Chicken Teriyaki | 11 oz meal | 270 | 6 | 20 | 3 | 37 | 600 | 17 | 3 | 37 | 2 1/2 | 2 1/2 carb, 2 lean meat |
| ✔Chicken Teriyaki w/Rice Bowl | 9.5 oz meal | 270 | 4 | 13 | 1 | 40 | 570 | 17 | 4 | 41 | 3 | 3 carb, 1 med-fat meat |
| ✔Mandarin Chicken | 10 oz meal | 280 | 3 | 7 | 0 | 35 | 520 | 20 | 4 | 44 | 3 | 3 carb, 2 very lean meat |
| ✔Sesame Chicken | 9.75 oz meal | 250 | 4 | 14 | 1 | 35 | 600 | 16 | 2 | 38 | 2 1/2 | 2 1/2 carb, 1 med-fat meat |
| ✔Sesame Chicken Shanghai | 12 oz meal | 300 | 5 | 15 | 1 | 40 | 550 | 24 | 6 | 40 | 2 1/2 | 2 1/2 carb, 2 lean meat |
| ✔Sweet and Sour Chicken | 11 oz meal | 360 | 7 | 17 | 3 | 45 | 360 | 20 | 5 | 53 | 3 1/2 | 3 1/2 carb, 2 lean meat |
| **King's Hawaiian** | | | | | | | | | | | | |
| Teriyaki Chicken Bowl | 1 bowl | 490 | 8 | 15 | 3 | 35 | 1420 | 20 | 3 | 85 | 5 1/2 | 5 1/2 strch, 1 med-fat meat, 1 fat |
| **Lean Cuisine** | | | | | | | | | | | | |
| ✔Café Classics, Oriental Beef | 9.3 oz meal | 240 | 4 | 15 | 2 | 30 | 590 | 17 | 2 | 35 | 2 | 2 carb, 2 lean meat |
| ✔Chicken Chow Mein w/Rice | 9 oz meal | 220 | 5 | 21 | 1 | 35 | 560 | 12 | 3 | 33 | 2 | 2 carb, 1 med-fat meat |
| ✔Mandarin Chicken | 9 oz meal | 250 | 4 | 14 | <1 | 25 | 590 | 15 | 3 | 38 | 2 1/2 | 2 1/2 carb, 1 med-fat meat |
| ✔Skillet Sensations, Beef Teriyaki & Rice | 12 oz meal | 280 | 3 | 10 | 1 | 25 | 700 | 14 | 5 | 48 | 3 | 3 carb, 1 lean meat |
| ✔Skillet Sensations, Chicken Oriental | 12 oz meal | 280 | 3 | 10 | <1 | 15 | 790 | 17 | 6 | 46 | 3 | 3 carb, 1 lean meat |

✔= Best Bet; NA = Not Available; Carb. Ch. = Carbohydrate Choices

| Oriental Meals/Entrees (Frozen) (Continued) | Serving Size | Cal. | Fat (g) | % Cal. Fat | Sat. Fat (g) | Chol. (mg) | Sod. (mg) | Pro. (g) | Fiber (g) | Carb. (g) | Carb. Ch. | Servings/Exchanges |
|---|---|---|---|---|---|---|---|---|---|---|---|---|
| ✓Teriyaki Stir-Fry | 10 oz | 290 | 4 | 12 | <1 | 25 | 590 | 17 | 4 | 48 | 3 | 3 carb, 1 med-fat meat |
| **Ling Ling** | | | | | | | | | | | | |
| ✓Potstickers | 5 pieces (5.4 oz) | 280 | 7 | 23 | 2 | 30 | 660 | 13 | 2 | 40 | 2 1/2 | 2 1/2 carb, 1 med-fat meat |
| **Marie Callender** | | | | | | | | | | | | |
| ✓Sweet & Sour Chicken | 14 oz meal | 570 | 15 | 25 | 3 | 40 | 700 | 23 | 7 | 86 | 6 | 6 carb, 1 med-fat meat, 2 fat |
| **Stouffer's** | | | | | | | | | | | | |
| Chicken Chow Mein w/Rice | 10.6 oz meal | 220 | 5 | 20 | 1 | 30 | 1420 | 13 | 0 | 33 | 2 | 2 carb, 1 med-fat meat |
| Skillet Sensations, Teriyaki Chicken | 12.5 oz meal | 340 | 3 | 8 | 1 | 30 | 1350 | 20 | 3 | 59 | 4 | 4 carb, 1 med-fat meat |
| **Uncle Ben's** | | | | | | | | | | | | |
| Chicken & Vegetable Rice Bowl | 12 oz | 360 | 5 | 13 | 2 | 25 | 1020 | 21 | 3 | 56 | 4 | 4 carb, 1 med-fat meat |
| Honey Ginger Chicken Noodle Bowl | 12 oz | 430 | 5 | 11 | 2 | 85 | 1700 | 25 | 3 | 69 | 4 1/2 | 4 1/2 carb, 2 lean meat |
| Orange Glazed Beef Noodle Bowl | 12 oz | 440 | 8 | 16 | 2 | 75 | 1020 | 26 | 4 | 70 | 4 1/2 | 4 1/2 carb, 2 med-fat meat |
| Spicy Beef & Broccoli Rice Bowl | 12 oz | 370 | 5 | 12 | 2 | 25 | 1550 | 21 | 1 | 62 | 4 | 4 carb, 1 med-fat meat |
| Spicy Thai Style Chicken Noodle Bowl | 12 oz | 400 | 8 | 18 | 5 | 80 | 980 | 21 | 6 | 60 | 4 | 4 carb, 1 med-fat meat, 1 fat |

| | | | | | | | | | | | |
|---|---|---|---|---|---|---|---|---|---|---|---|
| ✔ Sweet & Sour Chicken Rice Bowl | 12 oz | 360 | 3 | 8 | <1 | 30 | 620 | 17 | 2 | 65 | 4 | 4 carb, 1 lean meat |
| Teriyaki Chicken Rice Bowl | 12 oz | 380 | 4 | 10 | <1 | 25 | 1450 | 20 | 3 | 66 | 4 1/2 | 4 1/2 carb, 1 med-fat meat |

**Weight Watchers Smart Ones**

| | | | | | | | | | | | |
|---|---|---|---|---|---|---|---|---|---|---|---|
| ✔ Spicy Szechuan Style Vegetables & Chicken | 9 oz meal | 230 | 5 | 20 | 1 | 10 | 800 | 11 | 3 | 34 | 2 | 2 carb, 1 med-fat meat |

## PANCAKE MIX (AS PREPARED)

**Aunt Jemima**

| | | | | | | | | | | | |
|---|---|---|---|---|---|---|---|---|---|---|---|
| ✔ Pancake/Waffle Mix, Buckwheat | 1/4 cup | 120 | 1 | 8 | 0 | 0 | 560 | 5 | 4 | 22 | 1 1/2 | 1 1/2 strch |
| ✔ Pancake/Waffle Mix, Buttermilk | 1/3 cup | 190 | 2 | 10 | <1 | 10 | 480 | 6 | 2 | 31 | 2 | 2 strch |
| ✔ Pancake/Waffle Mix, Original | 1/3 cup | 150 | <1 | 6 | 0 | 0 | 620 | 4 | 1 | 28 | 2 | 2 strch |
| ✔ Pancake/Waffle Mix, Whole Wheat | 1/4 cup | 130 | <1 | 7 | 0 | 0 | 560 | 6 | 3 | 28 | 2 | 2 strch |
| ✔ Pancake/Waffle Mx, Regular | 1/3 cup | 190 | 2 | 9 | <1 | 15 | 470 | 6 | 1 | 39 | 2 1/2 | 2 1/2 strch |
| ✔ Pancakes From Mix, Reduced Calorie Buttermilk | 1/3 cup | 140 | 2 | 13 | <1 | 15 | 510 | 8 | 5 | 30 | 2 | 2 strch |

**Betty Crocker**

| | | | | | | | | | | | |
|---|---|---|---|---|---|---|---|---|---|---|---|
| ✔ Complete Buttermilk Pancake Mix | 1/3 cup/3 pancakes | 200 | 3 | 14 | <1 | 10 | 540 | 5 | 1 | 39 | 2 1/2 | 2 1/2 strch, 1 fat |

✔ = Best Bet; NA = Not Available; Carb. Ch. = Carbohydrate Choices

| Pancake Mix (As Prepared) (Continued) | Serving Size | Cal. | Fat (g) | % Cal. Fat | Sat. Fat (g) | Chol. (mg) | Sod. (mg) | Pro. (g) | Fiber (g) | Carb. (g) | Carb. Ch. | Servings/Exchanges |
|---|---|---|---|---|---|---|---|---|---|---|---|---|
| ✔Complete Original Pancake Mix | 1/3 cup/3 pancakes | 200 | 3 | 14 | 1 | 10 | 540 | 6 | 1 | 39 | 2 1/2 | 2 1/2 strch, 1 fat |
| **Bisquick** | | | | | | | | | | | | |
| ✔Shake 'N Pour Blueberry Pancake/Waffle Mix | 1/2 cup/3 pancakes | 210 | 4 | 17 | 1 | 0 | 640 | 6 | 1 | 40 | 2 1/2 | 2 1/2 strch, 1 fat |
| ✔Shake 'N Pour Buttermilk Pancake/Waffle Mix | 1/2 cup mix/3 pancakes | 200 | 3 | 14 | 1 | 0 | 680 | 7 | 1 | 38 | 2 1/2 | 2 1/2 strch, 1 fat |
| ✔Shake 'N Pour Original Pancake/Waffle Mix | 1/2 cup/3 pancakes | 210 | 4 | 17 | 1 | 0 | 710 | 5 | <1 | 39 | 2 1/2 | 2 1/2 strch, 1 fat |
| **Gold Medal/General Mills** | | | | | | | | | | | | |
| ✔Buttermilk Pancake Mix | 2 | 200 | 5 | 23 | 0 | 20 | 300 | 4 | 0 | 36 | 2 1/2 | 2 1/2 strch, 1 fat |
| **Robin Hood** | | | | | | | | | | | | |
| ✔Buttermilk Pancake Mix | 1/3 cup/3 pancakes | 180 | 3 | 15 | 1 | 0 | 510 | 5 | 1 | 31 | 2 | 2 strch, 1 fat |
| **PANCAKES (FROZEN)** | | | | | | | | | | | | |
| **Aunt Jemima** | | | | | | | | | | | | |
| ✔Microwave Pancakes, Blueberry | 3 | 210 | 4 | 17 | <1 | 20 | 670 | 6 | 2 | 40 | 2 1/2 | 2 1/2 strch, 1 fat |
| ✔Microwave Pancakes, Buttermilk | 3 | 210 | 4 | 17 | 1 | 20 | 600 | 6 | 2 | 40 | 2 1/2 | 2 1/2 strch, 1 fat |
| ✔Microwave Pancakes, Homestyle | 3 | 210 | 4 | 17 | <1 | 20 | 560 | 6 | 8 | 40 | 2 1/2 | 2 1/2 strch, 1 fat |

| Product | Amount | Cal. | Fat (g) | % Cal. Fat | Sat. Fat (g) | Chol. (mg) | Sod. (mg) | Carb. (g) | Fiber (g) | Prot. (g) | Carb. Ch. | Exchanges |
|---|---|---|---|---|---|---|---|---|---|---|---|---|
| ✔Microwave Pancakes, Low Fat | 3 | 150 | 2 | 12 | 0 | <5 | 530 | 30 | 8 | 5 | 2 | 2 strch |
| **Hungry Jack** | | | | | | | | | | | | |
| ✔Blueberry Microwave Pancakes | 2 | 155 | 2 | 12 | <1 | 5 | 370 | 30 | <1 | 3 | 2 | 2 strch |
| ✔Buttermilk Microwave Pancakes | 2 | 162 | 3 | 17 | <1 | 5 | 390 | 31 | <1 | 3 | 2 | 2 strch, 1 fat |
| ✔Mini Buttermilk Microwave Pancakes | 11 | 170 | 3 | 16 | <1 | 5 | 400 | 32 | <1 | 4 | 2 | 2 strch, 1 fat |
| ✔Original Microwave Pancakes | 3 | 162 | 3 | 17 | <1 | 5 | 365 | 31 | <1 | 3 | 2 | 2 strch, 1 fat |
| **Kellogg's Eggo** | | | | | | | | | | | | |
| ✔Buttermilk Pancakes | 3 | 270 | 8 | 27 | 2 | 15 | 610 | 44 | 1 | 7 | 3 | 3 strch, 2 fat |
| **Krusteaz** | | | | | | | | | | | | |
| ✔Blueberry Pancakes | 3 | 270 | 4 | 14 | 1 | 15 | 670 | 50 | 3 | 7 | 3 | 3 strch, 1 fat |
| ✔Buttermilk Pancakes | 3 | 280 | 4 | 13 | 1 | 10 | 710 | 52 | 3 | 8 | 3 1/2 | 3 1/2 strch, 1 fat |
| ✔Mini Pancakes | 6 | 110 | 2 | 12 | <1 | 0 | 300 | 22 | 1 | 3 | 1 1/2 | 1 1/2 strch |
| **PASTA (CANNED)** | | | | | | | | | | | | |
| **Chef Boyardee** | | | | | | | | | | | | |
| 99% Fat-Free Beef Ravioli | 1 cup | 190 | 1 | 5 | 0 | 15 | 1150 | 38 | 2 | 7 | 2 1/2 | 2 1/2 carb |
| ABC's & 123's Pasta in Cheese Sauce | 8.6 oz | 200 | 1 | 5 | 1 | 2 | 1020 | 42 | NA | 6 | 3 | 3 carb |
| ✔ABC's & 123's Pasta in Sauce | 7.5 oz | 160 | 1 | 6 | 1 | 2 | 830 | 31 | 3 | 5 | 2 | 2 carb |
| Beef Mini Ravioli | 9 oz | 240 | 5 | 18 | 2 | 18 | 1200 | 41 | 3 | 9 | 3 | 3 carb, 1 fat |

✔ = Best Bet; NA = Not Available; Carb. Ch. = Carbohydrate Choices

| Pasta (Canned) (Continued) | Serving Size | Cal. | Fat (g) | % Cal. Fat | Sat. Fat (g) | Chol. (mg) | Sod. (mg) | Pro. (g) | Fiber (g) | Carb. (g) | Carb. Ch. | Servings/Exchanges |
|---|---|---|---|---|---|---|---|---|---|---|---|---|
| Beef Ravioli | 8.7 oz | 230 | 5 | 20 | 2 | 15 | 1180 | 8 | 4 | 37 | 2 1/2 | 2 1/2 carb, 1 fat |
| ✔Beefaroni | 7.6 oz | 185 | 3 | 14 | 1 | 17 | 800 | 8 | 3 | 31 | 2 | 2 carb, 1 fat |
| Cheese Ravioli in Meat Sauce | 7.5 oz | 200 | 3 | 14 | NA | 10 | 1010 | 6 | NA | 37 | 2 1/2 | 2 1/2 carb, 1 fat |
| ✔Chef Jr., Pasta in Tomato & Cheese Sauce | 1 cup | 200 | <1 | 2 | 0 | <1 | 900 | 5 | 2 | 43 | 3 | 3 carb |
| ✔Chicken & Pasta | 7.5 oz | 180 | 2 | 10 | 1 | 15 | 850 | 10 | 1 | 30 | 2 | 2 carb |
| Chicken Ravioli | 7.5 oz | 180 | 4 | 20 | NA | 13 | 1100 | 7 | NA | 29 | 2 | 2 carb, 1 fat |
| Homestyle Cannelloni | 1 cup | 250 | 8 | 29 | 4 | 25 | 1090 | 11 | 2 | 31 | 2 | 2 carb, 1 med-fat meat, 1 fat |
| Homestyle Chicken Alfredo with Pasta | 1 cup | 250 | 12 | 43 | 6 | 60 | 970 | 10 | 1 | 24 | 1 1/2 | 1 1/2 carb, 1 med-fat meat, 1 fat |
| Homestyle Chicken Parmesan Pasta | 1 cup | 340 | 18 | 48 | 7 | 55 | 1210 | 12 | 3 | 31 | 2 | 2 carb, 1 med-fat meat, 3 fat |
| Homestyle Ravioli Primavera | 1 cup | 230 | 6 | 23 | 2 | 19 | 1090 | 7 | 3 | 40 | 2 | 2 carb, 1 fat |
| Lasagna | 1 cup | 270 | 10 | 33 | 5 | 25 | 830 | 9 | 2 | 36 | 2 1/2 | 2 1/2 carb, 2 fat |
| ✔Macaroni w/Cheese | 7.5 oz | 170 | 2 | 11 | 1 | 25 | 970 | 7 | 2 | 33 | 2 | 2 carb |
| Meatball Stew | 8 oz | 350 | 24 | 62 | NA | NA | 1315 | 9 | NA | 24 | 1 1/2 | 1 1/2 carb, 1 med-fat meat, 4 fat |
| Mini Ravioli | 1 cup | 240 | 7 | 26 | 3 | 20 | 1180 | 8 | 3 | 35 | 2 | 2 carb, 1 fat |

| | Serving Size | Cal. | Fat (g) | % Cal. Fat | Sat. Fat (g) | Chol. (mg) | Sod. (mg) | Prot. (g) | Fiber (g) | Carb. (g) | Carb. Ch. | Exchanges/Choices |
|---|---|---|---|---|---|---|---|---|---|---|---|---|
| Overstuffed Italian Sausage Ravioli | 1 cup | 290 | 4 | 12 | 2 | 15 | 1230 | 10 | 4 | 53 | 3 1/2 | 3 1/2 carb, 1 fat |
| Pasta Rings & Franks | 7.5 oz | 190 | 5 | 23 | 2 | 20 | 980 | 7 | 3 | 31 | 2 | 2 carb, 1 fat |
| Rigatoni | 7.5 oz | 210 | 6 | 26 | NA | 17 | 1080 | 8 | NA | 31 | 2 | 2 carb, 1 fat |
| Roller Coaster Pasta | 7.5 oz | 230 | 10 | 39 | 3 | 19 | 1070 | 7 | 3 | 28 | 2 | 2 carb, 2 fat |
| ✓ Sir Chomps Beef Ravioli | 7.5 oz | 170 | 3 | 15 | 1 | 15 | 690 | 7 | 4 | 32 | 2 | 2 carb, 1 fat |
| ✓ Sir Chomps Cheese Ravioli | 7.5 oz | 170 | 1 | 5 | 1 | 5 | 740 | 6 | 6 | 38 | 2 1/2 | 2 1/2 carb |
| Smurfs Pasta w/Meat Sauce | 7.5 oz | 230 | 5 | 44 | NA | 11 | 1160 | 9 | NA | 38 | 2 1/2 | 2 1/2 carb, 1 fat |
| Spaghetti w/Meatballs | 8.5 oz | 250 | 9 | 32 | 4 | 20 | 940 | 9 | 2 | 34 | 2 | 2 carb, 2 fat |
| **Chef Mate** | | | | | | | | | | | | |
| Italian Rotini & Meatballs | 1 cup | 270 | 11 | 37 | 4 | 20 | 1390 | 12 | 2 | 28 | 2 | 2 carb, 1 med-fat meat, 1 fat |
| Macaroni and Cheese | 1 cup | 280 | 11 | 35 | 6 | 30 | 1345 | 11 | 3 | 35 | 2 | 2 carb, 1 med-fat meat, 1 fat |
| Sausage 'N Shells | 1 cup | 380 | 28 | 66 | 9 | 55 | 990 | 15 | 1 | 19 | 1 | 1 carb, 2 med-fat meat, 4 fat |
| **Franco American** | | | | | | | | | | | | |
| Macaroni & Cheese | 7.4 oz | 170 | 6 | 32 | NA | NA | 1060 | 6 | NA | 24 | 1 1/2 | 1 1/2 carb, 1 fat |
| Spaghetti w/Meatballs | 7.4 oz | 220 | 9 | 37 | NA | NA | 950 | 9 | NA | 25 | 1 1/2 | 1 1/2 carb, 1 med-fat meat, 1 fat |

✓ = Best Bet; NA = Not Available; Carb. Ch. = Carbohydrate Choices

| Pasta (Canned) (Continued) | Serving Size | Cal. | Fat (g) | % Cal. Fat | Sat. Fat (g) | Chol. (mg) | Sod. (mg) | Pro. (g) | Fiber (g) | Carb. (g) | Carb. Ch. | Servings/Exchanges |
|---|---|---|---|---|---|---|---|---|---|---|---|---|
| Spaghetti w/Tomato-Cheese Sauce | 1 cup | 210 | 2 | 9 | 1 | 5 | 1020 | 7 | 3 | 41 | 3 | 3 carb |
| SpaghettiOs Raviolios | 1 cup | 230 | 4 | 16 | 2 | 10 | 1080 | 9 | 2 | 38 | 2 1/2 | 2 1/2 carb, 1 fat |
| SpaghettiOs w/Franks | 1 cup | 250 | 10 | 36 | 4 | 15 | 1190 | 9 | 5 | 30 | 2 | 2 carb, 2 fat |
| SpaghettiOs w/Meatballs | 1 cup | 240 | 8 | 30 | 4 | 20 | 1070 | 11 | 3 | 32 | 2 | 2 carb, 1 med-fat meat, 1 fat |
| ✓SpaghettiOs,Tomato & Cheese Sauce | 1 cup | 180 | 1 | 5 | <1 | 10 | 890 | 6 | 3 | 37 | 2 1/2 | 2 1/2 carb |
| **Progresso** | | | | | | | | | | | | |
| ✓Beef Ravioli | 1 cup | 260 | 5 | 17 | 2 | 5 | 940 | 9 | 4 | 45 | 3 | 3 carb, 1 fat |
| ✓Cheese Ravioli | 1 cup | 220 | 2 | 8 | 1 | <5 | 930 | 7 | 4 | 43 | 3 | 3 carb |
| **PASTA (DRY)** | | | | | | | | | | | | |
| **La Choy** | | | | | | | | | | | | |
| Chow Mein Noodles | 1/2 cup | 140 | 6 | 39 | 1 | 0 | 210 | 5 | 2 | 17 | 1 | 1 strch, 1 fat |
| Crispy Wide Noodles | 1/2 cup | 150 | 8 | 48 | 2 | 0 | 260 | 2 | 1 | 17 | 1 | 1 strch, 2 fat |
| ✓Rice Noodles | 1/2 cup | 125 | 3 | 22 | <1 | 0 | 365 | 2 | <1 | 22 | 1 1/2 | 1 1/2 strch, 1 fat |
| **PASTA (REFRIGERATED)** | | | | | | | | | | | | |
| **Di Giorno** | | | | | | | | | | | | |
| ✓Angel Hair Pasta | 2 oz (1 cup cooked) | 160 | 1 | 6 | 0 | 0 | 115 | 6 | 2 | 31 | 2 | 2 strch |
| ✓Fettuccine Pasta | 2.5 oz (1 cup cooked) | 200 | 2 | 9 | 0 | 0 | 140 | 8 | 2 | 38 | 2 1/2 | 2 1/2 strch |

| | Serving Size | Cal. | Fat (g) | % Cal. from Fat | Sat. Fat (g) | Chol. (mg) | Sod. (mg) | Carb. (g) | Fiber (g) | Prot. (g) | Carb. Ch. | Exchanges/Choices |
|---|---|---|---|---|---|---|---|---|---|---|---|---|
| ✔Herb Linguine Pasta | 2.5 oz (1 cup cooked) | 200 | 2 | 9 | 0 | 0 | 140 | 38 | 2 | 8 | 2 1/2 | 2 1/2 strch |
| Italian Sausage Ravioli in Green Bell Pepper Pasta | 1 1/4 cup | 340 | 12 | 32 | 6 | 55 | 570 | 45 | 3 | 14 | 3 | 3 carb, 1 med-fat meat, 1 fat |
| Light Cheese Stuffed Ravioli | 1 cup | 280 | 7 | 23 | 4 | 40 | 400 | 40 | 2 | 15 | 2 1/2 | 2 1/2 carb, 1 med-fat meat |
| ✔Linguine | 2.5 oz (1 cup cooked) | 200 | 2 | 9 | 0 | 0 | 140 | 38 | 2 | 8 | 2 1/2 | 2 1/2 strch |
| ✔Red Bell Pepper Fettuccine Pasta | 2.5 oz (1 cup cooked) | 200 | 2 | 9 | 0 | 0 | 140 | 38 | 2 | 8 | 2 1/2 | 2 1/2 strch |
| ✔Spinach Fettuccine Pasta | 2.5 oz (1 cup cooked) | 200 | 2 | 9 | 0 | 0 | 140 | 38 | 2 | 8 | 2 1/2 | 2 1/2 strch |
| Stuffed Pesto Tortelloni | 1 cup | 320 | 8 | 23 | 5 | 45 | 430 | 46 | 3 | 16 | 3 | 3 carb, 1 med-fat meat, 1 fat |
| Sun-Dried Tomato Stuffed Ravioli | 1 1/3 cup | 380 | 14 | 33 | 8 | 55 | 600 | 48 | 3 | 17 | 3 | 3 carb, 1 med-fat meat, 2 fat |
| Three Cheese Tortellini | 3/4 cup | 250 | 7 | 25 | 4 | 35 | 300 | 37 | 2 | 11 | 2 1/2 | 2 1/2 carb, 1 med-fat meat |
| **Digiorno Stuffed Pasta** | | | | | | | | | | | | |
| Beef & Roasted Garlic Tortellini | 1 cup | 340 | 11 | 29 | 4 | 50 | 390 | 46 | 1 | 14 | 3 | 3 strch, 1 med-fat meat, 1 fat |

✔ = Best Bet; NA = Not Available; Carb. Ch. = Carbohydrate Choices

| Pasta (Refrigerated) (Continued) | Serving Size | Cal. | Fat (g) | % Cal. Fat | Sat. Fat (g) | Chol. (mg) | Sod. (mg) | Pro. (g) | Fiber (g) | Carb. (g) | Carb. Ch. | Servings/Exchanges |
|---|---|---|---|---|---|---|---|---|---|---|---|---|
| Four Cheese Ravioli | 1 cup | 350 | 15 | 39 | 9 | 70 | 390 | 14 | 2 | 40 | 2 1/2 | 2 1/2 strch, 1 med-fat meat, 2 fat |
| Lemon Chicken Tortellini w/Black Pepper Pasta | 1 cup | 270 | 5 | 17 | 3 | 40 | 290 | 13 | 1 | 42 | 3 | 3 strch, 1 med-fat meat |
| Mozzarella Garlic Tortellini | 1 cup | 300 | 8 | 24 | 5 | 45 | 400 | 15 | 1 | 42 | 3 | 3 strch, 1 med-fat meat, 1 fat |
| Portabello Mushroom Tortellini | 1 cup | 310 | 7 | 20 | 5 | 40 | 490 | 13 | 3 | 48 | 3 | 3 strch, 1 med-fat meat |
| **Mallard's** | | | | | | | | | | | | |
| Gourmet Rainbow Tortellini | 1 cup | 250 | 5 | 18 | 3 | 45 | 330 | 11 | 2 | 39 | 2 1/2 | 2 1/2 strch, 1 fat |
| **Monterey Pasta Co.** | | | | | | | | | | | | |
| Tortellini Grandi, Italian Sausage | 1 cup | 300 | 7 | 21 | 3 | 45 | 300 | 14 | 2 | 43 | 3 | 3 strch, 1 med-fat meat |

## PASTA MEALS/ENTREES (DRY, AS PREPARED)

### Classico

| | Serving Size | Cal. | Fat (g) | % Cal. Fat | Sat. Fat (g) | Chol. (mg) | Sod. (mg) | Pro. (g) | Fiber (g) | Carb. (g) | Carb. Ch. | Servings/Exchanges |
|---|---|---|---|---|---|---|---|---|---|---|---|---|
| ✓It's Pasta Anytime, Penne w/ Tomato Italian Sausage Flavor Sauce | 15.25 oz meal | 540 | 8 | 13 | 1 | <1 | 850 | 17 | 8 | 100 | 6 1/2 | 6 1/2 carb, 2 fat |

| | Serving Size | Cal. | Fat (g) | % Cal. Fat | Sat. Fat (g) | Chol. (mg) | Sod. (mg) | Pro. (g) | Fiber (g) | Carb. (g) | Carb. Ch. | Exchanges |
|---|---|---|---|---|---|---|---|---|---|---|---|---|
| ✔It's Pasta Anytime, Penne w/ Tomato Mushroom Sauce | 15.25 oz meal | 530 | 8 | 14 | 1 | 0 | 960 | 16 | 8 | 99 | 6 1/2 | 6 1/2 carb, 2 fat |
| ✔It's Pasta Anytime, Spaghetti Pata w/Tomato Sauce | 15.25 oz meal | 550 | 8 | 13 | 1 | 0 | 890 | 16 | 8 | 103 | 7 | 7 carb, 2 fat |
| ✔It's Pasta Anytime, Tomato Beef Flavored Sauce | 15.25 oz meal | 540 | 8 | 13 | 2 | <1 | 890 | 17 | 8 | 101 | 7 | 7 carb, 2 fat |

## PASTA MEALS/ENTREES (FROZEN)

### Banquet

| | Serving Size | Cal. | Fat (g) | % Cal. Fat | Sat. Fat (g) | Chol. (mg) | Sod. (mg) | Pro. (g) | Fiber (g) | Carb. (g) | Carb. Ch. | Exchanges |
|---|---|---|---|---|---|---|---|---|---|---|---|---|
| Chicken Pasta Primavera | 9.5 oz dinner | 320 | 12 | 34 | 5 | 25 | 840 | 11 | 4 | 40 | 2 1/2 | 2 1/2 carb, 1 med-fat meat, 1 fat |
| Family Size Lasagna Roma | 8.3 oz | 280 | 10 | 32 | 6 | 45 | 630 | 14 | 4 | 34 | 2 | 2 carb, 1 med-fat meat, 1 fat |
| Family Size Lasagna w/Meat Sauce | 8 oz | 300 | 11 | 33 | 6 | 60 | 960 | 13 | 2 | 37 | 2 1/2 | 2 1/2 carb, 1 med-fat meat, 1 fat |
| Family Size Pasta & Italian Sausage | 8 oz | 340 | 20 | 53 | 8 | 35 | 920 | 12 | 3 | 28 | 2 | 2 carb, 1 med-fat meat, 3 fat |
| Fettuccine Alfredo | 9.5 oz dinner | 350 | 15 | 39 | 7 | 25 | 850 | 11 | 4 | 40 | 2 1/2 | 2 1/2 carb, 1 med-fat meat, 2 fat |

✔ = Best Bet; NA = Not Available; Carb. Ch. = Carbohydrate Choices

| Pasta Meals/Entrees (Frozen) (Continued) | Serving Size | Cal. | Fat (g) | % Cal. Fat | Sat. Fat (g) | Chol. (mg) | Sod. (mg) | Pro. (g) | Fiber (g) | Carb. (g) | Carb. Ch. | Servings/Exchanges |
|---|---|---|---|---|---|---|---|---|---|---|---|---|
| ✓Lasagna w/Meat Sauce | 9.5 oz dinner | 260 | 8 | 28 | 2 | 10 | 820 | 10 | 5 | 38 | 2 1/2 | 2 1/2 carb, 1 med-fat meat, 1 fat |
| Pasta w/White Cheddar Broccoli | 9.5 oz dinner | 320 | 11 | 31 | 6 | 15 | 810 | 11 | 4 | 48 | 3 | 3 carb, 1 med-fat meat, 1 fat |
| ✓Vegetable Lasagna | 10.5 oz dinner | 260 | 6 | 21 | 2 | NA | 850 | 11 | NA | 41 | 2 | 3 carb, 1 fat |
| **Budget Gourmet** | | | | | | | | | | | | |
| ✓Angel Hair Pasta | 8 oz meal | 230 | 5 | 20 | 2 | 10 | 430 | 8 | 3 | 38 | 2 1/2 | 2 1/2 carb, 1 fat |
| Fettuccine w/Meat Sauce | 10 oz dinner | 290 | 10 | 31 | NA | 25 | 980 | 16 | NA | 34 | 2 | 2 carb, 1 med-fat meat, 1 fat |
| Hearty Fettuccine Alfredo w/4 Cheese & Chicken | 14 oz meal | 520 | 25 | 43 | 9 | 135 | 1350 | 25 | 6 | 50 | 3 | 3 carb, 2 med-fat meat, 3 fat |
| ✓Hearty Pennini Pasta w/Chicken | 14 oz meal | 450 | 11 | 22 | 4 | 35 | 890 | 24 | 6 | 63 | 4 | 4 carb, 2 med-fat meat |
| Manicotti w/Meat Sauce | 10 oz meal | 450 | 26 | 53 | NA | 50 | 920 | 20 | NA | 33 | 2 | 2 carb, 2 med-fat meat, 3 fat |
| Pasta Shells & Beef | 10 oz meal | 340 | 14 | 37 | NA | 35 | 985 | 20 | NA | 34 | 2 | 2 carb, 2 med-fat meat, 1 fat |
| ✓Penne w/Tomato Sauce & Italian Sausage | 10 oz meal | 320 | 9 | 24 | 2 | 5 | 520 | 12 | NA | 53 | 3 1/2 | 3 1/2 carb, 2 fat |

| | Serving Size | Cal. | Fat (g) | % Cal. Fat | Sat. Fat (g) | Chol. (mg) | Sod. (mg) | Prot. (g) | Fiber (g) | Carb. (g) | Carb. Ch. | Exchanges/Choices |
|---|---|---|---|---|---|---|---|---|---|---|---|---|
| ✓Rigatoni in Cream Sauce | 10.8 oz meal | 290 | 7 | 22 | 3 | 30 | 710 | 19 | NA | 44 | 3 | 3 carb, 1 med-fat meat |
| ✓Spaghetti Marinara | 9.1 oz meal | 290 | 6 | 18 | 2 | 5 | 790 | 10 | 4 | 50 | 3 | 3 carb, 1 fat |
| ✓Special Solutions, Lasagna w/Meat Sauce | 10 oz meal | 250 | 7 | 25 | 3 | 30 | 690 | 15 | 3 | 31 | 2 | 2 carb, 1 med-fat meat |
| Three Cheese Lasagna | 10 oz dinner | 370 | 16 | 39 | 10 | 60 | 870 | 20 | 5 | 38 | 2 1/2 | 2 1/2 carb, 2 med-fat meat, 1 fat |
| ✓Ziti Parmesano | 8 oz meal | 260 | 7 | 24 | 2 | 10 | 550 | 11 | 4 | 39 | 2 1/2 | 2 1/2 carb, 1 med-fat meat |
| **Dining Lite** | | | | | | | | | | | | |
| Cheese Cannelloni | 9 oz meal | 310 | 9 | 26 | NA | 70 | 650 | 19 | NA | 38 | 2 1/2 | 2 1/2 carb, 2 med-fat meat |
| Fettuccine | 9 oz meal | 290 | 12 | 37 | NA | 35 | 1020 | 12 | NA | 33 | 2 | 2 carb, 1 med-fat meat, 1 fat |
| ✓Lasagna | 9 oz meal | 260 | 6 | 21 | NA | 30 | 800 | 14 | NA | 36 | 2 1/2 | 2 1/2 carb, 1 med-fat meat |
| Spaghetti w/Beef | 9 oz meal | 220 | 8 | 33 | NA | 20 | 440 | 12 | NA | 25 | 1 1/2 | 1 1/2 carb, 1 med-fat meat, 1 fat |

✓= Best Bet; NA = Not Available; Carb. Ch. = Carbohydrate Choices

## Healthy Choice

| Pasta Meals/Entrees (Frozen) (Continued) | Serving Size | Cal. | Fat (g) | % Cal. Fat | Sat. Fat (g) | Chol. (mg) | Sod. (mg) | Pro. (g) | Fiber (g) | Carb. (g) | Carb. Ch. | Servings/Exchanges |
|---|---|---|---|---|---|---|---|---|---|---|---|---|
| ✓Beef Macaroni | 8.5 oz | 220 | 4 | 16 | 2 | 20 | 450 | 12 | 5 | 34 | 2 | 2 carb, 1 med-fat meat |
| ✓Cheese Ravioli Parmigiana | 10.5 oz meal | 330 | 7 | 18 | 3 | 20 | 290 | 11 | 6 | 44 | 3 | 3 carb, 1 fat |
| ✓Chicken Fettuccine Alfredo | 8.5 oz meal | 280 | 7 | 23 | 3 | 40 | 410 | 22 | 3 | 35 | 2 | 2 carb, 2 lean meat |
| ✓Fettuccine Alfredo | 8 oz meal | 250 | 5 | 18 | 2 | 15 | 480 | 11 | 3 | 39 | 2 1/2 | 2 1/2 carb, 1 med-fat meat |
| ✓Lasagna Roma | 13.5 oz meal | 420 | 9 | 11 | 3 | 35 | 580 | 26 | 6 | 59 | 4 | 4 carb, 2 med-fat meat |
| Pasta Shells Marinara | 10.4 oz meal | 370 | 6 | 15 | 3 | 20 | 570 | 18 | 5 | 60 | 4 | 4 carb, 1 med-fat meat |
| Pasta Shells Marinara | 10.4 oz meal | 370 | 6 | 15 | 3 | 20 | 570 | 18 | 5 | 60 | 4 | 4 carb, 1 med-fat meat |
| ✓Penne Pasta w/Tomato Sauce | 8 oz meal | 230 | 5 | 20 | 1 | 10 | 490 | 9 | 5 | 36 | 2 1/2 | 2 1/2 carb, 1 fat |
| ✓Spaghetti and Sauce w/Seasoned Beef | 10 oz meal | 280 | 6 | 18 | 2 | 30 | 470 | 14 | 5 | 43 | 3 | 3 carb, 1 med-fat meat |
| ✓Three Cheese Manicotti | 11 oz meal | 300 | 9 | 27 | 3 | 35 | 550 | 15 | 5 | 40 | 2 1/2 | 2 1/2 carb, 1 med-fat meat, 1 fat |
| ✓Vegetable Pasta Italiano | 10 oz meal | 250 | 3 | 11 | 2 | 10 | 480 | 9 | 6 | 48 | 3 | 3 carb, 1 fat |
| Zucchini Lasagna | 13.5 oz meal | 280 | 4 | 13 | 3 | 10 | 310 | 13 | 5 | 47 | 3 | 3 carb, 1 med-fat meat |

## Kirkland Signature

| | | | | | | | | | | | | |
|---|---|---|---|---|---|---|---|---|---|---|---|---|
| 4 Cheese Ravioli | 5 oz | 310 | 12 | 35 | 6 | 45 | 800 | 17 | 6 | 37 | 2 1/2 | 2 1/2 carb, 1 med-fat meat, 1 fat |

## Lean Cuisine

| | | | | | | | | | | | | |
|---|---|---|---|---|---|---|---|---|---|---|---|---|
| ✔Alfredo Pasta Primavera | 10 oz meal | 290 | 7 | 21 | 3 | 10 | 570 | 11 | 3 | 46 | 3 | 3 carb, 1 fat |
| ✔Angel Hair Pasta | 10 oz meal | 260 | 5 | 17 | 1 | 0 | 470 | 9 | 2 | 46 | 3 | 3 carb, 1 fat |
| ✔Bow Tie Pasta & Creamy Tomato Sauce | 9.5 oz meal | 260 | 6 | 19 | 2 | 35 | 550 | 9 | 6 | 43 | 3 | 3 carb, 1 fat |
| ✔Cafe Classics-Cheese Lasagna w/Chicken Scaloppini | 10 oz meal | 290 | 8 | 25 | 2 | 30 | 590 | 21 | 3 | 33 | 2 | 2 carb, 2 med-fat meat |
| ✔Cheese & Spinach Manicotti | 15.5 oz meal | 370 | 8 | 19 | 2 | 35 | 850 | 25 | 8 | 50 | 3 | 3 carb, 2 med-fat meat |
| ✔Cheese Cannelloni | 9.1 oz meal | 230 | 4 | 16 | 2 | 15 | 570 | 20 | 3 | 28 | 2 | 2 carb, 1 med-fat meat |
| ✔Cheese Ravioli | 8.5 oz meal | 270 | 7 | 23 | 3 | 45 | 580 | 11 | 5 | 40 | 2 1/2 | 2 12/carb, 1 med-fat meat |
| ✔Chicken Lasagna | 10 oz | 270 | 8 | 27 | 3 | 35 | 590 | 19 | 5 | 30 | 2 | 2 carb, 2 med-fat meat |
| Classic Cheese Lasagna | 11.5 oz meal | 280 | 5 | 16 | 3 | 15 | 560 | 19 | 6 | 40 | 2 1/2 | 2 1/2 carb, 2 lean meat |
| ✔Fettuccine Alfredo | 9 oz meal | 300 | 7 | 21 | 3 | 15 | 550 | 12 | 2 | 47 | 3 | 3 carb, 1 med-fat meat |
| ✔Fettuccine Primavera | 10 oz meal | 270 | 7 | 23 | 3 | 15 | 580 | 13 | 4 | 38 | 2 1/2 | 2 1/2 carb, 1 med-fat meat |

✔ = Best Bet; NA = Not Available; Carb. Ch. = Carbohydrate Choices

| Pasta Meals/Entrees (Frozen) (Continued) | Serving Size | Cal. | Fat (g) | % Cal. Fat | Sat. Fat (g) | Chol. (mg) | Sod. (mg) | Pro. (g) | Fiber (g) | Carb. (g) | Carb. Ch. | Servings/Exchanges |
|---|---|---|---|---|---|---|---|---|---|---|---|---|
| ✓Hearty Portions, Jumbo Rigatoni w/Meatballs | 15.4 oz meal | 440 | 9 | 18 | 4 | 35 | 820 | 25 | 7 | 64 | 4 | 4 carb, 2 med-fat meat |
| Lasagna w/Meat Sauce | 10.5 oz meal | 290 | 6 | 19 | 4 | 25 | 560 | 21 | 4 | 37 | 2 1/2 | 2 1/2 carb, 2 lean meat |
| ✓Macaroni & Beef | 10 oz meal | 270 | 4 | 13 | 2 | 25 | 590 | 15 | 4 | 43 | 3 | 3 carb, 1 med-fat meat |
| ✓Penne Pasta w/Tomato Basil Sauce | 10 oz meal | 270 | 4 | 13 | 1 | 0 | 350 | 8 | 5 | 52 | 3 1/2 | 3 1/2 carb, 1 fat |
| ✓Spaghetti w/Meat Sauce | 11.5 oz meal | 290 | 5 | 16 | 2 | 20 | 570 | 11 | 7 | 50 | 3 | 3 carb, 1 med-fat meat |
| ✓Spaghetti w/Meatballs | 9.5 oz meal | 280 | 6 | 19 | 2 | 20 | 570 | 16 | 4 | 40 | 2 1/2 | 2 1/2 carb, 2 lean meat |
| ✓Vegetable Lasagna | 10.5 oz meal | 260 | 7 | 24 | 3 | 20 | 590 | 15 | 5 | 35 | 2 | 2 carb, 1 med-fat meat |
| **Marie Callender** | | | | | | | | | | | | |
| Cheese Ravioli in Marinara Sauce | 16 oz meal | 750 | 29 | 35 | 9 | 30 | 1070 | 25 | 11 | 96 | 6 1/2 | 6 1/2 carb, 1 med-fat meat, 5 fat |
| Chunky Tuna & Noodles | 12 oz meal | 960 | 35 | 33 | 18 | 55 | 1570 | 18 | 6 | 143 | 9 1/2 | 9 1/2 carb, 7 fat |
| Extra Cheese Lasagna | 15 oz meal | 590 | 27 | 41 | 13 | 50 | 1230 | 27 | 7 | 61 | 4 | 4 carb, 2 med-fat meat, 3 fat |
| Fettuccine Alfredo Supreme | 13 oz meal | 450 | 27 | 56 | 12 | 80 | 680 | 15 | 4 | 35 | 2 | 2 carb, 1 med-fat meat, 4 fat |
| Lasagna w/Meat Sauce | 15 oz meal | 630 | 31 | 44 | 15 | 75 | 1230 | 29 | 3 | 59 | 4 | 4 carb, 2 med-fat meat, 4 fat |

| Product | Serving Size | Cal. | Fat (g) | % Cal. Fat | Sat. Fat (g) | Chol. (mg) | Sod. (mg) | Prot. (g) | Fiber (g) | Carb. (g) | Carb. Ch. | Exchanges/Choices |
|---|---|---|---|---|---|---|---|---|---|---|---|---|
| Spaghetti & Meat Sauce | 17 oz meal | 670 | 25 | 34 | 4 | 35 | 1160 | 27 | 9 | 85 | 5 1/2 | 5 1/2 carb, 2 med-fat meat, 3 fat |
| **Michael Angelo's** | | | | | | | | | | | | |
| Eggplant Parmesan | 6 oz | 280 | 19 | 61 | 3 | 40 | 330 | 5 | 4 | 23 | 1 1/2 | 1 carb, 1 vegetable, 4 fat |
| Lasagna w/Meat Sauce | 1 cup | 410 | 22 | 48 | 8 | 80 | 640 | 25 | 0 | 28 | 2 | 2 carb, 3 med-fat meat, 1 fat |
| Stuffed Shells | 4 oz | 210 | 9 | 39 | 6 | 40 | 260 | 13 | 1 | 18 | 1 | 1 carb, 1 med-fat meat, 1 fat |
| ✓Vegetable Lasagna | 1 cup | 230 | 7 | 27 | 3 | 15 | 720 | 20 | 3 | 23 | 1 1/2 | 1 1/2 carb, 2 lean meat |
| **Morton** | | | | | | | | | | | | |
| Spaghetti w/Meat Sauce | 8.5 oz meal | 200 | 6 | 27 | 3 | 5 | 750 | 5 | 4 | 30 | 2 | 2 carb, 1 fat |
| **Pasta Prima** | | | | | | | | | | | | |
| ✓Spinach and Mozarella Ravioli Entrée | 1 cup | 200 | 5 | 23 | 2 | 27 | 390 | 9 | 4 | 29 | 2 | 2 carb, 1 med-fat meat |
| **Stouffer's** | | | | | | | | | | | | |
| Cheese Manicotti | 9 oz meal | 360 | 16 | 40 | 9 | 40 | 850 | 19 | 4 | 34 | 2 | 2 carb, 2 med-fat meat, 1 fat |
| Cheese Ravioli | 10.6 oz meal | 380 | 13 | 31 | 6 | 100 | 700 | 15 | 6 | 51 | 3 1/2 | 3 1/2 carb, 1 med-fat meat, 2 fat |

✓ = Best Bet; NA = Not Available; Carb. Ch. = Carbohydrate Choices

| Pasta Meals/Entrees (Frozen) (*Continued*) | Serving Size | Cal. | Fat (g) | % Cal. Fat | Sat. Fat (g) | Chol. (mg) | Sod. (mg) | Pro. (g) | Fiber (g) | Carb. (g) | Carb. Ch. | Servings/Exchanges |
|---|---|---|---|---|---|---|---|---|---|---|---|---|
| Fettuccine Alfredo | 10 oz | 460 | 23 | 45 | 13 | 70 | 910 | 16 | 3 | 47 | 3 | 3 carb, 1 med-fat meat, 4 fat |
| Fettuccine Primavera | 10 oz meal | 370 | 15 | 36 | 8 | 40 | 950 | 14 | 4 | 45 | 3 | 3 carb, 1 med-fat meat, 2 fat |
| Lasagna w/Meat Sauce | 10.5 oz meal | 370 | 14 | 34 | 7 | 45 | 1050 | 23 | 4 | 39 | 2 1/2 | 2 1/2 carb, 2 med-fat meat, 1 fat |
| Lasagna, Five-Cheese | 10.8 oz meal | 360 | 13 | 33 | 7 | 35 | 960 | 21 | 6 | 40 | 2 1/2 | 2 1/2 carb, 2 med-fat meat, 1 fat |
| Macaroni w/Beef | 11.5 oz meal | 420 | 20 | 43 | 8 | 50 | 1530 | 20 | 5 | 40 | 2 1/2 | 2 1/2 carb, 2 med-fat meat, 2 fat |
| Noodles Romanoff | 6 oz | 240 | 11 | 41 | 3 | 25 | 610 | 8 | 2 | 27 | 2 | 2 carb, 2 fat |
| Pasta Shells and American Cheese | 12 oz meal | 260 | 10 | 35 | 4 | 20 | 1190 | 11 | 2 | 31 | 2 | 2 carb, 1 med-fat meat, 1 fat |
| Spaghetti & Meatballs | 12.6 oz meal | 440 | 15 | 31 | 5 | 50 | 820 | 19 | 5 | 56 | 3 1/2 | 3 1/2 carb, 1 med-fat meat, 2 fat |
| Vegetable Lasagna | 10.5 oz meal | 440 | 20 | 41 | 8 | 35 | 1110 | 21 | 5 | 43 | 3 | 3 carb, 2 med-fat meat, 2 fat |

## Weight Watchers Smart Ones

| | Serving | Cal. | Fat (g) | % Cal. Fat | Sat. Fat (g) | Chol. (mg) | Sod. (mg) | Prot. (g) | Fiber (g) | Carb. (g) | Carb. Ch. | Exchanges/Choices |
|---|---|---|---|---|---|---|---|---|---|---|---|---|
| ✔ Lasagna Bolognese | 9 oz meal | 240 | 3 | 11 | 1 | 10 | 560 | 13 | 4 | 43 | 3 | 3 carb, 1 med-fat meat |
| ✔ Ravioli Florentine | 8.5 oz meal | 220 | 5 | 21 | 2 | 20 | 510 | 9 | 3 | 34 | 2 | 2 carb, 1 med-fat meat |
| ✔ Three Cheese Ziti Marinara | 9 oz meal | 290 | 7 | 22 | 2 | 5 | 600 | 11 | 5 | 47 | 3 | 3 carb, 1 fat |
| ✔ Tuna Noodle Gratin | 9.5 oz meal | 270 | 6 | 20 | 2 | 25 | 670 | 13 | 2 | 40 | 2 1/2 | 2 1/2 carb, 1 med-fat meat |

## PASTA SALAD, DRY MIX (AS PREPARED)

### Kraft

| | Serving | Cal. | Fat (g) | % Cal. Fat | Sat. Fat (g) | Chol. (mg) | Sod. (mg) | Prot. (g) | Fiber (g) | Carb. (g) | Carb. Ch. | Exchanges/Choices |
|---|---|---|---|---|---|---|---|---|---|---|---|---|
| Classic Ranch w/Bacon | 3/4 cup | 350 | 22 | 57 | 4 | 10 | 480 | 7 | 2 | 32 | 2 | 2 strch, 4 fat |
| Creamy Caesar | 3/4 cup | 340 | 21 | 56 | 4 | 15 | 630 | 7 | 2 | 31 | 2 | 2 strch, 4 fat |
| ✔ Garden Primavera | 3/4 cup | 240 | 8 | 30 | 2 | <5 | 710 | 8 | 2 | 35 | 2 | 2 strch, 2 fat |
| Herb and Garlic | 3/4 cup | 280 | 14 | 45 | 2 | 0 | 670 | 6 | 2 | 34 | 2 | 2 strch, 3 fat |
| ✔ Italian (97% Fat-Free) | 3/4 cup | 190 | 2 | 10 | 1 | <5 | 740 | 8 | 2 | 35 | 2 | 2 strch |
| Parmesan Peppercorn | 3/4 cup | 360 | 23 | 58 | 4 | 15 | 570 | 7 | 2 | 29 | 2 | 2 strch, 5 fat |

## PASTA SAUCE (CAN OR JAR)

### Classico

| | Serving | Cal. | Fat (g) | % Cal. Fat | Sat. Fat (g) | Chol. (mg) | Sod. (mg) | Prot. (g) | Fiber (g) | Carb. (g) | Carb. Ch. | Exchanges/Choices |
|---|---|---|---|---|---|---|---|---|---|---|---|---|
| Alfredo | 1/4 cup | 110 | 10 | 82 | 5 | 50 | 480 | 2 | 0 | 3 | 0 | 2 fat |
| ✔ Fire Roasted Tomato & Garlic | 1/2 cup | 60 | 1 | 15 | 0 | 0 | 500 | 2 | 2 | 10 | 1/2 | 1/2 carb |
| Florentine Spinach & Cheese | 1/2 cup | 80 | 5 | 56 | 1 | <5 | 490 | 3 | 2 | 8 | 1/2 | 1/2 carb, 1 fat |

✔= Best Bet; NA = Not Available; Carb. Ch. = Carbohydrate Choices

| Pasta Sauce (Can or Jar) (*Continued*) | Serving Size | Cal. | Fat (g) | % Cal. Fat | Sat. Fat (g) | Chol. (mg) | Sod. (mg) | Pro. (g) | Fiber (g) | Carb. (g) | Carb. Ch. | Servings/Exchanges |
|---|---|---|---|---|---|---|---|---|---|---|---|---|
| Four Cheese | 1/2 cup | 80 | 4 | 45 | 1 | <5 | 500 | 2 | 1 | 8 | 1/2 | 1/2 carb, 1 fat |
| ✓Italian Sausage with Peppers & Onions | 1/2 cup | 70 | 3 | 39 | 1 | 10 | 500 | 3 | 2 | 8 | 1/2 | 1/2 carb, 1 fat |
| ✓Portabello Mushroom | 1/2 cup | 70 | 2 | 26 | 0 | 0 | 420 | 2 | 2 | 11 | 1 | 1 carb |
| Roasted Garlic Alfredo | 1/4 cup | 110 | 10 | 82 | 5 | 50 | 460 | 2 | 0 | 3 | 0 | 2 fat |
| Spicy Tomato & Pesto | 1/2 cup | 90 | 5 | 50 | 1 | 0 | 530 | 3 | 2 | 9 | 1/2 | 1/2 carb |
| Sun Dried Tomato Alfredo | 1/4 cup | 110 | 9 | 74 | 5 | 40 | 450 | 2 | 0 | 4 | 0 | 2 fat |
| ✓Sweet Basil Marinara | 1/2 cup | 70 | 2 | 26 | 0 | 0 | 500 | 2 | 2 | 11 | 1 | 1 carb |
| ✓Tomato & Basil | 1/2 cup | 50 | 1 | 18 | 0 | 0 | 390 | 2 | 2 | 9 | 1/2 | 1/2 carb |
| **Contadina** | | | | | | | | | | | | |
| Deluxe Marinara Sauce | 1/2 cup | 73 | 4 | 49 | <1 | 0 | 469 | 2 | 2 | 9 | 1/2 | 1/2 carb, 1 fat |
| ✓Pasta-Ready Tomatoes & 3 Cheeses | 1/2 cup | 70 | 2 | 26 | <1 | 4 | 490 | 2 | 2 | 10 | 1/2 | 1/2 carb |
| Pasta-Ready Tomatoes & Mushrooms | 1/2 cup | 50 | 1 | 18 | 0 | 0 | 641 | 1 | 1 | 9 | 1/2 | 1/2 carb |
| Pasta-Ready Tomatoes & Olives | 1/2 cup | 60 | 2 | 30 | 0 | 0 | 641 | 1 | 1 | 8 | 1/2 | 1/2 carb |
| Pasta-Ready Tomatoes & Red Pepper | 1/2 cup | 60 | 2 | 30 | 0 | 0 | 691 | 1 | 1 | 8 | 1/2 | 1/2 carb |
| **Healthy Choice** | | | | | | | | | | | | |
| ✓Extra Chunky Garlic & Onion Pasta Sauce | 1/2 cup | 40 | 0 | 0 | 0 | 0 | 350 | 2 | NA | 10 | 1/2 | 1/2 carb |
| ✓Extra Chunky Mushroom Pasta Sauce | 1/2 cup | 45 | 0 | 0 | 0 | 0 | 350 | 2 | NA | 10 | 1/2 | 1/2 carb |

| Product | Serving | Cal. | Fat (g) | % Cal. Fat | Sat. Fat (g) | Chol. (mg) | Sod. (mg) | Prot. (g) | Fiber (g) | Carb. (g) | Carb. Ch. | Exchanges |
|---|---|---|---|---|---|---|---|---|---|---|---|---|
| ✔ Pasta Sauce w/Garlic & Herbs | 1/2 cup | 40 | 1 | 23 | NA | 0 | 350 | 2 | NA | 9 | 1/2 | 1/2 carb |
| ✔ Traditional Pasta Sauce | 1/2 cup | 40 | 1 | 23 | NA | 0 | 380 | 2 | NA | 9 | 1/2 | 1/2 carb |
| **Newman's Own** | | | | | | | | | | | | |
| Mushroom Marinara | 1/2 cup | 60 | 2 | 30 | 0 | 0 | 590 | 2 | 3 | 9 | 1/2 | 1/2 carb |
| Tomato & Fresh Basil | 1/2 cup | 100 | 5 | 45 | <1 | 0 | 590 | 1 | 5 | 15 | 1 | 1 carb, 1 fat |
| Tomato, Pepper's & Spices | 1/2 cup | 60 | 2 | 30 | 0 | 0 | 590 | 2 | 3 | 9 | 1/2 | 1/2 carb |
| **Prego** | | | | | | | | | | | | |
| Marinara Sauce | 1/2 cup | 100 | 6 | 54 | 2 | 0 | 620 | 1 | 1 | 10 | 1/2 | 1/2 carb, 1 fat |
| ✔ Spaghetti Sauce, All Varieties (Avg) | 1/2 cup | 100 | 3 | 27 | 1 | 0 | 455 | 2 | 3 | 17 | 1 | 1 carb, 1 fat |
| Xtra Chunky Spaghetti Sauce, All Varieties (Avg) | 1/2 cup | 120 | 5 | 38 | 1 | 0–5 | 510 | 2 | 3 | 17 | 1 | 1 carb, 1 fat |
| **Progresso** | | | | | | | | | | | | |
| Authentic Alfredo Sauce | 1/2 cup | 200 | 15 | 68 | 10 | 50 | 850 | 8 | 1 | 7 | 1/2 | 1/2 carb, 1 med-fat meat, 3 fat |
| Authentic Marinara Sauce | 1/2 cup | 100 | 4 | 36 | 1 | <5 | 590 | 4 | 3 | 12 | 1 | 1 carb, 1 fat |
| Marinara Sauce | 1/2 cup | 80 | 5 | 56 | <1 | <5 | 480 | 2 | 2 | 8 | 1/2 | 1/2 carb, 1 fat |
| Meat Flavored Pasta Sauce | 1/2 cup | 100 | 5 | 45 | 1 | 5 | 610 | 4 | 3 | 12 | 1 | 1 carb, 1 fat |
| Spaghetti Sauce | 1/2 cup | 100 | 5 | 45 | 1 | <5 | 620 | 3 | 2 | 12 | 1 | 1 carb, 1 fat |

✔ = Best Bet; NA = Not Available; Carb. Ch. = Carbohydrate Choices

| Pasta Sauce (Can or Jar) (Continued) | Serving Size | Cal. | Fat (g) | % Cal. Fat | Sat. Fat (g) | Chol. (mg) | Sod. (mg) | Pro. (g) | Fiber (g) | Carb. (g) | Carb. Ch. | Servings/Exchanges |
|---|---|---|---|---|---|---|---|---|---|---|---|---|
| **Ragu** | | | | | | | | | | | | |
| Cheese Creations, Classic Alfredo | 1/4 cup | 110 | 10 | 82 | 4 | 25 | 340 | 1 | 0 | 3 | 0 | 2 fat |
| Cheese Creations, Double Cheddar | 1/4 cup | 100 | 9 | 81 | 4 | 25 | 490 | 2 | 0 | 3 | 0 | 2 fat |
| Cheese Creations, Roasted Garlic Parmesan | 1/4 cup | 110 | 10 | 82 | 3 | 20 | 340 | 2 | 0 | 3 | 0 | 2 fat |
| Chunky Gardenstyle Garden Combination | 1/2 cup | 110 | 3 | 25 | 0 | 0 | 520 | 2 | 2 | 18 | 1 | 1 carb, 1 fat |
| Chunky Gardenstyle Mushroom & Green Pepper | 1/2 cup | 100 | 3 | 27 | 0 | 0 | 580 | 3 | 2 | 17 | 1 | 1 carb, 1 fat |
| Chunky Gardenstyle Super Garlic | 1/2 cup | 90 | 2 | 20 | 0 | 0 | 550 | 2 | 2 | 16 | 1 | 1 carb |
| Flavored with Meat | 1/2 cup | 80 | 4 | 45 | <1 | <5 | 800 | 2 | 2 | 8 | 1/2 | 1/2 carb, 1 fat |
| Mushroom | 1/2 cup | 70 | 3 | 39 | 0 | 0 | 790 | 2 | 2 | 8 | 1/2 | 1/2 carb, 1 fat |
| Robusto Classic Italian Meat | 1/2 cup | 90 | 4 | 40 | 1 | 0 | 710 | 3 | 2 | 9 | 1/2 | 1/2 carb, 1 fat |
| Robusto Roasted Garlic | 1/2 cup | 90 | 3 | 30 | 0 | 0 | 540 | 2 | 2 | 12 | 1 | 1 carb, 1 fat |
| Robusto Sweet Italian & Cheese | 1/2 cup | 100 | 5 | 45 | 2 | 5 | 670 | 4 | 3 | 11 | 1 | 1 carb, 1 fat |
| Robusto Tomato, Garlic & Onion | 1/2 cup | 110 | 3 | 25 | 0 | 0 | 520 | 2 | 2 | 18 | 1 | 1 carb, 1 fat |
| Traditional | 1/2 cup | 70 | 3 | 39 | 0 | 0 | 820 | 2 | 2 | 8 | 1/2 | 1/2 carb, 1 fat |

**Weight Watchers**

| | Serving Size | Calories | Fat (g) | % Calories from Fat | Saturated Fat (g) | Cholesterol (mg) | Sodium (mg) | Carbohydrate (g) | Fiber (g) | Protein (g) | Carbohydrate Choices | Exchanges |
|---|---|---|---|---|---|---|---|---|---|---|---|---|
| ✓Pasta Sauce w/Mushrooms | 1/3 cup | 40 | 0 | 0 | 0 | 0 | 430 | 9 | NA | 1 | 1/2 | 1/2 carb |

## PASTA SAUCE (REFRIGERATED)

**Di Giorno Stuffed Pasta**

| | Serving Size | Calories | Fat (g) | % Calories from Fat | Saturated Fat (g) | Cholesterol (mg) | Sodium (mg) | Carbohydrate (g) | Fiber (g) | Protein (g) | Carbohydrate Choices | Exchanges |
|---|---|---|---|---|---|---|---|---|---|---|---|---|
| Alfredo Sauce | 1/4 cup | 180 | 18 | 90 | 7 | 25 | 600 | 3 | 0 | 3 | 0 | 4 fat |
| Basil Pesto Sauce | 1/4 cup | 320 | 31 | 87 | 6 | 15 | 320 | 0 | 2 | 7 | 0 | 1 med-fat meat, 1 fat |
| Four Cheese Sauce | 1/4 cup | 160 | 15 | 84 | 7 | 30 | 410 | 3 | 0 | 5 | 0 | 1 med-fat meat, 2 fat |
| Garlic Pesto Sauce | 1/4 cup | 340 | 33 | 87 | 7 | 15 | 540 | 5 | 0 | 7 | 0 | 1 med-fat meat, 6 fat |
| Light Alfredo Sauce | 1/4 cup | 140 | 10 | 64 | 7 | 30 | 600 | 9 | 0 | 5 | 1/2 | 1/2 carb, 1 med-fat meat, 1 fat |
| ✓Marinara Sauce | 1/2 cup | 70 | 0 | 0 | 0 | 0 | 220 | 15 | 2 | 2 | 1 | 1 carb |
| ✓Plum Tomato & Mushroom Sauce | 1/2 cup | 60 | 0 | 0 | 0 | 0 | 260 | 13 | 2 | 2 | 1 | 1 carb |
| Plum Tomato Cream Sauce | 1/2 cup | 160 | 13 | 73 | 7 | 40 | 370 | 8 | 2 | 3 | 1/2 | 1/2 carb, 3 fat |
| Roasted Red Bell Pepper Cream Sauce | 1/4 cup | 140 | 10 | 64 | 6 | 35 | 510 | 8 | 0 | 4 | 1/2 | 1/2 carb, 2 fat |

**Monterey Pasta CO.**

| | Serving Size | Calories | Fat (g) | % Calories from Fat | Saturated Fat (g) | Cholesterol (mg) | Sodium (mg) | Carbohydrate (g) | Fiber (g) | Protein (g) | Carbohydrate Choices | Exchanges |
|---|---|---|---|---|---|---|---|---|---|---|---|---|
| Pesto Sauce | 1/4 cup | 210 | 19 | 81 | 4 | 10 | 300 | 5 | <1 | 7 | 0 | 1 med-fat meat, 3 fat |
| Sun Dried Tomato Cream Sauce | 1/2 cup | 280 | 27 | 87 | 17 | 100 | 420 | 7 | 0 | 3 | 1/2 | 1/2 carb, 5 fat |

✓= Best Bet; NA = Not Available; Carb. Ch. = Carbohydrate Choices

## PASTA SIDE DISHES (DRY, AS PREPARED)

| Product | Serving Size | Cal. | Fat (g) | % Cal. Fat | Sat. Fat (g) | Chol. (mg) | Sod. (mg) | Pro. (g) | Fiber (g) | Carb. (g) | Carb. Ch. | Servings/Exchanges |
|---|---|---|---|---|---|---|---|---|---|---|---|---|
| **Betty Crocker** | | | | | | | | | | | | |
| Bowl Appetit, Pasta Alfredo | 1 bowl | 360 | 11 | 28 | 4 | 15 | 890 | 14 | 1 | 51 | 3 1/2 | 3 1/2 carb, 1 med-fat meat, 1 fat |
| Bowl Appetit, Tomato Parmesan Penne | 1 bowl | 350 | 8 | 21 | 2 | 5 | 890 | 12 | 3 | 57 | 4 | 4 carb, 2 fat |
| Creamy Garlic & Herb Rotini | 1 cup | 360 | 16 | 40 | 4 | 5 | 840 | 10 | 1 | 44 | 3 | 3 carb, 3 fat |
| Creamy Homestyle Chicken Pasta | 1 cup | 210 | 4 | 17 | 1 | 10 | 730 | 9 | 1 | 36 | 2 1/2 | 2 1/2 carb, 1 fat |
| Garlic Alfredo Fettuccine | 1 cup | 340 | 13 | 34 | 4 | 10 | 840 | 11 | 1 | 45 | 3 | 3 carb, 3 fat |
| Roasted Chicken Vegetable Penne | 1 cup | 240 | 7 | 26 | 1 | 5 | 860 | 8 | 2 | 39 | 2 1/2 | 2 1/2 carb, 1 fat |
| Three Cheese Gemelli Pasta | 1 cup | 330 | 12 | 33 | 4 | 15 | 930 | 12 | 1 | 47 | 3 | 3 carb, 2 fat |
| Tomato Parmesan Pasta | 1 cup | 260 | 10 | 35 | 2 | 0 | 840 | 6 | 1 | 37 | 2 1/2 | 2 1/2 carb, 2 fat |
| **Kraft Noodle Classics** | | | | | | | | | | | | |
| Cheddar Cheese | 1 cup | 400 | 19 | 43 | 5 | 70 | 760 | 13 | 1 | 47 | 3 | 3 strch, 1 med-fat meat, 3 fat |
| Savory Chicken | 1 cup | 340 | 13 | 34 | 3 | 55 | 1370 | 10 | 2 | 46 | 3 | 3 strch, 3 fat |
| **Kraft Spaghetti Classics** | | | | | | | | | | | | |
| Creamy Garlic & Herb Rotini | 1 cup | 360 | 16 | 40 | 4 | 5 | 840 | 10 | 1 | 44 | 3 | 3 carb, 3 fat |
| ✔Mild Italian | 1 cup | 240 | 3 | 11 | 1 | <5 | 850 | 11 | 3 | 46 | 3 | 3 strch, 1 fat |

| | Serving | Cal | Fat (g) | % Cal Fat | Sat Fat (g) | Chol (mg) | Sod (mg) | Carb (g) | Fiber (g) | Prot (g) | Carb Choices | Exchanges |
|---|---|---|---|---|---|---|---|---|---|---|---|---|
| Spaghetti w/Meat Sauce | 1 cup | 330 | 10 | 27 | 4 | 15 | 810 | 47 | 3 | 11 | 3 | 3 strch, 2 fat |
| ✓ Tangy Italian | 1 cup | 240 | 2 | 8 | <1 | 0 | 830 | 46 | 3 | 11 | 3 | 3 strch |
| ✓ Zesty Cheese | 1 cup | 240 | 2 | 8 | 1 | 5 | 800 | 46 | 3 | 11 | 3 | 3 strch |

**Lipton**

| | Serving | Cal | Fat (g) | % Cal Fat | Sat Fat (g) | Chol (mg) | Sod (mg) | Carb (g) | Fiber (g) | Prot (g) | Carb Choices | Exchanges |
|---|---|---|---|---|---|---|---|---|---|---|---|---|
| Alfredo Noodles & Sauce | 2/3 cup | 250 | 7 | 25 | 4 | 75 | 940 | 39 | 2 | 10 | 2 1/2 | 2 1/2 strch, 1 fat |
| Beef Noodles & Sauce | 1/3 cup | 230 | 4 | 16 | 1 | 60 | 840 | 43 | 2 | 8 | 3 | 3 strch, 1 fat |
| Butter Herb Noodles & Sauce | 2/3 cup | 250 | 7 | 25 | 4 | 65 | 710 | 42 | 2 | 9 | 3 | 3 strch, 1 fat |
| Chicken Broccoli Noodles & Sauce | 1/2 cup | 230 | 4 | 16 | 2 | 65 | 740 | 41 | 2 | 9 | 3 | 3 strch, 1 fat |
| Creamy Tomato Parmesan Noodles & Sauce | 2/3 cup | 240 | 5 | 19 | 3 | 10 | 830 | 41 | 2 | 8 | 3 | 3 strch, 1 fat |
| Parmesan Noodles & Sauce | 2/3 cup | 250 | 8 | 29 | 4 | 70 | 750 | 37 | 2 | 10 | 2 1/2 | 2 1/2 strch, 2 fat |
| Roasted Garlic & Olive Oil Pasta Spirals & Sauce | 1/2 cup | 220 | 3 | 12 | <1 | 0 | 810 | 42 | 2 | 8 | 3 | 3 strch, 1 fat |
| Sour Cream & Chives Noodles & Sauce | 1/2 cup | 260 | 8 | 28 | 5 | 70 | 800 | 41 | 2 | 8 | 3 | 3 strch, 2 fat |
| Zesty Cheddar Pasta & Sauce | 1/2 cup | 240 | 5 | 19 | 2 | 10 | 820 | 42 | 2 | 9 | 3 | 3 strch, 1 fat |

## PASTA SIDE DISHES (FROZEN)

**Budget Gourmet**

| | Serving | Cal | Fat (g) | % Cal Fat | Sat Fat (g) | Chol (mg) | Sod (mg) | Carb (g) | Fiber (g) | Prot (g) | Carb Choices | Exchanges |
|---|---|---|---|---|---|---|---|---|---|---|---|---|
| Macaroni & Cheese | 5.3 oz | 210 | 8 | 34 | NA | 25 | 370 | 23 | 1 | 9 | 1 1/2 | 1 1/2 carb, 1 med-fat meat, 1 fat |

✓ = Best Bet; NA = Not Available; Carb. Ch. = Carbohydrate Choices

| Pasta Side Dishes (Frozen) (*Continued*) | Serving Size | Cal. | Fat (g) | % Cal. Fat | Sat. Fat (g) | Chol. (mg) | Sod. (mg) | Pro. (g) | Fiber (g) | Carb. (g) | Carb. Ch. | Servings/Exchanges |
|---|---|---|---|---|---|---|---|---|---|---|---|---|
| **Green Giant** | | | | | | | | | | | | |
| Pasta Accent-Creamy Cheddar | 2 1/2 cup | 250 | 8 | 29 | 3 | 5 | 700 | 9 | 5 | 36 | 2 1/2 | 2 strch, 1 vegetable, 1 fat |
| Pasta Accent-Primavera | 2 1/4 cup | 290 | 9 | 28 | 3 | 5 | 530 | 12 | 4 | 39 | 2 1/2 | 2 strch, 2 vegetable, 2 fat |
| Pasta Accents-Alfredo | 2 cups | 210 | 8 | 34 | 3 | 5 | 480 | 9 | 4 | 25 | 1 1/2 | 1 1/2 strch, 1 vegetable, 2 fat |
| Pasta Accents Vegetables, Florentine | 2 cups | 310 | 9 | 26 | 3 | 7 | 910 | 13 | 5 | 44 | 3 | 2 carb, 2 vegetable, 2 fat |
| Pasta Accents Vegetables, Garlic | 2 cups | 260 | 10 | 35 | 5 | 15 | 640 | 7 | 12 | 36 | 2 1/2 | 2 1/2 strch, 2 fat |
| Pasta Accents Vegetables, Oriental | 2 1/2 cup | 260 | 10 | 35 | 4 | 20 | 580 | 8 | 4 | 35 | 2 | 2 strch, 1 vegetable, 2 fat |
| Pasta Accents-White Cheddar | 1 3/4 cup | 270 | 9 | 30 | 3 | 10 | 750 | 9 | 3 | 37 | 2 1/2 | 2 strch, 1 vegetable, 2 fat |
| **Michael Angelo's** | | | | | | | | | | | | |
| Antipasto Pasta Salad | 4 oz | 250 | 16 | 58 | 6 | 25 | 690 | 8 | 5 | 18 | 1 | 1 carb, 1 vegetable, 3 fat |

| | | Cal | Fat (g) | Carb (g) | Fiber (g) | Sodium (mg) | Protein (g) | Sat Fat (g) | Carb (g) | Carb. Ch. | Exchanges |
|---|---|---|---|---|---|---|---|---|---|---|---|
| **PASTRIES (FROZEN)** | | | | | | | | | | | |
| **Pepperidge Farm** | | | | | | | | | | | |
| Puff Pastry Sheets | 1/6 sheet | 170 | 11 | 58 | 3 | 0 | 200 | 3 | <1 | 14 | 1 | 1 carb, 2 fat |
| **PASTRIES (READY-TO-EAT)** | | | | | | | | | | | |
| **Entenmann's** | | | | | | | | | | | |
| Apple Puffs Pastry | 1 | 260 | 12 | 42 | 3 | 0 | 220 | 2 | 1 | 36 | 2 1/2 | 2 1/2 carb, 2 fat |
| Cheese Crumb Danish | 1 slice | 200 | 9 | 41 | 4 | 40 | 190 | 4 | <1 | 25 | 1 1/2 | 1 1/2 carb, 2 fat |
| Chocolate Eclairs | 1 | 250 | 9 | 32 | 2 | 70 | 220 | 3 | 0 | 44 | 3 | 3 carb, 2 fat |
| ✔Fat-Free Black Forest Pastry | 1 slice | 130 | 0 | 0 | 0 | 0 | 115 | 3 | 2 | 32 | 2 | 2 carb |
| ✔Fat-Free Apricot Pastry | 1 | 150 | 0 | 0 | 0 | 0 | 110 | 3 | <1 | 34 | 2 | 2 carb |
| ✔Fat-Free Cinnamon Apple Twist Pastry | 1 slice | 150 | 0 | 0 | 0 | 0 | 110 | 3 | <1 | 35 | 2 | 2 carb |
| ✔Fat-Free Lemon Twist Pastry | 1 slice | 130 | 0 | 0 | 0 | 0 | 190 | 2 | 1 | 29 | 2 | 2 carb |
| ✔Fat-Free Raspberry Cheese Pastry | 1 slice | 140 | 0 | 0 | 0 | 0 | 110 | 3 | 1 | 32 | 2 | 2 carb |
| ✔Fat-Free Raspberry Twist Pastry | 1 slice | 140 | 0 | 0 | 0 | 0 | 180 | 1 | 1 | 32 | 2 | 2 carb |
| Pecan Danish Pastry Ring | 1 slice | 250 | 15 | 54 | 3 | 30 | 160 | 3 | 1 | 25 | 1 1/2 | 1 1/2 carb, 3 fat |
| Raspberry Danish Pastry Twist | 1 slice | 220 | 11 | 45 | 4 | 20 | 170 | 3 | <1 | 27 | 2 | 2 strch, 2 fat |
| **Otis Spunkmeyer** | | | | | | | | | | | |
| Breakfast Claws | 1 | 240 | 12 | 45 | 4 | 10 | 180 | 3 | <1 | 30 | 2 | 2 carb, 2 fat |

✔= Best Bet; NA = Not Available; Carb. Ch. = Carbohydrate Choices

| Pastries (Ready-to-Eat) (*Continued*) | Serving Size | Cal. | Fat (g) | % Cal. Fat | Sat. Fat (g) | Chol. (mg) | Sod. (mg) | Pro. (g) | Fiber (g) | Carb. (g) | Carb. Ch. | Servings/Exchanges |
|---|---|---|---|---|---|---|---|---|---|---|---|---|
| **Pepperidge Farm** | | | | | | | | | | | | |
| Apple Danish | 1 | 210 | 9 | 39 | 3 | 15 | 190 | 4 | 2 | 29 | 2 | 2 strch, 2 fat |
| Apple Dumplings Puff Pastry | 1 | 290 | 11 | 34 | 3 | 0 | 160 | 3 | 3 | 44 | 3 | 3 strch, 2 fat |
| Apple Mini Turnovers | 1 | 140 | 8 | 51 | 2 | 0 | 80 | 2 | 1 | 15 | 1 | 1 strch, 2 fat |
| Apple Turnover w/Vanilla Icing | 1 | 380 | 14 | 33 | 3 | 0 | 190 | 3 | 2 | 53 | 3 1/2 | 3 1/2 strch, 3 fat |
| Cheese Danish | 1 | 230 | 11 | 43 | 4 | 55 | 230 | 6 | 1 | 25 | 1 1/2 | 1 1/2 strch, 2 fat |
| Cherry Mini Turnovers | 1 | 140 | 8 | 51 | 2 | 0 | 70 | 2 | 1 | 16 | 1 | 1 strch, 2 fat |
| Cherry Turnover w/Vanilla Icing | 1 | 340 | 13 | 34 | 3 | 0 | 200 | 4 | 3 | 51 | 3 1/2 | 3 1/2 strch, 3 fat |
| Raspberry Danish | 1 | 210 | 9 | 39 | 3 | 15 | 190 | 4 | 2 | 29 | 2 | 2 strch, 2 fat |
| **Pillsbury** | | | | | | | | | | | | |
| Apple Turnover | 1 | 170 | 8 | 42 | 2 | 0 | 310 | 2 | <1 | 23 | 1 1/2 | 1 1/2 strch, 2 fat |
| Cherry Turnover | 1 | 180 | 8 | 40 | 2 | 0 | 310 | 2 | 0 | 24 | 1 1/2 | 1 1/2 strch, 2 fat |
| **PEANUT BUTTER** | | | | | | | | | | | | |
| **(Generic)** | | | | | | | | | | | | |
| Peanut Butter, Chunky | 1 Tbsp | 94 | 8 | 77 | 2 | 0 | 78 | 4 | 1 | 4 | 0 | 1 med-fat meat, 1 fat |
| Peanut Butter, Natural, Salted | 1 Tbsp | 94 | 8 | 77 | 1 | 0 | 40 | 4 | 1 | 3 | 0 | 1 med-fat meat, 1 fat |
| Peanut Butter, Natural, Unsalted | 1 Tbsp | 94 | 8 | 77 | 1 | 0 | <1 | 4 | 1 | 3 | 0 | 1 med-fat meat, 1 fat |
| Peanut Butter, Smooth | 1 Tbsp | 94 | 8 | 77 | 2 | 0 | 77 | 4 | <1 | 3 | 0 | 1 med-fat meat, 1 fat |

| | Serving | Cal. | Fat (g) | % Cal. Fat | Sat. Fat (g) | Chol. (mg) | Sod. (mg) | Prot. (g) | Fiber (g) | Carb. (g) | Carb. Ch. | Exchanges/Choices |
|---|---|---|---|---|---|---|---|---|---|---|---|---|
| Reduced Fat Peanut Butter | 2 Tbsp | 190 | 12 | 57 | 3 | 0 | 210 | 8 | 2 | 15 | 1 | 1 carb, 1 med-fat meat, 1 fat |
| **PICKLE RELISH** | | | | | | | | | | | | |
| **(Generic)** | | | | | | | | | | | | |
| ✔Hotdog Relish | 1 Tbsp | 14 | <1 | 0 | 0 | 0 | 167 | <1 | <1 | 0 | | free |
| ✔Sweet Pickle Relish | 1 Tbsp | 20 | <1 | 0 | <1 | 0 | 124 | 1 | <1 | 5 | 0 | free |
| **Green Giant** | | | | | | | | | | | | |
| ✔Corn Relish, Canned | 1 Tbsp | 20 | 0 | 0 | 0 | 0 | 40 | 0 | 0 | 5 | 0 | free |
| **PICKLES** | | | | | | | | | | | | |
| **(Generic)** | | | | | | | | | | | | |
| Dill Pickle | 1 | 12 | <1 | 0 | 0 | 0 | 833 | <1 | <1 | 3 | 0 | free |
| Dill Pickle Slices | 10 | 11 | <1 | 0 | 0 | 0 | 769 | <1 | <1 | 3 | 0 | free |
| Sour Pickle | 1 | 4 | <1 | 0 | 0 | 0 | 423 | <1 | <1 | <1 | 0 | free |
| Sweet Pickle | 1 | 41 | <1 | 0 | <1 | 0 | 329 | <1 | 1 | 11 | 1 | 1 carb |
| **PIE (FROZEN)** | | | | | | | | | | | | |
| **Banquet** | | | | | | | | | | | | |
| Apple Pie | 1/5 pie | 300 | 13 | 39 | 6 | 5 | 370 | 2 | 1 | 42 | 3 | 3 carb, 3 fat |
| Banana Pie | 1/3 pie | 350 | 21 | 54 | 5 | <5 | 290 | 2 | 1 | 39 | 2 1/2 | 2 1/2 carb, 4 fat |
| Cherry Pie | 1/5 pie | 290 | 14 | 43 | 6 | 10 | 310 | 2 | 1 | 39 | 2 1/2 | 2 1/2 carb, 3 fat |

✔ = Best Bet; NA = Not Available; Carb. Ch. = Carbohydrate Choices

| Pie (Frozen) (Continued) | Serving Size | Cal. | Fat (g) | % Cal. Fat | Sat. Fat (g) | Chol. (mg) | Sod. (mg) | Pro. (g) | Fiber (g) | Carb. (g) | Carb. Ch. | Servings/Exchanges |
|---|---|---|---|---|---|---|---|---|---|---|---|---|
| Chocolate Pie | 1/3 pie | 360 | 20 | 50 | 5 | <5 | 240 | 2 | 1 | 43 | 3 | 3 carb, 4 fat |
| Coconut Pie | 1/3 pie | 350 | 20 | 51 | 6 | <5 | 250 | 2 | 1 | 39 | 2 1/2 | 2 1/2 carb, 4 fat |
| Lemon Pie | 1/3 pie | 360 | 20 | 50 | 5 | <5 | 240 | 2 | 1 | 43 | 3 | 3 carb, 4 fat |
| Peach Pie | 1/5 pie | 270 | 13 | 43 | 6 | 5 | 340 | 2 | 1 | 36 | 2 1/2 | 2 1/2 carb, 3 fat |
| **Mrs. Smith's** | | | | | | | | | | | | |
| Apple Pie in Minutes 8″ | 1/8 pie | 210 | 9 | 39 | 2 | 0 | 250 | 2 | 1 | 29 | 2 | 2 carb, 2 fat |
| Blueberry Pie in Minutes 8″ | 1/8 pie | 220 | 9 | 37 | 2 | 0 | 240 | 2 | NA | 32 | 2 | 2 carb, 2 fat |
| Cappuccino | 1/9 pie | 360 | 19 | 48 | 14 | 0 | 160 | 3 | 1 | 44 | 3 | 3 carb, 4 fat |
| Cherry Pie in Minutes 8″ | 1/8 pie | 220 | 9 | 37 | 2 | 0 | 200 | 2 | NA | 32 | 2 | 2 carb, 2 fat |
| Cookies & Cream Lemony Lemon | 1/6 pie | 370 | 20 | 49 | 11 | 0 | 150 | 3 | <1 | 46 | 3 | 3 carb, 4 fat |
| Cookies & Cream Smores Pie | 1/6 pie | 410 | 20 | 44 | 12 | 0 | 230 | 4 | 2 | 54 | 4 | 4 carb, 4 fat |
| Deep Dish Apple Crumb | 1/10 pie | 340 | 14 | 37 | 3 | 0 | 300 | 2 | 2 | 52 | 3 1/2 | 3 1/2 carb, 3 fat |
| Dutch Apple Crumb | 1/8 pie | 360 | 16 | 40 | 3 | 0 | 360 | 3 | 2 | 52 | 3 1/2 | 3 1/2 carb, 3 fat |
| French Silk Chocolate | 1/9 pie | 560 | 40 | 64 | 24 | 80 | 330 | 4 | 1 | 48 | 3 | 3 carb, 4 fat |
| Key Lime | 1/9 pie | 420 | 19 | 41 | 12 | 0 | 210 | 7 | <1 | 56 | 4 | 4 carb, 4 fat |
| Lemon Meringue Pie in Minutes 8″ | 1/8 pie | 210 | 5 | 21 | NA | NA | 130 | 2 | NA | 38 | 2 1/2 | 2 1/2 carb, 1 fat |
| Peach Pie in Minutes 8″ | 1/8 pie | 210 | 9 | 39 | 2 | 0 | 190 | 2 | 0 | 29 | 2 | 2 carb, 2 fat |
| Pecan Pie in Minutes 8″ | 1/8 pie | 330 | 13 | 36 | 2 | 35 | 200 | 3 | NA | 51 | 3 1/2 | 3 1/2 carb, 3 fat |

| | Serving | Cal. | Fat (g) | % Cal. Fat | Sat. Fat (g) | Chol. (mg) | Sod. (mg) | Prot. (g) | Fiber (g) | Carb. (g) | Carb. Ch. | Exchanges |
|---|---|---|---|---|---|---|---|---|---|---|---|---|
| Pumpkin Pie in Minutes 8" | 1/8 pie | 190 | 6 | 28 | 2 | 35 | 230 | 3 | NA | 30 | 2 | 2 carb, 1 fat |
| **Sara Lee** | | | | | | | | | | | | |
| Apple | 1/8 pie | 340 | 16 | 42 | 4 | 0 | 310 | 3 | 1 | 46 | 3 | 3 carb, 3 fat |
| Blueberry | 1/8 pie | 360 | 15 | 38 | 4 | 0 | 340 | 3 | 2 | 54 | 3 1/2 | 3 1/2 carb, 3 fat |
| Cherry | 1/8 pie | 330 | 15 | 41 | 4 | 0 | 290 | 3 | 2 | 46 | 3 | 3 carb, 3 fat |
| French Silk Pie | 1/5 pie | 460 | 28 | 55 | 16 | 10 | 320 | 5 | 3 | 46 | 3 | 3 carb, 6 fat |
| Peach | 1/8 pie | 330 | 13 | 35 | 3 | 0 | 250 | 3 | 2 | 50 | 3 1/2 | 3 1/2 carb, 3 fat |
| Pumpkin | 1/8 pie | 260 | 11 | 38 | 3 | 30 | 460 | 4 | 2 | 37 | 2 1/2 | 2 1/2 carb, 2 fat |
| Raspberry | 1/8 pie | 380 | 19 | 45 | 5 | <5 | 330 | 3 | 2 | 48 | 3 | 3 carb, 4 fat |
| Tangy Lemon Meringue | 1/6 pie | 310 | 8 | 23 | 4 | 0 | 230 | 2 | 2 | 58 | 4 | 4 carb, 2 fat |
| Tropical Coconut Cream | 1/5 pie | 450 | 26 | 52 | 14 | <5 | 260 | 4 | 3 | 51 | 3 1/2 | 3 1/2 carb, 5 fat |
| **PIE (READY-TO-EAT)** | | | | | | | | | | | | |
| **Entenmann's** | | | | | | | | | | | | |
| Coconut Custard Pie | 1 slice | 340 | 19 | 50 | 8 | 135 | 310 | 7 | 1 | 35 | 2 | 2 carb, 4 fat |
| ✔ Fat-Free Cherry Beehive Pie | 1 slice | 270 | 0 | 0 | 0 | 0 | 310 | 3 | 1 | 64 | 4 | 4 carb |
| Homestyle Apple Pie | 1 slice | 300 | 14 | 42 | 4 | 0 | 300 | 2 | 2 | 42 | 3 | 3 carb, 3 fat |
| Lemon Pie | 1 slice | 340 | 17 | 45 | 5 | 45 | 420 | 3 | <1 | 45 | 3 | 3 carb, 3 fat |

✔ = Best Bet; NA = Not Available; Carb. Ch. = Carbohydrate Choices

| Product | Serving Size | Cal. | Fat (g) | % Cal. Fat | Sat. Fat (g) | Chol. (mg) | Sod. (mg) | Pro. (g) | Fiber (g) | Carb. (g) | Carb. Ch. | Servings/Exchanges |
|---|---|---|---|---|---|---|---|---|---|---|---|---|
| **PIE CRUST (FROZEN)** | | | | | | | | | | | | |
| **Mrs. Smith's** | | | | | | | | | | | | |
| Pie Shells | 1/8 pie shell | 80 | 5 | 56 | 1 | 0 | 105 | 1 | NA | 8 | 1/2 | 1/2 carb, 1 fat |
| **PIE CRUST MIX (AS PREPARED)** | | | | | | | | | | | | |
| **Betty Crocker** | | | | | | | | | | | | |
| ✔Italian Herb Pizza Crust (Pouch) | 1/4 crust | 160 | 2 | 11 | <1 | 0 | 350 | 4 | 1 | 32 | 2 | 2 carb |
| Pie Crust Mix | 1/8 of 9 crust | 110 | 8 | 65 | 2 | 0 | 150 | 1 | 0 | 9 | 1/2 | 1/2 carb, 2 fat |
| ✔Pizza Crust (Pouch) | 1/4 crust | 160 | 2 | 11 | <1 | 0 | 340 | 4 | 1 | 33 | 2 | 2 carb |
| **Robin Hood** | | | | | | | | | | | | |
| ✔Pizza Crust Mix | 1/4 crust | 160 | 2 | 11 | <1 | 0 | 340 | 4 | 1 | 33 | 2 | 2 carb |
| **PIE FILLING** | | | | | | | | | | | | |
| **Libby's** | | | | | | | | | | | | |
| ✔Apple Pie Filling | 1/3 cup | 80 | 0 | 0 | 0 | 0 | 10 | 0 | 0 | 20 | 1 | 1 carb |
| ✔Blueberry Pie Filling | 1/3 cup | 80 | 0 | 0 | 0 | 0 | 0 | 0 | 1 | 19 | 1 | 1 carb |
| ✔Cherry Pie Filling | 1/3 cup | 90 | 0 | 0 | 0 | 0 | 0 | 0 | 0 | 22 | 1 1/2 | 1 1/2 carb |
| **PITA BREAD** | | | | | | | | | | | | |
| **Wholesome Choice** | | | | | | | | | | | | |
| ✔Mini Pita Pocket Bread | 1 | 71 | 0 | 0 | 0 | 0 | 142 | 3 | <1 | 15 | 1 | 1 strch |

| | Serving Size | Cal. | Fat (g) | % Cal. Fat | Sat. Fat (g) | Chol. (mg) | Sod. (mg) | Carb. (g) | Fiber (g) | Prot. (g) | Carb. Ch. | Exchanges |
|---|---|---|---|---|---|---|---|---|---|---|---|---|
| ✓ White Pita Pocket Bread | 1 | 150 | 1 | 6 | 0 | 0 | 290 | 30 | 2 | 3 | 2 | 2 strch |
| **PIZZA (FROZEN, 12")** | | | | | | | | | | | | |
| **Celeste** | | | | | | | | | | | | |
| Cheese Pizza | 1/4 pizza | 315 | 17 | 49 | 7 | 20 | 690 | 28 | 2 | 14 | 2 | 2 carb, 1 med-fat meat, 2 fat |
| Deluxe Pizza | 1/4 pizza | 380 | 22 | 52 | 7 | 20 | 87– | 29 | 3 | 16 | 2 | 2 carb, 2 med-fat meat, 3 fat |
| Pepperoni Pizza | 1/4 pizza | 370 | 21 | 51 | 7 | 15 | 940 | 29 | 2 | 15 | 2 | 2 carb, 1 med-fat meat, 3 fat |
| Sausage Pizza | 1/4 pizza | 375 | 22 | 53 | 7 | 15 | 900 | 30 | 3 | 16 | 2 | 2 carb, 1 med-fat meat, 3 fat |
| Supreme Pizza | 1/4 pizza | 380 | 24 | 57 | 7 | 15 | 970 | 29 | 3 | 17 | 2 | 2 carb, 2 med-fat meat, 3 fat |
| **Di Giorno Rising Crust** | | | | | | | | | | | | |
| Four Cheese | 1/6 pizza | 320 | 11 | 31 | 6 | 25 | 870 | 39 | 3 | 16 | 2 1/2 | 2 1/2 carb, 1 med-fat meat, 1 fat |
| Italian Sausage | 1/6 pizza | 360 | 14 | 35 | 7 | 35 | 1000 | 40 | 3 | 18 | 2 1/2 | 2 1/2 carb, 2 med-fat meat, 1 fat |

✓ = Best Bet; NA = Not Available; Carb. Ch. = Carbohydrate Choices

## Pizza (Frozen, 12") (Continued)

| | Serving Size | Cal. | Fat (g) | % Cal. Fat | Sat. Fat (g) | Chol. (mg) | Sod. (mg) | Pro. (g) | Fiber (g) | Carb. (g) | Carb. Ch. | Servings/Exchanges |
|---|---|---|---|---|---|---|---|---|---|---|---|---|
| Pepperoni | 1/6 pizza | 370 | 16 | 39 | 8 | 35 | 1080 | 18 | 3 | 40 | 2 1/2 | 2 1/2 carb, 2 med-fat meat, 1 fat |
| Supreme | 1/6 pizza | 380 | 17 | 40 | 8 | 40 | 1100 | 18 | 3 | 40 | 2 1/2 | 2 1/2 carb, 2 med-fat meat, 1 fat |
| Three Meat | 1/6 pizza | 380 | 16 | 38 | 8 | 40 | 1100 | 19 | 3 | 40 | 2 1/2 | 2 1/2 carb, 2 med-fat meat, 1 fat |
| Vegetable | 1/6 pizza | 310 | 10 | 29 | 5 | 20 | 830 | 15 | 3 | 41 | 2 1/2 | 2 1/2 carb, 1 med-fat meat, 1 fat |
| **Jack's Great Combinations** | | | | | | | | | | | | |
| Bacon Cheeseburger | 1/4 pizza | 360 | 18 | 45 | 9 | 45 | 770 | 20 | 2 | 31 | 2 | 2 carb, 2 med-fat meat, 2 fat |
| Pepperoni | 1/4 pizza | 410 | 19 | 42 | 9 | 40 | 830 | 19 | 3 | 42 | 3 | 3 carb, 2 med-fat meat, 2 fat |
| Pepperoni & Mushroom | 1/4 pizza | 340 | 16 | 42 | 7 | 35 | 740 | 17 | 2 | 32 | 2 | 2 carb, 2 med-fat meat, 1 fat |
| Sausage | 1/4 pizza | 390 | 18 | 45 | 8 | 40 | 700 | 18 | 3 | 40 | 2 1/2 | 2 1/2, 2 med-fat meat, 2 fat |

| | Serving | Cal. | Fat (g) | % Cal. Fat | Sat. Fat (g) | Chol. (mg) | Sod. (mg) | Prot. (g) | Fiber (g) | Carb. (g) | Carb. Ch. | Exchanges |
|---|---|---|---|---|---|---|---|---|---|---|---|---|
| Sausage & Pepperoni | 1/4 pizza | 350 | 19 | 49 | 8 | 40 | 770 | 17 | 3 | 29 | 2 | 2 carb, 2 med-fat meat, 2 fat |
| Supreme | 1/4 pizza | 350 | 18 | 46 | 8 | 40 | 750 | 17 | 2 | 30 | 2 | 2 carb, 2 med-fat meat, 2 fat |
| **Jack's Naturally Rising Pizza** | | | | | | | | | | | | |
| Bacon Cheeseburger | 1/6 pizza | 350 | 15 | 39 | 7 | 40 | 680 | 18 | 3 | 35 | 2 | 2 carb, 2 med-fat meat, 1 fat |
| Canadian Style Bacon | 1/6 pizza | 280 | 9 | 29 | 5 | 30 | 590 | 16 | 2 | 34 | 2 | 2 carb, 1 med-fat meat, 1 fat |
| Cheese | 1/6 pizza | 290 | 10 | 31 | 6 | 25 | 500 | 15 | 2 | 35 | 2 | 2 carb, 1 med-fat meat, 1 fat |
| Pepperoni | 1/6 pizza | 350 | 16 | 41 | 8 | 40 | 710 | 17 | 2 | 35 | 2 | 2 carb, 2 med-fat meat, 1 fat |
| Pepperoni Supreme | 1/6 pizza | 340 | 16 | 42 | 8 | 35 | 670 | 16 | 2 | 34 | 2 | 2 carb, 1 med-fat meat, 2 fat |
| Sausage | 1/6 pizza | 340 | 15 | 40 | 7 | 35 | 600 | 17 | 2 | 34 | 2 | 2 carb, 2 med-fat meat, 1 fat |
| Sausage & Pepperoni | 1/6 pizza | 360 | 17 | 43 | 8 | 40 | 680 | 17 | 2 | 34 | 2 | 2 carb, 2 med-fat meat, 1 fat |

✔ = Best Bet; NA = Not Available; Carb. Ch. = Carbohydrate Choices

| Pizza (Frozen, 12") (Continued) | Serving Size | Cal. | Fat (g) | % Cal. Fat | Sat. Fat (g) | Chol. (mg) | Sod. (mg) | Pro. (g) | Fiber (g) | Carb. (g) | Carb. Ch. | Servings/Exchanges |
|---|---|---|---|---|---|---|---|---|---|---|---|---|
| Spicy Italian Sausage | 1/6 pizza | 330 | 14 | 38 | 7 | 40 | 680 | 17 | 2 | 34 | 2 | 2 carb, 2 med-fat meat, 1 fat |
| The Works | 1/6 pizza | 330 | 14 | 38 | 7 | 35 | 580 | 16 | 2 | 34 | 2 | 2 carb, 1 med-fat meat, 1 fat |
| **Jack's Original** | | | | | | | | | | | | |
| Canadian Style Bacon | 1/4 pizza | 280 | 10 | 32 | 5 | 30 | 620 | 16 | 2 | 31 | 2 | 2 carb, 1 med-fat meat, 1 fat |
| Cheese | 1/3 pizza | 360 | 13 | 33 | 7 | 30 | 650 | 19 | 3 | 41 | 3 | 3 carb, 1 med-fat meat, 2 fat |
| Hamburger | 1/4 pizza | 300 | 14 | 42 | 7 | 35 | 580 | 16 | 2 | 28 | 2 | 2 carb, 1 med-fat meat, 2 fat |
| Pepperoni | 1/4 pizza | 330 | 15 | 41 | 7 | 35 | 700 | 16 | 2 | 31 | 2 | 2 carb, 1 med-fat meat, 2 fat |
| Sausage | 1/4 pizza | 300 | 14 | 42 | 7 | 30 | 580 | 15 | 2 | 28 | 2 | 2 carb, 1 med-fat meat, 2 fat |
| Spicy Italian Sausage | 1/4 pizza | 290 | 13 | 40 | 6 | 35 | 650 | 15 | 2 | 29 | 2 | 2 carb, 1 med-fat meat, 2 fat |

## Pappalo's

| Product | Amount | Cal. | Fat (g) | % Cal. Fat | Sat. Fat (g) | Chol. (mg) | Sod. (mg) | Prot. (g) | Fiber (g) | Carb. (g) | Carb. Choices | Exchanges/Choices |
|---|---|---|---|---|---|---|---|---|---|---|---|---|
| Combination Sausage & Pepperoni Traditional Crust Pizza | 1/4 pizza | 360 | 12 | 30 | 6 | 45 | 730 | 23 | 4 | 40 | 2 1/2 | 2 1/2 carb, 2 med-fat meat |
| French Bread Cheese Pizza | 1 piece | 360 | 15 | 38 | NA | NA | 830 | 16 | NA | 40 | 2 1/2 | 2 1/2 carb, 1 med-fat meat, 2 fat |
| French Bread Combination Pizza | 1 piece | 430 | 21 | 44 | NA | NA | 1120 | 19 | NA | 41 | 3 | 3 carb, 1 med-fat meat, 3 fat |
| French Bread Pepperoni Pizza | 1 piece | 410 | 20 | 44 | NA | NA | 1130 | 16 | NA | 41 | 3 | 3 carb, 1 med-fat meat, 3 fat |
| French Bread Sausage Pizza | 1 piece | 410 | 18 | 41 | NA | NA | 1000 | 18 | NA | 41 | 3 | 3 carb, 1 med-fat meat, 3 fat |
| ✓Pepperoni Pizza Traditional Crust Pizza | 1/4 pizza | 350 | 11 | 29 | 5 | 45 | 700 | 22 | 4 | 40 | 2 1/2 | 2 1/2 carb, 2 med-fat meat |
| Sausage Pizza Traditional Crust Pizza | 1/4 pizza | 350 | 12 | 31 | 6 | 40 | 600 | 22 | 4 | 39 | 2 1/2 | 2 1/2 carb, 2 med-fat meat |
| Supreme Traditional Crust Pizza | 1/4 pizza | 350 | 12 | 31 | 6 | 45 | 640 | 22 | 4 | 38 | 2 1/2 | 2 1/2 carb, 2 med-fat meat |
| Three Cheese Traditional Crust Pizza | 1/4 pizza | 310 | 7 | 21 | 4 | 30 | 440 | 20 | 4 | 41 | 3 | 3 carb, 2 lean meat |

✓ = Best Bet; NA = Not Available; Carb. Ch. = Carbohydrate Choices

| Pizza (Frozen, 12") (Continued) | Serving Size | Cal. | Fat (g) | % Cal. Fat | Sat. Fat (g) | Chol. (mg) | Sod. (mg) | Pro. (g) | Fiber (g) | Carb. (g) | Carb. Ch. | Servings/Exchanges |
|---|---|---|---|---|---|---|---|---|---|---|---|---|
| **Red Baron** | | | | | | | | | | | | |
| Bake to Rise Four Cheese | 1/6 pizza | 340 | 13 | 34 | 6 | 25 | 800 | 17 | 2 | 40 | 2 1/2 | 2 1/2 carb, 1 med-fat meat, 2 fat |
| Bake to Rise Pepperoni | 1/6 pizza | 330 | 13 | 35 | 5 | 25 | 930 | 17 | 2 | 38 | 2 1/2 | 2 1/2 carb, 1 med-fat meat, 2 fat |
| Bake to Rise Special Deluxe | 1/6 pizza | 340 | 14 | 37 | 5 | 25 | 920 | 18 | 2 | 39 | 2 1/2 | 2 1/2 carb, 2 med-fat meat, 1 fat |
| Bake to Rise Supreme | 1/6 pizza | 340 | 14 | 37 | 5 | 25 | 900 | 17 | 2 | 38 | 2 1/2 | 2 1/2 carb, 1 med-fat meat, 2 fat |
| Cheese Pizza | 1/5 pizza | 350 | 17 | 45 | 8 | 30 | 680 | 16 | 2 | 33 | 2 | 2 carb, 1 med-fat meat, 2 fat |
| Classic Four Cheese | 1/4 pizza | 420 | 22 | 47 | 10 | 35 | 800 | 19 | 1 | 37 | 2 1/2 | 2 1/2 carb, 2 med-fat meat, 2 fat |
| Classic Pepperoni Pizza | 1/4 pizza | 440 | 25 | 51 | 9 | 35 | 1020 | 17 | 2 | 37 | 2 1/2 | 2 1/2 carb, 1 med-fat meat, 4 fat |
| Classic Sausage & Pepperoni | 1/5 pizza | 360 | 21 | 53 | 7 | 30 | 800 | 14 | 1 | 30 | 2 | 2 carb, 1 med-fat meat, 3 fat |

| | Serving | Cal. | Fat (g) | % Cal. Fat | Sat. Fat (g) | Chol. (mg) | Sod. (mg) | Prot. (g) | Fiber (g) | Carb. (g) | Carb. Ch. | Exchanges/Choices |
|---|---|---|---|---|---|---|---|---|---|---|---|---|
| Classic Supreme | 1/5 pizza | 350 | 20 | 51 | 7 | 25 | 760 | 14 | 2 | 30 | 2 | 2 carb, 1 med-fat meat, 3 fat |
| Combination Pizza | 1/5 pizza | 340 | 18 | 47 | 7 | 25 | 690 | 14 | 2 | 31 | 2 | 2 carb, 1 med-fat meat, 3 fat |
| Mexican Style Supreme | 1/5 pizza | 360 | 22 | 55 | 9 | 40 | 620 | 13 | 2 | 27 | 2 | 2 carb, 1 med-fat meat, 3 fat |
| Sausage Combination Pizza | 1/5 | 340 | 18 | 48 | 7 | 25 | 690 | 14 | 2 | 31 | 2 | 2 carb, 1 med-fat meat, 3 fat |
| **Spago** | | | | | | | | | | | | |
| 5 Grain Whole Wheat Pizza, Artichoke Hearts | 2.7 oz | 170 | 7 | 37 | NA | NA | NA | 8 | NA | 19 | 1 | 1 carb, 1 med-fat meat |
| 5 Grain Whole Wheat Pizza, Spicy Chicken | 2.7 oz | 180 | 8 | 40 | NA | 25 | 320 | 9 | NA | 18 | 1 | 1 carb, 1 med-fat meat, 1 fat |
| **Stouffer's** | | | | | | | | | | | | |
| French Bread Cheese Pizza | 5.2 oz | 370 | 16 | 39 | 27 | 15 | 880 | 14 | 3 | 43 | 3 | 3 carb, 1 med-fat meat, 2 fat |
| French Bread Double Cheese Pizza | 6 oz | 430 | 21 | 44 | 7 | 20 | 990 | 17 | 3 | 44 | 3 | 3 carb, 2 med-fat meat, 2 fat |
| French Bread Garden Vegetable Pizza | 5.8 oz | 350 | 12 | 31 | 5 | 10 | 500 | 12 | 3 | 48 | 3 | 3 carb, 2 fat |

✔ = Best Bet; NA = Not Available; Carb. Ch. = Carbohydrate Choices

| Pizza (Frozen, 12") (*Continued*) | Serving Size | Cal. | Fat (g) | % Cal. Fat | Sat. Fat (g) | Chol. (mg) | Sod. (mg) | Pro. (g) | Fiber (g) | Carb. (g) | Carb. Ch. | Servings/Exchanges |
|---|---|---|---|---|---|---|---|---|---|---|---|---|
| French Bread Pepperoni Pizza | 5.6 oz | 430 | 20 | 42 | 8 | 15 | 990 | 16 | 3 | 46 | 3 | 3 carb, 1 med-fat meat, 3 fat |
| French Bread Sausage Pizza | 6 oz | 420 | 18 | 39 | 7 | 20 | 1260 | 17 | 3 | 48 | 3 | 3 carb, 2 med-fat meat, 2 fat |
| French Bread Three Meat Pizza | 6.3 oz | 460 | 21 | 41 | 8 | 35 | 1200 | 20 | 5 | 48 | 3 1/2 | 3 1/2 carb, 1 med-fat meat, 3 fat |
| **Tombstone** | | | | | | | | | | | | |
| Bacon Cheeseburger Pizza | 4.7 oz | 330 | 16 | 44 | 7 | 40 | 730 | 17 | NA | 29 | 2 | 2 carb, 2 med-fat meat, 1 fat |
| Canadian Bacon Pizza | 3.6 oz | 230 | 10 | 39 | 4 | 25 | 580 | 12 | NA | 23 | 1 1/2 | 1 1/2 carb, 1 med-fat meat, 1 fat |
| Cheese Pizza | 3.4 oz | 230 | 10 | 40 | 4 | 25 | 460 | 11 | NA | 23 | 1 1/2 | 1 1/2 carb, 1 med-fat meat, 1 fat |
| Four Cheese Special Order Pizza | 4.3 oz | 300 | 14 | 42 | 6 | 35 | 630 | 15 | NA | 28 | 2 | 2 carb, 1 med-fat meat, 2 fat |
| Hamburger Pizza | 3.7 oz | 250 | 12 | 43 | 5 | 30 | 570 | 13 | NA | 23 | 1 1/2 | 1 1/2 carb, 1 med-fat meat, 1 fat |

| | Serving | Cal. | Fat (g) | % Fat | Sat. Fat (g) | Chol. (mg) | Sod. (mg) | Carb. (g) | Fiber (g) | Prot. (g) | Carb. Ch. | Exchanges/Choices |
|---|---|---|---|---|---|---|---|---|---|---|---|---|
| ✓Light Chicken Deluxe | 3.7 oz | 180 | 4 | 20 | 1 | 15 | 440 | 13 | 2 | 23 | 1 1/2 | 1 1/2 carb, 1 med-fat meat |
| ✓Light Vegetable Pizza | 4.3 oz | 230 | 7 | 27 | 3 | 10 | 420 | 12 | NA | 30 | 2 | 2 carb, 1 med-fat meat |
| Pepperoni Pizza | 3.6 oz | 260 | 14 | 47 | 5 | 30 | 620 | 12 | NA | 23 | 1 1/2 | 1 1/2 carb, 1 med-fat meat, 2 fat |
| Sausage & Pepperoni Pizza | 3.7 oz | 260 | 13 | 45 | 5 | 30 | 640 | 13 | NA | 23 | 1 1/2 | 1 1/2 carb, 1 med-fat meat, 2 fat |
| Sausage Pizza | 3.7 oz | 240 | 11 | 41 | 4 | 30 | 590 | 13 | NA | 23 | 1 1/2 | 1 1/2 carb, 1 med-fat meat, 1 fat |
| Supreme Light Pizza | 4.5 oz | 250 | 9 | 32 | NA | 20 | 630 | 15 | NA | 29 | 2 | 2 carb, 1 med-fat meat, 1 fat |

## Tombstone Double Top

| | Serving | Cal. | Fat (g) | % Fat | Sat. Fat (g) | Chol. (mg) | Sod. (mg) | Carb. (g) | Fiber (g) | Prot. (g) | Carb. Ch. | Exchanges/Choices |
|---|---|---|---|---|---|---|---|---|---|---|---|---|
| Pepperoni | 1/6 pizza | 340 | 19 | 50 | 9 | 45 | 810 | 18 | 2 | 24 | 1 1/2 | 1 1/2 carb, 2 med-fat meat, 2 fat |
| Sausage | 1/6 pizza | 320 | 17 | 48 | 9 | 40 | 760 | 18 | 2 | 25 | 1 1/2 | 1 1/2 carb, 2 med-fat meat, 1 fat |
| Sausage & Pepperoni | 1/6 pizza | 340 | 19 | 50 | 9 | 45 | 820 | 19 | 2 | 25 | 1 1/2 | 1 1/2 carb, 2 med-fat meat, 2 fat |

✔ = Best Bet; NA = Not Available; Carb. Ch. = Carbohydrate Choices

| Pizza (Frozen, 12") (Continued) | Serving Size | Cal. | Fat (g) | % Cal. Fat | Sat. Fat (g) | Chol. (mg) | Sod. (mg) | Pro. (g) | Fiber (g) | Carb. (g) | Carb. Ch. | Servings/Exchanges |
|---|---|---|---|---|---|---|---|---|---|---|---|---|
| Supreme | 1/6 pizza | 330 | 18 | 49 | 9 | 40 | 780 | 18 | 2 | 25 | 1 1/2 | 1 1/2 carb, 2 med-fat meat, 2 fat |
| Two Cheese | 1/5 pizza | 380 | 19 | 45 | 11 | 50 | 760 | 22 | 2 | 29 | 2 | 2 carb, 2 med-fat meat, 2 fat |
| **Tombstone Light** | | | | | | | | | | | | |
| ✓Supreme | 1/5 pizza | 270 | 9 | 30 | 4 | 20 | 720 | 17 | 3 | 30 | 2 | 2 carb, 2 med-fat meat |
| ✓Vegetable | 1/5 pizza | 240 | 7 | 26 | 3 | 10 | 500 | 14 | 3 | 31 | 2 | 2 carb, 1 med-fat meat |
| **Tombstone Original** | | | | | | | | | | | | |
| Canadian Style Bacon | 1/4 pizza | 350 | 14 | 36 | 7 | 35 | 890 | 20 | 3 | 36 | 2 1/2 | 2 1/2 carb, 2 med-fat meat, 1 fat |
| Deluxe | 1/5 pizza | 310 | 14 | 41 | 6 | 30 | 690 | 15 | 3 | 29 | 2 | 2 carb, 2 med-fat meat, 1 fat |
| Extra Cheese | 1/4 pizza | 350 | 15 | 39 | 8 | 30 | 680 | 18 | 3 | 35 | 2 | 2 carb, 2 med-fat meat, 1 fat |
| Hamburger | 1/5 pizza | 310 | 15 | 44 | 7 | 29 | 670 | 15 | 2 | 29 | 2 | 2 carb, 1 med-fat meat, 2 fat |
| Pepperoni | 1/4 pizza | 400 | 21 | 47 | 9 | 40 | 930 | 19 | 3 | 35 | 2 | 2 carb, 2 med-fat meat, 2 fat |

| | | | | | | | | | | | |
|---|---|---|---|---|---|---|---|---|---|---|---|
| Sausage | 1/5 pizza | 300 | 14 | 42 | 6 | 30 | 680 | 15 | 2 | 29 | 2 | 2 carb, 1 med-fat meat, 2 fat |
| Sausage & Mushroom | 1/5 pizza | 300 | 14 | 42 | 6 | 30 | 680 | 15 | 3 | 29 | 2 | 2 carb, 1 med-fat meat, 2 fat |
| Sausage & Pepperoni | 1/5 pizza | 320 | 16 | 45 | 7 | 30 | 740 | 15 | 2 | 29 | 2 | 2 carb, 1 med-fat meat, 2 fat |
| Supreme | 1/5 pizza | 320 | 16 | 45 | 7 | 30 | 730 | 15 | 2 | 29 | 2 | 2 carb, 1 med-fat meat, 2 fat |

## Tombstone Oven Rising Crust

| | | | | | | | | | | | |
|---|---|---|---|---|---|---|---|---|---|---|---|
| Italian Sausage | 1/6 pizza | 320 | 13 | 37 | 6 | 30 | 700 | 16 | 2 | 35 | 2 | 2 carb, 1 med-fat meat, 2 fat |
| Pepperoni | 1/6 pizza | 340 | 15 | 40 | 7 | 35 | 750 | 17 | 2 | 34 | 2 | 2 carb, 2 med-fat meat, 1 fat |
| Supreme | 1/6 pizza | 320 | 14 | 39 | 6 | 30 | 720 | 16 | 2 | 34 | 2 | 2 carb, 1 med-fat meat, 2 fat |
| Three Cheese | 1/6 pizza | 320 | 13 | 37 | 8 | 35 | 580 | 16 | 2 | 34 | 2 | 2 carb, 1 med-fat meat, 2 fat |
| Three Meat | 1/6 pizza | 340 | 15 | 40 | 7 | 35 | 750 | 17 | 2 | 34 | 2 | 2 carb, 2 med-fat meat, 1 fat |

✔ = Best Bet; NA = Not Available; Carb. Ch. = Carbohydrate Choices

| Pizza (Frozen, 12") (*Continued*) | Serving Size | Cal. | Fat (g) | % Cal. Fat | Sat. Fat (g) | Chol. (mg) | Sod. (mg) | Pro. (g) | Fiber (g) | Carb. (g) | Carb. Ch. | Servings/Exchanges |
|---|---|---|---|---|---|---|---|---|---|---|---|---|
| **Tombstone Thin Crust** | | | | | | | | | | | | |
| Four Meat Combo | 1/4 pizza | 380 | 23 | 54 | 10 | 45 | 890 | 19 | 2 | 26 | 2 | 2 carb, 2 med-fat meat, 3 fat |
| Italian Sausage | 1/4 pizza | 370 | 22 | 54 | 10 | 45 | 840 | 18 | 2 | 26 | 2 | 2 carb, 2 med-fat meat, 2 fat |
| Pepperoni | 1/4 pizza | 400 | 25 | 56 | 11 | 50 | 920 | 18 | 2 | 25 | 1 1/2 | 1 1/2 carb, 2 med-fat meat, 3 fat |
| Supreme | 1/4 pizza | 380 | 22 | 52 | 10 | 45 | 840 | 18 | 2 | 26 | 2 | 2 carb, 2 med-fat meat, 2 fat |
| Supreme Taco | 1/4 pizza | 370 | 23 | 56 | 11 | 50 | 740 | 16 | 2 | 27 | 2 | 2 carb, 1 med-fat meat, 4 fat |
| Three Cheese | 1/4 pizza | 360 | 21 | 53 | 11 | 45 | 690 | 19 | 2 | 25 | 1 1/2 | 1 1/2 carb, 2 med-fat meat, 2 fat |
| **Totinos** | | | | | | | | | | | | |
| Party Pizza, Combination Family | 1/3 pizza | 400 | 18 | 41 | 4 | 20 | 990 | 17 | 3 | 47 | 3 | 3 carb, 1 med-fat meat, 3 fat |
| Party Pizza, Sausage Family | 1/3 pizza | 410 | 18 | 40 | 4 | 15 | 870 | 16 | 4 | 48 | 3 | 3 carb, 1 med-fat meat, 3 fat |

| | | | | | | | | | | | |
|---|---|---|---|---|---|---|---|---|---|---|---|
| Select Pizza, Supreme | 1/3 pizza | 345 | 18 | 47 | 7 | NA | 770 | 17 | NA | 29 | 2 | 2 carb, 2 med-fat meat, 2 fat |
| Select Pizza, Two Cheese & Pepperoni | 1/3 pizza | 365 | 20 | 49 | 8 | NA | 825 | 16 | NA | 30 | 2 | 2 carb, 2 med-fat meat, 2 fat |
| Party Pizza, Canadian Bacon | 1/2 pizza | 330 | 13 | 35 | 2 | 10 | 860 | 15 | 3 | 42 | 3 | 3 carb, 1 med-fat meat, 2 fat |
| Party Pizza, Cheese | 1/2 pizza | 290 | 10 | 31 | 3 | 15 | 530 | 13 | 2 | 40 | 2 1/2 | 2 1/2 carb, 1 med-fat meat, 1 fat |
| Party Pizza, Pepperoni | 1/2 pizza | 380 | 19 | 45 | 4 | 15 | 980 | 14 | 3 | 41 | 3 | 3 carb, 1 med-fat meat, 3 fat |

## PIZZA (REFRIGERATED)

### San Francisco Foods

| | | | | | | | | | | | |
|---|---|---|---|---|---|---|---|---|---|---|---|
| Pepperoni Calzone | 1/2 calzone | 340 | 17 | 45 | 6 | 30 | 860 | 14 | 2 | 32 | 2 | 2 carb, 1 med-fat meat, 2 fat |
| Supreme Stuffed Pizza | 1/4 pizza | 400 | 17 | 38 | 6 | 30 | 880 | 15 | 3 | 46 | 3 | 3 carb, 1 med-fat meat, 2 fat |

## PIZZA CRUST MIX (REFRIGERATED)

### Pillsbury

| | | | | | | | | | | | |
|---|---|---|---|---|---|---|---|---|---|---|---|
| ✔Pizza Crust Dough | 1 slice | 150 | 2 | 12 | 0 | 0 | 380 | 5 | 4 | 9 | 1/2 | 1/2 strch |

✔ = Best Bet; NA = Not Available; Carb. Ch. = Carbohydrate Choices

| Product | Serving Size | Cal. | Fat (g) | % Cal. Fat | Sat. Fat (g) | Chol. (mg) | Sod. (mg) | Pro. (g) | Fiber (g) | Carb. (g) | Carb. Ch. | Servings/Exchanges |
|---|---|---|---|---|---|---|---|---|---|---|---|---|
| **PIZZA CRUST MIX (DRY, AS PREPARED)** | | | | | | | | | | | | |
| **Chef Boyardee** | | | | | | | | | | | | |
| ✓Quick & Easy Pizza Crust Mix | 1/3 cup | 160 | 2 | 11 | 0 | 0 | 330 | 5 | 1 | 30 | 2 | 2 carb |
| **PIZZA KITS** | | | | | | | | | | | | |
| **Chef Boyardee** | | | | | | | | | | | | |
| ✓Cheese Pizza Kit | 1 slice of 12 pizza | 310 | 8 | 23 | 2 | 5 | 920 | 10 | 2 | 50 | 3 | 3 carb, 2 fat |
| **PIZZA SAUCE** | | | | | | | | | | | | |
| **Contadina** | | | | | | | | | | | | |
| ✓All Purpose Pizza Sauce | 1/4 cup | 25 | 0 | 0 | 0 | 0 | 20 | 1 | 1 | 6 | 1/2 | 1/2 carb |
| ✓Chunky Pizza Sauce & 3 Cheeses | 1/4 cup | 35 | <1 | 26 | 0 | 0 | 190 | 1 | 1 | 5 | 1/2 | 1/2 carb |
| ✓Chunky Pizza Sauce & Mushrooms | 1/4 cup | 30 | 0 | 0 | 0 | 0 | 290 | 1 | 1 | 5 | 1/2 | 1/2 carb |
| ✓Chunky Pizza Sauce, Basic | 1/4 cup | 27 | <1 | 33 | 0 | 0 | 250 | <1 | 1 | 4 | 1/2 | 1/2 carb |
| ✓Deluxe Pizza Sauce | 1/4 cup | 30 | 1 | 30 | 0 | 2 | 120 | 1 | 1 | 5 | 1/2 | 1/2 carb |
| ✓Fully Prepared Pizza Sauce | 1/4 cup | 25 | 0 | 0 | 0 | 0 | 270 | 1 | 1 | 6 | 1/2 | 1/2 carb |
| ✓Pizza Sauce w/Basil | 1/4 cup | 25 | 0 | 0 | 0 | 0 | 20 | 1 | 1 | 6 | 1/2 | 1/2 carb |
| ✓Pizza Sauce w/Cheese | 1/4 cup | 30 | 1 | 30 | 0 | 0 | 350 | 1 | 1 | 4 | 0 | 1/2 carb |
| ✓Pizza Sauce w/Pepperoni | 1/4 cup | 30 | 1 | 30 | 0 | 0 | 360 | 1 | 1 | 4 | 0 | 1/2 carb |
| ✓Pizza Sauce, Original | 1/4 cup | 25 | <1 | 36 | 0 | 0 | 300 | 1 | 1 | 4 | 0 | 1/2 carb |

| Product | Serving | Cal. | Fat (g) | % Cal. Fat | Sat. Fat (g) | Chol. (mg) | Sod. (mg) | Prot. (g) | Fiber (g) | Carb. (g) | Carb. Ch. | Exchanges |
|---|---|---|---|---|---|---|---|---|---|---|---|---|
| ✔ Pizza Sauce, Squeeze | 1/4 cup | 38 | 2 | 47 | 0 | 0 | 385 | 1 | 1 | 6 | 1/2 | 1/2 carb |
| ✔ Pizza Squeeze Sauce, Italian Cheese | 1/4 cup | 30 | <1 | 30 | 0 | 0 | 380 | <1 | | 4 | 0 | 1/2 carb |
| **Progresso** | | | | | | | | | | | | |
| ✔ Pizza Sauce | 1/4 cup | 20 | 0 | 0 | 0 | 0 | 170 | <1 | 1 | 4 | 0 | free |
| **PIZZA SNACKS (FROZEN)** | | | | | | | | | | | | |
| **Jack's Pizza Bursts** | | | | | | | | | | | | |
| Pepperoni | 6 pieces | 260 | 14 | 49 | 5 | 20 | 560 | 9 | 2 | 25 | 2 | 2 carb, 3 fat |
| Sausage | 6 pieces | 250 | 12 | 43 | 4 | 20 | 490 | 8 | 2 | 25 | 2 | 2 carb, 2 fat |
| Sausage & Pepperoni | 6 pieces | 250 | 12 | 43 | 4 | 20 | 500 | 8 | 2 | 26 | 2 | 2 carb, 2 fat |
| Supercheese | 6 pieces | 250 | 12 | 43 | 5 | 20 | 460 | 9 | 2 | 25 | 2 | 2 carb, 2 fat |
| Supreme | 6 pieces | 250 | 13 | 47 | 4 | 20 | 520 | 8 | 2 | 26 | 2 | 2 carb, 3 fat |
| **Michael Angelo's** | | | | | | | | | | | | |
| ✔ Sausage Mini Calzones | 1 | 70 | 2 | 26 | <1 | 10 | 100 | 3 | 2 | 12 | 1 | 1 carb |
| **Ore Ida** | | | | | | | | | | | | |
| Bagel Bites, Cheese, Sausage, Pepperoni | 4 pieces | 200 | 6 | 27 | 3 | 15 | 620 | 8 | 1 | 27 | 2 | 2 carb, 1 fat |
| **Totinos** | | | | | | | | | | | | |
| Hamburger Pizza Rolls | 10 | 230 | 10 | 39 | NA | NA | 415 | 9 | NA | 26 | 2 | 2 carb, 1 med-fat meat, 1 fat |

✔ = Best Bet; NA = Not Available; Carb. Ch. = Carbohydrate Choices

| Pizza Snacks (Frozen) *(Continued)* | Serving Size | Cal. | Fat (g) | % Cal. Fat | Sat. Fat (g) | Chol. (mg) | Sod. (mg) | Pro. (g) | Fiber (g) | Carb. (g) | Carb. Ch. | Servings/Exchanges |
|---|---|---|---|---|---|---|---|---|---|---|---|---|
| ✓Pepperoni Pizza Rolls | 10 | 385 | 19 | 25 | 5 | 31 | 865 | 14 | 2 | 39 | 2 1/2 | 2 1/2 carb, 1 med-fat meat, 3 fat |
| Sausage Pizza Rolls | 10 | 350 | 15 | 39 | 3 | 25 | 630 | 14 | 3 | 40 | 2 1/2 | 2 1/2 carb, 1 med-fat meat, 2 fat |
| **PIZZA, SINGLE SERVING (FROZEN)** | | | | | | | | | | | | |
| **Celeste** | | | | | | | | | | | | |
| Cheese Pizza-For-One | 1 | 500 | 25 | 45 | 11 | 40 | 1070 | 21 | 4 | 48 | 3 | 3 carb, 2 med-fat meat, 3 fat |
| Deluxe Pizza | 1 | 580 | 32 | 49 | 10 | 20 | 1290 | 23 | 4 | 51 | 3 1/2 | 3 1/2 carb, 2 med-fat meat, 4 fat |
| Pepperoni Pizza-For-One | 1 | 545 | 30 | 49 | 9 | 20 | 1290 | 20 | 4 | 50 | 3 | 3 carb, 2 med-fat meat, 4 fat |
| Sausage Pizza-For-One | 1 | 570 | 32 | 50 | 10 | 20 | 1300 | 23 | 4 | 49 | 3 | 3 carb, 2 med-fat meat, 4 fat |
| Supreme Pizza-For-One | 1 | 680 | 39 | 52 | 12 | 20 | 1590 | 27 | 5 | 54 | 3 1/2 | 3 1/2 carb, 2 med-fat meat, 6 fat |
| Vegetable Pizza-For-One | 1 | 490 | 26 | 48 | NA | NA | 1200 | 20 | NA | 44 | 3 | 3 carb, 2 med-fat meat, 3 fat |

| | Serving Size | Cal. | Fat (g) | % Cal. Fat | Sat. Fat (g) | Chol. (mg) | Sod. (mg) | Carb. (g) | Fiber (g) | Pro. (g) | Carb. Ch. | Exchanges/Choices |
|---|---|---|---|---|---|---|---|---|---|---|---|---|
| **Healthy Choice** | | | | | | | | | | | | |
| ✔ Cheese French Bread Pizza | 6 oz pizza | 340 | 5 | 13 | 2 | 15 | 480 | 51 | 5 | 22 | 3 1/2 | 3 1/2 carb, 2 lean meat |
| ✔ French Bread Pizza, Pepperoni | 6 oz pizza | 340 | 5 | 13 | 2 | 20 | 580 | 49 | 6 | 24 | 3 | 3 carb, 2 lean meat |
| ✔ French Bread Pizza, Vegetable | 6 oz pizza | 280 | 4 | 13 | 2 | 10 | 480 | 44 | 5 | 17 | 3 | 3 carb, 1 med-fat meat |
| **Lean Cuisine** | | | | | | | | | | | | |
| French Bread Pizza, Cheese | 6 oz pizza | 320 | 7 | 20 | 4 | 15 | 580 | 48 | 4 | 15 | 3 | 3 carb, 2 lean meat |
| ✔ French Bread Pizza, Deluxe | 8.1 oz pizza | 300 | 6 | 18 | 3 | 25 | 590 | 46 | 4 | 16 | 3 | 3 carb, 3 lean meat |
| ✔ French Bread Pizza, Pepperoni | 5.3 oz pizza | 310 | 7 | 20 | 3 | 20 | 590 | 46 | 3 | 15 | 3 | 3 carb, 2 med-fat meat |
| French Bread Pizza, Sun Dried Tomatoes | 5.3 oz pizza | 340 | 8 | 21 | 5 | 20 | 580 | 48 | 3 | 19 | 3 | 3 carb, 2 med-fat meat |
| **Pappalo's** | | | | | | | | | | | | |
| Pizza-For-One Deep Dish Pepperoni | 1 | 525 | 19 | 33 | 7 | 38 | 985 | 65 | 3 | 23 | 4 | 4 carb, 2 med-fat meat, 2 fat |
| Pizza-For-One Pepperoni | 1 | 525 | 20 | 34 | 7 | 38 | 985 | 65 | 3 | 23 | 4 | 4 carb, 2 med-fat meat, 2 fat |
| **Red Baron** | | | | | | | | | | | | |
| Deep Dish 2 Meat Trio Pizza Singles | 6 oz | 460 | 26 | 51 | 8 | 25 | 950 | 42 | 2 | 16 | 3 | 3 carb, 1 med-fat meat, 4 fat |

✔ = Best Bet; NA = Not Available; Carb. Ch. = Carbohydrate Choices

| Pizza, Single Serving (Frozen) (Continued) | Serving Size | Cal. | Fat (g) | % Cal. Fat | Sat. Fat (g) | Chol. (mg) | Sod. (mg) | Pro. (g) | Fiber (g) | Carb. (g) | Carb. Ch. | Servings/Exchanges |
|---|---|---|---|---|---|---|---|---|---|---|---|---|
| Deep Dish Cheese Pizza Singles | 1 | 460 | 23 | 48 | 9 | 20 | 760 | 15 | 2 | 41 | 3 | 3 carb, 1 med-fat meat, 4 fat |
| Deep Dish Combination Pizza Singles | 1 | 490 | 26 | 51 | 9 | 25 | 970 | 16 | 2 | 41 | 3 | 3 carb, 1 med-fat meat, 4 fat |
| Deep Dish Pepperoni Pizza Singles | 1 | 530 | 31 | 53 | 11 | 35 | 90 | 18 | 2 | 47 | 3 | 3 carb, 1 med-fat meat, 5 fat |
| Deep Dish Supreme Pizza Singles | 6 oz | 460 | 27 | 53 | 9 | 25 | 890 | 16 | 2 | 40 | 2 1/2 | 2 1/2 carb, 1 med-fat meat, 4 fat |
| Deep Dish Vegetable Supreme Pizza Single | 6 oz | 440 | 24 | 49 | 8 | 20 | 790 | 16 | 2 | 20 | 1 1/2 | 1 1/2 carb, 2 med-fat meat, 3 fat |
| **Tombstone** | | | | | | | | | | | | |
| Pizza for One, Extra Cheese | 7 oz | 520 | 28 | 48 | 13 | 50 | 940 | 26 | 3 | 41 | 3 | 3 carb, 2 med-fat meat, 4 fat |
| Pizza For One, Pepperoni | 7 oz | 550 | 32 | 52 | 14 | 55 | 1160 | 25 | 3 | 41 | 3 | 3 carb, 3 med-fat meat, 3 fat |
| Pizza for One, Supreme | 7.7 oz | 550 | 32 | 52 | 14 | 55 | 1090 | 24 | 3 | 42 | 3 | 3 carb, 2 med-fat meat, 4 fat |

## Tombstone for One, 1/2 Less Fat

| | | | | | | | | | | | |
|---|---|---|---|---|---|---|---|---|---|---|---|
| Cheese | 1 pizza | 360 | 10 | 25 | 5 | 20 | 940 | 23 | 3 | 43 | 3 | 3 carb, 2 med-fat meat |
| ✔Vegetable | 1 pizza | 360 | 9 | 23 | 4 | 10 | 860 | 21 | 5 | 48 | 3 | 3 carb, 2 med-fat meat |

### Totinos

| | | | | | | | | | | | |
|---|---|---|---|---|---|---|---|---|---|---|---|
| Pizza-For-One, Combination | 1 | 290 | 16 | 50 | 4 | 15 | 730 | 10 | 1 | 26 | 2 | 2 carb, 1 med-fat meat, 2 fat |
| Pizza-For-One, Pepperoni | 1 | 290 | 16 | 50 | 4 | 15 | 700 | 10 | 1 | 26 | 2 | 2 carb, 1 med-fat meat, 2 fat |

### Weight Watchers Smart Ones

| | | | | | | | | | | | |
|---|---|---|---|---|---|---|---|---|---|---|---|
| ✔Deluxe Combination Pizza | 6.6 oz | 380 | 11 | 26 | 5 | 40 | 550 | 21 | 6 | 52 | 3 1/2 | 3 1/2 carb, 1 med-fat meat, 1 fat |

## POCKET SANDWICHES (FROZEN)

### Chef America/Big Stuffs

| | | | | | | | | | | | |
|---|---|---|---|---|---|---|---|---|---|---|---|
| Cheese Steak | 5.5 oz | 440 | 19 | 39 | 10 | 60 | 900 | 18 | 1 | 48 | 3 | 3 carb, 1 med-fat meat, 3 fat |
| Ham & Cheese | 5.5 oz | 420 | 16 | 33 | 6 | 50 | 1010 | 19 | 4 | 50 | 2 1/2 | 2 1/2 carb, 2 med-fat meat, 2 fat |
| Pepperoni Pizza | 5.5 oz | 440 | 19 | 39 | 7 | 60 | 900 | 17 | 4 | 50 | 3 | 3 carb, 1 med-fat meat, 3 fat |

✔ = Best Bet; NA = Not Available; Carb. Ch. = Carbohydrate Choices

| Pocket Sandwiches (Frozen) *(Continued)* | Serving Size | Cal. | Fat (g) | % Cal. Fat | Sat. Fat (g) | Chol. (mg) | Sod. (mg) | Pro. (g) | Fiber (g) | Carb. (g) | Carb. Ch. | Servings/Exchanges |
|---|---|---|---|---|---|---|---|---|---|---|---|---|
| **Chef America/Croissant Pockets** | | | | | | | | | | | | |
| ✔Chicken, Broccoli & Cheddar | 4.6 oz | 290 | 9 | 28 | 4 | 40 | 660 | 13 | 2 | 38 | 2 1/2 | 2 1/2 carb, 1 med-fat meat, 1 fat |
| Egg, Sausage & Cheese | 4.6 oz | 340 | 15 | 38 | 6 | 95 | 740 | 12 | 2 | 39 | 2 1/2 | 2 1/2 carb, 1 med-fat meat, 2 fat |
| Ham & Cheddar | 4.6 oz | 320 | 12 | 34 | 6 | 45 | 790 | 14 | 2 | 39 | 2 1/2 | 2 1/2 carb, 1 med-fat meat, 1 fat |
| Pepperoni Pizza | 4.6 oz | 360 | 16 | 39 | 7 | 40 | 800 | 14 | 3 | 41 | 3 | 3 carb, 1 med-fat meat, 2 fat |
| Philly Steak & Cheese | 4.6 oz | 350 | 16 | 40 | 8 | 50 | 790 | 15 | 2 | 37 | 2 1/2 | 2 1/2 carb, 1 med-fat meat, 2 fat |
| Supreme Pizza | 4.6 oz | 390 | 20 | 46 | 8 | 40 | 790 | 13 | 3 | 40 | 2 1/2 | 2 1/2 carb, 1 med-fat meat, 3 fat |
| Turkey & Ham w/Swiss | 4.6 oz | 290 | 10 | 31 | 4 | 40 | 730 | 14 | 2 | 37 | 2 1/2 | 2 1/2 carb, 1 med-fat meat, 1 fat |
| **Chef America/Deli Stuffs** | | | | | | | | | | | | |
| Cheese Steak | 4.6 oz | 350 | 14 | 37 | 7 | 45 | 680 | 15 | 3 | 40 | 2 1/2 | 2 1/2 carb, 1 med-fat meat, 2 fat |

| | Serving | | | | | | | | | | Carb. Ch. | |
|---|---|---|---|---|---|---|---|---|---|---|---|---|
| Ham & Cheese | 4.6 oz | 340 | 13 | 35 | 7 | 50 | 650 | 15 | 3 | 41 | 3 | 3 carb, 1 med-fat meat, 2 fat |
| Pepperoni Pizza | 4.6 oz | 350 | 14 | 37 | 6 | 35 | 660 | 14 | 3 | 41 | 3 | 3 carb, 1 med-fat meat, 2 fat |

### Chef America/Hot Pockets

| | Serving | | | | | | | | | | Carb. Ch. | |
|---|---|---|---|---|---|---|---|---|---|---|---|---|
| ✓Barbeque | 4.6 oz | 330 | 11 | 30 | 5 | 25 | 790 | 13 | 1 | 45 | 3 | 3 carb, 1 med-fat meat, 1 fat |
| Beef & Cheddar | 4.6 oz | 350 | 16 | 43 | 9 | 45 | 610 | 15 | 3 | 36 | 2 1/2 | 2 1/2 carb, 1 med-fat meat, 2 fat |
| Beef Fajita | 4.6 oz | 340 | 14 | 38 | 8 | 40 | 680 | 14 | 5 | 39 | 2 1/2 | 2 1/2 carb, 1 med-fat meat, 2 fat |
| Chicken & Cheddar w/Broccoli | 4.6 oz | 300 | 10 | 30 | 5 | 40 | 510 | 13 | 2 | 40 | 2 1/2 | 2 1/2 carb, 1 med-fat meat, 1 fat |
| Ham 'N Cheese | 4.6 oz | 320 | 12 | 34 | 6 | 40 | 620 | 14 | 3 | 39 | 2 1/2 | 2 1/2 carb, 1 med-fat meat, 1 fat |
| Meatballs w/Mozzarella | 4.6 oz | 320 | 11 | 31 | 6 | 30 | 620 | 15 | 4 | 39 | 2 1/2 | 2 1/2 carb, 1 med-fat meat, 1 fat |
| Pepperoni & Sausage | 4.6 oz | 330 | 14 | 36 | 6 | 35 | 510 | 13 | 4 | 33 | 2 | 2 carb, 1 med-fat meat, 2 fat |

✓= Best Bet; NA = Not Available; Carb. Ch. = Carbohydrate Choices

| Pocket Sandwiches (Frozen) (*Continued*) | Serving Size | Cal. | Fat (g) | % Cal. Fat | Sat. Fat (g) | Chol. (mg) | Sod. (mg) | Pro. (g) | Fiber (g) | Carb. (g) | Carb. Ch. | Servings/Exchanges |
|---|---|---|---|---|---|---|---|---|---|---|---|---|
| Pepperoni Pizza | 4.6 oz | 350 | 15 | 40 | 7 | 40 | 640 | 13 | 4 | 41 | 3 | 3 carb, 1 med-fat meat, 2 fat |
| Sausage Pizza | 4.6 oz | 340 | 15 | 38 | 7 | 35 | 550 | 14 | 3 | 37 | 2 1/2 | 2 1/2 carb, 1 med-fat meat, 2 fat |
| Turkey & Ham w/Cheese | 4.6 oz | 300 | 11 | 30 | 6 | 40 | 600 | 14 | 4 | 35 | 2 | 2 carb, 1 med-fat meat, 1 fat |
| **Chef America/Hot Pockets Pizza Mini's** | | | | | | | | | | | | |
| Double Cheese | 3 oz | 240 | 9 | 33 | 4 | 15 | 430 | 7 | 3 | 32 | 2 | 2 carb, 2 fat |
| Pepperoni | 3 oz | 250 | 11 | 40 | 4 | 15 | 500 | 7 | 3 | 31 | 2 | 2 carb, 2 fat |
| Pepperoni & Sausage | 3 oz | 230 | 9 | 35 | 3 | 15 | 460 | 8 | 4 | 31 | 2 | 2 carb, 2 fat |
| Sausage | 3 oz | 230 | 8 | 35 | 3 | 15 | 490 | 8 | 4 | 31 | 2 | 2 carb, 2 fat |
| **Chef America/Hot Pockets Toaster Breaks** | | | | | | | | | | | | |
| Double Cheese Pizza | 2.1 oz | 190 | 9 | 42 | 3 | 10 | 240 | 5 | 1 | 22 | 1 1/2 | 1 1/2 carb, 2 fat |
| Grilled Cheese Melt | 2.2 oz | 210 | 10 | 43 | 4 | 15 | 300 | 5 | 1 | 24 | 1 1/2 | 1 1/2 carb, 2 fat |
| Ham & Cheese Melt | 2.2 oz | 180 | 8 | 44 | 3 | 10 | 330 | 4 | 1 | 22 | 1 1/2 | 1 1/2 carb, 2 fat |
| Pepperoni Pizza | 2.1 oz | 200 | 10 | 45 | 4 | 10 | 350 | 5 | 2 | 21 | 1 1/2 | 1 1/2 carb, 2 fat |
| Philly Steak & Cheese Melt | 2.2 oz | 190 | 10 | 47 | 4 | 10 | 370 | 5 | 1 | 20 | 1 1/2 | 1 1/2 carb, 2 fat |
| Sausage & Pepperoni Pizza | 2.1 oz | 180 | 8 | 39 | 3 | 10 | 350 | 5 | 1 | 22 | 1 1/2 | 1 1/2 carb, 2 fat |

## Chef America/Lean Pockets

| | | | | | | | | | | | |
|---|---|---|---|---|---|---|---|---|---|---|---|
| Chicken Broccoli Supreme | 4.6 oz | 270 | 7 | 22 | 4 | 30 | 510 | 12 | 2 | 37 | 2 1/2 | 2 1/2 carb, 1 med-fat meat |
| ✔Chicken Fajita | 4.6 oz | 270 | 7 | 22 | 3 | 30 | 580 | 11 | 5 | 41 | 3 | 3 carb, 1 med-fat meat |
| ✔Chicken Parmesan | 4.6 oz | 280 | 7 | 21 | 3 | 25 | 490 | 14 | 3 | 41 | 3 | 3 carb, 1 med-fat meat |
| ✔Ham & Cheddar | 4.6 oz | 270 | 7 | 22 | 3 | 30 | 670 | 13 | 2 | 40 | 2 1/2 | 2 1/2 carb, 1 med-fat meat |
| ✔Pepperoni Pizza Deluxe | 4.6 oz | 270 | 7 | 22 | 3 | 35 | 580 | 15 | 3 | 37 | 2 1/2 | 2 1/2 carb, 1 med-fat meat |
| ✔Philly Steak & Cheese | 4.6 oz | 260 | 7 | 23 | 3 | 30 | 560 | 15 | 1 | 35 | 2 | 2 carb, 1 med-fat meat |
| ✔Turkey & Ham w/Cheddar | 4.6 oz | 270 | 7 | 22 | 3 | 35 | 700 | 14 | 1 | 41 | 3 | 3 carb, 1 med-fat meat |
| ✔Turkey, Broccoli & Cheese | 4.6 oz | 250 | 7 | 24 | 3 | 35 | 540 | 12 | 4 | 35 | 2 | 2 carb, 1 med-fat meat |

## Michael Angelo's

| | | | | | | | | | | | |
|---|---|---|---|---|---|---|---|---|---|---|---|
| Italian Style | 1 (8 oz) | 600 | 25 | 38 | 12 | 55 | 1590 | 27 | 5 | 66 | 4 1/2 | 4 1/2 carb, 2 med-fat meat, 3 fat |
| Meatball Calzones | | | | | | | | | | | | |

## Ore Ida

| | | | | | | | | | | | |
|---|---|---|---|---|---|---|---|---|---|---|---|
| ✔Baked BBQ Sauce w/Beef Pocket | 5 oz | 350 | 11 | 28 | 3 | 20 | 580 | 14 | 2 | 48 | 3 | 3 carb, 1 med-fat meat, 1 fat |

✔ = Best Bet; NA = Not Available; Carb. Ch. = Carbohydrate Choices

| Pocket Sandwiches (Frozen) (*Continued*) | Serving Size | Cal. | Fat (g) | % Cal. Fat | Sat. Fat (g) | Chol. (mg) | Sod. (mg) | Pro. (g) | Fiber (g) | Carb. (g) | Carb. Ch. | Servings/Exchanges |
|---|---|---|---|---|---|---|---|---|---|---|---|---|
| ✔Chicken Broccoli Cheese Pocket | 5 oz | 330 | 11 | 30 | 3 | 30 | 590 | 14 | 3 | 43 | 3 | 3 carb, 1 med-fat meat, 1 fat |
| ✔Chicken Fajita Pocket | 4 oz | 250 | 8 | 29 | 2 | 10 | 390 | 11 | 3 | 35 | 2 | 2 carb, 1 med-fat meat, 1 fat |
| Fried Beef Cheddar Pocket | 6 oz | 440 | 24 | 49 | 7 | 55 | 760 | 18 | 2 | 36 | 2 1/2 | 2 1/2 carb, 2 med-fat meat, 3 fat |
| Ham & Cheese Pocket | 5 oz | 370 | 15 | 36 | 6 | 35 | 880 | 14 | 3 | 46 | 3 | 3 carb, 1 med-fat meat, 2 fat |
| Pepperoni Pizza Pocket | 6 oz | 510 | 26 | 46 | 7 | 35 | 1040 | 19 | 4 | 50 | 3 | 3 carb, 1 med-fat meat, 4 fat |
| Pizza Deluxe Pocket | 5 oz | 400 | 19 | 42 | 7 | 40 | 590 | 18 | 3 | 39 | 2 1/2 | 2 1/2 carb, 2 med-fat meat, 2 fat |
| ✔Turkey Swiss Broccoli Pocket | 6 oz | 380 | 14 | 33 | 5 | 35 | 690 | 18 | 3 | 49 | 3 | 3 carb, 1 med-fat meat, 2 fat |
| **Red Baron** | | | | | | | | | | | | |
| Pizza Pouches, Ham & Cheese | 1 | 355 | 17 | 43 | 6 | 40 | 1050 | 15 | NA | 36 | 2 1/2 | 2 1/2 carb, 1 med-fat meat, 2 fat |

# POPCORN (READY-TO-EAT)

| | | | | | | | | | | | |
|---|---|---|---|---|---|---|---|---|---|---|---|
| **Cracker Jacks** | | | | | | | | | | | |
| ✔Fat-Free Butter Toffee | 3/4 cup | 110 | 0 | 0 | 0 | 0 | 85 | 1 | 1 | 26 | 2 | 2 carb |
| ✔Fat-Free Caramel | 3/4 cup | 110 | 0 | 0 | 0 | 0 | 70 | <1 | 1 | 26 | 2 | 2 carb |
| ✔Original | 1/2 cup | 120 | 2 | 15 | 0 | 0 | 70 | 2 | 1 | 23 | 1 1/2 | 1 1/2 carb |
| **Estee** | | | | | | | | | | | | |
| ✔Caramel Popcorn | 1 cup | 120 | 2 | 15 | 0 | 0 | 90 | <1 | 1 | 26 | 2 | 2 carb |
| **Franklin** | | | | | | | | | | | | |
| Crunch 'N Munch | 2/3 cup | 150 | 6 | 36 | 2 | 5 | 170 | 2 | <1 | 22 | 1 1/2 | 1 1/2 carb, 1 fat |
| **Frito-Lay** | | | | | | | | | | | | |
| Chester's Butter Popcorn | 3 cups | 160 | 12 | 68 | 2 | 0 | 330 | 2 | 3 | 15 | 1 | 1 strch, 2 fat |
| ✔Chester's Caramel Craze Popcorn | 3/4 cup | 130 | 2 | 14 | 0 | 0 | 220 | 1 | 1 | 27 | 2 | 2 strch |
| Chester's Cheddar Cheese Popcorn | 3 cups | 190 | 13 | 62 | 3 | 0 | 300 | 3 | 3 | 17 | 1 | 1 strch, 3 fat |
| Smartfood Butter Popcorn | 3 cups | 150 | 9 | 54 | 2 | 5 | 240 | 2 | 1 | 15 | 1 | 1 strch, 2 fat |
| ✔Smartfood Low-Fat Toffee Crunch Popcorn | 3/4 cup | 110 | 1 | 8 | 0 | 0 | 220 | 1 | 1 | 25 | 1 1/2 | 1 1/2 strch |
| Smartfood Reduced-Fat Butter Popcorn | 3 1/3 cups | 130 | 4 | 28 | <1 | 0 | 410 | 3 | 4 | 21 | 1 1/2 | 1 1/2 strch, 1 fat |

✔= Best Bet; NA = Not Available; Carb. Ch. = Carbohydrate Choices

| Popcorn (Ready-to-Eat) (Continued) | Serving Size | Cal. | Fat (g) | % Cal. Fat | Sat. Fat (g) | Chol. (mg) | Sod. (mg) | Pro. (g) | Fiber (g) | Carb. (g) | Carb. Ch. | Servings/Exchanges |
|---|---|---|---|---|---|---|---|---|---|---|---|---|
| Smartfood Reduced-Fat White Cheddar Cheese Popcorn | 3 cups | 140 | 6 | 39 | 2 | <5 | 280 | 4 | 3 | 19 | 1 | 1 strch, 1 fat |
| Smartfood White Cheddar Cheese Popcorn | 2 cups | 190 | 12 | 57 | 3 | 5 | 310 | 3 | 2 | 17 | 1 | 1 strch, 2 fat |
| **Health Valley** | | | | | | | | | | | | |
| ✔Fat-Free Caramel Corn Puffs | 1 oz | 100 | 0 | 0 | 0 | 0 | 45 | 3 | <1 | 21 | 1 1/2 | 1 1/2 strch |
| ✔Fat-Free Caramel Corn Puffs, Apple Cinnamon | 1 oz | 100 | 0 | 0 | 0 | 0 | 50 | 3 | <1 | 21 | 1 1/2 | 1 1/2 strch |
| **Planters** | | | | | | | | | | | | |
| ✔Fat-Free Fiddle Faddle | 1 cup | 110 | 0 | 0 | 0 | 0 | 210 | 2 | NA | 28 | 2 | 2 carb |
| Fiddle Faddle | 3/4 cup | 150 | 7 | 42 | 3 | 10 | 180 | 2 | 1 | 20 | 1 | 1 carb, 1 fat |
| **POPCORN CAKES** | | | | | | | | | | | | |
| **Orville Redenbacher's** | | | | | | | | | | | | |
| ✔Mini Popcorn Cakes, All Varieties (Avg) | 6 | 60 | <1 | 0 | 0 | 0 | 30 | 2 | 1 | 13 | 1 | 1 carb |
| ✔Popcorn Cake, All Varieties (Avg) | 2 | 65 | 1 | 14 | <1 | 0 | 55 | 1 | 1 | 15 | 1 | 1 carb |
| **Quaker** | | | | | | | | | | | | |
| ✔Caramel Corn Cakes | 1 | 50 | 0 | 0 | 0 | 0 | 25 | 1 | 0 | 11 | 1 | 1 carb |
| ✔White Cheddar Popcorn Cakes | 1 | 45 | <1 | 20 | 0 | 0 | 130 | 1 | 0 | 8 | 1/2 | 1/2 carb |

# POPCORN, MICROWAVE (AS PREPARED)

| | Serving | Cal. | Fat (g) | % Cal. Fat | Sat. Fat (g) | Chol. (mg) | Sod. (mg) | Carb. (g) | Fiber (g) | Pro. (g) | Carb. Ch. | Exchanges |
|---|---|---|---|---|---|---|---|---|---|---|---|---|
| **Betty Crocker** | | | | | | | | | | | | |
| ✓94% Fat-Free Butter | 6 cups | 110 | 2 | 16 | 0 | 0 | 230 | 23 | 4 | 4 | 1 1/2 | 1 1/2 carb |
| Cheddar Cheese | 5 cups | 150 | 10 | 60 | 3 | 0 | 230 | 16 | 3 | 3 | 1 | 1 carb, 2 fat |
| ✓Light Butter | 6 cups | 120 | 5 | 38 | 1 | 0 | 290 | 20 | 3 | 4 | 1 | 1 carb, 1 fat |
| Light Natural | 6 cups | 130 | 5 | 35 | 1 | 0 | 260 | 20 | 3 | 3 | 1 | 1 carb, 1 fat |
| ✓Movie Theater Butter | 1 cup | 40 | 3 | 68 | <1 | 0 | 55 | 3 | <1 | <1 | 0 | 1 fat |
| Natural | 4 cups | 150 | 10 | 60 | 3 | 0 | 280 | 16 | 3 | 3 | 1 | 1 carb, 2 fat |
| **Frito-Lay** | | | | | | | | | | | | |
| Chester's Microwave Butter Popcorn | 5 cups | 200 | 12 | 54 | 2 | 0 | 300 | 22 | 3 | 4 | 1 1/2 | 1 1/2 strch, 2 fat |
| **Jolly Time** | | | | | | | | | | | | |
| Blast O Butter | 3 1/2 cups | 150 | 11 | 66 | 3 | 0 | 340 | 19 | 3 | 9 | 1 | 1 carb, 2 fat |
| **Orville Redenbacher's** | | | | | | | | | | | | |
| Butter | 4 cups | 160 | 12 | 68 | 3 | 0 | 390 | 17 | 2 | 4 | 1 | 1 carb, 2 fat |
| Cheddar Butter | 3 cups | 150 | 12 | 72 | 3 | 0 | 290 | 12 | 2 | 3 | 1 | 1 carb, 2 fat |
| Homestyle | 4 1/2 cups | 170 | 12 | 64 | 3 | 0 | 330 | 18 | 2 | 4 | 1 | 1 carb, 2 fat |
| Light Butter | 4 cups | 110 | 5 | 41 | 1 | 0 | 330 | 19 | 3 | 4 | 1 | 1 carb, 1 fat |
| Movie Theater Butter | 4 cups | 170 | 12 | 64 | 3 | 0 | 360 | 16 | 2 | 4 | 1 | 1 carb, 2 fat |
| Ultimate Butter | 4 cups | 160 | 12 | 68 | 3 | 0 | 440 | 15 | 2 | 4 | 1 | 1 carb, 2 fat |

✓ = Best Bet; NA = Not Available; Carb. Ch. = Carbohydrate Choices

| Popcorn, Microwave (As Prepared) (Continued) | Serving Size | Cal. | Fat (g) | % Cal. Fat | Sat. Fat (g) | Chol. (mg) | Sod. (mg) | Pro. (g) | Fiber (g) | Carb. (g) | Carb. Ch. | Servings/Exchanges |
|---|---|---|---|---|---|---|---|---|---|---|---|---|
| **Pop-Secret** | | | | | | | | | | | | |
| ✓94% Fat-Free Natural | 6 cups | 110 | 2 | 16 | 0 | 0 | 230 | 4 | 4 | 23 | 1 1/2 | 1 1/2 carb |
| Butter | 4 cups | 150 | 10 | 60 | 3 | 0 | 210 | 3 | 3 | 16 | 1 | 1 carb, 2 fat |
| ✓Homestyle | 1 cup | 35 | 3 | 77 | <1 | 0 | 25 | <1 | <1 | 4 | 0 | 1 fat |
| ✓Jumbo Pop Butter | 1 cup | 40 | 3 | 68 | <1 | 0 | 50 | <1 | <1 | 4 | 0 | 1 fat (3 cups=1 strch, 2 fat) |
| ✓Jumbo Pop Movie Theater | 1 cup | 40 | 3 | 68 | <1 | 0 | 55 | <1 | <1 | 4 | 0 | 1 fat (3 cups=1 strch, 2 fat) |
| ✓Real Land O Lakes Real Butter | 1 cup | 35 | 3 | 77 | <1 | 0 | 60 | <1 | <1 | 4 | 0 | 1 fat (3 cups=1 strch, 2 fat) |

## PORK MEALS/ENTREES (FROZEN)

### Armour Classics

| | Serving Size | Cal. | Fat (g) | % Cal. Fat | Sat. Fat (g) | Chol. (mg) | Sod. (mg) | Pro. (g) | Fiber (g) | Carb. (g) | Carb. Ch. | Servings/Exchanges |
|---|---|---|---|---|---|---|---|---|---|---|---|---|
| Ham Steak | 10.75 oz dinner | 270 | 7 | 24 | NA | 50 | 1320 | 15 | NA | 36 | 2 1/2 | 2 1/2 carb, 1 med-fat meat |

### Banquet

| | Serving Size | Cal. | Fat (g) | % Cal. Fat | Sat. Fat (g) | Chol. (mg) | Sod. (mg) | Pro. (g) | Fiber (g) | Carb. (g) | Carb. Ch. | Servings/Exchanges |
|---|---|---|---|---|---|---|---|---|---|---|---|---|
| Boneless Pork Rib | 10 oz dinner | 400 | 19 | 43 | 8 | 45 | 1070 | 17 | 4 | 40 | 2 1/2 | 2 1/2 carb, 1 med-fat meat, 3 fat |

| Products | Serving Size | Cal. | Fat (g) | % Cal. Fat | Sat. Fat (g) | Chol. (mg) | Sod. (mg) | Pro. (g) | Fiber (g) | Carb. (g) | Carb. Ch. | Exchanges/Choices |
|---|---|---|---|---|---|---|---|---|---|---|---|---|
| Extra Helping Boneless Pork Riblet | 15.3 oz dinner | 720 | 40 | 50 | 15 | 80 | 1590 | 27 | 7 | 62 | 4 | 4 carb, 2 med-fat meat, 6 fat |
| Family Size Potato, Ham & Broccoli Au Gratin | 5.2 oz dinner | 210 | 13 | 56 | 5 | 30 | 970 | 7 | 2 | 16 | 1 | 1 carb, 1 med-fat meat, 2 fat |
| Pasta w/Italian Sausage & Peppers | 9.5 oz dinner | 300 | 12 | 36 | 4 | 15 | 760 | 10 | 6 | 39 | 2 1/2 | 2 1/2 carb, 1 med-fat meat, 1 fat |
| Pork Cutlet | 10.25 oz dinner | 420 | 25 | 54 | 7 | 38 | 1060 | 11 | 4 | 38 | 2 1/2 | 2 1/2 carb, 1 med-fat meat, 4 fat |
| **Healthy Choice** | | | | | | | | | | | | |
| ✔Bowl Creations, Roasted Potatoes w/Ham | 8.5 oz bowl | 200 | 3 | 14 | 2 | 30 | 600 | 17 | 6 | 26 | 2 | 2 carb, 2 very lean meat |
| ✔Hearty Handfuls, Ham & Cheese | 6.1 oz meal | 320 | 5 | 14 | 2 | 25 | 590 | 19 | 4 | 50 | 3 | 3 carb, 1 med-fat meat |
| ✔Herb Breaded Pork Patty | 8 oz meal | 280 | 6 | 18 | 3 | 30 | 570 | 18 | 4 | 38 | 2 1/2 | 2 1/2 carb, 2 lean meat |
| **Lean Cuisine** | | | | | | | | | | | | |
| ✔Café Classics, Honey Roasted Pork | 9.5 oz meal | 250 | 6 | 22 | 3 | 45 | 590 | 17 | 3 | 32 | 2 | 2 carb, 2 lean meat |
| **Marie Callender** | | | | | | | | | | | | |
| Country Fried Pork Chop | 15 oz meal | 540 | 28 | 46 | 9 | 65 | 2240 | 23 | 8 | 50 | 3 | 3 carb, 2 med-fat meat, 4 fat |

✔= Best Bet; NA = Not Available; Carb. Ch. = Carbohydrate Choices

| Pork, Meals/Entrees (Frozen) (*Continued*) | Serving Size | Cal. | Fat (g) | % Cal. Fat | Sat. Fat (g) | Chol. (mg) | Sod. (mg) | Pro. (g) | Fiber (g) | Carb. (g) | Carb. Ch. | Servings/Exchanges |
|---|---|---|---|---|---|---|---|---|---|---|---|---|
| Honey Roasted Ham Steak | 14 oz meal | 490 | 13 | 24 | 7 | 80 | 2310 | 29 | 5 | 63 | 4 | 4 carb, 2 med-fat meat, 1 fat |
| Linguine & Italian Sausage | 15 oz meal | 710 | 36 | 46 | 16 | 30 | 1330 | 26 | 8 | 70 | 4 1/2 | 4 1/2 carb, 2 med-fat meat, 5 fat |
| **Stouffer's** | | | | | | | | | | | | |
| Homestyle Breaded Port Cutlet | 10 oz meal | 420 | 23 | 49 | 10 | 50 | 1280 | 26 | 4 | 27 | 2 | 2 carb, 3 med-fat meat, 2 fat |
| Pork and Roasted Potatoes | 15.4 oz meal | 540 | 17 | 28 | 6 | 70 | 1480 | 28 | 8 | 68 | 4 1/2 | 4 1/2 carb, 2 med-fat meat, 1 fat |
| **Swanson** | | | | | | | | | | | | |
| Boneless Pork Ribs | 10.5 oz meal | 470 | 19 | 36 | 7 | 30 | 900 | 16 | 5 | 58 | 4 | 4 carb, 1 med-fat meat, 3 fat |
| **Swanson Hungry-Man** | | | | | | | | | | | | |
| Boneless Pork Rib | 14.1 oz meal | 750 | 37 | 44 | 13 | 85 | 1440 | 29 | 9 | 74 | 5 | 5 carb, 2 med-fat meat, 5 fat |

## PORK, FULLY COOKED (FROZEN)

| | Serving Size | Calories | Fat (g) | % Calories from Fat | Saturated Fat (g) | Cholesterol (mg) | Sodium (mg) | Carbohydrate (g) | Fiber (g) | Protein (g) | Carb. Ch. | Exchanges |
|---|---|---|---|---|---|---|---|---|---|---|---|---|
| **Homestyle Menu** | | | | | | | | | | | | |
| Country Style Ribs in Hickory BBQ Sauce | 3 oz | 160 | 7 | 39 | 3 | 50 | 650 | 14 | 0 | 9 | 1/2 | 1/2 carb, 2 lean meat |
| **Jimmy Dean** | | | | | | | | | | | | |
| Pork Roast in Bourbon Sauce, Fully Cooked | 5 oz | 300 | 12 | 36 | 4 | 100 | 380 | 35 | 1 | 11 | 1 | 1 carb, 5 lean meat |
| **Lloyd's BBQ Co.** | | | | | | | | | | | | |
| Pork Spareribs, Fully Cooked | 3 ribs w/5 oz sauce | 380 | 27 | 64 | 11 | 65 | 920 | 20 | 1 | 20 | 1 | 1 carb, 3 med-fat meat, 2 fat |

## POTATO SIDE DISHES (DRY, AS PREPARED)

| | Serving Size | Calories | Fat (g) | % Calories from Fat | Saturated Fat (g) | Cholesterol (mg) | Sodium (mg) | Carbohydrate (g) | Fiber (g) | Protein (g) | Carb. Ch. | Exchanges |
|---|---|---|---|---|---|---|---|---|---|---|---|---|
| **Betty Crocker** | | | | | | | | | | | | |
| Au Gratin Potatoes | 1/2 cup | 150 | 6 | 36 | 2 | 5 | 600 | 22 | 1 | 3 | 1 1/2 | 1 1/2 carb, 1 fat |
| Broccoli Au Gratin Potatoes (Homestyle) | 1/2 cup | 140 | 6 | 39 | 2 | <5 | 530 | 21 | 2 | 3 | 1 1/2 | 1 1/2 carb, 1 fat |
| Butter & Herb Mashed Potatoes | 1/2 cup | 160 | 8 | 45 | 2 | 5 | 470 | 20 | 1 | 3 | 1 | 1 carb, 2 fat |
| Cheddar & Bacon Potatoes | 1/2 cup | 150 | 6 | 36 | 2 | <5 | 650 | 21 | 1 | 3 | 1 1/2 | 1 1/2 strch, 1 fat |
| Cheddar & Sour Cream Potatoes | 1/2 cup | 130 | 3 | 21 | 1 | <5 | 570 | 25 | 1 | 3 | 1 1/2 | 1 1/2 carb, 1 fat |
| Cheddar Cheese Potatoes (Homestyle) | 1/2 cup | 120 | 3 | 23 | 1 | <5 | 600 | 21 | 1 | 4 | 1 1/2 | 1 1/2 carb, 1 fat |
| Cheesy Scalloped Potatoes (Homestyle) | 1/2 cup | 140 | 6 | 39 | 2 | <5 | 540 | 21 | 3 | 3 | 1 1/2 | 1 1/2 carb, 1 fat |
| Chicken & Herb Mashed Potatoes | 1/2 cup | 150 | 7 | 42 | 2 | <5 | 520 | 21 | 1 | 3 | 1 1/2 | 1 1/2 carb, 1 fat |

✔= Best Bet; NA = Not Available; Carb. Ch. = Carbohydrate Choices

| Potato Side Dishes (Dry, As Prepared) (Continued) | Serving Size | Cal. | Fat (g) | % Cal. Fat | Sat. Fat (g) | Chol. (mg) | Sod. (mg) | Pro. (g) | Fiber (g) | Carb. (g) | Carb. Ch. | Servings/Exchanges |
|---|---|---|---|---|---|---|---|---|---|---|---|---|
| Chicken & Vegetable Potatoes | 2/3 cup | 160 | 6 | 34 | 2 | <5 | 560 | 4 | 2 | 24 | 1 1/2 | 1 1/2 carb, 1 fat |
| Four Cheese Mashed Potatoes | 1/2 cup | 150 | 7 | 42 | 2 | <5 | 570 | 3 | 2 | 20 | 1 | 1 carb, 1 fat |
| Hash Brown Potatoes | 1/2 cup | 190 | 8 | 38 | 2 | 0 | 620 | 3 | 3 | 30 | 2 | 2 carb, 2 fat |
| Hearty Beef Mashed Potatoes & Gravy | 3/4 cup | 170 | 7 | 37 | 2 | 0 | 720 | 3 | 1 | 24 | 1 1/2 | 1 1/2 carb, 1 fat |
| Julienne Potatoes | 1/2 cup | 150 | 6 | 36 | 2 | <5 | 630 | 3 | 1 | 21 | 1 1/2 | 1 1/2 carb, 1 fat |
| Mashed Potato Buds | 2/3 cup | 160 | 8 | 45 | 2 | <5 | 460 | 3 | 1 | 19 | 1 1/2 | 1 1/2 carb, 2 fat |
| Potatoes, Cheesy Scalloped, Homestyle | 1/2 cup | 140 | 6 | 39 | 2 | <5 | 540 | 3 | 3 | 21 | 1 1/2 | 1 1/2 strch, 1 fat |
| Ranch Potatoes | 1/2 cup | 160 | 6 | 34 | 2 | <5 | 610 | 3 | 2 | 25 | 1 1/2 | 1 1/2 carb, 1 fat |
| Roasted Chicken Mashed Potatoes & Gravy | 3/4 cup | 180 | 7 | 35 | 2 | <5 | 680 | 3 | 1 | 25 | 1 1/2 | 1 1/2 carb, 1 fat |
| Roasted Garlic Mashed Potatoes | 1/2 cup | 150 | 8 | 48 | 2 | <5 | 400 | 3 | 2 | 19 | 1 1/2 | 1 1/2 carb, 2 fat |
| Scalloped Potatoes | 1/2 cup | 160 | 6 | 34 | 2 | <5 | 610 | 3 | 1 | 23 | 1 1/2 | 1 1/2 carb, 1 fat |
| Sour Cream & Chives Mashed Potatoes | 1/2 cup | 150 | 7 | 42 | 2 | 5 | 440 | 3 | 1 | 21 | 1 1/2 | 1 1/2 carb, 1 fat |
| Sour Cream 'n Chive Potatoes | 1/2 cup | 160 | 7 | 39 | 2 | 5 | 600 | 3 | 2 | 22 | 1 1/2 | 1 1/2 carb, 1 fat |
| Three Cheese Potatoes | 1/2 cup | 150 | 6 | 36 | 2 | <5 | 600 | 3 | 2 | 23 | 1 1/2 | 1 1/2 carb, 1 fat |
| Twice Baked Cheddar & Bacon Potatoes | 2/3 cup | 210 | 11 | 47 | 3 | 85 | 580 | 6 | 1 | 22 | 1 1/2 | 1 1/2 carb, 2 fat |

# POTATO SIDE DISHES (FROZEN)

| | Serving Size | Cal. | Fat (g) | % Cal. Fat | Sat. Fat (g) | Chol. (mg) | Sod. (mg) | Carb. (g) | Fiber (g) | Prot. (g) | Carb. Ch. | Exchanges/Choices |
|---|---|---|---|---|---|---|---|---|---|---|---|---|
| **Boston Market** | | | | | | | | | | | | |
| Garlic Dill New Potatoes | 1/2 cup | 130 | 6 | 41 | 1 | 0 | 450 | 2 | 1 | 18 | 1 | 1 carb, 1 fat |
| Mashed Potatoes | 1/2 cup | 180 | 9 | 45 | 3 | 10 | 520 | 3 | 1 | 23 | 1 1/2 | 1 1/2 carb, 2 fat |
| **Budget Gourmet** | | | | | | | | | | | | |
| Potato & Broccoli w/Cheese Sauce | 10.5 oz meal | 300 | 10 | 30 | 4 | 30 | 740 | 13 | NA | 40 | 2 1/2 | 2 1/2 carb, 1 med-fat meat, 1 fat |
| **Ore Ida** | | | | | | | | | | | | |
| ✔ Homestyle Potato Wedges w/skin | 3 oz | 110 | 3 | 25 | <1 | 0 | 15 | 2 | 2 | 19 | 1 | 1 strch, 1 fat |
| ✔ Mashed Potatoes, As Prepared | 2/3 cup | 90 | 2 | 20 | 1 | <5 | 150 | 1 | 1 | 16 | 1 | 1 strch |
| Topped Baked Potato, Broccoli & Cheese | 1 | 310 | 8 | 23 | 4 | 15 | 810 | 11 | 5 | 47 | 3 | 3 strch, 2 fat |
| Twice Baked Potato, Cheddar Cheese | 1 | 180 | 7 | 35 | 2 | 5 | 430 | 4 | 2 | 25 | 1 1/2 | 1 1/2 strch, 1 fat |
| **Stouffer's** | | | | | | | | | | | | |
| Potatoes Au Gratin | 4.6 oz | 150 | 5 | 30 | 4 | 15 | 510 | 6 | 3 | 20 | 1 | 1 carb, 1 fat |
| Scalloped Potatoes | 4.6 oz | 140 | 6 | 39 | 1 | <5 | 450 | 4 | 2 | 17 | 1 | 1 carb, 1 fat |
| **TGI Fridays** | | | | | | | | | | | | |
| Potato Skins, Cheddar & Bacon Stuffed | 3 pieces | 250 | 17 | 61 | 7 | 40 | 510 | 10 | 4 | 15 | 1 | 1 carb, 1 med-fat meat, 2 fat |

✔ = Best Bet; NA = Not Available; Carb. Ch. = Carbohydrate Choices

| Product | Serving Size | Cal. | Fat (g) | % Cal. Fat | Sat. Fat (g) | Chol. (mg) | Sod. (mg) | Pro. (g) | Fiber (g) | Carb. (g) | Carb. Ch. | Servings/Exchanges |
|---|---|---|---|---|---|---|---|---|---|---|---|---|
| **POTATO SIDE DISHES (REFRIGERATED)** | | | | | | | | | | | | |
| **Fresh Selections** | | | | | | | | | | | | |
| Garlic Mashed Potatoes, Fully Cooked | 1/2 cup | 150 | 8 | 48 | 2 | 5 | 250 | 3 | 1 | 18 | 1 | 1 strch, 2 fat |
| **PRETZELS** | | | | | | | | | | | | |
| **Estee** | | | | | | | | | | | | |
| ✓Dutch Pretzels | 2 | 130 | 1 | 7 | 0 | 0 | 40 | 3 | 1 | 26 | 2 | 2 strch |
| ✓Unsalted Pretzels | 23 | 120 | 1 | 8 | 0 | 0 | 30 | 3 | 1 | 25 | 1 1/2 | 1 1/2 strch |
| **Frito-Lay** | | | | | | | | | | | | |
| ✓Rold Gold Fat-Free Cheddar Cheese Pretzels | 1 oz | 110 | 0 | 0 | 0 | 0 | 440 | 3 | 1 | 23 | 1 1/2 | 1 1/2 strch |
| ✓Rold Gold Fat-Free Honey Mustard Pretzels | 1 oz | 110 | 0 | 0 | 0 | 0 | 380 | 3 | 1 | 23 | 1 1/2 | 1 1/2 strch |
| Rold Gold Pretzels, Crispy Thins | 1 oz | 110 | 2 | 16 | 0 | 0 | 670 | 3 | 1 | 22 | 1 1/2 | 1 1/2 strch |
| Rold Gold Pretzels, Fat-Free Sticks | 1 oz | 110 | 0 | 0 | 0 | 0 | 530 | 3 | 1 | 23 | 1 1/2 | 1 1/2 strch |
| Rold Gold Pretzels-Fat-Free Thins | 1 oz | 110 | 0 | 0 | 0 | 0 | 520 | 2 | 1 | 24 | 1 1/2 | 1 1/2 strch |
| ✓Rold Gold Pretzels-Fat-Free Tiny Twists | 1 oz | 100 | 0 | 0 | 0 | 0 | 420 | 3 | 1 | 23 | 1 1/2 | 1 1/2 strch |
| Rold Gold Pretzel Rods | 1 oz | 110 | 1 | 8 | 0 | 0 | 610 | 3 | 1 | 22 | 1 1/2 | 1 1/2 strch |
| ✓Rold Gold Sour Dough Nuggets | 1 oz | 110 | 0 | 0 | 0 | 0 | 330 | 2 | 1 | 24 | 1 1/2 | 1 1/2 strch |
| **Franklin** | | | | | | | | | | | | |
| ✓Crunch 'N Munch Toffee Pretzels | 12 | 120 | 1 | 8 | 0 | 0 | 200 | 1 | 0 | 25 | 1 1/2 | 1 1/2 carb |

## PUDDING MIX (AS PREPARED)

### Jell-O

| | Serving | Cal. | Fat (g) | % Cal. Fat | Sat. Fat (g) | Chol. (mg) | Sod. (mg) | Prot. (g) | Fiber (g) | Carb. (g) | Carb. Ch. | |
|---|---|---|---|---|---|---|---|---|---|---|---|---|
| ✔ Cook/Serve Pudding w/2% milk, Chocolate | 1/2 cup | 150 | 3 | 18 | 2 | 10 | 170 | 5 | <1 | 28 | 2 | 2 carb, 1 fat |
| ✔ Cook/Serve Pudding w/2% Milk, Vanilla | 1/2 cup | 140 | 3 | 19 | 2 | 10 | 200 | 4 | 0 | 26 | 2 | 2 carb, 1 fat |
| ✔ Instant Pudding w/Skim Milk Fat-Free, Chocolate | 1/2 cup | 140 | 0 | 0 | 0 | <5 | 410 | 5 | <1 | 31 | 2 | 2 carb |
| ✔ Instant Pudding w/Skim Milk Fat-Free, Vanilla | 1/2 cup | 140 | 0 | 0 | 0 | <5 | 410 | 4 | 0 | 29 | 2 | 2 carb |
| ✔ Instant Pudding w/Skim Milk Fat/Sugar Free, Vanilla | 1/2 cup | 70 | 0 | 0 | 0 | <5 | 400 | 4 | 0 | 12 | 1 | 1 carb |
| ✔ Instant Pudding w/Skim Milk-Fat/Sugar Free, Choc. | 1/2 cup | 80 | 0 | 0 | 0 | <5 | 390 | 5 | <1 | 14 | 1 | 1 carb |
| ✔ Instant Pudding/Pie Filling w/2% Milk, Chocolate | 1/2 cup | 160 | 3 | 17 | 2 | 10 | 470 | 4 | <1 | 31 | 2 | 2 carb, 1 fat |
| ✔ Instant Pudding/Pie Filling w/2% milk, Vanilla | 1/2 cup | 150 | 3 | 18 | 2 | 10 | 410 | 4 | 0 | 29 | 2 | 2 carb, 1 fat |

✔= Best Bet; NA = Not Available; Carb. Ch. = Carbohydrate Choices

# PUDDING SNACKS

| Product | Serving Size | Cal. | Fat (g) | % Cal. Fat | Sat. Fat (g) | Chol. (mg) | Sod. (mg) | Pro. (g) | Fiber (g) | Carb. (g) | Carb. Ch. | Servings/Exchanges |
|---|---|---|---|---|---|---|---|---|---|---|---|---|
| **Hunt's** | | | | | | | | | | | | |
| Snack Pack Chocolate Pudding | 4 oz | 160 | 6 | 34 | 2 | 0 | 180 | 2 | 0 | 25 | 1 1/2 | 1 1/2 carb, 1 fat |
| ✓Snack Pack Light Chocolate Pudding | 4 oz | 100 | 2 | 18 | NA | 0 | 120 | 3 | 0 | 20 | 1 | 1 carb |
| ✓Snack Pack Tapioca Pudding | 4 oz | 95 | <1 | 9 | 0 | 0 | 185 | 2 | 0 | 21 | 1 1/2 | 1 1/2 carb |
| Snack Pack Vanilla Pudding | 4 oz | 160 | 6 | 34 | 2 | 0 | 140 | 2 | 0 | 25 | 1 1/2 | 1 1/2 carb, 1 fat |
| **Jell-O** | | | | | | | | | | | | |
| Handi-Snacks Vanilla Pudding | 1 | 120 | 4 | 30 | 1 | 0 | 150 | 1 | 0 | 22 | 1 1/2 | 1 1/2 carb, 1 fat |
| ✓Pudding Snack Fat-Free Chocolate | 1 | 100 | 0 | 0 | 0 | 0 | 190 | 3 | <1 | 23 | 1 1/2 | 1 1/2 carb |
| ✓Pudding Snack Fat-Free Chocolate Vanilla Swirl | 1 | 100 | 0 | 0 | 0 | 0 | 210 | 3 | <1 | 23 | 1 1/2 | 1 1/2 carb |
| Pudding Snack Vanilla Chocolate Swirl | 1 | 160 | 5 | 28 | 2 | 0 | 180 | 3 | 0 | 27 | 2 | 2 carb, 1 fat |
| Pudding Snacks Chocolate | 1 | 160 | 5 | 28 | 2 | 0 | 190 | 3 | 0 | 28 | 2 | 2 carb, 1 fat |
| Pudding Snacks Tapioca | 1 | 140 | 4 | 26 | 2 | 0 | 160 | 2 | 0 | 26 | 2 | 2 carb, 1 fat |
| Pudding Snacks Vanilla | 1 | 160 | 5 | 28 | 2 | 0 | 170 | 2 | 0 | 25 | 1 1/2 | 1 1/2 carb, 1 fat |
| **Kraft** | | | | | | | | | | | | |
| Handi-Snacks Pudding, Chocolate | 1 | 130 | 4 | 28 | 1 | 0 | 125 | 2 | <1 | 23 | 1 1/2 | 1 1/2 carb, 1 fat |
| **Ultra Slim Fast** | | | | | | | | | | | | |
| ✓Pudding, All Varieties (Avg) | 4 oz | 100 | 1 | 9 | NA | 0 | 235 | 2 | 2 | 21 | 1 1/2 | 1 1/2 carb |

## QUICHE (FROZEN)

### Nancy's

| Product | Serving Size | Cal. | Fat (g) | % Cal. Fat | Sat. Fat (g) | Chol. (mg) | Sod. (mg) | Carb. (g) | Fiber (g) | Prot. (g) | Carb. Ch. | Exchanges/Choices |
|---|---|---|---|---|---|---|---|---|---|---|---|---|
| Quiche Broccoli Cheddar | 1 | 430 | 26 | 54 | 12 | 140 | 710 | 34 | 2 | 16 | 2 | 2 carb, 1 med-fat meat, 4 fat |
| Quiche Florentine | 1 | 440 | 26 | 53 | 12 | 180 | 620 | 35 | 1 | 18 | 2 | 2 carb, 2 med-fat meat, 3 fat |
| Quiche Lorraine | 1 | 490 | 29 | 53 | 13 | 195 | 860 | 34 | 1 | 24 | 2 | 2 carb, 3 med-fat meat, 3 fat |
| Quiche Monterey | 1 | 470 | 29 | 56 | 14 | 165 | 710 | 34 | 1 | 18 | 2 | 2 carb, 2 med-fat meat, 4 fat |

## RICE

### La Choy

| Product | Serving Size | Cal. | Fat (g) | % Cal. Fat | Sat. Fat (g) | Chol. (mg) | Sod. (mg) | Carb. (g) | Fiber (g) | Prot. (g) | Carb. Ch. | Exchanges/Choices |
|---|---|---|---|---|---|---|---|---|---|---|---|---|
| Fried Rice | 4 oz | 195 | <1 | 5 | <1 | 0 | 835 | 44 | 2 | 4 | 3 | 3 strch |

### Minute Rice

| Product | Serving Size | Cal. | Fat (g) | % Cal. Fat | Sat. Fat (g) | Chol. (mg) | Sod. (mg) | Carb. (g) | Fiber (g) | Prot. (g) | Carb. Ch. | Exchanges/Choices |
|---|---|---|---|---|---|---|---|---|---|---|---|---|
| ✓ Brown Rice, Whole-Grain, Instant, Cooked | 2/3 cup | 170 | 2 | 11 | 0 | 0 | 10 | 34 | 2 | 4 | 2 | 2 strch |
| ✓ Rice, Boil in Bag, Cooked | 1 cup | 190 | 0 | 0 | 0 | 0 | 10 | 42 | <1 | 4 | 3 | 3 strch |
| ✓ White Rice, Instant, Cooked | 3/4 cup | 160 | 0 | 0 | 0 | 0 | 5 | 36 | <1 | 3 | 2 1/2 | 2 1/2 strch |

✓= Best Bet; NA = Not Available; Carb. Ch. = Carbohydrate Choices

## Rice (*Continued*)

| | Serving Size | Cal. | Fat (g) | % Cal. Fat | Sat. Fat (g) | Chol. (mg) | Sod. (mg) | Pro. (g) | Fiber (g) | Carb. (g) | Carb. Ch. | Servings/Exchanges |
|---|---|---|---|---|---|---|---|---|---|---|---|---|
| **Uncle Ben's** | | | | | | | | | | | | |
| ✔Boil-In-Bag Converted Rice | 1 cup | 190 | <1 | 5 | 0 | 0 | 0 | 4 | 1 | 44 | 3 | 3 strch |
| ✔Converted Rice | 1 cup | 170 | 0 | 0 | 0 | 0 | 0 | 4 | 1 | 38 | 2 1/2 | 2 1/2 strch |
| ✔Instant Long-Grain Rice | 1 cup | 190 | <1 | 5 | 0 | 0 | 15 | 3 | 1 | 43 | 3 | 3 strch |
| ✔Instant Whole-Grain Brown Rice | 1/2 cup | 90 | 1 | 10 | 0 | 0 | 11 | 2 | 1 | 21 | 1 1/2 | 1 1/2 strch |
| ✔Original Brown Rice | 2/3 cup | 130 | 1 | 7 | 0 | 0 | 0 | 3 | 1 | 27 | 2 | 2 strch |
| **RICE CAKES** | | | | | | | | | | | | |
| **Quaker** | | | | | | | | | | | | |
| ✔Crispy Mini's Rice Cakes, BBQ | 10 | 70 | 2 | 26 | 0 | 0 | 140 | 1 | 0 | 12 | 1 | 1 carb |
| ✔Crispy Mini's Rice Cakes, Honey Nut | 8 | 60 | 0 | 0 | 0 | 0 | 90 | 1 | 0 | 15 | 1 | 1 carb |
| ✔Mini Rice Cakes, All Varieties (Avg) | 7–9 | 60 | 1 | 15 | 0 | 0 | 45–210 | 1 | 0 | 13 | 1 | 1 strch |
| ✔Rice Cakes, All Varieties (Avg) | 1 | 50 | <1 | 0 | 0 | 0 | 0–130 | 1 | 0 | 10 | 1 | 1 strch |
| ✔Rice Cakes, Salt Free | 1 | 35 | 0 | 0 | 0 | 0 | 0 | 1 | 0 | 7 | 1/2 | 1/2 strch |
| **RICE SIDE DISHES (CANNED)** | | | | | | | | | | | | |
| **Old El Paso** | | | | | | | | | | | | |
| Spanish Rice | 1 cup | 130 | 1 | 7 | 0 | 0 | 1340 | 3 | 2 | 28 | 2 | 2 carb |

## RICE SIDE DISHES (DRY, AS PREPARED)

| | Serving | Cal. | Fat (g) | % Cal. Fat | Sat. Fat (g) | Chol. (mg) | Sod. (mg) | Prot. (g) | Fiber (g) | Carb. (g) | Carb. Ch. | Exchanges |
|---|---|---|---|---|---|---|---|---|---|---|---|---|
| **Betty Crocker** | | | | | | | | | | | | |
| Bowl Appetit, Cheddar Broccoli Rice | 1 bowl | 300 | 8 | 24 | 3 | 10 | 990 | 8 | 1 | 52 | 3 1/2 | 3 1/2 carb, 2 fat |
| Bowl Appetit, Herb Chicken Vegetable Rice | 1 bowl | 260 | 4 | 14 | <1 | 20 | 850 | 8 | 1 | 50 | 3 | 3 carb, 1 fat |
| Cheddar & Broccoli Rice | 1 cup | 310 | 10 | 29 | 3 | 10 | 950 | 7 | 1 | 48 | 3 | 3 carb, 2 fat |
| Chicken Herb Rice | 1 cup | 270 | 5 | 17 | 1 | 5 | 870 | 6 | 1 | 48 | 3 | 3 carb, 1 fat |
| Creamy Herb Risotto | 1 cup | 320 | 12 | 34 | 4 | 5 | 810 | 5 | 0 | 49 | 3 | 3 carb, 2 fat |
| Garden Vegetable Pilaf | 1 cup | 240 | 6 | 23 | 1 | <5 | 840 | 6 | 2 | 43 | 3 | 3 carb, 1 fat |
| ✔ Herb Rice & Barley Medley | 1/3 cup | 180 | 1 | 5 | 0 | 0 | 480 | 5 | 3 | 39 | 2 1/2 | 2 1/2 carb |
| Long Grain & Wild Rice Pilaf | 1 cup | 220 | 5 | 21 | 1 | 0 | 580 | 5 | 1 | 40 | 2 1/2 | 2 1/2 carb, 1 fat |
| ✔ Rice & Barley Medley | 1/3 cup | 180 | 1 | 5 | 0 | 0 | 480 | 6 | 3 | 39 | 2 1/2 | 2 1/2 carb |
| Southwestern Rice | 1 cup | 250 | 6 | 22 | 1 | 0 | 950 | 5 | 2 | 45 | 3 | 3 carb, 1 fat |
| **Lipton** | | | | | | | | | | | | |
| Cheddar Broccoli Rice & Sauce | 1/2 cup | 230 | 3 | 12 | 2 | 5 | 940 | 7 | 1 | 46 | 3 | 3 strch, 1 fat |
| Chicken Flavor Rice & Sauce | 1/2 cup | 230 | 3 | 12 | 1 | 5 | 890 | 7 | 1 | 45 | 3 | 3 strch, 1 fat |
| Rice & Sauce Medley | 1/2 cup | 220 | 3 | 12 | <1 | 5 | 800 | 7 | 2 | 44 | 3 | 3 strch, 1 fat |
| Southwestern Chicken Rice & Sauce | 1/2 cup | 210 | 2 | 9 | 0 | 0 | 770 | 5 | 1 | 47 | 3 | 3 strch |
| Spanish Rice & Sauce | 1/2 cup | 220 | 2 | 8 | 0 | 0 | 830 | 6 | 2 | 47 | 3 | 3 strch |

✔ = Best Bet; NA = Not Available; Carb. Ch. = Carbohydrate Choices

| Rice Side Dishes (Dry, As Prepared) (Continued) | Serving Size | Cal. | Fat (g) | % Cal. Fat | Sat. Fat (g) | Chol. (mg) | Sod. (mg) | Pro. (g) | Fiber (g) | Carb. (g) | Carb. Ch. | Servings/Exchanges |
|---|---|---|---|---|---|---|---|---|---|---|---|---|
| Teriyaki Rice & Sauce | 1/2 cup | 220 | 2 | 8 | 0 | 0 | 840 | 5 | 1 | 45 | 3 | 3 strch |
| **Minute Rice** | | | | | | | | | | | | |
| Seasoned Long Grain & Wild Rice | 1 cup | 230 | <1 | 4 | 0 | 0 | 950 | 6 | 1 | 50 | 3 | 3 strch |
| **Old El Paso** | | | | | | | | | | | | |
| Cheesy Mexican Rice | 2 1/2 cups | 290 | 6 | 19 | 2 | <5 | 820 | 4 | 2 | 55 | 4 | 4 carb, 1 fat |
| Spanish Rice | 2 1/2 cup | 280 | 5 | 16 | 5 | 0 | 870 | 5 | 2 | 55 | 4 | 4 carb, 1 fat |
| **Rice-A-Roni** | | | | | | | | | | | | |
| Beef Flavored | 1 cup | 310 | 9 | 26 | 2 | 0 | 1160 | 7 | 2 | 52 | 3 1/2 | 3 1/2 strch, 2 fat |
| Chicken Flavored | 1 cup | 310 | 9 | 26 | 2 | 0 | 980 | 7 | 2 | 52 | 3 1/2 | 3 1/2 strch, 2 fat |
| Fried Rice | 1 cup | 320 | 11 | 31 | 2 | 0 | 1530 | 6 | 2 | 51 | 3 1/2 | 3 1/2 strch, 1 fat |
| **Uncle Ben's** | | | | | | | | | | | | |
| Chicken Vegetable Blend Long-Grain Rice | 1/2 cup | 200 | 2 | 9 | <1 | 5 | 620 | 5 | 1 | 42 | 3 | 3 strch |
| ✔ Herb Risotto | 1 cup | 200 | <1 | 5 | 0 | 0 | 470 | 4 | 0 | 44 | 3 | 3 strch |
| Long Grain Rice & Wild Chicken Stock Sauce | 1/2 cup | 190 | 1 | 5 | <1 | 0 | 670 | 5 | 1 | 41 | 3 | 3 strch |
| Original Recipe Wild Rice | 1 cup | 190 | <1 | 5 | 0 | 0 | 620 | 6 | 1 | 41 | 3 | 3 strch |
| Specialty Blends Pilaf | 1 cup | 200 | <1 | 5 | 0 | 0 | 630 | 4 | 1 | 44 | 3 | 3 strch |

| | Serving | Cal. | Fat (g) | % Cal. Fat | Sat. Fat (g) | Chol. (mg) | Sod. (mg) | Prot. (g) | Fiber (g) | Carb. (g) | Carb. Ch. | Exchanges |
|---|---|---|---|---|---|---|---|---|---|---|---|---|
| Three Cheese Long-Grain Rice & Vermicelli / Rice & Vermicelli | 1 cup | 200 | 3 | 14 | 1 | 5 | 770 | 5 | 1 | 41 | 3 | 3 strch |
| **RICE SIDE DISHES (FROZEN)** | | | | | | | | | | | | |
| **Green Giant** | | | | | | | | | | | | |
| Rice & Broccoli | 10 oz meal | 320 | 12 | 34 | 4 | 15 | 1000 | 8 | 2 | 44 | 3 | 3 strch, 2 fat |
| Rice Medley | 10 oz | 240 | 3 | 11 | 2 | 5 | 880 | 6 | 3 | 46 | 3 | 3 carb, 1 fat |
| Rice Pilaf | 10 oz | 230 | 3 | 12 | 2 | 5 | 1020 | 6 | 3 | 44 | 3 | 3 carb, 1 fat |
| **RICOTTA CHEESE** | | | | | | | | | | | | |
| **(Generic)** | | | | | | | | | | | | |
| ✔ Fat-Free Ricotta Cheese | 1/4 cup | 45 | 0 | 0 | 0 | 10 | 120 | 7 | 0 | 3 | 0 | 1 very lean meat |
| Part-Skim Ricotta Cheese | 1/4 cup | 80 | 5 | 56 | 3 | 25 | 150 | 7 | 0 | 2 | 0 | 1 med-fat meat |
| **RISOTTO (DRY, AS PREPARED)** | | | | | | | | | | | | |
| **Betty Crocker** | | | | | | | | | | | | |
| Creamy Herb Risotto | 1 cup | 320 | 12 | 34 | 4 | 5 | 810 | 5 | 0 | 49 | 3 | 3 carb, 2 fat |
| **SALAD DRESSING** | | | | | | | | | | | | |
| **Benecol** | | | | | | | | | | | | |
| Creamy Italian | 2 Tbsp | 100 | 10 | 90 | 2 | 0 | 170 | 0 | 0 | 3 | 0 | 2 fat |
| French | 2 Tbsp | 130 | 11 | 76 | 2 | 0 | 170 | 0 | 0 | 6 | 0 | 1/2 carb, 2 fat |
| Ranch | 2 Tbsp | 130 | 13 | 90 | 2 | 0 | 250 | 0 | 0 | 3 | 0 | 3 fat |

✔ = Best Bet; NA = Not Available; Carb. Ch. = Carbohydrate Choices

| Salad Dressing (*Continued*) | Serving Size | Cal. | Fat (g) | % Cal. Fat | Sat. Fat (g) | Chol. (mg) | Sod. (mg) | Pro. (g) | Fiber (g) | Carb. (g) | Carb. Ch. | Servings/Exchanges |
|---|---|---|---|---|---|---|---|---|---|---|---|---|
| **Estee** | | | | | | | | | | | | |
| ✔Creamy French Style | 2 Tbsp | 10 | 0 | 0 | 0 | 0 | 80 | 0 | 0 | 0 | 0 | free |
| ✔Italian Dressing | 2 Tbsp | 5 | 0 | 0 | 0 | 0 | 80 | 0 | 0 | 0 | 0 | free |
| **Good Seasons (as prepared from mix)** | | | | | | | | | | | | |
| Cheese Garlic | 2 Tbsp | 140 | 16 | 100 | 3 | 0 | 330 | 0 | 0 | 1 | 0 | 3 fat |
| Garlic & Herbs | 2 Tbsp | 140 | 15 | 96 | 2 | 0 | 340 | 0 | 0 | 1 | 0 | 3 fat |
| Gourmet Caesar | 2 Tbsp | 150 | 16 | 96 | 3 | 0 | 300 | 0 | 0 | 3 | 0 | 3 fat |
| Gourmet Parmesan Italian | 2 Tbsp | 150 | 16 | 96 | 3 | 0 | 330 | 0 | 0 | 2 | 0 | 3 fat |
| Honey French | 2 Tbsp | 160 | 15 | 84 | 2 | 0 | 250 | 0 | 0 | 5 | 0 | 3 fat |
| ✔Honey French, Fat-Free | 2 Tbsp | 20 | 0 | 0 | 0 | 0 | 250 | 0 | 0 | 5 | 0 | free |
| Honey Mustard | 2 Tbsp | 150 | 15 | 90 | 2 | 0 | 240 | 0 | 0 | 3 | 0 | 3 fat |
| ✔Honey Mustard, Fat-Free | 2 Tbsp | 20 | 0 | 0 | 0 | 0 | 280 | 0 | 0 | 5 | 0 | free |
| Italian | 2 Tbsp | 140 | 15 | 96 | 2 | 0 | 320 | 0 | 0 | 1 | 0 | 3 fat |
| ✔Italian, Fat-Free | 2 Tbsp | 10 | 0 | 0 | 0 | 0 | 290 | 0 | 0 | 3 | 0 | free |
| Italian, Reduced Calorie, All Varieties (Avg) | 2 Tbsp | 50 | 5 | 90 | 1 | 0 | 270 | 0 | 0 | 2 | 0 | 1 fat |
| Mexican Spice | 2 Tbsp | 140 | 14 | 96 | 3 | 0 | 310 | 0 | 0 | 2 | 0 | 3 fat |
| Mild Italian | 2 Tbsp | 150 | 15 | 90 | 3 | 0 | 370 | 0 | 0 | 2 | 0 | 3 fat |
| Oriental Sesame | 2 Tbsp | 150 | 16 | 96 | 3 | 0 | 360 | 0 | 0 | 3 | 0 | 3 fat |

| | | | | | | | | | | | |
|---|---|---|---|---|---|---|---|---|---|---|---|
| Roasted Garlic | 2 Tbsp | 150 | 15 | 90 | 2 | 0 | 340 | 0 | 0 | 2 | 0 | 3 fat |
| ✓Zesty Herb, Fat-Free | 2 Tbsp | 10 | 0 | 0 | 0 | 0 | 260 | 0 | 0 | 2 | 0 | free |
| Zesty Italian | 2 Tbsp | 140 | 15 | 96 | 2 | 0 | 220 | 0 | 0 | 1 | 0 | 3 fat |

**Kraft**

| | | | | | | | | | | | |
|---|---|---|---|---|---|---|---|---|---|---|---|
| Bacon & Tomato | 2 Tbsp | 140 | 14 | 90 | 3 | <5 | 280 | <1 | 0 | 2 | 0 | 3 fat |
| Buttermilk Ranch | 2 Tbsp | 150 | 16 | 96 | 3 | <5 | 240 | 0 | 0 | 1 | 0 | 3 fat |
| Caesar Italian | 2 Tbsp | 100 | 10 | 90 | 2 | 0 | 480 | <1 | 0 | 2 | 0 | 2 fat |
| Caesar Ranch | 2 Tbsp | 110 | 11 | 90 | 2 | 10 | 290 | 1 | 0 | 1 | 0 | 2 fat |
| Catalina French | 2 Tbsp | 120 | 10 | 75 | 2 | 0 | 390 | 0 | 0 | 7 | 1/2 | 1/2 carb, 2 fat |
| Catalina w/Honey | 2 Tbsp | 130 | 11 | 76 | 2 | 0 | 320 | 0 | 0 | 7 | 1/2 | 1/2 other CHO, 2 fat |
| Coleslaw Salad Dressing | 2 Tbsp | 130 | 11 | 76 | 2 | 15 | 410 | 0 | 0 | 7 | 1/2 | 1/2 carb, 2 fat |
| Creamy French | 2 Tbsp | 160 | 15 | 84 | 3 | 0 | 270 | 0 | 0 | 5 | 0 | 3 fat |
| Creamy Garlic | 2 Tbsp | 110 | 11 | 90 | 2 | 0 | 360 | 0 | 0 | 2 | 0 | 2 fat |
| Creamy Italian | 2 Tbsp | 110 | 11 | 90 | 2 | 0 | 250 | 0 | 0 | 2 | 0 | 2 fat |
| Cucumber Ranch | 2 Tbsp | 140 | 15 | 96 | 2 | 0 | 220 | 0 | 0 | 2 | 0 | 3 fat |
| ✓Fat-Free Blue Cheese | 2 Tbsp | 45 | 0 | 0 | 0 | 0 | 360 | 0 | 1 | 11 | 1 | 1 carb |
| ✓Fat-Free Caesar Italian | 2 Tbsp | 25 | 0 | 0 | 0 | 0 | 480 | <1 | 0 | 4 | 0 | free |
| ✓Fat-Free Catalina | 2 Tbsp | 35 | 0 | 0 | 0 | 0 | 320 | 0 | <1 | 8 | 1/2 | 1/2 carb |
| ✓Fat-Free French | 2 Tbsp | 45 | 0 | 0 | 0 | 0 | 300 | 0 | <1 | 11 | 1 | 1 carb |

✓= Best Bet; NA = Not Available; Carb. Ch. = Carbohydrate Choices

| Salad Dressing (*Continued*) | Serving Size | Cal. | Fat (g) | % Cal. Fat | Sat. Fat (g) | Chol. (mg) | Sod. (mg) | Pro. (g) | Fiber (g) | Carb. (g) | Carb. Ch. | Servings/Exchanges |
|---|---|---|---|---|---|---|---|---|---|---|---|---|
| ✔Fat-Free Honey Dijon | 2 Tbsp | 45 | 0 | 0 | 0 | 0 | 330 | 0 | 1 | 10 | 1/2 | 1/2 carb |
| ✔Fat-Free Italian Dressing | 2 Tbsp | 20 | 0 | 0 | 0 | 0 | 430 | 0 | 0 | 4 | 0 | free |
| ✔Fat-Free Peppercorn Ranch | 2 Tbsp | 45 | 0 | 0 | 0 | 0 | 330 | 0 | <1 | 11 | 1 | 1 carb |
| ✔Fat-Free Ranch | 2 Tbsp | 50 | 0 | 0 | 0 | 0 | 350 | 0 | <1 | 11 | 1 | 1 carb |
| ✔Fat-Free Red Wine Vinegar Dressing | 2 Tbsp | 15 | 0 | 0 | 0 | 0 | 410 | 0 | 0 | 3 | 0 | free |
| ✔Fat-Free Thousand Island | 2 Tbsp | 40 | 0 | 0 | 0 | 0 | 280 | 0 | 1 | 9 | 1/2 | 1/2 carb |
| Honey Dijon | 2 Tbsp | 110 | 10 | 82 | 2 | 0 | 210 | 0 | 0 | 6 | 1/2 | 1/2 carb, 2 fat |
| House Italian | 2 Tbsp | 120 | 12 | 90 | 2 | <5 | 240 | 0 | 0 | 2 | 0 | 2 fat |
| Lightly Done Right Raspberry Vinaigrette | 2 Tbsp | 60 | 4 | 60 | 0 | 0 | 270 | 0 | 0 | 5 | 0 | 1 fat |
| Lightly Done Right, Catalina | 2 Tbsp | 80 | 5 | 56 | 0 | 0 | 400 | 0 | 0 | 9 | 1/2 | 1/2 carb, 1 fat |
| Lightly Done Right, Classic Caesar | 2 Tbsp | 70 | 6 | 77 | 1 | 10 | 330 | <1 | 0 | 3 | 0 | 1 fat |
| Lightly Done Right, Italian | 2 Tbsp | 50 | 5 | 90 | 0 | 0 | 230 | 0 | 0 | 2 | 0 | 1 fat |
| Lightly Done Right, Ranch | 2 Tbsp | 80 | 7 | 79 | <1 | 10 | 300 | 0 | 0 | 3 | 0 | 1 fat |
| Lightly Done Right, Red Wine Vinegar | 2 Tbsp | 50 | 5 | 90 | 0 | 0 | 310 | 0 | 0 | 3 | 0 | 1 fat |
| Peppercorn Ranch | 2 Tbsp | 170 | 18 | 95 | 3 | 10 | 270 | 0 | 0 | 1 | 0 | 4 fat |
| Presto Italian | 2 Tbsp | 90 | 9 | 90 | 2 | 0 | 310 | 0 | 0 | 2 | 0 | 2 fat |
| Ranch Dressing | 2 Tbsp | 170 | 18 | 95 | 3 | 10 | 280 | 0 | 0 | 1 | 0 | 4 fat |
| Roka Brand Blue Cheese | 2 Tbsp | 130 | 13 | 90 | 3 | <5 | 310 | <1 | <1 | 2 | 0 | 3 fat |

| | Serving | Cal. | Fat (g) | % Cal. from Fat | Sat. Fat (g) | Chol. (mg) | Sod. (mg) | Fiber (g) | Pro. (g) | Carb. (g) | Carb. Ch. | Servings/Exchanges |
|---|---|---|---|---|---|---|---|---|---|---|---|---|
| Russian | 2 Tbsp | 130 | 10 | 69 | 2 | 0 | 310 | 0 | 0 | 10 | 1/2 | 1/2 carb, 2 fat |
| Sour Cream & Onion Ranch | 2 Tbsp | 170 | 18 | 95 | 3 | 10 | 250 | 0 | 0 | 1 | 0 | 4 fat |
| Taste of Life, Country Ranch | 2 Tbsp | 60 | 5 | 75 | 0 | 0 | 250 | 0 | 0 | 4 | 0 | 1 fat |
| Taste of Life, Garden Italian | 2 Tbsp | 50 | 5 | 90 | 0 | 0 | 300 | 0 | 0 | 5 | 0 | 1 fat |
| Taste of Life, Honey Catalina | 2 Tbsp | 80 | 5 | 56 | 0 | 0 | 290 | 0 | 0 | 8 | 0 | 1/2 carb, 1 fat |
| Taste of Life, Tomato & Garlic | 2 Tbsp | 60 | 5 | 75 | 0 | 0 | 240 | 0 | 0 | 4 | 0 | 1 fat |
| Thousand Island | 2 Tbsp | 110 | 10 | 82 | 2 | 10 | 310 | 0 | 0 | 5 | 0 | 2 fat |
| Thousand Island & Bacon | 2 Tbsp | 130 | 12 | 83 | 2 | 0 | 200 | 0 | 0 | 5 | 0 | 3 fat |
| Zesty Italian | 2 Tbsp | 110 | 11 | 90 | 1 | 0 | 540 | 0 | 0 | 2 | 0 | 2 fat |
| **Kraft Seven Seas** | | | | | | | | | | | | |
| Chunky Blue Cheese | 2 Tbsp | 130 | 13 | 90 | 3 | <5 | 310 | <1 | <1 | 2 | 0 | 3 fat |
| Classic Caesar | 2 Tbsp | 100 | 10 | 90 | 2 | 0 | 480 | <1 | 0 | 2 | 0 | 2 fat |
| Creamy Italian | 2 Tbsp | 120 | 12 | 90 | 2 | 0 | 510 | 0 | 0 | 1 | 0 | 3 fat |
| ✔Fat-Free Ranch | 2 Tbsp | 45 | 0 | 0 | 0 | 0 | 330 | 0 | 1 | 11 | 1 | 1 carb |
| ✔Fat-Free Creamy Italian | 2 Tbsp | 50 | 0 | 0 | 0 | 0 | 330 | 0 | <1 | 12 | 1 | 1 carb |
| ✔Fat-Free Red Wine Vinegar | 2 Tbsp | 15 | 0 | 0 | 0 | 0 | 410 | 0 | 0 | 3 | 0 | free |
| Green Goddess | 2 Tbsp | 130 | 13 | 98 | 2 | 0 | 260 | 0 | 0 | 1 | 0 | 3 fat |
| Herb Vinaigrette | 2 Tbsp | 140 | 15 | 96 | 2 | 0 | 250 | 0 | 0 | <1 | 0 | 3 fat |
| Herbs & Spices | 2 Tbsp | 90 | 9 | 90 | 1 | 0 | 290 | 0 | 0 | 1 | 0 | 2 fat |

✔= Best Bet; NA = Not Available; Carb. Ch. = Carbohydrate Choices

| Salad Dressing (*Continued*) | Serving Size | Cal. | Fat (g) | % Cal. Fat | Sat. Fat (g) | Chol. (mg) | Sod. (mg) | Pro. (g) | Fiber (g) | Carb. (g) | Carb. Ch. | Servings/Exchanges |
|---|---|---|---|---|---|---|---|---|---|---|---|---|
| Honey Mustard | 2 Tbsp | 110 | 10 | 82 | 2 | 0 | 210 | 0 | 0 | 6 | 1/2 | 1/2 carb, 2 fat |
| Ranch | 2 Tbsp | 160 | 17 | 96 | 3 | <5 | 260 | 0 | 0 | 2 | 0 | 3 fat |
| Red Wine Vinegar & Oil | 2 Tbsp | 90 | 9 | 90 | 1 | 0 | 500 | 0 | 0 | 2 | 0 | 2 fat |
| Reduced Fat Creamy Italian | 2 Tbsp | 60 | 5 | 75 | 1 | 0 | 500 | 0 | 0 | 2 | 0 | 1 fat |
| Reduced Fat Italian Olive Oil | 2 Tbsp | 45 | 4 | 80 | 0 | 0 | 460 | 0 | 0 | 2 | 0 | 1 fat |
| Reduced Fat Red Wine Vinegar & Oil | 2 Tbsp | 45 | 4 | 80 | 0 | 0 | 320 | 0 | 0 | 3 | 0 | 1 fat |
| Reduced Fat Viva Italian | 2 Tbsp | 45 | 4 | 80 | 0 | 0 | 320 | 0 | 0 | 2 | 0 | 1 fat |
| Two-Cheese Italian | 2 Tbsp | 70 | 7 | 90 | 1 | 0 | 240 | 0 | 0 | 3 | 0 | 1 fat |
| Viva Italian | 2 Tbsp | 90 | 9 | 90 | 1 | 0 | 370 | 0 | 0 | 2 | 0 | 2 fat |
| Viva Russian | 2 Tbsp | 150 | 16 | 96 | 3 | 0 | 210 | 0 | 0 | 3 | 0 | 3 fat |
| **Marie's** | | | | | | | | | | | | |
| Buttermilk Ranch Dressing/Dip | 2 Tbsp | 180 | 18 | 90 | 3 | 15 | 230 | 0 | 0 | 4 | 0 | 3 fat |
| Chunky Blue Cheese Dressing/Dip | 2 Tbsp | 180 | 19 | 95 | 4 | 15 | 170 | 1 | 0 | 3 | 0 | 4 fat |
| Cole Slaw Dressing | 2 Tbsp | 150 | 13 | 78 | 2 | 10 | 210 | 0 | 0 | 6 | 1/2 | 1/2 carb, 3 fat |
| Creamy Ranch Dressing/Dip | 2 Tbsp | 190 | 20 | 95 | 3 | 15 | 170 | <1 | 0 | 3 | 0 | 4 fat |
| ✔Fat-Free Honey Dijon Vinaigrette | 2 Tbsp | 50 | 0 | 0 | 0 | 0 | 125 | 0 | 0 | 11 | 1 | 1 carb |
| Honey Mustard Dressing/Dip | 2 Tbsp | 160 | 15 | 84 | 2 | 5 | 160 | 0 | <1 | 8 | 1/2 | 1/2 carb, 3 fat |

| | Serving Size | Calories | Fat (g) | % Cal. from Fat | Sat. Fat (g) | Chol. (mg) | Sod. (mg) | Carb. (g) | Prot. (g) | Carb. Ch. | Exchanges |
|---|---|---|---|---|---|---|---|---|---|---|---|
| ✓Light & Zesty White Wine Vinaigrette | 2 Tbsp | 40 | 0 | 0 | 0 | 0 | 270 | 10 | 0 | 1/2 | 1/2 carb |
| ✓Lite & Zesty Herb Vinaigrette | 2 Tbsp | 30 | 0 | 0 | 0 | 0 | 260 | 8 | 0 | 1/2 | 1/2 carb |
| ✓Lite & Zesty Italian Vinaigrette | 2 Tbsp | 35 | 0 | 0 | 0 | 0 | 270 | 8 | 0 | 1/2 | 1/2 carb |
| Low Calorie-Dressing/Dip-Blue Cheese | 2 Tbsp | 100 | 7 | 63 | 1 | 10 | 250 | 7 | 1 | 1/2 | 1/2 carb, 1 fat |
| Low Calorie-Dressing/Dip-Creamy Ranch | 2 Tbsp | 100 | 7 | 63 | <1 | 5 | 240 | 7 | 1 | 1/2 | 1/2 carb, 1 fat |
| ✓Low Fat Creamy Blue Cheese | 2 Tbsp | 45 | 2 | 40 | 0 | 0 | 270 | 7 | 0 | 1/2 | 1/2 carb |
| Low Fat Creamy Italian Herb | 2 Tbsp | 40 | 2 | 45 | 0 | 0 | 290 | 6 | 0 | 1/2 | 1/2 carb |
| ✓Low Fat Creamy Parmesan | 2 Tbsp | 45 | 2 | 40 | 0 | 0 | 270 | 7 | <1 | 1/2 | 1/2 carb |
| ✓Low Fat Zesty Ranch | 2 Tbsp | 45 | 2 | 40 | 0 | 0 | 330 | 7 | 0 | 1/2 | 1/2 carb |
| Parmesan Ranch Dressing/Dip | 2 Tbsp | 180 | 19 | 95 | 3 | 15 | 160 | 3 | <1 | 0 | 4 fat |
| Poppyseed Dressing/Dip | 2 Tbsp | 150 | 12 | 72 | 2 | 10 | 200 | 8 | 0 | 1/2 | 1/2 carb, 2 fat |
| Sour Cream & Dill Dressing/Dip | 2 Tbsp | 190 | 20 | 95 | 3 | 15 | 160 | 3 | 0 | 0 | 4 fat |
| Tangy French Dressing/Dip | 2 Tbsp | 130 | 11 | 76 | 2 | 0 | 260 | 8 | 0 | 1/2 | 1/2 carb, 2 fat |
| Thousand Island Dressing/Dip | 2 Tbsp | 240 | 23 | 86 | 4 | 20 | 320 | 7 | 0 | 1/2 | 1/2 carb, 5 fat |
| **Take Control** | | | | | | | | | | | |
| Blue Cheese | 2 Tbsp | 90 | 6 | 60 | 1 | 15 | 400 | 8 | 1 | 1/2 | 1/2 carb, 1 fat |
| Italian | 2 Tbsp | 50 | 4 | 72 | 0 | 5 | 290 | 5 | 0 | 0 | 1 fat |
| Reduced Fat Ranch | 2 Tbsp | 100 | 8 | 72 | 1 | 10 | 290 | 5 | 0 | 0 | 2 fat |

✓= Best Bet; NA = Not Available; Carb. Ch. = Carbohydrate Choices

| Salad Dressing (*Continued*) | Serving Size | Cal. | Fat (g) | % Cal. Fat | Sat. Fat (g) | Chol. (mg) | Sod. (mg) | Pro. (g) | Fiber (g) | Carb. (g) | Carb. Ch. | Servings/Exchanges |
|---|---|---|---|---|---|---|---|---|---|---|---|---|
| **Weight Watchers** | | | | | | | | | | | | |
| ✔Fat-Free Blue Cheese | 2 Tbsp | 16 | 0 | 0 | 0 | 0 | 110 | 0 | 0 | 2 | 0 | free |
| ✔Fat-Free Caesar | 2 Tbsp | 8 | 0 | 0 | 0 | 0 | 200 | 0 | 0 | 2 | 0 | free |
| ✔Fat-Free Creamy Italian | 2 Tbsp | 24 | 0 | 0 | 0 | 0 | 85 | 0 | 0 | 6 | 1/2 | 1/2 carb |
| ✔Fat-Free French | 2 Tbsp | 20 | 0 | 0 | 0 | 0 | 170 | 0 | 0 | 4 | 0 | free |
| ✔Fat-Free Russian Salad Dressing | 2 Tbsp | 8 | 0 | 0 | 0 | 0 | 120 | 0 | 0 | 2 | 0 | free |
| ✔Fat-Free Tomato Vinaigrette | 2 Tbsp | 16 | 0 | 0 | 0 | 0 | 150 | 0 | 0 | 4 | 0 | free |
| **Wishbone** | | | | | | | | | | | | |
| Caesar | 2 Tbsp | 155 | 16 | 93 | 2 | 2 | 495 | <1 | 0 | 2 | 0 | 3 fat |
| Chunky Blue Cheese | 2 Tbsp | 150 | 16 | 96 | 2 | 2 | 300 | <1 | 0 | 1 | 0 | 3 fat |
| Creamy Herbal | 2 Tbsp | 140 | 14 | 90 | NA | 0 | 455 | 0 | 0 | 2 | 0 | 3 fat |
| Creamy Italian | 2 Tbsp | 110 | 11 | 90 | 2 | 2 | 300 | <1 | 0 | 3 | 0 | 1 fat |
| Deluxe French | 2 Tbsp | 120 | 11 | 83 | 2 | 2 | 165 | <1 | 0 | 4 | 0 | 2 fat |
| ✔Fat-Free Blue Cheese | 2 Tbsp | 35 | 0 | 0 | 0 | 0 | 290 | 0 | 0 | 7 | 1/2 | 1/2 carb |
| ✔Fat-Free Italian | 2 Tbsp | 20 | 0 | 0 | 0 | 0 | 390 | 0 | 0 | 5 | 0 | free |
| ✔Fat-Free Thousand Island | 2 Tbsp | 35 | 0 | 0 | 0 | 0 | 290 | 0 | 0 | 9 | 1/2 | 1/2 carb |
| ✔Healthy Sensations Italian | 2 Tbsp | 12 | 0 | 0 | 0 | 0 | 280 | 0 | 0 | 2 | 0 | free |
| Italian | 2 Tbsp | 90 | 5 | 50 | 1 | 0 | 560 | 0 | 0 | 3 | 0 | 1 fat |

| | Amount | Cal. | Fat (g) | % Cal. Fat | Sat. Fat (g) | Chol. (mg) | Sod. (mg) | Prot. (g) | Fiber (g) | Carb. (g) | Carb. Ch. | Exchanges |
|---|---|---|---|---|---|---|---|---|---|---|---|---|
| Lite Caesar | 2 Tbsp | 60 | 5 | 75 | 1 | 0 | 410 | 1 | 0 | 3 | 0 | 1 fat |
| Lite Dijon Vinaigrette | 2 Tbsp | 60 | 5 | 75 | 1 | 0 | 410 | 0 | 0 | 3 | 0 | 1 fat |
| ✔Lite Italian | 2 Tbsp | 14 | <1 | 64 | 0 | 0 | 210 | <1 | 0 | 2 | 0 | free |
| Lite Ranch | 2 Tbsp | 100 | 9 | 81 | 4 | 5 | 300 | 0 | 0 | 5 | 0 | 2 fat |
| ✔Lite Sweet & Sour Spicy French | 2 Tbsp | 35 | 1 | 26 | 0 | 0 | 110 | 0 | 0 | 6 | 1/2 | 1/2 carb |
| Lite Thousand Island | 2 Tbsp | 70 | 4 | 51 | <1 | 20 | 200 | <1 | 0 | 6 | 1/2 | 1/2 carb, 1 fat |
| Olive Oil Italian | 2 Tbsp | 70 | 6 | 77 | 1 | 0 | 380 | 0 | 0 | 3 | 0 | 1 fat |
| Olive Oil Vinaigrette | 2 Tbsp | 60 | 4 | 60 | NA | 0 | 220 | 0 | 0 | 4 | 0 | 1 fat |
| Ranch | 2 Tbsp | 160 | 17 | 96 | 2 | 4 | 310 | <1 | 0 | 2 | 0 | 3 fat |
| Red Wine Vinegar | 2 Tbsp | 90 | 8 | 80 | 2 | 0 | 380 | 0 | 0 | 2 | 0 | 2 fat |
| Robusto Italian | 2 Tbsp | 90 | 9 | 90 | 1 | 0 | 580 | <1 | 0 | 4 | 0 | 2 fat |
| Russian | 2 Tbsp | 90 | 5 | 50 | <1 | 0 | 290 | <1 | 0 | 12 | 1 | 1 carb, 1 fat |
| Sante Fe | 2 Tbsp | 150 | 15 | 90 | 3 | 5 | 220 | 0 | 0 | 3 | 0 | 3 fat |

## SALAD MIXES (AS PREPARED)

### Betty Crocker

| | Amount | Cal. | Fat (g) | % Cal. Fat | Sat. Fat (g) | Chol. (mg) | Sod. (mg) | Prot. (g) | Fiber (g) | Carb. (g) | Carb. Ch. | Exchanges |
|---|---|---|---|---|---|---|---|---|---|---|---|---|
| ✔Suddenly Salad Garden | 3/4 cup | 140 | 1 | 6 | 0 | 0 | 520 | 5 | 2 | 28 | 2 | 2 carb |
| Italian 98% Fat-Free | | | | | | | | | | | | |
| Suddenly Salad, Caesar | 3/4 cup | 220 | 9 | 37 | 2 | 0 | 580 | 5 | 1 | 30 | 2 | 2 carb, 2 fat |

✔= Best Bet; NA = Not Available; Carb. Ch. = Carbohydrate Choices

| Salad Mixes (As Prepared) (Continued) | Serving Size | Cal. | Fat (g) | % Cal. Fat | Sat. Fat (g) | Chol. (mg) | Sod. (mg) | Pro. (g) | Fiber (g) | Carb. (g) | Carb. Ch. | Servings/Exchanges |
|---|---|---|---|---|---|---|---|---|---|---|---|---|
| Suddenly Salad, Classic Pasta | 3/4 cup | 250 | 8 | 29 | 1 | 0 | 910 | 7 | 2 | 38 | 2 1/2 | 2 1/2 carb, 2 fat |
| Suddenly Salad, Classic Salad | 3/4 cup | 250 | 8 | 29 | 1 | 0 | 910 | 7 | 2 | 38 | 2 1/2 | 2 1/2 carb, 2 fat |
| Suddenly Salad, Ranch & Bacon | 3/4 cup | 330 | 20 | 55 | 3 | 15 | 480 | 7 | 1 | 30 | 2 | 2 carb, 4 fat |
| Suddenly Salad, Roasted Garlic Parmesan | 3/4 cup | 260 | 11 | 38 | 2 | 10 | 770 | 7 | 1 | 33 | 2 | 2 carb, 2 fat |
| Tuna Helper, Pasta Salad | 2/3 cup | 380 | 27 | 64 | 3 | 10 | 730 | 10 | 1 | 26 | 2 | 2 carb, 1 med-fat meat, 4 fat |

## SALSA

### Breakstone

| | | | | | | | | | | | | |
|---|---|---|---|---|---|---|---|---|---|---|---|---|
| ✔Fat-Free Creamy Salsa Dip | 2 Tbsp | 20 | 0 | 0 | 0 | <5 | 240 | 1 | 0 | 3 | 0 | free |

### Eagle

| | | | | | | | | | | | | |
|---|---|---|---|---|---|---|---|---|---|---|---|---|
| ✔Salsa Dip | 2 Tbsp | 10 | 0 | 0 | 0 | 0 | 250 | 3 | 1 | 2 | 0 | free |

### Frito Lay/Tostitos

| | | | | | | | | | | | | |
|---|---|---|---|---|---|---|---|---|---|---|---|---|
| ✔Restaurant Style Salsa | 1/4 cup | 30 | 0 | 0 | 0 | 0 | 420 | <2 | <2 | 6 | 1/2 | 1 vegetable |
| ✔Salsa, Medium | 2 Tbsp | 40 | 2 | 45 | <1 | 5 | 65 | 1 | 1 | 5 | 1/2 | 1/2 carb |
| ✔Salsa-Mild/Medium/Hot | 1/4 cup | 30 | 0 | 0 | 0 | 0 | 520 | 2 | 2 | 6 | 1/2 | 1 vegetable |
| ✔Ultimate Garden Salsa | 1/4 cup | 30 | 0 | 0 | 0 | 0 | 460 | 2 | 2 | 6 | 1/2 | 1 vegetable |

### Kraft

| | | | | | | | | | | | | |
|---|---|---|---|---|---|---|---|---|---|---|---|---|
| ✔Fat-Free Salsa Dip | 2 Tbsp | 20 | 0 | 0 | 0 | <5 | 240 | 1 | 0 | 3 | 0 | free |

**Old El Paso**

| | Serving | | | | | | | | | | |
|---|---|---|---|---|---|---|---|---|---|---|---|
| ✔All Varieties (Avg) | 2 Tbsp | 10 | 0 | 0 | 0 | 155 | 0 | 0 | 2 | 0 | free |
| ✔Chunky Salsa Dip-Mild/Medium | 2 Tbsp | 15 | 0 | 0 | 0 | 230 | 1 | <1 | 3 | 0 | free |

**Ortega**

| | | | | | | | | | | | |
|---|---|---|---|---|---|---|---|---|---|---|---|
| ✔Salsa, All Varieties (Avg) | 2 Tbsp | 10 | 0 | 0 | 0 | 320 | 0 | 1 | 2 | 0 | free |

**Orval Kent**

| | | | | | | | | | | | |
|---|---|---|---|---|---|---|---|---|---|---|---|
| ✔Spicy Salsa w/Green Chili | 2 Tbsp | 10 | 0 | 0 | 0 | 180 | 0 | 0 | 2 | 0 | free |

**Pace**

| | | | | | | | | | | | |
|---|---|---|---|---|---|---|---|---|---|---|---|
| ✔Chunky Salsa | 2 Tbsp | 10 | 0 | 0 | 0 | 220 | 0 | 0 | 3 | 0 | free |

**Poore Brothers**

| | | | | | | | | | | | |
|---|---|---|---|---|---|---|---|---|---|---|---|
| ✔Roasted Red Pepper Salsa | 2 Tbsp | 10 | 0 | 0 | 0 | 190 | 0 | 0 | 3 | 0 | free |

**Que Bueno**

| | | | | | | | | | | | |
|---|---|---|---|---|---|---|---|---|---|---|---|
| ✔Salsa, All Varieties (Avg) | 1 Tbsp | 5 | 0 | 0 | 0 | 75 | 0 | 0 | <1 | 0 | free |

**Rosarita**

| | | | | | | | | | | | |
|---|---|---|---|---|---|---|---|---|---|---|---|
| ✔Salsa, All Varieties (Avg) | 2 Tbsp | 20 | <1 | 0 | 0 | 275 | 1 | 1 | 3 | 0 | free |
| ✔Taco Salsa, Mild | 3 Tbsp | 25 | 1 | 36 | 0 | 300 | 1 | 1 | 6 | 1/2 | 1/2 carb |

**Taco Bell Home Originals**

| | | | | | | | | | | | |
|---|---|---|---|---|---|---|---|---|---|---|---|
| ✔Smooth 'N Zesty Picanto Sauce, All Varieties (Avg) | 2 Tbsp | 15 | 0 | 0 | 0 | 190 | 0 | <1 | 3 | 0 | free |

✔ = Best Bet; NA = Not Available; Carb. Ch. = Carbohydrate Choices

| Salsa (*Continued*) | Serving Size | Cal. | Fat (g) | % Cal. Fat | Sat. Fat (g) | Chol. (mg) | Sod. (mg) | Pro. (g) | Fiber (g) | Carb. (g) | Carb. Ch. | Servings/Exchanges |
|---|---|---|---|---|---|---|---|---|---|---|---|---|
| ✓Thick 'N Chuncky Salsa, All Varieties (Avg) | 2 Tbsp | 15 | 0 | 0 | 0 | 0 | 260 | <1 | <1 | 2 | 0 | free |

## SANDWICH TOPPINGS

### Banquet

| | Serving Size | Cal. | Fat (g) | % Cal. Fat | Sat. Fat (g) | Chol. (mg) | Sod. (mg) | Pro. (g) | Fiber (g) | Carb. (g) | Carb. Ch. | Servings/Exchanges |
|---|---|---|---|---|---|---|---|---|---|---|---|---|
| Hot Sandwich Toppers, Creamed Beef | 4 oz | 120 | 6 | 45 | 3 | 25 | 700 | 7 | 0 | 8 | 1/2 | 1/2 carb, 1 med-fat meat |
| Hot Sandwich Toppers, Gravy & Salisbury Steak | 5 oz | 210 | 16 | 69 | 7 | 25 | 790 | 9 | 2 | 8 | 1/2 | 1/2 carb, 1 med-fat meat, 2 fat |
| ✓Hot Sandwich Toppers, Gravy & Sliced Beef | 4 oz | 70 | 2 | 26 | 1 | 25 | 440 | 8 | 0 | 5 | 0 | 1 lean meat |
| Hot Sandwich Toppers, Gravy & Sliced Turkey | 5 oz | 160 | 11 | 62 | 4 | 30 | 670 | 8 | 0 | 6 | 1/2 | 1/2 carb, 1 med-fat meat, 1 fat |

## SARDINES

### Underwood

| | Serving Size | Cal. | Fat (g) | % Cal. Fat | Sat. Fat (g) | Chol. (mg) | Sod. (mg) | Pro. (g) | Fiber (g) | Carb. (g) | Carb. Ch. | Servings/Exchanges |
|---|---|---|---|---|---|---|---|---|---|---|---|---|
| Sardines in Mustard Sauce | 3.8 oz can | 180 | 12 | 60 | 3 | 105 | 820 | 17 | 1 | 2 | 0 | 2 med-fat meat |
| Sardines in Soy Oil, Drained | 3.8 oz can | 220 | 16 | 65 | 4 | 100 | 310 | 18 | 0 | 1 | 0 | 2 high-fat meat |
| Sardines in Tomato Sauce | 3.8 oz can | 180 | 11 | 55 | 3 | 115 | 960 | 16 | 1 | 4 | 0 | 2 med-fat meat |

## SAUCES

| | Serving Size | Cal. | Fat (g) | % Cal. Fat | Sat. Fat (g) | Chol. (mg) | Sod. (mg) | Pro. (g) | Fiber (g) | Carb. (g) | Carb. Ch. | Exchanges/Choices |
|---|---|---|---|---|---|---|---|---|---|---|---|---|
| **(Generic)** | | | | | | | | | | | | |
| Soy Sauce | 1 Tbsp | 10 | <1 | 0 | 0 | <1 | 1028 | <1 | 0 | 2 | 0 | free |
| Tartar Sauce | 1 Tbsp | 74 | 8 | 100 | 1 | 7 | 99 | <1 | <1 | 0 | 0 | 2 fat |
| Teriyaki Sauce | 1 Tbsp | 15 | 0 | 0 | 0 | 0 | 690 | 1 | <1 | 3 | 0 | free |
| **Chef Mate** | | | | | | | | | | | | |
| Coney Island-Style Sauce | 1/4 cup | 76 | 5 | 59 | <1 | 2 | 383 | 2 | 1 | 6 | 1/2 | 1/2 carb, 1 fat |
| ✔ Creole Sauce | 1/4 cup | 25 | <1 | 36 | 0 | 0 | 340 | <1 | 0 | 4 | 0 | free |
| ✔ Hoisin Sauce | 1 Tbsp | 35 | <1 | 26 | 0 | 0 | 250 | <1 | 0 | 7 | 1/2 | 1/2 carb |
| ✔ Hot Dog Chili Sauce | 1/4 cup | 69 | 2 | 26 | <1 | 4 | 399 | 3 | 2 | 9 | 1/2 | 1/2 carb, 1 fat |
| ✔ Italian Sauce | 1/4 cup | 60 | 1 | 15 | <1 | 0 | 304 | 1 | <1 | 11 | 1 | 1 carb |
| ✔ Lemon Sauce | 2 Tbsp | 43 | <1 | 21 | 0 | 0 | 3 | <1 | 0 | 10 | 1/2 | 1/2 carb |
| Sloppy Joe Barbecue Sauce | 1/3 cup | 119 | 7 | 53 | 3 | 23 | 574 | 1 | <1 | 9 | 1/2 | 1/2 carb, 1 fat |
| ✔ Sweet & Sour Sauce | 2 Tbsp | 40 | <1 | 23 | <1 | 0 | 116 | <1 | <1 | 8 | 1/2 | 1/2 carb |
| ✔ Szechuan Sauce | 2 Tbsp | 42 | 2 | 43 | <1 | 0 | 436 | <1 | 0 | 6 | 1/2 | 1/2 carb |
| ✔ Teriyaki Sauce | 1 Tbsp | 20 | <1 | 45 | 0 | 0 | 159 | <1 | 0 | 4 | 0 | free |
| **Contadina** | | | | | | | | | | | | |
| Bolognese Sauce | 5 oz | 130 | 7 | 49 | 3 | 25 | 500 | 8 | NA | 0 | 0 | 1 med-fat meat |
| ✔ Sweet 'n Sour Sauce | 2 Tbsp | 40 | 1 | 23 | 0 | 0 | 115 | 0 | 0 | 8 | 1/2 | 1/2 carb |

✔ = Best Bet; NA = Not Available; Carb. Ch. = Carbohydrate Choices

| Sauces (*Continued*) | Serving Size | Cal. | Fat (g) | % Cal. Fat | Sat. Fat (g) | Chol. (mg) | Sod. (mg) | Pro. (g) | Fiber (g) | Carb. (g) | Carb. Ch. | Servings/Exchanges |
|---|---|---|---|---|---|---|---|---|---|---|---|---|
| **Del Monte** | | | | | | | | | | | | |
| Sloppy Joe Sauce | 1/4 cup | 70 | 0 | 0 | 0 | 0 | 680 | 1 | 0 | 16 | 1 | 1 carb |
| **Green Giant** | | | | | | | | | | | | |
| ✔Sloppy Joe Sandwich Sauce | 1/4 cup | 50 | <1 | 18 | <1 | 0 | 423 | 2 | 2 | 11 | 1 | 1 carb |
| **Hunt's** | | | | | | | | | | | | |
| ✔Alfresco Salsa, Medium | 2 Tbsp | 10 | 0 | 0 | 0 | 0 | 161 | <1 | <1 | 2 | 0 | free |
| ✔Chicken Sensations, All Flavors (Avg) | 1 Tbsp | 30 | 3 | 90 | <1 | 0 | 325 | <1 | <1 | 2 | 0 | 1 fat |
| ✔Homestyle Salsa, Medium | 2 Tbsp | 27 | <1 | 0 | 0 | 0 | 236 | 0 | <1 | 6 | 1/2 | 1/2 carb |
| ✔Pepper Sauce, Original & Hot | .1 tsp | 0 | 0 | 0 | 0 | 0 | 205 | 0 | 0 | <1 | 0 | free |
| ✔Picante Sauce, Medium | 2 Tbsp | 11 | <1 | 0 | 0 | 0 | 256 | <1 | <1 | 2 | 0 | free |
| ✔Steak Sauce | 1 Tbsp | 10 | <1 | 0 | 0 | 0 | 256 | <1 | <1 | 2 | 0 | free |
| **Kraft** | | | | | | | | | | | | |
| Cocktail Sauce | 1/4 cup | 60 | <1 | 0 | 0 | 0 | 800 | 1 | 1 | 13 | 1 | 1 carb |
| ✔Horseradish Sauce | 1 tsp | 20 | 0 | 0 | 0 | 0 | 35 | 0 | 0 | <1 | 0 | free |
| Sandwich Spread & Burger Sauce | 1 Tbsp | 50 | 4 | 72 | <1 | <5 | 105 | 0 | 0 | 3 | 0 | 1 fat |
| ✔Sweet & Sour Sauce | 2 Tbsp | 60 | 0 | 0 | 0 | 0 | 125 | 0 | 0 | 14 | 1 | 1 carb |
| **La Choy** | | | | | | | | | | | | |
| Chun King Hot Teriyaki Sauce | 1 Tbsp | 17 | 0 | 0 | 0 | 0 | 994 | 2 | 0 | 3 | 0 | free |

| | Serving | Cal. | Fat (g) | | | Sod. (mg) | | | Carb. (g) | Carb. Ch. | |
| --- | --- | --- | --- | --- | --- | --- | --- | --- | --- | --- | --- |
| ✔Light Teriyaki Sauce | 1 Tbsp | 18 | <1 | 0 | 0 | 439 | 1 | 0 | 4 | 0 | free |
| ✔Plum Sauce | 1 oz | 45 | <1 | 0 | 0 | 17 | <1 | NA | 11 | 1 | 1 carb |
| Stir Fry Mandarin Soy Sauce | 1/2 cup | 71 | <1 | 0 | 0 | 851 | 2 | 1 | 16 | 1 | 1 carb |
| ✔Stir Fry Sweet & Sour Sauce | 1 Tbsp | 26 | <1 | 0 | 0 | 59 | <1 | 0 | 7 | 1/2 | 1/2 carb |
| Stir Fry Szechuan Sauce | 1/2 cup | 73 | <1 | 12 | 0 | 612 | 3 | 2 | 16 | 1 | 1 carb |
| Stir Fry Teriyaki Sauce | 1/2 cup | 90 | <1 | 0 | 0 | 997 | 2 | 1 | 21 | 1 1/2 | 1 1/2 carb |
| ✔Teriyaki Sauce | 1 Tbsp | 17 | <1 | 0 | 0 | 917 | 1 | 0 | 3 | 0 | free |
| **Libby's** | | | | | | | | | | | |
| ✔Sloppy Joe Sauce | 1/3 cup | 45 | 0 | 0 | 0 | 430 | 1 | 1 | 10 | 1/2 | 1/2 carb |
| **Old El Paso** | | | | | | | | | | | |
| ✔Green Chili Enchilada Sauce | 1/4 cup | 30 | 2 | 60 | 0 | 330 | <1 | 0 | 3 | 0 | free |
| ✔Grilling Sauce, All Varieties (Avg) | 2 Tbsp | 60 | 0 | 0 | 0 | 380 | <1 | 0 | 14 | 1 | 1 carb |
| ✔Jalapeno Relish | 1 Tbsp | 5 | 0 | 0 | 0 | 110 | 0 | 0 | 1 | 0 | free |
| ✔Mild Enchilada Sauce | 1/4 cup | 30 | 2 | 60 | 0 | 190 | 0 | 0 | 4 | 0 | free |
| ✔Taco Sauce, All Varieties (Avg) | 1 Tbsp | 5 | 0 | 0 | 0 | 80 | 0 | 0 | 1 | 0 | free |
| ✔Tomatoes & Green Chilis | 1/4 cup | 10 | 0 | 0 | 0 | 300 | 0 | 0 | 2 | 0 | free |
| **Ortega** | | | | | | | | | | | |
| ✔Chile/Jalapeno Sauce/ Puree, All Varieties (Avg) | 1/4 cup | 15 | 0 | 0 | 0 | 0 | 1 | 0 | 3 | 0 | free |

✔= Best Bet; NA = Not Available; Carb. Ch. = Carbohydrate Choices

| Sauces (Continued) | Serving Size | Cal. | Fat (g) | % Cal. Fat | Sat. Fat (g) | Chol. (mg) | Sod. (mg) | Pro. (g) | Fiber (g) | Carb. (g) | Carb. Ch. | Servings/Exchanges |
|---|---|---|---|---|---|---|---|---|---|---|---|---|
| ✓Enchilada Sauce | 1 oz | 12 | 0 | 0 | 0 | 0 | 280 | 0 | 0 | 3 | 0 | free |
| ✓Picante Sauce, All Varieties (Avg) | 1 oz | 10 | 0 | 0 | 0 | 0 | 300 | 0 | 1 | 2 | 0 | free |
| Taco Sauce, All Varieties (Avg) | 1 oz | 10 | 0 | 0 | 0 | 0 | 610 | 0 | 0 | 3 | 0 | free |
| **Pancho Villa** | | | | | | | | | | | | |
| ✓Taco Sauce, Mild | 2 Tbsp | 15 | 0 | 0 | 0 | 0 | 170 | 0 | 0 | 3 | 0 | free |
| **Progresso** | | | | | | | | | | | | |
| Authentic White Clam Sauce | 1/2 cup | 150 | 10 | 60 | 2 | 20 | 710 | 9 | 0 | 5 | 0 | 1 med-fat meat, 1 fat |
| Creamy Clam Sauce | 1/2 cup | 110 | 6 | 49 | 2 | 10 | 440 | 5 | 0 | 8 | 1/2 | 1/2 carb, 1 fat |
| Lobster Sauce | 1/2 cup | 100 | 7 | 63 | 1 | 2 | 430 | 3 | 2 | 6 | 1/2 | 1/2 carb, 1 fat |
| ✓Red Clam Sauce | 1/2 cup | 60 | 1 | 15 | 0 | 10 | 350 | 4 | 1 | 8 | 1/2 | 1/2 carb, 1 very lean meat |
| White Clam Sauce | 1/2 cup | 140 | 10 | 64 | 2 | 15 | 510 | 7 | 0 | 5 | 0 | 1 med-fat meat, 1 fat |
| **Que Bueno** | | | | | | | | | | | | |
| ✓Enchilada Sauce | 1/2 cup | 60 | 2 | 30 | 0 | 0 | 320 | 2 | 1 | 8 | 1/2 | 1/2 carb |
| ✓Picante Sauce | 1 Tbsp | 5 | 0 | 0 | 0 | 0 | 130 | <1 | 0 | 1 | 0 | free |
| ✓Taco Sauce | 2 Tbsp | 15 | 0 | 0 | 0 | 0 | 130 | 0 | <1 | 3 | 0 | free |
| **Rosarita** | | | | | | | | | | | | |
| ✓Enchilada Sauce, Mild | 2.5 oz | 25 | 1 | 36 | 1 | 0 | 230 | 1 | 1 | 3 | 0 | free |

| | Serving Size | Cal. | Fat (g) | % Cal. Fat | Sat. Fat (g) | Chol. (mg) | Sod. (mg) | Carb. (g) | Fiber (g) | Prot. (g) | Carb. Ch. | Exchanges |
|---|---|---|---|---|---|---|---|---|---|---|---|---|
| ✔Zesty Jalapeno Picante Sauce | 2 Tbsp | 8 | <1 | 0 | 0 | 0 | 246 | 2 | | <1 | 0 | free |
| **Simmer Chef** | | | | | | | | | | | | |
| Creamy Mushroom Herb Sauce | 1/2 cup | 110 | 9 | 74 | 2 | 5 | 580 | 7 | 0 | 0 | 1/2 | 1/2 carb, 2 fat |
| Family Style Stroganoff Sauce | 1/2 cup | 110 | 7 | 57 | 5 | 5 | 760 | 8 | 1 | 2 | 1/2 | 1/2 carb, 1 fat |
| ✔Golden Honey Mustard Sauce | 1/2 cup | 150 | 2 | 12 | 0 | 0 | 400 | 30 | 1 | 1 | 2 | 2 carb |
| Hearty Onion Mushroom Sauce | 1/2 cup | 50 | 1 | 18 | 0 | 0 | 670 | 9 | 1 | 1 | 1/2 | 1/2 carb |
| Old Country Cacciatore Sauce | 1/2 cup | 110 | 4 | 33 | 4 | 0 | 540 | 15 | 2 | 2 | 1 | 1 carb, 1 fat |
| ✔Oriental Sweet & Sour Sauce | 1/2 cup | 110 | 1 | 8 | 0 | 0 | 280 | 23 | 0 | 0 | 1 1/2 | 1 1/2 carb |
| ✔Zesty Tomato Mexicali Sauce | 1/2 cup | 90 | 3 | 30 | 1 | 1 | 400 | 16 | 1 | 2 | 1 | 1 carb, 1 fat |
| **Tabasco** | | | | | | | | | | | | |
| ✔Pepper Sauce | 1 Tbsp | 2 | <1 | <1 | 0 | 0 | 87 | <1 | <1 | <1 | 0 | free |
| **Taco Bell Home Originals** | | | | | | | | | | | | |
| ✔Restaurant Hot Sauce | 1 tsp | 0 | 0 | 0 | 0 | 0 | 50 | 0 | 0 | 0 | 0 | free |
| ✔Taco Sauce, All Varieties (Avg) | 2 Tbsp | 15 | 0 | 0 | 0 | 0 | 160 | 3 | <1 | 0 | 0 | free |
| **SAUERKRAUT** | | | | | | | | | | | | |
| **(Generic)** | | | | | | | | | | | | |
| Sauerkraut, Canned | 1/2 cup | 22 | <1 | 0 | 0 | 0 | 780 | 5 | 3 | 1 | 0 | 1 vegetable |

✔ = Best Bet; NA = Not Available; Carb. Ch. = Carbohydrate Choices

## SAUSAGE

| Product | Serving Size | Cal. | Fat (g) | % Cal. Fat | Sat. Fat (g) | Chol. (mg) | Sod. (mg) | Pro. (g) | Fiber (g) | Carb. (g) | Carb. Ch. | Servings/Exchanges |
|---|---|---|---|---|---|---|---|---|---|---|---|---|
| **Libby's** | | | | | | | | | | | | |
| Chicken Vienna Sausage | 2 oz | 130 | 10 | 69 | NA | NA | 560 | 7 | 0 | 3 | 0 | 1 high-fat meat |
| Vienna Sausage | 2 oz | 160 | 15 | 84 | NA | NA | 330 | 6 | 0 | 1 | 0 | 1 high-fat meat, 1 fat |
| Vienna Sausage in BBQ Sauce | 2.5 oz | 180 | 15 | 75 | NA | NA | 420 | 8 | 0 | 2 | 0 | 1 high-fat meat, 1 fat |
| **Louis Rich** | | | | | | | | | | | | |
| Turkey & Cheddar Smoked Sausage | 2 oz | 95 | 6 | 57 | 2 | 35 | 540 | 9 | 0 | 2 | 0 | 2 lean meat |
| Turkey Polska Kielbasa Sausage | 2 oz | 80 | 4 | 45 | 2 | 40 | 495 | 9 | 0 | <1 | 0 | 1 med-fat meat |
| Turkey Sausage Links | 2 | 95 | 6 | 57 | 6 | 35 | 470 | 11 | 0 | <1 | 0 | 2 lean meat |
| Turkey Sausage-Smoked | 2 oz | 90 | 5 | 50 | 2 | 35 | 515 | 8 | 0 | 2 | 0 | 1 med-fat meat |
| **Oscar Mayer** | | | | | | | | | | | | |
| Beef Summer Sausage | 2 slices | 140 | 12 | 77 | 5 | 35 | 640 | 7 | 0 | 1 | 0 | 1 high-fat meat, 1 fat |
| Braunschweiger Spread-Liver Sausage | 2 oz | 190 | 17 | 81 | 6 | 90 | 630 | 8 | 0 | 2 | 0 | 1 high-fat meat, 2 fat |
| Braunschweiger-Liver Sausage | 1 slice | 100 | 9 | 81 | 3 | 50 | 320 | 4 | 0 | 1 | 0 | 1 high-fat meat |
| New England Brand Sausage | 2 slices | 60 | 3 | 45 | 1 | 25 | 570 | 8 | 0 | 1 | 0 | 1 lean meat |
| Pork Sausage Link | 2 | 170 | 15 | 79 | 5 | 40 | 410 | 9 | 0 | 1 | 0 | 2 high-fat meat |
| Smokie Links Sausage | 1 | 130 | 12 | 83 | 4 | 25 | 430 | 5 | 0 | 1 | 0 | 1 high-fat meat, 1 fat |
| Smokies Sausage-Little | 6 | 170 | 15 | 79 | 6 | 35 | 570 | 7 | 0 | 1 | 0 | 1 high-fat meat, 2 fat |

| Product | Amount | Cal. | Fat (g) | % Cal. Fat | Sat. Fat (g) | Chol. (mg) | Sod. (mg) | Carb. (g) | Fiber (g) | Prot. (g) | Carb. Ch. | Exchanges/Choices |
|---|---|---|---|---|---|---|---|---|---|---|---|---|
| Smokies-Little Cheese | 6 | 180 | 16 | 80 | 6 | 40 | 590 | 1 | 0 | 7 | 0 | 1 high-fat meat, 2 fat |
| Summer Sausage | 2 slices | 140 | 13 | 84 | 5 | 40 | 650 | 0 | 0 | 7 | 0 | 1 high-fat meat, 1 fat |
| **SEAFOOD (CANNED)** | | | | | | | | | | | | |
| **(Generic)** | | | | | | | | | | | | |
| Anchovies Rolled Fillets | 5 pieces | 25 | 2 | 72 | 0 | 12 | 980 | 0 | 0 | 3 | 0 | 1 fat |
| ✓ Crabmeat | 2 oz | 40 | 0 | 0 | 0 | 40 | 400 | 2 | 0 | 7 | 0 | 1 very lean meat |
| Sardines in Tomato Sauce | 1/4 cup | 80 | 4 | 45 | 2 | 36 | 170 | 1 | 1 | 10 | 0 | 1 med-fat meat |
| Smoked Oysters in Oil | 3 oz | 170 | 9 | 48 | 4 | 20 | 280 | 8 | <1 | 14 | 1/2 | 1/2 carb, 2 med-fat meat |
| **Progresso** | | | | | | | | | | | | |
| ✓ Minced Clams | 1/4 cup | 25 | 0 | 0 | 0 | 10 | 250 | 2 | 0 | 4 | 0 | 1 very lean meat |
| **SEAFOOD (FROZEN)** | | | | | | | | | | | | |
| **Mrs. Paul's** | | | | | | | | | | | | |
| Breaded Shrimp, Garlic & Herb | 1 | 340 | 15 | 39 | 3 | 910 | 910 | 33 | 3 | 19 | 2 | 2 carb, 2 med-fat meat, 1 fat |
| Breaded Shrimp, Special Recipe | 1 | 350 | 16 | 41 | 3 | 95 | 720 | 32 | 2 | 20 | 2 | 2 carb, 2 med-fat meat, 1 fat |
| Deviled Crabs | 3 oz | 180 | 9 | 45 | 3 | 25 | 540 | 19 | <1 | 7 | 1 | 1 carb, 1 med-fat meat, 1 fat |

✓ = Best Bet; NA = Not Available; Carb. Ch. = Carbohydrate Choices

| Seafood (Frozen) (*Continued*) | Serving Size | Cal. | Fat (g) | % Cal. Fat | Sat. Fat (g) | Chol. (mg) | Sod. (mg) | Pro. (g) | Fiber (g) | Carb. (g) | Carb. Ch. | Servings/Exchanges |
|---|---|---|---|---|---|---|---|---|---|---|---|---|
| **Sea Pak** | | | | | | | | | | | | |
| Oriental Breaded Butterfly Shrimp | 4 oz | 150 | 1 | 6 | 0 | 70 | 680 | 11 | 1 | 22 | 1 1/2 | 1 1/2 carb, 1 very lean meat |
| **Van De Kamp's** | | | | | | | | | | | | |
| Breaded Butterfly Shrimp | 7 | 300 | 15 | 45 | 3 | 80 | 610 | 10 | 3 | 30 | 2 | 2 carb, 1 med-fat meat, 2 fat |
| Breaded Popcorn Shrimp | 20 | 270 | 12 | 40 | 2 | 80 | 850 | 10 | 2 | 30 | 2 | 2 carb, 1 med-fat meat, 2 fat |
| Cheese & Crab Poppers | 4 | 320 | 16 | 45 | 7 | 35 | 800 | 17 | <1 | 27 | 2 | 2 carb, 2 med-fat meat, 1 fat |
| Crab Cakes | 1 | 170 | 9 | 48 | 2 | 15 | 460 | 6 | <1 | 17 | 1 | 1 carb, 2 fat |
| Stuffed Shrimp | 3 | 290 | 13 | 40 | 5 | 70 | 720 | 12 | <1 | 32 | 2 | 2 carb, 1 med-fat meat, 1 fat |

## SEAFOOD MEALS/ENTREES (FROZEN)

### Armour Classics Lite

| | Serving Size | Cal. | Fat (g) | % Cal. Fat | Sat. Fat (g) | Chol. (mg) | Sod. (mg) | Pro. (g) | Fiber (g) | Carb. (g) | Carb. Ch. | Servings/Exchanges |
|---|---|---|---|---|---|---|---|---|---|---|---|---|
| ✓Shrimp Creole Dinner | 11.25 oz dinner | 260 | 2 | 7 | NA | 45 | 900 | 6 | NA | 53 | 3 1/2 | 3 1/2 carb |

## Budget Gourmet

| | | | | | | | | | | | |
|---|---|---|---|---|---|---|---|---|---|---|---|
| Linguine w/Shrimp | 10 oz meal | 330 | 15 | 41 | NA | 75 | 1250 | 15 | NA | 33 | 2 | 2 carb, 1 med-fat meat, 2 fat |
| ✔Seafood Marinara | 11.5 oz meal | 320 | 9 | 25 | NA | 70 | 690 | 16 | NA | 43 | 3 | 3 carb, 1 med-fat meat, 1 fat |
| Seafood Newburg | 10 oz dinner | 350 | 12 | 31 | NA | 70 | 660 | 17 | NA | 43 | 3 | 3 carb, 1 med-fat meat, 1 fat |
| Shrimp & Fettuccine | 9.5 oz meal | 375 | 20 | 48 | NA | 145 | 660 | 10 | NA | 38 | 2 1/2 | 2 1/2 carb, 1 med-fat meat, 3 fat |
| ✔Shrimp w/ Scallops Marinara | 11.5 oz meal | 320 | 9 | 26 | NA | 70 | 690 | 16 | NA | 43 | 3 | 3 carb, 1 med-fat meat, 1 fat |

## Fan Sea Seafoods

| | | | | | | | | | | | |
|---|---|---|---|---|---|---|---|---|---|---|---|
| Crab Cakes Maryland Style | 1 | 150 | 8 | 48 | 1 | 60 | 360 | 11 | <1 | 10 | 1/2 | 1/2 carb, 1 med-fat meat, 1 fat |

## Fishery Products International

| | | | | | | | | | | | |
|---|---|---|---|---|---|---|---|---|---|---|---|
| Shrimp Scampi | 4 oz (8 shrimp) | 300 | 29 | 87 | 6 | 110 | 300 | 12 | 0 | 0 | 0 | 2 med-fat meat, 4 fat |

## Gourmet Dining

| | | | | | | | | | | | |
|---|---|---|---|---|---|---|---|---|---|---|---|
| ✔Shrimp Stir Fry Meal w/Sauce | 8 oz | 180 | 0 | 0 | 0 | 95 | 810 | 16 | 4 | 28 | 2 | 2 carb, 1 very lean meat |

✔= Best Bet; NA = Not Available; Carb. Ch. = Carbohydrate Choices

| Seafood Meals/Entrees (Frozen) (*Continued*) | Serving Size | Cal. | Fat (g) | % Cal. Fat | Sat. Fat (g) | Chol. (mg) | Sod. (mg) | Pro. (g) | Fiber (g) | Carb. (g) | Carb. Ch. | Servings/Exchanges |
|---|---|---|---|---|---|---|---|---|---|---|---|---|
| **Healthy Choice** | | | | | | | | | | | | |
| Shrimp & Vegetables | 11.8 oz meal | 270 | 6 | 20 | 3 | 50 | 580 | 15 | 6 | 39 | 2 1/2 | 2 1/2 carb, 1 med-fat meat |
| **Lean Cuisine** | | | | | | | | | | | | |
| ✔Café Classics, Shrimp and Angel Hair Pasta | 10 oz meal | 290 | 6 | 17 | 1 | 55 | 590 | 16 | 1 | 42 | 3 | 3 carb, 1 med-fat meat |
| **SHERBERT/SORBET** | | | | | | | | | | | | |
| **Ben & Jerry's** | | | | | | | | | | | | |
| ✔Lemon Swirl Sorbet | 1/2 cup | 120 | 0 | 0 | 0 | 0 | 15 | 0 | 9 | 30 | 2 | 2 carb |
| ✔Purple Passion Fruit Sorbet | 1/2 cup | 140 | 0 | 0 | 0 | 0 | 25 | 0 | 0 | 22 | 1 1/2 | 1 1/2 carb |
| **Dole** | | | | | | | | | | | | |
| ✔Nonfat Orange Sorbet | 1/2 cup | 110 | 0 | 0 | 0 | 0 | 9 | <1 | 0 | 28 | 2 | 2 carb |
| ✔Pineapple Nonfat Sorbet | 1/2 cup | 120 | <1 | 8 | NA | 0 | 11 | <1 | 0 | 28 | 2 | 2 carb |
| **Haagen Dazs** | | | | | | | | | | | | |
| ✔Nonfat Lemon Sorbet | 1/2 cup | 140 | 0 | 0 | 0 | 0 | 5 | 1 | 0 | 34 | 2 | 2 carb |
| Orange & Vanilla Sorbet | 1/2 cup | 190 | 8 | 38 | 0 | 0 | 35 | 3 | 0 | 27 | 2 | 2 carb, 2 fat |
| Raspberry Sorbet | 1/2 cup | 180 | 8 | 42 | 0 | 0 | 35 | 2 | 0 | 23 | 1 1/2 | 1 1/2 carb, 2 fat |

## SHORTENING

### Crisco

| | Serving Size | Cal. | Fat (g) | % Cal. Fat | Sat. Fat (g) | Chol. (mg) | Sod. (mg) | Prot. (g) | Fiber (g) | Carb. (g) | Carb. Ch. | Exchanges |
|---|---|---|---|---|---|---|---|---|---|---|---|---|
| Vegetable Shortening | 1 Tbsp | 110 | 12 | 98 | 3 | 0 | 0 | 0 | 0 | 0 | 0 | 2 fat |

## SNACK BARS

### Betty Crocker

| | Serving Size | Cal. | Fat (g) | % Cal. Fat | Sat. Fat (g) | Chol. (mg) | Sod. (mg) | Prot. (g) | Fiber (g) | Carb. (g) | Carb. Ch. | Exchanges |
|---|---|---|---|---|---|---|---|---|---|---|---|---|
| ✔Golden Grahams Treats, Peanut Butter Chocolate | 1 | 90 | 3 | 30 | <1 | 0 | 100 | 1 | 0 | 17 | 1 | 1 carb, 1 fat |
| Golden Grahams Treats, S'Mores Chocolate Chunk | 1 | 90 | 4 | 40 | 1 | 0 | 105 | 1 | 0 | 15 | 1 | 1 carb, 1 fat |
| ✔Sweet Rewards Fat-Free Bars, Blueberry w/Drizzle | 1 | 120 | 0 | 0 | 0 | 0 | 80 | 1 | <1 | 29 | 2 | 2 carb |
| ✔Sweet Rewards Fat-Free Bars, Double Fudge Supreme | 1 | 100 | 0 | 0 | 0 | 0 | 90 | 2 | 1 | 25 | 1 1/2 | 1 1/2 carb |

### Betty Crocker/Sweet Rewards

| | Serving Size | Cal. | Fat (g) | % Cal. Fat | Sat. Fat (g) | Chol. (mg) | Sod. (mg) | Prot. (g) | Fiber (g) | Carb. (g) | Carb. Ch. | Exchanges |
|---|---|---|---|---|---|---|---|---|---|---|---|---|
| ✔Fat-Free Snack Bar, Homestyle Brownie | 1 bar | 100 | 0 | 0 | 0 | 0 | 120 | 2 | 1 | 24 | 1 1/2 | 1 1/2 carb |
| ✔Fat-Free Snack Bar, Raspberry | 1 bar | 120 | 0 | 0 | 0 | 0 | 80 | 1 | <1 | 29 | 2 | 2 carb |
| ✔Fat-Free Snack Bar, Strawberry w/Drizzle | 1 bar | 120 | 0 | 0 | 0 | 0 | 80 | 1 | <1 | 29 | 2 | 2 carb |

### Clinical Products

| | Serving Size | Cal. | Fat (g) | % Cal. Fat | Sat. Fat (g) | Chol. (mg) | Sod. (mg) | Prot. (g) | Fiber (g) | Carb. (g) | Carb. Ch. | Exchanges |
|---|---|---|---|---|---|---|---|---|---|---|---|---|
| ✔Extend Bar, Peanut Butter Crunch | 1 | 160 | 3 | 17 | 0 | 0 | 85 | 4 | 0 | 30 | 2 | 2 carb, 1 fat |

✔ = Best Bet; NA = Not Available; Carb. Ch. = Carbohydrate Choices

| Snack Bars (*Continued*) | Serving Size | Cal. | Fat (g) | % Cal. Fat | Sat. Fat (g) | Chol. (mg) | Sod. (mg) | Pro. (g) | Fiber (g) | Carb. (g) | Carb. Ch. | Servings/Exchanges |
|---|---|---|---|---|---|---|---|---|---|---|---|---|
| **Estee** | | | | | | | | | | | | |
| ✔Rice Crunchie Bar, All Flavors (Avg) | 1 | 50 | 0 | 0 | 0 | 0 | 40 | 1 | <1 | 15 | 1 | 1 carb |
| **SNACK CAKES** | | | | | | | | | | | | |
| **Estee** | | | | | | | | | | | | |
| ✔Sugar-Free Mini Rice Cakes, All Flavors (Avg) | 5 | 60 | <1 | 15 | 0 | 0 | 20 | 1 | 5 | 14 | 1 | 1 carb |
| **Hostess** | | | | | | | | | | | | |
| Ding Dongs | 1 | 170 | 9 | 48 | 6 | 5 | 115 | 2 | 1 | 21 | 1 1/2 | 1 1/2 carb, 2 fat |
| Ho Ho's | 1 | 120 | 6 | 45 | 4 | 10 | 70 | 1 | <1 | 16 | 1 | 1 carb, 1 fat |
| Twinkies | 1 | 150 | 5 | 30 | 2 | 20 | 200 | 2 | <1 | 27 | 2 | 2 carb, 1 fat |
| **SNACK MIXES** | | | | | | | | | | | | |
| **Betty Crocker** | | | | | | | | | | | | |
| Chex Mix, Nacho Fiesta/Hot n' Spicy/ Traditional (Avg) | 2/3 cup | 130 | 4 | 28 | <1 | 0 | 385 | 2 | 2 | 22 | 1 1/2 | 1 1/2 carb, 1 fat |
| Chex Mix, Peanut Lovers/Bold Party Blend/Cheddar Cheese (Avg) | 1/2 cup | 140 | 6 | 39 | 1 | 0 | 355 | 3 | 2 | 20 | 1 | 1 carb, 1 fat |
| **Del Monte** | | | | | | | | | | | | |
| Sierra Trail Mix | 1/4 cup | 150 | 8 | 48 | 3 | 0 | 65 | 4 | 3 | 20 | 1 | 1 carb, 1 high-fat meat |

| Product | Serving | Cal. | Fat (g) | % Cal. Fat | Sat. Fat (g) | Chol. (mg) | Sod. (mg) | Prot. (g) | Fiber (g) | Carb. (g) | Carb. Ch. | Exchanges |
|---|---|---|---|---|---|---|---|---|---|---|---|---|
| ✓Yogurt Raisins, Strawberry/Vanilla | 0.9 oz bag | 110 | 3 | 25 | 3 | 0 | 40 | 2 | 0 | 20 | 1 | 1 carb, 1 fat |
| **Estee** | | | | | | | | | | | | |
| ✓Fruit & Nut Mix | 1/4 cup | 210 | 12 | 51 | 7 | <5 | 45 | 6 | 2 | 19 | 1 | 1 carb, 2 fat |
| **Gardetto's** | | | | | | | | | | | | |
| Chips & Twists Snack Mix, Sour Cream & Chive | 1/2 cup | 130 | 4 | 28 | 4 | <1 | 310 | 3 | 2 | 21 | 1 1/2 | 1 strch, 1 fat |
| Snak-ens Reduced Fat Snack Mix | 1/2 cup | 140 | 5 | 32 | 1 | 0 | 320 | 3 | 1 | 20 | 1 | 1 strch, 1 fat |
| Snak-ens Snack Mix, Original | 1/2 cup | 160 | 8 | 45 | 2 | 0 | 300 | 3 | 1 | 19 | 1 | 1 strch, 2 fat |
| **Pepperidge Farm** | | | | | | | | | | | | |
| Cheddar Goldfish Snack Mix | 1/2 cup | 160 | 7 | 39 | 2 | <5 | 370 | 3 | 1 | 19 | 1 | 1 strch, 1 fat |
| ✓Fat-Free Pretzel Goldfish Snack Mix | 1/2 cup | 100 | 0 | 0 | 0 | 0 | 400 | 3 | <1 | 21 | 1 1/2 | 1 1/2 strch |
| Garlic w/Bagel Chips Goldfish Snack Mix | 1/2 cup | 140 | 5 | 32 | <1 | 0 | 360 | 3 | 1 | 22 | 1 1/2 | 1 1/2 strch, 1 fat |
| Original Goldfish Snack Mix | 1/2 cup | 170 | 8 | 42 | 2 | <5 | 380 | 5 | 2 | 19 | 1 | 1 strch, 2 fat |
| Savory Goldfish Snack Mix | 1/2 cup | 150 | 7 | 42 | 1 | 0 | 380 | 3 | 1 | 20 | 1 | 1 strch, 1 fat |
| **Sunshine** | | | | | | | | | | | | |
| Cheez It Snack Mix | 1/2 cup | 130 | 5 | 35 | 1 | 0 | 330 | 3 | 2 | 21 | 1 1/2 | 1 1/2 strch, 1 fat |
| Cheez It Snack Mix, Big Crunch | 3/4 cup | 110 | 6 | 49 | 1 | 0 | 360 | 3 | <1 | 20 | 1 | 1 strch, 1 fat |
| Cheez It Snack Mix, Double Cheese | 3/4 cup | 110 | 5 | 41 | 1 | 0 | 450 | 3 | <1 | 19 | 1 | 1 strch, 1 fat |
| ✓Cheez It, Reduced-Fat Party Mix | 1/2 cup | 130 | 3 | 21 | <1 | 0 | 300 | 4 | 1 | 21 | 1 1/2 | 1 1/2 strch, 1 fat |

✓ = Best Bet; NA = Not Available; Carb. Ch. = Carbohydrate Choices

# SODA POP

| Product | Serving Size | Cal. | Fat (g) | % Cal. Fat | Sat. Fat (g) | Chol. (mg) | Sod. (mg) | Pro. (g) | Fiber (g) | Carb. (g) | Carb. Ch. | Servings/Exchanges |
|---|---|---|---|---|---|---|---|---|---|---|---|---|
| **(Generic)** | | | | | | | | | | | | |
| ✔Club Soda | 12 oz | 0 | 0 | 0 | 0 | 0 | 75 | 0 | 0 | 0 | 0 | free |
| ✔Cream Soda | 12 oz | 189 | 0 | 0 | 0 | 0 | 45 | 0 | 0 | 49 | 3 | 3 carb |
| ✔Ginger Ale Soda Pop | 12 oz | 124 | 0 | 0 | 0 | 0 | 26 | 0 | 0 | 32 | 2 | 2 carb |
| **7-Up** | | | | | | | | | | | | |
| ✔7-Up Soda Pop | 12 oz | 140 | 0 | 0 | 0 | 0 | 75 | 0 | 0 | 39 | 2 1/2 | 2 1/2 carb |
| **Barq's** | | | | | | | | | | | | |
| ✔Barq's Root Beer | 12 oz | 160 | 0 | 0 | 0 | 0 | 70 | 0 | 0 | 45 | 3 | 3 carb |
| **Citra** | | | | | | | | | | | | |
| ✔Citra Soda Pop | 12 oz | 150 | 0 | 0 | 0 | 0 | 60 | 0 | 0 | 36 | 2 1/2 | 2 1/2 carb |
| **Coca-Cola** | | | | | | | | | | | | |
| ✔Cherry Coke | 12 oz | 150 | 0 | 0 | 0 | 0 | 40 | 0 | 0 | 42 | 3 | 3 carb |
| ✔Coca-Cola Classic | 12 oz | 140 | 0 | 0 | 0 | 0 | 50 | 0 | 0 | 39 | 2 1/2 | 2 1/2 carb |
| ✔Diet Coke | 12 oz | 0 | 0 | 0 | 0 | 0 | 40 | 0 | 0 | 0 | 0 | free |
| **Dr. Pepper** | | | | | | | | | | | | |
| ✔Dr. Pepper Soda Pop | 12 oz | 150 | 0 | 0 | 0 | 0 | 55 | 0 | 0 | 40 | 2 1/2 | 2 1/2 carb |

### Fresca

| | | | | | | | | | |
|---|---|---|---|---|---|---|---|---|---|
| ✔Fresca Soda Pop | 12 oz | 0 | 0 | 0 | 35 | 0 | 0 | 0 | free |

### Minute Maid

| | | | | | | | | | |
|---|---|---|---|---|---|---|---|---|---|
| ✔Minute Maid Orange Soda Pop | 12 oz | 170 | 0 | 0 | 35 | 0 | 47 | 3 | 3 carb |

### Pepsi Cola

| | | | | | | | | | |
|---|---|---|---|---|---|---|---|---|---|
| ✔Diet Pepsi | 12 oz | 0 | 0 | 0 | 35 | 0 | 0 | 0 | free |
| ✔Mountain Dew Soda Pop | 12 oz | 170 | 0 | 0 | 70 | 0 | 46 | 3 | 3 carb |
| ✔Pepsi One | 12 oz | 0 | 0 | 0 | 45 | 0 | 0 | 0 | free |
| ✔Pepsi Soda Pop | 12 oz | 150 | 0 | 0 | 35 | 0 | 41 | 3 | 3 carb |
| ✔Wild Cherry Pepsi | 12 oz | 165 | 0 | 0 | 35 | 0 | 43 | 3 | 3 carb |

### Slice

| | | | | | | | | | |
|---|---|---|---|---|---|---|---|---|---|
| ✔Lemon Lime Soda Pop | 12 oz | 150 | 0 | 0 | 55 | 0 | 40 | 2 1/2 | 2 1/2 carb |
| ✔Orange Soda Pop | 12 oz | 190 | 0 | 0 | 55 | 0 | 50 | 3 | 3 carb |

### Sprite

| | | | | | | | | | |
|---|---|---|---|---|---|---|---|---|---|
| ✔Sprite Soda Pop | 12 oz | 140 | 0 | 0 | 70 | 0 | 38 | 2 1/2 | 2 1/2 carb |

### Sunkist

| | | | | | | | | | |
|---|---|---|---|---|---|---|---|---|---|
| ✔Orange Soda | 12 oz | 190 | 0 | 0 | 45 | 0 | 52 | 3 1/2 | 3 1/2 carb |

### TAB

| | | | | | | | | | |
|---|---|---|---|---|---|---|---|---|---|
| ✔TAB Soda Pop | 12 oz | 0 | 0 | 0 | 40 | 0 | 0 | 0 | free |

✔ = Best Bet; NA = Not Available; Carb. Ch. = Carbohydrate Choices

| Soda Pop (*Continued*) | Serving Size | Cal. | Fat (g) | % Cal. Fat | Sat. Fat (g) | Chol. (mg) | Sod. (mg) | Pro. (g) | Fiber (g) | Carb. (g) | Carb. Ch. | Servings/Exchanges |
|---|---|---|---|---|---|---|---|---|---|---|---|---|
| **Welch's** | | | | | | | | | | | | |
| ✓Grape Soda Pop | 12 oz | 190 | 0 | 0 | 0 | 0 | 55 | 0 | 0 | 51 | 3 1/2 | 3 1/2 carb |
| **SOUP (CANNED)** | | | | | | | | | | | | |
| **Campbells** | | | | | | | | | | | | |
| Vegetable Beef | 1 cup | 80 | 2 | 23 | <1 | 10 | 810 | 5 | 2 | 10 | 1/2 | 1/2 strch |
| 98% Fat-free Cream of Broccoli | 1 cup | 80 | 3 | 34 | 1 | 3 | 730 | 2 | 1 | 12 | 1 | 1 strch, 1 fat |
| 98% Fat-free Cream of Chicken | 1 cup | 80 | 3 | 34 | 2 | 10 | 830 | 3 | 0 | 10 | 1 | 1 strch, 1 fat |
| 98% Fat-Free Cream of Mushroom | 1 cup | 70 | 3 | 39 | 1 | 3 | 830 | 1 | 0 | 9 | 1/2 | 1/2 strch, 1 fat |
| Beef Consomme | 1 cup | 25 | 0 | 0 | 0 | 0 | 820 | 4 | 0 | 2 | 0 | 1 very lean meat |
| Black Bean | 1 cup | 120 | 2 | 15 | <1 | 0 | 1030 | 6 | 5 | 19 | 1 | 1 strch |
| Broccoli Cheese | 1 cup | 110 | 7 | 57 | 3 | 10 | 860 | 3 | 2 | 9 | 1/2 | 1/2 strch, 1 fat |
| Cheddar Cheese | 1 cup | 90 | 4 | 40 | 3 | 10 | 950 | 5 | 1 | 10 | 1/2 | 1/2 strch, 1 fat |
| Chicken & Stars | 1 cup | 70 | 2 | 26 | <1 | 1 | 1010 | 3 | 1 | 9 | 1/2 | 1/2 strch |
| Chicken Alphabet w/Vegetable | 1 cup | 80 | 2 | 23 | <1 | 10 | 880 | 4 | 1 | 11 | 1 | 1 strch |
| Chicken Dumpling | 1 cup | 80 | 3 | 34 | <1 | 125 | 1049 | 4 | 2 | 10 | 1/2 | 1/2 strch, 1 fat |
| Chicken Gumbo | 1 cup | 60 | 2 | 30 | <1 | 10 | 990 | 2 | 1 | 9 | 1/2 | 1/2 strch |
| Chicken Noodle | 1 cup | 70 | 2 | 26 | 1 | 15 | 980 | 3 | 1 | 9 | 1/2 | 1/2 strch, 1 fat |
| Chicken Vegetable | 1 cup | 80 | 2 | 23 | <1 | 10 | 940 | 3 | 2 | 12 | 1 | 1 strch |

| | Serving | Cal. | Fat (g) | % Cal. Fat | Sat. Fat (g) | Chol. (mg) | Sod. (mg) | Prot. (g) | Fiber (g) | Carb. (g) | Carb. Ch. | Exchanges |
|---|---|---|---|---|---|---|---|---|---|---|---|---|
| Chicken w/Rice | 1 cup | 70 | 3 | 39 | <1 | 3 | 940 | 3 | 0 | 9 | 1/2 | 1/2 strch, 1 fat |
| Chicken w/Wild Rice | 1 cup | 70 | 2 | 26 | <1 | 10 | 900 | 3 | 1 | 9 | 1/2 | 1 strch |
| Chicken Won Ton | 1 cup | 45 | <1 | 20 | 0 | 15 | 940 | 4 | 1 | 5 | 0 | 1 very lean meat |
| Chili Beef w/Bean | 1 cup | 170 | 5 | 26 | 3 | 15 | 910 | 7 | 4 | 24 | 1 1/2 | 1 1/2 strch, 1 fat |
| Chunky Beef | 10.8 oz | 180 | 6 | 30 | 2 | 20 | 1090 | 13 | 4 | 20 | 1 | 1 strch, 1 med-fat meat |
| Chunky Beef Pasta | 10.8 oz | 190 | 4 | 19 | 1 | 20 | 1200 | 16 | 3 | 23 | 1 1/2 | 1 1/2 strch, 2 lean meat |
| Chunky Beef w/Country Vegetable | 10.8 oz | 200 | 5 | 23 | 2 | NA | 1130 | 16 | 4 | 22 | 1 1/2 | 1 1/2 strch, 2 lean meat |
| Chunky Chicken Broccoli Cheese | 10.8 oz | 250 | 15 | 54 | 6 | 30 | 1400 | 11 | 1 | 17 | 1 | 1 strch, 1 med-fat meat, 2 fat |
| Chunky Chicken Corn Chowder | 10.8 oz | 310 | 19 | 55 | 9 | 30 | 1080 | 12 | 4 | 22 | 1 1/2 | 1 1/2 strch, 1 med-fat meat, 3 fat |
| Chunky Chicken Mushroom Chowder | 1 cup | 210 | 12 | 51 | 4 | 10 | 970 | 10 | 3 | 15 | 1 | 1 strch, 1 med-fat meat, 1 fat |
| Chunky Chicken Noodle | 1 cup | 160 | 4 | 23 | 1 | 25 | 1310 | 12 | 3 | 20 | 1 | 1 strch, 1 med-fat meat |
| Chunky Chicken Noodle w/Mushroom | 10.8 oz | 150 | 5 | 30 | 2 | 30 | 1150 | 14 | 1 | 13 | 1 | 1 strch, 1 med-fat meat |
| Chunky Chicken Rice | 1 cup | 140 | 3 | 19 | 1 | 18 | 840 | 25 | 2 | 18 | 1 | 1 strch, 3 lean meat |
| Chunky Chicken Vegetable | 1 cup | 130 | 3 | 21 | 2 | 20 | 950 | 9 | 3 | 12 | 1 | 1 strch, 1 lean meat |
| Chunky Chili Beef w/Beans | 11 oz | 300 | 7 | 21 | 2 | 20 | 1080 | 21 | 9 | 38 | 2 1/2 | 2 1/2 strch, 2 lean meat |
| Chunky Manhattan Clam Chowder | 1 cup | 130 | 4 | 28 | 1 | 5 | 900 | 6 | 3 | 20 | 1 | 1 strch, 1 fat |

✔ = Best Bet; NA = Not Available; Carb. Ch. = Carbohydrate Choices

| Soup (Canned) (Continued) | Serving Size | Cal. | Fat (g) | % Cal. Fat | Sat. Fat (g) | Chol. (mg) | Sod. (mg) | Pro. (g) | Fiber (g) | Carb. (g) | Carb. Ch. | Servings/Exchanges |
|---|---|---|---|---|---|---|---|---|---|---|---|---|
| Chunky Minestrone Soup | 1 cup | 140 | 5 | 32 | 2 | 5 | 800 | 5 | 2 | 22 | 1 1/2 | 1 1/2 strch, 1 fat |
| Chunky New England Clam Chowder | 10.8 oz | 300 | 18 | 54 | 7 | 15 | 1210 | 9 | 3 | 26 | 2 | 2 strch, 4 fat |
| Chunky Pepper Steak | 1 cup | 140 | 3 | 19 | 1 | 20 | 830 | 11 | 3 | 18 | 1 | 1 strch, 1 lean meat |
| Chunky Potato Ham Chowder | 10.8 oz | 270 | 18 | 60 | 9 | 25 | 1050 | 7 | 3 | 20 | 1 | 1 strch, 1 med-fat meat, 3 fat |
| Chunky Sirloin Burger w/Vegetables | 10.8 oz | 230 | 11 | 43 | 5 | 25 | 1160 | 12 | 5 | 25 | 1 1/2 | 1 1/2 strch, 1 med-fat meat, 1 fat |
| Chunky Split Pea n'Ham | 10.8 oz | 240 | 4 | 15 | 2 | 20 | 1400 | 18 | 4 | 33 | 2 | 2 strch, 2 lean meat |
| Chunky Steak Potato | 10.8 oz | 200 | 5 | 23 | 2 | 25 | 1100 | 15 | 4 | 24 | 1 1/2 | 1 1/2 strch, 2 lean meat |
| Chunky Stroganoff Beef | 10.8 oz | 310 | 16 | 46 | 6 | 45 | 1180 | 16 | 4 | 28 | 2 | 2 strch, 2 med-fat meat, 1 fat |
| Chunky Tortellini w/Chicken & Vegetable | 1 cup | 110 | 2 | 16 | <1 | 10 | 910 | 6 | 2 | 18 | 1 | 1 strch, 1 fat |
| Chunky Vegetable | 10.8 oz | 160 | 4 | 23 | 1 | 0 | 1090 | 4 | 5 | 28 | 2 | 2 strch, 1 fat |
| Cream Chicken Broccoli | 1 cup | 120 | 8 | 60 | 3 | 15 | 860 | 4 | 1 | 9 | 1/2 | 1/2 strch, 2 fat |
| Cream Chicken Mushroom | 1 cup | 120 | 8 | 60 | 3 | 15 | 860 | 4 | 1 | 9 | 1/2 | 1/2 strch, 2 fat |
| Cream Chicken Noodle | 1 cup | 130 | 7 | 48 | 2 | 15 | 800 | 5 | 2 | 12 | 1 | 1 strch, 1 fat |
| Cream of Asparagus | 1 cup | 90 | 4 | 40 | 1 | 5 | 860 | 3 | 1 | 11 | 1 | 1 strch, 1 fat |
| Cream of Broccoli | 1 cup | 100 | 6 | 54 | 3 | 3 | 770 | 2 | 1 | 9 | 1/2 | 1/2 strch, 1 fat |

|  | Amount |  |  |  |  |  |  |  |  |  |  | Exchanges/Choices |
| --- | --- | --- | --- | --- | --- | --- | --- | --- | --- | --- | --- | --- |
| Cream of Celery | 1 cup | 110 | 7 | 57 | 3 | 3 | 900 | 2 | 1 | 9 | 1/2 | 1/2 strch, 1 fat |
| Cream of Chicken | 1 cup | 130 | 8 | 55 | 3 | 10 | 890 | 3 | 1 | 11 | 1 | 1 strch, 2 fat |
| Cream of Mexlcan Pepper | 1 cup | 110 | 7 | 57 | 2 | 3 | 860 | 2 | 2 | 10 | 1/2 | 1/2 strch, 1 fat |
| Cream of Mushroom | 1 cup | 110 | 7 | 57 | 3 | 3 | 870 | 2 | 1 | 9 | 1/2 | 1/2 strch, 1 fat |
| Cream of Potato | 1 cup | 90 | 3 | 30 | 2 | 10 | 890 | 2 | 1 | 14 | 1 | 1 strch, 1 fat |
| Cream of Shrimp | 1 cup | 100 | 7 | 63 | 2 | 20 | 890 | 2 | 1 | 8 | 1/2 | 1/2 strch, 1 fat |
| Creamy Onion | 1 cup | 110 | 6 | 49 | 2 | 20 | 910 | 2 | 1 | 13 | 1 | 1 strch, 1 fat |
| Curly Noodle & Chicken Broth | 1 cup | 80 | 3 | 34 | <1 | 15 | 840 | 3 | 1 | 12 | 1 | 1 strch, 1 fat |
| Double Noodle & Chicken Broth | 1 cup | 100 | 3 | 27 | <1 | 15 | 810 | 4 | 2 | 15 | 1 | 1 strch, 1 fat |
| Fiesta Tomato | 1 cup | 70 | 0 | 0 | 0 | 0 | 860 | 1 | 1 | 16 | 1 | 1 strch |
| French Onion w/BeefStock | 1 cup | 70 | 3 | 39 | 0 | 3 | 980 | 2 | 1 | 10 | 1/2 | 1/2 strch, 1 fat |
| Golden Corn | 1 cup | 120 | 4 | 30 | 1 | 3 | 730 | 2 | 2 | 20 | 1 | 1 strch, 1 fat |
| Golden Mushroom | 1 cup | 80 | 3 | 34 | 1 | 5 | 930 | 2 | 1 | 10 | 1/2 | 1/2 strch, 1 fat |
| Green Pea | 1 cup | 180 | 3 | 15 | <1 | 5 | 890 | 9 | 5 | 29 | 2 | 2 strch, 1 fat |
| ✔ Healthy Request Chicken Broth | 1 cup | 20 | 0 | 0 | 0 | 0 | 480 | 3 | 0 | 1 | 0 | free |
| ✔ Healthy Request Chicken Noodle | 1 cup | 160 | 3 | 17 | 1 | 20 | 480 | 9 | 2 | 25 | 1 1/2 | 1 1/2 strch, 1 fat |
| ✔ Healthy Request Chicken Vegetable | 1 cup | 120 | 2 | 15 | <1 | 20 | 480 | 7 | 2 | 18 | 1 | 1 strch, 1 lean meat |
| ✔ Healthy Request Chicken w/Rice | 1 cup | 100 | 2 | 18 | <1 | 40 | 480 | 6 | 1 | 15 | 1 | 1 strch |
| ✔ Healthy Request Hearty Vegetable | 1 cup | 100 | 1 | 9 | 0 | 0 | 470 | 3 | 2 | 20 | 1 | 1 strch |

✔ = Best Bet; NA = Not Available; Carb. Ch. = Carbohydrate Choices

| Soup (Canned) *(Continued)* | Serving Size | Cal. | Fat (g) | % Cal. Fat | Sat. Fat (g) | Chol. (mg) | Sod. (mg) | Pro. (g) | Fiber (g) | Carb. (g) | Carb. Ch. | Servings/Exchanges |
|---|---|---|---|---|---|---|---|---|---|---|---|---|
| ✔Healthy Request Minestrone Soup | 1 cup | 120 | 2 | 15 | <1 | 3 | 480 | 4 | 3 | 24 | 1 1/2 | 1 1/2 strch |
| ✔Healthy Request Southwest-Style Vegetable | 1 cup | 140 | 1 | 6 | <1 | 0 | 480 | 5 | 5 | 28 | 2 | 2 strch |
| ✔Healthy Request Split Pea w/Ham | 1 cup | 170 | 3 | 16 | 1 | 15 | 480 | 9 | 4 | 27 | 2 | 2 strch, 1 fat |
| ✔Healthy Request Tomato Vegetable | 1 cup | 120 | 2 | 15 | <1 | 5 | 480 | 4 | 3 | 22 | 1 1/2 | 1 1/2 strch |
| ✔Healthy Request Turkey Vegetable Rice | 1 cup | 120 | 3 | 23 | 1 | 15 | 480 | 7 | 2 | 17 | 1 | 1 strch, 1 lean meat |
| ✔Healthy Request Vegetable Beef | 1 cup | 140 | 3 | 19 | 1 | 20 | 480 | 9 | 3 | 20 | 1 | 1 strch, 1 fat |
| ✔Healthy Request Zesty Penne Pasta | 1 cup | 90 | <1 | 10 | 0 | 5 | 470 | 4 | 2 | 17 | 1 | 1 strch |
| Hearty Vegetable w/Pasta | 1/2 cup | 90 | <1 | 10 | 0 | 0 | 830 | 2 | 2 | 18 | 1 | 1 strch |
| Home Cookin' Chicken Noodle | 1 cup | 130 | 3 | 21 | <1 | 0 | 750 | 3 | 4 | 24 | 1 1/2 | 1 1/2 strch, 1 fat |
| Home Cookin' Country Vegetable | 1 cup | 130 | 2 | 14 | 2 | 0 | 940 | 4 | 2 | 26 | 2 | 2 strch |
| Home Cookin' Hearty Lentil | 1 cup | 130 | <1 | 7 | <1 | 0 | 860 | 7 | 5 | 24 | 1 1/2 | 1 1/2 strch |
| Home Cookin' Italian Vegetable | 1 cup | 100 | 4 | 36 | 2 | 5 | 860 | 3 | 2 | 14 | 1 | 1 strch, 1 fat |
| Home Cookin' Minestrone | 1 cup | 120 | 2 | 15 | 1 | 5 | 990 | 4 | 3 | 19 | 1 | 1 strch |
| Home Cookin' Potato w/Roasted Garlic | 1 cup | 180 | 9 | 45 | 3 | 21 | 800 | 5 | 2 | 21 | 1 1/2 | 1 1/2 strch, 2 fat |
| Home Cookin' Split Pea w/Ham | 1 cup | 170 | 2 | 11 | <1 | 5 | 880 | 10 | 6 | 30 | 2 | 2 strch, 1 lean meat |
| Home Cookin' Tomato Garden | 1 cup | 150 | 4 | 24 | 2 | 5 | 900 | 5 | 4 | 27 | 2 | 2 strch, 1 fat |
| Italian Tomato Basil/Oregano | 1 cup | 100 | <1 | 9 | 0 | 0 | 820 | 2 | 2 | 23 | 1 1/2 | 1 1/2 strch |

| | Serving | Cal. | Fat (g) | % Cal. Fat | Sat. Fat (g) | Chol. (mg) | Sod. (mg) | Prot. (g) | Fiber (g) | Carb. (g) | Carb. Ch. | Exchanges |
|---|---|---|---|---|---|---|---|---|---|---|---|---|
| Manhattan Clam Chowder | 1 cup | 70 | 2 | 26 | <1 | 3 | 910 | 2 | 2 | 12 | 1 | 1 strch |
| Minestrone | 1 cup | 100 | 2 | 18 | <1 | 0 | 960 | 5 | 4 | 16 | 1 | 1 strch |
| Nacho Cheese Soup/Dip | 1 cup | 140 | 8 | 51 | 4 | 15 | 810 | 5 | 2 | 11 | 1 | 1 strch, 2 fat |
| New England Clam Chowder | 1 cup | 100 | 3 | 27 | 1 | 3 | 980 | 4 | 1 | 15 | 1 | 1 strch, 1 fat |
| Noodles & Ground Beef | 1 cup | 100 | 4 | 36 | 2 | 25 | 900 | 5 | 2 | 11 | 1 | 1 strch, 1 fat |
| Old-Fashioned Tomato Rice | 1 cup | 120 | 2 | 15 | <1 | 5 | 790 | 2 | 1 | 23 | 1 1/2 | 1 1/2 strch |
| Old-Fashioned Vegetable | 1 cup | 70 | 3 | 39 | <1 | 3 | 950 | 2 | 2 | 10 | 1/2 | 1/2 strch, 1 fat |
| Oyster Stew | 1 cup | 90 | 6 | 60 | 4 | 20 | 940 | 2 | 0 | 6 | 1/2 | 1/2 strch, 1 fat |
| Scotch Broth | 1 cup | 80 | 3 | 34 | 2 | 10 | 870 | 4 | 1 | 9 | 1/2 | 1/2 strch, 1 fat |
| Split Pea, Ham & Bacon | 1 cup | 180 | 4 | 20 | 2 | 3 | 860 | 10 | 5 | 28 | 2 | 2 strch, 1 fat |
| Tomato | 1 cup | 100 | 2 | 18 | 0 | 0 | 730 | 2 | 2 | 18 | 1 | 1 strch |
| Tomato Bisque | 1 cup | 130 | 3 | 21 | 2 | 5 | 900 | 2 | 2 | 24 | 1 1/2 | 1 1/2 strch, 1 fat |
| Turkey Noodle | 1 cup | 80 | 3 | 34 | <1 | 15 | 970 | 4 | 1 | 10 | 1/2 | 1/2 strch, 1 fat |
| Turkey Vegetable | 1 cup | 80 | 3 | 34 | <1 | 10 | 840 | 3 | 2 | 11 | 1 | 1 strch, 1 fat |
| Vegetable | 1 cup | 80 | 2 | 23 | <1 | 3 | 920 | 3 | 2 | 14 | 1 | 1 strch |
| Vegetarian Vegetable | 1 cup | 70 | <1 | 13 | 0 | 0 | 770 | 2 | 2 | 14 | 1 | 1 strch |
| **Health Valley** | | | | | | | | | | | | |
| ✔14-Garden Vegetable | 7.5 oz | 50 | 0 | 0 | 0 | 0 | 260 | 4 | 3 | 9 | 1/2 | 1/2 strch |
| ✔5-Bean Vegetable | 7.5 oz | 100 | 0 | 0 | 0 | 0 | 260 | 8 | 3 | 14 | 2 | 1 strch |

✔= Best Bet; NA = Not Available; Carb. Ch. = Carbohydrate Choices

| Soup (Canned) (*Continued*) | Serving Size | Cal. | Fat (g) | % Cal. Fat | Sat. Fat (g) | Chol. (mg) | Sod. (mg) | Pro. (g) | Fiber (g) | Carb. (g) | Carb. Ch. | Servings/Exchanges |
|---|---|---|---|---|---|---|---|---|---|---|---|---|
| ✔Beef Broth | 7.5 oz | 17 | 1 | 53 | 0 | 1 | 420 | 1 | 0 | 2 | 0 | free |
| ✔Black Bean & Vegetable | 7.5 oz | 70 | 0 | 0 | 0 | 0 | 250 | 9 | 17 | 9 | 1/2 | 1 1/2 strch, 1 very lean meat |
| ✔Chicken Broth | 1 cup | 35 | 2 | 51 | NA | 2 | 410 | 4 | 0 | 1 | 0 | free |
| ✔Country Corn & Vegetable | 1 cup | 80 | 0 | 0 | 0 | 0 | 240 | 6 | 5 | 17 | 1 | 1 strch |
| ✔Italian Minestrone | 7.5 oz | 80 | 0 | 0 | 0 | 0 | 290 | 8 | 4 | 12 | 1 | 1 strch, 1 very lean meat |
| ✔Lentil | 7.5 oz | 170 | 2 | 11 | 0 | 0 | 435 | 9 | 17 | 28 | 2 | 2 strch, 1 very lean meat |
| ✔Lentil & Carrot | 7.5 oz | 85 | 0 | 0 | 0 | 0 | 205 | 9 | 13 | 23 | 1 1/2 | 1 1/2 strch |
| ✔Pasta Cacciatore | 1 cup | 90 | 0 | 0 | 0 | 0 | 210 | 6 | NA | 19 | 1 | 1 strch |
| ✔Pasta Primavera | 1 cup | 80 | 0 | 0 | 0 | 0 | 210 | 8 | 11 | 21 | 1 1/2 | 1 1/2 strch, 1 very lean meat |
| ✔Pasta Romano | 1 cup | 140 | 0 | 0 | 0 | 0 | 250 | 10 | 13 | 32 | 2 | 2 strch, 1 very lean meat |
| ✔Rotini Vegetable Pasta | 1 cup | 100 | 0 | 0 | 0 | 0 | 290 | 4 | 4 | 20 | 1 | 1 strch |
| ✔Split Pea & Carrot | 7.5 oz | 80 | 0 | 0 | 0 | 0 | 290 | 9 | 13 | 17 | 1 | 1 strch, 1 very lean meat |
| ✔Tomato Vegetable | 1 cup | 75 | 0 | 0 | 0 | 0 | 225 | 6 | 5 | 16 | 1 | 1 strch |
| ✔Vegetable Barley | 7.5 oz | 85 | 0 | 0 | 0 | 0 | 185 | 6 | 4 | 18 | 1 | 1 strch |
| **Healthy Choice** | | | | | | | | | | | | |
| Bean & Ham | 1 cup | 166 | 1 | 5 | <1 | 4 | 980 | 9 | 7 | 31 | 2 | 2 strch, 1 lean meat |

| | Serving | Cal. | | | | | Sodium | | | Carb. Ch. | Exchanges |
|---|---|---|---|---|---|---|---|---|---|---|---|
| ✓Beef & Potato | 1 cup | 115 | 1 | 8 | <1 | 5 | 450 | 11 | <1 | 16 | 1 | 1 strch, 1 lean meat |
| ✓Broccoli Cheddar | 1 cup | 115 | 2 | 16 | 1 | <1 | 305 | 4 | 2 | 22 | 1 1/2 | 1 1/2 strch |
| ✓Chicken Alfredo w/Pasta | 1 cup | 130 | 2 | 14 | 1 | 10 | 335 | 2 | 2 | 17 | 1 | 1 strch, 1 lean meat |
| ✓Chicken Corn Chowder | 1 cup | 175 | 3 | 15 | 1 | 8 | 465 | 8 | 2 | 30 | 2 | 2 strch, 1 fat |
| ✓Chicken Pasta | 1 cup | 119 | 3 | 23 | 1 | 6 | 495 | 7 | 1 | 18 | 1 | 1 strch, 1 lean meat |
| ✓Chicken w/Rice | 1 cup | 120 | 2 | 15 | <1 | 6 | 325 | 9 | 3 | 19 | 1 | 1 strch, 1 lean meat |
| ✓Clam Chowder | 1 cup | 123 | 1 | 7 | <1 | 12 | 480 | 7 | 2 | 23 | 1 1/2 | 1 1/2 strch |
| ✓Country Vegetable | 1 cup | 110 | 1 | 8 | <1 | 0 | 455 | 5 | 3 | 24 | 1 1/2 | 1 1/2 strch |
| ✓Cream of Chicken w/Mushroom | 1 cup | 77 | <1 | 12 | <1 | 0 | 450 | 4 | <1 | 14 | 1 | 1 strch, 1 lean meat |
| ✓Cream of Mushroom | 1 cup | 55 | <1 | 16 | <1 | 2 | 480 | <1 | 3 | 13 | 1 | 1 strch |
| ✓Garden Vegetable | 1 cup | 110 | 1 | 8 | <1 | 0 | 455 | 5 | 6 | 22 | 1 1/2 | 1 1/2 strch |
| ✓Lentil | 1 cup | 135 | <1 | 7 | <1 | 0 | 470 | 10 | 5 | 28 | 2 | 2 strch |
| ✓Minestrone | 1 cup | 105 | 1 | 9 | <1 | 1 | 370 | 5 | 5 | 24 | 1 1/2 | 1 1/2 strch |
| ✓Old Fashioned Chicken Noodle | 1 cup | 137 | 3 | 20 | 1 | 9 | 400 | 9 | <1 | 19 | 1 | 1 strch, 1 lean meat |
| ✓Split Pea & Ham | 1 cup | 165 | 2 | 11 | <1 | 7 | 470 | 11 | 5 | 26 | 2 | 2 strch, 1 lean meat |
| ✓Tomato Garden | 1 cup | 80 | 1 | 11 | <1 | 0 | 300 | 2 | 3 | 18 | 1 | 1 strch |
| ✓Turkey w/Wild Rice | 1 cup | 70 | 1 | 13 | <1 | <5 | 405 | 9 | 3 | 9 | 1/2 | 1/2 strch, 1 very lean meat |

✔ = Best Bet; NA = Not Available; Carb. Ch. = Carbohydrate Choices

| Soup (Canned) (*Continued*) | Serving Size | Cal. | Fat (g) | % Cal. Fat | Sat. Fat (g) | Chol. (mg) | Sod. (mg) | Pro. (g) | Fiber (g) | Carb. (g) | Carb. Ch. | Servings/Exchanges |
|---|---|---|---|---|---|---|---|---|---|---|---|---|
| **Old El Paso** | | | | | | | | | | | | |
| Black Bean w/Bacon | 1 cup | 160 | 2 | 11 | <1 | 5 | 960 | 11 | 7 | 26 | 2 | 1 1/2 strch, 1 lean meat |
| Chicken Vegetable | 1 cup | 110 | 3 | 25 | <1 | 15 | 620 | 9 | 0 | 13 | 1 | 1 strch, 1 lean meat |
| Chicken w/Rice | 1 cup | 90 | 3 | 30 | <1 | 15 | 680 | 8 | 0 | 10 | 1/2 | 1/2 strch, 1 lean meat |
| Garden Vegetable | 1 cup | 110 | 3 | 25 | <1 | 3 | 710 | 5 | 0 | 17 | 1 | 1 strch, 1 fat |
| Hearty Beef | 1 cup | 120 | 3 | 23 | 2 | 25 | 690 | 10 | 0 | 14 | 1 | 1 strch, 1 lean meat |
| Hearty Chicken Noodle | 1 cup | 110 | 3 | 25 | 1 | 25 | NA | 9 | 0 | 10 | 1/2 | 1/2 strch, 1 lean meat |
| **Progresso** | | | | | | | | | | | | |
| 99% Fat-Free New England Clam Chowder | 1 cup | 130 | 2 | 14 | 0 | 5 | 700 | 5 | 1 | 22 | 1 | 1 strch |
| ✔99% Fat-free Beef Barley | 1 cup | 140 | 2 | 13 | 1 | 20 | 470 | 11 | 3 | 20 | 1 | 1 strch, 1 lean meat |
| 99% Fat-Free Chicken Noodle | 1 cup | 90 | 2 | 20 | 0 | 20 | 950 | 7 | 1 | 13 | 1 | 1 strch, 1 lean meat |
| 99% Fat-Free Chicken Rice w/Vegetables | 1 cup | 110 | 2 | 16 | 0 | 10 | 780 | 7 | 1 | 16 | 1 | 1 strch, 1 lean meat |
| ✔99% Fat-Free Lentil | 1 cup | 130 | 2 | 14 | 0 | 0 | 440 | 8 | 6 | 20 | 1 | 1 strch, 1 lean meat |
| 99% Fat-Free Minestrone | 1 cup | 130 | 2 | 14 | 0 | 0 | 710 | 7 | 4 | 23 | 1 1/2 | 1 1/2 strch |
| 99% Fat-Free Tomato Garden Vegetable | 1 cup | 100 | 2 | 18 | 0 | 0 | 660 | 3 | 2 | 19 | 1 | 1 strch |
| 99% Fat-Free Vegetable | 1 cup | 70 | 1 | 13 | 0 | 0 | 870 | 20 | 2 | 13 | 1 | 1 strch |
| Basil Rotini Tomato | 1 cup | 120 | 2 | 11 | <1 | <5 | 890 | 5 | 2 | 22 | 1 1/2 | 1 1/2 strch |
| Bean and Ham | 1 cup | 160 | 2 | 11 | <1 | 10 | 870 | 10 | 8 | 25 | 1 1/2 | 1 1/2 strch, 1 lean meat |

| | | | | | | | | | | | | |
|---|---|---|---|---|---|---|---|---|---|---|---|---|
| Beef Barley | 1 cup | 130 | 4 | 28 | 2 | 25 | 780 | 10 | 3 | 13 | 1 | 1 strch, 1 med-fat meat |
| Beef Minestrone | 1 cup | 140 | 3 | 19 | 1 | 10 | 970 | 10 | 3 | 18 | 1 | 1 strch, 1 med-fat meat |
| Beef Noodle | 1 cup | 140 | 4 | 26 | 2 | 30 | 950 | 13 | 1 | 15 | 1 | 1 strch, 1 med-fat meat |
| Beef Vegetable & Rotini | 1 cup | 130 | 3 | 21 | 1 | 25 | 780 | 13 | 4 | 14 | 1 | 1 strch, 1 med-fat meat |
| Chickarina | 1 cup | 130 | 5 | 35 | 2 | 20 | 1010 | 8 | <1 | 12 | 1 | 1 strch, 1 med-fat meat |
| Chicken & Wild Rice | 1 cup | 100 | 2 | 18 | 0 | 15 | 850 | 7 | 1 | 15 | 1 | 1 strch |
| Chicken Barley | 1 cup | 110 | 2 | 16 | 0 | 15 | 850 | 8 | 3 | 16 | 1 | 1 strch, 1 lean meat |
| Chicken Broth | 1 cup | 20 | 1 | 45 | 0 | 0 | 920 | 1 | 0 | 1 | 0 | free |
| Chicken Minestrone | 1 cup | 110 | 2 | 16 | 0 | 15 | 890 | 9 | 2 | 15 | 1 | 1 strch, 1 lean meat |
| Chicken Noodle | 1 cup | 90 | 2 | 20 | 0 | 25 | 950 | 9 | <1 | 9 | 1/2 | 1/2 strch, 1 lean meat |
| Chicken Rice & Vegetables | 1 cup | 90 | 2 | 20 | 0 | 10 | 890 | 6 | 1 | 13 | 1 | 1 strch, 1 lean meat |
| Chicken Vegetable | 1 cup | 90 | 2 | 20 | 0 | 15 | 820 | 7 | 2 | 13 | 1 | 1 strch, 1 lean meat |
| Clam & Rotini Chowder | 1 cup | 190 | 9 | 43 | 2 | 10 | 800 | 7 | 0 | 21 | 1 1/2 | 1 1/2 strch, 2 fat |
| Creamy Mushroom Chicken, 99% Fat-Free | 1 cup | 90 | 2 | 20 | <1 | 10 | 840 | 7 | 1 | 12 | 1 | 1 strch, 1 lean meat |
| Escarole in Chicken Broth | 1 cup | 25 | 1 | 36 | 0 | <5 | 930 | 1 | 1 | 3 | 0 | free |
| Green Split Pea | 1 cup | 170 | 3 | 16 | 1 | 5 | 870 | 10 | 5 | 25 | 1 1/2 | 1 1/2 strch, 1 fat |
| Hearty Black Bean, 99% Fat-Free | 1 cup | 170 | 2 | 11 | 0 | <5 | 730 | 8 | 10 | 30 | 2 | 2 strch |
| Hearty Chicken and Rotini | 1 cup | 90 | 2 | 20 | 0 | 15 | 970 | 8 | <1 | 12 | 1 | 1 strch, 1 very lean meat |
| Hearty Penne/Chicken Broth | 1 cup | 80 | 1 | 11 | 0 | 0 | 1020 | 4 | <1 | 14 | 1 | 1 strch |

✔ = Best Bet; NA = Not Available; Carb. Ch. = Carbohydrate Choices

| Soup (Canned) (*Continued*) | Serving Size | Cal. | Fat (g) | % Cal. Fat | Sat. Fat (g) | Chol. (mg) | Sod. (mg) | Pro. (g) | Fiber (g) | Carb. (g) | Carb. Ch. | Servings/Exchanges |
|---|---|---|---|---|---|---|---|---|---|---|---|---|
| Hearty Tomato | 1 cup | 100 | 2 | 18 | 0 | 0 | 800 | 2 | 1 | 19 | 1 | 1 strch |
| Homestyle Chicken & Vegetable | 1 cup | 90 | 2 | 20 | 0 | 15 | 900 | 7 | <1 | 11 | 1 | 1 strch, 1 lean meat |
| Lentil | 1 cup | 140 | 2 | 13 | 0 | 0 | 750 | 9 | 7 | 22 | 1 1/2 | 1 1/2 strch, 1 lean meat |
| Macaroni & Bean | 1 cup | 160 | 4 | 23 | 1 | <5 | 800 | 7 | 6 | 23 | 1 1/2 | 1 1/2 strch, 1 fat |
| Manhattan Clam Chowder | 1 cup | 110 | 2 | 16 | 0 | 3 | 710 | 12 | 3 | 11 | 1 | 1 strch, 1 lean meat |
| Meatballs & Pasta Pearls | 1 cup | 140 | 7 | 45 | 3 | 15 | 700 | 7 | 0 | 13 | 1 | 1 strch, 1 med-fat meat |
| Minestrone | 1 cup | 120 | 2 | 15 | 0 | 0 | 960 | 5 | 5 | 21 | 1 1/2 | 1 1/2 strch |
| ✔Minestrone Parmesan | 1 cup | 100 | 3 | 27 | <1 | 0 | 29 | 3 | 3 | 16 | 1 | 1 strch, 1 fat |
| New England Clam | 1 cup | 190 | 10 | 47 | 3 | 15 | 920 | 6 | 1 | 20 | 1 | 1 strch, 1 med-fat meat, 1 fat |
| Oregano Enee Italian Style Vegetable | 1 cup | 90 | 2 | 20 | 0 | 0 | 960 | 3 | 1 | 15 | 1 | 1 strch |
| Peppercorn Penne Vegetable | 1 cup | 100 | 1 | 9 | 0 | 0 | 920 | 3 | 2 | 20 | 1 | 1 strch |
| Potato Broccoli & Cheese | 1 cup | 160 | 6 | 34 | 2 | <5 | 960 | 5 | 1 | 21 | 1 1/2 | 1 1/2 strch, 1 fat |
| Roasted Garlic Pasta Lentil | 1 cup | 120 | 2 | 15 | 0 | 0 | 960 | 7 | 5 | 20 | 1 | 1 strch, 1 lean meat |
| Rotisserie Seasoned Chicken | 1 cup | 100 | 2 | 18 | 0 | 15 | 920 | 7 | 2 | 15 | 1 | 1 strch, 1 lean meat |
| Spicy Chicken & Penne | 1 cup | 110 | 2 | 16 | 0 | 0 | 950 | 9 | 1 | 14 | 1 | 1 strch, 1 lean meat |
| Split Pea w/Ham | 1 cup | 150 | 4 | 24 | 2 | 15 | 830 | 9 | 5 | 20 | 1 | 1 strch, 1 med-fat meat |
| Split Pea, 99% Fat-free | 1 cup | 170 | 2 | 11 | 2 | 0 | 620 | 10 | 5 | 29 | 2 | 2 strch, 1 lean meat |

| | | | | | | | | | | | |
|---|---|---|---|---|---|---|---|---|---|---|---|
| Tomato Basil | 1 cup | 100 | 2 | 18 | 0 | 0 | 790 | 2 | 1 | 19 | 1 | 1 strch |
| Tomato Soup | 1 cup | 100 | 2 | 18 | 0 | 0 | 790 | 2 | 1 | 19 | 1 | 1 strch |
| Tomato Vegetable | 1 cup | 90 | 2 | 20 | 0 | 0 | 990 | 3 | 4 | 15 | 1 | 1 strch |
| Tortellini/Chicken Broth | 1 cup | 70 | 2 | 26 | <1 | 10 | 970 | 3 | 2 | 10 | 1/2 | 1/2 strch |
| Turkey Rice w/Vegetables | 1 cup | 110 | 1 | 8 | 0 | 15 | 1040 | 7 | 1 | 18 | 1 | 1 strch, 1 very lean meat |
| Vegetable | 1 cup | 90 | 2 | 20 | <1 | <5 | 810 | 3 | 2 | 15 | 1 | 1 strch |

## SOUP MIX (AS PREPARED)

### Campbell's

| | | | | | | | | | | | |
|---|---|---|---|---|---|---|---|---|---|---|---|
| Chicken Noodle | 1 cup | 90 | 2 | 20 | <1 | 10 | 660 | 4 | 0 | 15 | 1 | 1 carb |
| Recipe Secrets Beef Onion | 1 cup | 25 | <1 | 36 | 0 | 0 | 610 | 1 | 0 | 5 | 0 | free |
| Recipe Secrets Onion | 1 cup | 20 | 0 | 0 | 0 | 0 | 610 | 0 | 0 | 4 | 0 | free |
| Recipe Secrets Onion-Mushroom | 1 cup | 30 | <1 | 30 | 0 | 0 | 640 | 1 | 0 | 5 | 0 | free |
| Recipe Secrets Savory Herb w/Garlic | 1 cup | 30 | 0 | 0 | 0 | 0 | 600 | 1 | <1 | 6 | 1/2 | 1/2 carb |

### Knorr

| | | | | | | | | | | | |
|---|---|---|---|---|---|---|---|---|---|---|---|
| Cream of Spinach | 1 cup | 70 | 3 | 39 | <1 | 0 | 760 | 2 | <1 | 10 | 1/2 | 1/2 carb, 1 fat |
| Creamy Chicken w/Rice | 1 cup | 90 | 3 | 30 | 2 | <1 | 860 | 3 | 0 | 14 | 1 | 1 carb, 1 fat |
| French Onion | 1 cup | 35 | 1 | 26 | <1 | 0 | 790 | 1 | 0 | 6 | 1/2 | 1/2 carb |
| Hot & Sour | 1 cup | 45 | 2 | 40 | <1 | 0 | 880 | 0 | 0 | 8 | 1/2 | 1/2 carb |
| Leek | 1 cup | 70 | 3 | 39 | 1 | <5 | 810 | 2 | 0 | 9 | 1/2 | 1/2 carb, 1 fat |

✔ = Best Bet; NA = Not Available; Carb. Ch. = Carbohydrate Choices

| Soup Mix (As Prepared) (Continued) | Serving Size | Cal. | Fat (g) | % Cal. Fat | Sat. Fat (g) | Chol. (mg) | Sod. (mg) | Pro. (g) | Fiber (g) | Carb. (g) | Carb. Ch. | Servings/Exchanges |
|---|---|---|---|---|---|---|---|---|---|---|---|---|
| Savory Chicken Noodle | 1 cup | 70 | 2 | 26 | 1 | 10 | 650 | 3 | 1 | 11 | 1 | 1 carb |
| Savory Minestrone | 1 cup | 100 | 2 | 18 | 1 | 0 | 810 | 2 | 3 | 18 | 1 | 1 carb |
| Tomato Basil | 1 cup | 80 | 3 | 34 | 1 | 0 | 920 | 2 | 0 | 13 | 1 | 1 carb, 1 fat |
| Tomato Beef | 1 cup | 60 | 2 | 30 | 1 | <5 | 1030 | 2 | 0 | 9 | 1/2 | 1/2 carb |
| Vegetable | 1 cup | 30 | <1 | 30 | 0 | 0 | 730 | 1 | 1 | 6 | 1/2 | 1/2 carb |
| **SOUP MIX, SINGLE SERVING (AS PREPARED)** | | | | | | | | | | | | |
| **Knorr Taste Break Soups** | | | | | | | | | | | | |
| Beef & Vegetable | 1 | 150 | 2 | 12 | 1 | 0 | 990 | 5 | 1 | 27 | 2 | 2 carb |
| Chicken w/Rice | 1 | 180 | 2 | 10 | <1 | 0 | 990 | 4 | 1 | 36 | 2 1/2 | 2 1/2 carb |
| Hearty Lentil | 1 | 200 | 1 | 5 | <1 | 0 | 820 | 10 | 5 | 38 | 2 1/2 | 2 1/2 carb |
| Navy Bean | 1 | 145 | 1 | 6 | 0 | 0 | 960 | 7 | 8 | 27 | 2 | 2 carb |
| Potato Leek | 1 | 150 | 4 | 24 | <1 | 0 | 990 | 2 | 1 | 27 | 2 | 2 carb, 1 fat |
| Red Bean Chili | 1 | 170 | 1 | 5 | 0 | 0 | 970 | 9 | 8 | 32 | 2 | 2 carb |
| Split Pea | 1 | 160 | <1 | 6 | 0 | 0 | 760 | 8 | 3 | 30 | 2 | 2 carb |
| Three Cheese Macaroni | 1 | 250 | 5 | 18 | 2 | 10 | 990 | 8 | 1 | 44 | 3 | 3 carb, 1 fat |
| Tomato Pasta | 1 | 170 | 2 | 11 | <1 | 0 | 820 | 5 | 0 | 34 | 2 | 2 carb |
| **Lipton Cup-A-Soup** | | | | | | | | | | | | |
| ✔Chicken Broth | 6 oz | 20 | 1 | 45 | 0 | 0 | 440 | 1 | 0 | 3 | 0 | free |

| | | | | | | | | | | | | |
|---|---|---|---|---|---|---|---|---|---|---|---|---|
| Chicken Noodle | 6 oz | 50 | 1 | 18 | 0 | 10 | 540 | 2 | 0 | 8 | 1/2 | 1/2 strch |
| Chicken Vegetable | 6 oz | 50 | 1 | 18 | 0 | 10 | 520 | 1 | 0 | 10 | 1/2 | 1/2 strch |
| Cream Chicken-Flavored Vegetable | 6 oz | 80 | 4 | 45 | 2 | 0 | 590 | 2 | NA | 10 | 1/2 | 1/2 strch, 1 fat |
| Cream of Chicken | 6 oz | 70 | 3 | 39 | 0 | NA | 640 | 12 | 0 | 3 | 1/2 | 1/2 strch, 1 fat |
| Cream of Mushroom | 6 oz | 60 | 2 | 30 | 0 | NA | 610 | 1 | 0 | 10 | 1/2 | 1/2 strch |
| Creamy Broccoli & Cheese | 6 oz | 70 | 3 | 39 | 2 | 0 | 540 | 2 | 1 | 9 | 1/2 | 1/2 strch, 1 fat |
| Green Pea | 6 oz | 80 | 1 | 11 | 0 | 0 | 520 | 4 | 3 | 12 | 1 | 1 strch |
| Hearty Chicken Supreme | 6 oz | 60 | 1 | 15 | 0 | 15 | 590 | 3 | 0 | 10 | 1/2 | 1/2 strch |
| Ring Noodle | 6 oz | 50 | 1 | 18 | 0 | 10 | 560 | 2 | 0 | 9 | 1/2 | 1/2 strch |
| ✓Spring Vegetable | 6 oz | 45 | 1 | 20 | 0 | 10 | 500 | 2 | 1 | 8 | 1/2 | 1/2 strch |
| Tomato | 6 oz | 90 | 1 | 10 | NA | 0 | 510 | 2 | NA | 20 | 1 | 1 strch |

## Maruchan Instant Lunch

| | | | | | | | | | | | | |
|---|---|---|---|---|---|---|---|---|---|---|---|---|
| Beef Ramen Noodles | 1 | 290 | 12 | 37 | 6 | 0 | 1260 | 7 | 2 | 38 | 2 1/2 | 2 1/2 carb, 2 fat |
| Cheddar Cheese Ramen Noodles | 1 | 340 | 16 | 42 | 7 | <5 | 1190 | 7 | 2 | 38 | 2 1/2 | 2 1/2 carb, 3 fat |
| Chicken Flavor Ramen Noodles | 1 | 280 | 12 | 39 | 6 | <5 | 1220 | 6 | 2 | 37 | 2 1/2 | 2 1/2 carb, 2 fat |
| Chicken Flavor w/Mushroom Ramen Noodles | 1 | 270 | 12 | 40 | 6 | 0 | 1380 | 6 | 5 | 35 | 2 | 2 carb, 2 fat |
| Creamy Pesto Ramen Noodles | 1 | 340 | 15 | 40 | 7 | <5 | 1320 | 7 | 2 | 37 | 2 1/2 | 2 1/2 carb, 3 fat |
| Ramen Noodles w/Shrimp | 1 | 290 | 12 | 37 | 6 | 10 | 1260 | 7 | 2 | 38 | 2 1/2 | 2 1/2 carb, 2 fat |

✓= Best Bet; NA = Not Available; Carb. Ch. = Carbohydrate Choices

| Soup Mix, Single serving (As Prepared) (*Continued*) | Serving Size | Cal. | Fat (g) | % Cal. Fat | Sat. Fat (g) | Chol. (mg) | Sod. (mg) | Pro. (g) | Fiber (g) | Carb. (g) | Carb. Ch. | Servings/Exchanges |
|---|---|---|---|---|---|---|---|---|---|---|---|---|
| **Nile Spice** | | | | | | | | | | | | |
| Black Bean | 1 | 170 | 2 | 11 | 0 | 0 | 640 | 12 | 12 | 36 | 2 1/2 | 2 1/2 carb |
| Chicken Vegetable | 1 | 110 | 2 | 16 | 1 | 0 | 670 | 4 | 2 | 21 | 1 1/2 | 1 1/2 carb |
| Lentil | 1 | 170 | 2 | 11 | 0 | 0 | 540 | 11 | 11 | 34 | 2 | 2 carb |
| Red Beans & Rice | 1 | 170 | 1 | 5 | 0 | 0 | 590 | 10 | 10 | 35 | 2 | 2 carb |
| Split Pea | 1 | 200 | 1 | 5 | 0 | 0 | 600 | 13 | 8 | 35 | 2 | 2 carb |
| ✓Sweet Corn Chowder | 1 | 110 | 2 | 16 | 1 | 5 | 400 | 3 | 3 | 22 | 1 1/2 | 1 1/2 carb |
| **SOUR CREAM** | | | | | | | | | | | | |
| **Breakstone** | | | | | | | | | | | | |
| Sour Cream | 2 Tbsp | 60 | 5 | 75 | 4 | 20 | 15 | <1 | 0 | 1 | 0 | 1 fat |
| ✓Sour Cream, Fat-Free | 2 Tbsp | 35 | 0 | 0 | 0 | <5 | 25 | 2 | 0 | 6 | 1/2 | 1/2 carb |
| Sour Cream, Reduced Fat | 2 Tbsp | 45 | 4 | 80 | 3 | 15 | 20 | 1 | 0 | 2 | 0 | 1 fat |
| **Knudson** | | | | | | | | | | | | |
| ✓Fat-free Sour Cream | 2 Tbsp | 35 | 0 | 0 | 0 | <5 | 25 | 2 | 0 | 6 | 1/2 | 1/2 carb |
| ✓Light Sour Cream | 2 Tbsp | 40 | 3 | 68 | 2 | 10 | 20 | 2 | 0 | 2 | 0 | 1 fat |
| **Sealtest** | | | | | | | | | | | | |
| Light Sour Cream | 2 Tbsp | 50 | 4 | 72 | 2 | 10 | 20 | 2 | 0 | 2 | 0 | 1 fat |
| Sour Cream | 2 Tbsp | 60 | 6 | 90 | 4 | 20 | 10 | 0 | 0 | 2 | 0 | 1 fat |

## SPAGHETTI SAUCE

### Campbells

| | | | | | | | | | | | |
|---|---|---|---|---|---|---|---|---|---|---|---|
| ✔ Italian Style Spaghetti Sauce | 1/2 cup | 50 | 0 | 0 | 0 | 360 | 2 | 2 | 12 | 1 | 1 carb |
| ✔ Marinara Homestyle Spaghetti Sauce | 1/2 cup | 40 | 0 | 0 | 0 | 360 | 2 | 2 | 10 | 1/2 | 1/2 carb |
| ✔ Mushroom Garlic Spaghetti Sauce | 1/2 cup | 50 | 1 | 0 | 0 | 330 | 2 | 2 | 11 | 1 | 1 carb |
| ✔ Mushroom Spaghetti Sauce | 1/2 cup | 50 | 1 | 18 | 0 | 330 | 2 | 2 | 11 | 1 | 1 1/2 carb |
| ✔ Traditional Spaghetti Sauce | 1/2 cup | 50 | 0 | 0 | 0 | 360 | 2 | 2 | 12 | 1 | 1 1/2 carb |
| ✔ Xtra Garlic Onion Spaghetti Sauce | 1/2 cup | 50 | 1 | 0 | 0 | 320 | 2 | 2 | 12 | 1 | 1 carb |

### Contadina

| | | | | | | | | | | | |
|---|---|---|---|---|---|---|---|---|---|---|---|
| ✔ Spaghetti Sauce | 1/2 cup | 90 | 2 | 20 | 0 | 440 | 2 | NA | 17 | 1 | 1 carb |
| ✔ Spaghetti Sauce w/Mushrooms | 1/2 cup | 90 | 2 | 20 | <1 | 430 | 2 | NA | 18 | 1 | 1 carb |

### Del Monte

| | | | | | | | | | | | |
|---|---|---|---|---|---|---|---|---|---|---|---|
| ✔ Spaghetti Sauce w/Garlic & Onion | 1/2 cup | 70 | 2 | 26 | 0 | 430 | 1 | NA | 10 | 1 | 1 carb |
| ✔ Spaghetti Sauce w/Meat | 1/2 cup | 70 | 2 | 26 | NA | 440 | 2 | NA | 9 | 1 | 1 carb |
| ✔ Spaghetti Sauce w/Mushrooms | 1/2 cup | 70 | 2 | 26 | NA | 440 | 1 | NA | 11 | 1 | 1 carb |
| ✔ Traditional Spaghetti Sauce | 1/2 cup | 70 | 2 | 26 | 0 | 430 | 1 | NA | 11 | 1 | 1 carb |

### Healthy Choice

| | | | | | | | | | | | |
|---|---|---|---|---|---|---|---|---|---|---|---|
| ✔ Spaghetti Sauce w/Mushrooms | 1/2 cup | 40 | 1 | 23 | 0 | 390 | 2 | NA | 9 | 1/2 | 1/2 carb |

✔ = Best Bet; NA = Not Available; Carb. Ch. = Carbohydrate Choices

| Spaghetti Sauce (Continued) | Serving Size | Cal. | Fat (g) | % Cal. Fat | Sat. Fat (g) | Chol. (mg) | Sod. (mg) | Pro. (g) | Fiber (g) | Carb. (g) | Carb. Ch. | Servings/Exchanges |
|---|---|---|---|---|---|---|---|---|---|---|---|---|
| ✓Spaghetti Sauce, Chunky Italian Vegetable | 1/2 cup | 40 | 0 | 0 | 0 | 0 | 350 | 1 | NA | 9 | 1/2 | 1/2 carb |
| **Hunt's** | | | | | | | | | | | | |
| Chunky Italian Style Vegetable Spaghetti Sauce | 1/2 cup | 64 | 3 | 42 | <1 | 0 | 616 | 3 | 3 | 9 | 1/2 | 1/2 carb, 1 fat |
| Classic Italian Spaghetti Sauce w/Parmesan | 1/2 cup | 60 | 2 | 30 | <1 | 0 | 550 | 3 | NA | 8 | 1/2 | 1/2 carb |
| Classic Italian Spaghetti Sauce w/Tomato & Basil | 1/2 cup | 50 | 2 | 36 | <1 | 0 | 550 | 1 | NA | 8 | 1/2 | 1/2 carb |
| Home Style Spaghetti Sauce | 1/2 cup | 60 | 2 | 30 | <1 | 0 | 530 | 2 | 2 | 10 | 1/2 | 1/2 carb, 1 fat |
| Old Country Spaghetti Sauce Flavored w/Meat | 1/2 cup | 70 | 3 | 39 | NA | 0 | 560 | 2 | NA | 10 | 1/2 | 1/2 carb, 1 fat |
| Old Country Spaghetti Sauce w/Garlic & Herbs | 1/2 cup | 80 | 2 | 23 | <1 | 0 | 560 | 2 | NA | 13 | 1 | 1 carb |
| Old Country Spaghetti Sauce w/Mushrooms | 1/2 cup | 53 | 3 | 51 | <1 | 0 | 542 | 2 | 3 | 7 | 1/2 | 1/2 carb, 1 fat |
| Old Country Traditional Spaghetti Sauce | 1/2 cup | 53 | 3 | 51 | <1 | 0 | 542 | 2 | 3 | 7 | 1/2 | 1/2 carb, 1 fat |
| Original Spaghetti Sauce w/Mushrooms | 1/2 cup | 70 | 2 | 26 | <1 | 0 | 560 | 2 | 2 | 12 | 1 | 1 carb |

| | Serving | Cal | Fat (g) | % Cal Fat | Sat Fat (g) | Chol (mg) | Sodium (mg) | Carb (g) | Fiber (g) | Pro (g) | Carb Ch. | Exchanges/Choices |
|---|---|---|---|---|---|---|---|---|---|---|---|---|
| Original Traditional Spaghetti Sauce | 1/2 cup | 70 | 2 | 26 | <1 | 0 | 530 | 2 | 2 | 12 | 1 | 1 carb |
| Spaghetti Sauce Flavored w/Meat | 1/2 cup | 70 | 2 | 26 | <1 | 2 | 570 | 2 | 2 | 12 | 1 | 1 carb |
| **SPORTS DRINKS** | | | | | | | | | | | | |
| **All-Sport** | | | | | | | | | | | | |
| ✔Sports Drink, All Varieties (Avg) | 8 oz | 70 | 0 | 0 | 0 | 0 | 60 | 0 | 0 | 20 | 1 | 1 carb |
| **Gatorade** | | | | | | | | | | | | |
| ✔Sports Drink, All Varieties (Avg) | 8 oz | 50 | 0 | 0 | 0 | 0 | 110 | 0 | 0 | 14 | 1 | 1 carb |
| **STEW (CANNED)** | | | | | | | | | | | | |
| **Chef Mate** | | | | | | | | | | | | |
| Beef Stew | 1 cup | 190 | 6 | 28 | 2 | 33 | 1190 | 15 | 3 | 19 | 1 | 1 strch, 2 med-fat meat |
| Corned Beef Hash | 1 cup | 485 | 30 | 56 | 13 | 90 | 1595 | 24 | 6 | 29 | 2 | 2 carb, 3 med-fat meat, 3 fat |
| **STUFFING MIX** | | | | | | | | | | | | |
| **Mrs. Cubbisons** | | | | | | | | | | | | |
| Cornbread Dressing | 3/4 cup | 130 | 1 | 7 | 0 | 0 | 600 | 4 | 2 | 25 | 1 1/2 | 1 1/2 strch |
| ✔Seasoned Dressing | 3/4 cup | 130 | 1 | 7 | 0 | 0 | 350 | 4 | 1 | 25 | 1 1/2 | 1 1/2 strch |
| **STUFFING MIX (AS PREPARED w/MARGARINE)** | | | | | | | | | | | | |
| **Butterball** | | | | | | | | | | | | |
| One Step Cornbread Stuffing | 1/2 cup | 150 | 3 | 18 | <1 | 0 | 590 | 4 | 3 | 29 | 2 | 2 strch, 1 fat |

✔ = Best Bet; NA = Not Available; Carb. Ch. = Carbohydrate Choices

| Stuffing Mix (As Prepared w/Margarine) (Continued) | Serving Size | Cal. | Fat (g) | % Cal. Fat | Sat. Fat (g) | Chol. (mg) | Sod. (mg) | Pro. (g) | Fiber (g) | Carb. (g) | Carb. Ch. | Servings/Exchanges |
|---|---|---|---|---|---|---|---|---|---|---|---|---|
| One Step Seasoned Stuffing | 1/2 cup | 160 | 3 | 17 | <1 | 0 | 600 | 4 | 4 | 30 | 2 | 2 strch, 1 fat |
| **Stove Top** | | | | | | | | | | | | |
| Chicken Flavor Stuffing Mix | 1/2 cup | 170 | 8 | 42 | 2 | 0 | 520 | 3 | <1 | 19 | 1 | 1 strch, 2 fat |
| Cornbread Flavor Stuffing Mix | 1/2 cup | 160 | 8 | 45 | 2 | 0 | 560 | 3 | 1 | 19 | 1 | 1 strch, 2 fat |
| Homestyle Herb | 1/2 cup | 170 | 8 | 42 | 2 | 0 | 500 | 3 | 1 | 19 | 1 | 1 strch, 2 fat |
| Long Grain & Wild Rice Stuffing Mix | 1/2 cup | 180 | 9 | 45 | 2 | 0 | 500 | 4 | <1 | 22 | 1 1/2 | 1 1/2 strch, 2 fat |
| Low Sodium Chicken Stuffing Mix | 1/2 cup | 180 | 9 | 45 | 2 | 0 | 340 | 4 | <1 | 21 | 1 1/2 | 1 1/2 strch, 2 fat |
| Microwave Chicken Stuffing | 1/2 cup | 160 | 7 | 39 | 2 | 0 | 480 | 4 | <1 | 20 | 1 | 1 strch, 1 fat |
| Microwave Corn Bread Stuffing Mix | 1/2 cup | 160 | 7 | 39 | 2 | 0 | 480 | 3 | <1 | 20 | 1 | 1 strch, 1 fat |
| Mushroom & Onion | 1/2 cup | 180 | 9 | 45 | 2 | 0 | 480 | 4 | <1 | 20 | 1 | 1 strch, 2 fat |
| San Francisco Stuffing Mix | 1/2 cup | 170 | 9 | 48 | 2 | 0 | 530 | 4 | 1 | 20 | 1 | 1 strch, 2 fat |
| Savory Herbs Stuffing Mix | 1/2 cup | 170 | 9 | 48 | 2 | 0 | 530 | 4 | 1 | 20 | 1 | 1 strch, 2 fat |
| Stuffing Mix for Beef | 1/2 cup | 180 | 9 | 45 | 2 | 0 | 540 | 4 | 1 | 22 | 1 1/2 | 1 1/2 strch, 2 fat |
| Stuffing Mix for Pork | 1/2 cup | 170 | 9 | 48 | 2 | 0 | 530 | 4 | 1 | 20 | 1 | 1 strch, 2 fat |
| Stuffing Mix for Turkey | 1/2 cup | 170 | 9 | 48 | 2 | 0 | 530 | 4 | <1 | 20 | 1 | 1 strch, 2 fat |
| **SWEET ROLLS (FROZEN)** | | | | | | | | | | | | |
| **Rhodes** | | | | | | | | | | | | |
| Anytime Caramel Rolls | 1 | 320 | 11 | 31 | 3 | 15 | 510 | 4 | 1 | 50 | 3 | 3 carb, 2 fat |

|  |  |  |  |  |  |  |  |  |  |  |  |  |
|---|---|---|---|---|---|---|---|---|---|---|---|---|
| Anytime Chocolate Cinnamon Swirls | 1 | 230 | 6 | 23 | <1 | 0 | 465 | 4 | 1 | 39 | 2 1/2 | 2 1/2 carb, 1 fat |
| Anytime Cinnamon Rolls | 1 | 230 | 6 | 23 | 0 | 0 | 465 | 4 | 1 | 39 | 2 1/2 | 2 1/2 carb, 1 fat |
| Anytime Orange Rolls | 1 | 220 | 5 | 21 | 0 | 0 | 465 | 4 | 1 | 39 | 2 1/2 | 2 1/2 carb, 1 fat |

## SWEET ROLLS (READY-TO-EAT)

### Aunt Fanny's

|  |  |  |  |  |  |  |  |  |  |  |  |  |
|---|---|---|---|---|---|---|---|---|---|---|---|---|
| Honey Bun, Applesauce | 1 | 330 | 17 | 46 | 4 | 0 | 300 | 6 | 1 | 43 | 3 | 3 strch, 3 fat |
| Honey Bun, Banana Cream | 1 | 350 | 18 | 46 | 4 | 0 | 290 | 5 | 2 | 32 | 2 | 2 strch, 4 fat |
| Honey Bun, Iced Honey | 1 | 350 | 18 | 46 | 4 | 0 | 290 | 5 | 2 | 32 | 2 | 2 strch, 3 fat |
| Honey Bun, Raspberry Filled | 1 | 350 | 17 | 44 | 5 | 0 | 290 | 5 | 2 | 45 | 3 | 3 strch, 3 fat |
| Honey Bun, Regular | 1 | 360 | 20 | 50 | 5 | 0 | 300 | 5 | 2 | 41 | 3 | 3 strch, 4 fat |
| Honey Bun, Vanilla Creme | 1 | 350 | 18 | 46 | 4 | 0 | 290 | 5 | 2 | 32 | 2 | 2 strch, 4 fat |

### Dolly Madison Bakery

|  |  |  |  |  |  |  |  |  |  |  |  |  |
|---|---|---|---|---|---|---|---|---|---|---|---|---|
| Cinnamon Sweet Rolls | 1 | 210 | 7 | 30 | 3 | 10 | 190 | 3 | 0 | 34 | 2 | 2 carb, 1 fat |
| Danish Rollers Sweet Rolls | 2 | 190 | 7 | 33 | 2 | 0 | 90 | 2 | <1 | 31 | 2 | 2 carb, 1 fat |

### Entenmann's

|  |  |  |  |  |  |  |  |  |  |  |  |  |
|---|---|---|---|---|---|---|---|---|---|---|---|---|
| ✔Cinnamon Rolls | 1/2 | 170 | 3 | 16 | <1 | 0 | 240 | 3 | 2 | 35 | 2 | 2 carb, 1 fat |
| ✔Fat-Free Apple Buns | 1 | 150 | 0 | 0 | 0 | 0 | 140 | 3 | 1 | 33 | 2 | 2 strch |
| ✔Fat-Free Blueberry Cheez Buns | 1 | 140 | 0 | 0 | 0 | 0 | 140 | 4 | 1 | 31 | 2 | 2 carb |
| ✔Fat-Free Pineapple Cheez Buns | 1 | 140 | 0 | 0 | 0 | 0 | 150 | 4 | <1 | 30 | 2 | 2 carb |

✔ = Best Bet; NA = Not Available; Carb. Ch. = Carbohydrate Choices

| Sweet Rolls (Ready-to-Eat) (*Continued*) | Serving Size | Cal. | Fat (g) | % Cal. Fat | Sat. Fat (g) | Chol. (mg) | Sod. (mg) | Pro. (g) | Fiber (g) | Carb. (g) | Carb. Ch. | Servings/Exchanges |
|---|---|---|---|---|---|---|---|---|---|---|---|---|
| ✓Fat-Free Raspberry Cheez Buns | 1 | 160 | 0 | 0 | 0 | 0 | 135 | 4 | 1 | 36 | 2 1/2 | 2 1/2 carb |
| ✓Fat-Free Cinnamon Raisin Buns | 1 | 160 | 0 | 0 | 0 | 0 | 125 | 3 | 1 | 36 | 2 1/2 | 2 1/2 carb |
| **Morton** | | | | | | | | | | | | |
| Honey Buns | 1 | 250 | 10 | 26 | 3 | 0 | 160 | 3 | <1 | 35 | 2 | 2 strch, 2 fat |
| Mini Honey Buns | 1 | 160 | 8 | 45 | 2 | 0 | 100 | 2 | 1 | 19 | 1 | 1 strch, 2 fat |
| **Pepperidge Farm** | | | | | | | | | | | | |
| Cinnamon Rolls | 1 | 250 | 12 | 43 | 3 | 15 | 220 | 4 | 2 | 33 | 2 | 2 strch, 2 fat |
| **Weight Watchers** | | | | | | | | | | | | |
| Glazed Cinnamon Rolls | 1 | 180 | 5 | 25 | 1 | 5 | 170 | 4 | NA | 31 | 2 | 2 carb, 1 fat |
| **SWEET ROLLS (REFRIGERATED)** | | | | | | | | | | | | |
| **Pillsbury** | | | | | | | | | | | | |
| Apple Cinnamon Sweet Roll w/Icing | 1 | 150 | 6 | 36 | 2 | 0 | 320 | 2 | <1 | 23 | 1 1/2 | 1 carb, 1 fat |
| Caramel Sweet Rolls | 1 | 170 | 7 | 37 | 2 | 0 | 330 | 2 | <1 | 24 | 1 1/2 | 1 1/2 carb, 1 fat |
| Cinnamon Rolls w/Icing | 1 | 150 | 6 | 36 | 2 | 0 | 340 | 2 | <1 | 23 | 1 1/2 | 1 1/2 carb, 1 fat |
| Orange Sweet Rolls w/Icing | 1 | 170 | 7 | 37 | 2 | 0 | 340 | 2 | <1 | 25 | 1 1/2 | 1 carb, 1 fat |
| Reduced Fat Cinnamon Rolls w/Icing | 1 | 140 | 4 | 26 | 1 | 0 | 340 | 2 | <1 | 24 | 1 1/2 | 1 1/2 strch, 1 fat |

| | Serving Size | Cal. | Fat (g) | % Cal. from Fat | Sat. Fat (g) | Chol. (mg) | Sod. (mg) | Prot. (g) | Fiber (g) | Carb. (g) | Carb. Ch. | Exchanges/Choices |
|---|---|---|---|---|---|---|---|---|---|---|---|---|
| **SYRUP** | | | | | | | | | | | | |
| **(Generic)** | | | | | | | | | | | | |
| ✔Lite Butter Pancake Syrup | 1/4 cup | 110 | 0 | 0 | 0 | | 130 | | 0 | 27 | 2 | 2 carb |
| ✔Lite Pancake Syrup | 1/4 cup | 110 | 0 | 0 | 0 | | 70 | | 0 | 27 | 2 | 2 carb |
| ✔Regular Pancake Syrup | 1/4 cup | 200 | 0 | 0 | 0 | | 40 | | 0 | 50 | 3 | 3 carb |
| **Cary's** | | | | | | | | | | | | |
| ✔Sugar Free Syrup | 1/4 cup | 35 | 0 | 0 | 0 | | 105 | | 0 | 9 | 1/2 | 1/2 carb |
| **Estee** | | | | | | | | | | | | |
| ✔Chocolate Syrup | 2 Tbsp | 15 | 0 | 0 | 0 | | 40 | | <1 | 5 | 1 | 1 carb |
| **TACO SHELLS** | | | | | | | | | | | | |
| **Old El Paso** | | | | | | | | | | | | |
| Mini Taco Shells | 7 | 150 | 7 | 42 | 1 | 0 | 130 | 2 | 2 | 19 | 1 | 1 strch, 1 fat |
| Super Taco Shells | 2 | 170 | 8 | 42 | 1 | 0 | 150 | 2 | 2 | 22 | 1 1/2 | 1 1/2 strch, 2 fat |
| Tostada Shells | 3 | 150 | 7 | 42 | 1 | 0 | 135 | 2 | 2 | 19 | 1 | 1 strch, 1 fat |
| White Corn Taco Shells | 3 | 150 | 7 | 42 | 1 | 0 | 135 | 2 | 2 | 19 | 1 | 1 strch, 1 fat |
| **Ortega** | | | | | | | | | | | | |
| Taco Shells | 2 | 140 | 7 | 45 | 1 | 0 | 200 | 2 | 2 | 20 | 1 | 1 strch, 1 fat |
| Tostada Shells | 2 | 150 | 8 | 48 | 2 | 0 | 190 | 2 | 2 | 18 | 1 | 1 strch, 2 fat |

✔= Best Bet; NA = Not Available; Carb. Ch. = Carbohydrate Choices

| Taco Shells (*Continued*) | Serving Size | Cal. | Fat (g) | % Cal. Fat | Sat. Fat (g) | Chol. (mg) | Sod. (mg) | Pro. (g) | Fiber (g) | Carb. (g) | Carb. Ch. | Servings/Exchanges |
|---|---|---|---|---|---|---|---|---|---|---|---|---|
| **Pancho Villa** | | | | | | | | | | | | |
| Taco Shells | 3 | 160 | 7 | 39 | 1 | 0 | 0 | 2 | 2 | 21 | 1 1/2 | 1 1/2 strch, 1 fat |
| **Rosarita** | | | | | | | | | | | | |
| Taco Shells | 2 | 110 | 4 | 33 | 1 | 0 | 100 | 2 | 2 | 17 | 1 | 1 carb, 1 fat |
| Tostada Shells | 2 | 120 | 5 | 38 | 1 | 0 | 35 | 2 | 0 | 20 | 1 | 1 carb, 1 fat |
| **Taco Bell Home Originals** | | | | | | | | | | | | |
| Taco Shells | 3 shells | 150 | 6 | 36 | 1 | 0 | 5 | 2 | 2 | 21 | 1 1/2 | 1 1/2 strch, 1 fat |
| **TARTAR SAUCE** | | | | | | | | | | | | |
| **Kraft** | | | | | | | | | | | | |
| Lemon Herb Tartar Sauce | 2 Tbsp | 150 | 16 | 96 | 3 | 15 | 170 | 0 | 0 | <1 | 0 | 3 fat |
| ✔Non-fat Tartar Sauce | 2 Tbsp | 25 | 0 | 0 | 0 | 0 | 200 | 0 | 0 | 5 | 0 | free |
| Tartar Sauce | 2 Tbsp | 90 | 9 | 90 | 2 | 10 | 170 | 0 | 0 | 4 | 0 | 2 fat |
| **TOASTER PASTRIES** | | | | | | | | | | | | |
| **Kellogg's** | | | | | | | | | | | | |
| PopTarts Pastry, All Varieties (Avg) | 1 | 200 | 5 | 23 | 2 | 0 | 185 | 2 | 1 | 38 | 2 1/2 | 2 1/2 strch, 1 fat |
| **Pillsbury** | | | | | | | | | | | | |
| Apple Toaster Strudel Pastries | 1 | 180 | 7 | 35 | 2 | 5 | 190 | 3 | 1 | 27 | 2 | 2 carb, 1 fat |
| Blueberry Toaster Strudel Pastries | 1 | 180 | 7 | 35 | 2 | 5 | 200 | 3 | 1 | 26 | 2 | 2 carb, 1 fat |

| | Serving | Cal. | Fat (g) | % Cal. from Fat | Sat. Fat (g) | Chol. (mg) | Sod. (mg) | Prot. (g) | Fiber (g) | Carb. (g) | Carb. Choices | Exchanges/Choices |
|---|---|---|---|---|---|---|---|---|---|---|---|---|
| Cherry Toaster Strudel Pastries | 1 | 180 | 7 | 35 | 2 | 5 | 200 | 3 | 1 | 27 | 2 | 2 carb, 1 fat |
| Cinnamon Toaster Strudel Pastries | 1 | 190 | 8 | 38 | 2 | 5 | 200 | 3 | 1 | 26 | 2 | 2 carb, 2 fat |
| Cream Cheese & Blueberry Toaster Strudel Pastries | 1 | 190 | 9 | 47 | 3 | 10 | 220 | 3 | 1 | 24 | 1 1/2 | 1 1/2 strch, 2 fat |
| Cream Cheese & Strawberry Toaster Strudel Pastries | 1 | 190 | 9 | 47 | 3 | 10 | 220 | 3 | 1 | 24 | 1 1/2 | 1 1/2 strch, 2 fat |
| Cream Cheese Toaster Strudel Pastries | 1 | 190 | 10 | 47 | 4 | 15 | 230 | 3 | 0 | 23 | 1 1/2 | 1 1/2 strch, 2 fat |
| French-Toast Toaster Strudel Pastries | 1 | 190 | 7 | 33 | 2 | 5 | 200 | 3 | 1 | 28 | 2 | 2 carb, 1 fat |
| Pop-Tarts Pastry Swirls, All Varieties (Avg) | 1 | 260 | 11 | 38 | 3 | 0 | 180 | 3 | 1 | 37 | 2 1/2 | 2 1/2 carb, 2 fat |
| Raspberry Toaster Strudel Pastries | 1 | 180 | 7 | 35 | 2 | 5 | 200 | 3 | 1 | 26 | 2 | 2 strch, 1 fat |
| Strawberry Toaster Strudel Pastries | 1 | 180 | 7 | 35 | 2 | 5 | 200 | 3 | 1 | 26 | 2 | 2 strch, 1 fat |

## TOFU

### (Generic)

| | Serving | Cal. | Fat (g) | % Cal. from Fat | Sat. Fat (g) | Chol. (mg) | Sod. (mg) | Prot. (g) | Fiber (g) | Carb. (g) | Carb. Choices | Exchanges/Choices |
|---|---|---|---|---|---|---|---|---|---|---|---|---|
| Tofu | 1/2 cup | 95 | 6 | 57 | <1 | 0 | 9 | 10 | 2 | 2 | 0 | 1 med-fat meat |

## TOMATO PRODUCTS (CANNED)

### Contadina

| | Serving | Cal. | Fat (g) | % Cal. from Fat | Sat. Fat (g) | Chol. (mg) | Sod. (mg) | Prot. (g) | Fiber (g) | Carb. (g) | Carb. Choices | Exchanges/Choices |
|---|---|---|---|---|---|---|---|---|---|---|---|---|
| ✓Crushed Tomatoes in Puree | 1/2 cup | 30 | 0 | 0 | 0 | 0 | 350 | 1 | 1 | 6 | 1/2 | 1 vegetable |
| ✓Italian (Pear) Tomatoes | 1/2 cup | 25 | 0 | 0 | 0 | 0 | 220 | 1 | 1 | 4 | 1/2 | 1 vegetable |
| ✓Italian Stewed Tomatoes | 1/2 cup | 50 | 1 | 18 | 0 | 0 | 260 | 1 | 1 | 8 | 1/2 | 1 vegetable |

✓= Best Bet; NA = Not Available; Carb. Ch. = Carbohydrate Choices

| Tomato Products (Canned) (Continued) | Serving Size | Cal. | Fat (g) | % Cal. Fat | Sat. Fat (g) | Chol. (mg) | Sod. (mg) | Pro. (g) | Fiber (g) | Carb. (g) | Carb. Ch. | Servings/Exchanges |
|---|---|---|---|---|---|---|---|---|---|---|---|---|
| ✓Italian Tomato Paste | 2 Tbsp | 35 | <1 | 0 | 0 | 0 | 290 | 1 | 1 | 7 | 1/2 | 1 vegetable |
| ✓Italian Tomato Sauce | 1/4 cup | 15 | 0 | 0 | 0 | 0 | 320 | <1 | 1 | 4 | 0 | 1 vegetable |
| ✓Mexican Stewed Tomatoes | 1/2 cup | 50 | 1 | 18 | 0 | 0 | 290 | 1 | 1 | 10 | 1/2 | 2 vegetable |
| Recipe Ready Tomatoes | 1/2 cup | 25 | <1 | 0 | 0 | 0 | 570 | 1 | 1 | 5 | 0 | 1 vegetable |
| ✓Stewed Tomatoes | 1/2 cup | 50 | 1 | 18 | 0 | 0 | 220 | 1 | 1 | 9 | 1/2 | 2 vegetable |
| ✓Thick & Zesty Tomato Sauce | 1/2 cup | 20 | 0 | 0 | 0 | 0 | 340 | 1 | 1 | 3 | 0 | 1 vegetable |
| ✓Tomato Paste | 2 Tbsp | 30 | 0 | 0 | 0 | 0 | 20 | 2 | 1 | 6 | 1/2 | 1 vegetable |
| ✓Tomato Puree | 1/4 cup | 20 | 0 | 0 | 0 | 0 | 15 | <1 | <1 | 4 | 0 | 1 vegetable |
| ✓Tomato Sauce | 1/4 cup | 15 | 0 | 0 | 0 | 0 | 280 | <1 | <1 | 3 | 0 | 1 vegetable |
| ✓Whole Peeled Tomatoes | 1/2 cup | 25 | 0 | 0 | 0 | 0 | 218 | 1 | 1 | 4 | 0 | 1 vegetable |
| **Libby's** | | | | | | | | | | | | |
| ✓Tomato Sauce | 1/4 cup | 20 | 0 | 0 | 0 | 0 | 280 | 0 | <1 | 4 | 0 | free |
| **TORTILLAS** | | | | | | | | | | | | |
| **Mission** | | | | | | | | | | | | |
| ✓96% Whole Wheat Tortilla | 1 | 140 | 3 | 19 | <1 | 0 | 380 | 4 | 2 | 26 | 2 | 2 carb, 1 fat |
| ✓98% Fat-Free Burrito-Size Flour Tortilla | 1 | 160 | <1 | 3 | 0 | 0 | 460 | 6 | 3 | 33 | 2 | 2 carb |
| Burrito-Size Flour Tortilla | 1 | 220 | 5 | 21 | 2 | 0 | 480 | 5 | 2 | 36 | 2 1/2 | 2 1/2 carb, 1 fat |
| ✓Fajita-Size Flour Tortilla | 1 | 110 | 3 | 25 | <1 | 0 | 240 | 2 | <1 | 19 | 1 | 1 carb, 1 fat |

| | Serving | Cal. | Fat (g) | % Fat | Sat. Fat (g) | Chol. (mg) | Sod. (mg) | Pro. (g) | Fiber (g) | Carb. (g) | Carb. Ch. | Exchanges |
|---|---|---|---|---|---|---|---|---|---|---|---|---|
| Gorditas Flour Tortilla | 1 | 180 | 5 | 25 | 2 | 0 | 510 | 5 | 1 | 28 | 2 | 2 carb, 1 fat |
| Soft Taco-Size Four Tortilla | 1 | 145 | 4 | 25 | 1 | 0 | 325 | 4 | 1 | 25 | 1 1/2 | 1 1/2 carb, 1 fat |
| ✔White Corn Tortilla | 2 | 100 | 2 | 18 | <1 | 0 | 25 | 2 | 1 | 18 | 1 | 1 carb |
| **Old El Paso** | | | | | | | | | | | | |
| Flour Tortilla | 1 | 130 | 4 | 28 | 1 | 0 | 290 | 3 | 0 | 21 | 1 1/2 | 1 1/2 strch, 1 fat |
| Soft Taco Tortillas | 2 | 160 | 5 | 28 | 1 | 0 | 350 | 3 | 0 | 26 | 2 | 2 strch, 1 fat |
| **TUNA (CANNED)** | | | | | | | | | | | | |
| **(Generic)** | | | | | | | | | | | | |
| Chunk Light Tuna in Vegetable Oil | 2 oz | 110 | 6 | 49 | 1 | 30 | 250 | 13 | 0 | 0 | 0 | 2 lean meat |
| ✔Chunk Light Tuna in Water | 2 oz | 60 | <1 | 0 | 0 | 30 | 250 | 13 | 0 | 0 | 0 | 2 very lean meat |
| ✔Low Sodium, Low Fat Chunk Light Tuna | 2 oz | 60 | <1 | 15 | 0 | 25 | 100 | 13 | 0 | 0 | 0 | 2 very lean meat |
| **Bumble Bee** | | | | | | | | | | | | |
| ✔Chunk Light Tuna in Water | 2.6 oz can | 70 | 1 | 13 | 0 | 40 | 350 | 15 | 0 | 0 | 0 | 2 very lean meat |
| ✔Solid Albacore Tuna in Water | 2.7 oz can | 90 | 1 | 10 | 0 | 35 | 350 | 20 | 0 | 0 | 0 | 3 very lean meat |
| **Star Kist** | | | | | | | | | | | | |
| ✔Chunk Light Tuna in Spring Water | 2.7 oz can | 80 | 1 | 11 | 0 | 40 | 350 | 18 | 0 | 0 | 0 | 3 very lean meat |
| No Drain Package, Chunk Light Tuna in Sunflower Oil | 1/4 cup | 110 | 6 | 49 | 1 | 30 | 250 | 12 | 0 | 0 | 0 | 2 lean meat |

✔ = Best Bet; NA = Not Available; Carb. Ch. = Carbohydrate Choices

| | Serving Size | Cal. | Fat (g) | % Cal. Fat | Sat. Fat (g) | Chol. (mg) | Sod. (mg) | Pro. (g) | Fiber (g) | Carb. (g) | Carb. Ch. | Servings/Exchanges |
|---|---|---|---|---|---|---|---|---|---|---|---|---|
| **Tuna (Canned) (Continued)** | | | | | | | | | | | | |
| ✔No Drain Package, Chunk White Albacore in Water | 1/4 cup | 70 | 1 | 13 | 0 | 25 | 250 | 15 | 0 | 0 | 0 | 2 very lean meat |
| ✔No Drain Package, Premium Chunk Light Tuna in Water | 1/4 cup | 60 | <1 | 15 | 0 | 30 | 250 | 13 | 0 | 0 | 0 | 2 very lean meat |
| ✔Solid White Albacore Tuna in Spring Water | 2.8 oz can | 100 | 1 | 9 | 1 | 35 | 350 | 21 | 0 | 0 | 0 | 3 very lean meat |
| **TURKEY (CANNED)** | | | | | | | | | | | | |
| **Swanson** | | | | | | | | | | | | |
| ✔Chunk White Turkey In Water | 2.5 oz | 80 | 1 | 11 | <1 | NA | 260 | 17 | 0 | 1 | 0 | 2 very lean meat |
| **TURKEY (FROZEN)** | | | | | | | | | | | | |
| **Louis Rich** | | | | | | | | | | | | |
| Breaded Turkey Nuggets | 4 | 310 | 18 | 52 | 4 | 45 | 760 | 16 | <1 | 16 | 1 | 1 carb, 2 med-fat meat, 2 fat |
| Turkey Patties | 1 | 115 | 6 | 47 | 2 | 70 | 340 | 19 | 0 | 0 | 0 | 2 lean meat |
| **TURKEY MEALS/ENTREES (FROZEN)** | | | | | | | | | | | | |
| **Armour Classics** | | | | | | | | | | | | |
| Turkey & Dressing Dinner | 11.5 oz dinner | 320 | 12 | 34 | NA | 50 | 1280 | 19 | NA | 34 | 2 | 2 carb, 2 med-fat meat |

## Banquet

| Product | Serving Size | Cal. | Fat (g) | % Cal. Fat | Sat. Fat (g) | Chol. (mg) | Sod. (mg) | Prot. (g) | Fiber (g) | Carb. (g) | Carb. Ch. | Exchanges/Choices |
|---|---|---|---|---|---|---|---|---|---|---|---|---|
| Extra Helping-Turkey & Gravy w/Dressing | 17 oz dinner | 630 | 32 | 46 | 5 | 80 | 2250 | 28 | 10 | 57 | 4 | 4 carb, 3 med-fat meat, 1 fat |
| Family Size Homestyle Gravy & Sliced Turkey | 4.8 oz | 150 | 11 | 67 | 4 | 35 | 670 | 8 | 1 | 5 | 0 | 1 med-fat meat, 1 fat |
| Honey Roast Turkey Breast | 9 oz dinner | 270 | 12 | 40 | 3 | 30 | 1310 | 11 | 4 | 29 | 2 | 2 carb, 1 med-fat meat, 1 fat |
| Turkey & Gravy w/Dressing | 9.25 oz dinner | 270 | 11 | 37 | 4 | 55 | 1060 | 14 | 3 | 30 | 2 | 2 carb, 2 med-fat meat |

## Boston Market

| Product | Serving Size | Cal. | Fat (g) | % Cal. Fat | Sat. Fat (g) | Chol. (mg) | Sod. (mg) | Prot. (g) | Fiber (g) | Carb. (g) | Carb. Ch. | Exchanges/Choices |
|---|---|---|---|---|---|---|---|---|---|---|---|---|
| Oven Roasted Turkey Medallions | 15.7 oz meal | 450 | 17 | 34 | 7 | 90 | 1820 | 33 | 3 | 40 | 2 1/2 | 2 1/2 carb, 4 lean meat |

## Budget Gourmet

| Product | Serving Size | Cal. | Fat (g) | % Cal. Fat | Sat. Fat (g) | Chol. (mg) | Sod. (mg) | Prot. (g) | Fiber (g) | Carb. (g) | Carb. Ch. | Exchanges/Choices |
|---|---|---|---|---|---|---|---|---|---|---|---|---|
| Dijon Turkey Breast | 11.2 oz meal | 340 | 12 | 32 | NA | 65 | 860 | 20 | NA | 37 | 2 1/2 | 2 1/2 carb, 2 med-fat meat |
| Sliced Turkey Breast | 11.1 oz meal | 290 | 9 | 28 | NA | 45 | 1200 | 16 | NA | 36 | 2 1/2 | 2 1/2 carb, 1 med-fat meat, 1 fat |
| Special Selections Turkey w/Scalloped Noodles | 9 oz meal | 440 | 20 | 41 | 10 | 115 | 840 | 19 | 2 | 44 | 3 | 3 carb, 1 med-fat meat, 3 fat |
| Turkey a la King w/Rice | 10 oz dinner | 390 | 18 | 42 | NA | 75 | 740 | 20 | NA | 36 | 2 1/2 | 2 1/2 carb, 2 med-fat meat, 2 fat |

✓ = Best Bet; NA = Not Available; Carb. Ch. = Carbohydrate Choices

| Turkey Meals/Entrees (Frozen) (*Continued*) | Serving Size | Cal. | Fat (g) | % Cal. Fat | Sat. Fat (g) | Chol. (mg) | Sod. (mg) | Pro. (g) | Fiber (g) | Carb. (g) | Carb. Ch. | Servings/Exchanges |
|---|---|---|---|---|---|---|---|---|---|---|---|---|
| **Healthy Choice** | | | | | | | | | | | | |
| ✔Bowl Creation, Turkey Divan | 9.5 oz bowl | 250 | 6 | 22 | 2 | 25 | 600 | 18 | 5 | 31 | 2 | 2 carb, 2 lean meat |
| ✔Country Inn Roast Turkey | 10 oz meal | 250 | 6 | 22 | 2 | 40 | 530 | 20 | 4 | 28 | 2 | 2 carb, 3 lean meat |
| ✔Country Roast Turkey w/Mushrooms | 8.5 oz meal | 230 | 5 | 20 | 2 | 45 | 440 | 19 | 2 | 26 | 2 | 2 carb, 2 lean meat |
| **Lean Cuisine** | | | | | | | | | | | | |
| ✔American Favorites, Roasted Turkey Breast | 9.8 oz meal | 270 | 3 | 10 | <1 | 20 | 590 | 13 | 5 | 49 | 3 | 3 carb, 2 lean meat |
| ✔Café Classics, Turkey Tenderloins | 9 oz meal | 240 | 5 | 17 | 1 | 30 | 590 | 14 | 5 | 37 | 2 1/2 | 2 1/2 carb, 1 med-fat meat |
| ✔Homestyle Turkey | 9.4 oz meal | 230 | 5 | 20 | 1 | 40 | 590 | 17 | 3 | 30 | 2 | 2 carb, 2 lean meat |
| ✔Roasted Turkey Breast | 14 oz meal | 350 | 6 | 15 | 1 | 25 | 840 | 24 | 8 | 49 | 3 | 3 carb, 2 lean meat |
| **Marie Callender** | | | | | | | | | | | | |
| ✔Grilled Turkey Breast & Rice Pilaf | 11.8 oz meal | 320 | 10 | 28 | 4 | 40 | 940 | 22 | 4 | 34 | 2 | 2 carb, 2 med-fat meat |
| Turkey w/Gravy & Dressing | 14 oz meal | 500 | 19 | 34 | 9 | 80 | 2040 | 31 | 4 | 52 | 3 1/2 | 3 1/2 carb, 3 med-fat meat, 1 fat |
| **Morton** | | | | | | | | | | | | |
| Gravy & Turkey w/Dressing Meal | 9 oz meal | 240 | 10 | 38 | 4 | 40 | 1200 | 10 | 4 | 27 | 2 | 2 carb, 1 med-fat meat, 1 fat |

| | Amount | Cal. | Fat (g) | % Fat Cal. | Sat. Fat (g) | Chol. (mg) | Sod. (mg) | Carb. (g) | Fiber (g) | Pro. (g) | Carb. Ch. | Exchanges |
|---|---|---|---|---|---|---|---|---|---|---|---|---|
| **Stouffer's** | | | | | | | | | | | | |
| Hearty Portions, Roast Turkey Breast | 16 oz | 490 | 20 | 37 | 6 | 35 | 1880 | 25 | 6 | 52 | 3 1/2 | 2 1/2 carb, 2 med-fat meat, 2 fat |
| Homestyle Roast Turkey | 9.6 oz meal | 310 | 13 | 38 | 6 | 50 | 930 | 22 | 3 | 27 | 2 | 2 carb, 2 med-fat meat, 1 fat |
| Turkey Tetrazzini | 10 oz meal | 360 | 17 | 43 | 7 | 55 | 1060 | 19 | 1 | 33 | 2 | 2 carb, 2 med-fat meat, 1 fat |
| **Swanson** | | | | | | | | | | | | |
| Stuffing Baked Turkey | 13.5 oz meal | 450 | 15 | 30 | 4 | 25 | 1080 | 20 | 5 | 59 | 4 | 4 carb, 1 med-fat meat, 2 fat |
| Turkey Breast | 11.8 oz meal | 330 | 6 | 16 | 1 | 40 | 1290 | 18 | 4 | 50 | 3 | 3 carb, 1 med-fat meat |
| **Swanson Hungry-Man** | | | | | | | | | | | | |
| Turkey w/Gravy and Stuffing | 16.8 oz meal | 500 | 15 | 27 | 4 | 50 | 1550 | 30 | 7 | 61 | 4 | 4 carb, 3 med-fat meat |

## VEAL MEALS/ENTREES (FROZEN)

| | Amount | Cal. | Fat (g) | % Fat Cal. | Sat. Fat (g) | Chol. (mg) | Sod. (mg) | Carb. (g) | Fiber (g) | Pro. (g) | Carb. Ch. | Exchanges |
|---|---|---|---|---|---|---|---|---|---|---|---|---|
| **Armour Classics** | | | | | | | | | | | | |
| Veal Parmigiana Dinner | 11.25 oz dinner | 400 | 22 | 50 | NA | 55 | 1220 | 18 | NA | 34 | 2 | 2 carb, 1 med-fat meat, 3 fat |

✓ = Best Bet; NA = Not Available; Carb. Ch. = Carbohydrate Choices

| Veal Meals/Entrees (Frozen) (Continued) | Serving Size | Cal. | Fat (g) | % Cal. Fat | Sat. Fat (g) | Chol. (mg) | Sod. (mg) | Pro. (g) | Fiber (g) | Carb. (g) | Carb. Ch. | Servings/Exchanges |
|---|---|---|---|---|---|---|---|---|---|---|---|---|
| **Banquet** | | | | | | | | | | | | |
| Family Size Veal Parmigiana Patties w/Tomato Sauce | 4.7 oz | 230 | 14 | 55 | 4 | 20 | 740 | 9 | 2 | 19 | 1 | 1 carb, 1 med-fat meat, 2 fat |
| Veal Parmigiana | 9 oz dinner | 360 | 19 | 48 | 6 | 25 | 960 | 13 | 7 | 35 | 2 | 2 carb, 2 med-fat meat, 2 fat |
| **Morton** | | | | | | | | | | | | |
| Veal Parmigiana w/Tomato Sauce | 8.8 oz meal | 280 | 15 | 48 | 5 | 25 | 950 | 8 | 4 | 30 | 2 | 2 carb, 3 fat |
| **Stouffer's** | | | | | | | | | | | | |
| Homestyle Veal Parmigiana | 11.6 oz meal | 430 | 17 | 36 | 5 | 80 | 1120 | 21 | 6 | 49 | 3 | 3 carb, 2 med-fat meat, 1 fat |
| **Swanson** | | | | | | | | | | | | |
| Veal Parmigiana | 11.3 oz meal | 390 | 18 | 42 | 8 | 85 | 1060 | 19 | 5 | 40 | 2 1/2 | 2 1/2 carb, 2 med-fat meat, 2 fat |
| **VEGETABLE JUICE (CANNED OR BOTTLED)** | | | | | | | | | | | | |
| **(Generic)** | | | | | | | | | | | | |
| ✓Tomato Juice | 1/2 cup | 21 | <1 | 0 | 0 | 0 | 440 | <1 | <1 | 5 | 0 | 1 vegetable |
| ✓Vegetable Juice | 1/2 cup | 23 | <1 | 0 | 0 | 0 | 442 | <1 | 1 | 6 | 1/2 | 1 vegetable |
| ✓Vegetable Juice Cocktail | 1/2 cup | 23 | <1 | 0 | <1 | 0 | 442 | <1 | 1 | 6 | 1/2 | 1 vegetable |

## Campbells

| | Serving | Cal. | Fat (g) | % Cal. Fat | Sat. Fat (g) | Chol. (mg) | Sod. (mg) | Pro. (g) | Fib. (g) | Carb. (g) | Carb. Ch. | Exchanges/Choices |
|---|---|---|---|---|---|---|---|---|---|---|---|---|
| Tomato Juice | 1 cup | 50 | 0 | 0 | 0 | 0 | 860 | 2 | 1 | 9 | 1/2 | 2 vegetable |
| V8 100% Vegetable Juice | 1 cup | 50 | 0 | 0 | 0 | 0 | 620 | 1 | 1 | 10 | 0 | 2 vegetable |
| V8 Picante Vegetable Juice | 1 cup | 50 | 0 | 0 | 0 | 0 | 680 | 2 | 1 | 10 | 1/2 | 2 vegetable |
| V8 Spicy Hot 100% Vegetable Juice | 1 cup | 50 | 0 | 0 | 0 | 0 | 780 | 2 | 1 | 10 | 1/2 | 2 vegetable |
| ✓V8-Light Tangy 100% Veg Juice | 1 cup | 60 | 0 | 0 | 0 | 0 | 340 | 2 | 1 | 11 | 1 | 2 vegetable |

## VEGETABLE MEALS/ENTREES (FROZEN)

### Budget Gourmet

| | Serving | Cal. | Fat (g) | % Cal. Fat | Sat. Fat (g) | Chol. (mg) | Sod. (mg) | Pro. (g) | Fib. (g) | Carb. (g) | Carb. Ch. | Exchanges/Choices |
|---|---|---|---|---|---|---|---|---|---|---|---|---|
| ✓Hearty Tex-Mex Rice & Beans | 14 oz meal; | 470 | 14 | 27 | 6 | 30 | 880 | 16 | 8 | 69 | 4 1/2 | 4 1/2 carb, 3 fat |

### Healthy Choice

| | Serving | Cal. | Fat (g) | % Cal. Fat | Sat. Fat (g) | Chol. (mg) | Sod. (mg) | Pro. (g) | Fib. (g) | Carb. (g) | Carb. Ch. | Exchanges/Choices |
|---|---|---|---|---|---|---|---|---|---|---|---|---|
| ✓Cheddar Broccoli Potatoes | 10.5 oz meal | 330 | 7 | 19 | 3 | 25 | 550 | 13 | 6 | 53 | 3 1/2 | 3 1/2 carb, 1 fat |
| ✓Garden Potato Casserole | 9.3 oz meal | 220 | 6 | 27 | 2 | 10 | 520 | 11 | 6 | 30 | 2 | 2 carb, 1 med-fat meat |

### Lean Cuisine

| | Serving | Cal. | Fat (g) | % Cal. Fat | Sat. Fat (g) | Chol. (mg) | Sod. (mg) | Pro. (g) | Fib. (g) | Carb. (g) | Carb. Ch. | Exchanges/Choices |
|---|---|---|---|---|---|---|---|---|---|---|---|---|
| Deluxe Cheddar Potato | 10.4 oz | 270 | 7 | 23 | 4 | 20 | 590 | 12 | 6 | 40 | 2 1/2 | 2 1/2 carb, 1 med-fat meat |
| ✓Stuffed Cabbage w/Whipped Potatoes | 9.5 oz meal | 170 | 5 | 26 | 2 | 15 | 380 | 8 | 5 | 24 | 1 1/2 | 1 1/2 carb, 1 med-fat meat |

✓ = Best Bet; NA = Not Available; Carb. Ch. = Carbohydrate Choices

| Vegetable Meals/Entrees (Frozen) (Continued) | Serving Size | Cal. | Fat (g) | % Cal. Fat | Sat. Fat (g) | Chol. (mg) | Sod. (mg) | Pro. (g) | Fiber (g) | Carb. (g) | Carb. Ch. | Servings/Exchanges |
|---|---|---|---|---|---|---|---|---|---|---|---|---|
| **Marie Callender** | | | | | | | | | | | | |
| Cheese, Broccoli & Bacon Topped Potato Wedges | 13 oz meal | 420 | 15 | 33 | 8 | 55 | 1480 | 20 | 7 | 50 | 3 | 3 carb, 2 med-fat meat, 1 fat |
| **Stouffer's** | | | | | | | | | | | | |
| ✔Stuffed Green Peppers | 10 oz meal | 200 | 5 | 23 | 2 | 20 | 820 | 11 | 3 | 27 | 2 | 2 carb, 1 med-fat meat |
| **Weight Watchers Smart Ones** | | | | | | | | | | | | |
| Sante Fe Style Rice & Beans | 10 oz meal | 300 | 8 | 24 | 4 | 20 | 620 | 12 | 6 | 49 | 3 | 3 carb, 1 med-fat meat, 1 fat |
| **VEGETABLE MEALS/ENTREES KITS (FROZEN, AS PREPARED)** | | | | | | | | | | | | |
| **Green Giant** | | | | | | | | | | | | |
| Create A Meal, Fajita Style | 10 oz | 430 | 16 | 33 | 6 | 70 | 1300 | 32 | 4 | 40 | 2 1/2 | 2 strch, 2 vegetable, 3 med-fat meat |
| **VEGETABLE SIDE DISHES (FROZEN)** | | | | | | | | | | | | |
| **Bird's Eye** | | | | | | | | | | | | |
| ✔Broccoli Stir Fry Vegetables | 3/4 cup | 45 | <1 | 0 | 0 | 0 | 34 | 3 | 4 | 9 | 1/2 | 2 vegetable |
| Chinese Stir Fry Vegetables | 1/2 cup | 36 | <1 | 0 | <1 | 0 | 540 | 2 | 2 | 8 | 1/2 | 1 vegetable |
| Creamed Spinach | 1/2 cup | 111 | 8 | 65 | 5 | 20 | 565 | 4 | 1 | 7 | 1/2 | 1 vegetable, 2 fat |
| ✔Deluxe Artichoke Hearts | 1/2 cup | 38 | <1 | 0 | <1 | 0 | 47 | 3 | 6 | 8 | 1/2 | 1 vegetable |

| | | | | | | | | | | | | |
|---|---|---|---|---|---|---|---|---|---|---|---|---|
| Japanese-Style Vegetables | 1/2 cup | 78 | 5 | 58 | 2 | 12 | 320 | 2 | 2 | 8 | 1/2 | 1 vegetable, 1 fat |
| ✔Pepper Stir Fry Vegetables | 3/4 cup | 29 | <1 | 0 | 0 | 0 | 21 | 3 | 3 | 6 | 1/2 | 1 vegetable |
| **Bird's Eye Classic** | | | | | | | | | | | | |
| ✔Broccoli w/Cauliflower, Carrot w/Butter | 1/2 cup | 55 | 2 | 33 | 1 | 5 | 240 | 2 | 3 | 8 | 1/2 | 2 vegetable |
| ✔Broccoli w/Cheese Sauce | 1/2 cup | 70 | 3 | 39 | 2 | 0 | 425 | 4 | 2 | 7 | 1/2 | 1 vegetable, 1 fat |
| ✔Cauliflower w/Cheese Sauce | 1/2 cup | 65 | 3 | 42 | 2 | 7 | 380 | 4 | 2 | 7 | 1/2 | 1 vegetable, 1 fat |
| ✔Peas & Potatoes in Cream Sauce | 1/2 cup | 75 | 2 | 24 | <1 | 4 | 380 | 4 | 3 | 12 | 1 | 1 strch |
| ✔Small Onions w/Cream Sauce | 1/2 cup | 60 | 2 | 30 | <1 | 4 | 325 | 2 | 2 | 10 | 1/2 | 2 vegetable |
| ✔Sweet Corn w/Butter Sauce | 1/2 cup | 115 | 3 | 23 | 1 | 5 | 216 | 3 | 2 | 23 | 1 1/2 | 1 1/2 strch, 1 fat |
| **Boston Market** | | | | | | | | | | | | |
| Creamed Spinach | 1/2 cup | 190 | 14 | 66 | 6 | 25 | 580 | 6 | 2 | 9 | 1/2 | 2 vegetables, 3 fat |
| **Budget Gourmet** | | | | | | | | | | | | |
| ✔Oriental Green Peas & Water Chestnuts | 5 oz | 120 | 3 | 25 | NA | 5 | 240 | 5 | NA | 15 | 1 | 1 carb, 1 fat |
| Spinach Au Gratin | 5.5 oz | 221 | 17 | 69 | 8 | 40 | 410 | 7 | 2 | 12 | 1 | 1 carb, 1 med-fat meat, 2 fat |
| **Gourmet Dining** | | | | | | | | | | | | |
| ✔Grilled Vegetable Medley, Fire Roasted | 3 oz | 20 | 0 | 0 | 0 | 0 | 15 | 1 | 2 | 5 | 0 | 1 vegetable |
| ✔Imperial Style Asian Blend | 3/4 cup | 30 | 0 | 0 | 0 | 0 | 25 | 1 | 2 | 5 | 0 | 1 vegetable |
| Stir Fry Vegetables | | | | | | | | | | | | |

✔ = Best Bet; NA = Not Available; Carb. Ch. = Carbohydrate Choices

| Vegetable Side Dishes (Frozen) (*Continued*) | Serving Size | Cal. | Fat (g) | % Cal. Fat | Sat. Fat (g) | Chol. (mg) | Sod. (mg) | Pro. (g) | Fiber (g) | Carb. (g) | Carb. Ch. | Servings/Exchanges |
|---|---|---|---|---|---|---|---|---|---|---|---|---|
| **Green Giant** | | | | | | | | | | | | |
| Broccoli in Cheese Sauce | 2/3 cup | 70 | 3 | 39 | 1 | <5 | 520 | 3 | 2 | 9 | 1/2 | 2 vegetable, 1 fat |
| ✔Broccoli Spears in Butter Sauce | 1/2 cup | 50 | 2 | 36 | 1 | <5 | 330 | 1.9 | 2 | 7 | 1/2 | 1 vegetable |
| ✔Broccoli-Cauliflower-Carrots in Butter Sauce | 3/4 cup | 60 | 2 | 30 | 1 | <5 | 300 | 2 | 2 | 8 | 1/2 | 2 vegetable |
| ✔Broccoli-Pasta-Sweet Peas in Butter Sauce | 3/4 cup | 70 | 2 | 26 | 2 | <5 | 280 | 3 | 2 | 11 | 1 | 1/2 strch, 1 vegetable |
| ✔Corn Niblets in Butter Sauce | 2/3 cup | 130 | 3 | 21 | 2 | <5 | 350 | 3 | 3 | 23 | 1 1/2 | 1 1/2 strch, 1 fat |
| ✔Cream Style Corn | 1/2 cup | 110 | 1 | 8 | 0 | 0 | 330 | 2 | 2 | 23 | 1 1/2 | 1 1/2 strch |
| Green Bean Casserole | 2/3 cup | 130 | 9 | 62 | 5 | 15 | 510 | 2 | 2 | 10 | 1/2 | 2 vegetable, 2 fat |
| Honey Glazed Carrots | 1 cup | 90 | 4 | 40 | <1 | 0 | 140 | <1 | 2 | 13 | 1 | 1/2 carb, 1 vegetable, 1 fat |
| ✔LeSueur Baby Peas & Butter Sauce | 3/4 cup | 100 | 2 | 18 | 2 | <5 | 370 | 5 | 16 | 16 | 1 | 1 strch |
| ✔LeSueur Baby Peas & Mushrooms | 3/4 cup | 60 | 0 | 0 | 0 | 0 | 105 | 4 | 4 | 10 | 1/2 | 2 vegetable |
| ✔Mixed Vegetables in Butter Sauce | 3/4 cup | 70 | 2 | 26 | 1 | <5 | 240 | 2 | 3 | 11 | 1 | 2 vegetable |
| ✔Select Amer. Mixtures-Broc/Waterchestnut Stir Fry | 2/3 cup | 25 | 0 | 0 | 0 | 0 | 30 | 1 | 2 | 5 | 0 | 1 vegetable |
| ✔Select American Mixtures, Broccoli/Carrots Skillet | 2/3 cup | 25 | 0 | 0 | 0 | 0 | 30 | 2 | 2 | 4 | 0 | 1 vegetable |

| | Amount | Cal. | Fat (g) | % Cal. Fat | Sat. Fat (g) | Chol. (mg) | Sod. (mg) | Carb. (g) | Fiber (g) | Pro. (g) | Carb. Ch. | Servings/Exchanges |
|---|---|---|---|---|---|---|---|---|---|---|---|---|
| ✓ Shoepeg White Corn in Sauce | 3/4 cup | 120 | 3 | 23 | 2 | 1 | 320 | 21 | 3 | 3 | 1 1/2 | 1 1/2 strch, 1 fat |
| ✓ Southwestern Style Corn | 3/4 cup | 90 | 1 | 10 | 0 | 0 | 130 | 18 | 1 | 3 | 1 | 1 strch |
| ✓ Sweet Peas in Butter Sauce | 3/4 cup | 100 | 2 | 18 | 2 | <5 | 400 | 16 | 5 | 4 | 1 | 1 strch |
| ✓ Vegetables Alfredo | 3/4 cup | 80 | 3 | 34 | 2 | 5 | 450 | 9 | 3 | 4 | 1/2 | 2 vegetable, 1 fat |
| Vegetables Teriyaki | 1 1/4 cup | 101 | <1 | 0 | 0 | 0 | 872 | 19 | 2 | 5 | 1 | 4 vegetable |

**Shanghai**

| | Amount | Cal. | Fat (g) | % Cal. Fat | Sat. Fat (g) | Chol. (mg) | Sod. (mg) | Carb. (g) | Fiber (g) | Pro. (g) | Carb. Ch. | Servings/Exchanges |
|---|---|---|---|---|---|---|---|---|---|---|---|---|
| ✓ Gourmet Stir-Fry International Vegetable Blend | 1 cup | 60 | 0 | 0 | 0 | 0 | 420 | 13 | 2 | 2 | 1 | 3 vegetables |

**Stouffer's**

| | Amount | Cal. | Fat (g) | % Cal. Fat | Sat. Fat (g) | Chol. (mg) | Sod. (mg) | Carb. (g) | Fiber (g) | Pro. (g) | Carb. Ch. | Servings/Exchanges |
|---|---|---|---|---|---|---|---|---|---|---|---|---|
| Corn Souffle | 4 oz | 170 | 7 | 37 | 2 | 55 | 540 | 21 | 1 | 5 | 1 1/2 | 1 1/2 carb, 1 fat |
| Cream Spinach | 4.5 oz | 160 | 12 | 68 | 4 | 15 | 380 | 8 | 2 | 4 | 1/2 | 1 vegetable, 2 fat |
| Green Bean Mushroom Casserole | 4 oz | 130 | 8 | 55 | 2 | 2 | 450 | 12 | 2 | 3 | 1 | 1 carb, 2 fat |
| Spinach Souffle | 4 oz | 150 | 10 | 60 | 2 | 120 | 480 | 9 | 0 | 6 | 1/2 | 1/2 carb, 1 med-fat meat, 1 fat |

## VEGETABLES (CANNED AND FROZEN)

**(Generic)**

| | Amount | Cal. | Fat (g) | % Cal. Fat | Sat. Fat (g) | Chol. (mg) | Sod. (mg) | Carb. (g) | Fiber (g) | Pro. (g) | Carb. Ch. | Servings/Exchanges |
|---|---|---|---|---|---|---|---|---|---|---|---|---|
| ✓ Asparagus Spears, Canned | 1/2 cup | 23 | <1 | 0 | <1 | 0 | 472 | 3 | 2 | 3 | 0 | 1 vegetable |
| ✓ Asparagus, Frozen | 1/2 cup | 23 | <1 | 0 | <1 | 0 | 3 | 4 | 3 | 2 | 0 | 1 vegetable |
| ✓ Bamboo Shoots, Canned | 1 cup | 25 | <1 | 0 | <1 | 0 | 9 | 4 | 2 | 2 | 0 | 1 vegetable |

| Vegetables (Canned and Frozen) (Continued) | Serving Size | Cal. | Fat (g) | % Cal. Fat | Sat. Fat (g) | Chol. (mg) | Sod. (mg) | Pro. (g) | Fiber (g) | Carb. (g) | Carb. Ch. | Servings/Exchanges |
|---|---|---|---|---|---|---|---|---|---|---|---|---|
| ✔Beans, Green or Wax, Canned | 1/2 cup | 14 | <1 | 0 | 0 | 0 | 171 | <1 | 1 | 3 | 0 | 1 vegetable |
| ✔Beets, Canned | 1/2 cup | 26 | <1 | 0 | 0 | 0 | 233 | <1 | 2 | 6 | 1/2 | 1 vegetable |
| ✔Broccoli Spears, Frozen | 1/2 cup | 26 | <1 | 0 | 0 | 0 | 22 | 3 | 3 | 5 | 0 | 1 vegetable |
| ✔Brussel Sprouts, Frozen, Cooked | 1/2 cup | 33 | <1 | 0 | <1 | 0 | 18 | 3 | 3 | 7 | 1/2 | 1 vegetable |
| ✔Carrots, Canned | 1/2 cup | 17 | <1 | 0 | 0 | 0 | 176 | <1 | 1 | 4 | 0 | 1 vegetable |
| ✔Cauliflower, Frozen, Cooked | 1/2 cup | 17 | <1 | 0 | 0 | 0 | 16 | 1 | 2 | 3 | 0 | 1 vegetable |
| ✔Corn On Cob-Frozen | 3 inch | 70 | <1 | 0 | 0 | 0 | 5 | 2 | 1 | 14 | 1 | 1 strch |
| ✔Corn, Canned | 1/2 cup | 83 | <1 | 0 | <1 | 0 | 286 | 3 | 6 | 20 | 1 | 1 strch |
| ✔Corn, Frozen, Cooked | 1/2 cup | 66 | <1 | 0 | 0 | 0 | 4 | 3 | 2 | 17 | 1 | 1 strch |
| ✔Green Beans, Frozen | 1/2 cup | 18 | <1 | 0 | 0 | 0 | 9 | <1 | 2 | 4 | 0 | 1 vegetable |
| ✔Green Peas Green, Canned | 1/2 cup | 59 | <1 | 0 | <1 | 0 | 186 | 4 | 4 | 11 | 1 | 1 strch |
| ✔Green Peas, Frozen | 1/2 cup | 62 | <1 | 0 | 0 | 0 | 70 | 4 | 4 | 11 | 1 | 1 strch |
| ✔Lima Beans, Frozen | 1/2 cup | 95 | <1 | 0 | <1 | 0 | 26 | 7 | 7 | 18 | 1 | 1 strch |
| ✔Mixed Vegetables w/Corn, Frozen | 1/2 cup | 40 | 0 | 0 | 0 | 0 | 40 | 2 | 2 | 9 | 1/2 | 1/2 strch |
| ✔Mixed Vegetables, Frozen | 2/3 cup | 60 | 0 | 0 | 0 | 0 | 35 | 2 | 3 | 12 | 1 | 1 carb |
| ✔Mixed Vegetables, No Corn, Peas, Pasta | 1/2 cup | 20 | 0 | 0 | 0 | 0 | 15 | 1 | 1 | 3 | 0 | 1 vegetable |
| ✔Mushrooms, Canned | 1/2 cup | 19 | <1 | 0 | 0 | 0 | 331 | 2 | 2 | 4 | 0 | 1 vegetable |
| ✔Okra, Frozen, Cooked | 1/2 cup | 34 | <1 | 0 | <1 | 0 | 3 | 2 | 3 | 8 | 1/2 | 1 vegetable |

| | Serving | Cal. | Fat (g) | % Cal. Fat | Sat. Fat (g) | Chol. (mg) | Sod. (mg) | Prot. (g) | Fiber (g) | Carb. (g) | Carb. Ch. | Exchanges/Choices |
|---|---|---|---|---|---|---|---|---|---|---|---|---|
| ✔ Spinach, Canned | 1/2 cup | 25 | <1 | 0 | 0 | 0 | 29 | 3 | 3 | 4 | 0 | 1 vegetable |
| ✔ Spinach, Frozen, Cooked | 1/2 cup | 27 | <1 | 0 | 0 | 0 | 82 | 3 | 3 | 5 | 0 | 1 vegetable |
| ✔ Succotash, Corn & Limas, Canned | 1/2 cup | 81 | <1 | 0 | 0 | 0 | 282 | 3 | 3 | 18 | 1 | 1 strch |
| ✔ Sweet Potatos, Canned | 1/2 cup | 92 | <1 | 0 | 0 | 0 | 53 | 2 | 3 | 22 | 1 1/2 | 1 1/2 strch |
| ✔ Tomatoes, Canned | 1/2 cup | 24 | <1 | 0 | 0 | 0 | 196 | 1 | 1 | 5 | 0 | 1 vegetable |
| ✔ Yellow Hominy, Canned | 1/2 cup | 58 | <1 | 0 | 0 | 0 | 168 | 2 | 2 | 12 | 1 | 1 strch |
| **Chef Mate** | | | | | | | | | | | | |
| Oriental Vegetables | 1 cup | 180 | 7 | 35 | 1 | 0 | 1410 | 3 | 3 | 27 | 2 | 2 carb, 1 fat |
| **Green Giant** | | | | | | | | | | | | |
| ✔ Butter Beans (Frozen) | 1/2 cup | 80 | 0 | 0 | 0 | 0 | 170 | 6 | 4 | 18 | 1 | 1 strch |
| ✔ Harvard Beets-Canned | 1/3 cup | 60 | 0 | 0 | 0 | 0 | 270 | <1 | 2 | 15 | 1 | 1/2 carb, 1 vegetable |
| ✔ Three Bean Salad-Canned | 1/2 cup | 90 | 0 | 0 | 0 | 20 | 490 | 3 | 4 | 20 | 1 | 1 strch |
| **Libby's** | | | | | | | | | | | | |
| ✔ Pumpkin, Solid Pack, Canned | 1/2 cup | 40 | <1 | 0 | 0 | 0 | 5 | 2 | 5 | 9 | 1/2 | 2 vegetable |
| **Mrs. Paul's** | | | | | | | | | | | | |
| ✔ Candied Sweet Potatoes | 1/2 cup | 276 | 1 | 3 | 0 | 0 | 110 | <1 | 2 | 67 | 4 1/2 | 4 1/2 carb |
| Old Fashioned Onion Rings | 2.5 oz | 200 | 10 | 45 | NA | NA | 365 | 3 | 1 | 24 | 1 1/2 | 1 1/2 carb, 2 fat |
| **Ore Ida** | | | | | | | | | | | | |
| ✔ Stew Vegetables | 2 oz | 35 | 0 | 0 | 0 | 0 | 45 | <1 | <1 | 7 | 1/2 | 1 vegetable |

✔= Best Bet; NA = Not Available; Carb. Ch. = Carbohydrate Choices

# VEGETABLES (FRESH PACKED)

## Fresh Express

| Product | Serving Size | Cal. | Fat (g) | % Cal. Fat | Sat. Fat (g) | Chol. (mg) | Sod. (mg) | Pro. (g) | Fiber (g) | Carb. (g) | Carb. Ch. | Servings/Exchanges |
|---|---|---|---|---|---|---|---|---|---|---|---|---|
| ✔American Salad Blend (Iceberg, Romaine, & Carrots) | 1 1/2 cups | 15 | 0 | 0 | 0 | 0 | 10 | 1 | 1 | 3 | 0 | 1 vegetable |
| ✔Angel Hair Cole Slaw | 1 cup | 20 | 0 | 0 | 0 | 0 | 15 | 1 | 2 | 5 | 0 | 1 vegetable |
| Caesar Salad Kit | 2 cups | 160 | 14 | 79 | 3 | 10 | 380 | 3 | 1 | 8 | 1/2 | 2 vegetables, 3 fat |
| Caesar Salad Kit w/Light Dressing | 2 cups | 100 | 7 | 63 | 2 | 10 | 360 | 2 | 1 | 8 | 1/2 | 2 vegetables, 1 fat |
| Caesar Supreme Salad Kit | 2 cups | 150 | 12 | 72 | 3 | 10 | 350 | 3 | 1 | 8 | 1/2 | 2 vegetables, 2 fat |
| Chicken Caesar Fresh Dinner-Size Salad | 3 cups | 260 | 18 | 62 | 4 | 50 | 940 | 14 | 1 | 12 | 1 | 2 vegetables, 1 med-fat meat, 2 fat |
| Chicken Caesar Fresh Lunch Salad | 1 pkg | 240 | 17 | 64 | 3 | 45 | 870 | 12 | 2 | 11 | 1 | 2 vegetables, 1 med-fat meat, 2 fat |
| Cole Slaw Kit | 2 cups | 120 | 8 | 60 | 1 | 5 | 135 | 1 | 2 | 12 | 1 | 2 vegetables, 2 fat |
| ✔Coleslaw Blend | 1 1/2 cups | 20 | 0 | 0 | 0 | 0 | 15 | 1 | 2 | 5 | 0 | 1 vegetable |
| ✔Double Carrots & Romaine Salad | 2 cups | 20 | 0 | 0 | 0 | 0 | 15 | 1 | 1 | 4 | 0 | 1 vegetable |
| ✔European Salad Blend (Romaine & Green Leaf) | 1 1/2 cups | 15 | 0 | 0 | 0 | 0 | 10 | 1 | 1 | 3 | 0 | 1 vegetable |

| | Amount | Cal. | Fat (g) | % Cal. Fat | Sat. Fat (g) | Chol. (mg) | Sod. (mg) | Carb. (g) | Fiber (g) | Pro. (g) | Carb. Ch. | Exchanges/Choices |
|---|---|---|---|---|---|---|---|---|---|---|---|---|
| ✓Fancy Field Greens Salad Blend (Romaine & Frisee) | 1 1/2 cups | 15 | 0 | 0 | 0 | 0 | 15 | 3 | 2 | 1 | 0 | 1 vegetable |
| ✓Hearts of Romaine Salad Blend | 1 1/2 cups | 15 | 0 | 0 | 0 | 0 | 5 | 2 | 1 | 5 | 0 | free |
| ✓Iceburg Garden Salad | 1 1/2 cups | 15 | 0 | 0 | 0 | 0 | 10 | 3 | 1 | 1 | 0 | 1 vegetable |
| ✓Iceburg Lettuce Shreds | 1 1/2 cups | 15 | 0 | 0 | 0 | 0 | 10 | 3 | 1 | 1 | 0 | 1 vegetable |
| ✓Italian Salad Blend (Romaine & Radicchio) | 1 1/2 cups | 15 | 0 | 0 | 0 | 0 | 10 | 2 | 1 | 1 | 0 | free |
| Oriental Salad Kit | 1 1/2 cups | 140 | 9 | 58 | 2 | 0 | 360 | 13 | 2 | 2 | 1 | 2 vegetables, 2 fat |
| Ranch Salad Kit | 2 cups | 140 | 11 | 71 | 2 | 10 | 300 | 6 | 1 | 2 | 1/2 | 1 vegetable, 2 fat |
| Ranch Salad Kit w/Light Dressing | 2 cups | 100 | 7 | 63 | 1 | 0 | 310 | 8 | 1 | 2 | 1/2 | 1 vegetable, 1 fat |
| ✓Real Bacon Crumblers Iceburg Salad | 2 cups | 35 | 1 | 26 | <1 | 5 | 260 | 3 | 1 | 4 | 0 | 1 vegetable |
| ✓Riviera Salad Blend (Butter Lettuce & Radicchio) | 1 1/2 cups | 10 | 0 | 0 | 0 | 0 | 5 | 2 | <1 | 1 | 0 | free |
| Romaine & Iceburg Garden Salad | 2 1/2 cups | 15 | 0 | 0 | 0 | 0 | 10 | 3 | 1 | 1 | 0 | 1 vegetable |
| ✓Spinach Salad | 1 1/2 cups | 40 | 0 | 0 | 0 | 0 | 160 | 10 | 5 | 2 | 1/2 | 2 vegetables |
| Taco Fiesta Salad Kit | 2 cups | 110 | 8 | 65 | 2 | 10 | 230 | 7 | 1 | 3 | 1/2 | 1 vegetable, 2 fat |
| Teriyaki Chicken Fresh Dinner-Size Salad | 4 cups | 260 | 16 | 55 | 3 | 30 | 820 | 9 | 1 | 6 | 1/2 | 2 vegetables, 1 med-fat meat, 2 fat |

✓ = Best Bet; NA = Not Available; Carb. Ch. = Carbohydrate Choices

| Vegetables (Fresh Packed) (*Continued*) | Serving Size | Cal. | Fat (g) | % Cal. Fat | Sat. Fat (g) | Chol. (mg) | Sod. (mg) | Pro. (g) | Fiber (g) | Carb. (g) | Carb. Ch. | Servings/Exchanges |
|---|---|---|---|---|---|---|---|---|---|---|---|---|
| Teriyaki Chicken Fresh Lunch Salad | 1 pkg | 250 | 16 | 58 | 3 | 25 | 800 | 11 | 2 | 17 | 1 | 3 vegetables, 1 med-fat meat, 2 fat |
| ✔Veggie Lover's Salad Blend (Carrots & Snow Peas) | 1 1/2 cups | 20 | 0 | 0 | 0 | 0 | 15 | 1 | 1 | 4 | 0 | 1 vegetable |
| **Ready Pac** | | | | | | | | | | | | |
| ✔Baby Spinach Salad | 4 cups | 20 | 0 | 0 | 0 | 0 | 65 | 2 | 2 | 3 | 0 | 1 vegetable |
| ✔Caesar Romaine Salad | 1 1/2 cups | 12 | 0 | 0 | 0 | 0 | 10 | 1 | <1 | 2 | 0 | free |
| ✔Chop Suey Mix | 1 1/2 cups | 15 | 0 | 0 | 0 | 0 | 35 | 1 | <1 | 3 | 0 | 1 vegetable |
| ✔Parisian Salad (Green Leaf Lettuce, Frisee, Radicchio & Shredded Carrots) | 2 cups | 12 | 0 | 0 | 0 | 0 | 30 | 1 | 1 | 2 | 0 | free |
| ✔Santa Barbara Salad (Escarole, Endive, Radicchio) | 3 1/2 cup | 15 | 0 | 0 | 0 | 0 | 20 | 1 | 2 | 3 | 0 | 1 vegetable |
| **VEGETABLES (FRESH)** | | | | | | | | | | | | |
| **(Generic)** | | | | | | | | | | | | |
| ✔Broccoli, Raw | 1 cup | 25 | <1 | 0 | 0 | 0 | 24 | 3 | 3 | 5 | 0 | 1 vegetable |
| ✔Carrots, Raw | 1 cup | 47 | <1 | 0 | 0 | 0 | 38 | 1 | 3 | 11 | 1 | 2 vegetable |
| ✔Cauliflower, Raw | 1 cup | 25 | <1 | 0 | 0 | 0 | 30 | 2 | 3 | 5 | 0 | 1 vegetable |
| ✔Celery, Raw | 1 cup | 19 | <1 | 0 | 0 | 0 | 104 | <1 | 2 | 4 | 0 | 1 vegetable |

## VEGETARIAN MEAT SUBSTITUTES

| Item | Serving | | | | | | | | | | | Exchanges |
|---|---|---|---|---|---|---|---|---|---|---|---|---|
| ✔Mushrooms, Raw | 1 cup | 18 | <1 | 0 | 0 | 0 | 3 | 2 | <1 | 3 | 0 | 1 vegetable |
| ✔Peppers, Green | 1 cup | 27 | <1 | 0 | 0 | 0 | 2 | <1 | 2 | 6 | 1/2 | 1 vegetable |
| ✔Tomatoes, Raw | 1 cup | 38 | <1 | 0 | 0 | 0 | 16 | 2 | 2 | 8 | 1/2 | 2 vegetable |

### Gardenburger

| Item | Serving | | | | | | | | | | | Exchanges |
|---|---|---|---|---|---|---|---|---|---|---|---|---|
| ✔Veggie Patties | 3.4 oz pattie | 180 | 4 | 20 | 2 | 30 | 430 | 10 | 6 | 25 | 1 1/2 | 1 1/2 carb, 1 med-fat meat |

### Green Giant

| Item | Serving | | | | | | | | | | | Exchanges |
|---|---|---|---|---|---|---|---|---|---|---|---|---|
| Harvest Burger, All Varieties (Avg) | 1 patty | 140 | 5 | 32 | 2 | 0 | 370 | 17 | 5 | 9 | 1/2 | 1/2 strch, 2 lean meat |

### Loma Linda

| Item | Serving | | | | | | | | | | | Exchanges |
|---|---|---|---|---|---|---|---|---|---|---|---|---|
| Big Franks, Canned | 1 | 110 | 7 | 57 | 1 | 0 | 240 | 10 | 2 | 2 | 0 | 1 med-fat meat |
| ✔Big Franks, Low-Fat, Canned | 1 | 80 | 3 | 34 | <1 | 0 | 220 | 11 | 2 | 3 | 0 | 2 very lean meat |
| Chik Nuggets, Frozen | 5 | 240 | 16 | 60 | 3 | 0 | 710 | 12 | 5 | 13 | 1 | 1 strch, 1 med-fat meat, 2 fat |
| Corn Dogs, Frozen | 1 | 150 | 4 | 24 | <1 | 0 | 500 | 7 | 3 | 22 | 1 1/2 | 1 strch, 1 med-fat meat |
| ✔Dinner Cuts, Canned | 2 slices | 90 | 2 | 20 | 1 | 0 | 500 | 17 | 2 | 3 | 0 | 2 very lean meat |
| Fried Chik'n/Gravy, Canned | 2 pieces | 160 | 10 | 56 | 2 | 0 | 440 | 12 | 2 | 4 | 0 | 2 med-fat meat |
| Linketts, Canned | 1 link | 70 | 5 | 64 | <1 | 0 | 160 | 7 | 1 | 1 | 0 | 1 med-fat meat |
| Little Links, Canned | 2 | 90 | 6 | 60 | 1 | 0 | 230 | 8 | 2 | 2 | 0 | 1 med-fat meat |

✔ = Best Bet; NA = Not Available; Carb. Ch. = Carbohydrate Choices

| Vegetarian Meat Substitutes (Continued) | Serving Size | Cal. | Fat (g) | % Cal. Fat | Sat. Fat (g) | Chol. (mg) | Sod. (mg) | Pro. (g) | Fiber (g) | Carb. (g) | Carb. Ch. | Servings/Exchanges |
|---|---|---|---|---|---|---|---|---|---|---|---|---|
| Nuteena, Canned | 3/8 inch slice | 160 | 13 | 73 | 5 | 0 | 120 | 6 | 2 | 6 | 1/2 | 1/2 strch, 1 med-fat meat, 2 fat |
| ✔Ocean Platter, Dry Mix | 1/3 cup | 90 | 1 | 10 | 0 | 0 | 450 | 14 | 4 | 8 | 1/2 | 1/2 strch, 2 very lean meat |
| ✔Patty Mix, Dry | 1/3 cup | 90 | 1 | 10 | 0 | 0 | 480 | 14 | 5 | 7 | 1/2 | 1/2 strch, 2 very lean meat |
| ✔Redi-Burger, Canned | 5/8 inch slice | 170 | 3 | 23 | <1 | 0 | 450 | 18 | 4 | 7 | 1/2 | 1/2 strch, 2 very lean meat |
| Sandwich Spread, Dry Mix | 1/4 cup | 80 | 5 | 56 | 1 | 0 | 260 | 4 | 3 | 7 | 1/2 | 1/2 strch, 1 fat |
| Savory Dinner Loaf Dry Mix, Dry Mix | 1/3 cup | 90 | 2 | 20 | 0 | 0 | 560 | 14 | 5 | 7 | 1/2 | 1/2 strch, 2 very lean meat |
| Swiss Stake, Canned | 1 | 120 | 6 | 45 | 1 | 0 | 430 | 9 | 4 | 8 | 1/2 | 1/2 strch, 1 med-fat meat |
| Tender Bits, Canned | 6 | 110 | 5 | 41 | <1 | 0 | 440 | 11 | 3 | 7 | 1/2 | 1/2 strch, 1 med-fat meat |
| Tender Rounds, Canned | 8 | 120 | 5 | 38 | 1 | 0 | 330 | 14 | 3 | 5 | 0 | 2 lean meat |
| ✔Vege-Burger, Canned | 1/4 cup | 70 | 2 | 26 | <1 | 0 | 115 | 11 | 2 | 2 | 0 | 1 lean meat |

| | | | | | | | | | | | | |
|---|---|---|---|---|---|---|---|---|---|---|---|---|
| ✔Vita-Burger Chunks, Dry | 1/4 cup | 70 | 1 | 13 | 0 | 0 | 350 | 10 | 3 | 6 | 1/2 | 1/2 strch, 1 very lean meat |
| ✔Vita-Burger Dry Granules | 3 Tbsp | 70 | 1 | 13 | 0 | 0 | 350 | 10 | 3 | 6 | 1/2 | 1/2 strch, 1 very lean meat |
| **Morningstar Farms** | | | | | | | | | | | | |
| America's Original Veggie Dog, Frozen | 1 | 80 | <1 | 11 | 0 | 0 | 580 | 11 | 1 | 6 | 1/2 | 1/2 strch, 1 very lean meat |
| ✔Better'n Burgers, Frozen | 1 | 80 | 0 | 0 | 0 | 0 | 360 | 13 | 3 | 6 | 1/2 | 1/2 strch, 1 very lean meat |
| ✔Better'n Eggs, Frozen | 1/4 cup | 20 | 0 | 0 | 0 | 0 | 90 | 5 | 0 | 0 | 0 | 1 very lean meat |
| ✔Breakfast Links, Frozen | 2 links | 60 | 2 | 30 | <1 | 0 | 340 | 8 | 2 | 2 | 0 | 1 lean meat |
| ✔Breakfast Patties, Frozen | 1 | 80 | 3 | 34 | <1 | 0 | 270 | 10 | 2 | 3 | 0 | 1 lean meat |
| ✔Breakfast Sandwich w/Scramblers/Patty/Cheese, Frozen | 1 | 280 | 3 | 10 | <1 | 10 | 1000 | 28 | 5 | 12 | 1 | 1 strch, 4 very lean meat |
| Breakfast Strips, Frozen | 2 strips | 60 | 5 | 75 | <1 | 0 | 220 | 2 | <1 | 2 | 0 | 1 fat |
| ✔Chik Nuggets, Frozen | 4 | 160 | 4 | 23 | <1 | 0 | 670 | 13 | 5 | 17 | 1 | 1 strch, 1 med-fat meat |
| Chik Patties, Frozen | 1 | 150 | 6 | 36 | 1 | 0 | 570 | 9 | 2 | 15 | 1 | 1 strch, 1 med-fat meat, 1 fat |
| Deli Franks, Frozen | 1 link | 110 | 7 | 58 | 1 | 2 | 524 | 10 | 3 | 3 | 0 | 1 med-fat meat |

✔ = Best Bet; NA = Not Available; Carb. Ch. = Carbohydrate Choices

| Vegetarian Meat Substitutes (*Continued*) | Serving Size | Cal. | Fat (g) | % Cal. Fat | Sat. Fat (g) | Chol. (mg) | Sod. (mg) | Pro. (g) | Fiber (g) | Carb. (g) | Carb. Ch. | Servings/Exchanges |
|---|---|---|---|---|---|---|---|---|---|---|---|---|
| ✔Garden Grille Patty, Frozen | 1 | 120 | 3 | 23 | 1 | <5 | 280 | 6 | 4 | 18 | 1 | 1 strch, 1 lean meat |
| ✔Garden Veggie Patty | 1 patty | 100 | 3 | 27 | <1 | 0 | 350 | 10 | 4 | 9 | 1/2 | 1/2 strch, 1 lean meat |
| Grillers, Frozen | 1 | 140 | 6 | 39 | 1 | 0 | 260 | 15 | 2 | 5 | 0 | 2 lean meat |
| ✔Ground Meatless, Frozen | 1/2 cup | 60 | 0 | 0 | 0 | 0 | 260 | 10 | 2 | 4 | 0 | 1 very lean meat |
| Harvest Burger Original, Frozen | 1 | 140 | 4 | 26 | 2 | 0 | 370 | 18 | 5 | 8 | 1/2 | 1/2 strch, 2 lean meat |
| MeatFree Corn Dog, Frozen | 1 | 150 | 4 | 24 | <1 | 0 | 500 | 7 | 3 | 22 | 1 1/2 | 1 1/2 strch, 1 med-fat meat |
| Meatless Buffalo Wings, Frozen | 5 | 200 | 9 | 41 | 2 | 0 | 730 | 13 | 3 | 16 | 1 | 1 strch, 1 med-fat meat, 1 fat |
| ✔Quarter Prime Patties, Frozen | 1 | 140 | 2 | 13 | 0 | 0 | 370 | 24 | 3 | 6 | 1/2 | 1/2 strch, 3 very lean meat |
| ✔Scramblers, Frozen | 1/4 cup | 35 | 0 | 0 | 0 | 0 | 95 | 6 | 0 | 2 | 0 | 1 very lean meat |
| ✔Spicy Black Bean Burger, Frozen | 1 patty | 110 | 1 | 8 | 0 | 0 | 470 | 11 | 5 | 16 | 1 | 1 strch, 1 very lean meat |
| ✔Stuffed Sandwich, Ham/Cheese Style, Frozen | 1 | 300 | 7 | 21 | 3 | 10 | 520 | 15 | 1 | 45 | 3 | 3 strch, 1 med-fat meat |
| ✔Stuffed Sandwich, Pepperoni Pizza Style, Frozen | 1 | 280 | 7 | 23 | 3 | 5 | 420 | 12 | 5 | 42 | 3 | 3 strch, 1 med-fat meat |

## Natural Touch

| | Serving Size | Calories | | | | | Sodium (mg) | | | | Carb. Ch. | Exchanges/Choices |
|---|---|---|---|---|---|---|---|---|---|---|---|---|
| Dinner Entrée, Frozen | 1 | 220 | 15 | 61 | 3 | 0 | 380 | 19 | 2 | 2 | 0 | 3 med-fat meat |
| ✔Garden Vege Patty, Frozen | 1 patty | 110 | 3 | 25 | <1 | 0 | 280 | 10 | 3 | 8 | 1/2 | 1/2 strch, 1 med-fat meat |
| Lentil Rice Loaf | 1 inch slice | 170 | 9 | 48 | 3 | 0 | 370 | 8 | 4 | 14 | 1 | 1 strch, 1 med-fat meat, 1 fat |
| Nine Bean Loaf | 1 inch slice | 160 | 8 | 45 | 2 | <5 | 350 | 8 | 5 | 13 | 1 | 1 strch, 1 med-fat meat, 1 fat |
| Okra Patty, Frozen | 1 patty | 110 | 5 | 41 | 1 | 0 | 360 | 11 | 3 | 4 | 0 | 2 lean meat |
| ✔Spicy Black Bean Burger, Frozen | 1 patty | 100 | 1 | 9 | 0 | 0 | 330 | 11 | 5 | 15 | 1 | 1 strch, 1 very lean meat |
| ✔Vegan Burger Crumbles, Frozen | 1/2 cup | 60 | 0 | 0 | 0 | 0 | 260 | 10 | 2 | 4 | 0 | 1 very lean meat |
| ✔Vegan Burger, Frozen | 1 patty | 70 | 0 | 0 | 0 | 0 | 370 | 11 | 3 | 6 | 1/2 | 1/2 strch, 1 very lean meat |
| ✔Vegan Sausage Crumbles, Frozen | 1/2 cup | 60 | 0 | 0 | 0 | 0 | 300 | 10 | 2 | 4 | 0 | 1 very lean meat |
| Vege Frank, Frozen | 1 | 100 | 6 | 54 | 1 | 0 | 470 | 10 | 2 | 2 | 0 | 1 med-fat meat |
| ✔Vegetarian Chili, Frozen | 1 cup | 170 | 5 | | 1 | 0 | 870 | 18 | 11 | 21 | 1 1/2 | 1 1/2 strch, 2 med-fat meat |

## Worthington

| | Serving Size | Calories | | | | | Sodium (mg) | | | | Carb. Ch. | Exchanges/Choices |
|---|---|---|---|---|---|---|---|---|---|---|---|---|
| Beef Style Meatless, Frozen | 3/8 inch slice | 110 | 7 | 57 | 1 | 0 | 620 | 9 | 3 | 4 | 0 | 1 med-fat meat |

✔ = Best Bet; NA = Not Available; Carb. Ch. = Carbohydrate Choices

| Vegetarian Meat Substitutes (*Continued*) | Serving Size | Cal. | Fat (g) | % Cal. Fat | Sat. Fat (g) | Chol. (mg) | Sod. (mg) | Pro. (g) | Fiber (g) | Carb. (g) | Carb. Ch. | Servings/Exchanges |
|---|---|---|---|---|---|---|---|---|---|---|---|---|
| Bolono, Frozen | 3 slices | 80 | 4 | 45 | 1 | 0 | 720 | 10 | 2 | 2 | 0 | 1 med-fat meat |
| Chicken, Sliced or Roll, Frozen | 2 | 80 | 5 | 56 | 1 | 0 | 370 | 9 | 2 | 1 | 0 | 1 med-fat meat |
| Chic-ketts, Frozen | 2 3/8 inch slices | 120 | 7 | 53 | 1 | 0 | 390 | 13 | 2 | 2 | 0 | 2 lean meat |
| ChikStiks, Frozen | 1 | 110 | 7 | 57 | 1 | 0 | 360 | 9 | 2 | 3 | 0 | 1 med-fat meat |
| Chili, Canned | 1 cup | 290 | 15 | 47 | 3 | 0 | 1130 | 19 | 9 | 21 | 1 1/2 | 1 1/2 strch, 2 med-fat meat, 1 fat |
| ✔Chili, Low Fat, Frozen | 1 cup | 170 | 1 | 5 | 0 | 0 | 870 | 18 | 11 | 21 | 1 1/2 | 1 1/2 strch, 2 very lean meat |
| ✔Choplets, Canned | 2 slices | 90 | 2 | 20 | 1 | 0 | 500 | 17 | 2 | 3 | 0 | 2 very lean meat |
| Corned Beef, Meatless | 4 slices | 140 | 9 | 58 | 2 | 0 | 520 | 10 | 2 | 5 | 0 | 1 med-fat meat, 1 fat |
| Country Stew, Canned | 1 cup | 210 | 9 | 34 | 1 | 0 | 830 | 13 | 5 | 20 | 1 | 1 strch, 1 med-fat meat, 1 fat |
| CrispyChik Patties, Frozen | 1 patty | 150 | 6 | 36 | 1 | 0 | 600 | 8 | 2 | 15 | 1 | 1 strch, 1 med-fat meat, 1 fat |
| ✔Cutlets, Canned | 1 slice | 70 | 1 | 13 | 0 | 0 | 340 | 11 | 2 | 3 | 0 | 2 very lean meat |
| ✔Diced Chik, Canned | 1/4 cup | 40 | 0 | 0 | 0 | 0 | 270 | 7 | 1 | 1 | 0 | 1 med-fat meat |
| ✔Dinner Roast, Frozen | 3/4 inch slice | 180 | 12 | 60 | 2 | 0 | 580 | 12 | 3 | 5 | 0 | 2 med-fat meat |

| Food | Serving | | | | | | | | | | | Exchanges |
|---|---|---|---|---|---|---|---|---|---|---|---|---|
| Fillets, Frozen | 2 | 180 | 10 | 50 | 2 | 0 | 750 | 16 | 4 | 8 | 1/2 | 1/2 strch, 2 med-fat meat |
| FriChik, Canned | 2 pieces | 120 | 8 | 60 | 1 | 0 | 430 | 10 | 1 | 0 | 0 | 1 med-fat meat, 1 fat |
| FriPats, Frozen | 1 patty | 130 | 6 | 42 | 1 | 0 | 320 | 14 | 3 | 4 | 0 | 2 lean meat |
| Golden Croquettes, Frozen | 4 | 210 | 10 | 43 | 2 | 0 | 600 | 14 | 3 | 14 | 1 | 1 strch, 2 med-fat meat |
| ✔Granburger, Dry | 3 Tbsp | 60 | <1 | 15 | 0 | 0 | 410 | 10 | 2 | 3 | 0 | 1 very lean meat |
| Leanies, Frozen | 1 link | 100 | 7 | 63 | 1 | 0 | 430 | 7 | 1 | 2 | 0 | 1 med-fat meat |
| ✔Multigrain Cutlet, Canned | 2 slices | 100 | 2 | 18 | <1 | 0 | 390 | 15 | 4 | 5 | 0 | 2 very lean meat |
| Numete , Canned | 3/8 inch slice | 130 | 10 | 69 | 3 | 0 | 270 | 6 | 3 | 5 | 0 | 1 med-fat meat, 1 fat |
| Prime Stakes, Canned | 1 | 120 | 7 | 53 | 1 | 0 | 440 | 10 | 4 | 4 | 0 | 1 med-fat meat, 1 fat |
| ✔Prosage Links, Frozen | 2 links | 60 | 3 | 45 | <1 | 0 | 340 | 8 | 2 | 2 | 0 | 1 lean meat |
| ✔Prosage Patties, Frozen | 1 patty | 80 | 3 | 34 | <1 | 0 | 300 | 9 | 2 | 3 | 0 | 1 lean meat |
| Prosage Roll, Frozen | 5/8 inch slice | 140 | 10 | 64 | 1 | 0 | 390 | 10 | 2 | 2 | 0 | 1 med-fat meat, 1 fat |
| Protose, Canned | 3/8 in slice | 130 | 7 | 48 | 1 | 0 | 280 | 13 | 3 | 5 | 0 | 2 lean meat |
| Salami, Meatless, Frozen | 3 slices | 130 | 8 | 55 | 1 | 0 | 800 | 12 | 2 | 2 | 0 | 2 med-fat meat |
| Saucettes, Canned | 1 link | 90 | 6 | 60 | 1 | 0 | 200 | 6 | 1 | 1 | 0 | 1 med-fat meat |
| Savory Slices, Canned | 3 slices | 150 | 9 | 36 | 4 | 0 | 540 | 10 | 3 | 6 | 1/2 | 1/2 strch, 1 med-fat meat, 1 fat |
| ✔Sliced Chik, Canned | 3 | 70 | 2 | 26 | <1 | 0 | 430 | 14 | 2 | 2 | 0 | 2 very lean meat |

✔= Best Bet; NA = Not Available; Carb. Ch. = Carbohydrate Choices

| Vegetarian Meat Substitutes (*Continued*) | Serving Size | Cal. | Fat (g) | % Cal. Fat | Sat. Fat (g) | Chol. (mg) | Sod. (mg) | Pro. (g) | Fiber (g) | Carb. (g) | Carb. Ch. | Servings/Exchanges |
|---|---|---|---|---|---|---|---|---|---|---|---|---|
| Smoked Beef Slices, Frozen | 6 slices | 120 | 6 | 45 | 1 | 0 | 730 | 11 | 3 | 6 | 1/2 | 1/2 strch, 1 med-fat meat |
| Smoked Turkey Slices, Frozen | 3 slices | 140 | 10 | 64 | 2 | 0 | 620 | 10 | 2 | 3 | 0 | 1 med-fat meat, 1 fat |
| Stakelets, Frozen | 1 | 140 | 8 | 51 | 1 | 0 | 480 | 12 | 2 | 6 | 1/2 | 1/2 strch, 2 med-fat meat |
| Stripples, Frozen | 2 strips | 60 | 5 | 75 | <1 | 0 | 220 | 2 | <1 | 2 | 0 | 1 fat |
| Super-Links, Canned | 1 link | 110 | 8 | 65 | 1 | 0 | 350 | 7 | 1 | 2 | 0 | 1 med-fat meat, 1 fat |
| Tuno, Drained, Canned | 1/3 cup | 80 | 4 | 45 | <1 | 0 | 380 | 7 | 1 | 4 | 0 | 1 med-fat meat |
| Tuno, Drained, Frozen | 1/2 cup | 80 | 6 | 68 | 1 | 0 | 290 | 6 | 1 | 2 | 0 | 1 med-fat meat |
| Turkee Slices, Canned | 3 slices | 170 | 12 | 64 | 2 | 0 | 580 | 13 | 2 | 3 | 0 | 2 med-fat meat, 1 fat |
| ✓Vegetable Skallops, Canned | 1/2 cup | 90 | 2 | 20 | <1 | 0 | 410 | 15 | 3 | 3 | 0 | 2 very lean meat |
| ✓Vegetable Steaks, Canned | 2 | 80 | 2 | 23 | <1 | 0 | 300 | 15 | 3 | 3 | 0 | 2 very lean meat |
| ✓Vegetarian Burger, Canned | 1/4 cup | 60 | 2 | 30 | 0 | 0 | 270 | 9 | 1 | 2 | 0 | 1 lean meat |
| Vegetarian Egg Rolls, Frozen | 1 | 180 | 8 | 40 | 2 | 0 | 380 | 6 | 2 | 20 | 1 | 1 strch, 2 fat |
| ✓Veja Links, Low Fat, Canned | 1 | 40 | 2 | 45 | 0 | 0 | 190 | 5 | 0 | 1 | 0 | 1 lean meat |
| ✓Veja-Links, Canned | 1 link | 50 | 3 | 54 | <1 | 0 | 190 | 5 | 0 | 1 | 0 | 1 lean meat |
| Wham, Frozen | 2 slices | 80 | 5 | 56 | 1 | 0 | 430 | 7 | 0 | 1 | 0 | 1 med-fat meat |

## WAFFLE MIX (AS PREPARED)

### Betty Crocker/General Mills

| | | | | | | | | | | | | |
|---|---|---|---|---|---|---|---|---|---|---|---|---|
| Belgian Waffle Mix | 1 | 370 | 17 | 41 | 9 | 130 | 1020 | 8 | 1 | 47 | 3 | 3 strch, 3 fat |

## WAFFLES (FROZEN)

### Aunt Jemima

| | | | | | | | | | | | | |
|---|---|---|---|---|---|---|---|---|---|---|---|---|
| ✓Microwave Waffles, Blueberry | 2 | 210 | 6 | 26 | 2 | <5 | 470 | 5 | 1 | 34 | 2 | 2 strch, 1 fat |
| ✓Microwave Waffles, Homestyle | 2 | 200 | 6 | 27 | 2 | <5 | 440 | 5 | 1 | 32 | 2 | 2 strch, 1 fat |

### Chef America

| | | | | | | | | | | | | |
|---|---|---|---|---|---|---|---|---|---|---|---|---|
| ✓Belgian Chef Waffles | 2.7 oz | 180 | 2 | 11 | 1 | 0 | 450 | 3 | 0 | 34 | 2 | 2 carb |

### Kellogg's Eggo

| | | | | | | | | | | | | |
|---|---|---|---|---|---|---|---|---|---|---|---|---|
| Apple Cinnamon Waffles | 2 | 200 | 7 | 32 | 2 | 20 | 400 | 5 | 2 | 30 | 2 | 2 strch, 1 fat |
| ✓Banana Bread Waffles | 2 | 190 | 6 | 28 | 1 | 0 | 280 | 5 | 2 | 30 | 2 | 2 strch, 1 fat |
| Blueberry Waffles | 2 | 200 | 7 | 32 | 2 | 20 | 420 | 5 | 1 | 30 | 2 | 2 strch, 1 fat |
| Buttermilk Waffles | 2 | 190 | 7 | 33 | 2 | 20 | 420 | 5 | 2 | 28 | 2 | 2 strch, 1 fat |
| Chocolate Chip Waffles | 2 | 200 | 7 | 32 | 2 | 15 | 380 | 4 | 1 | 32 | 2 | 2 strch, 1 fat |
| Cinnamon Toast Waffles | 2 | 290 | 10 | 31 | 3 | 25 | 480 | 5 | 1 | 46 | 3 | 3 strch, 2 fat |
| ✓Golden Oat Waffles | 2 | 140 | 3 | 19 | <1 | 0 | 270 | 5 | 3 | 26 | 2 | 2 strch, 1 fat |
| Homestyle Waffles | 2 | 190 | 7 | 33 | 2 | 20 | 440 | 5 | 2 | 29 | 2 | 2 strch, 1 fat |
| Honey & Nut Waffles | 2 | 220 | 9 | 37 | 2 | 20 | 390 | 6 | 2 | 30 | 2 | 2 strch, 2 fat |

✔ = Best Bet; NA = Not Available; Carb. Ch. = Carbohydrate Choices

| Waffles (Frozen) (Continued) | Serving Size | Cal. | Fat (g) | % Cal. Fat | Sat. Fat (g) | Chol. (mg) | Sod. (mg) | Pro. (g) | Fiber (g) | Carb. (g) | Carb. Ch. | Servings/Exchanges |
|---|---|---|---|---|---|---|---|---|---|---|---|---|
| ✔Low Fat Homestyle Waffles | 2 | 160 | 3 | 17 | <1 | 15 | 300 | 5 | 1 | 31 | 2 | 2 strch, 1 fat |
| ✔Low Fat Nutri-Grain Blueberry Waffles | 2 | 150 | 3 | 18 | <1 | 0 | 420 | 5 | 4 | 30 | 2 | 2 strch, 1 fat |
| ✔Low Fat Nutri-Grain Waffles | 2 | 140 | 3 | 19 | <1 | 0 | 430 | 5 | 3 | 28 | 2 | 2 strch, 1 fat |
| Minis Homestyle Waffles | 12 | 260 | 9 | 31 | 2 | 25 | 600 | 7 | 2 | 38 | 2 1/2 | 2 1/2 strch, 2 fat |
| ✔Nutri-Grain Mult-Bran Waffles | 2 | 160 | 5 | 28 | 1 | 0 | 360 | 5 | 5 | 29 | 2 | 2 strch, 1 fat |
| ✔Nutri-Grain Plain Waffles | 2 | 170 | 5 | 26 | 1 | 0 | 420 | 5 | 3 | 28 | 2 | 2 strch, 1 fat |
| ✔Special K Waffles | 2 | 120 | 0 | 0 | 0 | 0 | 280 | 6 | 1 | 26 | 2 | 2 strch |
| Strawbery Waffles | 2 | 200 | 7 | 32 | 2 | 20 | 420 | 5 | 2 | 30 | 2 | 2 strch, 1 fat |
| **Van's** | | | | | | | | | | | | |
| ✔Belgian Waffles | 2 | 146 | 4 | 25 | 0 | 0 | 92 | 5 | 2 | 24 | 1 1/2 | 1 1/2 carb, 1 fat |

## WHIPPED TOPPING

### Kraft/Cool Whip

| | Serving Size | Cal. | Fat (g) | % Cal. Fat | Sat. Fat (g) | Chol. (mg) | Sod. (mg) | Pro. (g) | Fiber (g) | Carb. (g) | Carb. Ch. | Servings/Exchanges |
|---|---|---|---|---|---|---|---|---|---|---|---|---|
| ✔Cool Whip Free Whipped Topping | 2 Tbsp | 15 | 0 | 0 | 0 | 0 | 5 | 0 | 0 | 3 | 0 | free |
| ✔Cool Whip Topping, Extra Creamy | 2 Tbsp | 30 | 2 | 60 | 2 | 2 | 5 | 0 | 0 | 2 | 0 | free |
| ✔Cool Whip Topping, Lite | 2 Tbsp | 20 | 1 | 45 | 1 | 1 | 0 | 0 | 0 | 2 | 0 | free |
| ✔Cool Whip Topping, Regular | 2 Tbsp | 25 | 2 | 72 | 2 | 0 | 0 | 0 | 0 | 2 | 0 | free |
| ✔Cool Whip Whipped Topping | 2 Tbsp | 25 | 2 | 72 | 2 | 0 | 0 | 0 | 0 | 2 | 0 | free |
| ✔Dairy Whip Whipped Light Cream | 2 Tbsp | 10 | 1 | 90 | <1 | <5 | 0 | 0 | 0 | <1 | 0 | free |